Interdisciplinary Economics

A major figure in economics, Kenneth E. Boulding shaped and in some instances pioneered debates in institutional economics, post-Keynesian economics, evolutionary economics, ecological economics, peace research, and conflict research, amongst others. These disciplines are well-developed by now, and so it may not be apparent what contributions Boulding has made. As the heterodoxy is developing increasingly feasible alternatives for the mainstream, and the mainstream is itself opening up and transforming, attention for Boulding's work will increase.

A growing number of economists, working inside and outside of academia (including those in business schools and independent research centres) seek to relate insights from the social sciences with those from physical and biological sciences. Boulding initiated and spurred such interdisciplinary approaches. At the same time, his early emphasis on the economy as a system, and on symbolic communication that sustains it, is reflected in cutting-edge work at the moment. Boulding combines these strands in his work. His ability not just to reach out to fields of studies adjacent to economics—colonizing them, à la Gary Becker, or cherry picking from and then misrepresenting them, à la George Akerlof—but rather to engage with these actively is the main theme of this volume.

A former president of the American Economic Association, Boulding's contributions are recognized in many other fields besides economics. He did, of course, make seminal contributions to Keynesian and institutional economics. Yet, a polymath, he helped found a number of research areas outside standard economics, most importantly of which are systems theory, conflict mediation, and ecological economics.

Wilfred Dolfsma is Chair of Innovation at the University of Groningen, the Netherlands.

Stefan Kesting is Teaching Fellow at the University of Leeds, England.

Routledge Studies in the History of Economics

1 **Economics as Literature**
Willie Henderson

2 **Socialism and Marginalism in Economics 1870–1930**
Edited by Ian Steedman

3 **Hayek's Political Economy**
The socio-economics of order
Steve Fleetwood

4 **On the Origins of Classical Economics**
Distribution and value from William Petty to Adam Smith
Tony Aspromourgos

5 **The Economics of Joan Robinson**
Edited by Maria Cristina Marcuzzo, Luigi Pasinetti and Alesandro Roncaglia

6 **The Evolutionist Economics of Léon Walras**
Albert Jolink

7 **Keynes and the 'Classics'**
A study in language, epistemology and mistaken identities
Michel Verdon

8 **The History of Game Theory, Vol 1**
From the beginnings to 1945
Robert W. Dimand and Mary Ann Dimand

9 **The Economics of W. S. Jevons**
Sandra Peart

10 **Gandhi's Economic Thought**
Ajit K. Dasgupta

11 **Equilibrium and Economic Theory**
Edited by Giovanni Caravale

12 **Austrian Economics in Debate**
Edited by Willem Keizer, Bert Tieben and Rudy van Zijp

13 **Ancient Economic Thought**
Edited by B. B. Price

14 **The Political Economy of Social Credit and Guild Socialism**
Frances Hutchinson and Brian Burkitt

15 **Economic Careers**
Economics and economists in Britain 1930–1970
Keith Tribe

16 **Understanding 'Classical' Economics**
Studies in the long-period theory
Heinz Kurz and Neri Salvadori

17 **History of Environmental Economic Thought**
E. Kula

18 **Economic Thought in Communist and Post-Communist Europe**
Edited by Hans-Jürgen Wagener

19 **Studies in the History of French Political Economy**
From Bodin to Walras
Edited by Gilbert Faccarello

20 **The Economics of John Rae**
Edited by O. F. Hamouda, C. Lee and D. Mair

21 **Keynes and the Neoclassical Synthesis**
Einsteinian versus Newtonian macroeconomics
Teodoro Dario Togati

22 **Historical Perspectives on Macroeconomics**
Sixty years after the 'General Theory'
Edited by Philippe Fontaine and Albert Jolink

23 **The Founding of Institutional Economics**
The leisure class and sovereignty
Edited by Warren J. Samuels

24 **Evolution of Austrian Economics**
From Menger to Lachmann
Sandye Gloria

25 **Marx's Concept of Money**
The God of Commodities
Anitra Nelson

26 **The Economics of James Steuart**
Edited by Ramón Tortajada

27 **The Development of Economics in Europe since 1945**
Edited by A. W. Bob Coats

28 **The Canon in the History of Economics**
Critical essays
Edited by Michalis Psalidopoulos

29 **Money and Growth**
Selected papers of Allyn Abbott Young
Edited by Perry G. Mehrling and Roger J. Sandilands

30 **The Social Economics of Jean-Baptiste Say**
Markets and virtue
Evelyn L. Forget

31 **The Foundations of Laissez-Faire**
The economics of Pierre de Boisguilbert
Gilbert Faccarello

32 **John Ruskin's Political Economy**
Willie Henderson

33 **Contributions to the History of Economic Thought**
Essays in honour of R. D. C. Black
Edited by Antoin E. Murphy and Renee Prendergast

34 Towards an Unknown Marx
A commentary on the manuscripts of 1861–63
Enrique Dussel

35 Economics and Interdisciplinary Exchange
Edited by Guido Erreygers

36 Economics as the Art of Thought
Essays in memory of G. L. S. Shackle
Edited by Stephen F. Frowen and Peter Earl

37 The Decline of Ricardian Economics
Politics and economics in post-Ricardian theory
Susan Pashkoff

38 Piero Sraffa
His life, thought and cultural heritage
Alessandro Roncaglia

39 Equilibrium and Disequilibrium in Economic Theory
The Marshall-Walras divide
Michel de Vroey

40 The German Historical School
The historical and ethical approach to economics
Edited by Yuichi Shionoya

41 Reflections on the Classical Canon in Economics
Essays in honour of Samuel Hollander
Edited by Sandra Peart and Evelyn Forget

42 Piero Sraffa's Political Economy
A centenary estimate
Edited by Terenzio Cozzi and Roberto Marchionatti

43 The Contribution of Joseph Schumpeter to Economics
Economic development and institutional change
Richard Arena and Cecile Dangel

44 On the Development of Long-run Neo-Classical Theory
Tom Kompas

45 F. A. Hayek as a Political Economist
Economic analysis and values
Edited by Jack Birner, Pierre Garrouste and Thierry Aimar

46 Pareto, Economics and Society
The mechanical analogy
Michael McLure

47 The Cambridge Controversies in Capital Theory
A study in the logic of theory development
Jack Birner

48 Economics Broadly Considered
Essays in honour of Warren J. Samuels
Edited by Steven G. Medema, Jeff Biddle and John B. Davis

49 Physicians and Political Economy
Six studies of the work of doctor-economists
Edited by Peter Groenewegen

50 **The Spread of Political Economy and the Professionalisation of Economists**
Economic societies in Europe, America and Japan in the nineteenth century
Massimo Augello and Marco Guidi

51 **Historians of Economics and Economic Thought**
The construction of disciplinary memory
Steven G. Medema and Warren J. Samuels

52 **Competing Economic Theories**
Essays in memory of Giovanni Caravale
Sergio Nisticò and Domenico Tosato

53 **Economic Thought and Policy in Less Developed Europe**
The nineteenth century
Edited by Michalis Psalidopoulos and Maria-Eugenia Almedia Mata

54 **Family Fictions and Family Facts**
Harriet Martineau, Adolphe Quetelet and the population question in England 1798–1859
Brian Cooper

55 **Eighteenth-Century Economics**
Peter Groenewegen

56 **The Rise of Political Economy in the Scottish Enlightenment**
Edited by Tatsuya Sakamoto and Hideo Tanaka

57 **Classics and Moderns in Economics, Volume I**
Essays on nineteenth and twentieth century economic thought
Peter Groenewegen

58 **Classics and Moderns in Economics, Volume II**
Essays on nineteenth and twentieth century economic thought
Peter Groenewegen

59 **Marshall's Evolutionary Economics**
Tiziano Raffaelli

60 **Money, Time and Rationality in Max Weber**
Austrian connections
Stephen D. Parsons

61 **Classical Macroeconomics**
Some modern variations and distortions
James C. W. Ahiakpor

62 **The Historical School of Economics in England and Japan**
Tamotsu Nishizawa

63 **Classical Economics and Modern Theory**
Studies in long-period analysis
Heinz D. Kurz and Neri Salvadori

64 **A Bibliography of Female Economic Thought to 1940**
Kirsten K. Madden, Janet A. Sietz and Michele Pujol

65 **Economics, Economists and Expectations**
From microfoundations to macroeconomics
Warren Young, Robert Leeson and William Darity Jnr.

66 **The Political Economy of Public Finance in Britain, 1767–1873**
Takuo Dome

67 **Essays in the History of Economics**
Warren J. Samuels, Willie Henderson, Kirk D. Johnson and Marianne Johnson

68 **History and Political Economy**
Essays in honour of P. D. Groenewegen
Edited by Tony Aspromourgos and John Lodewijks

69 **The Tradition of Free Trade**
Lars Magnusson

70 **Evolution of the Market Process**
Austrian and Swedish economics
Edited by Michel Bellet, Sandye Gloria-Palermo and Abdallah Zouache

71 **Consumption as an Investment**
The fear of goods from Hesiod to Adam Smith
Cosimo Perrotta

72 **Jean-Baptiste Say and the Classical Canon in Economics**
The British connection in French classicism
Samuel Hollander

73 **Knut Wicksell on Poverty**
No place is too exalted
Knut Wicksell

74 **Economists in Cambridge**
A study through their correspondence 1907–1946
Edited by M. C. Marcuzzo and A. Rosselli

75 **The Experiment in the History of Economics**
Edited by Philippe Fontaine and Robert Leonard

76 **At the Origins of Mathematical Economics**
The Economics of A. N. Isnard (1748–1803)
Richard van den Berg

77 **Money and Exchange**
Folktales and reality
Sasan Fayazmanesh

78 **Economic Development and Social Change**
Historical roots and modern perspectives
George Stathakis and Gianni Vaggi

79 **Ethical Codes and Income Distribution**
A study of John Bates Clark and Thorstein Veblen
Guglielmo Forges Davanzati

80 **Evaluating Adam Smith**
Creating the wealth of nations
Willie Henderson

81 **Civil Happiness**
Economics and human flourishing in historical perspective
Luigino Bruni

82 **New Voices on Adam Smith**
Edited by Leonidas Montes and Eric Schliesser

83 **Making Chicago Price Theory**
Milton Friedman–George Stigler correspondence, 1945–1957
Edited by J. Daniel Hammond and Claire H. Hammond

84 **William Stanley Jevons and the Cutting Edge of Economics**
Bert Mosselmans

85 **A History of Econometrics in France**
From nature to models
Philippe Le Gall

86 **Money and Markets**
A doctrinal approach
Edited by Alberto Giacomin and Maria Cristina Marcuzzo

87 **Considerations on the Fundamental Principles of Pure Political Economy**
Vilfredo Pareto
(Edited by Roberto Marchionatti and Fiorenzo Mornati)

88 **The Years of High Econometrics**
A short history of the generation that reinvented economics
Francisco Louçã

89 **David Hume's Political Economy**
Edited by Carl Wennerlind and Margaret Schabas

90 **Interpreting Classical Economics**
Studies in long-period analysis
Heinz D. Kurz and Neri Salvadori

91 **Keynes's Vision**
Why the great depression did not return
John Philip Jones

92 **Monetary Theory in Retrospect**
The selected essays of Filippo Cesarano
Filippo Cesarano

93 **Keynes's Theoretical Development**
From the tract to the general theory
Toshiaki Hirai

94 **Leading Contemporary Economists**
Economics at the cutting edge
Edited by Steven Pressman

95 **The Science of Wealth**
Adam Smith and the framing of political economy
Tony Aspromourgos

96 **Capital, Time and Transitional Dynamics**
Edited by Harald Hagemann and Roberto Scazzieri

97 **New Essays on Pareto's Economic Theory**
Edited by Luigino Bruni and Aldo Montesano

98 **Frank Knight & the Chicago School in American Economics**
Ross B. Emmett

99 **A History of Economic Theory**
Essays in honour of Takashi Negishi
Edited by Aiko Ikeo and Heinz D. Kurz

100 **Open Economics**
Economics in relation to other disciplines
Edited by Richard Arena, Sheila Dow and Matthias Klaes

101 **Rosa Luxemburg and the Critique of Political Economy**
Edited by Riccardo Bellofiore

102 **Problems and Methods of Econometrics**
The Poincaré lectures of Ragnar Frisch 1933
Edited by Olav Bjerkholt and Ariane Dupont-Keiffer

103 **Criticisms of Classical Political Economy**
Menger, Austrian economics and the German historical school
Gilles Campagnolo

104 **A History of Entrepreneurship**
Robert F. Hébert and Albert N. Link

105 **Keynes on Monetary Policy, Finance and Uncertainty**
Liquidity preference theory and the global financial crisis
Jorg Bibow

106 **Kalecki's Principle of Increasing Risk and Keynesian Economics**
Tracy Mott

107 **Economic Theory and Economic Thought**
Essays in honour of Ian Steedman
John Vint, J. Stanley Metcalfe, Heinz D. Kurz, Neri Salvadori and Paul Samuelson

108 **Political Economy, Public Policy and Monetary Economics**
Ludwig von Mises and the Austrian tradition
Richard M. Ebeling

109 **Keynes and the British Humanist Tradition**
The moral purpose of the market
David R. Andrews

110 **Political Economy and Industrialism**
Banks in Saint-Simonian economic thought
Gilles Jacoud

111 **Studies in Social Economics**
Leon Walras
Translated by Jan van Daal and Donald Walker

112 **The Making of the Classical Theory of Economic Growth**
Anthony Brewer

113 **The Origins of David Hume's Economics**
Willie Henderson

114 **Production, Distribution and Trade**
Edited by Adriano Birolo, Duncan Foley, Heinz D. Kurz, Bertram Schefold and Ian Steedman

115 **The Essential Writings of Thorstein Veblen**
Edited by Charles Camic and Geoffrey Hodgson

116 **Adam Smith and the Economy of the Passions**
Jan Horst Keppler

117 **The Analysis of Linear Economic Systems**
Father Maurice Potron's pioneering works
Translated by Christian Bidard and Guido Erreygers

118 **A Dynamic Approach to Economic Theory: Frisch**
Edited by Olav Bjerkholt and Duo Qin

119 **Henry A. Abbati: Keynes' Forgotten Precursor**
Serena Di Gaspare

120 **Generations of Economists**
David Collard

121 **Hayek, Mill and the Liberal Tradition**
Edited by Andrew Farrant

122 **Marshall, Marshallians and Industrial Economics**
Edited by Tiziano Raffaelli

123 **Austrian and German Economic Thought**
Kiichiro Yagi

124 **The Evolution of Economic Theory**
Edited by Volker Caspari

125 **Thomas Tooke and the Monetary Thought of Classical Economics**
Matthew Smith

126 **Political Economy and Liberalism in France**
The contributions of Frédéric Bastiat
Robert Leroux

127 **Stalin's Economist**
The economic contributions of Jenö Varga
André Mommen

128 **E.E. Slutsky as Economist and Mathematician**
Crossing the limits of knowledge
Vincent Barnett

129 **Keynes, Sraffa, and the Criticism of Neoclassical Theory**
Essays in honour of Heinz Kurz
Neri Salvadori and Christian Gehrke

130 **Crises and Cycles in Economic Dictionaries and Encyclopaedias**
Edited by Daniele Bensomi

131 **General Equilibrium Analysis: A Century After Walras**
Edited by Pascal Bridel

132 **Sraffa and Modern Economics, Volume I**
Edited by Roberto Ciccone, Christian Gehrke and Gary Mongiovi

133 **Sraffa and Modern Economics, Volume II**
Edited by Roberto Ciccone, Christian Gehrke and Gary Mongiovi

134 **The Minor Marshallians and Alfred Marshall: An Evaluation**
Peter Groenewegen

135 **Fighting Market Failure**
Collected essays in the Cambridge tradition of economics
Maria Cristina Marcuzzo

136 **The Economic Reader**
Edited by Massimo M. Augello and Marco E. L. Guido

137 **Classical Political Economy and Modern Theory**
Essays in honour of Heinz Kurz
Neri Salvadori and Christian Gehrke

138 **The Ideas of Ronald H. Coase**
Lawrence W. C. Lai

139 **Anticipating the Wealth of Nations**
Edited by Maren Jonasson and Petri Hyttinen, with an Introduction by Lars Magnusson

140 **Innovation, Knowledge and Growth**
Edited by Heinz D. Kurz

141 **A History of Homo Economicus**
The nature of the moral in economic theory
William Dixon and David Wilson

142 **The Division of Labour in Economics**
A history
Guang-Zhen Sun

143 **Keynes and Modern Economics**
Edited by Ryuzo Kuroki

144 **Macroeconomics and the History of Economic Thought**
Festschrift in honour of Harald Hagemann
Edited by Hagen M. Krämer, Heinz D. Kurz and Hans-Michael Trautwein

145 **French Liberalism in the 19th Century**
An anthology
Edited by Robert Leroux

146 **Subjectivisim and Objectivism in the History of Economic Thought**
Edited by Yukihiro Ikeda and Kiichiro Yagi

147 **The Rhetoric of the Right**
Language change and the spread of the market
David George

148 **The Theory of Value and Distribution in Economics**
Discussions between Pierangelo Garegnani and Paul Samuelson
Edited by Heinz Kurz

149 **An Economic History of Ireland since Independence**
Andy Bielenberg

150 **Reinterpreting the Keynesian Revolution**
Robert Cord

151 **Money and Banking in Jean-Baptiste Say's Economic Thought**
Gilles Jacoud

152 **Jean-Baptiste Say**
Revolutionary, entrepreneur, economist
Evert Schoorl

153 **Essays on Classical and Marxian Political Economy**
Samuel Hollander

154 **Marxist Political Economy**
Essays in retrieval: selected works of Geoff Pilling
Edited by Doria Pilling

155 **Interdisciplinary Economics**
Kenneth E. Boulding's engagement in the sciences
Edited by Wilfred Dolfsma and Stefan Kesting

Interdisciplinary Economics

Kenneth E. Boulding's engagement in the sciences

Edited by Wilfred Dolfsma and Stefan Kesting

Routledge
Taylor & Francis Group
LONDON AND NEW YORK

First published 2013
by Routledge
2 Park Square, Milton Park, Abingdon, Oxon OX14 4RN

Simultaneously published in the USA and Canada
by Routledge
711 Third Avenue, New York, NY 10017

Routledge is an imprint of the Taylor & Francis Group, an informa business

British Library Cataloguing in Publication Data
A catalogue record for this book is available from the British Library

Library of Congress Cataloging in Publication Data
Boulding, Kenneth E. (Kenneth Ewart), 1910–1993.
Interdisciplinary economics: Kenneth E. Boulding's engagement in the sciences/edited by Wilfred Dolfsma and Stefan Kesting.
pages cm.
1. Economics. 2. Social sciences. 3. Boulding, Kenneth E. (Kenneth Ewart), 1910–1993. I. Dolfsma, Wilfred. II. Kesting, Stefan, 1965–
III. Title.
HB171.B634 2012
330–dc23 2012043170

ISBN: 978-0-415-48347-6 (hbk)
ISBN: 978-0-203-52021-5 (ebk)

Typeset in Times New Roman
by Wearset Ltd, Boldon, Tyne and Wear

Printed and bound in the United States of America by Publishers Graphics, LLC on sustainably sourced paper.

Contents

Figures and tables

Figures

Tables

Contributors

Robert E. Babe is a Professor of Media Studies, University of Western Ontario, London Canada. *Media, Structures, and Power: The Robert E. Babe Collection*, was published by the University of Toronto Press in 2011.

John B. Davis is a Professor of Economics at Marquette University, United States, a Professor of Economics at the University of Amsterdam, Netherlands, and a Fellow of the Tinbergen Institute, Netherlands.

Wilfred Dolfsma, economist and philosopher, is a Professor of Strategy and Innovation at the University of Groningen School of Economics and Business and Corresponding Editor of the *Review of Social Economy.*

John Groenewegen is a Professor of Economics of Infrastructures at the University of Delft, Netherlands.

Keith Hartley is a defence economist and Emeritus Professor of Economics at the University of York and QinetiQ Visiting Fellow. Previously, he was Director of the Centre for Defence Economics at York and founding Editor of the journal *Defence and Peace Economics*. He has been adviser to the UN, European Commission, European Defence Agency, UK Government Departments and to the Parliamentary Defence Committee. He is the author of over 500 publications and reports and his recent books include *The Economics of Defence Policy* (Routledge, 2011) and *Handbook on the Economics of Conflict* (with Derek Braddon, Elgar, 2011). His current research interests include the economic impacts of defence spending, defence exports, collaboration and measuring defence output. He is writing a book on *The Economics of Aerospace Industries* (Elgar, forthcoming).

Stefan Kesting is a Teaching Fellow, head of second year and undergraduate programmes director at the economics division of the Leeds University Business School, UK. He has taught ethics and economics, and various other fields of economics and has written on gender, social, ecological, and institutional economics.

Arjo Klamer is a Professor of Cultural Economics at the Erasmus University. He has taught at various American universities and has written on the rhetoric and culture of economics as well as the economics of culture.

Thomas Marmefelt is an Associate Professor of Economics at the University of Södertörn, Sweden, and Adjunct Professor (Docent) of Economics, especially Evolutionary Economics, at Åbo Akademi University, Finland.

Andrew Mearman is an Associate Professor in Economics and Associate Head of Department for Economics at the Bristol Business School, University of the West of England, Bristol.

Deirdre Nansen McCloskey teaches Economics, History, English, and Communication at the University of Illinois in Chicago. Her latest book is *Bourgeois Dignity: Why Economics Can't Explain the Modern World* (2010).

Roberta Patalano is an Assistant Professor at Parthenope University, Naples. Her research activity is interdisciplinary and focuses on the intersection among economics, cognitive science, and psychoanalysis. Main publications include books and articles on imagination in social contexts, the mental roots of institutions, path dependence, and the process of change, both at individual and group level.

Joseph E. Pluta is a Professor of Economics at St. Edward's University in Austin, Texas. He is the author of 21 books and numerous articles in professional journals including the *Journal of Economic Issues*, *American Journal of Economics and Sociology*, *Southern Economic Journal*, *National Tax Journal*, *Public Finance/Finances Publiques*, *Public Finance Review*, *Development and Change*, and the *International Journal of Social Economics*. He has also published over 70 short stories.

Clive L. Spash is a Professor, Chair of Public Policy and Governance, at the Department of Socio-Economics, WU Vienna University of Economics and Business, Austria. He is an economist who writes, researches, and teaches on public policy with an emphasis on economic and environmental interactions. His main interests are interdisciplinary research on human behaviour, environmental values, and the transformation of the world political economy to a more socially and environmentally just system.

William Waller is a Professor of Economics and Director of Wine Studies at Hobart and William Smith Colleges, Geneva, New York, United States.

Robert C. Waters received his degree of Doctor of Business Administration (Business Economics) from the University of Southern California. He also holds an MBA and a BS in engineering from UCLA. Since 1979, he has been a member of the faculty of the George Washington University, initially as a Professor of Engineering Management, and in 2008 he became a Professor Emeritus. He was on the faculty of the Missouri University of Science and Technology, Rolla, and held management positions at TRW Systems and GE. His interests include history of engineering management, and the management, economics, and culture of technical organizations. He is a Fellow of the American Society of Engineering Management and an Associate Editor of the *Engineering Management Journal*.

Acknowledgements

The editors and publishers would like to thank the following for granting permission to reproduce material in this work:

The Kenneth Boulding Collection, Archives, University of Colorado at Boulder Libraries and the Bentley Historical Library, University of Michigan for permission to reproduce articles, book chapters, and poems by Kenneth E. Boulding.

The Association for Evolutionary Economics (AFEE) for permission to reprint several articles first published in the *Journal of Economic Issues*.

The Association for Social Economics (ASE) for permission to reprint several articles first published in the *Review of Social Economy*.

M.E. SHARPE, INC. and Paul Davidson for permission to reprint an article first published in the *Journal of Post Keynesian Economics*.

Elsevier for permission to reprint an article from *World Development*.

The Perseus Books Group for permission to reprint a chapter from: Babe, Robert E., *Communication and the Transformation of Economics: Essays in Information, Public Policy, and Political Economy, Critical Studies in Communication and in the Cultural Industries* (Boulder and Oxford: Harper Collins, Westview Press, 1995, pp. 159–178).

Edward Elgar, Sylvia Samuels, Steven G. Medema, and A. Allan Schmid for permission to reprint a chapter from: Samuels, Warren J., Medema, Steven G., and Schmid, A. Allan, *The Economy as a Process of Valuation* (Cheltenham, UK and Northampton, MA: Edward Elgar Publishing Ltd, pp. 299–327).

For various reasons, this project has had a rather long gestation process. Thanks to all colleagues who contributed to the book. We are most grateful to Simon Holt of Routledge for his strong interest in this book and his patience in seeing it through to completion, as well as to Joanne Hepworth for technical assistance and Katie Short for copy-editing. We would also like to thank all colleagues who gave us advice along the way. Our special thanks go to the participants at sessions at the ASE World Congress, at the ASSA meetings (in the programme of the Association for the Study of the Grants Economy), and particularly to Ted Tsukahara and Eleanor Brown.

We are also grateful to Auckland University of Technology for financial support and Professor Michel Renault at the University of Rennes for hosting

Stefan Kesting while he was working on the book during a study leave in 2010.

All poems, except the last one on page 23, come from *Beasts, Ballads, and Bouldingism* (Transaction Books, 1980). The last poem can be found in *Sonnets from Later Life 1981–93* (Pendle Hill, 1994).

Part I

Introduction

1 Boulding and interdisciplinary economics

Introduction to the volume

Wilfred Dolfsma and Stefan Kesting

Interdisciplinary social science

One reason for us to choose Kenneth Boulding as a focal point of attention in this volume is that his research and thinking is, in its very nature, one that engages, from a background in economics, with a wide range of disciplines in the social sciences and beyond. There has been much methodological discussion of late about how to conceptualize from a methodological point of view research that engages with other research traditions beyond discipline borders. Scientific disciplines develop along trajectories that have an internal logic, as Thomas Kuhn has argued (Kuhn 1962; Dosi 1982; Dolfsma & Welch 2009), yet may expect novelty and innovation to be instigated when insights from beyond its borders enter (cf. Dolfsma *et al.* 2011). Allowing such insights to intrude, possibly breaching what Thomas Kuhn has called a "protective belt" that actively defends core insights in a discipline from falsification, a process that involves active policing by the community (Gieryn 1999), is not obvious, despite the prodding by funding agencies. A major impetus for funding agencies to promote interdisciplinary research, besides a belief that new insights may thus be stimulated, is that such research is regarded as being more beneficial to society. The view of science as part of society, which this entails, is one that is wholeheartedly supported by Boulding.

Three figures may help to clarify what it can mean and entail for a particular science to relate to other sciences or reach beyond its own boundaries.

Using insights from two (or more) disciplines without actively bringing the two together to explore where they connect and really, substantively, complement each other would be a case of multidisciplinary research, as illustrated in Figure 1.1a. Actively exploring connections and exploiting complementarities, as illustrated in Figure 1.1b, would be characterized as interdisciplinary research. When insights are exchanged between two such science-systems, drawing on systems theory expounded, amongst others, by Luhmann (1995), one would expect that each of these systems will not remain unaltered, but influence each other. Both science a and science b, at least in the perception of the practitioners involved, will develop in a different way afterwards from how they would develop had they not actively been brought to engage with each other. The purview of each science changes as a result in the meantime.

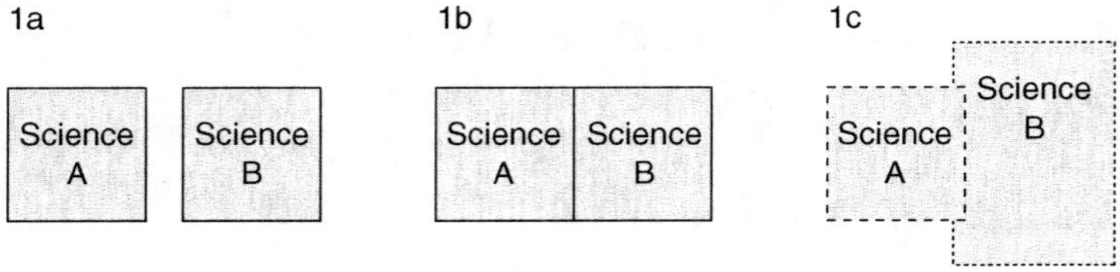

Figure 1.1 *a* Multidisciplinary research; *b* Interdisciplinary research; *c* Transdisciplinary research.

When the might of two separate disciplines is brought to bear, simultaneously, on a theme or domain where an academic issue is addressed, transdisciplinary research happens. Such transdisciplinary research does not hold concepts or approaches sacred just because a protective belt insulates them from scrutiny. Transdisciplinary research would appear to result most likely from research efforts to address a particular real-world problem, rather than from researchers looking around for a problem from the perspective of their discipline (cf. Phelps-Brown 1972). The latter is likely to result in what some call "blackboard economics/science" without regard for real-world problems or phenomena, or in A′–C′ economics (science) (see McCloskey 1994). The latter produces scientific "results" by ever so slightly changing the assumptions (A′) for a new model when compared to a previous model (A), to derive and publish slightly new conclusions (C′).

Transdisciplinary research pragmatically adopts concepts from any of the fields believed to be relevant, discusses the extent to which these are complementary and relevant to the study at hand, and applies these in the context of a particular problem. Concepts and relations between concepts may need to be re-considered as a result, however. Transdisciplinary research will also need to apply Occam's Razor to cut out what should be considered "noise" just as much as single-discipline research—it is not less scientific in this sense, and perhaps more so.

Kenneth Ewart Boulding

Mott authored an outstanding personal and academic biography of Kenneth Boulding soon after his death in 1993 in the *Economic Journal* (Mott 2000). Boulding's personal and academic lives are closely intertwined; his interdisciplinary approach in his scientific endeavors seems very much inspired by his personal experiences and convictions. While this volume primarily is meant to address interdisciplinary research in the social sciences in general and in economics in particular, Boulding is exemplary in what an interdisciplinary approach can lead to.

Kenneth Boulding's research can be characterized as much more than adopting two (or more) otherwise separate disciplines in the social sciences without relating the two or bringing them together. Rather than merely being multidisciplinary, as Figure 1.1a illustrates, Boulding actively aimed to engage different sciences by bringing them together to allow for cross-fertilization. This would seem to hold in particular for economics, sociology, and anthropology under the overarching frameworks of exchange theory and systems theory. In particular his emphasis on communication, one could claim, allows Boulding to bring disciplines to cross into each other's conceptual domains. Boulding did not opt for the easy imperialist approach of taking a given conceptual framework to "apply" it to a set of problems not normally considered by that discipline. Current practitioners in economics, and Gary Becker in particular, have been accused of imperialism of this kind (Swedberg 1990, 1990a). Rather, Boulding has adopted what may be called transdisciplinary research (Figure 1.1c)—his life-long project on the grants economy of love, threat, and exchange might best signify this.

In a way, however, Kenneth Boulding can be seen to have, almost single-handedly, created new fields of study that have grown into disciplines by themselves over the past decades. Most prominently among these are ecological and grants economics as well as peace and conflict studies.

Judged by the criterion of the amount of interdisciplinary research undertaken by an individual researcher, Boulding's research might well be characterized as extraordinarily interdisciplinary. For one, the area of overlap for him is very large. The rugged edges in Figure 1.2 suggest active engagement as well as involvement in the changing nature of boundaries between disciplines and newly emerging disciplines. Boulding has been much more willing and able than others to venture into areas well beyond what economists would normally dare. He has learned from that, no doubt, but has also *taught* many how to start and pursue such an endeavor.

While placing great emphasis on transferring knowledge and transforming it, Boulding has not been afraid of taking academic risks. Single-discipline research is relatively safe, as it will surely deliver novel insights, albeit of a more circumscribed nature. Single-discipline research is likely to be incremental, too. More radical research is, however, risky in itself. It might yield nothing new, and a proportion of the research that Boulding has been engaged in has not produced something to stand the test of time. More radical research may, however, also result in highly valuable insights and entirely novel and rich streams of research. In

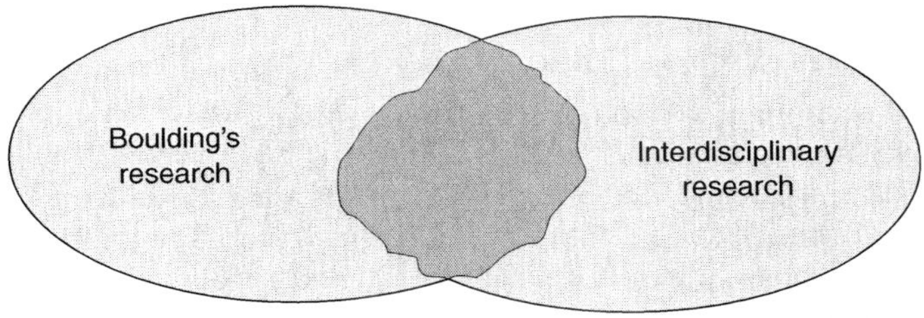

Figure 1.2 Interdisciplinary research by Boulding.

producing such insights and research streams, Boulding can be compared to Nobel Laureates. Maintaining such a research effort does mean that, personally, one must not be discouraged by just any sign of falsification. Fortunately, even the great philosopher of science Karl Popper has hinted that scientists may have to be stubborn at times (Popper 1976). Boulding may well have been stubborn to a degree, which is visible both in his overall goals and in his associative approach to reach those goals. While being stubborn enabled him to be productive, the associative approach has given some the impression of sloppiness. His approach to science, however, fitted with his view of how systems of knowledge develop and how communication occurs. After reviewing the different topics indicative of Boulding's interdisciplinary research, in this Introduction and the sections with chapters to come, an epilogue briefly assesses Boulding's contributions.

Choice of texts, choice of commentaries, and choice of commentators

We have chosen 13 different themes indicative of Boulding's approach to interdisciplinary social science and have included poems and drawings by Boulding for each section. Research straddling the academic disciplines in particular has left a mark long after Boulding actively contributed to it. It may be here, studying conflicts and peace, and the ecology (Kesting 2010), for instance, that he has been most influential. Where he focused on single-discipline research, such as his work on post-Keynesian economics (Canterbery 1994; Harcourt 1983; Wray 1997), his work has been less influential, it would seem. Some of the interdisciplinary research has not had much of an impact, or has had less of an impact than one would have expected. His Grants Economy project may have been too far ahead of its time and could find a more conducive audience ready to be persuaded by its strengths now that behavioral economics is "in the swim". We have thus chosen themes central to his work, characterizing its interdisciplinary nature.

While in most cases the choice for specific texts was quite obvious and will not rattle this volume's audience, other choices have been more difficult to make. Mostly this has been because the themes for which choices were more difficult to make were more central to the work of Boulding. He has thus written more and more extensively on them. Some of these texts will be better known to a wider audience than others, but these may not be the ones that best and most concisely characterize Boulding's work on the theme.

Systems theory is certainly Boulding's predominant framework of analysis. It may even be seen as *the* significant one which unifies and gives direction to all his work. It is therefore not surprising that the key text chosen for the part focusing on systems theory has a lot of similarities with the key text chosen for the part on the unity of social sciences. Because the systems approach was so important for Boulding overall, it surfaces in some of the other chapters of this book, too. We chose to reprint one of his foundational, very early articles on the matter (1956). The text provides a good introduction to his view on systems theory and his hopes of what it could achieve for the progress of science in general and social science in particular. Khalil's article (reprinted from 1996) can be read as a comment for this part because he concentrates on Boulding's *Ecodynamics*, which is a key element of his systems theory and which Khalil carefully distinguishes from evolutionary economics. Joseph Pluta, who has currently written on the topic, kindly agreed to write the comment for this part.

Unfortunately, what appears to be Boulding's direct statement to the topic of the unity of the social sciences in the pages of the journal *Human Organization* is just spontaneous and polite oral comment on Gunnar Myrdal's address to a meeting of the society of applied anthropology in 1975, and covers only one page in print. While three chapters in his book *Economics as a Science* definitely hold a lot of material for this part, it is too broad-ranging to be reprinted in this volume. The best text to represent his views on the relation between economics and other social sciences is, thus, his paper on the relations of economic, political, and social systems (1962a). Boulding's message is that all phenomena can be described as systems, each with different characteristics. This unifies the social and natural sciences in their attempt to analyze their specific subject areas. Social sciences are abstracting from and reducing the complexity of the social system of human history as a whole by breaking it up into manageable subsystems and dealing with each of those separately. The areas of social subsystems identified by Boulding (population, exchange, threat, and learning systems) create overlapping boundaries between disciplines in the social sciences. Moreover, they are not independent and constantly interact with each other. Hence, specialization in the social sciences is at once productive and dangerous. Thomas Marmefelt, an expert in the field, agreed to do the job. An earlier treatment of Boulding's interdisciplinary research focusing on structuralism was produced by Robert Solo (1997).

The presidential address, given at the annual meetings of the American Economic Association, is the definitive contribution by Boulding on morality (1969). It discusses the topic in both directions: the ethos of economics and its ethical critiques, as well as the contribution of economics to the moral sciences. The text touches upon quite a few other schemes in this book and includes some remarks on religion. The excellent commentary articles by Warren Samuels and John Davis thus also take a broad approach.

There are other short contributions by Boulding on ethics. This philosophical area was important for much of his work—this holds for his view of welfare and ecological economics (Kesting 2010), for instance, but also for his power theory. The text on legitimacy (1974) discusses the origin and basis of evaluating something as legitimate. This has a strong link to our moral values, but the text goes beyond the question of norms. Some of the reasons given by Boulding as to why we regard something as legitimate are more psychological, for instance. The three-page article on values (1978) presents a quite broad overview of the role of values in the social sciences and discusses their value base and values as an unavoidable object of study for them. However, it touches only in passing on economics.

Boulding elaborates on the importance of ethics for economics in *Economics as a Moral Science* (1970) and further in his texts on the relevance of legitimacy and value judgments (1974 and 1974a). Going through the history of economic thought, he demonstrates that all great economists of the past needed normative arguments to legitimate their economic theories. In his view, the price system is embedded in normative institutions and therefore based on value judgments. Welfare and social justice have to be seen as dynamic concepts and to be thoroughly founded on ethics.

The fact that Boulding's ethical beliefs were firmly grounded in religion comes through in chapter 15 of his book *Ecodynamics* (1978a), as well as in his text on the ethics of economic organization, written 25 years earlier (1953). It is quite significant for the strong link between religion and ethics in his thinking that a well-known professor of theology (Reinhold Niebuhr) wrote a commentary for Boulding's book on *The Organizational Revolution*.

The text on persuasion (1989), written for John Kenneth Galbraith's festschrift, is clearly Boulding's best and concise one on communicative action, though the theme of persuasion runs through the whole of his life's work. An earlier example is his short text on communication of legitimacy (1974b). With Robert Babe, we have an author who already commented on Boulding's theory of communication in 1995 and now kindly agreed to revisit this topic.

Power and Betterment in the Economy (1995) is more of an outline of Boulding's approach to welfare than an introduction to his power theory. *Power in Society* (1978b) is more suitable for this volume. It provides a good overview of his understanding of power and contains all the important features (threat, economic, integrative power, and the power to change the future, as well as the illusion or uncertainty of power) explored by him in great detail in his last book, *Three Faces of Power* (1990). Paul Streeten's article (1989) offers insights into Boulding's power theory. And Bill Waller provides links to *Three Faces of Power*, as well as an overview of the content of this book.

The 1991 article *What is Evolutionary Economics?* is certainly a proper choice for our volume. It is quite programmatic and one of Boulding's most recent papers on the theme of evolution. In it, he describes his systematic and dynamic view of natural and social (economic) systems. We found particularly his discussion of productivity, which he links to social learning, interesting. The paper links well with the one on culture in this book. Other important theoretical elements explained in the text are positive feedback, evolutionary/historical method, and punctuated equilibrium. Another article (1989a) featuring the aforementioned concept is much less theoretically clear. However, it presents similar arguments to the one chosen for this book, whilst focusing mainly on communalities between social and biological systems. Readers interested in this subject may want to take a look at the recently published collection on *Evolution, Order and Complexity* (2002). With the older comment by Dopfer (1994) and the brand new one written by Waters, we bring to bear two expert voices on Boulding's evolutionary theory.

We chose to print Boulding's 1977 article on American institutional economics in this volume. It is one of two critical accounts of this school by him.

There are twenty years of distance between these two papers, but interestingly his particular attitude towards institutional economics did not change. Both conclude that institutional economists asked the right questions in dissenting from mainstream economics, but did not come up with satisfying answers. Moreover, both articles emphasize and approve of the normative vantage point of institutional economic critique of neoclassical economics. Boulding clearly agrees that institutions and values matter.

Whilst the earlier 1957 article is still very relevant and readable today, two-thirds of it is mostly about what Boulding himself calls a "kind of 'Cook's Tour' of economic dissent" (1957: 8). This is surely of interest for the historian of economic thought because it provides interesting insights into American institutional economics' roots in and interconnections with European movements of economic dissent. It contains some intimate and witty portraits of Veblen, Commons, and Mitchell and a skeptical and quite critical evaluation of their contribution to economic theory, which is, according to Boulding, not much. In this article, he confesses: "In my student days I conceived an almost violent prejudice against institutionalism" (1957: 11), but at the end of the piece he agrees that his research program actually is that of an institutionalist.

The later 1977 article is a much better piece for this volume because it provides more extensive theoretical argument to provoke critical appraisal and comment. With its focus on neoclassical price theory and institutional critique thereof, it seems much more specialized at first glance. However, this focus is pointing directly to the main theoretical difference between the two schools. Boulding praises the analytical value of neoclassical theory in the first part, accusing its institutional critics of going too far in their negative account of it. He saves his critical broad-side to be fired for the second half of the paper. Still, Boulding tries to remain balanced in his account of both schools of thought. Unfortunately, he did not live long enough to write another piece on the topic in 1997. It would have certainly included what he thought of new institutional economics. Since John Groenewegen has just co-authored a textbook on institutional economics (2010), he is the perfect commentator for this part.

Though Boulding wrote extensively on economics as an ecological science (1970a, 1978c, 1981a) and contributed in a number of ways to the foundation of ecological economics, he is mainly known for his metaphor of the *Spaceship Earth* (1966). This is the reason why we reprinted this text as the starting point for rethinking his concepts and influence in the field. However, other texts, such as *Ecological Dynamics* (1978c), provide a much more detailed theoretical insight into his evolutionary concepts. Boulding wrote a comment himself, which is also reprinted here (1993). With Clive Spash, we are glad to have found a commentator who is not only a distinguished ecological economist, but also someone who has further explored precisely the themes and questions once initiated by Boulding.

The slightly older text from the *American Economic Review* (1970b) is mainly about economics as a particular subculture in itself and not on the significance of culture for the functioning of the economy and, thus, for economics as a research area. Building on this one (some similarities are apparent), the later text (1973) contains this perspective of the culture of economics, but also discusses the second aspect of culture as a significant field of research. Therefore, it is the much more relevant and interesting text for our book. Roberta Patalano discusses recent insights to allow for a critical reflection.

The (1981b) book chapter is reprinted here because it provides a concise and yet detailed introduction to Boulding's *Grants Economics*. Other relevant publications on the theme we chose not to include for various reasons. The article for the *Michigan Academician* (1969a) is a bit too concise and does not cover all the intriguing details of the concept. The three other texts, the one for the *American Economic Review* co-authored by Pfaff and Horvath (1972) and the two written ten years later about the pathologies of public grants (1982) and issues of innovation (1982a), discuss the concept itself only briefly and focus more on its practical and political implications and try to address critique. Randy Wray provided a detailed critical account of grants economics in 1994, which is definitely worth reprinting here, and Arjo Klamer kindly agreed to present us with a fresh account for this volume.

The volume covers two topics which seem even more related than others: "conflict" and "peace". However, they are also very specialized research areas of Boulding and actually each warrants a separate chapter in this book. Two of Boulding's texts are reprinted here to allow for proper engagement with his contributions in both related fields. Though the beautifully written article on the role of conflict in the dynamics of society appeared much later (1986) than chapter 15 in his book on the general theory of conflict and defense (1962c), it is rather similar in content to the longer and earlier text, which provides a more detailed and better overview of all the elements of Boulding's theory of conflict and its resolution. Therefore, this book chapter is also reprinted in this volume.

The article on the pure theory of death (1962) is founded on Boulding's systems theory and could provide a very nice introduction to that theme, but the text is of limited relevance today because it is very much a document of the time of the cold war and is written under the imminent threat of a nuclear war. Whilst the article on future directions in conflict and peace studies (1978d) critically reviews the achievements and flaws of the research in this area (too much emphasis on zero sum games and too much influence of ideology), it contains very little of Boulding's own contributions to peace studies. Hence, his text on the role of organized non-violence in achieving stable peace (1990a) found its way into this book. It has not lost any of its relevance today and remains thought-provoking. Keith Hartley, an economist specializing in peace and conflict studies, sheds new light on this area. The field also plays a major role in Anatol Rapoport's earlier account of Boulding's life achievements (1997), reprinted here.

The core text for the section on teaching economics is certainly Boulding's article on the content of textbooks (1988). Since he is dismissing his own textbooks (1950, 1959, 1966a) in this (1988) text, it is probably not worth reprinting parts from these. Nevertheless, there is much of interest in them (Wray 1997;

Figure 1.3 Kenneth E. Boulding.

McFarling 2002). Wray's account of Boulding's macroeconomics as a foundation for teaching is reprinted in this volume. As always, Boulding starts from a systems and evolutionary approach, and views standard textbooks from a dissident's perspective. The 1988 Boulding text is particularly useful for an understanding of his view on teaching economics because he provides an appendix to demonstrate how a dynamic and comparative historical as well as statistical analysis could be used as a teaching tool. In the 1988 article, he criticizes the neglect of dynamics and uncertainty in economics teaching. He also reviews and criticizes flow concepts and the problematic tools of indifference curves, identities, equilibrium, and statistical measures. An additional, short text could have, but has not, been included in this section: "Some Observations on the Learning of Economics" (1975a). It supplements the 1988 article quite nicely, and so does a chapter on appropriate methodologies for the study of the economy (1992). Boulding reflects on teaching methods and points out that stirring up the minds of students or creating what he calls "cognitive dissonance" in an interactive process of learning is of utter importance (see also 1974c). In Andrew Mearman, we found the appropriate commentator to critically review Boulding's recommendations on teaching (heterodox) economics.

The reprinted text on the future of economics (1986a) is clearly Boulding's best on this topic. He argues that economics tends to ignore some of the most important problems of the real world instead of engaging with them. He discusses major pathologies of epistemology. What we particularly like about this article is the turn in his definition of economics—from his earlier one based on "exchange" towards a new one founded on "provisioning". A similar kind of argument can be found in the last chapter (7) of his book *Economics as a Science* (1970c) and chapter 4 of his book *Evolutionary Economics* (1981). Building on her *How to Be Human though An Economist* (2000) and her Bourgeois Virtues project, Deirdre McCloskey comments on this subject.

To show Boulding's artistic side, we selected a poem, often accompanied by a little drawing by him, for each part in this book, taken mostly from a collection published in 1980.

References

Babe, R.E. (1995) "The Communication Theory of Kenneth E. Boulding", in: R.E. Babe, *Communication and the Transformation of Economics: Essays in Information, Public Policy, and Political Economy, Critical Studies in Communication and in the Cultural Industries*, Boulder and Oxford: Harper Collins, Westview Press, pp. 159–178.

Boulding, K.E. (1950) *A Reconstruction of Economics*, New York: Wiley & Sons.

Boulding, K.E. (1953) "Ethics in the Theory of Organization", Ch. 5 in: K.E. Boulding, *The Organizational Revolution: A Study in the Ethics of Economic Organization*, New York: Harper & Brothers, pp. 66–86.

Boulding, K.E. (1956) "General Systems Theory – The Skeleton of Science", *Management Science*, 2(3): 197–208.

Boulding, K.E. (1957) "A New Look at Institutionalism", *American Economic Review*, 47(2): 1–12.

Boulding, K.E. (1959) *Principles of Economic Policy*, London: Staples Press.

Boulding, K.E. (1962) "A Pure Theory of Death: Dilemmas of Defense Policy in a World of Conditional Viability", in: G.W. Baker and L.S. Cottrell (eds.), *Behavioral Science and Civil Defense*, Washington, DC: USGPO, pp. 53–69. Reprinted in: K.E. Boulding, *Beyond Economics – Essays on Society, Religion, and Ethics*, Ann Arbor: The University of Michigan Press, 1962, pp. 113–130.

Boulding, K.E. (1962a) "The Relations of Economic, Political, and Social Systems", *Social and Economic Studies* (Jamaica) (Dec. 1962), 11(4): 351–362. Reprinted as chapter 11 in: K.E. Boulding, *Beyond Economics – Essays on Society, Religion, and Ethics*, Ann Arbor: The University of Michigan Press, 1962, pp. 98–111.

Boulding, K.E. (1962c) "Conflict Resolution and Control", Ch. 15 in: K.E. Boulding, *Conflict and Defense: A General Theory*, Lanham: University Press of America, pp. 305–328.

Boulding, K.E. (1966) "The Economics of the Coming Spaceship Earth", first published in: K.E. Boulding, *Environmental Quality in a Growing Economy*, Baltimore: The Johns Hopkins University Press. Reprinted in: H.E. Daly and K.N. Townsend (eds.), *Valuing the Earth – Economics, Ecology, Ethics*, Cambridge, MA and London: The MIT Press, 1993, pp. 297–309.

Boulding, K.E. (1966a) *Economic Analysis*, latest edition, New York: Harper & Row.

Boulding, K.E. (1969) "Economics as a Moral Science", *The American Economic Review*, 59(1): 1–12, AEA presidential address.

Boulding, K.E. (1969a) "The Grants Economy", *Michigan Academician*, Winter, 1(1&2): 3–11. Reprinted in: K.E. Boulding, *The Collected Papers of Kenneth E. Boulding*, Vol. II, Boulder: Colorado Associated University Press, 1974, pp. 477–485.

Boulding, K.E. (1970) "Economics as a Moral Science", chapter 6 in: K.E. Boulding, *Economics as a Science*, New York: McGraw-Hill, pp. 117–138.

Boulding, K.E. (1970a) "Economics as an Ecological Science", chapter 2 in: K.E. Boulding, *Economics as a Science*, New York: McGraw-Hill, pp. 23–53.

Boulding, K.E. (1970b) "Is Economics Culture-Bound?", *American Economic Review*, 60(2): 402–411.

Boulding, K.E. (1970c) "Economics and the Future of Man", chapter 7 in: K.E. Boulding, *Economics as a Science*, New York: McGraw-Hill, pp. 139–157.

Boulding, K.E, Pfaff, M., and Horvath, J. (1972) "Grants Economics: A Simple Introduction", *American Economist*, 16(1): 19–28.

Boulding, K.E. (1973) "Towards the Development of a Cultural Economics", in: L. Schneider and C. M. Bonjean (eds.), *The Idea of Culture in the Social Sciences*. New York: Cambridge University Press, pp. 47–64.

Boulding, K.E. (1974) "The Legitimacy of Economics", reprinted in: K.E. Boulding, *The Collected Papers of Kenneth E. Boulding*, Vol. II, Boulder: Colorado Associated University Press, pp. 417–425.

Boulding, K.E. (1974a) "The Basis of Value Judgements in Economics", reprinted in: K.E. Boulding, *The Collected Papers of Kenneth E. Boulding*, Vol. II, Boulder: Colorado Associated University Press, pp. 397–414.

Boulding, K.E. (1974b) "The Communication of Legitimacy", in: K.E. Boulding, *The Collected Papers of Kenneth E. Boulding*, Vol. IV, Boulder: Colorado Associated University Press, pp. 239–243.

Boulding, K.E. (1974c) "Introducing Freshmen to the Social System", *American Economic Review*, 64(2): 414–419.

Boulding, K.E. (1975) A one-page comment on a presentation: The Unity of the Social

Sciences by Gunnar Myrdal, Plenary address, 34th Annual Meeting of the Society of Applied Anthropology, The Hague, Netherlands 1975, *Human Organisation*, 34(4): 327–332.

Boulding, K.E. (1975a) "Some Observations on the Learning of Economics", *American Economic Review*, 65(2): 428–430.

Boulding, K.E. (1977) "Prices and Institutions", *Journal of Economic Issues*, 11(4): 809–821.

Boulding, K.E. (1978) "Do the Values of Science Lead to a Science of Value?", *Social Science Quarterly*, 58(4): 548–550.

Boulding, K.E. (1978a) "Evolutionary Dynamics of Religion and Ethics", chapter 15 in: K.E. Boulding, *Ecodynamics – A New Theory of Societal Evolution*, Beverly Hills and London: Sage Publications, pp. 307–322.

Boulding, K.E. (1978b) "Power in Society", chapter 11 in: K.E. Boulding, *Ecodynamics – A New Theory of Societal Evolution*, Beverly Hills and London: Sage Publications, pp. 233–252.

Boulding, K.E. (1978c) "Ecological Dynamics", chapter 4 in: K.E. Boulding, *Ecodynamics – A New Theory of Societal Evolution*, Beverly Hills and London: Sage Publications, pp. 77–98.

Boulding, K.E. (1978d) "Future Directions in Conflict and Peace Studies", *Journal of Conflict Resolution*, 22(2): 342–354.

Boulding, K.E. (1980) *Beasts, Ballads, and Bouldingism*, London: Transaction Books.

Boulding, K.E. (1981) *Evolutionary Economics.* London: Sage, in particular: chapter 1 "The Basic Evolutionary Model", pp. 23–47, and chapter 2 "The Evolutionary Approach to Economic History", pp. 123–146.

Boulding, K.E. (1981a) "The Economics of Energy and Entropy in Evolutionary Perspective", chapter 5 in: K.E. Boulding, *Evolutionary Economics*, London: Sage, pp. 147–168.

Boulding, K.E. (1981b) "The Micro Theory of Grants and Granting Behavior", chapter 2 in: K.E. Boulding, *A Preface to Grants Economics: The Economy of Love and Fear*, New York: Praeger, pp. 15–34.

Boulding, K.E. (1982) "Pathologies of the Public Grants Economy", in: R.C.O. Matthews and G.B. Stafford (eds.), *The Grants Economy and Collective Consumption*, London: Macmillan Press, pp. 3–19, reprinted as chapter 11 in: K.E. Boulding (ed.), *Towards a New Economics: Critical Essays on Ecology, Distribution, and Other Themes*, Hants: Edward Elgar, 1992, pp. 143–157.

Boulding K.E. (1982a) "Innovation and the Grants Economy", in: S.B. Lundstedt and E.W. Colglazier, Jr. (eds.), *Managing Innovation: The Social Dimensions of Creativity Invention and Technology*, New York: Pergamon Press, reprinted as chapter 10 in: K.E. Boulding (ed.), *Towards a New Economics: Critical Essays on Ecology, Distribution, and Other Themes*, Hants: Edward Elgar, 1992, pp. 135–142.

Boulding, K.E. (1986) "The Role of Conflict in the Dynamics of Society", *Current Research on Peace and Violence*, 9(3): 98–102, reprinted in: K.E. Boulding (ed.), *Towards a New Economics: Critical Essays on Ecology, Distribution, and Other Themes*, Hants: Edward Elgar, 1992, pp. 190–197.

Boulding, K.E. (1986a) "What Went Wrong with Economics?", *American Economist*, Spring, 30: 5–12.

Boulding, K.E. (1988) "What Do We Want in an Economics Textbook?", *Journal of Economic Education*, 19(2): 113–132.

Boulding, K.E. (1989) "The Pathologies of Persuasion", in: S. Bowles, R. Edwards, and

W.G. Shepherd (eds.) *Unconventional Wisdom – Essays in Honor of John Kenneth Galbraith*, Boston: Houghton Mifflin Company, pp. 3–19.

Boulding, K.E. (1989a) "Punctiationalism in Societal Evolution", *Journal of Social and Biological Structures*, 12: 213–223.

Boulding, K.E. (1990) *Three Faces of Power*, Newbury Park, CA: Sage Publications.

Boulding, K.E. (1990a) "The Role of Organized Non-violence in Achieving Stable Peace", in: V.K. Kool (ed.), *Perspectives on Nonviolence*, Springer-Verlag: New York, pp. 3–13, reprinted as chapter 17 in: K.E. Boulding (ed.), *Towards a New Economics: Critical Essays on Ecology, Distribution, and Other Themes*, Hants: Edward Elgar, 1992, pp. 225–235.

Boulding, K.E. (1991) "What is Evolutionary Economics?", *Evolutionary Economics*, 1: 9–17.

Boulding, K. E. (1992) "Appropriate Methodologies for the Study of the Economy", chapter 7 in: K.E. Boulding (ed.), *Towards a New Economics: Critical Essays on Ecology, Distribution, and Other Themes*, Hants: Edward Elgar, pp. 98–112.

Boulding, K.E. (1993) "Spaceship Earth Revisited", in: H.E. Daly and K.N. Townsend (eds.), *Valuing the Earth – Economics, Ecology, Ethics*, Cambridge MA and London: The MIT Press, pp. 311–314.

Boulding, K.E. (1995) "Power and Betterment in the Economy", in: E. Boulding and K.E. Boulding (ed.), *The Future: Images and Processes*, Thousand Oaks, CA: Sage, pp. 57–75.

Boulding, K.E. (2002) *Evolution, Order and Complexity*, London and New York: Routledge.

Canterbery, E.R. (1994) "Boulding's T, Kaleckian Power, and Minsky's Fragility Hypothesis", *Journal of Economic Issues*, 28(4): 1227–1247.

Dolfsma, W. and Welch, P. (2009) "Paradigms and Novelty in Economics: The History of Economic Thought as a Source of Enlightenment", *American Journal of Economics and Sociology*, 68(5): 1085–1106.

Dolfsma, W., McMaster, R., and Finch, J. (2011) "Identifying Institutional Vulnerability: The Importance of Language, and System Boundaries", *Journal of Economic Issues*, 40(4): 805–818.

Dopfer, K. (1994) "Kenneth Boulding: A Founder of Evolutionary Economics", *Journal of Economic Issues*, 28(4): 1201–1204.

Dosi, G. (1982) "Technological Paradigms and Technological Trajectories: A Suggested Interpretation of the Determinants and Directions of Technical Change", *Research Policy*, 11(3): 147–162.

Gieryn, T.F. (1999) *Cultural Boundaries of Science: Credibility on the Line*, Chicago: University of Chicago Press.

Groenewegen, J., Spithoven, A., and Van den Berg, A. (2010) *Institutional Economics*, New York: Palgrave Macmillan.

Harcourt, G.C. (1983) "A Man of All Systems: Talking with Kenneth Boulding", *Journal of Post Keynesian Economics*, 6(1): 143–154.

Kesting, S. (2010) "Boulding's Welfare Approach of Communicative Deliberation", *Ecological Economics*, 69(5): 973–977.

Khalil, E.L. (1996) "Kenneth Boulding: Ecodynamist or Evolutionary Economist?", *Journal of Post Keynesian Economics*, 19(1): 83–100.

Kuhn, T.S. (1962) *The Structure of Scientific Revolutions*, Chicago: University of Chicago Press.

Luhmann, N. (1995) *Social Systems*, Stanford: Stanford University Press.

McCloskey, D.N. (1994) *Knowledge and Persuasion in Economics*, Cambridge: Cambridge University Press.

McCloskey, D.N. (2000) *How to Be Human Though an Economist*, Ann Arbor: The University of Michigan Press.

McFarling, B.R. (2002) "A Post Keynesian Appreciation of 'A Reconstruction of Economics'", *Journal of Post Keynesian Economics*, Summer, Vol. 24(4): 643–656.

Mott, T. (2000) "Kenneth Boulding, 1910–1993", *Economic Journal*, 110, June: F430–444.

Phelps-Brown, E.H. (1972) "The Underdevelopment of Economics", *Economic Journal*, 82(325): 1–10.

Popper, K. (1976 [1970]) "Normal Science and its Dangers", in: I. Lakatos and A. Musgrave (eds.), *Criticism and the Growth of Knowledge*, London: Cambridge University Press, pp. 51–58.

Rapoport, A. (1997) "Memories of Kenneth E. Boulding", *Review of Social Economy*, 55(4): 416–431.

Solo, R.A (1997) "Boulding among the Structuralists", *Review of Social Economy*, Winter, 55(4): 432–444.

Streeten, P. (1989) "Global Institutions for an Interdependent World", *World Development*, 17(9): 1349–59.

Swedberg, R. (1990) "The New 'Battle of Methods'", *Challenge*, 33(1): 33–38.

Swedberg, R. (1990a) "Socioeconomics and the New 'Battle of the Methods': Towards a Paradigm Shift", *Journal of Behavioral Economics*, 19(2): 141–154.

Wray, L.R. (1994) "Kenneth Boulding's Grants Economics", *Journal of Economic Issues*, December, 28(4): 1205–1225.

Wray, L.R. (1997) "Kenneth Boulding's Reconstruction of Macroeconomics", *Review of Social Economy*, Winter, 55(4): 445–463.

Poem

Homo Genius

The Homo Genius is so bright
He keeps himself awake at night,
But finds, before his life is done,
Two heads are not as good as one.

Part II

Systems theory

2 Key text: General systems theory

The skeleton of science[1]

Kenneth E. Boulding

General systems theory[2] is a name which has come into use to describe a level of theoretical model-building which lies somewhere between the highly generalized constructions of pure mathematics and the specific theories of the specialized disciplines. Mathematics attempts to organize highly general relationships into a coherent system, a system however which does not have any necessary connections with the "real" world around us. It studies all thinkable relationships abstracted from any concrete situation or body of empirical knowledge. It is not even confined to "quantitative" relationships narrowly defined—indeed, the development of a mathematics of quality and structure is already on the way, even though it is not as far advanced as the "classical" mathematics of quantity and number. Nevertheless, because in a sense mathematics contains all theories, it contains none; it is the language of theory, but it does not give us the content. At the other extreme, we have the separate disciplines and sciences, with their separate bodies of theory. Each discipline corresponds to a certain segment of the empirical world, and each develops theories which have particular applicability to its own empirical segment. Physics, chemistry, biology, psychology, sociology, economics, and so on, all carve out for themselves certain elements of the experience of man and develop theories and patterns of activity (research) which yield satisfaction in understanding, and which are appropriate to their special segments.

In recent years, increasing need has been felt for a body of systematic theoretical constructs which will discuss the general relationships of the empirical world. This is the quest of general systems theory. It does not seek, of course, to establish a single, self-contained "general theory of practically everything" which will replace all the special theories of particular disciplines. Such a theory would be almost without content, for we always pay for generality by sacrificing content, and all we can say about practically everything is almost nothing. Somewhere however between the specific that has no meaning and the general that has no content there must be, for each purpose and at each level of abstraction, an optimum degree of generality. It is the contention of the general systems theorists that this optimum degree of generality in theory is not always reached by the particular sciences. The objectives of general systems theory then can be set out with varying degrees of ambition and confidence. At a low level of ambition but with a high degree of confidence, it aims to point out similarities in the theoretical constructions of different disciplines, where these exist, and to develop theoretical models having applicability to at least two different fields of study. At a higher level of ambition, but with perhaps a lower degree of confidence, it hopes to develop something like a "spectrum" of theories—a system of systems which may perform the function of a "gestalt" in theoretical construction. Such "gestalts" in special fields have been of great value in directing research towards the gaps which they reveal. Thus the periodic table of elements in chemistry directed research for many decades towards the discovery of unknown elements to fill gaps in the table until the table was completely filled. Similarly a "system of systems" might be of value in directing the attention of theorists towards gaps in theoretical models, and might even be of value in pointing towards methods of filling them.

The need for general systems theory is accentuated by the present sociological situation in science. Knowledge is not something which exists and grows in the abstract. It is a function of human organisms and of social organization. Knowledge, that is to say, is always what somebody knows: the most perfect transcript of knowledge in writing is not knowledge if nobody knows it. Knowledge, however, grows by the receipt of meaningful information—that is, by the intake of messages by a knower which are capable of reorganizing his knowledge. We will quietly duck the question as to what reorganizations constitute "growth" of knowledge by defining "semantic growth" of knowledge as those reorganizations which can profitably be talked about, in writing or speech, by the Right People. Science, that is to say, is what can be talked about profitably by scientists in their role as scientists. The crisis of science today arises because of the increasing difficulty of such profitable talk among scientists as a whole. Specialization has outrun Trade, communication between the disciplines becomes increasingly difficult, and the Republic of Learning is breaking up into isolated subcultures with only tenuous lines of communication between them—a situation which threatens intellectual civil war. The reason for this breakup in the body of knowledge is that in the course of specialization the receptors of information themselves become specialized. Hence physicists only talk to physicists, economists to economists—worse still, nuclear physicists only talk to nuclear physicists and econometricians to econometricians. One wonders sometimes if science will not grind to a stop in an assemblage of walled-in hermits, each mumbling to himself words in a private language that only he can understand. In these days the arts may have beaten the sciences to this desert of mutual unintelligibility, but that may be merely because the swift intuitions of art reach the future faster than the plodding leg work of the scientist. The more science breaks into sub-groups, and the less communication is possible among the disciplines, however, the greater chance there is that the total growth of knowledge is being slowed down by the loss of relevant communications. The spread of specialized deafness means that someone who ought to know something that someone else knows is not able to find it out for lack of generalized ears.

It is one of the main objectives of general systems theory to develop these generalized ears, and by developing a framework of general theory to enable one specialist to catch relevant communications from others. Thus the economist who realizes the strong formal similarity between utility theory in economics and field theory in physics[3] is probably in a better position to learn from the physicists than one who does not. Similarly a specialist who works with the growth concept—whether the crystallographer, the virologist, the cytologist, the physiologist, the psychologist, the sociologist, or the economist—will be more sensitive to the contributions of other fields if he is aware of the many similarities of the growth process in widely different empirical fields.

There is not much doubt about the demand for general systems theory under one brand name or another. It is a little more embarrassing to inquire into the supply. Does any of it exist, and if so where? What is the chance of getting more of it and, if so, how? The situation might be described as promising and in ferment, though it is not wholly clear what is being promised or brewed. Something which might be called an "interdisciplinary movement" has been abroad for some time. The first signs of this are usually the development of hybrid disciplines. Thus physical chemistry emerged in the third quarter of the nineteenth century, social psychology in the second quarter of the twentieth. In the physical and biological sciences, the list of hybrid disciplines is now quite long—biophysics, biochemistry, and astrophysics are all well established. In the social sciences, social anthropology is fairly well established; economic psychology and economic sociology are just beginning. There are signs, even, that Political Economy, which died in infancy some hundred years ago, may have a rebirth.

In recent years, there has been an additional development of great interest in the form of "multisexual" interdisciplines. The hybrid disciplines, as their hyphenated names indicate, come from two respectable and honest academic parents. The newer interdisciplines have a much more varied and occasionally even obscure ancestry, and result from the reorganization of material from many different fields of study. Cybernetics, for instance, comes out of electrical engineering, neurophysiology, physics, and biology, with even a dash of economics. Information theory, which originated in communications engineering, has important applications in many fields stretching from biology to the social sciences. Organization theory comes out of economics, sociology, engineering, and physiology, and management science itself is an equally multidisciplinary product.

On the more empirical and practical side, the interdisciplinary movement is reflected in the development of interdepartmental institutes of many kinds. Some of these find their basis of unity in the empirical field which they study, such as institutes of industrial relations, of public administration, of international affairs, and so on. Others are organized around the application of a common methodology to many different fields and problems, such as the Survey Research Center and the Group Dynamics Center at the University of Michigan. Even more important than these visible developments, perhaps, though harder to perceive and identify, is a growing dissatisfaction in many departments, especially at the level of graduate study, with the existing traditional theoretical backgrounds for the empirical studies which form the major part of the output of Ph.D. theses. To take but a single example from the field with which I am most familiar. It is traditional for studies of labor relations, money and banking, and foreign investment to come out of departments of economics. Many of the needed theoretical models and frameworks in these fields, however, do not come out of "economic theory" as this is usually taught, but from sociology, social psychology, and cultural anthropology. Students in the department of economics, however, rarely get a chance to become acquainted with these theoretical models, which may be relevant to their studies, and they become impatient with economic theory, much of which may not be relevant.

It is clear that there is a good deal of interdisciplinary excitement abroad. If this excitement is to be productive, however, it must operate within a certain framework of coherence. It is all too easy for the interdisciplinary to degenerate into the undisciplined. If the interdisciplinary movement, therefore, is not to lose that sense of form and structure which is the "discipline" involved in the various separate disciplines, it should develop a structure of its own. This I conceive to be the great task of general systems theory. For the rest of this paper, therefore, I propose to look at some possible ways in which general systems theory might be structured.

Two possible approaches to the organization of general systems theory suggest themselves, which are to be thought of as complementary rather than competitive, or at least as two roads, each of which is worth exploring. The first approach is to look over the empirical universe and to pick out certain general phenomena which are found in many different disciplines, and to seek to build up general theoretical models relevant to these phenomena. The second approach is to arrange the empirical fields in a hierarchy of complexity of organization of their basic "individual" or unit of behavior, and to try to develop a level of abstraction appropriate to each.

Some examples of the first approach will serve to clarify it, without pretending to be exhaustive. In almost all disciplines, for instance, we find examples of populations—aggregates of individuals conforming to a common definition, to which individuals are added (born) and subtracted (die) and in which the age of the individual is a relevant and identifiable variable. These populations exhibit dynamic movements of their own, which can frequently be described by fairly simple systems of difference equations. The populations of different species also exhibit dynamic interactions among themselves, as in the theory of Volterra. Models of population change and interaction cut across a great many different fields—ecological systems in biology, capital theory in economics, which deals with populations of "goods," social ecology, and even certain problems of statistical mechanics. In all these fields, population change, both in absolute numbers and in structure, can be discussed in terms of birth and survival functions relating numbers of births and of deaths in specific age groups to various aspects of the system. In all these fields, the interaction of population can be discussed in terms of competitive, complementary, or parasitic relationships among populations of different species, whether the species consist of animals, commodities, social classes, or molecules.

Another phenomenon of almost universal significance for all disciplines is that of the interaction of an "individual" of some kind with its environment. Every discipline studies some kind of "individual"—electron, atom, molecule, crystal, virus, cell, plant, animal, man, family, tribe, state, church, firm, corporation, university, and so on. Each of these individuals exhibits "behavior," action, or change, and this behavior is considered to be related in some way to the environment of the individual—that is, with other individuals with which it comes into contact or into some relationship. Each individual is thought of as consisting of a structure or complex of individuals of the order immediately below it—atoms are an arrangement of protons and electrons; molecules of atoms; cells of molecules; plants, animals, and men of cells; social organizations of men. The "behavior" of each individual is "explained" by the structure and arrangement of the lower individuals of which it is composed, or by certain principles of equilibrium or homeostasis according to which certain "states" of the individual are "preferred." Behavior is described in terms of the restoration of these preferred states when they are disturbed by changes in the environment.

Another phenomenon of universal significance is growth. Growth theory is, in a sense, a subdivision of the theory of individual "behavior," growth being one important aspect of behavior. Nevertheless there are important differences between equilibrium theory and growth theory, which perhaps warrant giving growth theory a special category. There is hardly a science in which the growth phenomenon does not have some importance, and though there is a great difference in complexity between the growth of crystals, embryos, and societies, many of the principles and concepts which are important at the lower levels are also illuminating at higher levels. Some growth phenomena can be dealt with in terms of relatively simple population models, the solution of which yields growth curves of single variables. At the more complex levels, structural problems become dominant and the complex interrelationships between growth and form are the focus of interest. All growth phenomena are sufficiently alike however to suggest that a general theory of growth is by no means an impossibility.[4]

Another aspect of the theory of the individual and also of interrelationships among individuals which might be singled out for special treatment is the theory of information and communication. The information concept as developed by Shannon has had interesting applications outside its original field of electrical engineering. It is not adequate, of course, to deal with problems involving the semantic level of communication. At the biological level, however, the information concept may serve to develop general notions of structuredness and abstract measures of organization which give us, as it were, a third basic dimension beyond mass and energy. Communication and information processes are found in a wide variety of empirical situations, and are unquestionably essential in the development of organization, both in the biological and in the social world.

These various approaches to general systems through various aspects of the empirical world may lead ultimately to something like a general field theory of the dynamics of action and interaction. This, however, is a long way ahead.

A second possible approach to general systems theory is through the arrangement of theoretical systems and constructs in a hierarchy of complexity, roughly corresponding to the complexity of the "individuals" of the various empirical fields. This approach is more systematic than the first, leading towards a "system of systems." It may not replace the first entirely, however, as there may always be important theoretical concepts and constructs lying outside the systematic framework. I suggest below a possible arrangement of "levels" of theoretical discourse.

(i) The first level is that of the static structure. It might be called the level of frameworks. This is the geography and anatomy of the universe—the patterns of electrons around a nucleus, the pattern of atoms in a molecular formula, the arrangement of atoms in a crystal, the anatomy of the gene, the cell, the plant, the animal, the mapping of the earth, the solar system, the astronomical universe. The accurate description of these frameworks is the beginning of organized theoretical knowledge in almost any field, for without accuracy in this description of static relationships, no accurate functional or dynamic theory is possible. Thus the Copernican revolution was really the discovery of a new static framework for the solar system which permitted a simpler description of its dynamics.

(ii) The next level of systematic analysis is that of the simple dynamic system with predetermined, necessary motions. This might be called the level of clockworks. The solar system itself is of course the great clock of the universe from man's point of view, and the deliciously exact predictions of the astronomers are a testimony to the excellence of the clock which they study. Simple machines such as the lever and the pulley, even quite complicated machines like steam engines and dynamos, fall mostly under this category. The greater part of the theoretical structure of physics, chemistry, and even of economics falls into this category. Two special cases might be noted. Simple equilibrium systems really fall into the dynamic category, as every equilibrium system must be considered as a limiting case of a dynamic system, and its stability cannot be determined except from the properties of its parent dynamic system. Stochastic dynamic systems leading to equilibria, for all their complexity, also fall into this group of systems; such is the modern view of the atom and even of the molecule, each position or part of the system being given with a certain degree of probability, the whole nevertheless exhibiting a determinate structure. Two types of analytical method are important here, which we may call, with the usage of the economists, comparative statics and true dynamics. In comparative statics, we compare two equilibrium positions of the system under different values for the basic parameters. These equilibrium positions are usually expressed as the solution of a set of simultaneous equations. The method of comparative statics is to compare the solutions when the parameters of the equations are changed. Most simple mechanical problems are solved in this way. In true dynamics, on the other hand, we exhibit the system as a set of difference or differential equations, which are then solved in the form of an explicit function of each variable with time. Such a system may reach a position of stationary equilibrium, or it may not—there are plenty of examples of explosive dynamic systems, a very simple one being the growth of a sum at compound interest! Most physical and chemical reactions and most social systems do in fact exhibit a tendency to equilibrium—otherwise the world would have exploded or imploded long ago.

(iii) The next level is that of the control mechanism or cybernetic system, which might be nicknamed the level of the thermostat. This differs from the simple stable equilibrium system mainly in the fact that the transmission and interpretation of information is an essential part of the system. As a result of this, the equilibrium position is not merely determined by the equations of the system, but the system will move to the maintenance of any given equilibrium, within limits. Thus the thermostat will maintain any temperature at which it can be set; the equilibrium temperature of the system is not determined solely by its equations. The trick here of course is that the essential variable of the dynamic system is the difference between an "observed" or "recorded" value of the maintained variable and its "ideal" value. If this difference is not zero, the system moves so as to diminish it; thus the furnace sends up heat when the temperature is recorded as "too cold" and is turned off when the recorded temperature is "too hot." The homeostasis model, which is of such importance in physiology, is an example of a cybernetic mechanism, and such mechanisms exist through the whole empirical world of the biologist and the social scientist.

(iv) The fourth level is that of the "open system," or self-maintaining structure. This is the level at which life begins to differentiate itself from not-life: it might be called the level of the cell. Something like an open system exists, of course, even in physico-chemical equilibrium systems; atomic structures maintain themselves in the midst of a throughput of electrons, molecular structures maintain themselves in the midst of a throughput of atoms. Flames and rivers likewise are essentially open systems of a very simple kind. As we pass up the scale of complexity of organization towards living systems, however, the property of self-maintenance of structure in the midst of a throughput of material becomes of dominant importance. An atom or a molecule can presumably exist without throughput: the existence of even the simplest living organism is inconceivable without ingestion, excretion, and metabolic exchange. Closely connected with the property of self-maintenance is the property of self-reproduction. It may be, indeed, that self-reproduction is a more primitive or "lower level" system than the open system, and that the gene and the virus, for instance, may be able to reproduce themselves without being open systems. It is not perhaps an important question at what point in the scale of increasing complexity "life" begins. What is clear, however, is that by the time we have got to systems which both reproduce themselves and maintain themselves in the midst of a throughput of material and energy, we have something to which it would be hard to deny the title of "life."

(v) The fifth level might be called the genetic-societal level; it is typified by the plant, and it dominates the empirical world of the botanist. The outstanding characteristics of these systems are, first, a division of labor among cells to form a cell-society with differentiated and mutually dependent parts (roots, leaves, seeds, etc.) and, second, a sharp differentiation between the genotype and the phenotype, associated with the phenomenon of equifinal or "blueprinted" growth. At this level, there are no highly specialized sense organs and information receptors are diffuse and incapable of much throughput of information—it is doubtful whether a tree can distinguish much more than light from dark, long days from short days, cold from hot.

(vi) As we move upward from the plant world towards the animal kingdom, we gradually pass over into a new level, the "animal" level, characterized by increased mobility, teleological behavior, and self-awareness. Here we have the development of specialized information-receptors (eyes, ears, etc.) leading to an enormous increase in the intake of information; we have also a great development of nervous systems, leading ultimately to the brain, as an organizer of the information intake into a knowledge structure or "image." Increasingly as we ascend the scale of animal life, behavior is the response not to a specific stimulus but to an "image" or knowledge structure or view of the environment as a whole. This image is of course determined ultimately by information received into the organism; the relation between the receipt of information and the building up of an image, however, is exceedingly complex. It is not a simple piling up or accumulation of information received, although this frequently happens, but a structuring of information into something essentially different from the information itself. After the image structure is well established, most information received produces very little change in the image—it goes through the loose structure, as it were, without hitting it, much as a sub-atomic particle might go through an atom without hitting anything. Sometimes, however, the information is "captured" by the image and added to it, and sometimes the information hits some kind of a "nucleus" of the image and a reorganization takes place, with far reaching and radical changes in behavior in apparent response to what seems like a very small stimulus. The difficulties in the prediction of the behavior of these systems arise largely because of this intervention of the image between the stimulus and the response.

(vii) The next level is the "human" level, that is, of the individual human being considered as a system. In addition to all, or nearly all, of the characteristics of animal systems, man possesses self-consciousness, which is something different from mere awareness. His image, besides being much more complex than that even of the higher animals, has a self-reflexive quality—he not only knows, but knows that he knows. This property is probably bound up with the phenomenon of language and symbolism. It is the capacity for speech—the ability to produce, absorb, and interpret symbols, as opposed to mere signs, like the warning cry of an animal—which most clearly marks man off from his humbler brethren. Man is distinguished from the animals also by a much more elaborate image of time and relationship; man is probably the only organization that knows that it dies, that contemplates in its behavior a whole life span, and more than a life span. Man exists not only in time and space but in history, and his behavior is profoundly affected by his view of the time process in which he stands.

(viii) Because of the vital importance for the individual man of symbolic images and behavior based on them, it is not easy to separate clearly the level of the individual human organism from the next level, that of social organizations. In spite of the occasional stories of feral children raised by animals, man isolated from his fellows is practically unknown. So essential is the symbolic image in human behavior that one suspects that a truly isolated man would not be "human" in the usually accepted sense, though he would be potentially human. Nevertheless, it is convenient for some purposes to distinguish the individual human as a system from the social systems which surround him, and in this sense social organizations may be said to constitute another level of organization. The unit of such systems is not perhaps the person—the individual human as such—but the "role"—that part of the person which is concerned with the organization or situation in question, and it is tempting to define social organizations, or almost any social system, as a set of roles tied together with channels of communication. The interrelations of the role and the person, however, can never be completely neglected—a square person in a round role may become a little rounder, but he also makes the role squarer, and the perception of a role is affected by the personalities of those who have occupied it in the past. At this level, we must concern ourselves with the content and meaning of messages, the nature and dimensions of value systems, the transcription of images into a historical record, the subtle symbolizations of art, music, and poetry, and the complex gamut of human emotion. The empirical universe here is human life and society in all its complexity and richness.

(ix) To complete the structure of systems, we should add a final turret for transcendental systems, even if we may be accused at this point of having built Babel to the clouds. There are, however, the ultimates and absolutes and the inescapable unknowables, and they also exhibit systematic structure and relationship. It will be a sad day for man when nobody is allowed to ask questions that do not have any answers.

One advantage of exhibiting a hierarchy of systems in this way is that it gives us some idea of the present gaps in both theoretical and empirical knowledge. Adequate theoretical models extend up to about the fourth level, and not much beyond. Empirical knowledge is deficient at practically all levels. Thus, at the level of the static structure, fairly adequate descriptive models are available for geography, chemistry, geology, anatomy, and descriptive social science. Even at this simplest level, however, the problem of the adequate description of complex structures is still far from solved. The theory of indexing and cataloging, for instance, is only in its infancy. Librarians are fairly good at cataloguing books, chemists have begun to catalogue structural formulae, and anthropologists have begun to catalogue culture trails. The cataloguing of events, ideas, theories, statistics, and empirical data has hardly begun. The very multiplication of records, however, as time goes on will force us into much more adequate cataloguing and reference systems than we now have. This is perhaps the major unsolved theoretical problem at the level of the static structure. In the empirical field, there are still great areas where static structures are very imperfectly known, although knowledge is advancing rapidly, thanks to new probing devices, such as the electron microscope. The anatomy of that part of the empirical world which lies between the large molecule and the cell, however, is still obscure at many points. It is precisely this area, however—which includes, for instance, the gene and the virus—that holds the secret of life, and until its anatomy is made clear, the nature of the functional systems which are involved will inevitably be obscure.

The level of the "clockwork" is the level of "classical" natural science, especially physics and astronomy, and is probably the most completely developed level in the present state of knowledge, especially if we extend the concept to include the field theory and stochastic models of modern physics. Even here, however, there are important gaps, especially at the higher empirical levels. There is much yet to be known about the sheer mechanics of cells and nervous systems, of brains, and of societies.

Beyond the second level, adequate theoretical models get scarcer. The last few years have seen great developments at the third and fourth levels. The theory of control mechanisms ("thermostats") has established itself as the new discipline or cybernetics, and the theory of self-maintaining systems or "open systems" likewise has made rapid strides. We could hardly maintain, however, that much more than a beginning has been made in these fields. We know very little about the cybernetics of genes and genetic systems, for instance, and still less about the control mechanisms involved in the mental and social world. Similarly the processes of self-maintenance remain essentially mysterious at many points, and although the theoretical possibility of constructing a self-maintaining machine which would be a true open system has been suggested, we seem to be a long way from the actual construction of such a mechanical similitude of life.

Beyond the fourth level, it may be doubted whether we have as yet even the rudiments of theoretical systems. The intricate machinery of growth by which the genetic complex organizes the matter around it is almost a complete mystery. Up to now, whatever the future may hold, only God can make a tree. In the face of living systems, we are almost helpless; we can occasionally cooperate with systems which we do not understand: we cannot even begin to reproduce them. The ambiguous status of medicine, hovering as it does uneasily between magic and science, is a testimony to the state of systematic knowledge in this area. As we move up the scale, the absence of the appropriate theoretical systems becomes ever more noticeable. We can hardly conceive ourselves constructing a system which would be in any recognizable sense "aware," much less self-conscious. Nevertheless, as we move towards the human and societal level, a curious thing happens: the fact that we have, as it were, an inside track, and that we ourselves are the systems which we are studying, enables us to utilize systems which we do not really understand. It is almost inconceivable that we should make a machine that would make a poem: nevertheless, poems are made by fools like us by processes which are largely hidden from us. The kind of knowledge and skill that we have at the symbolic level is very different from that which we have at lower levels—it is like, shall we say, the "knowhow" of the gene as compared with the knowhow of the biologist. Nevertheless, it is a real kind of knowledge and it is the source of the creative achievements of man as artist, writer, architect, and composer.

Perhaps one of the most valuable uses of the above scheme is to prevent us from accepting as final a level of theoretical analysis which is below the level of the empirical world which we are investigating. Because, in a sense, each level incorporates all those below it, much valuable information and insights can be obtained by applying low-level systems to high-level subject matter. Thus most of the theoretical schemes of the social sciences are still at level (ii), just rising now to (iii), although the subject matter clearly involves level (viii). Economics, for instance, is still largely a "mechanics of utility and self interest," in Jevons' masterly phrase. Its theoretical and mathematical base is drawn largely from the level of simple equilibrium theory and dynamic mechanisms. It has hardly begun to use concepts such as information which are appropriate at level (iii), and makes no use of higher-level systems. Furthermore, with this crude apparatus, it has achieved a modicum of success, in the sense that anybody trying to manipulate an economic system is almost certain to be better off if he knows some economics than if he does not. Nevertheless, at some point progress in economics is going to depend on its ability to break out of these low-level systems, useful as they are as first approximations, and utilize systems which are more directly appropriate to its universe—when, of course, these systems are discovered. Many other examples could be given—the wholly inappropriate use in psychoanalytic theory, for instance, of the concept of energy, and the long inability of psychology to break loose from a sterile stimulus–response model.

Finally, the above scheme might serve as a mild word of warning even to management science. This new discipline represents an important breakaway from overly simple mechanical models in the theory of organization and control. Its emphasis on communication systems and organizational structure, on principles of homeostasis and growth, on decision processes under uncertainty, is carrying us far beyond the simple models of maximizing behavior of even ten years ago. This advance in the level of theoretical analysis is bound to lead to more powerful and fruitful systems. Nevertheless, we must never quite forget that even these advances do not carry us much beyond the third and fourth levels, and that in dealing with human personalities and organizations we are dealing with systems in the empirical world far beyond our ability to formulate. We should not be wholly surprised, therefore, if our simpler systems, for all their importance and validity, occasionally let us down.

I chose the subtitle of my paper with some eye to its possible overtones of meaning. General systems theory is the skeleton of science in the sense that it aims to provide a framework or structure of systems on which to hang the flesh and blood of particular disciplines and particular subject matters in an orderly and coherent corpus of knowledge. It is also, however, something of a skeleton in a cupboard—the cupboard in this case being the unwillingness of science to admit the very low level of its successes in systematization, and its tendency to shut the door on problems and subject matters which do not fit easily into simple mechanical schemes. Science, for all its successes, still has a very long way to go. General systems theory may at times be an embarrassment in pointing out how very far we still have to go, and in deflating excessive philosophical claims for overly simple systems. It also may be helpful, however, in pointing out to some extent where we have to go. The skeleton must come out of the cupboard before its dry bones can live.

Notes

1 This article was previously published in *Management Science*, 1956, Vol. 2(3), pp. 197–208.

2 The name and many of the ideas are to be credited to L. von Bertalanffy, who is not, however, to be held accountable for the ideas of the present author! For a general discussion of Bertalanffy's ideas, see *General System Theory: A New Approach to Unity of Science, Human Biology*, Dec. 1951, Vol. 23, pp. 303–361.

3 See A.G. Pikler, "Utility Theories in Field Physics and Mathematical Economics," *British Journal for the Philosophy of Science*, 1955, Vol. 5, pp. 47 and 303.

4 See "Towards a General Theory of Growth" by K.E. Boulding, *Canadian Journal of Economics and Political Science*, 19 Aug. 1953, pp. 326–340.

2a Commentary article: Kenneth Boulding

Ecodynamicist or evolutionary economist?[1]

Elias L. Khalil[2]

Kenneth Boulding had no trouble crossing the divides separating evolutionary biology, ecology, Keynesian economics, conflict studies, socioeconomics, and environmental economics. He was consumed by a love of knowledge and a passion for constructing a general theory of human behavior and social systems. This paper focuses only on the relevance of his employment of ecological principles to the understanding of socioeconomic dynamics. This should be relevant to economists who have recently become interested in chaos theory, nonlinear dynamics, and positive feedbacks (e.g., Day, 1982, 1983; Baumol and Quandt, 1985; Semmler, 1986; Barnett *et al.*, 1989; Baumol and Benhabib, 1989; Goodwin, 1990; Brock *et al.*, 1991; Benhabib, 1992; Bak *et al.*, 1993).[3]

The main thesis of the paper is that, while Boulding claimed to have offered an evolutionary account of economic change, he had mainly presented an ecological account of transformation of artifacts. The paper argues that there are at least two kinds of temporal change, noted by Nicholas Georgescu-Roegen, among others, that need to be distinguished in order to situate Boulding's contribution properly. One kind, studied by ecodynamics, examines transformations as exemplified by market fluctuations, where the principles of ecosystem equilibrium might be helpful. Another kind, studied by evolutionary theory, scrutinizes processes of development of economic organizations such as firms and national economies where the principles of evolutionary biology might be suitable.[4]

This paper maintains that, in order to make sense of Boulding, one must see his view of temporal change as within the ecodynamical research area, rather than within the evolutionary/developmental one. The two kinds of temporal change are not alternative perspectives of the same object but, rather, deal with two different objects. The two objects are not differentiated by evolutionary game theorists, who use the neoclassical optimization approach, and also by Schumpeterian and Keynesian economists, who stress nonergodic feedbacks (e.g., Arthur, 1989, 1990; Anderson *et al.*, 1988; Day and Chen, 1993; Radzicki, 1990; Rosser, 1991, 1992, 1993). Boulding himself is not clear about the difference between the two research areas in most, but not all, occasions. He confusingly appeals to developmental biology (the rise of an embryo from the fertilized egg) as a substantive heuristic of the production of goods and services. It is true that he does invoke organismic metaphors, Darwin's theory of natural selection, and terms such as "evolution" to describe the transmutation of knowledge and social organization (Boulding, 1981, 1989a). However, when Boulding goes beyond metaphors and offers insights about the role of knowledge and its transformation, he falls back onto the ecological dynamics framework.

On one occasion, Boulding recognizes that his ecodynamics is different from the evolutionary/organismic view.[5] In a reflection on his work, Boulding (1985–86, p. 3) notes the difference between two kinds of approaches in general systems theory. He identifies James Miller's 1978 volume as the epitome of that branch of general systems research interested in the physiology of social organization.[6] In contrast, Boulding locates his 1978 book as representing the other branch of general systems research, which is concerned with ecological and market dynamics. Boulding expresses the hope that these two branches of scientific discourse will be united in the future, since they seem "highly complementary."

The proposed distinction between ecodynamics and evolutionary economics can be related to Joseph Schumpeter's (1949) famous distinction between growth and economic development. Growth involves the quantitative measurement of change of capital stock, human labor, resources, and output. Schumpeter (1954) probably correctly maintained that equilibrium economics is legitimate if it is restricted to the study of growth. In contrast, development entails the study of how growth is related to the underpinning cultural and legal institutions, major technological paradigms, and the forms of business organization.

This paper maintains that, while the two modes of conception are radically different, they do not exclude each other, since each addresses a different phenomenon. It might be more beneficial, at least at the theoretical level, to keep them separate. However, they might be joined in the case of applied economics, where one cannot ignore how market interaction (ecodynamics) influences the path of evolution of the firm and the economic society at large. But economic theory would benefit from keeping, at first approximation at least, the two kinds of analyses apart. There is a great tendency to confuse them because of the temptation of Ockham's razor.[7]

The next section elucidates Boulding's basic concepts. The third section discusses Boulding's three sagas. This is followed by a section that argues that Boulding is not an evolutionary thinker but rather an ecodynamicist. We then show that ecodynamical change differs from evolutionary change by going back, via Georgescu-Roegen, to Aristotle's distinction between mechanical movement and development. The conclusion relates the distinction to the current confusion surrounding the notion of increasing returns as handled, among others, by Brian Arthur, Douglas North, and Paul Krugman.

Boulding's basic concepts

One can safely ignore Boulding's discussion in *Ecodynamics* of the evolution of the universe. But his discussion of population dynamics (ch. 3) and ecological dynamics (ch. 4) inform his categories more than his survey of biological evolution (ch. 5). This paper strictly reviews Boulding's categories concerning societal dynamics.

Artifacts

Boulding (1978, p. 121) argues that the key to the understanding of ecodynamics is the study of artifacts: "Social dynamics can be thought of primarily as the evolution of human artifacts." But he defines artifacts in a peculiar way:

> Human artifacts not only include material structures and objects, such as buildings, machines, and automobiles, but they also include organizations, organizational structures like extended families ... tribes, nations, corporations, churches, political parties, governments, and so on. Some of these may grow unconsciously, but they all originate and are sustained by the images in the human mind.
>
> (Boulding, 1978, p. 121)

Boulding seems to confuse tools, which are usually called artifacts, with organizations.[8] It is true that organizations, like tools, are made by and for humans. But there is one difference. The leader of an organization has to appeal to the members' loyalty to a common goal in order to keep the organization intact. This is not the case with the engineer in relation to the artifact he or she creates. Also, organizations are entities motivated by strategies that stand somewhat independently of the goals of the constitutive members (Khalil, 1996a). To wit, the existence of organizations does not usually depend on the identities of particular members. While IBM today is the same individual as IBM a half century ago, the people who comprise it have changed.

Boulding's definition of artifacts is even broader than that for organizations. He continues and states that human beings are also artifacts: "Even human beings themselves are in considerable part human artifacts, shaped by cultures in which they grow ... I am as much a human artifact as the chair I sit on and the house that shelters me" (Boulding, 1978, p. 122). Again, it is true that children, like tools, are shaped by socio-cultural variables. But children develop gradually into more autonomous persons with self-articulated goals, while tools cannot develop on their own. This is the case irrespective of the particular theory one holds with regard to the nature of human society.

Boulding even considers trees, horses, and grasses as "biological artifacts." But such organisms are not manipulated by external agencies, as is the case with tools employed by monkeys and humans. Likewise, it is baffling to dub rocks "geological artifacts." No active will has helped in the formation of rocks.

But Boulding's confusion dissipates once it is clear that he is not constructing an evolutionary theory. He is not interested in making distinctions between the *unit* of evolution (such as genome, organism, or troop of organisms), on the one hand, and the environment, on the other. Such a separation and the identification of the unit of evolution are at the heart of controversy in evolutionary biology

(Brandon and Burian, 1984).[9] Boulding is, rather, concerned with production activity, which underlies human artifacts and organisms (ecological artifacts): Both are produced by a plan, whether knowledge or DNA: "[T]he process by which a fertilized egg becomes a chicken is not essentially different from the process by which knowledge in the minds of automobile company members is transformed into an automobile" (Boulding, 1981, p. 25).

Boulding ignores the difference between the two products, organisms and tools, and dubs them "species." This would be a jumble if Boulding were interested in evolutionary phenomena, where he has to separate the organism from its environment. But it makes sense to ignore the distinction between the two, insofar as "ecological relationships" are the focus:

> Human artifacts enter into ecological relationships with each other and with biological artifacts. The automobile is competitive with the horse and has reduced its number.... It is a predator with regard to oil supplies because it is diminishing their quantity to the point where in a few decades both species face extinction.
>
> (Boulding, 1978, p. 122)

Boulding's treatment of resources, firms, organisms, and automobiles as logically equivalent "species" has obviously nothing to do with how biologists define "species."[10] The categories are, rather, lumped together as "artifacts" because of Boulding's particular ecodynamist question: What are the effects of the introduction of automobiles on the niches of rabbits, oil deposits, or railway companies? Or what are the consequences of air pollution on the population of eagles, pine trees, and houses? To answer these questions, one does not need to draw the familiar boundaries called by evolutionary theory among entities and their environment.

Human knowledge

Boulding makes an important qualification in his treatment of all forms within the ecological space as equivalent artifacts. He maintains that the introduction of the human brain on the stage of natural history has drastically changed the scene because of the image-making capacity of the brain to fantasize and act on new possibilities:

> It is this extraordinary capacity of the human brain for making images not only of the world outside it, which it sees as reality, but also, in fantasy, of innumerable worlds of the imagination, which distinguishes it from even the highest brains of nonhuman animals.
>
> (Boulding, 1978, p. 127)

For Boulding, the products of the human brain, human artifacts, are different from biological and physical artifacts. The brain generates knowledge on how to produce things that differs from inherited know-how, that is, the DNA. Such knowledge can imagine immediately its artifact, while the DNA cannot. Therefore, knowledge can manifest itself without the need for phenotype, while such phenotype is essential for the manifestation of the DNA genotype.

With the introduction of human knowledge, Boulding (1978) insists that "[i]t is important to recognize that there are two different genetic processes at work in the world." Nonhuman development is controlled by non-Lamarckian "biogenetic structure" of DNA (the genosphere), while human production operates according to Lamarckian "noögenetic structure" (the noösphere). The latter involves the neurological system, which makes it possible for higher organisms, and especially humans, to learn and transmit knowledge from one generation to the next. Such learning in human history becomes so dominant that the biogenetic structures cannot account for the variety of human artifacts.

While the idea of image or growth of knowledge makes Boulding come closer to evolutionary thinking, it does not make him an evolutionary thinker. For Boulding (1978, pp. 124–127), the creative act of the image in the production of artifacts still, to a great extent, parallels the biological production of organisms from fertilized eggs. The production of artifacts, such as automobiles, undergoes the steps of replication, recombination, redefinition, and realization. Replication entails the transmission of information via oral and written language. Recombination involves the joining of different competencies and specializations in, for example, the making of automobiles. Redefinition amounts to the introduction of technological innovation and discovery. Realization improves the system of communication transmitting directives on how to accomplish a plan. But there is one capacity not found in nonhuman spheres. It is the human mind's imaginative ability, which replaces the blind force of natural selection in the nonhuman sphere. The human mind has the "capacity for forming complex images of the future, as a product perhaps of the larger capacity of forming images of space and time" (p. 132).

Probably influenced by Auguste Comte, the nineteenth-century French philosopher, Boulding (1978, pp. 134 ff.) records the stages of development of the human mind from folk to literary and finally to scientific knowledge. Folk knowledge consists of images of ordinary life and the immediate sensations concerning one's environment. Literary-philosophical knowledge entails speculative stories about causes behind sensual experience. In contrast, scientific knowledge amounts to a system of organized learning in light of systematic observations and testing. The scientific enterprise has become a subculture in the past 500 years, certainly assisted by tools of measurement and technology.

Each stage in the development of human knowledge has ushered in a major expansion of human niches. While folk knowledge is associated with the paleolithic and early neolithic niches, literary-philosophic knowledge is related to the rise of civilization. Finally, the triumph of the scientific mind is accompanied by the commercial and industrial revolutions in Western Europe in the past few centuries.

Boulding's three sagas

Boulding maintains that human history can be understood as the incessant interaction of different artifacts. He presents three major clusters of such interactions, each of which is also composed of three other groupings (what he calls the "trinity of trinities" [1978, p. 211]).

The first cluster, or saga, consists of the interrelations of things, organizations, and people. The first artifact, "things," consists of raw, finished, and part-finished:

> material artifacts from a vast phylum of species beginning with the simplest stone tools and wooden sticks, going to fires, which we must count as human artifacts, skins, shelters, and bone implements, developing in an almost endless variety of forms of increasing complexity to the spacelab and the latest computer.
>
> (Boulding, 1978, p. 212)

The second artifact, "organizations," ranges from the human family to modern complex societies. Boulding insightfully notes that a key element in the explanation of the latter is the distinction between the person and the role:

> An organization can be defined as a structure of roles linked by lines of communication. The role rather than the person is the essential unit of the organization. Persons occupy roles and behave accordingly, but the same role may be occupied by different persons in succession or indeed occasionally by artifacts such as a machine.
>
> (Boulding, 1978, p. 212)

Finally, the third artifact, "people," introduces the element of population size into the ecological space. An excess amount of population or population movement induces technical and organizational changes, one of which was the neolithic revolution. People also form human capital, which accounts for the generation and transmission of knowledge. Such knowledge intermediates the interaction between organizations and things.

From the evolutionary standpoint, there is a difficulty with Boulding's thesis about the equivalency of people, organizations, and things. People, unlike organizations, cannot act as an individual because the category expresses merely the aggregation of body masses, not necessarily organized to attain a goal. Furthermore, things stand asymmetrically to persons and organizations. Organizations and persons can manipulate things, but things cannot manipulate organizations and persons. From the ecological standpoint, however, one might entertain the logical equivalency of organizations, people, and things. It is only from the viewpoint of ecological competition that Boulding can maintain that the interaction between things and organizations makes it "hard to say which is the leader in the movement":

> We certainly cannot take the simplistic view that it is always material artifacts which create the social organizations or that it is always the social organizations which create the material artifacts. Each reacts on the other in a constant process of positive feedback. Did agriculture produce the village or did the village produce agriculture? We do not really know.
>
> (Boulding, 1978, p. 215)

Boulding's second saga consists of knowledge, energy, and materials. The first category, "knowledge," plays a central role in Boulding's image. But he warns that we should not forget energy and matter as the substrate on which knowledge works. The trio of knowledge, energy, and matter are essential ingredients in the functioning of organizations and their ability to interact with the environment.

The third and most interesting saga is one of Boulding's major themes, which he introduced earlier in an article and elaborated later in a full-length book (Boulding, 1962, 1989b; see also Pfaff, 1976). It is about the dichotomous distinction among three systems that act as "social organizers" of the human ecology. They consist of the "threat system," "integrative system," and "exchange system." The threat system exemplifies political power; the integrative system represents one-way exchanges (gifts, philanthropy, and government transfers) that cement communal cohesion; and the exchange system is the sphere of economics proper. An important pulse in Professor Boulding's work is the containment of the threat system by expanding the integrative system.

Assessment

In Boulding's three sagas, "everything depends on everything else" (1978, p. 224). But the human capacity to produce images is the central actor in his human ecology—a thesis that can be traced back to his most read book, *The Image* (Boulding, 1956).

Boulding frequently described the mutation of knowledge as "evolutionary." But human knowledge, for Boulding, is ultimately an artifact no different from buildings and chairs. While he allows knowledge to change through learning, there is no criterion for its learning (like the neo-Darwinian optimization of fitness criterion [Khalil, 1993a, 1993b]), or for its progress. So the temporal change of human knowledge is basically the outcome of the human mind processing information as a result of its *symmetrical* interaction with people and chairs. This can make sense only if society is seen primarily as an ecosystem of externally related chairs and people. In this manner, learning is simply portrayed as self-feeding adjustment as the organism enters new experiences with its ecological surroundings.

One of Boulding's (1934) early publications, which put him on the map of economics, is a critique of Frank Knight's theory of capital using an ecological approach. Boulding borrows the population model from ecology in order to illustrate his theory of capital as a fund rather than a flow. Capital goods are presented as a population with different vintages; they enter and exit the capital fund like births and deaths of organisms in a population. Frank Knight (1935) made Boulding famous overnight when he published an article with the subtitle "Mr. Boulding and the Austrians." Boulding (1936) explicitly objected to Knight's theoretical treatment of capital as a flow that can be switched easily from one industry to another in response to changes of relative rates of profit. Boulding's thesis about the distinction between flow and fund persisted in his writings throughout his career (see Boulding, 1993). The thesis, which came to be called the balance sheet approach to national income accounts, permeates his most important contribution to economies, *A Reconstruction of Economics* (1950).[11]

If one subscribes to one thesis of the sociology of knowledge literature—namely, that one's early orientation lays the direction of one's path of intellectual development—then it is clear that Boulding's concepts of capital and national income accounts shaped his more elaborate vision of the transformation of artifacts in human ecology. The vision is not evolutionary for the simple reason that it lacks the identification of the unit of evolution. Such a lack was recognized by Boulding when he related the anecdote of the question of H.W.B. Joseph, his Oxford philosophy tutor in the 1930s: "What involves, Mr. Boulding, what evolves?" (see Siguenza, 1981, p. 146). Boulding's answer, that human artifacts from automobiles to knowledge are the units of "evolution," cannot be taken seriously. Boulding's concept of artifacts is so broad as to include everything in the ecological space. And for a unit of evolution to act as a unit, it must be separated from the environment—a position upon which neo-Darwinian and non-Darwinian (such as neo-Lamarckian [Khalil, 1992]) theorists concur (Brandon and Burian, 1984).

The unit of evolution has to be contrasted with an environment, possess a certain organic cohesiveness, and act according to a strategy in order for it to evolve. Automobiles and chairs do not qualify in any sense. They clearly lack organic connectedness and strategy. Furthermore, automobiles and human knowledge do not stand on the same logical plane. Only one presupposes the other. In addition, knowledge is not a purposeful unit; it is not even a unit. While knowledge can stand independently of its creators, as illustrated by printed matter and electronic data bases, it is meaningless independent of the receiving subject.

In order to account for the evolutionary process, evolutionary theory must start with units or individuals. Although the claim cannot be defended here, organizations as households, firms, and political communities are good candidates to be considered as individuals. In order to elucidate the cohesiveness of such units, the theory must start with the organic composition of the division of labor recognized by James Miller (1978).

Back to Aristotle via Georgescu-Roegen

Nicholas Georgescu-Roegen's distinction between two kinds of temporal change might shed some light on the fundamental difference between Boulding's ecodynamical and Miller's organic (evolutionary) kinds of temporal change.

Georgescu-Roegen (1971, p. 197) differentiates between "irreversible" and "irrevocable" change. Both are certainly "non-reversible" change in the sense that they are not like reversible phenomena that "follow the same course phase by phase in the reverse order," like the movement of a pendulum in a zero-friction container or the rolling of a billiard ball on a zero-friction surface.

The first kind of non-reversibility, "irreversibility," amounts to cyclical motion where the object "can return to any previously attained phase." Georgescu-Roegen illustrates irreversibility with the flow of vehicles in a traffic circle and the tree losing and gaining its leaves. Other examples abound, from the pace of the heartbeat to sleep and mood fluctuation.

In contrast, irrevocable motion involves "processes that cannot pass through a given state more than once." This includes the aging process that characterizes all living entities and technological development.[12] Irreversible dynamics is the result of statistical improbability, while the irrevocable process is the outcome of ontological impossibility. For example, a hurricane does not reverse its path because of complicated factors, but it is not impossible for it to do so. In contrast, it is impossible, even theoretically, to reverse the aging of cells and organisms.

Aristotle makes an important distinction that may shed light on Georgescu-Roegen's contrast between irreversibility and irrevocability. In book 5 of *The Physics*, Aristotle differentiates between movement (*kinesis*) and development (*metabolé*, which is about internal processes of change). It seems that movement depicts reversible/irreversible change, while development portrays irrevocable change. With regard to movement, "we may … add that the 'forms' and 'conditions' and 'place,' which are all goals of movement, are themselves without movement" (Aristotle, 1980, vol. 2, p. 11 [*Physics*, book 5, ch. 1, 224b, 5–15]). This is the case because "no quality or place or magnitude either causes movement or experiences it"; movement is merely the passing of a subject between a starting point and a goal, that is, between what Aristotle calls "contraries."

With regard to development, the form of the subject undergoes transitions as in genesis—what Aristotle calls the unqualified "coming into being." In unqualified transition, the form undergoes a mere negation from A to its contradictory not-A. In qualified transition, the form undergoes "'coming to be this or that' from being not this or that." "Thus the transition of x from 'not-white' to 'white' is a coming-to-be of *white*; whereas the transition of x from simple non-existence to existence is an unqualified coming into being" (Aristotle, 1980, p. 15).

Some of Aristotle's examples of development are obviously faulty—for example, when he considers the rise of temperature of a subject as "development"—similar to the perishing of an organism or the development of an oak tree from the seed. Nonetheless, his distinction of movement and development is important. The distinction amounts to the observation that development is about relations and "relations cannot 'move'": "From all this it follows that genesis cannot be a movement, for, if it were, the non-existent in its transit to existence would have to move" (Aristotle, 1980, p. 17). To start with, "anything that moves must have position, which the non-existent cannot have, since it is not anywhere." "Neither can perishing," likewise, "be a movement; for the opposite of a movement is either movement or rest, whereas the opposite of perishing is genesis" (p. 19).

It seems reasonable to identify "movement" with the issue of reversibility since it is with respect to external contraries or poles that do not move. Similarly, it appears convincing to identify development with irrevocability since it is about processes of form either coming into being or perishing. Such processes are irrevocable because they do not involve movement of the subject between external contraries, but rather the transition of form from what is potential to actual and into nonexistence.

Boulding's ecodynamics is obviously about a particular kind of change, namely, movement. It is not about the flourishing of capacity or development from the general to the particular. Insofar as the economy exhibits both kinds of change, it is erroneous to absorb Boulding's ecodynamics (and maybe equilibrium economics) within the paradigm of evolutionary economics.

Conclusion

This paper maintains that Boulding's theory of change is mainly ecological as opposed to evolutionary. The ecological/evolutionary divide runs along, respectively, the difference between the Keynesian multiplier-accelerator model that determines effective demand, on one hand, and the trajectory of technological/institutional regime underpinning production, on the other (Khalil, 1995a). The two kinds of change are confused probably because ecodynamical change and evolutionary change are characterized by recursive, nonergodic feedbacks. Stated simply, however, the ecodynamical/Keynesian type of change is about fluctuations around a trend, while the evolutionary type is about the trend itself. Thus, they are not alternative approaches. To distinguish them, I suggest calling the evolutionary kind of change "nonergodic development," while dubbing the ecodynamical kind of change "nonergodic dynamics."

Aside from other differences, the works of Brian Arthur (1989, 1990), Douglass North (1990, ch. 11), and Paul David (1985) generally exemplify the evolutionary approach concerning nonergodic development. Their work deals with how an initial investment in a certain, and maybe less efficient, technological/institutional framework makes it entrenched as a result of learning-by-doing and increasing returns. Thus, nonergodic development deals with the fundamental, underpinning process of division of labor in society.

In contrast, the ecodynamical approach concerning nonergodic dynamics focuses on market cumulative causation. Such self-feeding causation takes the form of spatial polarization as well as temporal fluctuation. The best-known work with regard to spatial polarization is Paul Krugman's (e.g., 1991) theory of geographical core/periphery bifurcation. Krugman traces the rise of core/periphery to increasing returns to the extent of production—an idea highlighted earlier by Allyn Young and Nicholas Kaldor. Krugman shows how highly fixed costs and costs of transportation induce firms to concentrate their investment in a few plants and in regions close to the population center. The move toward such a center spurs ecodynamical change, which makes the center more attractive to other firms—which prompts nonergodic, uneven regional growth.[13]

With regard to temporal fluctuation, David Levine's (1981) theory of the business cycle is a good example.[14] The theory shows how investments tend to be bunched together because economic activity feeds on itself: A rise in investment generates a boom, while a slowdown turns into a recession. The macro externality stems from ecodynamical interaction. The investment of one company is the particular demand facing other companies; it does not necessarily translate into a greater demand facing the company that made the initial investment.

There is one fundamental difference between the two kinds of nonergodic feedback. The evolutionary trend exhibits a *single* unfolding of the potentiality of the underpinning technological/institutional regime of production. The betterment of one group, region, or historical period arises from the creation of new wealth. Nonergodic development involves a positive-sum game. In contrast, the Keynesian ecodynamical fluctuation around the trend necessarily exhibits a *dual*-track activity (bifurcation). The growth of one region or income class is accomplished by impoverishing another region or income class. Or the overshooting of output beyond potential GDP entails the undershooting of output in the following temporal sequence. The Keynesian nonergodic dynamics of bifurcated feedbacks are by definition symmetrical and, hence, amount to a zero-sum game.

Boulding (1985–86) recognized the ecological/evolutionary dichotomy of theoretical tools. He would probably be ready to admit the limits of the ecodynamical view. It simply cannot explain the change of the fundamental technological/institutional regime of production. At best, it is about the ecodynamical change around the trend. Likewise, the evolutionary approach cannot account for the ecodynamical fluctuation of the market. The ecodynamical and evolutionary tools of analysis are distinct since they deal with different aspects of economic activity. Boulding has bequeathed for us, *inter alia*, the ever-pressing burden of resisting the temptation to allow one theoretical tool to swallow the other.

Notes

1 This article was previously published in *Journal of Post Keynesian Economics*, 1996, *19* (1), 83–100.

2 The author is Assistant Professor of Economics at Ohio State University and Visiting Scholar at the University of Chicago. He wishes to express appreciation for the comments of Mark Perlman, Richard Day, Warren Samuels, anonymous referees, and the technical help of Carole Brown and Beth Burns. He also appreciates the research support extended by the Alexander von Humboldt Foundation (Germany) and Ulrich Witt at the University of Freiburg. But none should be blamed for any remaining shortcomings.

3 Chaos theory, which focuses on sudden discontinuities, has even recently attracted the attention of some historians (Reisch, 1991; Roth, 1992; Beyerchen, 1992–93; cf. Khalil, 1995b).

4 To be clear, evolutionary biology should not be identified exclusively with the neo-Darwinian approach—as much as economics should not be delimited by the neoclassical paradigm. Evolutionary theory encompasses other traditions such as the neo-Lamarckian, developmental, autopoiesis, and structuralist ones (Khalil, 1993a, 1993b).

5 While the term "ecodynamics" is awkward, it is more appropriate than "ecological economics." The latter term has been appropriated by economists who apply the laws of thermodynamics and matter/energy influx, rather than the maximization of preferences, to the study of the *interface* of the economy and the environment. While Boulding (1966) is one of the founders of ecological economics, the subject matter of ecological economics is different from the modeling of the *internal* dynamics of the economy as an ecosystem.

6 In an encyclopedic volume, James Miller (1978) reviews the cross-level invariance of functions of organizations. He identified nineteen functions across seven levels of organizations. The suggested seven levels consist of the cell, organ, organism, group, organization, society, and supranational system. The nineteen functions include the reproducer, boundary, ingestor, distributor, converter, producer, matter-energy storage, extruder, motor, supporter, input transducer, internal transducer, channel/net, decoder, associator, memory, decider, encoder, and output transducer. For instance, the boundary function is performed at the seven levels, respectively, by the cell membrane, capsule of viscus, skin, sergeant-at-arms, and guards at the other levels. In the same order, the decider function is performed by the regulator gene, sympathetic fiber of the sinoatrial node of the heart, part of the cerebral cortex, head of family, executive office, national government, and council of ministers or government of supranational state. Thus, there are no functions at higher levels of organization that do not have parallel existence, even in a rudimentary fashion, at lower levels. This can be taken to mean, which cannot be demonstrated here, that there are no emergent novelties as we travel from lower to higher organizations. Instead, we witness the abstract elaboration of functions that can be found, although in more primordial forms, at lower levels.

7 I elaborate elsewhere on the distinction between the two phenomena that invoke the two kinds of theoretical tools (Khalil, 1990a, 1992, 1995b, 1996c). One phenomenon, called "natural complex," is about organizations such as firms and states and their developmental processes. The other, dubbed "natural system," is about structures such as market equilibrating patterns and their ecodynamics over time.

8 Friedrich Hayek also equates organizations with artifacts in his dichotomy between spontaneous order (*cosmos*) such as markets and designed order (*taxis*) in which he lumped firms, artifacts, and socialist economies (see Khalil, 1996b).

9 To be clear, neo-Darwinian theorists generally distinguish between the "unit of evolution," such as the population genetic pool, and the "unit of selection," which is debatable—whether it is exclusively the gene (Richard Dawkins) or it also includes the organism (Ernst Mayr), and further encompasses the group of organisms (David Wilson and Elliott Sober). But the distinction is specific to the neo-Darwinian framework and should not concern us here.

10 Stated briefly, there are two main views on the definition of species, the biological species concept and the morphological species concept. The former, identified with Ernst Mayr (1987), classifies organisms as part of the same species if they interbreed successfully. Obviously the definition runs into problems when it comes up against asexually reproducing species, conspecific organisms that are separated by geography, and fossil organisms (see Sreshefsky, 1992). In contrast, the morphological species concept (also known as the classical or typological concept), traced to Linnaeus (Carl von Linné), classifies organisms according to their apparent similarities. Obviously this runs into trouble when there is sharp sexual dimorphism (males look very different from females), when organisms belong to subspecies of same species, and when organisms belong to different species but have very similar morphology.

11 Four decades after the publication of *A Reconstruction of Economics*, Boulding writes:

> [T]he reconstruction [was] around two major theses. One was that capital was more important than income, especially from the point of view of the household, where the use of household capital is much more important than consumption.
>
> The second reconstruction was a macroeconomic theory of profits, originating from Keynes' *Treatise on Money* and his concept of the "widow's cruse." This is what in later years I came to call the "K Theory," as it originates in the work of Keynes, Kalecki, Kaldor, and Kenneth (myself).
>
> (Boulding, 1989c, p. 376; see Boulding, 1985, p. 5; Rimmer, 1989)

12 However, I dispute strongly whether the entropic degradation as described by the second law of thermodynamics fits in this category. I believe, but cannot demonstrate here, that the entropic change belongs to the irreversible category (Khalil, 1990b).

13 In this light, Krugman's (1991) appeal to the work of Brian Arthur's increasing returns is misguided. While both are interested in path-dependent change, Arthur and North are concerned as well with the evolutionary process of technological trajectory, not with the spontaneous rise of market structures.

14 Although David Levine, incidentally, mistook his theory of the business cycle for a theory of capital accumulation (Khalil, 1987).

References

Anderson, Philip W.; Arrow, K.J.; and Pines, David, eds. *The Economy as an Evolving Complex System.* Redwood City, CA: Addison-Wesley, 1988.

Aristotle. *The Physics*, 2 vols., trans. by Philip H. Wicksteed and Francis M. Cornford. Cambridge, MA: Harvard University Press; London: William Heinemann, 1980.

Arthur, W. Brian. "Competing Technologies, Increasing Returns, and Lack-in by Historical Events." *Economic Journal*, March 1989, *99*, 116–131.

Arthur, W. Brian. "Positive Feedbacks in the Economy." *Scientific American*, February 1990, *262* (2), 92–99.

Bak, Per; Chen, Kan; Scheinkman, José; and Woodford, Michael. "Aggregate Fluctuations from Independent Sectoral Shocks: Self-Organized Criticality in a Model of Production and Inventory Dynamics." *Ricerche Economiche*, March 1993, *47* (1), 3–30.

Barnett, William A.; Geweke, John; and Shell, Karl, eds. *Economic Complexity: Chaos, Sunspots, Bubbles and Nonlinearity*. Cambridge: Cambridge University Press, 1989.

Baumol, William J., and Quandt, Richard E. "Chaos Models and Their Implications for Forecasting." *Eastern Economic Journal*, January–March 1985, *11* (1), 3–15.

Baumol, William J., and Benhabib, Jess. "Chaos: Significance Mechanism and Economic Applications." *Journal of Economic Perspectives*, Winter 1989, *3* (1), 77–105.

Benhabib, Jess, ed. *Cycles and Chaos in Economic Equilibrium.* Princeton, NJ: Princeton University Press, 1992.

Beyerchen, Alan. "Clausewitz, Nonlinearity, and the Unpredictability of War." *International Security*, Winter 1992–93, *17* (3), 59–90.

Boulding, Kenneth E. "The Application of the Pure Theory of Population Change to the Theory of Capital." *Quarterly Journal of Economics*, August 1934, *48* (4), 645–666.

Boulding, Kenneth E. "Professor Knight's Capital Theory: A Note in Reply." *Quarterly Journal of Economics*, May 1936, *50* (3), 524–531.

Boulding, Kenneth E. *A Reconstruction of Economics*. New York: Wiley, 1950.

Boulding, Kenneth E. *The Image: Knowledge in Life and Society.* Ann Arbor, MI: University of Michigan Press, 1956.

Boulding, Kenneth E. "The Relations of Economic, Political and Social Systems." *Social and Economic Studies*, December 1962, *11*, 351–362.

Boulding, Kenneth E. "The Economics of the Coming Spaceship Earth." In Henry Jarrett (ed.), *Environmental Quality in a Growing Economy*. Baltimore: Johns Hopkins University Press, 1966.

Boulding, Kenneth E. *Ecodynamics: A New Theory of Societal Evolution*. Beverly Hills, CA: Sage, 1978.

Boulding, Kenneth E. *Evolutionary Economics*. Beverly Hills, CA: Sage, 1981.

Boulding, Kenneth E. "Puzzles over Distribution." *Challenge*, November–December 1985, *28* (5), 4–10.

Boulding, Kenneth E. "The Next Thirty Years in General Systems." *General Systems Yearbook*, 1985–86, *29*, 3–5.

Boulding, Kenneth E. "Punctuationalism in Societal Evolution." *Journal of Social and Biological Structures*, April–July 1989a, *12* (2–3), 213–223.

Boulding, Kenneth E. *Three Faces of Power*. Newbury Park, CA: Sage, 1989b.

Boulding, Kenneth E. "A Bibliographical Autobiography." *Banca Nazionale de Lavoro Quarterly Review*, December 1989c, *171*, 365–393.

Brandon, Robert N., and Burian, Richard M., eds. *Genes, Organisms, Populations: Controversies over the Units of Selection*. Cambridge, MA: MIT Press, 1984.

Brock, William A.; Hsieh, David A.; and LeBaron, Blake. *Nonlinear Dynamics, Chaos and Instability: Statistical Theory and Economic Evidence*. Cambridge, MA: MIT Press, 1991.

David, Paul A. "Clio and the Economics of QWERTY." *American Economic Review*, May 1985, *75* (2), 332–337.

Day, Richard H. "Irregular Growth Cycles." *American Economic Review*, June 1982, *72* (3), 406–414.

Day, Richard H. "The Emergence of Chaos from Classical Economic Growth." *Quarterly Journal of Economics*, 1983, *98*, 201–213.

Day, Richard H., and Chen, Ping, eds. *Nonlinear Dynamics and Evolutionary Economics*. New York: Oxford University Press, 1993.

Georgescu-Roegen, Nicholas. *The Entropy Law and the Economic Process*. Cambridge, MA: Harvard University Press, 1971.

Goodwin, Richard M. *Chaotic Economic Dynamics*. Oxford: Clarendon Press, 1990.

Khalil, E.L. "The Process of Capitalist Accumulation: A Review Essay of David Levine's Contribution." *Review of Radical Political Economics*, Winter 1987, *19* (4), 76–85.

Khalil, E.L. "Natural Complex vs. Natural System." *Journal of Social and Biological Structures*, February 1990a, *13* (1), 11–31.

Khalil, E.L. "Entropy Law and Exhaustion of Natural Resources: Is Nicholas Georgescu-Roegen's Paradigm Defensible?" *Ecological Economics*, 1990b, *2* (2), 163–178.

Khalil, E.L. "Economics and Biology: Eight Areas of Research." *Methodus*, December 1992, *4* (2), pp. 29–45.

Khalil, E.L. "Neo-classical Economics and Neo-Darwinism: Clearing the Way for Historical Thinking." In Ron Blackwell, Jaspal Chatha, and Edward J. Nell (eds.), *Economics as Worldly Philosophy*. London: Macmillan, 1993a, pp. 22–72.

Khalil, E.L. "Is Poincaréan Nonlinear Dynamics the Alternative to the Selection Theory of Evolution?" *Journal of Social and Evolutionary Systems*, November 1993b, *16* (4), 489–500.

Khalil, E.L. "Ecological Economics, Neoclassical Economics and the Technological/Institutional Regime of Production." *British Review of Economic Issues*, February 1995a, *17* (41), 41–70.

Khalil, E.L. "Nonlinear Thermodynamics and Social Science Modeling: Fad Cycles, Cultural Development and Identificational Slips." *American Journal of Economics and Sociology*, October 1995b, *54* (4), 423–438.

Khalil, E.L. "Organism and Organization." *Biology and Philosophy*, 1996a, *12* (1), 119–126.

Khalil, E.L. "Friedrich Hayek's Darwinian Theory of Evolution of Institutions: Two Problems." *Australian Economics Papers*, June 1996b, *35* (66), 183–201.

Khalil, E.L. "Nonlinear Dynamics vs. Development Processes: Two Kinds of Temporal Change." *Manchester School*, September 1996c, *64* (3), 309–322.

Knight, Frank. "The Theory of Investment Once More: Mr. Boulding and the Austrians." *Quarterly Journal of Economics*, November 1935, *50*, 1.

Krugman, Paul. *Geography and Trade*. Leuven, Belgium: Leuven University Press, jointly with Cambridge, MA: MIT Press, 1991.

Levine, David P. *Economic Theory, Volume 2: The System of Economic Relations as a Whole*. London: Routledge and Kegan Paul, 1981.

Mayr, Ernst. "The Ontological Status of Species: Scientific Progress and Philosophical Terminology." *Biology and Philosophy*, April 1987, *2*, 145–166.

Miller, James Grief. *Living Systems*. New York: McGraw-Hill, 1978.

North, Douglass C. *Institutions, Institutional Change and Economic Performance*. Cambridge: Cambridge University Press, 1990.

Pfaff, Martin, ed. *Frontiers in Social Thought: Essays in Honor of Kenneth E. Boulding*. Amsterdam: North-Holland, 1976.

Radzicki, Michael J. "Institutional Dynamics, Deterministic Chaos, and Self-Organizing Systems." *Journal of Economic Issues*, March 1990, *24* (1), 57–102.

Reisch, George A. "Chaos, History, and Narrative." *History and Theory*, 1991, *30* (1), 1–20.

Rimmer, Russell, J. "Boulding's Theory of Distribution in a Neo-Pasinetti Framework." *Cambridge Journal of Economics*, 1989, *13*, 453–458.

Rosser, Jr., J. Barkley. *From Catastrophe to Chaos: A General Theory of Economic Discontinuities*. Amsterdam: Kluwer Press, 1991.

Rosser, Jr., J. Barkley. "The Dialogue between the Economic and the Ecological Theories of Evolution." *Journal of Economic Behavior and Organization*, 1992, *17*, 195–215.

Rosser, Jr., J. Barkley. "Cycles and Evolution in Ecology and Economics." *Methodus*, June 1993, *5* (1), 101–103.

Roth, Randolph. "Is History a Process? Nonlinearity, Revitalization Theory, and the Central Metaphor of Social Science History." *Social Science History*, Summer 1992, *16* (2), 197–243.

Schumpeter, Joseph A. *The Theory of Economic Development: An Inquiry into Profits, Capital, Credit, Interest, and the Business Cycle*, trans. by Redvers Opie. Cambridge, MA: Harvard University Press, (1912) 1949. [Reprinted by Transaction Publishers, with a new introduction by John E. Elliott, 1989.]

Schumpeter, Joseph A. *History of Economic Analysis*. New York: Oxford University Press, 1954.

Semmler, Willi, ed. *Competition, Instability, and Nonlinear Cycles*. Proceedings of an International Conference, New School for Social Research, New York, March 1985. Berlin and New York: Springer-Verlag, 1986.

Siguenza, Manuel. "Review of Kenneth Boulding's *Ecodynamics*." *Journal of Economic Issues*, March 1981, *15* (1), 146–151.

Sreshefsky, Marc, ed. *The Units of Evolution: Essays on the Nature of Species*. Cambridge, MA: MIT Press, 1992.

2b Comment: Kenneth Boulding's skeleton of science and contemporary general systems theory

Joseph E. Pluta[1]

The scholarship of Kenneth Boulding has produced substantial contributions to several areas of knowledge, many of which are only peripherally related to the discipline of economics, his presumed academic specialty. Indeed, being confined to any single discipline was a constraint Boulding refused to accept at a time when economics often appeared more interested in turning inward rather than outward. By one account, Boulding "published more than a thousand items in thirty subject areas" (Solo 1994: 1188). Among his numerous achievements was his helping to establish the direction that a fledgling interdisciplinary pursuit called systems theory was to pursue.

Background

Boulding was one of the founders in 1956 of the Society for General Systems Research (SGSR), an organization that was renamed the International Society for Systems Science (ISSS) in 1988. Originally charged with developing theoretical systems that can be used in more than a single discipline, the ISSS has broadened its focus to include practical applications of systems techniques to problem solving. Boulding served as first president of the organization whose later presidents included such notable scholars as cultural anthropologist Margaret Mead, political scientist Bertram Gross, chemist Ilya Prigogine, and several other distinguished academics. Boulding also later served as president of the American Economic Association.

A society devoted to the study of systems was initially conceived in 1954 at the Stanford Center for Advanced Study in the Behavioral Sciences through the combined efforts of economist Boulding, biologist Ludwig von Bertalanffy, neuroscientist Ralph Gerard, and mathematician Anatol Rapoport. With the assistance of biologist James Grier Miller, SGSR was formally established as an affiliate of the American Association for the Advancement of Science two years later.

In his classic article on general systems theory (GST), Boulding proposed a social systems gravimeter, which he dubbed the "skeleton of science", comprised of nine levels of organization, each delineating an increasing level of complexity (Boulding 1956). He lamented at the time that theoretical models in

GST had yet to advance beyond the fourth level of his "skeleton" and were fairly rare even above the second level. General systems theorists, along with scholars in the sister disciplines that the original movement inspired, have clearly made progress during the past half century, both in terms of analytical rigor and in the application of their methods to a wide range of issues. Much of this work, however, still remains within the third and fourth levels of the Boulding gravimeter. This suggests that either modern GST may have paid limited attention to the Boulding framework or that the GST approach still has much to gain by developing and applying it.

The former conclusion may appear valid on two fronts. First, as has recently been noted, "Boulding never returned to the Skeleton in his later writings" (Wilby 2006: 698), the reason for which can only be speculated upon at this juncture.[2] Having done considerable work in systems theory later in his career, he likely chose to become more involved in new directions in which this work took him and simply allowed his original formulation of the concept to stand on its own. Of course, given Boulding's extensive scholarly interests, there is a limit to the research avenues that any scholar can pursue during the course of a highly productive lifetime.

Second, citations of Boulding in the work of some modern systems theorists (Radzicki 2003; Lane 2008; and Richardson 1999) have been relatively rare.[3] In much of the work of these and other writers, Boulding either is not cited at all or else is mentioned only briefly in passing. Perhaps there is still much in Boulding's early thought that contemporary writers can utilize. It is the latter argument that will be pursued here.

The skeleton

Table 2.1 summarizes Boulding's skeleton of science as originally described in his 1956 article, with selected updates from later researchers. Beginning with level 1, each consecutive level represents a higher degree of complexity and a more demanding challenge for interdisciplinary researchers. While acknowledging that "open systems" thinking had made dramatic strides at the third and fourth levels during the early 1950s, Boulding was quick to point out that "(a) dequate theoretical models extend up to about the fourth level, and not much beyond. Empirical knowledge is deficient at practically all levels" (Boulding 1956: 205). While empirical research over the past half century has improved upon the deficiencies Boulding noted in that area, many present-day systems theorists, despite the advances their interdisciplinary approach has achieved, still concur with his assessment of the inadequacy of theoretical models. As will be discussed below, their work in designing more sophisticated models continues.

More than a decade ago, a useful effort to reconceptualize the original hierarchy of the skeleton was undertaken (Mingers 1997). Among several suggested updates, two of the more significant were the distinction between living and nonliving systems, along with more explicit definition of a systems complexity scale that separates levels in the skeleton.

Table 2.1 The Boulding skeleton of science

Level	*Description*	*Characteristic*	*Example*	*Discipline*
1	Structures and frameworks	Static, spatial pattern	Picture, statue, jigsaw puzzle, atom, molecule	Descriptive elements of all disciplines
2	Clockworks	Predetermined dynamic motion	Clocks, machines, mechanics, solar system	Physics, astronomy, engineering, economics
3	Control mechanisms	Closed-loop control	Thermostat, homeostasis	Cybernetics, physiology
4	Open systems	Structurally self-maintaining	Cells, flames, rivers	Theory of metabolism
5	Genetic-societal systems	Society of cells, functional parts	Plants	Botany
6	Animals	Nervous system, self-awareness, mobility	Birds and beasts	Zoology
7	Humans	Knowledge, language, self-consciousness	Human beings	Biology, psychology, ecology, neurobiology
8	Socio-cultural systems	Roles, values, communication	Families, clubs, boy scouts	History, sociology, anthropology, psychology, economics, political science
9	Transcendental systems	Unanswerable questions	God?	Philosophy, religion

Sources: Adapted from Boulding (1956: 202–205) and updates from Mingers (1997: 306), Wilby (2005: 394), and Wilby (2006: 697).

Mingers' self-referential systems hierarchy is, among other things, an effort to move beyond Boulding's level 4. Self-referential systems involve human observation and self-consciousness, a step above the level of abstract interaction between animals that contain nervous systems. Much of the current GST literature is built around loop diagrams originally mentioned in Boulding's level 3. Some of the more sophisticated loop diagram models may be considered, at least theoretically, as reaching level 7 in the realignment offered by Mingers. In his conclusion, Mingers proposed greater reliance on circular systems and building on Boulding's original hierarchy.

More recently, additional attention has been drawn to the early work of Boulding by former ISSS president Jennifer Wilby, who concludes:

> Boulding's Skeleton does feel intuitively correct. The problem of increasing complexity in image, message filtering and observer-dependency at the higher levels of the Skeleton will continue to frustrate the search for a working, valuable, social-science gravimeter. It may also explain the lack of specific follow-up work on the Skeleton by Boulding and other writers in the field of general systems theory.... Further work on developing a social science gravimeter is needed in GST.
>
> (Wilby 2006: 699)

Unfortunately, some of the overviews of where GST has been and where it is going suggest that relatively few of its researchers are looking to Boulding for inspiration. Twenty five years ago, for example, in a thorough survey of obstacles facing GST and proposed solutions, Boulding received only minor mention (Troncale 1985). When this study was recently updated (Troncale 2009), Boulding was not mentioned at all. A research proposal for systems science only includes Boulding in a lengthy list of "twentieth-century experimenters" (Warfield 2003). A very recent overview of trends in GST mentions Boulding only as one of the founders of the Society for General Systems Research but does not cite any of his work (Drack and Schwarz 2010).[4] These surveys suggest that some generalists in the field who are calling for a reexamination of the direction of research, including a greater appreciation of the history of GST thought, seldom if ever point in the direction of Boulding's work.

For too many GST researchers today, Boulding merits only a passing and even a compulsory respectful footnote. In fact, more than one academic journal article in the field of GST exists where a work of Boulding is included in the list of references but he is not cited at all in the body of the text. One writer (Waters 2006) has speculated on possible reasons some of Boulding's work has been ignored in a number of different disciplines. He is also critical of a recent post-Keynesian analysis (Khalil 1996) for its assessment of Boulding. Khalil argued that Boulding's work was based more on principles rooted in ecology (ecodynamics) rather than in evolutionary economics. Waters finds the Khalil critique of Boulding to be narrow and unappreciative of Boulding's concept of knowledge. In terms of the argument presented here, Khalil does not mention the skeleton and says little in his critique that directly addresses the adequacy of Boulding's systems thinking.

Some promising research

And yet, some contemporary researchers do recognize the value of studying the history of GST, including the contributions of Boulding. In addition to the work of Mingers and Wilby mentioned above, one writer (Martinelli 2001) has recently proposed an application of Boulding's hierarchy to corporate managerial systems. Another (Georgiou 2010) has discussed Boulding's mathematics of information theory and his concept of human knowledge in a recent historically oriented article. Yet another (Jackson 2009) has demonstrated the importance of Boulding's hierarchy in the development of the theory and practice of operations research. A fourth study (Weaver 2002) has used the Boulding hierarchy to describe the production of artificially intelligent control programs in heating and cooling mechanisms. Some GST researchers, therefore, are aware that Boulding was there "back when it all began" and have genuinely built upon his early work.

Three of the more innovative adaptations of the original Boulding skeleton illustrate its potentially broad reach. In a highly creative yet analytically solid approach, one study (Sridhar and Camburn 1993) applies Boulding's hierarchy to the study of ethical behavior within giant corporations. In an important link with physical science, especially biology, a second work by Wilby applies Boulding's hierarchy to the study of emerging infectious diseases and argues that it can be used to improve the process of policy decisions in the area of public health (Wilby 2005). An approach with geographically broad implications (Ryan and Mothibi 2000) applies some of Boulding's later (mid-1960s) systems thinking to science and technology policy formulation problems in developing countries.

All of this work should eventually inspire further research that builds on the skeleton. In the interest of pointing the way toward possible future research ventures, some of the specific methodologies and research findings of the above work are worthy of closer examination.

For example, beginning with Boulding's skeleton, Martinelli compared characteristics of 18 separate hierarchies. Based on usefulness to corporate management, he drew upon the most relevant elements contained therein and constructed a new hierarchy combining portions of Boulding's first seven levels (up to the human level) (Martinelli 2001: 72). He further suggested ways his hierarchy could be enriched to accommodate specific corporate needs.

Wilby constructs a matrix to show that nearly every level of Boulding's skeleton can be used to categorize complex risk factors in emerging infectious diseases (Wilby 2005: 390). She argues that, even when single risk factors can be isolated, they must be studied using a multidisciplinary approach. By identifying relevant disciplines in each case, she is able to list those disciplines that were overlooked in a 1998 strategy document that assessed the threat and prevention of the spread of infectious diseases. The document was published by the US Center for Disease Control (CDC). In the Wilby study, the Boulding hierarchy is the centerpiece of the holistic analysis of CDC policy goals, with some disciplines being used at levels 7 and 8. As a result, it is possible to look beyond the scientific aspects of infectious diseases and include social, political, and human interest factors.

In their study of corporate ethics or the lack thereof, Sridhar and Camburn (1993) accept largely as is the first four levels of Boulding's hierarchy. They proceed to argue that much research on organizations, including the corporate structure, has been undertaken using the open systems approach of Boulding's level 4. They state further, however, that this level is inadequate for studying complex interactions among members of corporate organizations, including top-level management response to crises where ethical judgment is required.

After expanding the focus of levels 5 through 9 in the Boulding skeleton and redefining some terms, Sridhar and Camburn perform standard statistical tests on student perceptions of corporate response in five case studies: Arthur D. Little and toxic waste disposal, Burroughs Wellcome and the anti-AIDS drug called AZT, Drexel Burnham-Lambert and insider trading, the Lincoln Savings and Loan financial scandal, and the Miami Herald coverage of the extramarital affair involving US Senator Gary Hart. Each of these crises called into question organizational action or inaction.

Sridhar and Camburn conclude that the revised version of the Boulding hierarchy that they offer is better suited to the study of corporate ethics than previous attempts by organizational theorists, most of whom confine their analyses to the open systems approach of Boulding's level 4. Corporations in the Sridhar and Camburn study were viewed as more organic and more social entities where a more human-like set of qualities are marshaled in response to ethically dubious behavior.

The rigor vs. synthesis issue

GST has become more sophisticated in its techniques but also more fragmented. While the former is clearly a natural and generally desirable development, the latter has produced several branches of research teams not always cognizant of, or even interested in, what others are doing. Each branch, meanwhile, has produced a seemingly endless array of new terms with specific definitions, resulting in some controversy over what each of these terms means, how they can be used, and how important each is to the analysis in question. It is not unusual, for example, that a new methodology using a detailed set of newly defined terms is developed only to be ignored by others working in different branches of the GST tree. At some point, however, some synthesis of the best of these methodologies appears necessary while the least useful approaches (say, those with the fewest applications) are discarded or at least relegated secondary status.

Some of the problems of using the same terminology across traditional academic disciplines have been identified along with suggestions for minimizing reluctance to do so (Bailey 2001). Exporting both terms and concepts often still meets with resistance in the disciplines of both origin and destination. While Boulding certainly understood the need for overcoming this obstacle, it was primarily a hurdle he left for others to clear. In addition, he was so prolific at inventing new terms himself that he may have unintentionally contributed more to the problem than to its solution.

In some ways, modern GST has clearly moved beyond some of the constraints under which Boulding initially operated. Most notably, despite his contributions in the area of evolutionary economics (Boulding 1981) where the concept has always been held in extreme disfavor, Boulding initially appears to embrace the notion of equilibrium that the economics profession had "borrowed" from the physical sciences. His 1956 article explicitly states:

> In true dynamics ... we exhibit the system as a set of difference or differential equations, which are then solved in the form of an explicit function of each variable with time. Such a system may reach a position of stationary equilibrium, or it may not—there are plenty of examples of explosive dynamic systems, a very simple one being the growth of a sum at compound interest! Most physical and chemical reactions *and most social systems* do in fact exhibit a tendency to equilibrium—otherwise the world would have exploded or imploded long ago.
>
> (Boulding 1956: 203; italics added)

Despite his penchant for metaphor, Boulding at that time clearly endorsed use of the equilibrium concept in systems modeling. Modern GST theorists have chosen more dynamic methods, including complex diagrammatics originally developed under circular and cumulative causation (Pluta 2010). Later in life, Boulding himself became less enamored of the equilibrium concept, certainly as far as its application to systems thinking was concerned but also as a generally effective concept (Boulding 1978).

Drawing upon the early work of evolutionary economists (Veblen 1900; Myrdal 1944), researchers employing circular and cumulative causation are among the pioneers in the use of what present-day systems dynamicists call loop diagrams. Initially, these were developed as an alternative to equilibrium models, which are deficient because they suggest that changing a single variable moves the system to a new state of rest, that this new position is somehow benevolent or at least normal, and that change is one directional with no feedback effects. Loop diagrams allow for multiple interaction among variables within a system, explicitly recognize feedback effects, and openly acknowledge that a dynamic system may be moving toward either beneficial or harmful results. Loop diagrams today are more sophisticated than those originally used by evolutionary economists, although, once again, systems researchers often either ignore or downplay the early influence of evolutionary economists.[5]

One of the current branches of systems thinking is the open systems approach of post-Keynesian economics (Chick and Dow 2005; Chick 2004; and Loasby

2003). Recall from Table 2.1 that structurally self-maintaining open systems were a major feature of Boulding's level 4. Other than an occasional citation, however, few post-Keynesian authors acknowledge the influence of Boulding and explicit mention of the skeleton apparently does not exist in this literature. It should also be pointed out that the open systems methodology exemplifies only level 4 of the skeleton, while researchers in other branches of GST have laid claim to at least experimental work in levels 7 and 8.

Like others in the fragmented world of systems thinking, the post-Keynesians are engaged in a lively methodological debate over appropriate use of terms and the direction of their research. Compared to other systems theorists, the post-Keynesians are far more likely to draw on the circular and cumulative causation approach (Berger and Elsner 2007). More so than other schools of economic thought, post-Keynesians apply the open systems framework to key macroeconomic policy choices. Such a focus is especially useful since government policy (changes in tax rates, expenditure levels and priorities, regulation, and the money supply) affects both economic and noneconomic variables. Despite the wide range of issues it has addressed, post-Keynesian research provides little evidence of a sustained effort at synthesis with other systems thinkers.

One of the original goals of the systems movement was the unification of the sciences and the elimination of duplication that might be occurring simultaneously in different fields. Obviously, not only has this not happened but the road toward this achievement may also be getting longer. The fact that GST and its companion disciplines are still engaged in defining concepts and terms suggests how close to relative infancy this movement still resides.

In their rush to develop new methods, greater rigor, and wider applications, younger GST researchers have not always shown an appreciation for the historical origins of the movement. At the risk of overgeneralization, it might be mentioned that this is a characteristic shared by young scholars in many fields, most assuredly in economics and in a number of the physical sciences. In an effort to teach the latest analytical techniques, graduate programs are seldom guilty of overemphasizing the history of their disciplines.

The level of rigor found in much published GST research is indeed impressive and clearly has risen over the past three or four decades. This is especially evident in such journals as the *International Journal of General Systems*, *Cybernetics and Systems*, the *International Journal of Systems Science*, *Systems Research and Behavioral Science*, *Systemic Practice and Action Research*, and several others. The mathematical and technical sophistication displayed in models presented in these sources rivals that of most academic disciplines, certainly in the social sciences. Boulding himself no doubt would have appreciated and respected much of this work. He also, however, would have likely expressed concern that the level of analysis might be reducing rather than enhancing cross-disciplinary communication, which after all was a primary motivation behind the systems movement at its inception.

Rigor and synthesis, of course, need not be contradictory goals. Both can be achieved simultaneously but the process of doing so depends on the level of communication among leading researchers. Disciplinary boundaries must be broken down carefully, with conferences and continued published research the most likely vehicles. It would be difficult, and probably presumptuous, for someone like myself, who was not formally trained in systems theory, to offer any more in the way of recommendations. Leading researchers in GST are far more capable of leading the way. I would, however, like to offer one illustrative anecdote.

On three separate occasions, I did enjoy the distinct privilege of having lengthy one-on-one conversations with Kenneth Boulding in such disparate locations as Monterey, California; Georgetown, Texas; and Toronto, Canada. Each time, no matter what was being discussed, he inevitably returned to the importance of close communication among scholars in diverse disciplines. The story I remember best was his description of the economist who was building an elaborate econometric model encompassing dozens of quantifiable variables. At the conclusion of his research, the economist in the story stated proudly, almost arrogantly, that what remained to be done could be found in the discipline of political science if only someone there would expand upon *his* model.

With his characteristic warm smile, Boulding looked at me and stated: "But alas, the other chap wasn't there because he was busy building his own model that left out economic variables." No doubt he related similar stories to others and may have even published a version in one of his works of which I am not familiar. At the other extreme, as Boulding himself stated in 1956: "It is all too easy for the interdisciplinary to degenerate into the undisciplined" (Boulding 1956: 200). With slow but deliberate progress and, hopefully, with the advice of a wise sage like Boulding near at hand, systems thinking continues to work on avoiding both pitfalls.

Some possible refinements to the skeleton?

With the proliferation of data generation and collection in both the physical and the social sciences, it is not unreasonable to expect that greater empirical knowledge within levels 7 and 8 of the skeleton will soon be forthcoming. The traditional disciplines listed in Table 2.1 as representing levels 5 through 8 of the skeleton have clearly produced statistics not even imagined at the time the skeleton was initially conceived. Some of the methods developed in these areas clearly call for data to be subjected to testing.

It may be valuable at this point to reconsider how Boulding himself described the appropriate domain of his level 8. In his own words:

> ... it is convenient for some purposes to distinguish the individual human as a system from the social systems which surround him, and in this sense social organizations may be said to constitute another level of organization. The unit of such systems is not perhaps the person—the individual human as such—but the "role"—that part of the person which is concerned with the organization or situation in question, and it is tempting to define social

> organizations, or almost any social system, as a set of roles tied together with channels of communication.
>
> (Boulding 1956: 205)

Here Boulding the evolutionary economist is calling for systems theorists to study social organizations or humanly created institutions. A wider range of institutions (and the data they have spawned) than those listed as examples in Boulding's level 8 now provide added potential for those researching socio-cultural systems. Evolutionary economists define institutions as groupings of people with common behavior patterns (Pluta 2011: 204). Institutions include habits of thought (like custom and tradition), established social practices (like human behavior and family life), and forms of organization (like markets; business firms, large and small; banks; governments; and a legal system). Institutions are also considered to be established forms of ceremonial behavior.

Note the similarities in this definition of institutions to the description of organizations given by Mingers in his discussions of Boulding's level 8.

> ... Within such systems, regular patterns of behaviour emerge through the structural coupling between members. These can be described in terms such as rules, norms and patterns of meaning. Such Social Organizations can be highly diverse and ritualized, but once established are highly conservative since they generate, in their members, structural responses that generally conform to the prevailing relations.
>
> (Mingers 1997: 309)

The study of such entities within such traditional disciplines as economics, sociology, political science, history, anthropology, and psychology has been extensive over the past half century. No doubt, considerable duplication of effort has occurred. That fact alone speaks to the need for greater interdisciplinary effort.

Some steps in that direction have taken place, as is evident from such newly emerging fields as economic psychology, happiness research, cognitive science, sociobiology, and, to a lesser extent, behavioral economics. While interesting and clearly departing from the mainstream of several disciplines, most of these areas have seldom combined research methods of more than two (occasionally perhaps three) traditional disciplines. As such, they have fallen short of genuine systems thinking.

Traditional disciplines themselves are institutions. They are often static in their methods, past binding, resistant to change, authoritative (even dictatorial), ceremonial, and past-glorifying. They may even slow the speed with which new technical knowledge is introduced and human progress is achieved. Mainstream economics has certainly done this with its continued embrace of such dubious concepts as the invisible hand, consumer rationality, equilibrium, the marginal productivity theory, the inevitability of diminishing returns, and the fiction of pure competition.

Boulding and others in the systems thinking movement have taken a giant step in breaking down these and other traditional resistances to change. While much clearly remains to be done, the existence of data on many of the institutions mentioned above provides a potentially fruitful starting point for systems thinkers interested in exploring some of the higher levels of the skeleton. This is especially the case when one considers the wealth of data collected in recent decades on: corporations, including banks, small businesses, educational institutions, unions, religious organizations, government agencies, and even families. These databases have barely been tapped by researchers using a systems approach.

Summary and conclusions

Some contemporary systems theorists have chosen to ignore or at least downplay the early work of Kenneth Boulding. This group has advanced the level and scope of systems thinking by building more analytically sophisticated models and extending the range of issues that the interdisciplinary approach has addressed. Other contemporary researchers have made the Boulding skeleton the centerpiece of their pursuits. Some have adopted the skeleton largely as is and extended systems thinking above level 4 in the original hierarchy. Others have kept Boulding's first four levels intact while redefining the higher levels in ways that more suitably fit their particular research agendas.

Boulding constantly stressed communication across traditional academic disciplines as well as communication among systems thinkers. The former is still occurring with some regularity (even among groups that are not part of formal systems thinking), while the latter is often lacking as the movement has fragmented. Some systems theorists no longer feel comfortable even using the term GST and prefer monikers or nomenclature more in line with branches of the field in which they have done their own work.

Writing more than 20 years after outlining the rudiments of the skeleton, Boulding in his *Ecodynamics* presented a series of arguments for synthesis. Commenting on the book at the time of Boulding's death, one reviewer (Henderson 1995: 274) described this work "as the search for the all-by-all matrix". To make certain that general systems thinking does not move further from a full synthesis of disciplinary approaches today than it was in Boulding's day, the movement would do well to not lose sight of what originally motivated that "search".

Notes

1 Professor of Economics, St. Edward's University, Austin, Texas.
2 He does, however, speak of hierarchies in various systems (Boulding 1978). He also writes at length about many different aspects of his general systems theory in his later work (Boulding 1985, 1989).
3 The articles cited here are representative of some of the major contributions of these authors. All three have published a considerable amount in this field elsewhere. None of this work, however, draws substantially on the work of Boulding.
4 In all fairness, this article focuses primarily on the work of Ludwig von Bertalanffy, another pioneer in the field. It also calls for contemporary scholars to pay more

attention to the historical roots of the movement. The fact remains, however, that in this survey Boulding is virtually ignored.

5 For an excellent collection of articles on the historical roots as well as the applications of circular and cumulative causation, see Berger (2009).

References

Bailey, K.D. (2001) "Towards Unifying Science: Applying Concepts Across Disciplinary Boundaries", *Systems Research and Behavioral Science*, 18: 41–62.

Berger, S. (ed.) (2009) *The Foundations of Non-Equilibrium Economics: The Principle of Circular and Cumulative Causation*, London: Routledge.

Berger, S. and Elsner, W. (2007) "European Contributions to Evolutionary Institutional Economics: The Cases of Cumulative Circular Causation (CCC) and Open System Approach (OSA) – Some Methodological and Policy Implications", *Journal of Economic Issues*, 41: 529–537.

Boulding, K.E. (1956) "General Systems Theory: The Skeleton of Science", *Management Science*, 2: 197–208.

Boulding, K.E. (1978) *Ecodynamics: A New Theory of Societal Evolution*, Beverly Hills, CA: Sage.

Boulding, K.E. (1981) *Evolutionary Economics*, Beverly Hills, CA: Sage.

Boulding, K.E. (1985) *The World as a Total System*, Beverly Hills, CA: Sage.

Boulding, K.E. (1989) *Three Faces of Power*, Beverly Hills, CA: Sage.

Chick, V. (2004) "On Open Systems", *Brazilian Review of Political Economy*, 24: 1–16.

Chick, V. and Dow, S. (2005) "The Meaning of Open Systems", *Journal of Economic Methodology*, 12: 363–381.

Drack, M. and Schwarz, G. (2010) "Recent Developments in General System Theory", *Systems Research and Behavioral Science*, 27: 601–610.

Georgiou, I. (2010) "Seven and the Sausage Machine: Searching for Conclusions in Miller's 1956 Magical Paper", *Systems Research and Behavioral Science*, 27: 611–621.

Henderson, H. (1995) "An Appreciation of Kenneth Boulding", *Systems Research*, 12: 273–279.

Jackson, M.C. (2009) "Fifty Years of Systems Thinking for Management", *Journal of the Operational Research Society*, 60: 24–32.

Khalil, E.L. (1996) "Kenneth Boulding: Ecodynamicist or Evolutionary Economist?" *Journal of Post Keynesian Economics*, 19: 83–100.

Lane, D.C. (2008) "The Emergence and Use of Diagramming in System Dynamics: A Critical Account", *Systems Research and Behavioral Science*, 25: 3–23.

Loasby, B.J. (2003) "Closed Models and Open Systems", *Journal of Economic Methodology*, 10: 285–306.

Martinelli, D.P. (2001) "Systems Hierarchies and Management", *Systems Research and Behavioral Science*, 18: 69–82.

Mingers, J. (1997) "Systems Topologies in the Light of Autopoiesis: A Reconceptualization of Boulding's Hierarchy and a Typology of Self-Referential Systems", *Systems Research and Behavioral Science*, 14: 303–314.

Myrdal, G. (1944) *An American Dilemma*, New York: Harper and Brothers.

Pluta, J.E. (2010) "Evolutionary Alternatives to Equilibrium Economics: Some Suggested Applications", *American Journal of Economics and Sociology*, 69: 1155–1177.

Pluta, J.E. (2011) *Human Progress amid Resistance to Change*, Victoria, British Columbia: Freisen Press.

Radzicki, M.J. (2003) "Mr. Hamilton, Mr. Forrester, and a Foundation for Evolutionary Economics", *Journal of Economic Issues*, 37: 133–173.

Richardson, G.P. (1999) "Reflections for the Future of System Dynamics", *Journal of the Operational Research Society*, 50: 440–449.

Ryan, T.B. and Mothibi, J. (2000) "Towards a Systemic Framework for Understanding Science and Technology Policy Formulation Problems for Developing Countries", *Systems Research and Behavioral Science*, 17: 375–381.

Solo, R.A. (1994) "Kenneth Ewart Boulding: 1910–1993. An Appreciation", *Journal of Economic Issues*, 28: 1187–1200.

Sridhar, B.S. and Camburn, A. (1993) "Stages of Moral Development of Corporations", *Journal of Business Ethics*, 12: 727–739.

Troncale, L.R. (1985) "The Future of General Systems Research: Obstacles, Potentials, Case Studies", *Systems Research*, 2: 1–42.

Troncale, L.R. (2009) "Revisited: The Future of General Systems Research: Update on Obstacles, Potentials, Case Studies", *Systems Research and Behavioral Science*, 26: 553–561.

Veblen, T.B. (1900) "The Preconceptions of Economic Science", *Quarterly Journal of Economics*, 14: 240–269.

Warfield, J.N. (2003) "A Proposal for Systems Science", *Systems Research and Behavioral Science*, 20: 507–520.

Waters, R. (2006) "What Happened to Boulding's Evolutionary Economics?" *Journal of Economic Issues*, 40: 465–471.

Weaver, B. (2002) "Cutting the Apron Strings: Emerging Intelligent Process Control Systems", *Scientific Computing and Instrumentation*, 19: 18, 46.

Wilby, J.M. (2005) "Combining a Systems Framework with Epidemiology in the Study of Emerging Infectious Disease", *Systems Research and Behavioral Science*, 22: 385–398.

Wilby, J.M. (2006) "An Essay on Kenneth E. Boulding's General Systems Theory: The Skeleton of Science", *Systems Research and Behavioral Science*, 23: 695–699.

Poem

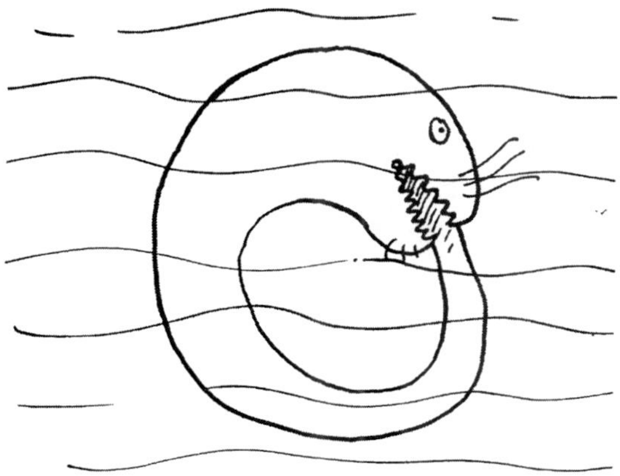

The Feedback

The Feedback lives upon its tail,
A source of food that cannot fail,
For Messages that bear repeat'n
Will grow as fast as they are eaten.

Part III

Unity of social sciences

3 Key text: The relations of economic, political, and social systems[1]

Kenneth E. Boulding

The raw material of social systems is the history of mankind. The record of history, however, is no more than raw material. In order to have knowledge of social systems, we must abstract out of the almost infinite complexity of this record those elements which exhibit enough regularity to be subject to analysis. Social systems, that is, are essentially abstractions from reality; without these abstractions, however, we cannot hope to understand reality. A system is anything that is not chaos, and even though history seems highly chaotic at times, we have an intuitive feeling that it is not pure chaos. If it is not chaos, there is system in it, and if there is system in it, there is some hope that the system may be perceived and understood.

All systems potentially consist of three elements, which might be labeled necessity, chance, and freedom. In the case of systems which have worked themselves through time into a virtual equilibrium, the elements of chance and freedom are practically non-existent and the element of necessity is all that remains. The solar system is a good case in point. In the formation of this system, there may well have been important elements of chance which determined how many planets there should be, how large they should be, and in what orbits they should lie. In so far as the system was created, it will have elements of freedom in it also, but this we must leave to the theologians. At present, however, the elements of chance and freedom have almost been eliminated, with the notable exception now of political astronomy. It is necessity that rules the stars or, at least, the planets. Their orbits can be described by difference or differential equations of only the second order. Given the position of the solar system yesterday and today, we can theoretically find an equation which will predict exactly its position tomorrow; given today and tomorrow, we can then predict the next day, and so on indefinitely into the future. It is this stability in the relationship between the positions of the system in successive time periods which constitutes *necessity* in mechanical systems and which gives us, therefore, the power of prediction. We can predict eclipses because they belong to a system in which the elements of chance and freedom are almost wholly eliminated.

As we move from the physical into the biological systems, the element of chance becomes more important in the dynamic process. We cannot predict the life history of an infant of any kind in the way that we can predict the movement of the planets. We can predict a limited range of life histories but we cannot tell in advance out of this limited range which one will be realized. We know that a kitten will not grow up into a dog, but his life history as a cat has many possible variations, none of which can be predicted in advance. It may be a hungry alley cat or a sleek house cat; it may be ferocious or gentle, depending on its experiences. In a living organism, we may, perhaps, regard its genetic constitution as embodying the element of necessity in its development, for its genetic constitution is something which it cannot change. Its development depends also, however, on environmental factors, some of which may be subject to necessity but many of which can only be attributed to chance. Systems of this kind are called "stochastic" systems and they are by no means absent even in physics. As we move from the physical through the biological into the social sciences, however, the stochastic element becomes more and more important. Such systems may be expressed by stochastic equations in which there is some random component; money invested at a constant rate of interest in a safe bank grows, according to a simple law of necessity, at a constant rate of growth. Money invested in speculative enterprises grows according to a stochastic system. There may be a constant growth component in it, but from day to day or from year to year a number is picked, as it were, out of a hat and added or subtracted. The actual day-to-day course of the system, therefore, is fundamentally unpredictable, even though the general tenor of its way may be predicted.

The third component of general systems, freedom, is virtually unknown at the physical level except in mixed socio-physical systems. It begins to become important as we reach the higher organisms in biology and it becomes of great importance in social systems. By freedom I mean that element which is introduced into the system by the existence of knowledge structures, or images, and especially by the existence of an image of the future. Freedom is the process by which an image of the future is consciously realized. If I am in Jamaica in December, 1961, it is not because of any mechanical necessity, such as that which moves the planets, for my movements are too complex to be described by differential equations, except, perhaps, of an infinite degree. Nor is it satisfactory to explain my appearance in Jamaica on the grounds that my movements constitute a random walk. I may flatter myself, but I am pretty sure that my movements around the face of the earth do not have the mathematical characteristics of a purely random path, that is, a path in which the direction, extent, and changes of movement are determined by the throw of the dice. The mere fact that I return home again occasionally is sufficient to destroy the random walk explanation, simply because a random walker returns home much less often than I do. There must, therefore, be some other explanation of my movements, and this can only be found in the fact that I have an image of the future at any moment of time and that I tend to act in such a way as to make the future conform to my image. If my image of the future involves going to Jamaica in December, 1961, sometime before this date I will make preparations; I will buy a plane ticket; at the right time I will go to the airport, get on the plane, and eventually arrive in Jamaica. There are, of course, stochastic elements in this process which may interrupt it; I may have a heart attack, the plane may crash, or the world may come to an end; these stochastic elements, however, lurk in every system, but it is one of the great objects of knowledge to lessen their incidence and to lower their probability.

We must recognize, therefore, that in any system which has an important element of freedom in it, knowledge about the system always changes it. We run into this even in the physical sciences in the famous Heisenberg principle, according to which the attempt to inform ourselves about the position or velocity of an electron changes its position or velocity. As we move towards the social sciences, knowledge about the system and information collected from the system becomes a more and more important part of the system itself. This does not mean, however, that knowledge is impossible or that the systems are uncontrollable. Indeed, the possibility of control of social systems arises only as knowledge about them increases. I am by no means a Marxist and, indeed, I regard Marxism as a very dangerous simplification of social dynamics, but I have a lot of sympathy with what Engels called the "leap from necessity into freedom." We begin to make this leap when our knowledge of social systems rises to the point at which some sort of control becomes possible so that the future is no longer solely in the hands of necessity and chance. We can then form images of the future of society as well as of our own personal lives which have some chance of coming about, a chance which is great enough to make it worthwhile pursuing conscious efforts towards the future that we have in mind. The more inaccurate our knowledge of the social system, of course, the less the element of freedom in it; we may think that we are directing our actions towards a certain future when, in fact, our actions have the effect of taking us away from this future rather than towards it. Nevertheless, the idea that we can plan for a future of society as well as in our own personal lives is, perhaps, one of the most important ideas of the nineteenth century, and it is an idea that we owe in no small measure to Marx himself.

If we are going to reduce the almost inconceivable complexity of human history to manageable, systematic form, we must break up the social system, at least conceptually, into sub-systems, recognizing, of course, but at the same time keeping in the back of our minds, the fact that these sub-systems are not independent and that they constantly interact with each other. A large number of these sub-systems may be identified, but I propose to discuss only four of them which I regard of primary importance. These four I shall label population systems, exchange systems, threat systems, and learning systems. In all of these, we can trace the same three general elements of necessity, chance, and freedom.

In population systems we consider, first of all, the total stock of all those objects or items which are significant from the point of view of social systems. We may consider also the composition of the stock, that is, its division into various significant categories. Then we consider the dynamics of the stock, that is, its change through time, as this is determined by additions to and subtractions from the stock. The fundamental law of necessity in such a system is that the increase in any stock over a period of time must be equal to the additions to the stock less the subtractions from it, or "births" into it minus "deaths" out of it. This identity is a mechanical necessity which can be avoided neither by chance nor by freedom.

The most significant population system is, of course, the population of human beings themselves. It is possible to make projections of human population and its distribution by area, race, sex, or any other composition by assuming fairly simple relationships between births, deaths, immigration, emigration, and so on into the various groups. These projections represent the element of necessity in population systems; they all take the form of saying that, if certain parameters of the system remain the same, then its course will be as projected. These projections, however, are not predictions, because of the chance elements in the system. The parameters themselves, such as the age-specific birth and death rates, are always subject to unpredictable change, and those who believed that the population projections were, in fact, predictions have been grievously disappointed by the experience of the last twenty-five years. Nevertheless, the projections are important, for they give us the range of possible futures and they enable us to make propositions of the form, "If there is no change in these parameters, then the future will be like this." We can say, for instance, to use a very crude example, that if the population of Jamaica continues to increase at its present rate, it will double, roughly, every forty years. Population systems also enable us to make projections about the distribution and composition of populations. Cohort analysis enables us to predict, within reasonable margins of error, what the age composition of the population is likely to be in the future. In the United States, for instance, the fact that there were so many more babies born in the forties than there were in the thirties has now created a crisis in the educational system because of the distortion in the age distribution of the population. This is a crisis which was both predictable and predicted. On the other hand, it is extremely dangerous to assume that birth and death rates will continue at present rates or will follow any prescribed course into the future. The failure of the population predictions of the forties was based largely on this mistake.

It is not only to human populations, however, that population analysis applies. It can be applied to anything which has a stock and which has additions to or subtractions from that stock. It can be applied, therefore, to the whole world of capital goods and of commodities; it can be applied even to such things as ideas and images. The famous proposition that capital can only increase if production exceeds consumption is identical in form with the basic identity of all population analysis. A good deal of the theory of economic development rests on this identity. The rate of capital accumulation can be increased only by increasing production or by diminishing consumption. Frequently, the latter is the only alternative open. So we run into the iron law of development; that development implies parsimony, whether involuntary or imposed.

It is clear that population systems broadly interpreted cover a large part of the field of social dynamics; nevertheless, they do not cover it all. As we move from demography into economics, for instance, we find that the concept of exchange becomes more and more important. Exchange systems may, perhaps, be regarded as a sub-division of population systems as they essentially involve the redistribution of existing stocks of things among people. Exchange systems, however, have peculiarities of their own, which perhaps justify their classification as a special sub-system. Exchange is a basic form of human interaction; it is basic, not only to economic life, but also to all social relationships, such as marriage, friendship, and all kinds of collective action. We think of it fundamentally as an exchange of "goods" and its basic proposition is, "I will do something good for you if you will do something good for me." It is a positive-sum game in which all parties can be better off, but it is also a curious mixture of cooperative and competitive elements. It is cooperative in so far as there is gain to both parties; it is competitive in so far as the distribution of this gain depends on the terms of trade, that is, on the ratio of exchange, in that the ratio of exchange makes one party relatively better off and one party relatively worse off than they were before.

Exchange systems can become seriously disturbed by changes in the medium of exchange. Inflation or deflation in the monetary system, for instance, disturbs the whole system of exchange because of the fact that many exchange relationships involve a time interval between one transaction and its reciprocal transactions. Exchange, of course, always consists of two transfers or transactions, but these do not have to occur at the same time. In a debt relationship, for instance, or in the implicit exchange among the generations in which the middle aged support the young in expectation that they themselves will be supported when they are old, and support the old in repayment of the support that they received when they were young, there is a substantial time interval between one transfer and the transfer which completes the exchange. If, in the interval, there is a general social change, for instance, in the price level, the whole system of transfers over time is disturbed. Inflation discriminates against the creditors, deflation against the debtors, and economic development can easily discriminate against the generation that initiates it. Marriage and friendship both may be wrecked by disappointment in deferred exchange, though in this case, the commodity may simply be affection or approval. Political parties and political structures, likewise, are involved in this time exchange; a political party makes promises and, if these are not fulfilled, the voters may take their revenge at the next election. The whole dynamics of population systems themselves are profoundly affected by the operations of the exchange system. Thus, the great depression in the United States, which resulted fundamentally from a breakdown in the exchange system, had profound effects on the birth rate, on future populations, and on the accumulation of capital.

Exchange systems, again, have certain elements of necessity in them. The relative price structure, for instance, is not arbitrary and cannot be changed at will without severe repercussions on the society. The closer we get to perfect competition, the greater the element of necessity in the system and the more all-pervasive and compelling is the "law of supply and demand." We cannot force the price structure away from some equilibrium position without producing serious consequences in the way of shortages and surpluses of commodities. As we move towards monopoly, and especially towards oligopoly or bilateral-monopoly, however, the element of chance in the system becomes more important. Where we have bargaining, there will be a range of prices at which a bargain may be struck, but there is no way of predicting in advance where within this range the bargain will actually be found. Under these circumstances, there is a genuinely stochastic element in the dynamics of a price system which cannot be neglected. There are also, however, elements of freedom in it. The equilibrium price structure is not an absolute necessity; it can be changed under appropriate governmental action and pressure. Within limits, the consequences of these distortions can be predicted, and the control of the price system may well be an instrument by which we move towards some image of the future. We may wish, for instance, to make vice expensive and virtue cheap, and we may be able to do this both through the tax system and through direct prohibitions or encouragements. We may look into the future and decide that some commodity, for instance, water, which is plentiful now, is going to be scarce in the future. We may wish, therefore, to distort the present price system in order to anticipate the future scarcity. The present price system, for instance, affects the course of future technology; if we make something expensive, it is likely to be economized. This is one argument, for instance, for distorting the price system in favor of higher money wages. Then a "disequilibrium" system would create dynamic change. Even though high wages create unemployment, it may be better to have unemployment than low wages because, if labor is scarce, it will be economized and it is the economizing of labor which constitutes the essence of economic development. These elements of freedom in the price system are not well understood or worked out, but they undoubtedly exist, and the more explicit we can be about them, the better our policy is likely to be. The argument that the price system must lie wholly in the realm of necessity is not, I think, acceptable to modern ears.

We have still by no means encompassed all the relationships of society and here, again, even though what I have called "threat systems" may be viewed as a special case of exchange systems, they nevertheless present so many peculiarities that they deserve to be singled out for special treatment. An exchange system is based on a transfer of goods, a threat system on the transfer of "bads." An exchange system, as we have seen, is based on the proposition, "If you do something good for me, I will do something good for you." A threat system is based on the proposition, "If you do not do something good for me, I will do something bad for you." Threat systems are the basis of politics as exchange systems are the basis of economics. Political power fundamentally is based on threats. Actual political life, however, is made up of a curious mixture of exchange systems and threat systems. In part, and perhaps in the largest part, government is always by consent, that is, by exchange. We give up some of our personal sovereignty to the state, as we give up some of our personal income in taxation because we feel that the state does something for us in exchange. It gives us protection, identification, an enlarged personality, and other benefits and, in so far as it does this, the system may quite properly be regarded as a system of exchange. This, however, is not the whole story. Man early discovered that threats were a powerful method of social organization. We can, indeed, conceive of classical civilization as essentially a threat system based on the fact that, with the invention of agriculture, the food producer produced more than he could eat himself or, rather, than he needed to eat himself, and that with the food surplus the ruler was able to feed an army or a coercive organization which would then compel the food producer to give up the food that would feed the agent that coerced him. As long as this is unchallenged, this is a very stable social system. As the civilizations of the Mayans and of Mohenjodaro testify, the threat, of course, need not always be a physical one. It can also be spiritual. Many of the early civilizations seem to have been based on spiritual threats, that is, on the capacity of a priesthood to threaten people with spiritual damnation, if they did not turn over their food surpluses to the social organization.

Slavery in the early colonial system was a good example of the threat system in an almost pure form. With the surplus which the slave produced over his subsistence, the master could employ a coercive power with which he could threaten the slave's life. As long as the slave preferred slavery to death, and as long as the master was able and willing to use the means of coercion at his disposal, the system continued. The demise of the system occurred, not so much because of any internal instability, but because of the fact that both its moral and its economic base were eroded by the development of more profitable systems of social organization, namely, a system of exchange. An exchange system is fundamentally more productive than a threat system simply because the exchange of goods encourages the production of goods, whereas the threat of ill discourages the production of goods. While a one-sided threat system is internally stable, threat systems in themselves develop instability because of the fact that they become not one-sided but bi-lateral. The proposition, "If you do not do good to me, I will do bad to you" becomes "If you do bad to me, I will do bad to you." It is hard to keep a monopolistic threat system intact, and, against one threat system, another threat system tends to be aroused. Threat systems, therefore, constantly decline into war systems or deterrence systems which seem to have an inherent instability in them. This is the main reason for the rise and fall of civilizations, and the long cycles which have characterized human development for the last 5,000 years. We are now at the extreme end of this period in which the threat system has become so universal that it threatens to destroy us all.

Any account of social dynamics would be incomplete if it did not include learning systems. Learning, of course, is involved in all the other systems but here, again, it has peculiarities of its own which make it desirable to single it out. A learning system may be defined broadly as a social process by which the image of the world possessed by the individuals of the society comes to change. At each moment, each individual has an image of the world which includes an image of space, of time, of the past and the future, of his role in society, of things that are expected of him, the things he expects of others, his obligations and his rights, and so on. This image largely determines his behavior. If people find themselves in situations where their behavior does not reinforce their image, then either their image must change or they will find themselves in a new situation. If a man thinks he is Napoleon and acts as if he were Napoleon, when in fact he is not, he will soon find himself segregated in a mental hospital in which his role is acceptable. We might add that if he thinks he is Napoleon when he is Napoleon, he finds himself at Saint Helena. Society moves and changes by an enormous interaction of images, behaviors, disappointments, role fulfillments or unfulfillments, and the constant interaction of images on society and society on the images.

The most significant thing that has happened, perhaps in the whole history of mankind, is the formalization and systemization of the learning process itself in what we know as science. This has resulted in an enormous acceleration of change in the image. In folk culture, the image is very resistant to change. If messages are received which are inconsistent with the image, they are generally rejected. Because of this stability in the image, a primitive society in which the processes of learning are not specialized, provided that it is left to itself, is likely to be very stable and will reproduce itself generation after generation. The specialization of the learning process has introduced an enormous dynamic into human society in the last 400 years and has now placed us in a pace of social change so rapid that now we go through in a single year a change in the basic parameters of the social system at least equivalent to what took 100 years in the age of classical civilization.

This specialization of the learning system offers both great hope and great danger to mankind. It offers hope because it is only out of this specialization that we can hope to understand the nature of social systems and, hence, move from the realm of necessity into the realm of freedom. It is only by the specialized activities of the knowledge seekers, especially in the social sciences, that we can hope to understand the social system sufficiently well to be able to control it and to be able to move into a positive image of the future through our own volition and policy. Otherwise, we are merely slaves of necessity or victims of chance. On the other hand, the very specialization of the learning process and the rapidity of change make it all the more difficult to understand and especially to get widespread understanding of the nature of the change itself. Let us imagine what the world would be like if the parameters of the physical systems in which we operate changed as rapidly and as unpredictably as the parameters of the social systems. Suppose, for instance, that on Monday the gravitational constant was low, whereas on Tuesday it was high; we would literally never know how to get out of bed. On Monday, we fly through the window and Tuesday we crack our head on the floor. To live at all in a world like this we would have to have an elaborate system of scientific information; we would have to have a gravimeter by the bedside to tell us before we even got up whether to make a desperate leap or a gentle movement.

This, however, is precisely the fix we are in in social systems. Their significant parameters, such as, for instance, the price level, the productivity of labor, the range of the deadly missile, or the proportion of communications received outside the family, change constantly and often with great rapidity. Under these circumstances, it is extremely difficult to know how to operate and it is not surprising that we make serious mistakes. Under these circumstances too, however, it is all the more important to devise accurate and unbiased methods of sifting information and of condensing information into forms which are readily appreciated. We desperately need a social systems-equivalent of the gravimeter by the bedside. In economics, we have this to some extent in the form of national income statistics. It was still possible in the United States in 1931 to argue about whether there was a depression or not. Today, we cannot have a turndown for two or three months without this fact coming to the attention of all the significant decision-makers in this society. In international systems, we have not yet reached this position; we have, in fact, a system of information which is almost designed to be corrupted. Both diplomats and intelligence agencies produce an extremely biased picture of the truth, by nature of the social system which they themselves inhabit, and until we can get more accurate and more "scientific" information in international systems, the chance of handling them well is very slim.

In religious systems, in family life, and in the broader learning process by which the images, skills, and ideas of society move from one year to the next, our information processes are not organized at all. Because of this, public expenditures, especially in the field of health, education, and welfare, are usually made very inefficiently. In the United States, at any rate, we seem to have a very fundamental principle, that while we are willing to spend a lot of money to see that public funds are spent honestly, we will not spend a dollar to see that they are spent wisely. Until this situation is rectified, one must remain highly skeptical about the advantages of any substantial expansion in the public sector, even in the most developed economies of the capitalist world. As a corollary, one might say that there is no socialist country in which an expansion of the private market sector would not result in a marked increase in economic efficiency, even though this might not result in the desired rate of social change.

I should, perhaps, add a fifth system to the four I have already outlined, though I am hesitant to do this because we understand so little about it. The four systems outlined above, however, do not encompass an important social phenomenon which could variously be described as social integration, affection, altruism, or even by the simple word "love." Love systems are those in which the individual comes to identify his own desires with those of another. These are important in the explanation of the institution of the family, of the church, and of nationalism, of the phenomena of philanthropy and self-sacrifice, and of all those areas of life where we do not merely exchange or threaten but in which we *identify*. A sense of identification, of course, participates in both exchange and threat systems; the love of country, like the love of a spouse, has elements of exchange in it or perhaps even of threat. These elements do not encompass the whole picture, however, and I suspect that we have to include an autonomous element of integration if we are to obtain a full description of social systems.

The complaint may be made with some justice that I have not dealt adequately with the title of the paper, in that my classification and hierarchy of systems does not correspond closely to the division between the economic, the political, and the social. My only defense to this charge is that I believe that the distinctions I have made are more elemental and important than the usual distinctions on which the customary division of the social sciences are based. It is true, of course, that economic systems concentrate around the phenomenon of exchange, and, if we like, we can identify exchange systems with economics. Economic systems cannot wholly be understood, however, apart from the economic operations of the government, especially through the systems of unilateral transfers in taxes and subsidies. In order to understand this element in the economic system, we have to invoke either threat systems or love systems. The budgets of states are arrived at by an extremely complex process of exchange, threat, and philanthropy; the same is true, as a matter of fact, for the budget of individuals.

Similarly, even though we may wish to make a certain identification of political science with threat systems, these also do not quite encompass its traditional field. Government is by consent as well as by threat; in order to explain government by consent we have to introduce either exchange systems or love systems. We consent also because we identify our own interest with those of the coercer. Even in international relations where we might suppose that threat systems reign supreme, we find that there are examples of the systems of stable peace, for instance, between the United States and Canada, in which the threat system has been so completely overlaid by other relationships that it has ceased to be important or, at least, visible.

Social systems are less clearly demarcated traditionally from political or economic systems. This has always caused difficulties, for the sociologist has never quite decided whether he is studying everything about the social system or whether he has a demarcated field within it. Sociologists like George Homans attempt to make exchange the basis of all social relationship. I suspect this is quite inadequate and that, even in the most elementary forms of social interaction, threat systems and love systems are important and that all these, of course, exist in the setting of population systems and learning systems. It would certainly be tidy if the sociologist could be designated to study love systems as the core of his discipline, that is, the systems by which integration takes place. To put the matter in another way, the principal subject of sociology would then be alienation, which is, of course, the opposite of integration. This division of labor is probably too tidy and most sociologists would object to it. However, it does seem to me that the problem of how, in the course of social interaction, we learn or fail to learn to identify with other people and with other organizations is peculiar to the "sociological" part of social systems.

As for the interaction among these various systems, it would take, of course, a large volume even to summarize them. I will take but a single example from the problem of economic development. Economic development as a process can be described fairly accurately by means of population systems. Its principal measure is the increase in *per capita* income, which is, of course, the birth rate of commodities per person or the amount of commodities to which the average individual gives birth in the course of a year's activity. There is a somewhat mechanical economic theory of economic development which is essentially an application of population analysis, arising out of the assumption that income is a function of total capital and that the increase in capital is a function of the differences in income and consumption. This mechanical theory, however, is descriptive rather than predictive. In order to give it flesh and blood, we must have some notion about the role of the exchange system, especially as reflected in the price structure, in this process. We must know also something about the role of threat systems, that is, the possibility of the use of coercive power. On the whole, it may be said that the capitalist development rests on exchange systems and socialist development on the threat systems, but this, as usual, is too simple a point of view and many modifications would have to be made. It can be said also, I suspect, that a prerequisite of economic development is a certain minimum of social integration. Economic development always involves costs to certain parts of the population. It is a painful process which may involve a gross injustice to a whole generation who sacrifice for growth in order that the next generation or so may enjoy the benefits. Such a system is impossible unless there is a strong sense of social identification. In traditional capitalism, the sense of identification is supposed to be found through the family. The present generation is expected to be parsimonious because the parents identify with the children or even the great-grandchildren who will enjoy the fruits of the parsimony. The family, that is, is a love system extending through time. Socialist development attempts to expand this sense of identification to the whole society, at least as embodied in the élite party. There is a thin dividing line, however, between love systems and threat systems and there is a constant tendency for one to pass into the other. Thus, capitalist development has seldom proceeded very far without the exercise of police power, and socialist development seems to be even more dependent on coercion, as the record of Stalin shows. It is in the study of the subtle interweaving of these various systems of society, therefore, that the best hope of understanding social systems and, therefore, ultimately, their control lies.

Note

1 This article was previously published in *Social and Economic Studies* (Jamaica), December 1962, 11(4): 351–362, and was reprinted as chapter 12 in K.E. Boulding, *Beyond Economics – Essays on Society, Religion, and Ethics*, Ann Arbor: The University of Michigan Press, pp. 98–111.

3a Commentary article: Boulding among the structuralists[1]

Robert A. Solo

The character of structuralism is given as studies of systems of perception wherein the author interposes an organizing element between observation and perception. The organizing element for Piaget is the cognitive structure, for Foucault the epistime, for Kuhn the paradigm, for Solo ideology, and for Boulding the image. The idea and significance of "the image" in Boulding's book *The Image* is analyzed and the place of that work in Boulding's grand project, to create a universal science, is indicated.

Structuralism

In this essay, I will locate and discuss the place and work of Kenneth Boulding as a "structuralist," in relation to that of Jean Piaget, Michel Foucault, and Thomas Kuhn, alike regarded as preeminent among structuralists; to these names I humbly add my own. Piaget wrote as a psychologist, Foucault and Kuhn as historians and philosophers of science, and I as an institutional economist.

I must at once enter a disclaimer. It is not clear to me that structuralism can be understood as a field of study or as a philosophy or as a school of thought, though Jean Piaget tried to make it into all three. If there is a structuralist school, it is not one that Boulding, Foucault, Kuhn, or myself ever attended. In the preface to his most famous work, *The Order of Things*, the redoubtable Michel Foucault remarks acidly:

> In France certain half-witted "commentators" persist in labeling me a structuralist … I have been unable to get it into their tiny minds that I have used none of the methods, concepts or key terms that characterize structural analysis.
>
> … There may well be certain similarities between the work of the structuralists and my own work. It would hardly behoove me, of all people, to claim that my discourse is independent of the conditions and rules of which I am very largely unaware, and which determine other work that is being done today.
>
> (1970: xiv)

I agree with Foucault in that I do not associate structuralism with any particular theory or philosophy but I do believe that those "certain similarities" to which he refers constitutes the spontaneous emergence of a distinctive and significant category of thought that I will refer to as structuralist. Structuralist thought can be characterized as follows:

All structuralist works are studies of the system (or systems) of perception. And they all share an approach to the analysis of such systems. Traditionally we think of perception as a one-on-one relationship equating the observed and the perceived. The structuralist interposes between the observation and the perception an organizing element that controls (screen, shapes) the perception of the observed and that hence determines consequent thought and behavior. The originality and distinctive character of any particular brand of structuralism lies in the nature of the organizing element that it would interpose between observation and perception. Jean Piaget called his organizing element "cognitive structure," hence the name "structuralism."

In what follows, the structuralist inquiry will be illustrated and elaborated upon with reference to the work of Piaget, Foucault, Kuhn, Solo, and later, Boulding.

Piaget

Psychologists have long been interested in the process of learning, especially the extraordinary and critical early learning by children. It was thought that children learned in a continuous and cumulative process of observing and absorbing, watching, remembering, imitating. Piaget interposed between observation and perception a genetically determined, layered series of what he called "cognitive structures." Each cognitive structure lays out a distinctive and bounded potential for learning within a determined level of conceptualization and comprehension. Each cognitive structure is a prerequisite to and opens the way for the succeeding cognitive structure that enables another, more encompassing level of conceptualization and comprehension. And so on in a series that constitutes the genetically determined hierarchy of development. Thus:

> Piaget uncovers in his studies of child learning a sequential emergence of explicable, identifiable cognitive structures, formations within the unconscious that put boundaries upon observation and awareness and determines the possibilities of and the character of thought.
>
> The infant in its groping realizes the geography of the blanket and the space of the crib. Within the frame of that momentous realization it is able to observe, in quite a new way the events of the world. On the basis of that fundamental discovery of the nature of space, another cognitive structure can emerge through the questing volition of the mind. Another continent of reality is discovered in the realization of continuities extraneous to the reach of its own sight and sensation, that the toy tucked under the blanket before the nap will be there upon waking and that all other things have a life or

> existence continuing outside and apart from the mind's eye. In the frame of that cognitive structure, making sights and sensations into independent things and existences, patterns of relationships between those objects and existences can be observed and thought upon.
>
> (Solo 1993: 25)

Kuhn

Children learn, and societies learn. I think it is fair to say that, in the modern world, science and scientific advance are understood as at least the prime species of social learning. Science and scientific advance as a process of social learning, as it is described in the logical positivism of Karl Popper, is very much like the process of child learning as propounded by psychology before Piaget. It was understood as a continuous and cumulative process of learning through observation, trial, and error. Popper postulates a process wherein accepted theory and hypotheses are constantly subjected to the test of prediction. Whatever fails that test is thereby by "falsified" and must be discarded. Thence a breach is created in the seamless horizon of science. The energies of scientists rush in to fill the breach in a process of search and discovery to the end of formulating a theory that overcomes that specific failure in prediction while explaining and predicting all that could be explained and predicted before. Given the ever-expanding reach and scope of scientific inquiry forever opening new areas of phenomena against which the laws of science must be tested, new failures of prediction are inevitable. Theories will be falsified and inadequacies of the existing structure of science will be thus uncovered, and the energies of science will again rush in to overcome the failure in prediction with another transformation of the body of theory that restores its full capacity to explain and predict. Thus science operates as a cumulative and continuous movement toward a complete and perfect grasp of physical reality.

> The neo-classical view of science projects the image of rational man onto a continuum of centuries. An endless indefatigable, unilinear learning process produces an accumulating fund of information, ever increasing in breadth and in the precision with which it follows the contours of reality. As does the rational mind, science operates through perpetually testing its ideas against the experience of reality. When an established theory, extended beyond its powers to comprehend and explain observed phenomena, fails the test of prediction, it is rejected. In its place a new theory is installed, one that cannot be so refuted within the present range of information, until once more the quest for information goes beyond the power of theory to explain and to predict. That theory, in its turn, is refuted, discarded, replaced by another more adequate theory. So the process continues in the unending construction of a more encompassing system of scientific laws.
>
> (Solo 1993: 28)

Thomas Kuhn challenged and denied this neoclassical view of science as a cumulative and continuous learning process and offered a different conception of "scientific advance." As Piaget interposed cognitive structures as the organizing element that contained, directed, shaped, and set the boundaries of individual perception and learning. Thomas Kuhn interposes the "the paradigm" as the organizing element that contains, directs, shapes, and sets the boundaries of disciplinary perception in the process of social learning. The paradigm is the perceptual framework within which a particular scientific inquiry or discipline operates, and from which that inquiry or discipline derives its focus and coherence.

The paradigm embodies a given set of related generalizations, and theories, attitudes and expectations, conventional assumptions, and model experiments, with these as parameters that delimit the boundaries of perception. Within those boundaries, scientific activity can proceed in the positivist mode, formulating theories, submitting them to the test of prediction and taking predictive failures into account in the design of future research. Such science operating within the boundaries of the paradigm can bear good fruit and register genuine scientific progress. The science practiced and performed within the boundaries of the paradigm, Kuhn called "normal science" and normal science, says Kuhn, is what "all scientists do most of the time and what some scientists do all of the time."

The paradigm that encloses each of the disciplines of science and that contains, shapes, and limits the thought and endeavors of all those who operate within that discipline is itself resistant to challenge and change. It does not vanish and wither away at the touchstone of predictive failure. It does not accept for itself the test of predictive failure. Rather it exists as an island of order in a sea of contradiction and anomalies. Its central precepts and its boundary assumptions are immune from its own machinery of test and discard. It can generate a bounded progress from within itself, but it cannot by its own rules transcend itself and escape its own boundaries. Yet it is precisely in transcending the paradigm and escaping its boundaries that what we consider the great advances of science occur. Thus the history of scientific advance appears as a series of leaps from one paradigm to another. The process of breakthrough, escaping the boundaries and transcending the enclosure of a discipline to create an alternative outlook and the basis for the formation of a rival paradigm (which will in turn exist as an island in a sea of anomalies and contradictions), Kuhn calls "revolutionary science." Thus understood science as a process of social learning ceases to be unilinear and cumulative. Nor can we speak of scientific advance with the old certainty. Certainly science changes but whether those changes are to be regarded as an advance or not becomes a matter not of proof but rather of intuition and judgment.

It should not be difficult for us to understand and appreciate Kuhn's arguments in the light of our experience qua economists with the ups and downs of and the shifts in the prevailing perceptions between the three coexisting paradigms in economics: the neoclassical, the Keynesian, and the Marxist. Nor have we any definitive explanation of what brings about the formation and disposition, the acceptance and the discard of the paradigm. The nature of Kuhn's "revolutionary science" remains a mystery. And the same is true when we look to the cause of basic change in the organizing element in any of the systems of perception introduced by the structuralists.

Foucault

Michel Foucault postulates an organizing element determining the character of collective perception that goes deeper than Piaget's cognitive structures, and deeper than Kuhn's paradigm. He seeks for and identifies time-defined prisms of perception that he calls the "epistime," which at some subconscious and yet universal level casts a unique and particular light on every endeavor of science and in every facet of art and every facet of endeavor of the time. In so doing, it defines an era. In ways and for reasons that are not yet explained, prisms of perceptions come and go; and when they go and when they come all phenomena will be seen in a different light. As a consequence, there will be revolutionary changes across the board, in every facet of science, in every facet of art. And these many, revolutionary changes will, in their essence, be the same change, reflecting (and revealing) the same shift in an underlying vision of things. For example, the theories of Marx and Darwin are worlds apart. Yet in essence they are the same theory, the same vision of boundless and bloody evolutionary struggle.

In support of his thesis, Foucault produces a massive analytic. It is focused on the history of exemplar sciences (those concerned with living things, with language, with the economy, with disease, and with insanity) from the period of the Renaissance to the modern epoch. At successive points in history, he goes to the prevailing character of these sciences at the time to show their fundamental commonality and hence to uncover and reveal the episteme as the organizing element of perception underlying them all. Then comes the quick collapse of that episteme and its sudden replacement by another that works its way up from deep layers of the subconscious into a revolutionary transformation of inquiry on living things, on language, and on the economy, exemplifying the birth of a new collective perception shared and made manifest in each of the aforementioned areas of inquiry.

Do other avant-garde movements like "deconstruction" reflect the same epistemic change? They too focus on systems of perception. While the structuralist goes from the event, observed and interpreted via the systems of perception, and inscribed as the text, the deconstructionist goes from the text deconstructed to determine and perhaps to challenge the perceptions it reflects.

Solo

I have qua structuralist interposed ideology as the organizing element of individual and collective perceptions, with ideology defined as:

> any set of the individual's ideas concerning what is … and what should be … with respect to a field of choice and action. Ideology is the individual's

> notion of what should be done, framed necessarily within his conception of what is possible.
>
> Without an ideology suited to the problem or question at issue, there can be no coherent choice or purposeful action.... Nor is the need for ideology singular, any more than there is but a single field of choice and action ... and for any or each of these fields of choice and action, a different and distinct set of ideas and values may be brought to bear.... Choice and action operate by reference to an ideological complex, or to a cluster of ideologies.
>
> (Solo 1974: 1–2)

> Ideologies die. They vanish and are forgotten. But there can be no end to ideology itself, for ideology is a functional necessity. It is the interface of the psychic and social systems. It is man's window on his world.
>
> (1974: 18)

The Political Authority and the Market System (Solo 1974), focusing on the American experience, attempts among other things to explain

1 the creation and transformation of ideology;
2 the operation of the American political system in the interplay of the Congress as an agency of "composite choice" where the role of ideology is peripheral and transient and of the Supreme Court as an agency of authoritative choice where ideology plays the central role; and
3 in these terms to explain the development of American Economic policy and the development of American Constitutional Law over the past two centuries.

Boulding

After spending the 1954–1955 academic year at the Center for Advanced Study in the Behavioral Sciences at Stanford University, with eleven months of "vigorous interaction, both playful and serious, with a group of thirty six able social and biological scientists," while still in a state of "intellectual exaltation," Kenneth Boulding "dictated, in uninterrupted composition, *The Image*."

The Image is a beautiful little book, indeed a work of art, and the one that Boulding himself considers to be his best and most successful. It is also his only specifically structuralist work. It conceives everyman's system of perception with an image of "all the mind knows," as the organizing element that even as it recreates itself through observing and learning serves to screen and control the new inflow of impression and information and to orient and direct behavior and response. Kenneth Boulding displays before us that latent image of "all that I know" unrolling under the impulsion of whim or will:

> I know where I am. I see before me ... the red roofs of the campus of Stanford University, beyond that the ... bare golden hills of the Hamilton Range

… have a picture of the earth as round. I visualize it as a globe.… Looking further I visualize the globe as a small speck circling around a bright star … not only located in space. I am located in time. I know I came to California about a year ago and am leaving in about three weeks.… I have a picture in my mind of the formation of the earth, of the long history of geological time, of the brief history of man … I am … located in a field of personal relations.… I know to some extent who I am … a professor … I will go into a classroom and begin to speak and nobody will be surprised.… I am located in a world of nature, in a world of how things operate … when I get to my car there are some things I must do to start it … Finally I am located in a world of subtle intimations and emotions. I am sometimes elated, sometimes a little depressed, sometimes happy, sometimes sad.… What I am talking about is what I believe to be true; my subjective knowledge. It is this Image that largely governs my behavior. In about an hour I will rise … drive down to my home, play with the children, have supper, perhaps read a book, go to bed.… *The first proposition of this book, therefore is that behavior depends on the image.*

What, however, determines the image? That is the central question of this work.… The image is built up as a result of all the past experiences of the possessor of the image … there is a constant stream of messages entering the organism from the senses.… As a child grows his image of the world expands … every time a message reaches him his image is likely to be changed in some degree by it, and as his image is changed his behavior will be changed likewise.… *The meaning of a message is the change which it produces in the image.* When a message hits an image … the image … may change … in some rather regular and well defined way.… There is, however, a third type of change of the image that might be described as a revolutionary change. Sometimes a message hits some sort of nucleus or supporting structure in the image and the whole thing changes in a quite radical way … our image is in itself resistant to change. When it receives messages that conflict with it, its first impulse is to reject them as in some sense untrue … then one day we receive a message which overthrows our previous image and we revise it completely. The person, for instance, whom we saw as a trusted friend is now seen to be a hypocrite and deceiver … a certain difference between the image which I have of physical objects in space and time and the valuations which I put on these objects. The image of value is concerned with the *ratings* of the various parts of our image of the world, according to some scale of betterness or worseness.… We change these scales of valuation in response to messages received much as we change our image of the world around us … a "devout" psychologist will resist strongly any evidence of extrasensory perception, because to accept it would overthrow his whole image of the universe … for any individual organism or organization, there are no such things as "facts." There are only messages filtered through a changeable value system.… Part of our image of the world is the belief that this image is shared by other people like

> ourselves who are also part of our image of the world.... If a group of people are in a room together their behavior clearly shows they all think they are in the same room. It is this shared image which is "public knowledge" ... groups of individuals do not merely share messages that come to them from nature. They also initiate and receive messages themselves.... It is discourse or conversation that makes the human image "public" in a way that the image of no lower animal can possibly be.... In my theoretical system the scientific method merely stands as one among the many methods whereby images change and develop. The development of images is part of the culture or of the subculture in which they are developed.... Science is a subculture among subcultures. It can claim to be useful.... It cannot claim to give validity ... my theory might well be called an organic theory of knowledge.... We do not have to conceive of the knowledge structure as a physical chemical structure. It can be inferred from the behavior of the organism.... When I say the knowledge is an organic structure, I mean that it follows principles of growth and development similar to those with which we are familiar in complex organisms and organizations. ... Growth takes place through a kind of metabolism.... An active internal organizing principle much as a gene is a principle or entity organizing the growth of bodily structures ... an inward teacher imposing its own form and "will" on the less formed matter around it.
>
> (Boulding 1961: 3–19)

I apologize for the brevity of this message and for the piecemeal, bitty-bit manner in which it was delivered, but I hope that it conveys to you the character of Boulding's "image" and the role "image" plays in his system of perception. Boulding goes on "to discuss the growth of images, both public and private, in individuals, in organizations, in society, and even, with some trepidation among the lower forms of life" (1961: 19).

He regards any escape from entropy and chaos as an "organization" and he proposes a hierarchy of organization in terms of the increasingly central role of the image, going from static structures, i.e. things, bodies, trees, roads, houses, planets, in their aspect of being "just there" for us. At the next level, organization is the predetermined dynamics of the "clockwork.... The great clock of course is the solar system endlessly repeating its complex motions in the majestic wheel of the firmament." The third level of organization Boulding called "thermostats" where an image and a value scale is built into the machine *Image ex Machina.* The thermometer has its image of a universe of temperatures, its scale of values, its temperature ideal, *too warm, not warm enough, just right*, and its messages communicating with the heater, *turn it up, turn it down, turn on, shut off.*

I found Boulding's section on thermostats provocative and highly intriguing. That we have created the machine in our own image, and made the world of machines into a reflection of our own world, has a mythic quality with an echo from Genesis. The material on the biological level of life is truly amazing. One senses that this is an area on which Boulding has been cogitating for decades, his own ideas building, his excitement mounting, his enthusiasm fresh, his new image ready to burst forth. Here he is not reviewing old knowledge to show the links of its acquisition with the image. Here rather we stand beside Boulding as his own comprehension grows. In a word, we are not moving away from acquired knowledge that has been used to exemplify facets of the image. We are moving toward new conceptions that the use of the image serves to express and explore. And in fact the material developed in the chapter on the biological level of life casts a long shadow ahead. It is the seed that will flower two decades later in Boulding's *Ecodynamics* as a revolutionary reconceptualization of the theory of evolution.

Boulding finds his fourth stage in the organization of the living cell as a self-maintaining system capable of metabolism, digestion, excretion, and reproduction: "Its behavior cannot be understood unless it is assumed that in some sense it has 'knowledge'—that it interprets the information it receives into the form of a knowledge structure." At the fifth level of organization is the plant with its "society of cells" or its cell societies, each of which receives something from the others and gives something to the others in ways that support the continued existence of them all, with messages from their environment built into an image. "The plant 'knows' when it is time to put out its leaves, to flower, to fruit, and to die." At the sixth level of organization, that of the animal, with an enormous increase in the capacity to take in and absorb information, with increased complexity of the image, and a greatly increased capacity to learn in a learning that can directly reshape the image and the behavior of the organism.

> The seventh level of organization is that of the human being … it is the capacity for organizing information into large and complex images that is the chief glory of our species.… We not only know, but we know that we know. This reflective character of the human image is unique … man is capable of "rational behavior," that is to say, his response is not to an immediate stimulus but to an image of the future filtered through an elaborate value system … Man's image is also characterized by a phenomenal capacity for internal growth and development quite independent of messages received from the outside.… This property of the "imagination" is also responsible for the greatest achievements of man.

In the exercise of this imagination he can build organizations that transcend individual mortality as open systems of roles and niches with individuals hired and fired, living and dying as their throughput.

Thus the image "is clearly present even at the very earliest stages of life. It grows in importance and complexity as we ascend the biological ladder. It is of overwhelming importance in the interpretation of human behavior and the dynamics of society" (Boulding 1961: 19–31).

Piaget wrote as a psychologist, Foucault and Kuhn as historians of science, I as an economist; all of us developed our structuralist ideas and applied our structuralist perceptions within the frame of our professional paradigms. Not Kenneth Boulding! *The Image* was written and remains entirely apart from and outside of his economics. Understanding structuralism in the study of the systems of perception, including the perceptions of self-perception, *The Image* is perhaps the purest and broadest expression of the structuralist idea.

The creation of this isolated masterpiece is not untypical in Boulding's career. With his eagle's vision he was always far ahead of his time. In the distance he spied out bountiful potentials. The crowd was far behind. He hacked out a path to those potentials. He designed and created prototypes, and some in the crowd looked on with admiration, even amazement, but they stayed behind, preferring the familiarity and security of the trenches to the bright new fields into which he would lead them. Nor was Boulding troubled by their reluctance, for he was driven by another and higher aspiration. This was to create a universal science, with *The Image* playing a central role in that project.

After he had established his mastery of neoclassical and Keynesian economics and had transcended their boundaries, he sought step by step to create a universal science. His effort to create a universal science can be understood as having three phases. The first to create a general science to encompass and account for the interaction and interdependence of physical, natural, and social entities. The second to develop a general theory of learning, knowledge, and behavior in the psychic domain. The third to conceptualize biological, societal, and physical evolution and change in the universe at large.

Boulding took a step in fulfillment of the first phase of this agenda with his *Reconstruction of Economics* (1950), with its blueprint and a prototype for the transformation of economics into a universal theory of ecology, whose laws would cover the interaction and interdependence of all physical, natural, and social entities.

The Image, which is the subject of this essay, relates to the second phase of the grand project. There Boulding goes directly to the mind, central system of perception and warehouse of images, those "images in the mind to which all of us are chained." In it Boulding laid the basis for a universal theory of learning, knowledge, organization, and behavior.

His last great work, *Ecodynamics: A New Theory of Societal Evolution*, which covers the spheres of "societal evolution and its biological corollary" and of "physical dynamics and evolution," would be the third and culminating phase of the grand project. It is an enormous work that offers a new critique and a fascinating reconception of biological evolution, and an awesome and prophetic vision of a future that merges the dangers implicit in biological, geological, sociological trends and evolution, and the options for political choice and action.

In the nine brilliant concluding chapters of *The Image*, Boulding elaborated upon and developed the implications of this theory with respect to the Biological Level of Life, to Man and Society, to the Public Image, to the Sociology of Knowledge, to Economic Life, to the Political Process, to History, and to Philosophy. And if these chapters say a lot about the world, they also tell us much about Boulding's own, personal image of the world in the mid-1950s.

To the degree that their focus is on the natural world, these closing chapters of *The Image* surprise and excite us. Not so with the chapters on the social sciences and the humanities. Of course there is wisdom, insight, and novelty in every one of them, but one senses that by now the author has become a little weary with matters on which he has already had his say. He uses them now as a reference base to illustrate in concrete ways the uses and the potentials of the image. His treatment of philosophy, for example, is simply to use the ideas of the image to cast (justifiable) doubt on the value of conventional epistemology, and indeed on the idea of "scientific truth." I was especially disappointed with his chapter on the economic life. There he ridicules the use of certain images associated with the theory of utility maximization and the indifference curve. I have no quarrel with what he says. I was troubled by what he failed to say. He bushwhacked the theory where I would have expected a frontal assault. With his work on the theory of organization and with his development of the "public image" he had the weapons for a frontal assault. He could have gone to the decision-making crux of the economy where the formation of a public image in the realm of a quasi-political bureaucracy roamed over by the free-wheeling buccaneers has replaced the ownership-based power and the individualized choice of the traditional entrepreneur. Kenneth Boulding was himself too chained to the images of neoclassical theory ever to attack theory at its roots.

This was a time of transition, and Boulding's *The Image* is a model of that transition of thought with its sometimes incongruous intermingling of the old and the new. Like all great creative thinkers, he never fully assimilated into his image the forward leaps of his thinking. Thus, for example, while he regarded Freud with a certain awe, and spoke of the subconscious with ponderous respect, and foresaw the psychoanalytic record as a sort of data base for the new science of Eiconics he proposed, no element of the unconscious mind enters into his analytic. He is in essence a man of the enlightenment. In his own thinking, and in thinking about thought, and about learning, he is an unreconstructed rational individualist. With all his immense erudition, the work of the structuralists, who had so much to say to him, passed him by. Which is too bad. Piaget would certainly have changed his image of learning, and particularly of child learning. Kuhn and Foucault would have changed his idea of science and of scientific advance, and would have given him the sense of deeper directives in the formation of images than the messages of which he speaks.

Not only for what it says but also for what it fails to say, for what it takes into and for what it leaves out of account, for what it knows and for what it does not know, Kenneth Boulding's *The Image* is a personal document but also is an historical artifact, and ought also to be studied as such. It is an artifact that offers an indelible insight into the population of images existing as the living reality of a moment in history. The world of *The Image* as of when it was written was quite a hopeful one. War was over. We were getting down to business, normal life returning. The war was remembered but its awesome demons had gone; nor does *The Image* convey any fear that they would soon return. There is no hint of clouds on the horizon. There is no word of a drug culture sweeping its world, nor of a vast opulence, nor of a vast poverty with the poor and homeless spread out like a blanket of misery on city streets. Nor evidently was didactic feminism yet in the saddle, for Kenneth Boulding speaks without shame of Man as the symbol of humanity. Nor had Boulding's America become the one superpower, the only big bully on the block.

In any case, to read *The Image* now or a hundred years from now is again to touch the hand and to be warmed by the spirit of a greatness that refuses to diminish.

Note

1 This article was previously published in *Review of Social Economy*, Winter 1997, 55(4): 432–444.

References

Boulding, Kenneth E. (1950) *Reconstruction of Economics*, New York: John Wiley & Sons.

Boulding, Kenneth E. (1961) *The Image*, Ann Arbor: University of Michigan Press.

Boulding, Kenneth E. (1978) *Ecodynamics: A New Theory of Societal Evolution*, Beverly Hills, CA: Sage Publications.

Foucault, Michel (1970) *The Order of Things*, New York: Random House.

Kuhn, Thomas S. (1962) *The Structure of Scientific Revolutions*, Chicago: University of Chicago Press.

Piaget, Jean (1967) *Logique et connaisance scientifique*, Paris: Gallimard.

Piaget, Jean (1971) *Structuralism*, New York: Harper Torchbooks.

Solo, Robert (1974) *The Political Authority and the Market System*, Cincinnati: South-Western Pub. Co.

Solo, Robert (1991) *The Philosophy of Science and Economics*, London: Macmillan.

Solo, Robert (1993) [1975] "What is Structuralism? Piaget's Epistemology and the Varieties of Structuralist Thought," in Warren J. Samuels (ed.), *The Chicago School of Political Economy*, New Brunswick, NJ: Transaction Publishers.

3b Comment: Social dynamics, evolution, and the unity of social sciences

Kenneth Boulding in the light of Friedrich von Hayek and John Searle

Thomas Marmefelt

Introduction

The unity of social sciences becomes apparent when studying social dynamics. In his important article, 'The Relations of Economic, Political, and Social Systems', Kenneth Boulding (1962) establishes the unity of social sciences as emerging from the interdependence between various systems shaping social dynamics: the population, exchange, threat, learning, and love systems. The basic idea is interdependent social systems, reflecting Boulding the systems theorist. His emphasis is upon the interdependence of and interaction between systems; in fact he anticipates his own thought on social evolution, elaborated in his later book *Ecodynamics: A New Theory of Societal Evolution* (Boulding, 1978). There, the focus is upon interdependent processes: 'The watchword of evolution is interaction, not causation. It is therefore a pluralistic interpretation to the core, even though we recognize that some processes frequently dominate others' (Boulding, 1978, p. 211). Hence, Boulding the theorist of social evolution stresses interdependence and interaction. The unity of social sciences essentially follows from the interactive nature of social dynamics, between various social systems, but more fundamentally between cognition and institutions. Marmefelt (2009) shows that Kenneth Boulding and Friedrich von Hayek, as evolutionary economists, develop theories of social evolution that put learning at the very core, while philosopher John Searle finds the origin of social institutions in collective intentionality and the assignment of status function. This chapter studies the importance of cognition and institutions in social dynamics.

As evolutionary economists, both Hayek and Boulding were highly multidisciplinary and they brought various disciplines together into a unity; Boulding having the most comprehensive view, bringing the various pieces of Hayek's theory on social evolution together. While Hayek (1952) considers a mental map reproducing the physical order in the sensory order, Boulding (1978) refers to images, when dealing with cognition. Hayek's mental map can be understood as the individual's current set of Boulding's images. Marmefelt (2009) stresses this complementarity between Boulding and Hayek in their thought on social evolution. This chapter studies Boulding's thought on social dynamics from a system theoretic approach, thus stressing the role of interacting social systems (Boulding, 1962) in societal evolution (Boulding, 1978) and its legacy to the social sciences compared with the thought of Hayek and Searle.

Cognition and institutions in Boulding's analysis of social systems

Boulding (1962, p. 531) considers systems as the absence of chaos, involving three elements: necessity, chance, and freedom. The combination of these three elements reflects cognition and institutions. He starts with the necessity of mechanical systems and points out the greater importance of chance in biological systems. For a living organism, Boulding (p. 352) regards 'its genetic constitution as embodying the elements of necessity', but he stresses that its development depends also 'on environmental factors, some of which may be subject to necessity, but many of which can only be attributed to chance'.

The latter he defines as 'stochastic' systems and he points out that the stochastic element increases when going 'from the physical through the biological to the social sciences'. This means that a defining characteristic of social sciences is that they study systems with a strong stochastic element. The fundamental problem is to understand the behavior of interacting agents facing behavioral uncertainty. Institutions, defined as rules of conduct, emerge because they reduce behavioral uncertainty. They may not turn chance into necessity, but they could, at least, decrease the element of chance into the direction of necessity by turning uncertainty into risk, thus keeping the stochastic element within bounds. Hence, the social sciences deal with institutions.

Money is an important institution, facilitating coordination like language. Boulding (1962, p. 352) considers necessity and chance when it comes to growth of money invested, which is governed by necessity when invested in a safe bank deposit at a constant rate of interest and by chance when invested in speculative enterprises. Relevant institutions here would be moral norms and banking institutions restricting speculation, thus reducing chance. Davidson (1978, 1982, 1987) argues similarly that the institution of explicit money contracts matters in a nonergodic, i.e. uncertain, world.[1] Forward money contracts provide legal assurance when the production process is long and future supply and demand are not statistically predictable (Davidson, 1987, p. 150).

Turning from economics to political science, the European Union as peace project, integrating European countries to prevent war, or constitutional arrangements keeping the power balance stable between ethnic communities in multiethnic countries are important institutions. Turning to sociology, institutions would reduce chance by promoting integration rather than alienation. Boulding (1962, p. 352) considers the principal subject of sociology to be alienation as opposite to integration. Nevertheless, this involves the achievement through institutions of some balance between necessity and chance. Consequently, social scientists study institutions to find out whether there is a balance between necessity and chance in social dynamics. However, there is a third component to consider. When Boulding considers the third component of general systems, namely freedom, he turns to the effects of knowledge. 'By freedom I mean that element which is introduced into the system by the existence of knowledge structures, or images, and especially by the existence of an image of the future' (Boulding, 1962, p. 352).

When bringing in knowledge structures or images, Boulding essentially considers cognition and human cognitive capabilities to control social dynamics. He argues that we begin to make the leap from necessity to freedom 'when our knowledge of social systems rises to the point at which some sort of control becomes possible so that the future is no longer solely in the hands of necessity and chance' (p. 353). He points out that the element of freedom depends upon the accuracy of our knowledge of the social system.

Consequently, our capability to form correct images of society is crucial to our capability to control social dynamics. The high degree of complexity in social dynamics makes total control, representing a case with pure freedom without both chance and necessity, impossible, while some degree of partial control would be within reach of human cognitive capabilities. Ultimately, the element of control depends upon our capability to form correct images of highly complex social systems, concerning both composition and dynamics, thus making communication crucial. Hence, we should focus upon symbolic communication and interpersonal relations, in order to understand how images of large, complex systems are formed. However, while Boulding's (1978) evolutionary analysis addresses communication and the formation of large, complex systems, Boulding's (1962) analysis of the social system considers a breakup of the social system, at least conceptually into subsystems.

Boulding and the components of the social system

Boulding (1962) defines four systems of primary importance to the social system: population systems, exchange systems, threat systems, and learning systems, later adding a fifth system: love systems. In population systems, he considers the composition and dynamics of the stock of items significant in social systems, such as human beings, capital goods, commodities, and ideas and images. Essentially, this means that population dynamics is used as an overall conceptual tool. Population analysis, he argues, opens up for making projections of human population, but these 'are not predictions because of the chance elements in the system' (p. 354). He states also that capital accumulation can be understood in terms of population analysis.

According to Boulding, exchange systems involve elements of population systems and they may even 'be regarded as a sub-division of population systems as they essentially involve the redistribution of existing stocks of things', but they 'have peculiarities of their own' (p. 355). Exchanges influence the population dynamics of commodities, but also of capital goods and ideas. Using the analogy of birds building their nests, we may think in terms of the exchange system nesting in and shaping the population system, like birds in their own nests. Exchange is the fundamental form of social interaction to Boulding, who essentially argues that social life is extended exchange, going beyond economic relations. 'Exchange is a basic form of human interaction; it is basic, not only to economic life, but also to all social relationships, such as marriage, friendship, and all kinds of collective action' (Boulding, 1962, p. 355). Exchange is to him both 'a positive-sum game' and 'a curious mixture of cooperative and competitive elements'. The idea of exchange being a positive-sum game relates to his work on grants economics.

Boulding (1973, p. 25) defines reciprocity as mutual grants, i.e. mutual, unconditional one-way transfers, and argues that exchange 'almost always develops originally out of reciprocity'. Grants are by nature unconditional one-way transfers. If person A gives a gift of value V to person B without asking for anything in return, then A gives a grant to B. If B gives some other gift of value V to A without asking for anything in return, then B gives a grant to A. However, since A and B both give gifts of equal value to each other, there are mutual grants between A and B, thus establishing reciprocity. This is all unconditional. By contrast, exchange is a conditional two-way transfer. If A gives to B something of value V, on the condition that B gives something of the same value in return and B does it, then A and B conduct an exchange. Boulding makes, thus, a distinction between reciprocity and exchange. He states that grants induce sacrifice that yields community, identity, and commitment, something which exchange is unable to do due to its involving so little sacrifice (pp. 27f.). Hence, the balance between grants and exchange may increase the relative importance of cooperative elements of exchange, thus reducing behavioral uncertainty, a transformation of chance into necessity. Considering interpersonal relations, Adam Smith's (1759) notion of fellow-feeling comes into mind. It means that we, through imagination, are able to place ourselves in the situation of our fellow humans. We are, thus, able to understand how other people feel, which is a prerequisite for reciprocity. As Sugden (2005, p. 70) argues, recurrent interpersonal interactions tend to endow corresponding sentiments with normative status, thus maintaining trust and reciprocity. An important implication of fellow-feeling is a sense of fairness, which strengthens the cooperative element of exchange. This creates interdependence between exchange systems and love systems, which we will deal with later.

Returning to Boulding's analysis of the social system, exchange systems can be seriously disturbed by changes in the medium of exchange, where inflation discriminates against creditors and deflation against debtors, according to Boulding (1962, p. 355). Horwitz (2000) considers inflation and deflation as monetary disequilibria that disturb the capital structure of the economy, giving a more erroneous capital structure because they cause relative prices to change and render economic calculation more difficult. This gives interdependence between exchange systems and learning systems, which we will deal with later. Monetary disequilibria are expressions of chance, while monetary equilibrium expresses necessity in terms of having relative prices reflecting the real economy. The relative price structure involves, to Boulding (1962, p. 356), necessity, as the relative price structure cannot be changed without severe repercussions to society. A monetary regime maintaining monetary equilibrium would, therefore, be an institution that transforms chance into necessity. Hence, a well-functioning price mechanism reflects necessity given by monetary equilibrium. Boulding (1962, p. 356) points out that necessity prevails under perfect competition, while monopoly and oligopoly make chance important, and that freedom opens up for government control that distorts the equilibrium price structure.

The threat system may, however, be regarded as a special case of exchange systems, but it is based upon transfer of bads, unlike the exchange system, which is based upon the transfer of goods, according to Boulding (pp. 356f.). This means that the threat system is linked to the exchange system in a similar way as the exchange system is linked to the population system; the threat system nesting in and shaping the exchange system. Hence, the threat system is nested in and shapes the exchange system. He argues that political power is based upon threats, while actual political life is made up of 'a curious mixture of exchange systems and threat systems' (p. 357). However, the role of exchange in politics is, as Boulding points out, an outcome of government being based upon consent, which is fundamental to democracy, which means that there is a social contract between political leaders and citizens. As Boulding argues, we give up some personal sovereignty and pay taxes because we perceive that we receive something in return. We can view that in terms of political enterprises, which have taxes as source of finance and provide public services appreciated by a sufficient number of taxpayers, in a similar way as market enterprises, which have loanable funds as source of finance and provide goods and services appreciated by a sufficient number of consumers.

The links between political and market enterprises in an economy is studied within fiscal sociology, as developed by Wagner (2007), who views the state as an arena of interaction, like the market, thus applying catallactics, the study of the market order, to the state as well as the market, since both the state and the market are characterized by the same economizing logic and social processes, and he points out that taxation provides the equity of political enterprises. Wagner argues that fiscal phenomena emerge through social interaction, like market phenomena, and that the state budget is an outcome of an evolutionary process rather than construction. He regards both the state and the market as emergent orders with their own set of enterprises, connected through links between market enterprises and political enterprises. This is the idea behind his notion of the conjunctive economy, in which these two types of enterprises are connected with each other in networks, thus uniting market and state, thereby going beyond simple dichotomies of market versus state, as opposed to the disjunctive economy, where political enterprises are connected to each other in one network and market enterprises to each other in a separate network. Rather than merely regarding the market as embedded in society, like Dolfsma *et al.* (2005), Wagner's (2007) conjunctive economy implies that both the state and the market are embedded in society. Consequently, the exchange element upon which fiscal sociology is based provides durable links between political and market enterprises, thus making the economic and political systems interdependent, but investors in political enterprises differ from those in market enterprises. Wagner (2007, p. 107) argues that taxation provides the equity of political enterprises, so investors in political enterprises are compelled, while investors in market enterprises are contractual. Taxpayers are obliged to pay taxes, even if they fund political enterprises they do not support, while market investors are free to choose what market enterprises to fund among those they support. For our analysis, that taxation makes taxpayers compelled investors in political enterprises implies that they are subject to the threat system as well as the exchange system, rather than being voluntary contractual investors, like those in market enterprises, who are subject to the exchange system only. There is an element of threat to the investors in the political enterprises, which illustrates Boulding's claim that politics combines exchange and threat. As taxpayers, people may ask for something in return in terms of public policies, but they may not choose what policies to finance.

Boulding (1962, pp. 357f.) favors the exchange system as being more productive and stable:

> An exchange system is fundamentally more productive than a threat system simply because the exchange of goods encourages the production of goods, whereas the threat of ill discourages the production of goods. [...] Threat systems, therefore, constantly decline into war systems or deterrence systems which seem to have an inherent instability in them.

Hence, political systems are more stable the stronger the element of exchange is, i.e. the more political systems are like economic systems, whose fundamental similarity is the main argument of fiscal sociology. The state as well as the market are orders subject to social theorizing, as they both are outcomes of social interaction, so both the state and the market belong to the exchange system, thus reducing the threat system. Yet, there remains some coercion in the state, which constitutes an element of threat. Nevertheless, Boulding makes an important point by highlighting the exchange element in politics.

Now, turning to cognition, Boulding (p. 358), when considering the learning system, states that learning 'is involved in all the other systems', by which he means all the other social systems, but with 'peculiarities of its own' and he defines the learning system 'as a social process by which the image of the world possessed by individuals of the society comes to change'. First, the links between the learning system and all other social systems involve the learning system nesting in and shaping all other social systems; so the learning system shapes the population, exchange, and threat systems as well as the love system, which we will deal with later. We may think in terms of a bird that builds four nests. Second, this hints at the links between cognition and institutions. Boulding considers learning as the change of images when new information arrives. If institutional reality does not fit the image of institutions, then the image should change, otherwise a new, unexpected situation arrives.

According to Boulding, people have to change their image in situations where their behavior does not reinforce their image, or they will find themselves in a new situation, so there is 'constant interaction of images on society and society on the images'. Hence, institutions, the rules of conduct, interact continually with cognition in the form of images. For Searle (2005, p. 14), the assignment of status function has the form 'X counts as Y in C', e.g. US dollar bank notes count as money in the United States. In order to see the links between institutions as rules of behavior and cognition as image, we may use a similar form of formalization. Dolfsma *et al.* (2011) add individual H, Language L, and society S, but the individual remains a black box. Following Boulding, the focus should be on images.

An institution can be seen as having the form: 'in situation *S* do action *A*'. It is based upon the image that '*A* is appropriate when *S*' and the image that 'the situation is *S* rather than ~*S*'. If *A* is successful, then this reinforces the images that '*A* is appropriate when *S*' and that 'the situation is *S* rather than ~*S*', thus maintaining the institution 'in situation *S* do action *A*'. If *A* no longer works, then this induces a shift in the image that '*A* is appropriate when *S*' and/or the image that 'the situation is *S* rather than ~*S*'. The former undermines the image that '*A* is appropriate when *S*' and thereby weakens the institution 'in situation *S* do action *A*', unlike the latter. Hence, when *A* is unsuccessful, the viability of institution 'in situation *S* do action *A*' depends on the relative share of the image 'the situation must be ~*S*'.

According to Boulding, science as formalization and specialization of the learning process is perhaps the most significant event in human history, which has greatly increased the acceleration of change in the image. As learning means the change in image in the light of new information and science accelerates learning, science accelerates the rate of change in the image. Science has, therefore, contributed to understanding the nature of social systems, thus inducing a shift from necessity to freedom. Science may inform us whether the situation is *S* or ~*S*. Nevertheless, Boulding (1962, p. 359) also stresses that 'the very specialization of the learning process and the rapidity of change make it all the more difficult to understand and especially to get widespread understanding of the nature of the change itself'.

Essentially, what Boulding addresses here is the impossibility of even the greatest minds in the world to grasp more than a very small fraction of human knowledge, a fraction that decreases faster as the growth of human knowledge accelerates. On the one hand, more human knowledge allows for more control, but on the other hand, the fraction of human knowledge available to a single mind becomes increasingly smaller. This puts issues of communication and coordination at the very core of social dynamics and thereby the social sciences. The study of communication and coordination in various social systems brings unity to the social sciences. Consider the mode of communication and coordination in the threat system and exchange system, respectively. Should we rely on centralized coordination by the state or decentralized coordination by the market, relying on communication through market prices rather than language? May the state control social dynamics? In fact, Boulding (p. 359) is 'highly skeptical about the advantages of any substantial expansion of the public sector', as long as we are willing to spend a lot of money to make sure public funds are spent honestly, but nothing to make sure they are spent wisely. Correct book-keeping receives a lot of attention, unlike the achievements in terms of human development, when it comes to fields, to which a positive value is attributed. Boulding refers to public expenditure in health, education, and welfare, which are areas for which a higher expenditure is generally considered positive, but little attention is given to what these expenditures actually achieve in terms of the quality of those public services. Furthermore, Boulding (p. 360) states that 'there is no socialist country in which an expansion of the private market sector would not result in a marked increase in economic efficiency, even though this might not result in the desired rate of social change'. Thus, he holds the market economy to be more efficient than the planned economy. Hence, communication through market prices and decentralized coordination through the market process are required.

Boulding anticipates the benefits of transition from a planned economy to a market economy, in general, but also some post-socialist transition problems. While a market economy emerges bottom-up, post-socialist transition as of 1989 has been top-down, thus neglecting the great importance of civil society that guides the market to be an instrument to do the morally good.

Civil society is a small-group order, in which morality emerges. According to Heyne (1985, p. 478), there are personal elements that nurture the moral rules upon which rule-coordinated capitalist societies are founded. These personal elements can be found in small-group communities. Along the lines of economic personalism, Santelli *et al.* (2002) argue that the small-group order of family, friends, church, and colleagues with whom one shares traditions, moral values, and plans for the future creates a difference between self-interest and selfishness. They point out that selfishness means goals being pursued without any concern given to others, while self-interest involves a small-group order, in which people are cooperative to pursue their own interests. A self-interested person takes, unlike a selfish one, the interests of others into account, because cooperation with them is required. These small-group orders originate in civil society.

Marmefelt (2007) points out that civil society relies upon what Brennan and Pettit (2004) call the intangible hand and that the intangible hand reconciles self-esteem with esteem received from others, thus inducing the performance of individual moral duties, because norms are formed that yield reciprocal sympathy. In addition to the invisible hand of the market, there is a visible hand of hierarchies, or organizations. These organizations have been designed for specific purposes, while orders emerge through human interaction, but without having a specific purpose themselves. The latter are held together by norms enforced by an intangible hand, because people seek esteem. Brennan and Pettit find the dichotomy of the invisible hand of the market and what they call the iron hand of law and administration misconceived. In contrast, Brennan and Pettit argue that the intangible hand makes people act to receive esteem and avoid disesteem, and they attribute the forces of esteem to civil society. However, they neglect self-esteem. There may be a desire for praiseworthiness as well as a desire for praise. Praiseworthiness is to be worthy of praise and refers to a personal quality, while a person may receive praise from others, which is interpersonal. Adam Smith's (1759) impartial spectator induces humans to see themselves from a third-person perspective. Following Smith, Pelligra (2005) argues that our conscience induces us to follow our desire to be praiseworthy, even when there is no possibility of being praised. Smith (1759) defines sympathy as fellow-feeling, which means that humans take the interests of others into account, i.e. they are self-interested, but not selfish. Norms give fellow-feeling among humans belonging to a community, thus defining a level of reciprocal sympathy, a measure of the general fellow-feeling in a community. Culture provides a level of reciprocal sympathy, so the utility of two interacting agents include not only their own utility, but also the utility of the other in a reciprocal way, and, referring to Hayek (1979), the exchange society and the coordination through the market process depend on gradually evolved moral beliefs (Marmefelt, 2007).

Following Röpke (1958 [1998, p. 98]), the market economy requires the existence of 'a society in which certain fundamentals are respected and color the whole network of social relationships', including individual effort and responsibility, absolute norms and values, independence based on ownership, prudence and daring, and calculating and saving. According to Gregg (2010), Röpke made an effort to ground the market economy upon Christian humanism. Gregg (pp. 176ff.) argues that the dehumanization of theoretical economics, on the level of economic policy, undermines a society's ability to uphold liberty and order, because centralized compulsion expands at the expense of economic liberty, thus opening up for government intervention, while the welfare state, which takes responsibility for everyone's happiness, gives rise to soft despotism. Röpke's position, combining liberty and order, implies a free market economy with a strong civil society giving order. We may extend Wagner's (2007) analysis, where the state and the market are the two arenas of interaction in society, called the public square and the market square, respectively, by adding civil society as a third arena of interaction, called the civic square, in which civic enterprises are established. Consequently, we may think in terms of a conjunctive economy with civic, market, and political enterprises, in the sense of interdependent undertakings, which are connected both between and within the three squares of society: the civic, market, and public squares. Civil society can be understood as the integrative structures that emerge from a shared identity.

Actually, Boulding (1962, p. 360) considers civil society as integrative structures in the form of the love system, which is a source of identification that yields social integration, as there are areas in life which 'we do not merely exchange or threaten but in which we *identify*'. This is in line with the common definition of civil society, as the sector of society that is neither state nor market. Boulding argues that a sense of identification 'participates in both exchange and threat systems', but he suspects that we must 'include an autonomous element of integration if we are to obtain a full description of social systems'. He points out that 'the love of country, like the love of a spouse, has elements of exchange in it or perhaps even of threat', but he adds 'an autonomous element of integration' (p. 360). The strong links between exchange and love systems can be seen in Boulding's (1973, p. 25) comparison of exchange (two-way transfers formalized by contract) and reciprocity (mutual grants), involving integrative aspects. Exchange is a formalization of reciprocity (p. 26), so we may think in terms of the love system nesting in and shaping the exchange system strongly, but to some extent also the threat system. Hence, the love system nests in and shapes especially the exchange system, but also the threat system.

In fact, Boulding anticipates his own evolutionary analysis (Boulding, 1978), elaborating on the love system that he then calls the integrative system, which he gives a fundamental role in bonding. We shall consider that more in the next section. Nevertheless, Boulding (1962, pp. 361f.) links identification in traditional capitalism with the family, which he views as 'a love system extending through time', while he argues that socialism tries to 'expand this sense of identification to the whole society, at least as embodied in the élite party'.

However, the division of labor between the love system and the threat system is an open issue to Boulding.

> There is a thin dividing line, however, between love systems and threat systems and there is a constant tendency for one to pass into the other. Thus, capitalist development has seldom proceeded very far without the exercise of police power, and socialist development seems to be even more dependent on coercion, as the record of Stalin shows.
>
> (Boulding, 1962, p. 362)

Consequently, understanding and thereby control of social systems require, according to Boulding, 'the study of the subtle interweaving of these various systems of society'. We may think in terms of a three-level architecture of the social system. At the first level, the threat system shapes the exchange system, which shapes the population system. At the second level, the love system shapes the exchange and threat systems. Finally, at the third level, the learning system shapes all the other social systems. Hence, the learning system becomes fundamental to society, because it shapes all the other social systems. Figure 3b.1 shows society as nested social systems, where arrows denote the direction by which a social system is nested in and shaping another social system and a double arrow denotes the force of nesting and shaping to be a strong one.

Boulding (1973) argues that all societies are defined by a point combining threat, love, and exchange, and that the proportions of these three social organizers have changed during human history, but he also points out that the love system sustains the exchange system. In other words, the exchange system is dependent on the love system, so that the love system nests in and shapes the exchange system. Benevolence among people gives rise to reciprocity, which creates community, identity, and commitment, and exchange arises out of reciprocity, thus illustrating the love system nesting in and shaping the exchange

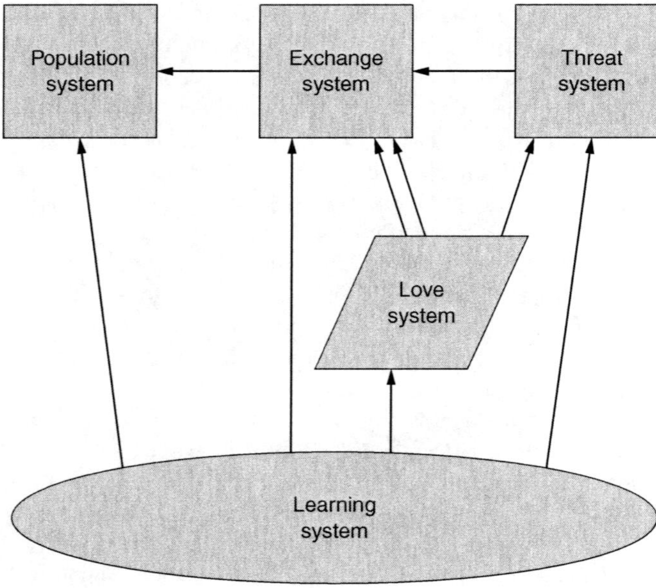

Figure 3b.1 Society as nested social systems.

system. He argues that exchange requires integrative networks and he prefers a society combining reciprocity and exchange (pp. 110ff.), thus providing the mechanism that makes the market embedded in society. Civil society provides the morality of the market. To the casual reader, this ends the story, but we have to consider cognition. As the learning system shapes all the other social systems, including the love system, learning is crucial to the love system as well as the exchange, threat, and population systems. In fact, Boulding anticipates his own evolutionary analysis, by giving learning a fundamental role in social dynamics. In Boulding's (1978) evolutionary analysis, the exchange, threat, and integrative (love) systems provide the bonding structure, while learning is fundamental to explain the population dynamics of human artifacts.

Boulding's evolutionary analysis in the light of Hayek and Searle

Boulding (1978, p. 13) defines evolution as 'primarily a process in genetic structure, which [he has] called "know-how"'. He stresses 'the structure's ability to "instruct"; that is, to be a code of selection according to a program'. By doing so, Boulding puts the learning system and the knowledge structure at the very core. In addition, he relates learning to the increasing complexity of structure. Turning from Boulding the system theorist to Boulding the theorist of social evolution, the learning system is transformed to the very driving force of evolution, which continually increases complexity of structure.

> [W]hat happens in the evolution of chemical elements from hydrogen to uranium is increasing complexity of structure, which has many parallels to the increase in complexity of the genetic structure in biological evolution or the knowledge structure in societal evolution.
>
> (Boulding, 1978, p. 32)

> When we get to societal evolution the paramount role of knowledge is very clear. All human artifacts originate in human knowledge. Just as the biosphere could not have produced a human being ten million years ago because it did not have the know-how, the social system could not have produced an automobile a hundred years ago because it did not have the know-how.
>
> (p. 33)

Consequently, evolution is a process in knowledge and the social system evolves through human learning, which gives a continually increasing complexity of knowledge structure and thereby a continually increasing complexity of society. The mechanism by which knowledge operates, Boulding (p. 34) finds in production, where knowledge directs energy to transform materials. Hayek also stresses the importance of the accumulation of knowledge to social evolution, in which society is a spontaneously evolved order. This is based on both the innate, genetically inherited rules of human behavior and the learnt, culturally transmitted rules of human conduct (Hayek, 1967, p. 78, 1973, p. 74). The latter rules matter to civilization, which brings a more complex human society with more complex coordination patterns. Indeed, Hayek (1979, pp. 160f.) argues that coordination of groups larger than hunting and gathering bands requires a cultural evolution of learnt rules. Hence, the learnt rules become increasingly important with the increasing complexity of human societies. According to Hayek (1973, p. 44), a social order requires only that people follow some rules when they respond individually to the particular circumstances. An order evolves through an evolutionary selection of abstract rules, which are applicable to all circumstances, in contrast to concrete rules that guide organizations with specific purposes. In an order, Hayek argues (1976, p. 15), justice requires that rules which command general assent are discovered, in order to settle different views of particulars. Particular cases have to be judged according to the same abstract rules that have evolved as generally accepted.

Like Boulding, who considers exchange more productive and stable than threat, as we already have seen, Hayek's (1976) market order or catallaxy involves a wealth-creating game that increases the prospects of participants to satisfy their needs.

> It is thus a wealth-producing game because it supplies to each player information which enables him to provide for needs of which he has no

> direct knowledge and by the use of means of the existence of which without it he would have no cognizance, thus bringing about the satisfaction of a greater range of needs than would otherwise be possible.
>
> (Hayek, 1976, p. 115)

According to McCann (2004), in classical liberal philosophy, individuals are socially embedded and community reflects that mutual interests and shared values serve an integrative function, and in this philosophy, McCann finds Hayek to be a representative of what he calls communitarian liberalism, where responsibility and obligation, and the onus of social disapproval compel rational action to pursue socially acceptable ends.[2] As Lavoie and Chamlee-Wright (2000, p. 118) argue, profit opportunities emerge as culturally embedded individuals engage in fragmented efforts of interpretation. In fact, they combine cognition and morality, so that learning is subject to a cultural context. They point out that business decisions are 'more like complex readings in which the business person negotiates the search for profits with the search for socially beneficial action' (pp. 120f.). In other words, when business people are involved in adjusting their image of profit opportunities through market interaction, they take the norms of the community into account. Because business people are culturally embedded, they try to reconcile making profit with moral responsibility, according to the norms of the specific culture to which they belong, illustrating how the integrative (love) system shapes the exchange system, while the learning system shapes them both.

When we move from social dynamics with interacting social systems to social evolution, Boulding (1978, p. 41) sees a shift from stable to changing parameters, thus preventing mechanical projection into the future. Referring to the Heisenberg principle, Boulding argues that, in social systems, a prediction of the future that is believed will change the future itself (p. 42). Instead, he points out that the failure of predictions or expectations causes a change in our image of the world, but although we only learn from failure, we may not always learn the right thing (p. 42). Nevertheless, he finds that we are, from our experience as humans, more able to sample social than physical systems with some degree of confidence. Humans are insiders of social systems, but not of physical systems, so they learn from personal experience of social interaction, which they cannot do in physical systems because they are outsiders. The fact that social systems developed later than physical systems and involve more complexity is irrelevant because humans know more about the social systems in which they are involved, like they know more about the present and recent past than about the distant past, although social systems have become more complex over time.

> Our knowledge of social systems, therefore, while it is in many ways inaccurate, is not likely to be grossly overturned by new discoveries. Even the folk knowledge in social systems in which ordinary daily life is based in earning, spending, learning, adjusting, organizing, managing, childrearing, politicking, and so on, is not grossly dissimilar from the sophisticated

> images of the social system derived from the social sciences, even though it is built upon the very imperfect samples of personal experiences.
>
> (pp. 43f.)

By contrast, he points out that our image of the astronomical universe is subject to revolutionary changes through new data. Boulding points out that we know more about the origin of any social institution than we do about the origin of the human race, and more about the origin of the human race than about the origin of the moon (p. 44). Why? Folk images evolve through a shared history of social interaction, both personal history and the history of preceding generations. Learning through social interaction is social learning, which means that humans change their images by communicating with others through language or money prices (Marmefelt, 2012). When people make exchanges, they observe the morality of other agents and assess what exchanges are possible, thus assessing the current link between the integrative (love) system and exchange system in the light of the past. Readings, or interpretations, are made within a cultural context, which provides shared meanings, along the lines of Lavoie and Chamlee-Wright (2000). The shared images constitute shared images, or folk images, which have evolved through social learning. Fairly reliable folk images of social systems and institutions evolve through continual social interaction.

As Boulding (1978, pp. 43f.) argues, the social sciences are relatively secure because there is folk knowledge about social systems and institutions. Social scientists are culturally and socially embedded, and their embeddedness provides them with background knowledge, in the sense that they have the folk images that can explain behavioral patterns that emerge as social facts. By contrast, physicists do not have inside experience as particles. Given that fairly reliable images of social systems and institutions evolve through social learning and that social scientists, who as insiders of social systems participate in social interaction out of which these images evolve, and they know these images, we may, therefore, argue that the social sciences benefit from elaborated images of social systems and institutions, in contrast to the physical sciences concerning physical systems. Social learning provides social scientists with fairly reliable folk images of social systems and institutions. Hence, the role of social learning in providing fairly good knowledge about social systems and institutions implies that the role of cognition and communication is crucial for social scientists in their pursuit to understand the evolution and functioning of social institutions. We have to go deeper than just connected systems.

Social learning, as learning through social interaction, occurs in different social contexts in complex societies. Cognition and symbolic communication operate in the exchange, threat, and love systems. What people learn from their social interactions shapes their expectations, decisions, and actions. It is essential to social scientists to understand the mechanisms of cognition and symbolic communication. Symbolic communication is essential to all social interaction, but it is subject to distortions of images through persuasion. As Boulding (1978, p. 226) argues, what he calls symbolic systems are part of the techniques of persuasion, which occur in different social contexts and social processes, be it the formation of business contracts and political agreements, or group dynamics, where group members persuade according to some evolving median norm. Although, Boulding (p. 44) stresses that physical, biological, and social evolution 'involves the increase in the number and complexity of individual structures', social phenomena involve human agency based upon human cognition and communication, ultimately upon social learning.

Boulding's folk knowledge is what Hayek (1945 [1948, pp. 80–83]) calls the knowledge of the particular circumstances of time and place, which is dispersed among individuals, in contrast to general, scientific knowledge. The image of the social system is based upon fragmented, local knowledge, which is subject to learning that benefits from communication uniting the fragments of knowledge. As Marmefelt (2009, p. 66) argues:

> Hayek (1945 [1948, pp. 86ff.]) points out that the function of the price system is to communicate information, thus using the knowledge of many people, while Boulding (1978, p. 128) stresses the importance of language as a means of communication that is used to form images of large, complex, and integrated systems unknown from personal experience.

Hence, the study of social learning processes becomes crucial to achieve unity of social sciences. Social learning may indeed influence population dynamics in the realm of social systems.

Compare Boulding the system theorist with Boulding the theorist of social evolution. Recall that the learning system shapes all the other social systems, according to Boulding (1962). However, as evolutionary theorist, he substitutes societal evolution, in which learning is its core, for his systems theory, where the learning system shapes all the other social systems. In addition, Boulding, as evolutionary theorist, substitutes population dynamics in social evolution for the population system as social system. Boulding (1978, pp. 136ff.) stresses that humans are niche-expanders, creating niches into which they expand, and that accumulation of folk knowledge has been crucial. What does population dynamics mean? Boulding's population dynamics involve entry and exit, while equilibrium population is reached when entry equals exit. He considers a population as a stock of species with throughput of the items that constitute species by conforming to a common definition (pp. 54ff.), and he argues that a population has an age composition so that aging characterizes the items that make up the population (p. 57). Hence, items are born, live, and finally die. In the equilibrium population model, the birth rate and the death rate are equal (pp. 58f.), and this equilibrium population Boulding (p. 62) defines as a 'niche'. A population expanding into a niche starts having a rapid growth rate, which declines and eventually becomes zero, when the equilibrium population is reached (p. 63). As the population of the final level of complexity, he considers the population of human artifacts, involving things, organizations, and people, for which equilibrium populations can be found.

In fact, Boulding (pp. 121f.) interprets human history as the evolution of human artifacts, such as material structures and objects, and organizations and organizational structures, but even human beings themselves, in the sense that they are shaped by their culture, and all of them originate and are sustained by the images in the human mind. He thinks primarily of social dynamics as the evolution of human artifacts. Naturally, human artifacts involve human knowledge, while learning plays a crucial role behind the evolution of human artifacts. Humans have to learn how to produce and use artifacts, so without learning artifacts would not evolve. Even an artifact produced by accident involves learning. Consequently, knowledge, or know-how, provides the key to Boulding's notion of evolution, and the fundamental similarity he sees between biological and social evolution. He stresses the similarity between biological and social evolution because he sees mutation and learning as genetic changes in biology and society.

> Just as there is the biosphere or genetic know-how in the biosphere, so there is a noosphere of human knowledge in the sociosphere. The noosphere is the totality of the cognitive content, including values of all human nervous systems, plus the prosthetic devices by which this system is extended and integrated in the form of libraries, computers, telephones, post offices, and so on.
>
> (p. 122)

Hence, cognition is the very core of social dynamics as evolution of human artifacts. While the 'biogenetic structure takes place through mutation', Boulding argues that there is a '"noogentic structure" within the nervous systems of organisms, which is transmitted to offspring by a learning process' (p. 123). Biological evolution and social evolution have, thus, the same structure, involving know-how that changes.

Turning to human cognition, a comparison between Hayek and Boulding provides some insights of the nature of learning and its biological foundations. In Hayek's (1952) sensory order, the map 'reproduces some of the relations which exist in certain parts of the physical world' (p. 109), while Boulding (1978, p. 200) argues that species of ideas, images, affections, and symbols interact in the integrative system. Marmefelt (2009, p. 66) shows that there are fundamental similarities between Hayek's notion of map and Boulding's notion of image. First, the mental reproductions of the physical world, made by means of Hayek's map, correspond to Boulding's images in the human mind, so that Hayek's map may be seen as a set of Boulding's images. Second, Hayek (1952, pp. 115ff.) sees the map as an apparatus of classification, by which a sequence of individual mental images results from streams of impulses. Third, this phenomenal order is based on the neural order of the nervous system that brings in the impulses that, through classification, becomes represented in the sensory order.

Consequently, what Boulding (1978) calls noosphere builds upon the biosphere. He finds that the human brain really makes a difference. The human mind, which yields the sensory order, builds upon the capacity of the human brain, out of which the neural order develops, in the sense of providing the mental capacity to form images. The neural order originates in the capacity of the human brain because the mental capacity of the brain gives the opportunity space of possible neural orders.

> It is the extraordinary capacity of the human brain for making images not only of the world outside it, which it sees as reality, but also, in fantasy, of innumerable worlds of imagination, which distinguishes it from even the highest brains of non-human animals.
>
> (Boulding, 1978, p. 127)

Hence, human imagination is decisive for the human capability of exercising some degree of control over social dynamics as evolution of human artifacts.

The casual reader may want to stop here, but the mechanisms of cognition and symbolic communication, and the mechanisms by which cognition and symbolic communication shape social systems, remain to be analyzed, in particular how they operate to establish some control of the overall social system. Boulding stresses that language is a distinctive human artifact that gives 'extraordinary power of communicating into the future', which 'binds the whole human race, or at least large portions of it, together as if it were in a single mind', while 'the human mind can form images of large, complex, and integrated systems of which it has no personal experience through the magic of human language and other forms of communication' (p. 128). Therefore, cognition and communication allow some control of the overall social system. Language allows the formation of images of complex systems, such as the social system, and the communication necessary for that purpose. According to Boulding, decisions are choices made by humans and decisions become increasingly important as complex images of the future evolve (p. 132), but human learning as the capacity to change images in light of further information is more important (p. 133), in which symbolic communication is used to convey information.

Language is the fundamental means of symbolic communication, and thereby an important tool for social learning. Searle (2005) gives the symbolizing function of language a crucial role in the evolution of social institutions, using the concepts of consciousness and intentionality to characterize the mind. He considers consciousness a biological phenomenon because conscious processes are biological processes, while conscious experiences are represented as shifts and changes in the structure of the field of consciousness. Searle considers intentionality as subjective states, such as beliefs and desires, intentions and perceptions, loves and hates, and fears and hopes that relate a person to the rest of the world. Having a good map, referring to Hayek, or good images, referring to Boulding, is essential to what Searle calls the satisfaction of intentional states (Marmefelt, 2009, p. 67). Searle (2005) accounts for social phenomena by using the notion of collective intentionality, which arises whenever people cooperate. Institutions require, besides collective intentionality, the assignment of status function, and language is crucial as fundamental institution, according to Searle, because institutions require the imposition of status functions and the ability to impose status functions requires language, in itself an institution, or at least a language-like capacity for symbolization. There are symbols that may help us recognize institutions. Searle (2005) argues that the provision of status indicators that help us recognize that an object has a status function is an institutional function of language.

Consequently, Boulding's evolutionary perspective in the light of Hayek and Searle involves population dynamics, where humans create niches into which they can expand, facilitated by learning, to a large extent social, because it is based upon social interaction and symbolic communication, by means of language and money prices that give an appropriate map or set of images, while language provides a foundation for all other institutions.

The three remaining social systems, which Boulding (1978, pp. 139f.) considers as the social organizers, are: the threat relationship, the exchange relationship, and the integrative relationship (love). In his system-theoretic analysis, Boulding (1962) considers the first two, but does not really elaborate on the love system. In his evolutionary analysis, Boulding (1978) analyzes the integrative system thoroughly. The integrative system is more fundamental and of most interest here because fairly reliable images of social systems and institutions evolve out of the symbolic communication and social learning within the integrative system.

While threat is a reluctant bond and exchange is a loose and temporary bond, the integrative relationship is a pure bond (p. 222). Boulding argues that species of ideas, images, valuations, affections, and symbols interact in the integrative system (p. 200). The central organizer in the integrative system is, to Boulding, the image of identity (pp. 190f.), while the integrative system has symbols as messengers and is dominated by emotive symbols (p. 197). The image of identity is based upon symbols that are revealed only through communication because identity requires that at least two persons share the same image of the self, as member of a family, profession, nation, etc. According to Boulding, the 'whole vast world of symbols that makes up the complex image of human identity is a subterranean ecosystem, hidden beneath the hard surface of skulls, apparent only when it results in communications and records of communications' (p. 199). Hence, symbolic communication and social learning are crucial to the dynamics of the integrative system. Symbolic communication and social learning may induce exchange or threat. Boulding points out that perceived patterns of personal identities yield patterns of benevolence and malevolence; the former inducing exchange and the latter threat (pp. 191f.). Hence, symbolic communication shapes the integrative system directly and thereby the exchange and threat systems indirectly.

Symbolic communication gives social learning its key role in social dynamics. Indeed, Boulding explains the evolution of the integrative system by social learning, in the form of acculturation, by which children learn from their parents and other elders.

> The key to the evolution of the integrative system, therefore, is first the process by which a human being learns throughout the whole life; and second the process by which the culture and knowledge structure of the society is transmitted to a growing child, which anthropologists tend to call 'acculturation' and sociologists 'socialization'.
>
> (p. 201)

Consequently, symbolic communication and social learning are crucial to the evolution of the integrative system, involving fairly reliable images of social systems and institutions, thereby shaping the evolution of the exchange and threat systems through patterns of benevolence and malevolence.

Conclusion

In his analysis of the social system, Boulding considers a breakup of it, at least conceptually, into subsystems as a way to develop an understanding of the social system, which is necessary to exercise some degree of control of social dynamics. This venture gives unity of social sciences, if we focus upon the underlying mechanisms rather than mere connections between systems. Social dynamics involve interaction between social systems, but more fundamentally between cognition and institutions. Social scientists study institutions to find out whether there is a balance between necessity and chance in social dynamics, while the element of freedom depends upon the accuracy of our knowledge of the social system, that is, our capability to form correct images of society, which is crucial to our capability to partly control some elements of social dynamics. He considers the subsystems of the social system: population systems, exchange systems, threat systems, learning systems, and love systems. They involve different social sciences that are united by Boulding's focus on the interweaving of the various systems of society, the social systems. His social system theory addresses the exchange, threat, and love systems as connected orders, in which we may observe interlinked market, political, and civic enterprises that interact. Boulding's five social systems are nested in and shape other social systems: the threat system shapes the exchange system, the exchange system shapes the population system, and the love system shapes especially the exchange system but also the threat system, while the learning system plays a fundamental role, as it shapes all the four other systems, thus being the crucial link for the unity of social sciences.

In his evolutionary analysis, Boulding addresses communication and the formation of large, complex systems. Learning becomes the very core as he views evolution as a process in knowledge or know-how, thus making learning the very driving force of evolution. Regarding humans as niche-expanders, Boulding also turns away from the population system to population dynamics, where an equilibrium population defines a niche. The population of human artifacts is at the final level of complexity and he views human history as the evolution of human artifacts, all originating and being sustained by the images in the human mind, and social dynamics as the evolution of human artifacts. Hence, cognition plays a crucial role in the evolution of human artifacts.

Hayek also stresses the importance of the accumulation of knowledge to social evolution. Boulding's folk knowledge corresponds to Hayek's knowledge of the particular circumstances of time and place. When turning to cognition, Boulding's notion of image corresponds to Hayek's map. Cognition and communication allow some control of the social system. Both Boulding and Hayek see the mind as a cultural phenomenon, based upon the biological phenomenon, the human brain. This they share with Searle, who goes from consciousness as a biological phenomenon to intentionality as a cultural one, founding social institutions on collective intentionality and the assignment of status function, thus making language or language-like symbolism necessary. While Searle considers language as the fundamental institution, Boulding finds it necessary to form images of large, complex, and integrated systems.

Boulding's evolutionary analysis involves population dynamics, where humans create niches into which they can expand, and learning, making that possible. This learning is to a large extent social, being based upon social interaction and symbolic communication. The threat, exchange, and integrative systems remain as the three social organizers. The integrative system is based upon the image of identity, while symbolic communication and social learning are crucial not only to the dynamics of the integrative (love) system, but also to the dynamics of the entire bonding structure because the pattern of benevolence and malevolence that emerges in the integrative system induces a combination of exchange and threat. Hence, the dynamics of the integrative system shape the dynamics of both the exchange and the threat systems through symbolic communication and social learning. Consequently, the unity of the social sciences is to be found in cognition and communication, especially social learning and symbolic communication, as the foundation of social institutions.

Acknowledgement

I thank the editors for their comments.

Notes

1 Davidson (1987, p. 148) defines uncertainty in terms of nonergodic stochastic processes, where calculation of space or time averages based on past data is unable to supply a statistically reliable estimate of either the current space average or the future space or time averages. He points out that when people face an uncertain, i.e. nonergodic, future, they try to form sensible expectations that rely on the existence of social institutions, such as contracts and money. Davidson (1982–83) points out that the economic process is nonergodic because it moves in historical time and that economic agents destroy any ergodic stochastic processes when they make crucial decisions, along the lines of Shackle (1955).

2 Hayek's social order involves social embeddedness of markets. To Hayek, society is an overall spontaneous order, in which the market is a specific spontaneous order. This means a spontaneous order version of Polanyi's (1944) social embeddedness of

markets. Boulding (1973, p. 94) criticizes Paretian welfare economics for neglecting benevolence, while Hayek (1976, p. 5) argues that general welfare is the abstract order that assists in the pursuit of a great variety of individual purposes. Yeager (2001) points out that indirect utilitarianism involves a broader notion of self-interest that goes beyond selfishness, and Marmefelt (2007) that integrative structures are spontaneously organized within civil society that provides a foundation of the market order, yielding reciprocal sympathy that contributes to the spontaneous emergence of learning networks.

References

Boulding, K.E. (1962) 'The Relations of Economic, Political and Social Systems', *Social and Economic Studies*, 11: 351–362.

Boulding, K.E. (1973) *The Economy of Love and Fear: A Preface to Grants Economics*, Belmont, CA: Wadsworth Publishing Company.

Boulding, K.E. (1978) *Ecodynamics: A New Theory of Societal Evolution*. Beverly Hills, CA: Sage.

Brennan, G., and Pettit, P. (2004) *The Economy of Esteem: An Essay on Civil and Political Society*, Oxford: Oxford University Press.

Davidson, P. (1978) *Money and the Real World*, 2nd edition, London: Macmillan.

Davidson, P. (1982) *International Money and the Real World*, London: Macmillan.

Davidson, P. (1982–83) 'Rational Expectations: A Fallacious Foundation for Studying Crucial Decision-Making Processes', *Journal of Post Keynesian Economics*, 5: 182–198.

Davidson, P. (1987) 'Sensible Expectations and the Long-Run Non-Neutrality of Money', *Journal of Post Keynesian Economics*, 10: 146–153.

Dolfsma, W., Finch, J., and McMaster, R. (2005) 'Market and Society: How Do They Relate, and How Do They Contribute To Welfare?', *Journal of Economic Issues*, 39: 347–356.

Dolfsma, W., Finch, J., and McMaster, R. (2011) 'Identifying Institutional Vulnerability: The Importance of Language and System Barriers', *Journal of Economic Issues*, 45: 805–818.

Gregg, S. (2010) *Wilhelm Röpke's Political Economy*, Cheltenham and Northampton, MA: Edward Elgar.

Hayek, F.A. von (1945) 'The Use of Knowledge in Society', *American Economic Review*, 35: 519–530, reprinted in Hayek, F.A. von (1948) *Individualism and Economic Order*, Chicago: University of Chicago Press.

Hayek, F.A. von (1952) *The Sensory Order: An Inquiry into the Foundations of Theoretical Psychology*, Chicago: University of Chicago Press.

Hayek, F.A. von (1967) *Studies in Philosophy, Politics, and Economics*, Chicago: University of Chicago Press.

Hayek, F.A. von (1973 [1982]) *Law, Legislation, and Liberty: A New Statement of the Liberal Principles of Justice and Political Economy* (vol. 1: Rules and Order), London: Routledge and Kegan Paul.

Hayek, F.A. von (1976 [1982]) *Law, Legislation, and Liberty: A New Statement of the Liberal Principles of Justice and Political Economy* (vol. 2: The Mirage of Social Justice), London: Routledge and Kegan Paul.

Hayek, F.A. von (1979 [1982]) *Law, Legislation, and Liberty: A New Statement of the Liberal Principles of Justice and Political Economy* (vol. 3: The Political Order of a Free People), London: Routledge and Kegan Paul.

Heyne, P. (1985) 'The Concept of Economic Justice in Religious Discussion', in Block, W., Brennan, G., and Elzinga, K. (eds.), *Morality of the Market: Religious and Economic Perspectives*, The Fraser Institute, Vancouver, 463–482.

Horwitz, S. (2000) *Microfoundations and Macroeconomics: An Austrian Perspective*, London and New York: Routledge.

Lavoie, D.C., and Chamlee-Wright, E. (2000) *Culture and Enterprise: The Development, Representation, and Morality of Business*, A Cato Institute Book, London and New York: Routledge.

Marmefelt, T. (2007) 'Civil Society Formation and Global Exchange: Lithuania, Sweden, the Baltic Sea Area, and the World', *Indian Journal of Economics & Business*, Symposium on Economic Development, Transition Economics, and Globalization: Austrian and Public Choice Perspectives, Special Issue: 109–127.

Marmefelt, T. (2009) 'Human Knowledge, Rules, and the Spontaneous Evolution of Society in the Social Thought of Darwin, Hayek, and Boulding', *Journal of Economic Behavior & Organization*, 71: 62–74.

Marmefelt, T. (2012) 'Emergent Money and Economic Cycles: A Social Learning Perspective', in Tavidze, A. (ed.), *Progress in Economics Research. Volume 26*, New York: Nova Science Publishers, 31–57.

McCann, R. (2004) *Individualism and Economic Order: The Social Element in Liberal Thought*, London and New York: Routledge.

Pelligra, V. (2005) 'Under Trusting Eyes: The Responsive Nature of Trust', in Gui, B., and Sugden, R. (eds.) *Economics and Social Interaction: Accounting for Interpersonal Relations*, Cambridge: Cambridge University Press, 105–124.

Polanyi, K. (1944) *The Great Transformation*, Boston: Beacon Hill.

Röpke, W. (1958 [1998]) *Jenseits von Angebot und Nachfrage*, reprinted in Quinn, D. (ed.), *A Humane Economy: The Social Framework of the Free Market*, Wilmington, DE: ISI Books.

Santelli, A.J., Sikkenga, J., Sirico, R.A., Yates, S., and Zúñiga, G. (2002) *The Free Person in the Free Economy: A Personalist View of Market Economies*, Lanham, MD: Lexington Books.

Searle, J.R. (2005) 'What Is an Institution?' *Journal of Institutional Economics*, 1: 1–22.

Shackle, G.L.S. (1955) *Uncertainty in Economics*, Cambridge: Cambridge University Press.

Smith, A. (1759 [1976]) *The Theory of Moral Sentiments*, Oxford: Clarendon Press.

Sugden, R. (2005) 'Fellow-Feeling', in Gui, B., and Sugden, R. (eds.) *Economics and Social Interaction: Accounting for Interpersonal Relations*, Cambridge: Cambridge University Press, 52–75.

Wagner, R.E. (2007) *Fiscal Sociology and the Theory of Public Finance*, Cheltenham and Northampton, MA: Edward Elgar.

Yeager, L.B. (2001) *Ethics as Social Science: The Moral Philosophy of Social Cooperation*, Cheltenham: Edward Elgar.

Poem

The Bleary Dither

I'm glad I'm not a Bleary Dither:
He knows not why, or whence, or whither,
Or how, or when, or who, or where;
His mind is neither here nor there.

Part IV

Economics and morality

4 Key text: Economics as a moral science[1]

Kenneth E. Boulding

Adam Smith, who has strong claim to being both the Adam and the Smith of systematic economics, was a professor of moral philosophy and it was at that forge that economics was made. Even when I was a student, economics was still part of the moral sciences tripos at Cambridge University. It can claim to be a moral science, therefore, from its origin, if for no other reason. Nevertheless, for many economists the very term "moral science" will seem like a contradiction. We are strongly imbued today with the view that science should be *wertfrei* and we believe that science has achieved its triumph precisely because it has escaped the swaddling clothes of moral judgment and has only been able to take off into the vast universe of the "is" by escaping from the treacherous launching pad of the "ought." Even economics, we learn in the history of thought, only became a science by escaping from the casuistry and moralizing of medieval thought. Who, indeed, would want to exchange the delicate rationality of the theory of equilibrium price for the unoperational vaporings of a "just price" controversy? In the battle between mechanism and moralism, generally mechanism has won hands down, and I shall not be surprised if the very title of my address does not arouse musty fears of sermonizing in the minds of many of my listeners.

Let me first explain, then, what I mean by moral and by moral science. A moral, or ethical proposition, is a statement about a rank order of preference among alternatives, which is intended to apply to more than one person. A preference which applies to one person only is a "taste." Statements of this kind are often called "value judgments." If someone says, "I prefer A to B," this is a personal value judgment, or a taste. If he says, "A is better than B," there is an implication that he expects other people to prefer A to B also, as well as himself. A moral proposition then is a "common value."

Every culture, or subculture, is defined by a set of common values, that is, generally agreed upon preferences. Without a core of common values, a culture cannot exist, and we classify society into cultures and subcultures precisely because it is possible to identify groups who have common values.

Most tastes are in fact also common values and have been learned by the process by which all learning is done, that is, by mutation and selection. The most absurd of all pieces of ancient wisdom is surely the Latin tag *de gustibus non disputandum*. In fact, we spend most of our lives disputing about tastes. If we want to be finicky about definitions, we might turn the old tag around and say where there is disputing, we are not talking about tastes. Nevertheless, even personal tastes are learned, in the matrix of a culture or a subculture in which we grow up, by very much the same kind of process by which we learn our common values. Purely personal tastes, indeed, can only survive in a culture which tolerates them, that is, which has a common value that private tastes of certain kinds should be allowed.

One of the most peculiar illusions of economists is a doctrine that might be called the Immaculate Conception of the Indifference Curve, that is, that tastes are simply given, and that we cannot inquire into the process by which they are formed. This doctrine is literally "for the birds," whose tastes are largely created for them by their genetic structures, and can therefore be treated as a constant in the dynamics of bird societies. In human society, however, the genetic component of tastes is very small indeed. We start off with a liking for milk, warmth, and dryness and a dislike for being hungry, cold, and wet, and we do have certain latent drives which may guide the formation of later preferences in matters of sex, occupation, or politics, but by far and away the largest part of human preferences are learned, again by means of a mutation-selection process. It was, incidentally, Veblen's principal, and still largely unrecognized, contribution to formal economic theory, to point out that we cannot assume that tastes are given in any dynamic theory, in the sense that in dynamics we cannot afford to neglect the processes by which cultures are created and by which preferences are learned.

I am prepared indeed to go much further and to say that no science of any kind can be divorced from ethical considerations, as defined above. The propositions of science are no more immaculately conceived than the preferences of individuals. Science is a human learning process which arises in certain subcultures in human society and not in others, and a subculture, as we have seen, is a group of people defined by the acceptance of certain common values, that is, an ethic which permits extensive communication among them.

The scientific subculture is no exception to this rule. It is characterized by a strong common value system. A high value, for instance, is placed on veracity, on curiosity, on measurement, on quantification, on careful observation and experiment, and on objectivity. Without this common value structure, the epistemological process of science would not have arisen; indeed it did not arise in certain societies where conditions might otherwise have been favorable but where some essential common values of the scientific subcultures did not exist. The question as to exactly what values and ethical propositions are essential to the scientific subculture may be in some dispute. The fact that there are such values cannot be disputed. It is indeed one of the most perplexing questions in intellectual history as to why the scientific subculture developed in the time and place that it did in Western Europe. The common values that are prerequisite to it are rather rare among human subcultures. The common values, for instance, of the military or the people that run the international system are quite different from those of science. In this sense, therefore, science has an essential ethical basis.

This means that even the epistemological content of science, that is, what scientists think they know, has an ethical component. The proposition, for instance, that water consists of two molecules of hydrogen and one of oxygen is not usually thought of as a proposition with high ethical content. Nevertheless, any student in chemistry who decides that he prefers to think of hydrogen as dephlogisticated water will soon find out that chemistry is not just a matter of personal taste. The fact that there is no dispute going on about any particular scientific proposition does not mean to say that it is a matter of taste; it simply means that the dispute about it has been resolved through the application of certain common values and ethical presuppositions.

There is, however, a fundamental sense in which the epistemological process even in the physical and biological sciences is now running into situations which have strong ethical implications outside the scientific subculture. The myth that science is simply discovering knowledge about an objectively unchangeable world may have had some validity in the early stages of science but, as the sciences develop, this myth becomes less and less valid. The learning process of science is now running into two serious difficulties. The first might be called the generalized Heisenberg principle. When we are trying to obtain knowledge about a system by changing its inputs and outputs of information, these inputs and outputs will change the system itself, and under some circumstances they may change it radically. My favorite illustration of the Heisenberg principle is that of a man who inquires through the door of the bedroom where his friend is sick, "How are you?" whereupon the friend replies "Fine," and the effort kills him. In the social sciences of course the generalized Heisenberg principle predominates because knowledge of the social sciences is an essential part of the social system itself, hence objectivity in the sense of investigating a world which is unchanged by the investigation of it is an absurdity.

The second difficulty is that, as science develops, it no longer merely investigates the world; it creates the world which it is investigating. We see this even in the physical sciences where the evolution of the elements has now been resumed in this part of the universe after some six billion years. We are increasingly going to see this in the biological sciences, which will only find out about the evolutionary process by actively engaging in it, and changing its course. In the social sciences one can defend the proposition that most of what we can really know is what we create ourselves and that prediction in social systems can be achieved only by setting up consciously created systems which will make the predictions come true. Knowledge of random systems can only be obtained by destroying them, that is, by taking the randomness out of them. There is a great deal of evidence, for instance, that the fluctuations of prices in organized commodity or security markets are essentially random in nature. All we can possibly discover therefore by studying these fluctuations is what bias there might be in the dice. If we want to predict the future of prices in such a market we will have to control it, that is, we will have to set up a system of counterspeculation which will guarantee a given future course of prices. The gold standard is a primitive example of such a system in which it is possible to predict that the price of gold will lie within the gold points as long as the system remains intact. Similarly, we can predict the inside temperature of a house with an effective furnace and thermostat much better than we can predict the outside temperature, simply because we control one and not the other.

We cannot escape the proposition that as science moves from pure knowledge towards control, that is, towards creating what it knows, what it creates becomes a problem of ethical choice, and will depend upon the common values of the societies in which the scientific subculture is embedded, as well as of the scientific subculture. Under these circumstances, science cannot proceed at all without at least an implicit ethic, that is, a subculture with appropriate common values. The problem exists in theory even in what might be described as the objective phase of science, that is, the phase in which it is simply investigating "what is," because the question of the conditions under which ignorance is bliss is not an empty one. The assumption which is almost universal in academic circles that ignorance cannot possibly be bliss might under some circumstances be proved wrong by the very methods of science itself. As long as science is investigating an unchanging world, however, this problem does not become acute, for if knowledge does not change the world, then all ignorance does for us is to prevent us from satisfying our idle curiosity. When, however, knowledge changes the world, the question of the content of the common values, both of the subculture which is producing knowledge and of the total society in which that subculture is embedded, becomes of acute importance. Under these circumstances, the concept of a value-free science is absurd, for the whole future of science may well rest in our ability to resolve the ethical conflicts which the growth of knowledge is now creating. Science could create an ethical dynamic which would bring it to an end.

Let us return then to economics as a moral science, not merely in the sense in which all science is "affected with an ethical interest," but in the quite specific sense of asking whether economics itself can be of assistance in resolving ethical disputes, especially those which arise out of the continued increase of knowledge. Economics specializes in the study of that part of the total social system which is organized through exchange and which deals with exchangeables. This to my mind is a better definition of economics than those which define it as relating to scarcity or allocation, for the allocation of scarce resources is a universal problem which applies to political decisions and political structures through coercion, threat, and even to love and community, just as it does to exchange. I have elsewhere distinguished three groups of social organizers which I have called the threat system, the exchange system, and the integrative system. Economics clearly occupies the middle one of these three. It edges over towards the integrative system insofar as it has some jurisdiction over the study of the system of one-way transfers of exchangeables, which I have called the "grants economy," for the grant, or one-way transfer, is a rough measure of an integrative relationship. On the other side, economics edges towards an area between the threat system and the exchange system which might be described as the study of strategy or bargaining.

To complete the circle there is also an area, between the threat system and the integrative system, of legitimated threat, which is the principal organizer of political activity and the main subject matter of political science. All these systems are linked together dynamically through the process of human learning, which is the main dynamic factor in all social systems. Part of this learning process is the learning of common values and moral choices, without which no culture and no social system is possible. The process by which we learn our preference structures indeed is a fundamental key to the total dynamics of society.

Economics, as such, does not contribute very much to the formal study of human learning, though some philosophical economists, like Frederick Hayek (1945), have made some interesting contributions to this subject. Our main contribution as economists is in the description of what is learned; the preference functions which embody what is learned in regard to values, and the production functions which describe the results of the learning of technology. We may not have thought much about the genetics of knowledge, but we have thought about its description, and this is a contribution not to be despised.

Thus, economics suggests the proposition that actual choices depend not only on preferences but on opportunities, and that under some circumstances quite small changes in either preferences or opportunities may result in large changes in actual choices made. This proposition applies just as much to ethical choices and common values as it does to private tastes. It throws a good deal of light also on what might be called the evolutionary ecology of ethical systems. Successful ethical systems tend to create subcultures, and these subcultures tend to perpetuate and propagate the ethical systems which created them. This principle helps to explain the persistent division of mankind into sects, nations, and ideological groups. If we were to map the ethical preference systems of the individuals who comprise mankind, we would not find a uniform distribution but we would find a very sharp clustering into cultures and subcultures with relatively empty spaces between the clusters. All the members of a single sect, for instance, tend to think rather alike in matters of ethical judgment and differentiate themselves sharply from the ethical judgments of other sects. Individuals tend to be attracted to one or another of these clusters, leaving the social space between them relatively empty, like space between the stars. The reasons for this phenomenon lie deep in the dynamics of the human learning process, for our preferences are learned mainly from those with whom we have the most communication. This principle accounts for the perpetuation of such clusters, though it does not necessarily account for their original formation, which exhibits many puzzling phenomena. The splitting of these clusters in a kind of mitosis is also an important and very puzzling phenomenon. Once we realize, however, that these are highly sensitive systems, as economic analysis suggests, we can see how wide divergences might arise. Thus, the actual difference in preferences and even opportunities between, shall we say, the socialist countries and the capitalist countries, may in fact be quite small, but this difference is enough to produce a very wide difference in the choices made.

Economics has made its own attempt to solve some of the problems involved in the moral judgment in what we know as welfare economics. I believe this attempt has been a failure, though a reasonably glorious one, and we should take a brief look at it. Welfare economics attempts to ask the question, "What do we mean when we say that one state of a social system is better than another in strictly economic terms?" The most celebrated answer given is the Paretian optimum, which states in effect that Condition A of a social system is economically superior to Condition B, if nobody feels worse off in A than in B, and if at least one person feels better off. "Better off" or "worse off" are measured of course by preferences, so that we could restate the condition as saying that State A is superior to State B if one or more persons prefer A and if nobody prefers B. If we permit internal redistributions within the system, that is, compensation, the range of possible superior states is considerably broadened. From this simple principle a wide range of applications has been found possible in a stirring intellectual drama which might well be subtitled "Snow White (the fairest of all) and the Seven Marginal Conditions."

Many, if not most, economists accept the Paretian optimum as almost self-evident. Nevertheless, it rests on an extremely shaky foundation of ethical propositions. The more one examines it, for instance, the more clear it becomes that economists must be extraordinarily nice people even to have thought of such a thing, for it implies that there is no malevolence anywhere in the system. It implies, likewise, that there is no benevolence, the niceness of economists not quite extending as far as good will. It assumes selfishness, that is, the independence of individual preference functions, such that it makes no difference to me whether I perceive you as either better off or worse off. Anything less descriptive of the human condition could hardly be imagined. The plain fact is that our lives are dominated by precisely this interdependence of utility functions which the Paretian optimum denies. Selfishness, or indifference to the welfare of others, is a knife edge between benevolence on the one side and malevolence on the other. It is something that is very rare. We may feel indifferent towards those whom we do not know, with whom we have no relationships of any kind, but towards those with whom we have relationships, even the frigid relationship of exchange, we are apt to be either benevolent or malevolent. We either rejoice when they rejoice, or we rejoice when they mourn.

The almost complete neglect by economists of the concepts of malevolence and benevolence cannot be explained by their inability to handle these concepts with their usual tools. There are no mathematical or conceptual difficulties involved in inter-relating utility functions, provided that we note that it is the perceptions that matter (Boulding, 1962). The familiar tools of our trade, the indifference map, the Edgeworth box, and so on, can easily be expanded to include benevolence or malevolence, and indeed without this expansion many phenomena, such as one-way transfers, cannot be explained. Perhaps the main explanation of our neglect of these concepts is the fact that we have concentrated so heavily on exchange as the object of our study, and exchange frequently takes place under conditions of at least relative indifference or selfishness, though I argue that there is a minimum degree of benevolence even in exchange, without which it cannot be legitimated and cannot operate as a social organizer. We exchange courtesies, smiles, the time of day, and so on, with the clerk in the store, as well as exchanging money for commodities. The amount of benevolence which exchangers feel towards each other need not be large, but a certain minimum is essential. If exchangers begin to feel malevolent towards each other, exchange tends to break down, or can only be legitimated under conditions of special ritual, such as silent trade or collective bargaining.

Nevertheless, economists can perhaps be excused for abstracting from benevolence and malevolence, simply because their peculiar baby, which is exchange, tends to be that social organizer which lies between these two extremes, and which produces, if not selfishness, at least low levels of malevolence and benevolence. The threat system constantly tends to produce malevolence simply because of the learning process which it engenders. A threatener may begin by feeling benevolent towards the threatened—"I am doing this for your own good"—but threats almost invariably tend to produce malevolence on the part of the threatened towards the threatener, and this is likely to produce a type of behavior which will in turn produce malevolence on the part of the threatener towards the threatened. This can easily result in a cumulative process of increasing malevolence, which may or may not reach some kind of equilibrium. The breakup of communities into factions and into internal strife frequently follows this pattern. At the other end of the scale, the integrative system tends to produce benevolence and those institutions which are specialized in the integrative system, such as the family, the church, the lodge, the club, the alumni association, and so on, tend also to create and organize benevolence, even beyond the circle of their members. This is partly because benevolence seems to be an important element in establishing a satisfactory personal identity, especially after the threat system has been softened by the development of exchange. Those who live under threat, who generally occupy the lower end of the social scale, as well as those who live by threat at the upper end, tend to find their personal identities through malevolence and through the development of counterthreat or through the displacement of hatred onto weaker objects, such as children and animals. Once this state is passed, however, and society is mainly organized by exchange, there seems to be a strong tendency to move towards the integrative system and the integrative institutions. The Rotary Club is a logical extension of a business-oriented society, but it is not one that would necessarily have occurred to economists.

Oddly enough, it is not welfare economics, with its elegant casuistry, subtle distinctions, and its ultimately rather implausible recommendations, which has made the greatest impact on the development of common values and ethical propositions. The major impact of economics on ethics, it can be argued, has come because it has developed broad, aggregative concepts of general welfare which are subject to quantification. We can see this process going right back to Adam Smith, where the idea of what we would today call per capita real income as the principal measure of national well-being has made a profound impact on subsequent thinking and policy. The development of the concept of a gross national product and its various modifications and components as statistical measures of economic success, likewise, has had a great impact in creating common values for the objectives of economic policy. Another, less fortunate, example of a measure which profoundly affected economic policy was the development of the parity index by the Bureau of Agricultural Economics in the United States Department of Agriculture. As a measure of the terms of trade of agriculture, this became an important symbol. "A hundred per cent of parity" became the avowed goal of agricultural policy, even though there is very little reason to suppose that the terms of trade of a given historic period, in this case the period 1909–14, have any ultimate validity as an ideal. Because of differing rates of change in productivity in different parts of the economy, we should expect the terms of trade of different sectors to change. If, for instance, productivity in agriculture rises faster than in the rest of the economy, as it has done in the last thirty years, we would expect the terms of trade of agriculture to "worsen" without any worsening of the incomes of farmers, and without any sense of social injustice.

Even though economic measurement may be abused, its effect on the formation of moral judgments is great, and on the whole I believe beneficial. The whole idea of cost–benefit analysis, for instance, in terms of monetary units, say "real" dollars of constant purchasing power, is of enormous importance in the evaluation of social choices and even of social institutions. We can grant, of course, that the "real" dollar, which is oddly enough a strictly imaginary one, is a dangerously imperfect measure of the quality of human life and human values. Nevertheless, it is a useful first approximation, and in these matters of evaluation of difficult choices it is extremely useful to have some first approximation that we can then modify. Without this, indeed, all evaluation is random selection by wild hunches. It is true, of course, that cost–benefit analysis of all sorts of things, whether of water projects, other pork barrel items, or in more recent years weapon systems, can be manipulated to meet the previous prejudices of people who are trying to influence the decisions. Nevertheless, the fundamental principle that we should count all costs, whether easily countable or not, and evaluate all rewards, however hard they are to evaluate, is one which emerges squarely out of economics and which is at least a preliminary guideline in the formation of the moral judgment, in what might be called the "economic ethic."

Nevertheless, the economic ethic, or the total cost–benefit principle, is subject to sharp challenge. Two principal criticisms have been made of it, the first of which I think is probably not valid, and the second of which may be valid under limited circumstances. The criticism that I think is not valid is that cost–benefit analyses in particular, or economic principles in general, imply selfish motivation and an insensitivity to the larger issues of malevolence, benevolence, the sense of community, and so on. It is quite true, as shown above, that economists have neglected the problem of malevolence and benevolence. Nevertheless, our attitudes towards others can be measured at least as well as we can measure other preferences, either by some principle of "revealed preference" or by direct questioning. It is entirely within the competence of economics, for instance, to develop a concept of the "rate of benevolence," which is the quantity of exchangeables, as measured in real dollars, which a person would be willing to sacrifice in order to contemplate an increase of one real dollar in the welfare of another person. If the rate of benevolence is zero, of course, we have indifference or pure selfishness; if the rate of benevolence is negative we have malevolence, in which case people need compensation in order to contemplate without loss the increased welfare of an enemy, or in reverse would be willing to damage themselves in order to damage another. The rate of malevolence then would be the amount in real dollars one would be prepared to damage one's self in order to damage another person to the extent of one dollar. These rates of malevolence incidentally are frequently quite high. It apparently costs the United States about four dollars to do one dollar's worth of damage in Vietnam, in which case our rate of benevolence towards North Vietnam is at least minus four. In determining cost–benefit analysis we can easily include rates of benevolence and malevolence, adding the benefits and subtracting the costs to those towards whom we are benevolent, multiplied of course by the rate of benevolence, and subtracting the benefits and adding the costs, similarly modified, to those towards whom we are malevolent.

The concept of a rate of benevolence, incidentally, is at least a partial solution to the perplexing question of interpersonal comparisons of utility around which economists have been doing a ritual dance for at least three generations. Any decision involving other people obviously involves these interpersonal comparisons. They are made, of course, inside the mind of the decision-maker and what his rates of benevolence or malevolence are likely to be is determined by the whole social process in which he is embedded. Surely something can be said about this. We are, for instance, likely to be more benevolent to people who are going to vote for us and perhaps malevolent to people who are going to vote against us. The economic theory of democracy indeed, as developed by Anthony Downs and others, is a very good example of what I have sometimes called "economics imperialism," which is an attempt on the part of economics to take over all the other social sciences.

The second attack on the "economic ethic" is more fundamental and harder to repulse. This is the attack from the side of what I have elsewhere called the "heroic ethic" (Boulding, 1968). In facing decisions, especially those which involve other people, as virtually all decisions do, we are faced with two very different frameworks of judgment. The first of these is the economic ethic of total cost–benefit analysis. It is an ethic of being sensible, rational, whatever we want to call it. It is an ethic of calculation. We cannot indeed count the cost without counting. Hence, it is an ethic which depends on the development of measurement and numbers, even if these are ordinal numbers. This type of decision-making, however, does not exhaust the immense complexities of the human organism, and we have to recognize that there is in the world another type of decision-making, in which the decision-maker elects something, not because of the effects that it will have, but because of what he "is," that is, how he perceives his own identity. This "heroic" ethic takes three major forms—the military, the religious, and the sporting.

The heroic ethic "theirs not to reason why, theirs but to do and die" is so fundamental to the operation of the military that attempts to apply an economic ethic to it in the form of cost–benefit analysis or programmed budgeting, or even strategic science as practiced by Herman Kahn, T.C. Schelling, or even Robert McNamara, are deeply threatening to the morale and the legitimacy of the whole military system. Religion, likewise, is an essentially heroic enterprise, even though there is a strong streak of spiritual cost–benefit analysis in it. The enormous role which religion has played in the history of mankind, for good or ill, is based on the appeal which it has to the sense of identity and the sense of the heroic even in ordinary people. "Here I stand and I can do no other," said Luther; "To give and not to count the cost, to labor and ask for no reward" is the prayer of St. Francis. "Do your own thing" is the motto of our new secular Franciscans, the Hippies. In our national religion, President Kennedy said, "Ask not what your country can do for you, ask only what you can do for your country." We find the same principle in poetry, in art, in architecture, which are constantly striving to disengage themselves from the chilling embrace of cost–benefit analysis. I cannot resist quoting here in full what has always seemed to me one of the finest expressions in English poetry of the heroic critique of economics—Wordsworth's extraordinary sonnet on King's College Chapel, Cambridge (Ecclesiastical Sonnet, Number XLIII):

> INSIDE OF KING'S COLLEGE CHAPEL, CAMBRIDGE
> Tax not the royal Saint with vain expense,
> With ill-matched aims the Architect who planned—
> Albeit labouring for a scanty band
> Of white-robed Scholars only—this immense
> And glorious Work of fine intelligence!
> Give all thou canst; high Heaven rejects the lore
> Of nicely-calculated less or more;
> So deemed the man who fashioned for the sense
> These lofty pillars, spread that branching roof
> Self-poised, and scooped into ten thousand cells,
> Where light and shade repose, where music dwells
> Lingering—and wandering on as loth to die;
> Like thoughts whose very sweetness yieldeth proof
> That they were born for immortality.

Okay, boys, bring out your cost–benefit analysis now! There is a story, for the truth of which I will not vouch, that Keynes once asked the chaplain of King's College if he could borrow the chapel for a few days. The chaplain was overjoyed at this evidence of conversion of a noted infidel until it turned out that Keynes had got stuck with a load of wheat in the course of his speculations in futures contracts and wanted to use the chapel for storage.

The "lore of nicely-calculated less or more," of course, is economics. I used to think that high heaven rejected this because its resources were infinite and therefore did not need to be economized. I have since come to regard this view as theologically unsound for reasons which I cannot go into here, but also for a more fundamental reason. High heaven, at least as it exists and propagates itself in the minds of men, is nothing if not heroic. The power of religion in human history has arisen more than anything from its capacity to give identity to its practitioners and to inspire them with behavior which arises out of this perceived identity. In extreme form, this gives rise to the saints and martyrs of all faiths, religious or secular, but it also gives rise to a great deal of quiet heroism, for instance, in jobs, in marriage, in child rearing, and in the humdrum tasks of daily life, without which a good deal of the economy might well fall apart.

A good deal of the criticism of economics from both left and right arises from dissatisfaction with its implied neglect of the heroic. There is a widespread feeling that trade is somehow dirty, and that merchants are somewhat undesirable characters, and that especially the labor market is utterly despicable as constituting the application of the principle of prostitution to virtually all areas of human life. This sentiment is not something which economists can neglect. We have assumed all too easily in economics that because something paid off it was therefore automatically legitimate. Unfortunately, the dynamics of legitimacy are more complex than this. Frequently it is negative pay-offs, that is, sacrifices, rather than positive payoffs which establish legitimacy. It has been the precise weakness of the institutions that we think primarily of as economic, that is, associated with exchange, such as the stock market, the banking system, organized commodity markets, and so on, as Schumpeter pointed out, that they easily lose their legitimacy if they are not supported by other elements and institutions in the society which can sustain them as integral parts of a larger community. On the right also we find nationalists, fascists, and the military, attacking the economic man and economic motivation from the point of view of the heroic ethic. It is a wonder indeed that economic institutions can survive at all, when economic man is so universally unpopular. No one in his senses would want his daughter to marry an economic man, one who counted every cost and asked for every reward, was never afflicted with mad generosity or uncalculating love, and who never acted out of a sense of inner identity and indeed had no inner identity even if he was occasionally affected by carefully calculated considerations of benevolence or malevolence. The attack on economics is an attack on calculatedness and the very fact that we think of the calculating as cold suggests how exposed economists are to romantic and heroic criticism.

My personal view is that, especially at his present stage or development, man requires both heroic and economic elements in his institutions, in his learning processes and in his decision-making, and the problem of maintaining them in proper balance and tension is one of the major problems of maturation, both of the individual person and of societies. Economic man is a clod, heroic man is a fool, but somewhere between the clod and the fool, human man, if the expression may be pardoned, steers his tottering way.

Let me conclude by stealing another idea from economics and applying it to general moral science. This is the concept of a production function, some sort of limited relationship between inputs and outputs as expressed in the great biblical principle that grapes are not gathered from thorns, or figs from thistles (Matthew 7:16). There are production functions not only for grapes and figs, but also for goods and bads, and indeed for the ultimate Good. We dispute about what is good, about what outputs we want as a result of the inputs we put in. We dispute also, however, about the nature of the production functions themselves, what inputs in fact will produce what outputs. In the case of physical production functions, the problems can be resolved fairly easily by experimenting, even though there are some pretty doubtful cases, as in the case of cloud seedings, which do not seem to be demonstrably more effective than rain dances. In the case of moral production functions, however, the functions themselves are much in dispute, and there may indeed be more disputation about the production functions than there is about the nature of the desired outputs themselves. I was impressed some years ago, when engaged in a long, arduous seminar with some young Russians and young Americans, with how easy it was to agree on ultimate goals, even across these widely divergent ideologies, and how extraordinarily hard it was to agree about the inputs which are likely to produce these ultimate goals.

There is a problem here in human learning of how do we get to know the moral production functions in the complex melee of social, political, and economic life, when it seems to be pervaded throughout with a note of almost cosmic irony in which almost everything we do turns out differently from what we expect because of our ignorance, so that both the bad and the good we do is all too often unintentional. I cannot solve this epistemological problem in one short paper, but I recommend it as a major intellectual challenge to the moral sciences. What I am concerned with here is economics as an input into this moral production function. Does economics, as George Stigler has suggested, make people conservative (Stigler, 1959)? If so, it is perhaps because it simply points out the difficulties and dangers of heroic action and makes people appreciate the productivity of the commonplace, of exchange and finance, of bankers and businessmen, even of the middle class which our heroic young so earnestly despise. Perhaps this is why so many young radicals today have abandoned economics as a poisoned apple of rationality which corrupts the pure and heroic man of their identities and sympathies. Economics is a reconciler, it brings together the ideologies of East and West, it points up the many common problems which they have, it is corrosive of ideologies and disputes that are not worth their costs. Even as it acts as a reconciler, however, does it not undermine that heroic demand for social mutation which will not be stilled in the voices of our young radicals?

I confess I have been deeply disturbed when I have asked myself these questions and I have no easy answers to them. Nevertheless, I am not sorry that I became an economist, for to belong to a body of people who have never even thought of introducing malevolence into their social theory is somehow in this day and age a little cheering. The anxieties, the moral anguish, and the intense dispute which has racked the American Economic Association this year and which is symbolized by the question as to whether we should move our meeting from Chicago is symptomatic of the fact that not even the study of economics can turn people into purely economic men. Strangely enough it was the mathematical economists and econometricians who were most heroically moved by a sense of outrage against their personal identity, and who were least affected by the cost–benefit analysis. In this year of crisis, I have also learned something about myself—that it is easier to make heroic decisions as a member of the committee than it is as a sole decision-maker and that heroism is much less appropriate in political than it is in personal decisions. The lessons of this year, therefore, are that the study of economics does not produce clods, even if perhaps the American Economic Association does not produce undue heroics. So we can hope at least that economics is one of the inputs that helps to make us human. If so, the benefits of this strange activity will be well worth its undoubted cost, even if in our heroic mood we dare not calculate them.

Note

1 Presidential address delivered at the Eighty-first meeting of the American Economic Association, Chicago, Illinois, December 29, 1968. This address will be listed as Publication 122 of the Institute of Behavioral Science, University of Colorado. This article was previously published in *The American Economic Review*, 1969, 59(1), 1–12.

References

Boulding, K.E., "Notes on a Theory of Philanthropy," in F.G. Dickinson, ed., *Philanthropy and Public Policy*, National Bureau of Economic Research, New York, 1962.

Boulding, K.E., "Ethical Dilemmas in Religion and Nationalism," lecture at the New York Ethical Society, April 18, 1968.

Hayek, F.A. von, "The Use of Knowledge in Society," *The American Economic Review*, Sept. 1945, 35, 519–727.

Stigler, G. J., "The Politics of Political Economists," *Quarterly Journal of Economics*, Nov. 1959, 73, 522–32.

4a Commentary article: Kenneth Boulding's *The Image* and contemporary discourse analysis[1]

Warren J. Samuel

After reading Veblen, one can never quite see a university campus or an elaborate house in just the same light as before.

(Kenneth Boulding, *The Image*, p. 9)

We must always operate with the concept of an inventory of images and we can never replace this inventory by a single image, not even that of the most important person in the organization.

(p. 63)

One of the most noticeable trends in history has been the rise of manifest images about history itself.

(p. 126)

Introduction

Economics has, in the last decade, experienced a post-modernist turn. For most intents and purposes the critical episode in this development was publication by Donald McCloskey of his article on the rhetoric of economics in the *Journal of Economic Literature* (McCloskey 1983). His article vastly expanded the horizons and sensitivities of both economic methodologists and economists with other specialties.

The origins of post-modernism reside in the remote past but include work in the sociology of knowledge, the role of values and ideology in economics, and so on. At the level of general philosophy, Immanuel Kant persuaded many that reality, or whatever went by that name, could not conclusively be directly approached or experienced by human beings—that the human mind and its creations, such as techniques of analysis, both mediated and generated perception. Ludwig Wittgenstein in his later work convinced many that language did not bear any necessary relation to the object of language, say, reality. The development of logical empiricism led to the gradual realizations (1) that logic could at best lead only to conclusions which were validly derived from premises and not necessarily true (in the sense of accurate description and/or correct explanation), (2) that there were severe limitations to empiricism, and (3) that there were severe limitations to the conclusions drawn from the application of data in the testing of hypotheses even with a refutation principle.

Truth, or hard truth or Truth with a capital T, became increasingly difficult to conceptualize and perhaps impossible to achieve in practice. At the same time, emphasis on the substantive impacts of language led to an emphasis on the rhetorical rather than the truth-value meaning of propositions and theories. Furthermore, criticism of prescriptivist epistemology developed from both within philosophy of science and epistemology themselves and the growing analysis of discourse and language and of the sociology of science.

One upshot of these developments in economics was the combination of continued attention to the credentials, however limited, which statements purporting to be knowledge might carry, and newly established attention to the rhetorical, or storytelling, character of the statements quite independent of their putative truth value, whatever their credentials. Epistemology had been joined by discourse analysis.

One facet of these developments, harkening back to Kant, was the identification and the questioning of the ontological meaning of statements and the object of theories. Philosophical and scientific realism could not be summarily dismissed but claims of ontological pre-eminence, as the basis of putatively scientific stories, carried less-persuasive power.

At any rate, these developments—as well as long-standing concerns about ideology, metaphysics, paradigms, worldviews, ultimate faith presuppositions or preconceptions, and *Weltanschauungen*, coupled with developments within linguistics itself—have led to more narrowly focused attention being given to the putative definitions of reality and of values generated by or reflected in the economic theories of all schools of thought. A considerable diminution has taken place in the conceit or hubris characterizing the attitudes which analysts display in upholding and advancing their theories, though some unquestionably remains. Much of this has been the result of significantly greater attention being given to the economic theory of a school as a particular mode of discourse and, in the terminology of Thomas Kuhn, the paradigm ensconced therein.

All this has constituted a major transformation in the perspective taken by many economists of the ideas which constitute the substance of their professional, and perhaps also personal, life. And it clearly traces back to the initial work of McCloskey—as well as to the work of others, such as Arjo Klamer—and reposes in a now substantial literature.

McCloskey, however, was not the first professional economist to identify and emphasize the linguistic/hermeneutic/discursive nature of economic theories. One could probably list several dozen who earlier had serious intuitions about and/or wrote directly on the topic, going back at least as far as Adam Smith.

For example, a once well-known attempt to penetrate the mysteries of economics as language was made by L.M. Fraser in his 1947 book, *Economic Thought and Language.*

Less appreciated in regard to its analysis of economic discourse is John R. Commons's *Legal Foundations of Capitalism*. Here is early and remarkably sophisticated attention to considerations of language and of how words, as artifacts, encapsulate changing interpretations of experience and of values. Commons adopted a social constructivist and not a representational conception of language. 'Words, price and numbers', he wrote:

> are nominal and not real. They are signs and symbols needed for the operation of the working rules. Yet each is the only effective means by which human beings can deal with each other securely and accurately with regard to the things that are real. But each may be insecure and inaccurate.
>
> (Commons 1924, p. 9)

Certain words embody and give effect to theories—for example, of property, liberty and value—which are sometimes erected into metaphysical and ontological absolutes, but, however held, serve as the basis for the formulation and reformulation of rights, duties and so on. Commons also writes, 'Ideals are ideas projected into the future by means of symbols' (p. 349). The symbols are for the most part linguistic. It is out of these processes that both the economic system known as capitalism emerged and evolved and the words themselves are given ascriptive meaning.

The language Commons uses to discuss language is remarkably close to present-day usage.

Commons focuses on the reinterpretation of legal and constitutional terms by the courts, especially the Supreme Court, as a result of which concepts such as property and liberty have been redefined, giving effect to new theories thereof. Changes in legal semantics thus incorporate more or less subtle but typically cumulatively important changes in law and therefore in relative rights, opportunities, exposures and immunities. Commons also indicates the privileging of certain selective specifications of concepts like private property as natural and therefore antecedent to and independent of government, in contrast to the actual process of the human social construction of property as an institution, although those selective privilegings function as part of that process.

Commons devotes enormous attention to the critical role of legal terms and to the important consequences of changes in their meanings and definitions. He principally emphasizes the growth of the legal definition of property to include incorporeal and intangible property, the transformation of the meaning of property from use-value and exchange-value (and the correlative change from an emphasis on one's own use to others' potential use and the role of withholding). Changes in the legal definition of property were a function of changes in judicial theories of property and liberty, all involving words with socioeconomic consequences. He writes that 'when property began to yield exchange-value as well as use-value, the term "uses" was simply enlarged by the courts to include it' (p. 113). '[M]odern business is conducted and ... American legislatures, executives and inferior courts are held in conformity to the Constitution of the United States ... as latterly interpreted by the Supreme Court' (p. 7). Commons indicates the process and results of selectively privileging certain specifications of property and other terms (such as the police power, pp. 35–6) as natural and therefore antecedent to and independent of government, in contrast to the actual process of the human social construction of property utilizing language.

Commons is a social constructivist with regard to both jurisprudence (the language and meanings of law) and language in general. Changes in definition are in part the means whereby both legislature and, especially, the courts can legislate (make law); such changes in definition, Commons writes, 'are of course not arbitrary. They spring from new conditions. Yet they are discretionary' (p. 356). Legal change for Commons is more than a matter of changing conditions; it is also a matter of changed perceptions and evaluations of experience, for example, changes in which/whose customs the courts will embody in law and enforce on others, and so on. Changing definitions can arise from new conditions but conditions can be variably experienced and evaluated, depending upon purposes and values, so that even new conditions can be variably interpreted and lead to different changes in language or no change. All this is central to the social reconstruction of reality.

Commons rejects the 'illusion of certainty'—given, for example, by natural law and natural rights doctrines—which

> [give] rise to metaphysical 'entities' and 'substances' conceived as existing apart from and independent of the behavior of officials and citizens.... These illusions naturally arise from the hopes and fears of mankind which substitute wishes for behavior. We conceive that what we wish is the reality, the real thing. Thus rights and duties also, like the state, are given the illusion of a reality existing apart from the conduct of officials
>
> (pp. 124, 125)

Commons's point is that 'The state is what its officials do' (p. 122). Legal rights and duties are none other than the probability that officials will act in a certain way respecting the claims that citizens make against each other (p. 125).

This is all empirical rather than metaphysical or mythic, though Commons is obviously aware of the use of such ideas for legitimation and psychic balm. He emphasizes that preconceived absolutes have been revised through the device of changing the definitions of terms. These changing definitions revise the mode of discourse, and therefore of perception, and permit both (1) adjustment to and revision of the socially constructed reality and (2) psychic balm, a sense of the predetermined to accompany the reality of change:

> A change in definitions is such a simple and natural way of changing the constitution from what it is to what it ought to be, and the method is so universal and usually so gradual in all walks of life, that the will of God, or the will of the People, or the Corporate will, scarcely realizes what has happened. The method is, indeed, that common-sense device whereby man can go on believing in unchanging entities, and yet be practical.
>
> (p. 373)

Commons's total model of legal–economic change is vast and complex. Part of it amounts to the dualism that generalized perceptions of legal–economic reality (for present purposes, Kuhn's 'paradigm') through language influence behavior and policy and thereby the social construction of reality and, also through language, are the result of changes in the social construction of reality (in both senses, that of the literal creation of social reality and its interpretation).

A well-known economist with unquestionable credentials as an economic theorist who both emphasized and analyzed the semantics of economics was Fritz Machlup. Thus, in his *Economic Semantics* (1963; reprinted 1991), Machlup explored semantic issues in economic methods, value theory, macroeconomic theory and policy, and methodology. And throughout a number of writings, he examined the social nature of knowledge, in part, as encapsulated in discourse.[2]

Ben Ward's *What's Wrong with Economics?*—a considerably neglected 1972 work, neglected perhaps because of its title, which correctly conveys its deep criticism of neoclassicism as well as Marxism—contains several direct and pointed analyses of language. Ward rejects the idea that language necessarily has a representational relation with reality. (Ward distinguishes between the connotative and the performative aspects or roles of language [pp. 208–9].) For him, communication is a function of the web of mutual understandings. '[F]acts, theories and values are inextricably intertwined in communication—scientific or otherwise' (Ward 1972, p. 114). 'Meaning ... [is] a function of context as well as of structure and the meaning of individual words and phrases' (p. 112). Positivism has failed because 'of what is now known about the nature of language, not to mention what is known about the actual behavior of scientists' (p. 115). The formation and use of language is part of the interactive and social process of internal change in human development.

Ward calls attention to the socializing role of language, the development of language and the interpretation of experience influenced by language (p. 122). He also calls attention to how myth-building, ensconced in language, involves giving 'a hard surface to a soft reality' and the tendency of the world to adopt itself to the needs of expertise, also ensconced in language (p. 158).

Perhaps Ward's most dramatic and prescient argument follows from his identification of the ubiquity of interpretation and of interpretation as a mix of fact, theory and values, as well as from his emphasis on the operative importance of persuasiveness relative to truth. The argument is that economics is largely a set of stories and the practice of economics is that of storytelling. His position is encapsulated in the statement that 'the basic methodological element in economics, and all social science, is not the study but the story' (p. 190).

Yet, argues Ward, economic theory fails to deal with communication; in part, it fails to deal with the dissemination of worldview or with the network of commitments and the socialization of individuals generated by all sorts of communication modes. Indeed, 'The issue of manipulation of individuals through socialization by family and school and profession and media cannot be discussed in terms of a model that does not admit the possibility of such manipulation' (p. 205).

One of the most acute and wide-ranging yet integrated analyses is found in Kenneth Boulding's *The Image*, published in 1956. The objective of this chapter is to consider and understand what Boulding had to say in relation to present-day post-modern interests and thereby to understand that book as a significant precursor and contribution to the contemporary study of rhetoric of economics, broadly defined. Whereas for Commons, for example, the *transaction* is the fundamental unit of analysis, for Boulding, the *image* is the fundamental element of analysis, in two models which are, in matters linguistic and otherwise, much more supplementary than contradictory, if the latter at all.

Boulding's own statement of objective in *The Image* is worth noting:

> It is the purpose of this work, therefore, to discuss the growth of images, both private and public, in individuals, in organizations, in society at large, and even with some trepidation, among the lower forms of life. Only thus can we develop a really adequate theory of behavior.
>
> (p. 18)

Boulding's theory of the image will be considered as follows: Section 2 examines the nature of the image in relation to knowledge and truth; Section 3 identifies what he has to say regarding the role of the image; Section 4 treats the origins and dynamics of image change; Section 5 examines the linguistic character of the image; Section 6, the relation of the image to informational systems and other structures; Section 7 records what Boulding had to say on the relations of economics and the image, including but going beyond the general notion that economics as a discipline is a set of images.

In *The Image*, Boulding advanced three lines of argument relevant to this chapter: (1) the definitional role of language—the definition of reality and of values represented by words—ensconced within the images on which people predicate action; (2) the interpretive structures resident deep within language (in the manner of Benjamin Whorf, Jean Piaget, Claude Levi-Strauss, Thomas Kuhn, Noam Chomsky and Michel Foucault[3]); and (3) the relevance of truth as a consideration but the arguably greater empirical prevalence of the interpretive rhetorical or discursive formulations embodied within images.

Two preliminary notices: first, I shall discuss what Boulding has to say in *The Image* only in regard to discourse analysis; of course, there is more than that in the book. To a considerable extent, I will let Boulding speak for himself, so that my image of his image of the image does not overly intervene—though it obviously is impossible to fully escape that situation.

Nature of the image in relation to knowledge and truth

The image is, for Boulding, a theoretical construct for which he here endeavors to provide an explanation. Although he does not come right out and say so, it may be presumed that the image of the image itself is subject to his theory of the image; that is, that his idea and theory are self-referential. This is an important matter, warranting a brief initial digression.

Boulding himself uses certain terms reflective of certain images he either has or wants to convey. For example:

> [T]here is an orderly development in the public image as recorded in the transcript of successive civilizations and generations.... The over-all development ... is neither random nor haphazard.
>
> (p. 77; see also p. 78: 'The relational image likewise exhibits an orderly development through time')

> We may perhaps hazard the suggestion that there is some optimum degree of feedback from the lower to the higher roles...
>
> (p. 100)

> The real question at issue is, whether the process will be improved by being made more self-conscious.
>
> (pp. 159–60)

The concepts of '*orderly* development', '*optimum* degree' and '*improved*' each require subjective judgment; it is a matter of the hermeneutics of image choice rather than the application of a conclusive transcendent, independently given test. Self-referentiality or self-reflexivity is derivative of Boulding's own arguments that his theory is an image of the image and that 'images can only be compared with images' (p. 165): his theory of the image is itself an image and must be treated in the same way as other images. Self-referentiality surfaces, for example, in the inexorable necessity of choice between levels of discourse (pp. 167–70; discussed below). It especially arises in his position on skepticism (pp. 171–5, discussed below in the concluding section). The theory of the image being itself an image, it must be subject to its own theory. Nowhere does Boulding explicitly say this, but it is strongly implicit. Of course, Boulding's theory of the image maintains neither that every implication of an image necessarily follows nor that an image must be entirely consistent. The issue certainly remains open, though on the basis of personal knowledge—yes, image—of Boulding, it would seem that he would accept if not insist on self-referentiality.

The image is a mental picture of understanding (pp. 3–4). It is a result of the gathering and organizing of information (p. 35 and passim), that is, of learning, with (very importantly) the gathering and organizing itself influenced by controlling images. The image may be more or less coherent (p. 10; also see below). The image may be of facts and/or of values (p. 11 and passim). 'Value images ... consist ... of a "posture" which in a sense summarizes an extremely complex network of alternatives and situations.... [In the case of Christianity, it is] a whole attitude toward life and the universe' (p. 110).

Some images are of 'real' things, ' "real" in the sense that they are not products of our imagination, that they would continue to exist "outside" us, even if we disappeared from the scene' (p. 52). Boulding explicitly begs 'the whole philosophical question of idealism versus realism' but does distinguish between furniture and utensils and the 'dreams, imaginings, fairy stories, legends [that are] perceived as unreal, as not having any existence outside of the human image' (p. 52). He also seems to effectively distinguish between simple things, like furniture, and conceptual(ized) things, like the economic system, as well as things, like capital, which can be conceptualized in different ways. For the important concerns of the social and natural sciences, the role of imagination is critical.

It is very important to Boulding to recognize that the image may be taken as knowledge but that image as putative knowledge may not carry acceptable epistemological credentials and that, indeed, the image as putative knowledge may not constitute truth (Truth).[4]

> What I have been talking about is knowledge. Knowledge, perhaps, is not a good word for this. Perhaps one would say my *Image* of the world. Knowledge has an implication of validity, of truth. What I am talking about is what I believe to be true; my subjective knowledge. It is this Image that largely governs my behavior.
>
> (pp. 5–6)

Apropos of the Kantian position, one reads Boulding saying that 'We now know that what used to be regarded as primary sense data are in fact highly learned interpretations' (p. 50).

For Boulding, there are (with regard to nonsimple things, such as furniture) 'no such things as "facts". There are only messages filtered through a changeable value system' (p. 14, about which more below); indeed, 'it is not the message that is important but the transformation of the image which it produces' (p. 90). Images are not, or need not be, purely private; shared image structures constitute culture (and variegated shared image structures constitute varying subcultures) (pp. 14–15; p. 49: 'The relational image varies greatly from culture to culture, and even within subcultures within the same general society'). Society is composed of images but it is also 'a process of modification of images through messages' (p. 107). One aspect of this process is people's 'intense hatred … of multidimensional value orderings' (p. 111), the latter relating to the plurality of co-existing images and the fact that each person 'perceives … from his own position' and therefore different persons 'do not each receive the same messages' (p. 132).

Science itself is a mode of image formation, however much accompanied by the conceit of 'truth'. Although 'It is the peculiar glory of science that it has systematized the growth of the relational image within its subculture in a way that enables it to tread lightly over the relational quicksands of common sense', it is also true that

> Science … buys its success at a price; indeed at a high price. The price is a severe limitation of its field of inquiry and a value system which is as

> ruthless in its own way in the censoring of messages as the value system of primitive man. Messages which will not conform to the subculture are condemned as illusion.
>
> (p. 71)

Science is thus also a matter of sociology:

> Most epistemological systems seek some philosopher's stone by which statements may be tested in order to determine the 'truth,' that is, their correspondence to outside reality. I do not claim to have any such philosopher's stone, not even the touchstone of science. I have, of course, as great respect for science and scientific method—for careful observation, for planned experience, for the testing of hypotheses and for as much objectivity as semirational beings like ourselves can hope to achieve. In my theoretical system, however, the scientific method merely stands as one among many of the methods whereby images change and develop. The development of images is part of the culture or the subculture in which they are developed, and it depends upon all the elements of that culture or subculture. Science is a subculture among subcultures. It can claim to be useful. I may claim rather more dubiously to be good. It cannot claim to give validity.
>
> (p. 16)

Boulding summarizes by saying that 'my theory might well be called an organic theory of knowledge. Its most fundamental proposition is that knowledge is what somebody or something knows, and that without a knower, knowledge is an absurdity' (p. 16).

With its source in the subjective value system, the meaning of an image is a function of its generative value system. Boulding engages in a number of distinctions. In several chapters (2, 3 and 4) he identifies several levels of organization of the image. He distinguishes between their different natures, structures, degrees of complexity and degrees of sophistication (pp. 48, 95), that is, degrees of informational importance. He explores the relation of the image to complex sensory structures (p. 24). He also writes about imagination, 'self-consciousness, time-boundedness, images of the past, of the future, of causality, of relationship' (pp. 29–30). He is especially concerned with the temporal, spatial and relational elements of structures of the image (p. 25: 'Closely associated with the time structure of his image is the image of the structure of relationships. Because we are aware of time, we are also aware of cause and effect, of contiguity and succession, of cycles and repetition'). There also are personal, valuational and affectional images as well as divisions of the image into conscious, unconscious areas and the dimensions of, first, degrees of certainty and uncertainty, or clarity and vagueness;[5] second, reality and unreality; and third, private and public (pp. 47–8, 98, 123, 132 and passim). In addition, Boulding distinguishes between latent and manifest (concept of) images (pp. 83ff., 116ff.); the relative stability and instability of the image (p. 108); whether the image is pathological or beneficial (pp. 79, 111); truth and distortion (see below); security and insecurity as a consequence of images held, as in international relations (p. 112); mechanical, quasi-mechanical and organic models or images (pp. 121ff. and passim); and official (formal) and informal (p. 142).

The idea of the pathological is raised by Boulding at several points. He writes that

> it is often the most successful images that become the most dangerous. The image becomes institutionalized in the ceremonial and coercive institutions of society. It acquires thereby a spurious stability. As the world moves on, the image does not.
>
> (p. 79)

> An image which is about to collapse of its own weight is frequently supported far beyond its time by the efforts of misguided people to push it over. The attacks of the reformers produce defensive mechanisms on the part of the holders of the image. It is identified in the value system with other dearly held values and hence, any messages inconsistent with it are rejected.
>
> (p. 122)

Messages can engender vicious circles (p. 91) or vicious processes (p. 112), one example of which is the mutual creation of degenerative images of each other by the United States and the USSR during the Cold War (p. 114).

Other points that Boulding makes about the image include: (1) that 'The image is always the property of the individual persons, not of the organization' (p. 28; see also p. 54); (2) that only 'a very small part of our image is exposed to our internal view at any time' (p. 53); and, *inter alia*, (3) that 'We must always operate with the concept of an inventory of images and we can never replace this inventory by a single image, not even that of the most important person in the organization' (p. 63)—another way in which Boulding rejects the idea that there necessarily must be one correct image, an argument which suggests that he held his own theory of the image in a self-reflexive, or self-referential, way.

Boulding returns to the question of truth in the final chapter, 'The Image and Truth: Some Philosophical Implications'. Here he argues several things. One is that his theory of the image 'is consistent with a great number of philosophical positions regarding the ultimate nature of truth and our perception of it' and that he is not 'committed to any particular epistemology' (p. 165).[6] Another is that

> the problem of truth and validity cannot be solved completely, if what we mean by the truth of an image is its correspondence with some reality in the world outside it. The difficulty with any correspondence theory of truth ... is that images can only be compared with images. They can never be compared with any outside reality.[7] ... We can never examine the correspondence of the image with reality, whether in the field or value or in the field of fact.
>
> (pp. 165, 174–5)

A third is his rejection of the positive/normative dichotomy, saying that

> The theory of the image is distinctly unfriendly to the position that facts and values are quite distinct, that facts are a proper subject for scientific study, whereas values are not, that facts are objective and values are subjective. In the theory of the image, images of fact and images of value are alike present in the image.
>
> (p. 173)

Perhaps the most suggestive discussion relates to the several levels of discourse which Boulding identifies as pertaining to the truth of a statement, including:

1 'If I say that your image is not true, I may simply mean that it is not the same as mine' (p. 167);
2 that 'it is not the same as the public image of our subculture' (p. 167); or
3 that the meaning of truth is its survival value, as measured by its own stability *or* by 'the ability which it confers for survival on the organism possessing it'—apropos of which Boulding notes that 'it can be argued with alarming cogency that lies are frequently more stable and have a better survival value than the truth' (p. 168); or
4 that it means 'an orderly development of the image ... Truth ever eludes our grasp, but we are always moving asymptotically toward it' (p. 169); or
5 that it is 'something which comes to us with authority. It is part of our image of society that there are some people who know things and some people who don't' (p. 170).

This latter means that among the images held by people are those which legitimize the positions of authority of those who can then legitimize other images.

The role of the image

The fundamental role of the image is to define the world. The image is the basic, final, fundamental, controlling element in all perception and thought. It largely governs our definition of reality, substantively and normatively, in part as to what is actual and what is possible. In a very pregnant sense, 'persons themselves are to a considerable extent what their images make them' (p. 71).[8] It therefore largely governs behavior: 'It is this Image that largely governs my behavior' (p. 6). 'The behavior is response to an image, not a response to a stimulus, and without the concept of an image the behavior cannot possibly be understood' (p. 43). More specifically, the image, comprehended in an information-flow model, serves a message-control function:

> between the incoming and outgoing messages lies the great intervening variable of the image. The outgoing messages are the result of the image, not

> the result of the incoming messages. The incoming messages only modify the outgoing messages as they succeed in modifying the image.
>
> (p. 28)

More generally, as an analytical tool,

> the *concept* [italics added] of the image becomes an increasingly important part of any theoretical model, and the image itself becomes increasingly complex.... It is of overwhelming importance in the interpretation of human behavior and of the dynamics of society.
>
> (p. 31)

If the image is as important as Boulding says it is, no less could be the case.

The image is also involved in the joint socialization of the individual and legitimation of the status quo. Whereas 'an enormous number of aspects of life and experience can be recorded directly[,] ... large parts of the image ... can only be transcribed in symbolic form' (p. 65). This latter is particularly the case with individual socialization,[9] 'detailed images of role expectations' and 'what might be called symbolic or personalized images of institutions themselves' (p. 109). Thus 'The ceremonial life of society largely centers around the reinforcement of the acquired value system' (p. 73). The question arises, of course, as to the 'reality' of the social value system in contrast to its selective portrayal if not distortion of matters; that is, the question of the difference between education and propaganda, into each of which symbolism and image enters heavily. Boulding's position is indicated in his treatment of nationalism:

> One of the main purposes of national education is to distort the image of time and space in the interests of the nation.[10] The school atlases have one's own nation large and others small. The school history books have the history of one's own nation large and of others small. It is the history teachers above all who create the image of the Englishman, the German, the American, or the Japanese. This also is an important source of war.
>
> ...The task of the historian is always to make bricks without straw, to make what he believes are correct images of the past from an extremely imperfect sample of recorded data. It is no wonder that history is so phenomenally subject to abuse, that it becomes the agent of propaganda, and also that it is so continually being rewritten.
>
> (pp. 68, 69)

The problem, of course, is that Boulding does not herein subscribe to any epistemological position which would serve as a means enabling him to conclusively distinguish between truth and distortion. One almost reads Boulding as saying that the category of truth does not apply to socialization and legitimation—though he would also likely say that effective socialization and legitimation requires some modicum of truth.

The origin and dynamics of the image

The image, as an ongoing matter, emerges from a person's selectively perceived experience of events (p. 6). Aside from the sources of the origin of experience themselves and the context of experience itself, the key is selective perception inasmuch as perception selects what is experienced. Ensconced, therefore, within the forgoing is a dual relationship: the image is a function of experience *and* experience is a function of the image insofar as experience is controlled by selective perception. The image is part of—and changes within—an ongoing process in which experience and image and selective perception coevolve.

Boulding distinguishes between images of 'fact' and of 'value' (p. 11):

> there is a certain difference between the image which I have of physical objects in space and time and the valuations which I put on these objects or on the events which concern them .. although ... the process by which we obtain an image of values is not very different from the process whereby we obtain an image of fact, there is clearly a difference between them.
>
> (p. 11)

Boulding says further both that 'It is almost certain that most people possess not merely one scale of valuation but many scales for different purposes' and that 'the value scales of any individual or organization are perhaps the most important single element determining the effect of the messages it receives on its image of the world' (p. 12). So the image itself is a product of a process of mediation—of experience, or messages—by the value system.

Even at the level of simple or supposedly simple sense perception we are increasingly discovering that the message which comes through the senses is itself mediated through a value system. We do not perceive our sense data raw; they are mediated through a highly learned process of interpretation and acceptance (pp. 13–14).

Moreover, 'What this means is that for any individual organism or organization, there are no such things as "facts." There are only messages filtered through a changeable value system'[11] (p. 14). People do not respond to stimuli alone but 'to an image of the future filtered through an elaborate value system' (p. 26). Thus does Boulding repeat the main point: 'the basic pattern of image formation: messages filtered through a value system' (p. 39).

Boulding stresses learning, especially in higher organisms. But imagination also has a role (pp. 24, 26–7). Any image can be extended. A person is 'capable of organizing his own experience in ways that will extend the image further. This is the essence of science and the scientific method' (p. 26). New messages can led to

> symbolic changes in my image, changes which refer not to the immediate universe around me but to the whole content of my imagination. It is this

> symbolic image and the communications which establish it and which change it which constitutes the peculiar quality of human society.
>
> (p. 44)

Earlier in this paragraph Boulding remarks that 'It is this ability to proliferate and elaborate the image into a symbolic universe that is the peculiarity and the glory of man' (p. 44).

Moreover, human beings possess self-consciousness, which is to say that they can form images of their images (pp. 25, 45, 61). Consciousness 'is intimately connected with the symbolic process and ... is profoundly affected by disturbances of the symbolic process' (pp. 45–6).

Education performs the role of social control and is a principal source of the value image: 'Education in most societies is a matter of harnessing the biological drives in the interests of establishing [and reinforcing] the value system of a society.... The ceremonial life of society largely centers around the reinforcement of the acquired value system' (pp. 72–3).

Boulding gives pride of historical primacy to organized religion:[12] 'All cultures of the past have crystallized and nucleated around their religion because it is the religion which supplies the manifest image of their destiny toward which they feel themselves to be drawn' (p. 127). Moreover, 'There seems to be a great deal of evidence ... that nonreligious ideologies are incapable of providing the kind of manifest image of life, history, and purpose which are satisfying to the masses of mankind' (p. 128).

A mutual relation therefore exists between images and perceived experience. Changing experience alters the image.

> Every time a message reaches him his image is likely to be changed in some degree by it, and as his image is changed his behavior patterns will be changed likewise.
>
> We must distinguish carefully between the image and the messages that reach it. The messages consist of *information* in the sense that they are structured experiences. The *meaning of a message is the change which it produces in the image.*
>
> (p. 7; italics in original)

The arrival of a message can result in no change of the image, a change 'in some rather regular and well-defined way that might be described as simple addition' (p. 7), a revolutionary reorganization of the image, an increase or decrease in the uncertainty of the image[13] (pp. 10, 52) or, as already noted, an extension of the image.

Images are more or less stable and resistant to change (p. 13; apropos of homeostasis, see p. 21). Logical consistency and aesthetics are involved (p. 13). In addition, 'Images of the future must be held with a degree of uncertainty' (p. 11). Changes in the value system, as the mediating mechanism, also occur (p. 14). Stability is always relative (p. 49). There is learning; conscious, unconscious and subconscious (p. 53), though 'Rational behavior is that which is governed by the part of the image which is accessible to consciousness. What is usually called irrational behavior, in fact, follows the same principles' (p. 54).

Among the sources of change identified by Boulding are (1) learning processes, including ceremonial, formal and face-to-face and from 'poets, historians,[14] writers, and cartoonists' (pp. 54–5, 73, 114 and passim); (2) generational change (pp. 56, 104); (3) societal and organizational diversity and change, including change in power structure,[15] which helps account, for example, for changes in whose private image counts for more in the formation of the public image (pp. 57, 79); and (4) the activity and impact of charismatic persons.

This last is taken up by Boulding in a manner reminiscent of the ideas of Max Weber, Friedrich von Wieser and Joseph A. Schumpeter: 'To a very large extent change in the image comes about through the impact on society of unusually creative, charismatic, or prophetic individuals' (p. 75); 'Great men ennoble the roles which they take; little men debase them' (p. 104). Yet Boulding is aware that 'Sometimes it is not the single individual but rather the chance combination of individuals which produces the striking effect' (p. 76). This itself is one example of Boulding's use of the principle of unintended and unforeseen consequences. Actually nothing less than that can be expected from his model of general interaction. At other points, therefore, he writes that 'When … consequences are reflected in information fed back to us, we find very often that feedback does not confirm the original image' (p. 115); that 'the image itself is continually modified by the disappointment and surprises involved in the feedback' (p. 123; see also p. 105; that 'It is the fall of the ideal image that leads to the collapse of empires and the decay of cultures, yet how little we know about the forces which support or destroy these powerful beings' (p. 145);[16] and, *inter alia*, that 'The extraordinary rapidity with which images have changed in the last two hundred years is perhaps mainly a [unforeseen and unintended] result of increased communications among previously isolated subcultures' (p. 146). It may also enter his treatment of nonlogical factors (p. 168).

Image change is affected, too, by waves of optimism and pessimism (pp. 89, 125).

Image change is path dependent: 'everything builds on what has gone before' (p. 95): 'our very message input depends to a considerable extent upon our existing value structure … the way in which the total image grows determines or at least limits the directions of future growth' (p. 174).

The enormous complexity of the dynamics (social change) of image formation is indicated in the following sample quotations:

> [T]he general view of the social process … developed in these chapters … sees the whole movement of society as a process of image-formation under the stimulus of messages transmitted by networks of communication…
>
> (p. 98)

> If discussion is to be a successful process of decision-making it must exhibit a degree of convergence toward common images of the whole organization.
>
> (p. 101)

> [T]he political process ... is not ... the summation of fixed individual preferences but is the process of the mutual modification of images both relational and evaluational in the course of mutual communication, discussion, and discourse.
>
> (pp. 102–3)

> [T]he communication networks of organizations affect not only the distribution of images of the role but also affect the value structures of the individuals concerned.... The dynamics of political life can be interpreted largely in terms of the interaction of two processes. The first is the process whereby political images are created and distributed among the individuals of a society. The second is the process whereby specialized skills and knowledge are distributed among the people of the society. The political image is essentially an image of roles.
>
> (p. 103)

> [T]here is no mechanical process of overthrow of one class by the one below it. Instead, there is a much more complex process whereby the dynamics of the political image and of the distribution of skill and knowledge interact.
>
> (p. 107)

And, apropos of the Greek conception of rhetoric:

> Changes in the image as a result of symbolic intercourse would depend, of course, on the skill of the communicators as well as on the initial situation [path dependence]. The whole art of persuasion is the art of perceiving the weak spots in the images of others and of prying them apart with well-constructed symbolic messages.
>
> (p. 134; this statement in particular is reminiscent of Pareto's idea of the selective invocation of derivations (rationalizations) in the mobilization of political psychology; see Samuels 1974)

Finally, Boulding identifies three stages of the image: belief, belief in believing, and not believing:

> In the first stage, we find that people believe in it. This is the unselfconscious stage. People think of themselves, for instance, as Americans, or as British, or as Germans, without ever questioning the notion. In the second stage, people believe in believing in it. They see the world as divided into nations. They see, however, that they might just as well have

> been something else from what they are. Once the image has reached this stage it is a short step to not believing in it at all. The same history is repeated in many religions.
>
> (pp. 61–2)

The linguistic character of the image

Images are linguistic phenomena for mankind. Language is the material of images. Having an image, reducing it to words, talking about it—all this involves the use of language. We really do have a 'universe of discourse', even if there are 'many such universes of discourse' (p. 15).

> The human organism is capable not only of having an image of the world, but of talking about it. This is the extraordinary gift of language.... It is discourse or conversation which makes the human image public in a way that the image of no lower animal can possible be.
>
> (p. 15)

> It is the capacity for organizing information into large and complex images which is the chief glory of our species ... our capacity for language and for record.
>
> (p. 25)

> It is this capacity for language which is the most essential difference between man and all other organisms.
>
> (p. 43)

> The study of man is the study of talk. Human society is an edifice spun out of the tenuous webs of conversation.
>
> (p. 45)

Boulding uses the terminology of linguistics when he writes that messages can be divided into signs and symbols but models them in his own way. 'A sign is a message which alters the image of the immediate universe around the organism.' But a symbol need not have any effect on that image:

> It does produce an effect, however, of what might be called the image of the image, on the image of the future, on the image of the past, on the image of the potential or even the image of the impossible.

Thus,

> When I hear someone speaking to me the noise of his words is a sign. It changes or confirms my image of his presence in the room with me.... If, however, he is talking in a language I understand there are symbolic changes

> in my image, changes which refer not to the immediate universe around me but to the whole content of my imagination.
>
> (p. 44)

Hence the importance of written records, in the 'more intellectual subcultures in which images tend to be verbalized and recorded in the form of transcripts' (p. 143). As already indicated, because of its greater definitional technical sophistication and subtlety, 'As science becomes more and more sophisticated, it becomes further divorced from the popular images and less capable of influencing them' (p. 49).

The image is very much a linguistic phenomenon. Which is to say that our definitions of the world are driven, to no small degree, by the language we comprehend—albeit, as also already indicated, at various different levels of discourse (pp. 167–71).

But the creation of specialized languages can create barriers to communication and to the delivery and reception of messages. Each intellectual discipline, divided into university departments, has 'not only an image of its own but also a language of its own' (p. 137), such that

> The universe of discourse is crumbling into a multiverse, and in one's more depressed moments one looks forward to a time when the progress of science will grind to a standstill in a morass of mutual incomprehensibility. Out of our intellectual pride, we may be building a new Tower of Babel.
>
> (p. 139)

Relation of the image to informational systems and other structures

Messages or informational systems are simultaneously the genesis, the result and the context of the image. Moreover, the image itself is a message-control device, part of the complex origins and dynamics of change of the image itself:

> between the incoming and outgoing messages lies the great intervening variable of the image. The outgoing messages are the result of the image, not the result of the incoming messages. The incoming messages only modify the outgoing messages as they succeed in modifying the image.
>
> (p. 28)

The capacity to process information is critical (p. 40), as is the position governing perception of the message (pp. 132–3 and passim).

The image is a function of information flow and mediation by the image itself. But it is also a function of cultural and subcultural structures. For example, science is a particular subculture, filtering messages through its value system, such that Boulding writes, rather bluntly, that

> Science ... represents the most sophisticated attempt to deal with the relational image. Even here, however, relational images arise through strong filtering of messages through the value structure of the scientific subculture. There are many areas of experience which are not respectable for scientists to study and which they investigate with grave risks to their reputations.
>
> (p. 50)

Thus Boulding finds that

> it is common to find that what looks like a change in the value image is actually a change in the position of the individual in the field of the image in general ... much more the result of a difference in the position of the individual in the field rather than a difference in the value ordering itself.
>
> (p. 51; the discussion interestingly points to an alternative interpretation of demand theory from that in which demand changes only as a result of relative prices)

Along a difference line, discussing individual roles in organizations and their change on the basis of individual images, Boulding notes that 'The individual ... never merely passively fits a role. He reorganizes the role itself through the operation of his own peculiar images' (p. 60). Apropos of the epigram about the ubiquity of inventories of images and the consequent need in organizations to choose among them (p. 63), it becomes clear that the operative image is in part a function of the structure of power which determines both what/whose images are relevant and which will be selected (as in the production possibility curve in which power helps govern which values will be on the axes—that is, on the menu of choice—as well as both preferences and their weighting).

Boulding defines subculture as 'a group of people sharing a public image' (p. 133). Changing structures lead to changes in images and to image systems, and vice versa.

Science is comprehended as a subculture requiring freedom and uncoerciveness (p. 80), and he warns of the danger that the social and behavioral sciences 'can all too easily play into the hands of the manipulators' (p. 80), so that their contribution to the study and formation of images can be coopted by social and economic power players for their own ends. (On the danger from within economics, see below.)

Economics and the image

The forgoing implies that economics as an intellectual discipline is very much a matter of images and especially the images given effect and/or raised by its terminology. It presumably can also be said of economics that it is both the cause and the consequence of greater complexity and that its complex and even contradictory images reflect that situation (pp. 31, 40–1).

Boulding suggests that the specific terminology of economics is a product of the image (and vice versa, of course). This surely is implicit in his statement that 'the physical capital of a society must be regarded as the result of the structuring of the material substance by an image' (p. 58)—an implication reinforced when one considers the different images of capital embodied in different theories of capital, commencing at least since the late nineteenth century, in the great capital controversies.

Boulding also uses a metaphor from economics when he writes of 'the stock of images in a society' (pp. 54ff.) as if it were a form of cultural capital.

At any rate, Boulding laments that 'economists have badly [and strangely, p. 149] neglected the impact of information and knowledge structures on economic behavior and processes' (p. 82). It is probably the case that the overall neglect is less now than in 1956 but little progress relative to opportunity has been accomplished along Boulding's lines. His conclusion that 'There is a large field of investigation open … in the general area of the nature of economic perception, information, images, and transformation of the image' (p. 86) remains true today.

More specifically, Boulding argues that the information needs of economic actors under imperfect competition are different and far greater than in competitive markets (p. 85). The problem of oligopoly requires resort to 'the idea of an image and … the modification of the image by messages' (p. 92). The stability or stickiness of prices (which he refers to as 'well-known') 'may have much more to do with the uncertain nature of the image involved than with any ideal of maximizing behavior' (p. 86). The same is true of price warfare (p. 112). Uncertainty is treated throughout the book.

Boulding acknowledges economically self-justifying and self-defeating images (pp. 124–5). He believes that 'The Malthusian process can be modified substantially by an expansion of the image of the procreative process' (p. 121).

He points to threshold and related effects: 'These transformations of the economic image and the subsequent revolutions in behavior seem to come very suddenly. They often represent, however, the culmination of long processes' (p. 87).

He points to the role of oversimplifying symbolic images in economic affairs, especially with regard to values (p. 110). The stock market is discussed as an institution to which symbolic meaning is frequently attached (p. 89).

His strongest assertions have to do with economic dynamics. He argues that 'The process of reorganization of economic images through messages is the key to the understanding of economic dynamics' (p. 90). Not surprisingly, 'The problem of the transformation of images' is held to be 'of great importance in the theory of economic development' (p. 93). Technical change is a matter of changes of the image and 'is always propagated by the methods by which images are propagated' (p. 121);

> The history of the technological revolution [in the Industrial Revolution] must be written largely in terms of the dynamics of the image—the image of change as a good and desirable thing introduced by the various religious

> reformations, and the image of an orderly universe whose secret relations might be explored by experiment and observation.[17]
>
> (p. 122)

But, again, economics has neglected the image:

> it is possible to develop quite elaborate abstract models without the explicit concepts of the image … [But] if this abstraction is to go beyond the level of very first approximation, we must introduce the image-forming process in society. If we are to have a theory of economic behavior or a theory of economic dynamics an explicit recognition of the importance of the image is necessary.
>
> (p. 97)

Two other contexts in which economics is discussed are worth noting. In one he applies to economics insights into 'the shady side of "professional ethics"'. He writes that: 'Every profession and craft which has a self-conscious image of itself in the minds of its members is to some extent a conspiracy against the public' (pp. 140–1, the language echoing similar words of Adam Smith regarding businessmen). This caution notwithstanding, Boulding discusses Eiconics—his name for the systematic and self-conscious study of the image—in economizing terms:

> Any economizing of learning … is highly desirable. Eiconics may be more of a contribution to this restructuring of the universe of knowledge than it is a new science in the sense in which the old sciences are sciences. If a single theoretical principle can be shown to apply over a wide area of the empirical world, this is economy in the learning process.
>
> (p. 163)

Conclusion

Several principal findings by Boulding stand out and are significant to the conduct of economic inquiry. One is that most if not all of our putative knowledge is a function of images rather than any direct representation of 'economic reality', whatever that term may be taken to mean. The image may be taken to be knowledge but it cannot, on epistemological terms, be treated conclusively as truth. What we take as 'facts' are due more to the image system in which they appear than, in any necessary way, to the object of inquiry (which may itself be illusory; images can be had of what does not exist as well as of selective aspects of things) or to 'truth' (or Truth). Another is that at the heart of social dynamics is the process wherein both perception is influenced by image and image is influenced by perception. The general equilibrium, or general interdependence, character of the image and its context is critical to what Boulding has to say. Whether one prefers to approach the matter from such dichotomies as truth and falsity, rational and irrational, and so on, images are both independent and dependent variables in the complex cumulative-causation processes of cultural change. Boulding's work, in this respect, is a call to study the factors and forces governing the transformation of images.

Commons's model and Boulding's model are much more supplementary than contradictory. Indeed, inasmuch as Commons emphasizes the complex processes through which conceptions of public purpose are worked out, as part of the crux of legal–economic history and the legal foundations of capitalism, it is not too much to say that at the core of varying specifications of public purpose are varying images of what the economy is all about, including images of value (desirability, reasonableness) and possibility. Conversely, one can interpret Boulding's model of the image as particularly significant in comprehending the legal–economic nexus and its operation but also as, to some extent, driven by the operation of the legal–economic nexus.

Boulding's theory of the image is, however, directly in conflict with the Chicago idea that behavioral change responds only (is it too strong to say that?) from changes in relative prices operating in the context of given preferences.

Recognition of the image operative in any particular situation enables the recognizer to transcend or to escape from hitherto/otherwise uncontemplated beliefs and understandings. In such a manner does the idea, that is, the image, of the image enable its own transcendence. Alas, the hitherto unrecognized image may now be replaced by another image, to which the same process of discovery may again have to apply. Yet this may well be the only way in which the normative and other premises and presumptions that drive policy conclusions can be identified, albeit in a never-ending stream.

In his review of *The Image*, John Maurice Clark raised two questions. The first is, 'who would check the eiconist's own images of the images he is studying?' The second has to do with the threat which Boulding's analysis represented to positivism (in a manner and to an effect similar to that posed by those who stressed the importance of ideology, values and, in Joseph Schumpeter's sense, vision). Clark's is the conventional response. After responding to the first question by saying that technical specialists can do the checking, he writes:

> If so, the net effect should be useful, making our images more objective by promoting an understanding and discounting of subjective elements. Similarly, though Boulding may seem to be stressing as unavoidable the commingling of images of 'fact' (or how things work) with images of value (of how we like the way they work), I should like to think that in a more deliberate study he would handle this question so as to reduce wishful thinking rather than encourage it.
>
> (Clark 1957, p. 263)

I suspect that Boulding would reverse the charge of wishful thinking, holding that it applies to those who think that technical and other work can eliminate the social constructivism that is ensconced in images, and that such work at best would involve the replacement of one image with another. For Boulding, more is involved than the mixing of the normative with the positive:[18] our very cognition is rendered inescapably problematic if not relative. The anonymous reviewer in the *Times Literary Supplement* (1957, p. 155) thus gives Boulding's answer with regard to the question of skepticism: 'His answer is that we can study images without committing ourselves to any tests of ultimate validity.' This apparently would not be good enough for Clark. That it is not good enough for most people is suggested by the fate among economists which has obviously befallen Vilfredo Pareto's argument, that belief systems (akin to Boulding's images) are the product of nonrational processes. The rationality assumption has been effectively protected.

Interestingly, Charles Morris, the sociologist, in his review of the book, noted, first, that Boulding had in effect combined others' theories of the executive, information and feedback mechanisms; and, second, that the concept of the image becomes a principle of organization. He then suggests that the concept could become 'an instance of his [Boulding's] own thesis' (Morris 1957, p. 601) if he would use it as a device to further integrate into his analysis the work of still other writers.

Eiconics has become neither a household name nor the designation of a university program or department. But hermeneutics, deconstruction, social linguistics and other approaches to the analysis of human discourse and belief systems have become central to what is often called post-modernism and to the study of economics as a rhetorical or discursive system of messages and conversation.

The controversial reception given to these approaches suggests that Boulding may have correctly anticipated a central problem inhibiting the reception of Eiconics. The recognition of Eiconics in economics and the other social sciences would be tantamount to the recognition that human beliefs are largely insubstantial images.[19] It would therefore be seen as a threat to political legitimation of the status quo and the psychic balm which offers security and certitude against ambiguity and open-endednesss, each of which is important for both individuals and societies.[20] It would also threaten both discursive legitimation and criticism of every status quo (threatening criticism insofar as it is ostensibly based on substantive, nonimaged grounds). It would threaten psychic balm because of the philosophical skepticism to which, as Boulding recognized, it would tend to lead:

> The question must be faced … whether the theory of the image does not move us in the direction of a philosophical skepticism more devastating even than that of Hume.… the communication and information theorist dissolves the hard fact into messages filtered through a value system. Like Hume, we pale before the abyss of skepticism toward which our logic leads us relentlessly but from which we draw back horrified, incredulous at incredulity.… From the abyss of reason we turn again to clutch at the slender rope of faith. Faiths are the genes of society. Their operation is as potent and as mysterious as that of the gene in biology.
>
> (pp. 171–2)

Be that as it may, it would seem that the philosophical positions manifest by Boulding's *The Image* echo lines of reasoning which have erratic histories but have been building at least since Kant and especially since Wittgenstein. Moreover, the problem of skepticism versus legitimation is not unique to Eiconics; it has arisen throughout the history of the social sciences.

The Image is quintessential Kenneth Boulding. Some of it is superficial and overreaching. Some of it is straightforward declaration of interpretation. Some of it approaches breathless affirmation. But much of it is very suggestive and stimulating. Much of it deals, in its own way, with very deep questions—questions which the social sciences in general and economics in particular tend to ignore and even obfuscate. And much if not all of this has to do with the symbolic structure of society and the language in which it is embedded—what Boulding called *the image*. As Robert Solo has written, *The Image* is Boulding's 'finest and most important book'. In it, Boulding:

> develops the implications and consequences of his theory of the image for biological behavior, the theory of organization, the sociology of knowledge, the operations of an economy, the political process, epistemology, and ethics. It is, all in all, a brilliant *tour de force*.
>
> (Solo 1984, pp. 466–7)

Notes

1 This article was previously published in W. Samuels, S.G. Medema and A.A. Schmid (eds.), *The Economy as a Process of Valuation*, Cheltenham: Edward Elgar, 1997, pp. 299–327.

2 Machlup's ideas are considered in Langlois (1985), Kirzner (1985) and Samuels (1985). For the comparable views of John Kenneth Galbraith, see Samuels (1984).

3 The contemporaneous development of and common emphasis on the image in Boulding's and most of the others' work is stressed by Solo (1994, p. 30).

4 With regard to whether simple organisms 'know', follow instinct, or exercise motor responses, see pp. 32ff.

5 Apropos of the American presidency, Boulding writes that 'An image of this role is present in the minds of millions of Americans in greater or less degree of clarity. It is not only present, it is accepted, that is, it is placed high on the value scale' (p. 104). In later years Boulding might have written that the image of the 'imperial presidency' was bound up with that of an imperial/superpower United States.

6 Virgil C. Aldrich, in his review of *The Image* in the *Journal of Philosophy*, points out a wide range of philosophical treatments clearly paralleling Boulding's (Aldrich 1957). He also points to the ambivalence in Boulding's treatment of positivism or science. Hortense Powdermaker, in her review published in *American Anthropologist*, also points to certain work done by anthropologists and political scientists, as well as problems with Boulding's view of science (Powdermaker 1957). Boulding's intention for the concept of the image to be integrative is reflected in the wide range of journals in which the book was reviewed.

7 Boulding continues:

> The difficulty with the coherence theory of truth, on the other hand, is that the coherence or consistency of the image is simply not what we mean by its truth.... We have no real guarantee that the 'outside' to which the image is supposed to

> correspond, is itself consistent and coherent; indeed, there are philosophers, like the existentialists, who argue that it is not, that the real world outside us is in fact a mass of inconsistencies and absurdities and is in a very real sense nonsense. The consistency and coherence which we pretend to detect in it, they argue, is merely a fashion of our own minds.
>
> (pp. 165–6)

to which Boulding might well have added 'and reified by words'.

8 This statement is reminiscent of Frank Knight's dictum that the ultimate product of the economy is people.

9 '[T]he symbolic messages which are issued from individuals in the group reflect in some degree the image which they possess, and these messages when received by other individuals in the group confirm the image which is held by the recipient' (p. 133).

10 Boulding arguably should have written 'in the interests of certain selected images of the nation'.

11 The text continues:

> This statement may sound rather startling. It is inherent, however, in the view which I have been propounding. This does not mean, however, that the image of the world possessed by an individual is a purely private matter or that all knowledge is simply subjective knowledge, in the sense in which I have used the word.... It follows ... that if a group of people are to share the same image of the world, or to put it more exactly, if the various images of the world which they have are to be roughly identical, and if this group of people are exposed to much the same set of messages in building up images of the world, the value systems of all individuals must be approximately the same.
>
> (pp. 14–15)

12 It is not inapposite to note that the concept of the Invisible Hand, so fundamental to the history of economic thought and the status with which certain economic ideas are held, was borrowed from religion—though the hand is not always, is indeed only rarely, identified as that of a deity.

13 Boulding also contrasts two opposing tendencies, one leading to greater chaos, the other to greater organization (p. 19). As already noted, he writes that 'the concept of the image becomes an increasingly important part of any theoretical model, and the image itself becomes increasingly complex' (p. 31). He notes that the step from botanical to zoological levels, from chemical to electrical levels,

> represents an enormous increase in the possibility of receiving, transmitting, storing, and organizing information. It represents, therefore, a tremendous potential increase in the size and complexity of the image, an increase which to date reaches its highest development in man.
>
> (p. 40)

Heterogenity of the putative object of inquiry and of putative information, that is, of messages, coupled with selective perception abetted by multiplicity of perspectives or standpoints, leads inevitably to diversity of images and thereby to a decrease in certitude and an increase in uncertainty.

14 'There is some truth in the claim that nations are the creation of their historians—it is the image of the past that gives rise both to the image of the present and of the future' (p. 114).

15 There is not much explicit discussion of power in *The Image* but there is more here than in Boulding's other early books. One exception is his statement that: 'There is a very real dilemma of power in society in that the images which are useful in gaining power are seldom useful in exercising it wisely or in keeping it' (p. 109). I have

particular reference to the absence of direct confrontation by Boulding with the process of working out answers to such questions as to what constitutes 'orderly', 'optimal', 'improved' and 'pathological'—concepts, discussed above in regard to the problem of self-referentiality, with respect to which his linguistic constructions sometimes lead him to treat those concepts as independently given—and to the question of the role of power structure in sorting out whose images will count. Apropos of the latter, Boulding does write that:

> We are also interested not only in how public decisions are made, but in who makes them. We are interested in what determines the structure of powerful roles in society and we are also interested in the processes by which these roles are filled.
>
> (pp. 98–9)

16 One example: it is generally agreed that the reluctance of Soviet leaders to use force to suppress the movements for Baltic independence in 1991 derived in part from the shocks to their image consequent to widespread learning about the origins of Soviet occupation and absorption of the Baltic states.

17 Boulding is critical of Marx for his 'monstrous' theory of value (p. 145) but not of his view that 'the history of ideas was a sort of caboose attached to the great steam engine of technological development and class struggle' (p. 15) as part of one strand of the sociology of knowledge.

18 By comparison, in a review published in *Christian Century*, Niels C. Nielsen, Jr., asserts that 'Boulding's analysis skirts the problem of the normative and descriptive in the social sciences' (Nielsen 1957, p. 562). Noting that Boulding shows 'how much persons are determined by what they think they are—in short, measured by their own image' and 'stresses personal rather than power factors in his analysis of government' (p. 561), as well as showing 'that thought is radically perspectival in every area' (p. 562), Nielsen laments that: 'He really gives us no answer to the question of the validity of the images' (p. 561).

19 Thurman Arnold was also one who recognized that economics, law and other disciplines largely deal with symbols (for present purposes, the equivalent to Boulding's images) which, while socially functional, lack (ontological and other) substance. Vilfredo Pareto was another. See Samuels (1974, 1979).

20 This seems to be part of what Boulding meant when he referred to the 'relational quicksands of common sense' (p. 71).

References

Aldrich, Virgil C. (1957), Book Review, *Journal of Philosophy*, vol. 54 (May), pp. 365–7.

Anonymous (1957), Book Review, *Times Literary Supplement*, 15 March, p. 155.

Boulding, Kenneth E. (1956), *The Image*, Ann Arbor, MI: University of Michigan Press.

Clark, John Maurice (1957), Book Review, *Journal of Political Economy*, vol. 65 (July), p. 263.

Commons, John R. (1924), *Legal Foundations of Capitalism*, New York: Macmillan.

Fraser, Lindley M. (1947), *Economic Thought and Language*, London: Black.

Kirzner, Israel M. (1985), Comment on R.N. Langlois 'From the Knowledge of Economics to the Economics of Knowledge: Fritz Machlup on Methodology and on the "Knowledge Society"', *Research in the History of Economic Thought and Methodology*, vol. 3, pp. 237–41.

Langlois, Richard N. (1985), 'From the Knowledge of Economics to the Economics of Knowledge: Fritz Machlup on Methodology and on the "Knowledge Society"', *Research in the History of Economic Thought and Methodology*, vol. 3, pp. 225–35.

Machlup, Fritz (1963), *Essays in Economic Semantics*, Englewood Cliffs, NJ: Prentice-Hall.

Machlup, Fritz (1991), *Economic Semantics*, New Brunswick, NJ: Transaction.

McCloskey, Donald N. (1983), 'The Rhetoric of Economics', *Journal of Economic Literature*, vol. 21 (June), pp. 481–517.

Morris, Charles (1957), Book Review, *American Sociological Review*, vol. 22 (Fall), pp. 600–1.

Nielsen, Niels G., Jr. (1957), Book Review, *Christian Century*, vol. 74 (May), pp. 561–2.

Powdermaker, Hortense (1957), Book Review, *American Anthropologist*, vol. 59 (August), pp. 718–19.

Samuels, Warren J. (1974), *Pareto on Policy*, New York: Elsevier.

Samuels, Warren J. (1979), 'Legal Realism and the Burden of Symbolism: The Correspondence of Thurman Arnold', *Law and Society Review*, vol. 13, pp. 997–1011.

Samuels, Warren J. (1984), 'Galbraith on Economics as a System of Professional Belief', *Journal of Post Keynesian Economics*, vol. 7, pp. 61–76.

Samuels, Warren J. (1985), 'Machlup on Knowledge: Science, Subjectivism and the Social Nature of Knowledge', *Research in the History of Economic Thought and Methodology*, vol. 3, pp. 243–55.

Solo, Robert A. (1984), 'Solo on Boulding', in Henry W. Spiegel and Warren J. Samuels (eds.), *Contemporary Economists in Perspectives*, Vol. 2, Greenwich, CT: JAI Press.

Solo, Robert A. (1994), 'Kenneth Ewart Boulding', in Geoffrey M. Hodgson, Warren J. Samuels and Marc R. Tool (eds.), *The Elgar Companion to Institutional and Evolutionary Economics*, Vol. 1, Brookfield, VT: Edward Elgar.

Ward, Benjamin (1972), *What's Wrong with Economics?*, New York: Basic Books.

4b Comment: Kenneth Boulding as a moral scientist

John B. Davis[1]

Kenneth Boulding's AEA presidential address argued that economics is a moral science. His view derived from his general systems theory thinking, his three systems view of human society, and his early contributions to evolutionary economics. Boulding's argument that economics could not be value-free should be distinguished from other well-known views of economics as a moral science, such as Gunnar Myrdal's. This paper discusses the development and nature of Boulding's thinking about economics as a moral science in the larger context of his thinking.

> The concept of a value-free science is absurd.
>
> (Boulding, 1969, p. 4)

Locating Boulding's critique of value-free economics

Kenneth Boulding presented his famous "Economics as a Moral Science" paper (Boulding, 1969) that rejected the idea that economics is value-free as his Presidential Address to the American Economic Association in December 1968 at the height of the war in Vietnam. Understanding something about Boulding's personal history and circumstances will help us to understand what lay behind his thinking. The previous year, when he had moved to the University of Colorado, some members of the University Board of Regents had opposed his appointment because Boulding had been involved in arranging a teach-in against the war when he was at the University of Michigan. But Boulding said of this: "They thought I was a dangerous radical. Actually, I am a dangerous conservative" (Mott, 2000, p. F436).[2] Indeed, the next year Boulding accepted the post of faculty advisor to the campus Republican club at Colorado and changed his voter registration to Republican—which he retained until the early 1980s when Ronald Reagan began a new arms build-up, and he then changed his registration to Democratic. So Boulding was not left-wing in his politics nor involved in the radical economics of the time. In fact he was always hostile to Marx's theory of capitalism and its emphasis on class conflict. What he did feel strongly about was the cause of peace, having become a Quaker early in life, and having been active throughout his career in a variety of ways in the cause of peace. Moreover, he himself saw peace and conflict resolution research as his largest area of work (Boulding, 1989) and regarded his involvement in the founding of the *Journal of Conflict Resolution* and the International Peace Research Association as important lifetime achievements.

This tells us, then, one thing about the thinking behind Boulding's Address and famous paper and critique of economics, namely, that it did not spring from the radical, Marxist, or neo-Marxist view of the time that standard economics was essentially as an expression of capitalist ideology. Indeed, Boulding was well known in the profession for having written a fairly conventional economics text, *Economic Analysis* (1941), and he never hesitated to say that economics was a legitimate science. His complaint, rather, was that it had mistakenly come to be seen as a value-free science when it should rather have been seen as a moral science in the tradition of Adam Smith and Alfred Marshall. Thus the conventional view in the economics profession when he gave his 1968 Address, that economics had advanced by purging values from the subject, was for him a retrograde development and a decline rather than an improvement in the scientific character of economics. Economics was consequently not only a science in his estimation, but a science which could not function properly when investigated without attention to the values that he believed inevitably operated within it. What did he mean by this? A second important clue lies in the fact that Boulding did not believe that economics was exceptional in this regard. His view, then, was also not the well-known critique of the idea of a value-free economics others had recently advanced (e.g., Myrdal, 1953, 1958). Myrdal's view was that economics and the social sciences in general were unavoidably value-laden, because in contrast with the natural sciences they involved human actors. Rather he believed that "no science of any kind can be divorced from ethical considerations" (Boulding, 1969, p. 2). That is, he held that all science is inescapably value-laden.

Yet even this view of science does not get us entirely to what was behind Boulding's thinking, since he also denied that value-ladenness was even something especially characteristic of the scientific process. Rather his larger view was that science was only one dimension of human culture, and that human culture in general was always guided and sustained by values.

> Science is a human learning process which arises in certain subcultures in human society and not in others, and a subculture as we have seen is a group of people defined by acceptance of certain common values, that is, an ethic which permits extensive communication between them.
>
> (Ibid.)

The common value system of science is indeed distinctive in various ways from the common value systems of other human subcultures. In the sciences, high value is "placed on veracity, on curiosity, on measurement, on quantification, on careful observation and experiment, and on objectivity" without which "the epistemological process of science would not have arisen" (Ibid.), and the common values of other subcultures, such as the military, were clearly quite different. But for Boulding the main point is that all human activities are types of culture, and thus necessarily value-laden. Culture, he believed, is distinctive of human life, takes on many forms, and is always structured by values appropriate to our activities in the many different domains of life. Thus to understand Boulding's critique of economics as a moral science and as a value-laden activity we need to understand something about his view of culture. Here, however, we find ourselves needing to look more deeply into the foundations of Boulding's thinking in connection with his broad systems theory approach or general systems theory way of looking at the world, which represented an intellectual commitment for him equal to his commitment to peace.

General systems theory and the impossibility of personal tastes

From early in his career at the University of Michigan, Boulding was first active in a transdisciplinary general systems theory movement that aimed to explain the world in a holistic, non-mechanistic manner in terms of entire systems of relationships. Many people contributed to postwar general systems theory, which is often identified with one of its pre-eminent proponents, Ludwig von Bertalanffy (cf. 1968, 1974; László, 1972). However, Boulding's involvement in the movement should not be underestimated, since Bertalanffy, Anatol Rapoport, Ralph Gerard, and Boulding together established the Society for General Systems Research in 1954 (renamed the International Society for Systems Science in 1988), and Boulding remained committed to a systems approach throughout his career. The basic conception general systems theory involves is that phenomena in all domains of life are interconnected through sets of relationships that exhibit common patterns and properties that can be observed across the different sciences. The major concern its proponents had was that the different sciences had become too narrowly focused on their separate concerns and subjects, and that greater attention to shared constructs, principles, and properties, even if abstractly represented, would make desirable communication between scientists more possible. This did not imply that all sciences should be reduced to general systems accounts; rather the view was that the different sciences retained their specific areas of investigation while they simultaneously exhibited similar systemic features. Thus general systems theorists argued for framing the specific areas of investigation in different sciences, where possible, by consideration of shared cross-science general structures in the interest of promoting development across and within the different sciences. In this sense, general systems theory was a version of the classic unity of science view that science advances through increasing unification (cf. Oppenheim and Putnam, 1958).

Boulding made such an argument in his own early contribution to the approach, "General Systems Theory: The Skeleton of Science," where he argued, for example, that:

> a specialist who works with the growth concept—whether the crystallographer, the virologist, the cytologist, the psychologist, the sociologist or the economist—will be more sensitive to the contributions of other fields if he is aware of the many similarities of the growth process in widely different empirical fields.
>
> (1956, p. 198)

It is interesting, then, that we can see this same point in his American Economics Association Presidential Address in regard to the many subcultures that make up human society. Subcultures are always defined in terms of the sets of common values that people accept and rely on for communication within them. Though two sciences, say economics and immunology, might appear to be very different from one another, they can nonetheless be understood to be similar systems in that both rely on sets of shared values that structure communication of scientists in each field. Thus Boulding's point that economics is value-laden was not just that this is true of economics as it is true of other sciences; his general systems view of the world was that value-ladenness was one of the fundamental cross-science general structures that we ought to investigate to promote development within the different sciences.

We can see more of what was involved in this view if we look more closely at Boulding's early general systems thinking. Thus when it came to the question of how one should go about explaining general systems, Boulding believed that one approach proceeded by arranging particular empirical fields in a hierarchy of increasing complexity, which corresponded to the increasing complexity of the "individuals" studied in different types of scientific research.[3] His own method of classification had nine hierarchical levels or categories of increasing complexity: frameworks, clockworks, thermostats, cells, plants, animals, human beings, social organizations, and transcendental systems. I do not attempt to review the rationales he employed for this particular ordering and classification, but rather try to draw out the thread he employs to explain increasing system complexity beginning with thermostats, since he repeatedly across his career tended to ground his thinking in the idea of systems that maintained some sort of balance.[4] Thermostats, then, are types of systems that possess self-control mechanisms or function as self-organizing cybernetic systems; that is, they tend to work to maintain equilibrium states. After thermostats in Boulding's ordering are living versions of such systems, namely, cells which are systems open to their environment that also function as self-maintaining structures. In this respect they are characteristic of life in its most basic form. As we then move on from plants to animals in Boulding's hierarchy we move from systems with advanced self-organizing divisions of labor to systems that also use this property to achieve mobility and self-awareness. Human beings among animals in addition possess self-consciousness, which goes beyond simple self-awareness. Social organizations then use these principles to self-organize and structure collections of people by roles with channels of communication. Finally, transcendental systems, despite being concerned with "unknowables" and absolutes, also exhibit systematic self-reproducing structures and relationships.

What we see here, then, is not only a hierarchical organization of systems of increasing complexity, but a view of all systems as homeostatic in nature. That is, Boulding's general systems view was grounded in the idea that a system has an integrity and cohesiveness that derives from its self-regulating and self-organizing properties. This goes beyond the simpler holism idea that systems can be associated with observable sets of interconnected relationships in that it ascribes an active principle to such systems that ensures their continued functioning as systems per se. Of course by the standards of much science of his time, and especially economics, where more mechanical views of the world were central, this sort of ascription of an inherent active principle would have seemed implausible and unjustified.[5] But Boulding and the general systems movement were in fact part of a much larger development in postwar ideas that would come to have tremendous impact on human society in subsequent decades, namely, the idea of cybernetic systems, such as emerged in the technology of computers, which, as originally conceived by such individuals as Alan Turing, Norbert Wiener, William Ross Ashby, Warren McCulloch, Margaret Mead, and John von Neumann, relied on and shared the same view of holistic systems as self-regulating and self-organizing (see Heims, 1993). Boulding and others in the general systems theory movement were well aware of this development and saw themselves as contributing to a general philosophy to explain it. So when he gave his famous Presidential Address, he may well have believed himself a fore-runner bringing general systems theory into economics.

From this vantage point, then, let us further appraise Boulding's critique of economics as a value-free subject, recalling his special emphasis on culture. A main focus of this critique is the economist's standard view of taste—a view Boulding wonderfully castigated as "the Immaculate Conception of the Indifference Curve" (1969, p. 2). Thus, what is his view of this idea of a preference or a taste?

> Let me first explain, then, what I mean by moral and moral science. A moral or ethical proposition is a statement about a rank order of preference among alternatives, which is intended to apply to more than one person. A preference which applies to one person only is a taste. Statements of this kind are often called "value judgments." If someone says, "I prefer A to B," this is a personal value judgment, or a taste. If he says, "A is better than B," there is an implication that he expects other people to prefer A to B also, as well as himself. A moral proposition then is a "common value."
>
> (Ibid., p. 1)

Thus the standard view of a preference or a taste is as a purely personal value judgment, whereas a moral proposition which is shared by people relies on a "common value." But Boulding rejects this simple opposition and argues that the idea of a truly personal taste makes no sense, since:

> personal tastes are learned, in the matrix of a culture or a subculture in which we grow up, by very much the same kind of process by which we learn our common values. Purely personal tastes, indeed, can only survive in a culture which tolerates them, that is, which has a common value that private tastes of certain kinds should be allowed.
>
> (Ibid.)

The illusion that tastes are purely private is thus what Boulding calls the "Immaculate Conception of the Indifference Curve." In effect, for him, all tastes were in some degree endogenous to a system of common values.

We can now see, then, in light of Boulding's general systems thinking, just why he regarded the economist's idea of purely personal (or exogenous) tastes as nonsensical. Values that arise in cultures or subcultures always depend upon common values—even where they allow space for autonomy of "private" tastes—because they function as principles that enable those cultures or subcultures to self-organize and self-regulate themselves. The notion that tastes might play a role independent of the homeostatic self-maintenance of a culture was accordingly inconsistent with his understanding of how a culture functioned as a system. Cultures were not collections of elements mechanically linked to one another, but holistic structures that were self-sustaining in virtue of active integrating principles. Values and value judgments play this active role in integrating human systems. Consequently personal tastes always depend on common values. They cannot be understood as disconnected collections of phenomena; nor can an economics meant to explain the world scientifically base itself on this particular view of taste. Indeed, a scientific economics is necessarily a systems-based economics.

These are thus the foundations of Boulding's critique of economics as a value-free science. Yet his views about general systems continued to develop in the years before his Presidential Address in ways that tell us more about his thinking about economics as a moral science. Accordingly I turn to his later general systems view that all societies are organized through a combination of three specific types of systems, the threat (or fear), exchange, and integrative (or love) systems, and then use this further thinking to re-appraise his critique of economics.

The three systems of social organization

Boulding's thinking is often linked to the idea of a grants economy, where a grant is a unilateral transfer. The origin of the idea, however, was Boulding's prior intuition that social organizations could be understood to be integrative systems in which conflict between people could function in a constructive way (Mott, 1992). A grant, then, is a key measure of an integrative system in virtue of its character as something quantifiable. But Boulding developed reservations about this conception when he realized that grants could be given for different reasons. As he understood it, they could be given out of love or fear, and so given the contrary nature of love and fear, it was not entirely clear just what an integrative system was. Were both motives integrating? What was the nature of an integrative system then? For a time, Boulding simply enlarged his view of what an integrative system was, to include not only these motives (or drives) but other ones as well. But this seems to have complicated his claim that integrative systems had a special nature, and he so later came to differentiate three main kinds of systems of social organization according to their dominant motives—the threat, exchange, and integrative systems—where the motive of fear is especially characteristic of the first and the motive of love is especially characteristic of the last, while arguing that all societies could be explained by the combination of these three broad systems.[6]

This three-system differentiation came out clearly, then, in Boulding's 1969 Presidential Address in connection with his characterization of economics as a moral science.

> I have elsewhere distinguished three groups of social organizers which I have called the threat system, the exchange system, and the integrative system. Economics clearly occupies the middle one of these three. It edges over towards the integrative system insofar as it has some jurisdiction over the study of the system of one-way transfers of exchangeables, which I have called the "grants economy," for a grant, or one-way transfer, is a rough measure of an integrative relationship. On the other side, economics edges towards an area between the threat system and the exchange system which might be described as the study of strategy or bargaining.
>
> (1969, p. 4)

Economics, then, was not solely located in the exchange system, but interacted with both of the other two systems as well.[7] At the same time, Boulding thought that defining economics as studying exchange and exchangeables was a better definition than the traditional allocation of scarce resources definition, in that it gave economics a relatively distinct domain of concern of its own—the allocation of scarce resources being an activity carried out in political processes as well.

But his key argument regarding the nature of economics as a moral science went back to his overall general systems view that different systems shared important commonalities with one another. Thus while economics was a relatively distinct subject matter concerned with the system of exchange, it contained within it elements from each of the other two systems, just as they contained within them elements of exchange. This comes out clearly in Boulding's critique of welfare economics and the idea of a Paretian optimum.

> Many, if not most, economists accept the Paretian optimum as almost self-evident. Nevertheless, it rests on an extremely shaky foundation of ethical propositions. The more one examines it, for instance, the more clear it becomes that economists must be extraordinarily nice people even to have

> thought of such a thing, for it implies that there is no malevolence anywhere in the system. It implies, likewise, that there is no benevolence, the niceness of economists not quite extending as far as good will. It assumes selfishness, that is, the independence of individual preference functions, such that it makes no difference to me whether I perceive you as either better off or worse off.
>
> (Ibid., p. 5)

Malevolence and benevolence, of course, are alternative terms for fear and love, the motives most characteristic, respectively, of the threat/fear and integrative/love systems. Economists, Boulding argues, avoid recognizing the role these motives play in economic life by their narrow view of preferences as selfish, or as rather purely self-regarding. The problem, however, is that thinking in this way misrepresents the true nature of human preferences.

> The plain fact is that our lives are dominated by precisely this interdependence of utility functions which the Paretian optimum denies. Selfishness, or indifference to the welfare of others, is a knife edge between benevolence on the one side and malevolence on the other. It is something that is very rare.
>
> (Ibid., p. 6)

It is very rare, we may add, because on Boulding's systems view economics continually edges over to the threat/fear and integrative/love systems. Economics, it follows, has been cast by contemporary economists as a value-free science precisely because they have ignored these connections the system of exchange has to these two other systems, and that the three systems combine to explain human social organization. On the one hand, he allows, this oversight is understandable, and

> economists can perhaps be excused for abstracting from benevolence and malevolence, simply because their peculiar baby, which is exchange, tends to be that social organizer which lies between these two extremes, and which produces, if not selfishness, at least low levels of malevolence and benevolence.
>
> (Ibid.)

On the other hand, Boulding argues, economists have also long had at their disposal adequate tools for explaining benevolence and malevolence in the form of the externality concept, and ought not be excused for continuing to neglect these motives.

> The almost complete neglect by economists of the concepts of malevolence and benevolence cannot be explained by their inability to handle these concepts with their usual tools. There are no mathematical or conceptual

> difficulties involved in inter-relating utility functions, provided that we note that it is the perceptions that matter.... The familiar tools of our trade, the indifference map, the Edgeworth box, and so on, can easily be expanded to include benevolence and malevolence, and indeed without this expansion many phenomena, such as one-way transfers, cannot be explained.
>
> (Ibid.)

Thus we see again that Boulding's position is that economics is actually less scientific when it ignores moral values in economic life since it then fails to adequately explain human behavior. A moral science of economics—one that clearly recognizes the common value systems that operate throughout life—is therefore the only truly scientific economics.

Boulding goes on to build on this idea by identifying several areas of achievement in the history of economics where important ethical propositions were successfully established.

> The major impact of economics on ethics, it can be argued, has come because it has developed broad, aggregative concepts of general welfare which are subject to quantification. We can see this process going right back to Adam Smith, where the idea of what we call today per capital real income, as the principal measure of national well-being, has made a profound impact on subsequent thinking and policy.
>
> (Ibid., p. 7)

Other such concepts are the parity index used in terms of trade analysis and cost–benefit analysis. These broad, aggregative sorts of measures, Boulding argues, presuppose that the exchange system occupies a place in a world made up of other systems as well, and that they jointly explain social organization. So despite economists' conviction that they have freed economics from ethical reasoning, and are engaged in value-free investigation, in fact they have long practiced economics as a moral science, and are well recognized for doing so.

This still does not quite give Boulding's full view of the role played by ethics in economics, however, since it fails to sufficiently emphasize the single most important commonality operating within and across all social systems. "All these systems are linked together dynamically through the process of human learning which is the main dynamic factor in all social systems" (Ibid., p. 4). While economists, then, have contributed little to the explanation of learning, it is interesting that they have nonetheless made a contribution to the subject of learning in the form of a "description of what is learned; the preference functions which embody what is learned in regard to values, and the production functions which describe the results of the learning of technology" (Ibid.). This then implies that "actual choices depend not only on preferences but on opportunities, and that under some circumstances quite small changes in either preferences or opportunities may result in large changes in actual choices made" (Ibid., pp. 4–5). We enter, therefore, a further dimension of Boulding's thinking—one in which he was quite original among economists—namely his evolutionary view of the world and in particular in the current context "what might be called the evolutionary ecology of ethical systems" (Ibid., p. 5). Thus to see the last piece in Boulding's view of economics as a moral science we turn to his evolutionary thinking.

Boulding's evolutionary thinking

Boulding's evolutionary thinking had roots in his early ideas but matured considerably after his AEA Presidential Address (Boulding, 1978, 1981, 1991).[8] At the same time, his strong emphasis in the Address on learning provides an important indication of how his thinking would subsequently develop. What he would basically argue was that any system contains seeds of its own transformation or future genesis, and that this works through a learning process. Thus going back to an earlier interest in income distribution, he first argued that "land, labor, and capital are not factors of production, but factors of *distribution*" in the sense that they also function as " 'know-how', materials, and energy" that will guide future methods of production (Mott, 2000, p. F438). As Boulding himself put it:

> It is much more accurate to identify the factors of production as know-how (that is genetic information structure), energy, and materials, for, as we have seen, all processes of production involve the direction of energy by some know-how toward the selection, transportation, and transformation of the materials into the product.
>
> (1981, p. 27)

This effectively meant that we need to see economies as being like single organisms in that they are more than just collections of resources that get mechanically combined in production, and they need to be understood as containing active principles that enable them to self-reproduce themselves as entire systems. Or, as his general systems thinking had earlier emphasized, economic systems are homeostatic systems that maintain a self-sustaining balance through processes of change—albeit as also part of larger evolutionary processes that include societal evolution and natural evolutionary processes.[9]

From this perspective, we accordingly ought to look at economic systems as occupying successive stages of development, with one system giving rise to the next, and with human production capacities continually increasing via cumulative learning processes that reinforce economic development across economic systems through time. This was the lesson Boulding took from his understanding of the long history of human society, a process he later summarized as follows: "There are positive feedback processes here: the more we know, the easier it is to know more; the more we make, the easier it is to make more; the richer we are, the easier it is to get richer" (1991, p. 14). Yet despite this apparent continuity in human history, Boulding also held a punctuated equilibrium evolutionary view of change in which improbable events and sometimes even catastrophic ones explain much of how the future replaces the past (Ibid., p. 13). This then implied for him an important methodological lesson. On the assumption that learning generates information and that information by nature must be new and surprising, it follows that "exact prediction is impossible" (Ibid., p. 16). This of course goes against conventional economics' usual emphasis on prediction as the measure of good theory (Friedman, 1953), and also conflicts with its representation of the economy as highly determinate. But how, then, do we responsibly organize production and economies with an eye to the future?

The answer, it seems fair to say, is that we must rely on those systems of common values Boulding had singled out in his Presidential Address to provide us future direction. There he had indeed referred to an "evolutionary ecology of ethical systems" (1969, p. 5). "Successful ethical systems tend to create subcultures, and these subcultures tend to perpetuate and propagate the ethical systems which created them" (Ibid.). That is, common value systems also evolve and develop as a key form of human learning, building on the past in a cumulative way while providing interpretation of the possibilities the future creates. As such they are essential to how economies operate, and accordingly need to be central to the explanations economics provides.

Note that this argument for understanding economics as a moral science is built on but also goes significantly beyond his moral science argument based on his systems approach. There he argued that common value systems are pervasive in human systems of social organization, and that no single system, such as the exchange system, can be properly understood without attention to them. Here, from his more evolutionary point of view, Boulding makes a strong claim about the nature of the active principle in economic systems responsible for their holistic character. That is, it is the human propensity or capacity (he does not say which) to form ethical judgments that makes the universe of ethical values a driving and organizing force in human life. In an important sense, then, Boulding comes full circle from his early general systems view, answering a question which he had previously left largely unaddressed: what are the active principles that give human social organization its system-like quality? Among these, preeminently, are human values.

Boulding's particular view of economics as a moral science

Boulding was unhesitating in his belief that economics is a moral science, and with his general systems approach he offered an original way of arguing that we ought to treat it as such. His view was not one formulated in terms of a theory of ideology as a value-based superstructural accompaniment of forms of production. It was also not a semantical or conceptual approach—a value-ladenness type of view—that claims that science at the level of language or theory cannot abstract from the domain of value. Rather Boulding worked from a particular view of the relationship between economic life and ethical life, whereby the latter, as understood in terms of common values, permeates the former. At the same time, in his later three systems thinking about social organization, he adopted a modified view of this permeation thesis, since there he allows for a relative autonomy of the economic world in that the system of exchange only "edges" onto the threat/fear and integrative/love systems. In this respect, his view comes closer to that of others who have argued that the economic world is at least a relatively value-free domain that nonetheless has value-based boundaries operating upon it set out by the normative concerns of society (cf. Finn, 2006). This suggests that there is something of a tension in Boulding's view of economics as a moral science between the permeation thesis and the relative autonomy view that calls for final comment.

One interpretation to consider, then, is that the particular set of common values that operates in economics as a domain investigating the system of exchange is what economists would call methodological values. These are shared value assumptions about how the specific subject matter of economics ought to be explained and include such concerns as choice of the subject matter to be investigated, the methods to be used in this investigation, and the criteria, standards, and norms that ought to be used to assess and judge the results of this investigation (see Boumans and Davis, 2010, pp. 170ff.). Consider the choice of subject matter. Whether economics aims to explain, say, individual choice behavior or income distribution would reflect the normative goals of economists, but what they say then ultimately about these subjects could still be thought value-free. Economics would then not be an entirely value-free science. But this would still be compatible with saying that economics is concerned with the system of exchange, albeit one that sometimes "edges" over toward systems whose sciences are concerned with subject matters that are clearly value-laden (for example, political science in the threat/fear system).

Alternatively, we could ask whether we believe Boulding's arguments treat the subject matter of economics itself as normative. That is, do the common values he believes operate in any culture, including that of economics, invariably extend to the content of that culture itself, and not just to the ways and methods people have of doing things? Here, it seems, we must note an important idea running from his early general systems view of systems as hierarchically structured to his later evolutionary thinking. What we find in both instances is the idea that what follows at one stage is presupposed in some cumulative fashion by what precedes it at an early stage. On this conception, then, value permeation must be thought pervasive throughout all more complex differentiated systems, whatever their relative autonomy, because they all derive from more primitive systems which were themselves governed by sets of common values. Thus the long history of the world is a history of the emergence of increasingly complex values systems specialized in ever greater ways, and the social world as made up of three different systems of social organization is no less the outcome of a history of human development reflecting common values.

It may appear to economists, then, that the domain of exchange is relatively autonomous so that their values are restricted to their methods of investigation and scientific practices, but Boulding, it seems, would have argued more strongly that the subject itself economists investigate is deeply permeated by common values. Thus common values are pervasive throughout all aspects of a culture or science, and do not just act as boundary conditions upon it. There is an irony in this conclusion, however. It is that the development of increasingly complex systems, a process which Boulding would have expected to continue, always makes the common values from which such systems derive and upon which they depend more distant and difficult to recognize. It was consequently left to individuals such as himself, Boulding would presumably have said, to remind economists of what economics has forgotten, namely, that economics is ultimately a moral science.

Notes

1 Thanks go to Geoff Hodgson, Tracy Mott, and Randy Wray for comments on an earlier version of this paper.
2 The biographical material in this paragraph is drawn from Mott (2000).
3 The other main approach was "to look over the empirical universe and to pick out certain general *phenomena* which are found in many different disciplines, and to seek to build up general theoretical models relevant to these phenomena" (1956, p. 200). Boulding adopted this approach in his later systems theory argument that there are three main systems of social organization, as discussed below.
4 See Wray (1990) on Boulding's preoccupation with balance sheets and stocks. An important aspect of the balance sheet for Boulding was that it always included a "bottom line" of net worth (cf. Boulding, 1991, p. 10).
5 Though of course this is precisely what the invisible hand idea involves!
6 Thus it seems fair to say he turned to his second approach for understanding general systems, which was "to look over the empirical universe and to pick out certain general *phenomena* which are found in many different disciplines, and to seek to build up general theoretical models relevant to these phenomena" (1956, p. 200).
7 Boulding wrote before game theory and the subject of strategy and bargaining became an important part of mainstream economics, so his view that economics "edges towards an area between the threat system and the exchange system" was prescient. However, his grants economy view, associated with how economics "edges over towards the integrative system" failed to become a significant part of mainstream economics, and where it did develop it departed little from conventional neoclassical thinking (cf. Wray, 1994, pp. 1212ff.).
8 It is worth noting here the close affinity between Boulding's subsequent evolutionary thinking and that of Nicholas Georgescu-Roegen, who gave his AEA Ely lecture in the year after Boulding's Presidential Address (Georgescu-Roegen, 1970).
9 Here we see Boulding's preference for Alfred Marshall's biological thinking as a basis for understanding economics as a moral science.

References

Bertalanffy, Ludwig von (1968) *General System Theory: Foundations, Development, Applications*, New York: George Braziller; revised edition 1976.

Bertalanffy, Ludwig von (1974) *Perspectives on General System Theory*, ed. Edgar Taschdjian, New York: George Braziller.

Boulding, Kenneth (1941) *Economic Analysis*, New York: Harper & Brothers, 2nd ed., 1948, 3rd ed., 1955, 4th ed., 1966.

Boulding, Kenneth (1956) "General Systems Theory: The Skeleton of Science," *Management Science*, 2 (3, April): 197–208.

Boulding, Kenneth (1969) "Economics as a Moral Science," *American Economic Review*, 59 (1): 1–12.

Boulding, Kenneth (1978) *Ecodynamics: A New Theory of Societal Evolution*, Beverly Hills, CA: Sage.

Boulding, Kenneth (1981) *Evolutionary Economics*, Beverly Hills, CA: Sage.

Boulding, Kenneth (1989) "A Bibliographical Autobiography," *Banca Nazionale del Lavoro Quarterly Review*, 171: 365–93.

Boulding, Kenneth (1991) "What Is Evolutionary Economics?" *Journal of Evolutionary Economics*, 1: 9–17.

Boumans, Marcel and John Davis (2010) *Economic Methodology: Understanding Economics as a Science*, London: Palgrave Macmillan.

Finn, Daniel (2006) *The Moral Ecology of Markets: Assessing Claims about Markets and Justice*, Cambridge: Cambridge University Press.

Friedman, Milton (1953) *Essays in Positive Economics*, Chicago: University of Chicago Press.

Georgescu-Roegen, Nicholas (1970) "The Economics of Production," *American Economic Review*, 60: 1–9.

Heims, Steve (1993) *Constructing a Social Science for Postwar America: The Cybernetics Group, 1946–1953*, Cambridge, MA: MIT Press.

László, Ervin, ed. (1972) *The Relevance of General Systems Theory: Papers Presented to Ludwig Von Bertalanffy on His Seventieth Birthday*, New York: George Braziller.

Mott, Tracy (1992) "Kenneth Boulding Interviewed by Tracy Mott 28–29 March 1991," *Review of Political Economy*, 4 (3): 341–74.

Mott, Tracy (2000) "Kenneth Boulding, 1910–1993," *Economic Journal*, 110 (June): F430–44.

Myrdal, Gunnar (1953) *The Political Element in the Development of Economic Theory*, trans. Paul Streeten, London: Routledge.

Myrdal, Gunnar (1958) *Value in Social Theory*, ed. and intro. Paul Streeten, London: Routledge.

Oppenheim, Paul and Hilary Putnam (1958) "Unity of Science as a Working Hypothesis," *Minnesota Studies in the Philosophy of Science*, II: 3–36.

Wray, L. Randall (1990) "Boulding's Balloons: A Contribution to Monetary Theory," *Journal of Economic Issues*, 24 (4): 1–20.

Wray, L. Randall (1994) "Kenneth Boulding's Grants Economics," *Journal of Economic Issues*, 28 (4): 1205–225.

Poem

Freedom is what's inside the fence
Of Morals, Money, Law, and Sense,
And we are free, if this is wide
(Or nothing's on the other side).
We come to Politics (and Sin)
When Your fine freedoms fence Me in,
And so through Law we come to be
Curtailing Freedom – to be free.

Principles of Economic Policy,
1958, p. 110

Part V

Communication/persuasion

5 Key text: The pathologies of persuasion[1]

Kenneth E. Boulding

Persuasion as a critical but neglected element in social systems

Persuasion is a human relationship of great universality and significance. It is surprising, therefore, that it has been so much neglected, both by social scientists and by moral philosophers. Nowhere in the social sciences do we find anything that looks like a general theory of persuasion as a social relationship. In the study of rhetoric and in the underworld of what used to be called speech departments, we find a certain classical literature, going back at least to Aristotle, on the art of persuasion, the various techniques which may be used, and so on. We find something of this also in modern psychology, especially in applied psychology. What we do not find is much discussion of the role of persuasion in the total social system, or even its role in the total decision-making process, either in the organization or in the person.

Yet it is clear that persuasion plays a crucial role in all social systems, that without it society probably could not exist. It forms the matrix, indeed, within which other social organizers, such as the threat system and the exchange system, are able to come into being. Unless we can persuade someone that a threat is credible, or that an offer to exchange is genuine, neither threats nor exchange can serve to organize social relations and role structures. At the level of the integrative system, also, it is clear that persuasion plays an absolutely crucial role in the awakening of love, in the development of community, honor, sacrifice, legitimacy, and in the whole development of the human identity. People become lovers, spouses, citizens, church members, party members, employees or employers, mainly because they are persuaded to do so by their own minds, by other people, or perhaps by circumstances.

To be persuaded, indeed, is a wider concept than to persuade. We are persuaded that there is a force of gravity the first time we take a fall. All sorts of information input, both verbal and nonverbal, take part in the persuasion process. To persuade, however, as a human activity, is to add messages, which again may be either verbal or nonverbal, to the vast input of another person in the hope of "changing the mind." Persuasion is a part of the human learning process, and the human learning process is the essence of the social dynamics of society. In the light of its crucial importance, it is all the more astonishing that this phenomenon should have been so long neglected.

Persuasion ignored by economics and the other social sciences

Economics knows little of persuasion, which has seldom emerged from the practically oriented, earthy underworld of marketing into the empyrean ether of economic theory. Economic man never has to be persuaded to do anything, just as he never has to learn anything because he knows everything already. He makes his maximizing choices in the light of a given value system, a known set of choices, and a known set of consequences. How he learned all this the economist never inquires. What I have elsewhere called the doctrine of the "immaculate conception of the indifference curve" is so firmly established in economics that it is a very rare economist indeed who questions it. There are hints indeed in Adam Smith's *Wealth of Nations* (1937) that people learn to be what they are and that the differences between the philosopher and the porter, in preferences no doubt as well as in abilities, depend on their life experiences, that is, on their total input of information, rather than on their genetic heritage.

Of the twentieth-century economists, I can think of only three who have ever raised the question as to how people are persuaded to have the preferences they do: Thorstein Veblen, especially in *The Theory of the Leisure Class* (1937), recognized very clearly that preferences are learned from the subculture in which they operate; John Kenneth Galbraith suggests that businesses themselves help to create the preferences which enable them to survive in the market (Galbraith, 1967); and I should modestly add myself to this distinguished but not very persuasive company (Boulding, 1969).

The general assumption of economic theory, therefore, that there is an equilibrium set of prices which can be derived from the existing preferences of individuals and the production functions of commodities seems to be true only in short periods, for as we consider the total dynamics of society the impact of the price structure on preferences may be just as important as the impact of preferences on the price structure. However, Veblen also remained in the underworld of institutional economics, and the mainstream of economic theory flowed on cheerfully into a vast slough called "welfare economics," which is based solidly on the principle that nobody is ever persuaded of anything and nobody ever learns anything. The very concept of the Paretian optimum, that *summum bonum* of welfare economics, implies that all preferences are given and all utilities are independent, so that everybody is selfish and exhibits neither malevolence nor benevolence, envy or pride, or indeed any of the seven deadly sins, nor of course do they exhibit any of the corresponding virtues (Boulding, 1987). The only place for economic man indeed is limbo. He is too virtuous for hell and not virtuous enough for heaven.

Of the other social sciences, psychology has probably made the largest contribution to the study of persuasion, especially through the theory of the

Errata: ***Interdisciplinary Economics*** **(978-0-415-48347-6)**

The author of Chapter 4a (pages xvi and 126–152) should be:

Warren J. Samuels

subconscious. We are all familiar with the doctrine that the prune is a witch. All this, however, is rather superficial, simply because our ignorance of the humane learning process is enormous. One should not scold psychologists; they are like the rest of us, doing their little best, but they are faced with a system of almost inconceivable complexity. The human nervous system has about ten billion neurons, so that its capacity is of the order of two to the ten billionth power. A system of such enormous complexity cannot be reduced to explicit formulations and it is not surprising, therefore, that psychology retreats into animal behavior.

Sociology, which should perhaps have had a theory of persuasion at its very core, has neglected the problem even more single-mindedly than the economists. There is, of course, a literature on socialization and on child development and on the learning of roles, but the part played by persuasion in all this is very rarely recognized. The moral philosophers have neglected the problem in any systematic sense, again with remarkable unanimity. I know of no systematic treatise on this subject. And while this may only reflect my own ignorance, if any such cases exist they have certainly not made very much impact.

Persuasion in the learning process

The concept of persuasion, like all other important concepts, has fuzzy edges. We are faced with a spectrum of phenomena rather than with a clear-cut boundary which divides what is persuasion from what is not. At its widest definition, we could include in persuasion almost the whole of the human learning process and a good deal of animal learning as well. The learning process consists of the modification of what might be called the internal universe, or the image of the world which is possessed by the knower. This modification takes place in a number of different ways. It takes place partly through the internal generation of messages and images in the imagination. The knowledge structure is changing all the time because of the enormous internal activity of the nervous system within which it is embodied.

The earlier concept of the mind as a kind of *tabula rasa*, on which the messages coming in from the outside world through the senses were simply imprinted, is now seen to be hopelessly inadequate. Even in modern perception theory, the mind is now seen as an enormously active organization constantly producing vast numbers of images, even at the unconscious level. The senses, and the information coming in from them, act much more as critics than as authors. This is not to deny, of course, that we do receive imprints from the senses, but for perception, and still more for an increase in knowledge to take place, the inputs from the senses must be processed through a huge active system, the nature of which at the moment we are only just beginning to understand. It is not a mere quirk of language, therefore, to say that I am "persuaded" that I am now sitting on the porch at my cabin, looking at a blue sky flecked with clouds, at rocks and pine trees, at rough furniture, and at the Dictaphone which I am using. I am persuaded of all this because I have an input through my eyes and from other sense preceptors which persuade me, that is, change my knowledge structure in the direction of accepting the image of the real world around me. When the senses no longer persuade, the person is in real trouble. I can imagine a pink elephant sitting in front of me. As I have a good imagination, I can imagine it in considerable detail, but my senses inform me that it is not there. If I were drunk, or still more, schizophrenic, my senses would lose their power of persuasion and I would be at the mercy of my imagination, and I might see the pink elephant.

Knowledge consists partly in the memories and the internal records of perception, but it involves much more than a simple roster of memories. It involves, for instance, the perception of regularities in the perceived world. This is true even at the level of what I have called "folk knowledge," the kind of knowledge we acquire in the ordinary business of life. I am able to get out of bed in the morning because I have learned the regularities in the law of gravity, which have been somehow coded into my nervous system, into my muscles, and the rest of me. Without the knowledge of such regularities, that is, of laws, action would be impossible. I have suggested elsewhere that if the gravitational constant was in fact not constant, we would find it extremely difficult to learn how to get out of bed in the morning or how to do any of the commonest activities of daily life.

At the more sophisticated level of scientific knowledge, of course, these laws and regularities become explicit. They are embodied in mathematical formulae, from which precise images of the future are derived than can then be tested. The testing process, however, is crucial to the development of knowledge of all kinds. It involves having some sort of image of the regularities of the world; it involves making an inference from these images, that is, a prediction about the future; it involves observing the future as the present passes over and it becomes the past; and it involves comparing the image of the future as we had it in the past with the image of the same thing after it has become the past. If there is a mismatch between the image of the future as we hold it in the past and the image of the same thing as we remember it after it has occurred, then there has to be some sort of reorganization. These reorganizations can be of many kinds, some of which produce more knowledge than others. Without mismatch, however, there can be no learning, though what we learn and whether what we learn is true is not determined by the mismatch alone, but by our reactions to it.

Ethics as persuasion about valuations

Ethics begins to come into the picture when we consider that some part of our knowledge structure is a set of values or preferences. Some such assumption as this is absolutely necessary to the theory of choice, for choice involves contemplating at least two alternative futures over which we have some control and selecting one of them. The moment we make a selection we have in effect made a value ordering. We have decided that the future that we chose is "better" than the future that we did not. I have sometimes accused decision theory of being merely a set of mathematical variations on the theme that "everybody does what he thinks best at the time," but even so, the concept of "best" involves a scalar ordering of the world in some kind of scale of better or worse. Usually this need only be an ordinal scale, that is, we have to order possible alternatives—first, second, third—but we do not have to measure the value of each alternative in a cardinal number, although there are situations in which cardinality of value measurement may be necessary.

Ordering the world on a scale of better or worse is something that we do all the time, and it is something that we have to *learn* how to do. In some cases, values are "learned" genetically, that is, are built into the structure of the nervous system by the genes as they organize the phenotype. This seems particularly true of the insects, who learn very little, if anything, in their lifetimes. The behavior of the ant is governed by quite a complex value system. It "chooses" some objects rather than others, some directions rather than others, even though its activity also seems to have a large random component. These choices, however, are not learned, but are presumably built into the nervous system of the ant by its genetic code. Birds, likewise, have preferences that are mainly genetic. Orioles prefer other orioles and oriole nests to robins and robins' nests, but this preference does not seem to be learned much from their life experience.

There are some kinds of learning even in the birds, for instance, in bird song, some of which has to be learned, some of which is genetically controlled. As we move into the mammals, especially as we move toward humans, the learning component in the development of value orderings increases until in humans it becomes completely dominant. The human being starts out with certain primitive genetic values determined by the structure and composition of the baby's nervous system as it is created by the genetic code, but his genetic value system is extremely elementary and almost the whole preference structure of the adult has been learned. Even many things that we previously thought of as instinct, such as sex, are in fact very largely learned, even though the genetically created physical structure of the nervous system introduces certain predispositions into the learning process.

It is clear, therefore, that just as we are persuaded that the world around us is what we think it is, so we are persuaded of our values. An American is persuaded to be an American by his upbringing and by the innumerable information inputs which he has perceived. In much the same way, the average Russian is persuaded to be a Russian. The whole process of socialization, as the sociologists call it, indeed, is nothing more than an elaborate piece of persuasion, simply because it is a learning process.

The persuader–persuadee relation as part of human learning

This may, however, be carrying the concept of persuasion too far. As noted earlier, to be persuaded is not the same thing at all as to persuade. Persuasion, in the active sense of persuading, is by no means coextensive with the learning process. It is indeed only a part of it, and perhaps quite a small part of it at that. It is with this part, however, that we are most concerned in this paper. Here we are concerned with the persuader rather than with the persuaded, with those who seek to influence rather than those who are influenced. Even when we narrow the concept down to this point, however, we still find that it includes a very large area of human relationships in social life. We can think indeed of at least five areas of social life where the relationship between an active persuader and a more passive persuadee is an essential element in the system.

We start first of all with the family. Each spouse is constantly trying to persuade the other to do something or to believe something which he or she prefers. In a successful marriage presumably some kind of an equilibrium is reached fairly soon between the spouses, after which relatively little persuasion takes place, because the tastes of the parties are similar enough so that they are not a severe source of discord. In the relations of parents with children, however, persuasion goes on constantly and intensely. The value structure of the child, particularly, is open to parental persuasion, simply because of the basic relationship of dependency. Persuasion is frequently at a rather unconscious level, as, for instance, in the learning of language. However, a child growing up in an English-speaking home is easily persuaded to learn English, and one who grows up in a French-speaking home similarly is persuaded to learn French.

In the institutions of formal education, it is clear that persuasion is a major enterprise. In the classroom the teacher takes an active role in trying to transmit certain knowledge structures from his own nervous system to the nervous systems of the students. All the arts of persuasive rhetoric indeed are part of the stock in trade of the good teacher, whose success may be judged by the amount of persuasion that he manages to perform. Here persuasion becomes a good deal more conscious than it is in the family, where the child often grows up persuaded more by what the parents are than by what they consciously do.

As we move from education into religion, the role of persuasion becomes even more prominent. The sermon is almost the ideal type of the persuasive rhetorical exercise. The architecture of the church, the stained-glass windows, the symbolism of the ritual are all means of persuasion, designed to change the mind of the visitor or the participant in directions which the church quite self-consciously desires. It is not surprising, therefore, that children growing up in a Christian community easily become Christian; those growing up in a Buddhist community become Buddhists.

An interesting question is that of the extent to which art from different cultures should be regarded as persuasive in its essential character. A great deal of art clearly is persuasive. The Ravenna mosaics, medieval stained glass, the Gothic cathedral, the Palladian temple, the state capital, the triumphal arch, Collegiate Gothic, fashionable paintings, and fine clothes ... all carry persuasive messages. In the last century a certain feeling has grown up in the artistic community that to use art for persuasive purposes, especially for the persuasive purposes of other people, is in some sense prostitution. This is the movement of "art for art's sake." Even here, however, unless the artist is performing a purely individual act, which hardly deserves the name of art, he is presumably seeking to persuade the viewer of the art at least to enjoy it and appreciate it.

Politics is another area of life where persuasion is of enormous importance. This is true even in the most dictatorial regime. Indeed, frequently the more dictatorial the regime, the more effort has to be put into propaganda and persuasion. The cynical arts of Madison Avenue pale almost into bland virtue beside the persuasive activities of Goebbels or the persuasive appeal of Mao's "Little Red Book," both of which ended up in the garbage can. In democratic societies, of course, the rhetoric of politics is almost wholly the rhetoric of persuasion. The major activity of all candidates for office consists largely of attempts to change the value preferences of the voters in their favor. It is a nice question as to whether Billy Graham or Ronald Reagan is more skilled at persuasive rhetoric, but from this point of view they are clearly birds of a feather.

Finally, we come to the uses of persuasion in business and economic life. This constitutes a major part of industrial relations on the one hand and marketing on the other. The economist's ideal type, the seller in perfect competition, facing a market which will take any quantity of what he has to sell at a price that he cannot himself determine, is described unflatteringly in the marketing literature as an "order taker." The wheat farmer and the gold miner may indeed conform to this ideal type. Over the whole range of manufacturing and service industries, however, imperfect competition is the rule and imperfect competition almost always implies marketing, that is, positive activity devoted specifically to increasing the demand for the product. All of this falls under the head of persuasion, that is, activity devoted to changing the image of the world and especially the values of preference orderings in the minds of somebody else—Galbraith's "revised sequence" (Galbraith, 1967).

Industrial relations can be thought of as marketing in the labor market and involves a great deal of persuasion on both sides. Bargaining of any kind, and collective bargaining in particular, has to be visualized as an exercise in mutual persuasion, to the point where both parties are persuaded to accept the bargain on the same terms. Within organizations, also, a great deal of persuasion has to go on in order to get people to accept the role to which they are assigned in the hierarchy. Indeed, I suspect that the further up the hierarchy one goes, the more time is spent on persuasion, even in hierarchies which appear at first sight to be highly authoritarian and dictatorial. Even the Pope must persuade the cardinals; the cardinals, the archbishops; the archbishops, the bishops and the priests; and the priests, the laity. In military organizations as well, an enormous amount of persuasion goes on. Otherwise there would not be so many meetings. The committee indeed is the altar at which the rites of persuasion are mainly performed. Show me an organization without committees and you will show me one without persuasion. The persuasive activities of more powerful people may be more mixed with threat, and those of less powerful people more dependent on rhetoric, but naked threat is rarely effective, and even threat has to be clothed in the language of persuasion.

The "production function" of persuasion

Let us now look briefly at what might be called the "production function" of the persuasion enterprise, that is, what inputs into it produce what outputs, particularly from the point of view of the persuader. It is clear that the immediate product of the persuader is information of some kind, whether this is an advertisement, a speech, a sermon, a poem, a piece of architecture, or a punch to the jaw. The persuader's special production function is that which involves the inputs of resources which are necessary to produce a given output of information. Information, however, is only an intermediate product; the final product is the change in the knowledge structure or the value structure in the nervous system of the persuadee. This is much more difficult to estimate.

We might postulate certain very rough aggregate parameters of this system: first, the ratio of information output of the persuader to the value of the resources used; second, the ratio of the change in the knowledge structure of the persuadee per unit of information received; and third, the value of this perceived change in the mind of the persuader. The decision as to whether it is worthwhile to try to persuade somebody clearly depends on the ratio between the value in the mind of the persuader of the change that he believes will take place in the mind of the persuadee, to the value of the inputs which the persuader has to employ in producing the information, or whatever it is that will produce this change. This, of course, is a statement of the obvious, as cost–benefit analysis usually is. It does point up the fact, however, that in this calculation there are enormous uncertainties. Persuasion indeed is one of the most uncertain of all the operations of the human mind. The persuader may have a pretty fair idea what his output is costing him. He usually has very little idea as to the impact of this output of information on the mind of the persuadee. Under these circumstances, we would not be surprised to find that the persuasion industry, if we call it that, is subject to all sorts of nonrational phenomena, such as rules of thumb (a given percentage of sales spent for advertising), habits (preachers go on preaching sermons long after they have had any effect), and waves of fashion as we find them in advertising, in education, and elsewhere.

Any theory of persuasion obviously has to revolve around the study of these highly uncertain production functions. Thus, the theory of operant conditioning assumes that persuasion is accomplished by the association of some kind of reward with the change which the persuader is going to bring about. This, in effect, supposes that persuasion is closely related to the phenomenon of exchange. The persuader achieves an objective by rewarding the persuadee for the changes which he is trying to bring about. Operant conditioning tends to assume that the rewards have to be almost immediate and have to be clearly related in the mind of the persuadee with the change which is taking place in him.

No one could doubt, of course, that these processes do take place, and that the rewards play an important part in the learning process. Nevertheless, the weakness of this kind of theory (also, I suspect, of the practice based on it) is that it assumes that the human mind, and especially the human value structure, is almost indefinitely malleable. Its malleability, however, has sharp limits. There are limitations imposed, for instance, by the genetic composition of an individual's nervous system. We are not going to be able to persuade a person who is genetically tone deaf to respond to any kind of music, simply because he cannot differentiate one note from another, no matter what the reward structure. It is no use rewarding him for Beethoven and penalizing him for rock if he cannot tell one from the other. This is merely an extreme case of a general problem of the ability to discriminate. In obvious physiological cases such as tone deafness and color blindness, the nonmalleability of the system is fairly clear. There may, however, be much more subtle failures of discrimination of which we are now barely aware. Discrimination in the bad sense of the word, for instance, such as stereotyping and racial and religious discrimination, is often the result of a failure to discriminate in the good sense, in the sense, for instance, that we say that people have discriminating tastes. This in turn is a basic failure in the learning process. Why this happens and how it happens, however, I think we do not really understand.

We might perhaps postulate a concept of a "persuadability gradient," or perhaps since elasticity is such a good word in economics, we might almost call it the "elasticity of persuadability." Some people are very firm in their opinions and values and are very hard to persuade; other people are indeed malleable and are easy to persuade. Again, I think we really do not know what makes the difference. It certainly has something to do, in the mathematical sense, with the "strength" of the orderings of a person's value system. A person who has strong orderings, who always knows whether he prefers A to B, is apt to be less persuadable than somebody who has weak orderings and does not really care whether he has A or B. This is a personality trait which seems to have been studied very little by psychologists. Just how it is learned, or whether indeed it has any genetic base, is, again, something that we do not know.

The problem is enormously complicated by the fact that we are not dealing here with easily quantifiable inputs and outputs, but rather with complex multidimensional structures in which the structure and composition, or inputs or outputs, may have much more significance than any simple measure of quantity. The psychology of persuasion has, of course, some wisdom about these matters. We are all familiar, for instance, with the principle of association, the logic of which is highly dubious, the psychology of which may have some truth in it. Thus, the syllogism "sex is agreeable, I see an advertisement with a pretty girl smoking a cigarette, therefore cigarettes must be agreeable" must be an example of one of a large class of false syllogisms. In the psychology of persuasion, however, this kind of false logic seems to be very successful, and it is perhaps the first major principle of the rhetoric of persuasion. Jones has a kind face, kind faces are good, therefore Jones would make a good mayor, is the sort of logic which all too often guides the voters.

The pathologies of persuasion in the creation of error

Finally, we come to the title of this paper: What about "the pathologies of persuasion"? The greatest pathology of persuasion is that it may produce error, that is, images in the minds of the persuaded that do not correspond to something in the real world. If I am persuaded by a charismatic preacher that I can jump off the Empire State Building and fly, and I try it, my disillusionment will end very rapidly. Unfortunately, many erroneous images are not so easily tested. Rain dances are sometimes followed by rain; development policies are sometimes followed by development; revolutions occasionally, though very rarely, improve a society; a criminal justice system may even reduce crime. Nevertheless, as we move into complex systems, the problems of testing become acute. It becomes easy to persuade people of things that are not so, often to their severe detriment. The things that the human race has believed that are not so would fill a very large encyclopedia.

We see this persistence of error as a result of persuasive skills even in scholarly knowledge. Alchemy lasted for a very long time, and even now persists in a few underworlds, in spite of the fact that the elements are not earth, air, fire, and water. Even chemists at one time believed in phlogiston. A pattern of believing plausible but hard-to-test images of the world, what Kuhn has called "normal science" (Kuhn, 1962), has been quite common, even in the history of the physical sciences, still more so in the case of the social sciences. Marxism has persisted for well over a hundred years now on a large scale, in spite of the fact that "classes" are heterogeneous aggregates, about as useful in understanding the real complexities of social interaction as the alchemist's elements were for chemistry.

Mainline economics, as defined, say, by most of the Nobel Prize winners, is not in much better shape. The younger generation has gotten trapped in a set of mathematical and statistical variations on models which are not really adequate to describe the complexity of social life, especially in the modern world. The pathology of persuasion here is the persuasiveness of the Ph.D. committee, which is pretty powerful in persuading younger people to develop eloquent elaborations on the mistakes of their elders. As Lester C. Thurow, one of the few younger economists who has not lost interest in the real world, says of John Kenneth Galbraith in his delightful article in *The New Palgrave*: "His books have been written always in the form of verbally persuasive economic tracts, without a hint of mathematics" (1987, p. 455). Why, then, have these verbally persuasive tracts failed to persuade? The economics profession has gone deeper and deeper into its mathematical and statistical morass, with its eighteenth-century mathematics and nineteenth-century statistics, quite inappropriate to investigating a system, which, like most systems in the real world, is fundamentally topological and structural rather than numerical and algebraic. Even though it is true that all knowledge is gained by the orderly loss of information, most statistical analysis throws away the essential information, especially information about extreme positions of systems, which is necessary to fulfill an understanding of complexity. Mainline economics for the last fifty years now has been in a condition of "normal science," becoming increasingly remote from the realities of the world, with evidence accumulating against the existing models. It seems to be time for a scientific revolution. Perhaps this can only be done, however, by a topological mathematician using a mathematics which still remains to be written in the twenty-first century.

Economics, of course, is not the only victim of pathological persuasive systems. International and strategic studies have built a huge fairy tale on models of deterrence and threat power, which are wholly inappropriate to the nuclear age. Psychology is only now beginning to recover from behaviorism, with its absurd denial of the capacity of humans to have knowledge about their own consciousness. Even in the physical sciences, geology, which resisted the enormous evidence in favor of plate tectonics and continental drift for a generation or more, finally succumbed in the face of some overwhelming evidence on the mid-Atlantic rift. Now what used to be heresy has become orthodoxy.

Pathologies of persuasion in marketing

We are fairly familiar with the pathologies of persuasion in advertising and marketing. Cigarette advertising is a classic case, where people are being persuaded to shorten their own lives. Persuasions that lead to addictions are perhaps the most pathological, addictions being the satisfaction of certain desires in which the satisfaction increases the future desire. Tobacco, alcohol, and drugs are obvious examples. Some forms of radicalism, conservatism, fundamentalism, and the desire for power may be even more dangerous, as they are addictive mental states.

Even though there is no addiction, there may be dishonesty in persuasion both at the marketing level and at the political, religious, and even academic levels. But there are certain offsetting factors here. The fact that liars can be found out does give an important modicum of truth to the old saying that honesty is the best policy. Even if it is only the reputation for honesty, that it is the best policy, still, such a reputation can be destroyed by a single instance of being found out. This is as true of politicians and preachers as it is of business people.

One pathology of the persuasive system which is perhaps harder to deal with, perhaps because it is hard to identify, is what might be called "vulgarization." When the persuasive powers of the artist and architect are directed toward bishops and princes, the very smallness of the subculture may result in beauty. However, when the powers of persuasion are democratized, they may degenerate into kitsch or mere functionalism, like modern architecture. I am not sure that this is a serious problem, but it cannot be wholly brushed aside.

We are reminded constantly nowadays that we are moving into an information age. I suspect this really started with DNA. Nevertheless, the information industry is increasing very rapidly as a percentage of the total economy. This may mean that persuasion becomes a larger and larger part of social activity and the pathologies of persuasion become more and more important. In simpler societies, where a large part of human activity consisted of growing things and making things, persuasion was not so important, though it certainly began to increase with the rise of civilization, empires, and organized religions. In the world of the future, persuasion may become increasingly important and the pathologies of persuasion all the more dangerous.

Remedies for the pathologies of persuasion

The question of the remedies for the pathologies of persuasion, therefore, becomes increasingly important as time goes on, and the situation is not at all clear. Here again, one of Galbraith's great concepts, "countervailing power," is at least a wedge to enter into a rather impenetrable problem. There are undoubtedly countervailing powers to pathologies of persuasion. We see this, for instance, in the tremendous development of citizen initiatives, the development of the environmental movement, the consumer movement, innumerable private organizations to check on the sins both of corporate business and of government. The computer age seems to be generating an enormous spread of person-to-person communication, as evidenced, for instance, by the "minitel" system in France, the development of worldwide computer networks such as BITNET, the enormous rise of private citizen diplomacy and local government diplomacy undermining the almost inherently pathological persuasion system of the national state. The increase of diversity within such organizations as the Catholic Church, and now the Soviet Union and China, and even the large corporations is a straw in the wind which suggests that the pathologies of persuasion are not wholly incurable and that the very technology of information itself provides a countervailing power.

Just what countervailing power countervails against, however, is not always clear. The power of trade unions may countervail against unorganized labor and household purchases rather than against the employer. Protests against apartheid may actually strengthen it. Protest in many fields has often backfired. Even the Prohibition movement was a countervailing power against the liquor industry, but created a still greater countervailing power for the moderate drinkers and probably did less to solve the alcoholism problem than Alcoholics Anonymous does. There is a large field of study opening up here, also one which is by no means devoid of hope. Galbraith's persuasive economic tracts and other voices in the wilderness may still turn out to be really persuasive, and in that there is much hope for the future.

Notes

1 This article was previously published in *Unconventional Wisdom – Essays in Honor of John Kenneth Galbraith*, S. Bowles, R. Edwards, and W.G. Shepherd, eds., Boston: Houghton Mifflin Company, 1989, pp. 3–19.

References

Boulding, Kenneth E., "Economics as a Moral Science," *American Economic Review*, 59, no. 1, March 1969: 1–12.

Boulding, Kenneth E., "The Economics of Pride and Shame," *Atlantic Economic Journal*, 15, no. 1, March 1987: 10–19.

Galbraith, John Kenneth, *The New Industrial State*, Boston: Houghton Mifflin, 1967.

Kuhn, Thomas S., *The Structure of Scientific Revolutions*, Chicago: University of Chicago Press, 1962.

Smith, Adam, *The Wealth of Nations*, New York: Random House/Modern Library, 1937.
Thurow, Lester, "John Kenneth Galbraith," in *The New Palgrave: A Dictionary of Economics*, vol. 2; ed. John Eatwell, New York: Stockton Press, 1987.
Veblen, Thorstein, *The Theory of the Leisure Class*, New York: Random House/Modern Library, 1937.

5a Commentary article: The communication theory of Kenneth E. Boulding[1]

Robert E. Babe

In the act of creation, a man brings together two facets of reality and, by discovering a likeness between them, suddenly makes them one.

Jacob Bronowski ([1956] 1972)

Kenneth E. Boulding (1910–1993)—poet, peace activist, environmentalist, Quaker, co-founder of general systems theory—was author of more than thirty books, many of them positioning information/communication at the very heart of an innovative, evolutionary economics. Of them all perhaps the most significant were *The Image*, the book he felt to be his most influential, completed by dictation in but nine days, and *Ecodynamics*, which he termed his "manifesto about the universe" (Boulding, 1992, p. 81).

Born in Liverpool, England to a working class family,[2] Boulding studied first at Oxford, then at the University of Chicago under Frank Knight, and briefly at Harvard under Joseph Schumpeter. Another important influence was sociologist Robert Park, whom he met while teaching at Fisk University. Boulding recounted how a "half-hour conversation [with Park] about social ecology … quite changed my life, beginning my interest in ecological and evolutionary theory" (Boulding, 1992, p. 74).

Never earning an advanced degree, Boulding nonetheless was recipient or more than thirty honorary degrees. He taught at universities in some seven countries and served as president of six learned societies, including the American Economics Association and the Society for General Systems Research, of which he was co-founder. Through his life and works Boulding maintained passionately that "There is such a thing as human betterment—a magnificent, multidimensional, complex structure—a cathedral of the mind—and [that] human decisions should be judged by the extent to which they promote it" (Boulding, 1992, p. 83).[3]

If Malthus sowed seeds for an evolutionary economics, and if Veblen interleaved expansive notions of communication into economics, thereby inaugurating evolutionary and institutional economics, Kenneth Boulding was the one most fully to isolate and explore *information* as an agent of economic organization, change and development.

Production as communication

Production

For Kenneth Boulding, *production*, "whether of a chicken from an egg or a house from a blueprint," is a process whereby "some kind of information or knowledge structure is able to direct *energy* toward the transportation, transformation, or rearrangement of *materials* into less probable structures than those existing at the start of the process" (Boulding, 1978, pp. 12, 34; emphasis added). When a seed germinates in the ground, for example, its informational structure (DNA) utilizes and directs stored energy to draw selectively upon nutrients or "building materials" in the soil to produce its *phenotype* (the plant). Likewise for animals, *genomes* (that is, the total inherited genetic information) utilize energy and materials in directing processes of growth and development. Similarly, a housing contractor studies a blueprint, and from the knowledge or instructions embedded therein (the analogue of a genome) utilizes energy to assemble construction materials, which he/she rearranges to produce a more complex or improbable structure than had existed previously.

For Boulding, production is defined as the realization of phenotypes from genotypes (Boulding, 1981, p. 25), and for him it is not merely metaphorical to view genes as *knowing how* to construct organisms out of surrounding materials. Rather, he affirmed,

> There is clearly know-how in the genome, not only how to make a leg but how to make it the right length and how to stop building when it is long enough; these are pretty subtle instructions, especially for anything as speechless as DNA, which does not seem to have much capacity beyond four-letter-words.
>
> (Boulding, 1978, p. 106)

In Boulding's eyes, while there are important similarities between organic and inorganic processes of production, there are also important differences. Genes, for example, while imparting organization to surrounding materials and constructing organisms out of them, are themselves slow to change. ("The gene," he joked, "is a wonderful teacher; it is, however, a very poor learner.") According to present theory (as distinct from those implicit in the works of Lamarck),[4] genes "learn" nothing and change only through "chance" (i.e., unexplained or unexplainable mutations).

By contrast, many organic *phenotypes* do learn, which is to say that interactions with their environment change their images or knowledge structures, i.e., the informational patterns encoded in their nervous systems. Boulding believed that growth in the knowledge possessed by phenotypes follows a pattern "closely related to the life pattern itself." Since knowledge is a structure, he explained, its "present form always limits its possibilities of growth,… [resulting in] the phenomenon of 'readiness' for certain kinds of knowledge at different stages of life" (Boulding, [1966] 1995, p. 14).

In addition to organic genomes and learned structures, Boulding viewed material artifacts also as constituting knowledge structures. Human artifacts (or "social species," as Boulding often referred to them) are produced by applying human learning and energy to matter; they therefore embody and manifest human knowledge. Just as the genome "in a favorable environment is capable of creating a teleological process to produce the appropriate phenotype" (Boulding, 1970, pp. 21–2), so too can human knowledge in a favorable environment produce artifacts, or social species. In both instances, improbable informational structures (or "know-how") direct "energy toward the transportation and transformation of materials into equally improbable structures of the phenotype or product" (Boulding, 1978, p. 106). So universal indeed is this process of production that Boulding, as we saw previously, recommended replacing economics' traditional triad of land–labor–capital as prototypical factors of production with the triad, energy–materials–information.[5] According to Boulding, economics' traditional classification is far too "imprecise."[6]

All production, whether organic or inorganic, according to Boulding, entails *selections*. Through sequences of behavior, knowledge structures "recognize" and correct divergence between actual and ideal states (Boulding, 1978, p. 108). These sequences he referred to as homeostatic or cybernetic mechanisms. Embryology is the study of such mechanisms in developing organisms, but for Boulding analogous are conscious processes of human decision-makers when producing social species. Decision-makers, Boulding wrote, bring mental contexts or "images" to production processes. These images are comprised of two parts, the first being a system of ideal values, goals or preferred states, and the second a notion of actual values or of actual states. The goal of decision-makers is always to reduce differences between the two images (Boulding, 1958, p. 93).[7]

Production of artifacts ("social species")

Boulding distinguished among three main types of human artifacts or "social species," namely *material artifacts*, that is material structures and objects such as buildings, machines and automobiles; *organizational structures*, that is human institutions, ranging from extended families and hunting bands to transnational corporations, governments and churches; and *biological artifacts*, under which heading Boulding included not only plants and animals altered by domestication, selective breeding and genetic engineering, but as well human beings.

Humans, Boulding declared, are to a considerable extent artifactual. While every person is, of course, produced *biologically* in accordance with information inherent to the genetic structure of the original fertilized egg, people are "produced" also in the cultural sense of acquiring learned images, knowledge, language skills, and so forth (Boulding, 1981, p. 24). Moreover "there is also an important internal learning process in which human beings help to create themselves" (Boulding, 1985, p. 72).

Despite remarkable similarities between biological and social processes of production, there are also, however, important differences. Whereas biological reproduction (birth) is occasioned by sexual union between two members of the same species, production of artifacts stems from "intercourse among a large number of artifacts of different kinds." Automobiles, for example, are compound entities consisting of myriad parts, each with its own informational ("genetic") structure. Whereas biological populations tend, eventually at least, toward zero growth in accordance with the Malthusian Population Principle and the "law of diminishing growth,"[8] no such tendency is apparent, according to Boulding, for human artifacts (social species) due to their multiparental, asexual origin (Boulding, 1978, p. 68).[9] Furthermore, unlike biogenetic information, knowledge of how to produce social species exists outside the phenotype, for instance, as blueprints, plans, templates, maps, chemical equations, books and in human memory; Boulding averred that this "extrinsic nature of the genome" permits and encourages rapid evolution, adding that specialized components of artifacts are particularly subject to continuous change as humans focus attention and work upon them (Boulding, 1981, p. 26).

A further important dissimilarity between organic and social processes of production concerns the introduction, reintroduction or perhaps affirmation[10] of "teleological" elements in evolutionary processes. Noogenetic[11] processes of teaching and learning, while in some ways similar to biogenetic processes of mutation and selection, were for Boulding unique in terms of obvious or manifest deliberation and purposefulness. "The human race," he wrote, "is not merely pushed by past events or present circumstances, but it is also pulled by its own images of the future into a future" (Boulding, 1978, p. 132). Humans, in other words, are "niche-expanders," unlike most other organisms that usually simply occupy niches and expand to fill them up.

Communication

Communication, for Boulding, is "any process that transfers some kind of significant structure or pattern from one system to another" (Boulding, 1985, p. 133). Physical systems (such as air, light, wires, paper, cables, invisible portions of the electromagnetic spectrum, and so forth) are "agents of communication," enabling this transfer. Communication takes place when images or information structures, encoded by physical carriers, reach their destination.

Production for Boulding, then, is a *communicatory* process. Production entails an image or information structure being "carried over" so as to bring about a higher order of complexity elsewhere. In *biogenetic production*, genetic information (or "know-how") is transmitted by genes from one generation to the next. In *noogenetic production*, "learned structures in central nervous systems or their equivalents … [are transmitted] by a learning process" (Boulding, [1979] 1995, p. 27). Parallels to the thought of Veblen in these matters are readily apparent.

Information, whether transmitted biogenetically or noogenetically, can be subject to alteration in transmission, a change often termed *evolution*. Boulding defined evolution as "a process of cumulative change of know-how" (Boulding, [1983] 1995, p. 47). *Biogenetic evolution* occurs when genetic information (or know-how) undergoes mutation, the mutant phenotype then being subject to selection processes in its environment. *Noogenetic evolution*, on the other hand, occurs when knowledge transmitted from one generation to another undergoes change and becomes subject to cognitive social selection processes (Boulding, [1979] 1995, p. 27).

For Boulding, "because human knowledge creates know-how—and know-how is the genetic factor of production that produces human artifacts—the growth of knowledge has irreversible effects" (Boulding, [1983] 1995, p. 51). Boulding saw the cumulative growth in know-how as constituting a primary explanation of "time's arrow," that is, the unidirectional or non-reversible property of time.

Social species and the ecosystem

Organic species and social species alike constitute components of *ecosystems*, defined by Boulding as "interacting populations of different species in which the birth and death rates of each population are a function of its own size and the size of the other populations with which it is in contact" (Boulding, 1985, pp. 23–4). Species, whether organic or social, occupy *niches*, defined by Boulding as the equilibrium populations of phenotypes in their ecosystems (Boulding, [1979] 1995, p. 27).

Social species are similar to organic species in the sense that both are "selected" for occupancy of niches. Commodities, for instance, at any moment have a population or stock that increases through production and decreases through consumption and, like biological species, they interact continuously, influencing each other's birth, growth and death rates.

Modes of species' interaction are various. Petroleum and automobiles, for Boulding, are in continuous symbiotic interaction, whereas inter-city trains and buses tend to interact competitively. Social artifacts may also be competitive with organic species (for example, automobiles with horses), or cooperative with them (for instance, chemical fertilizers with domesticated crops). Boulding also analyzed predator–prey relations and host–parasite relations (Boulding, [1962] 1963).

For him, "the fundamental principle of ecological evolution" is that "everything depends on everything else." This, he wrote, means that "there is no such thing as 'environment,' if by this we mean a surrounding system that is independent of what goes on inside it" (Boulding, 1978, pp. 224, 31).

Commoditized and non-commoditized species

Commoditized and non-commoditized species (whether biological or social), while alike in engaging in ecological interaction, differ by definition in the extent to which the price system, at least directly, mediates their ecological interactions. According to Boulding, "the niche of a commodity is determined mainly by the demand for it—that is, the willingness of people to purchase it" (Boulding, 1981,

p. 61), whereas the niche for non-commoditized biological species is determined by their ability to produce surviving offspring. The distinction, however, is by no means absolute: non-commoditized biological species are increasingly subject to ecological pressures stemming from markets; chain saws displace non-commoditized species living in rain forests, for example. "Environmental economists" recommend in principle that all non-commoditized species should be made over into commoditized species.

Information and knowledge structures

The information concept

We have seen how Boulding characterized production as the activation or functioning of a knowledge structure to bring about a more improbable material structure than had existed at the start of the process. Production, then, entails communication, since production means the carrying-over of a knowledge structure to a new location, and the fulfillment of its potential there. Utilizing potential inhering in knowledge structures does not necessarily mean, however, simply "the mechanical following of a previously known plan with all the potential present at the beginning." It can entail also "the creation of new potential under the stimulus of events that could not be predicted" (Boulding, [1983] 1995, p. 42).

Knowledge structures, or know-how, relate closely to *information* of course, and Boulding's typification of information contributes to our understanding of the correspondence between production and communicatory processes. "Information is not," he wrote, "a simple physical event such as a noise or a shape on a piece of paper." Rather, "it is an event in a context." And the context is the thing that really determines the significance, that is, the meaning or information-content, of the event (Boulding, 1958, p. 89).

Conceptually there are at least two contexts to consider in order to discern how meaning or significance is gleaned from stimuli, messages or events. One concerns the physical stimuli surrounding the information or event in question. "A word is not so much a *thing* as a *place* in a sentence," wrote Boulding (1958, p. 88); a word's meaning depends upon its context in its own sentence, and upon its place within the larger message or system of messages. Likewise, the "meaning" of a gene (the effect it produces) depends upon the complete genome.

Second, message recipients bring context to messages and events. Messages, comprised of signs and symbols, are decoded by means of the particular language or decoding system that the message recipient applies to them. Codes or languages, however, are social construction ("institutions," or "habits of thought," in Veblen's terms). A given symbol, therefore, can connote different meanings to different message recipients, depending upon which "language" or "dialect" the particular respondent applies to it, which will depend *inter alia* upon the culture or subculture within which the message recipient is immersed, and as well on his/her unique life experiences.

According to Boulding, therefore, information distinguishes *living* processes from purely mechanical ones. Whereas in mechanical processes a particular physical event always produces identical responses, for living systems there can be "varying responses to constant physical stimuli, depending on the 'significance' of the stimuli in an informational setting" (Boulding, 1958, p. 87). Boulding maintained that mainstream economics is too mechanical in its interpretation of life processes; consequently, he upbraided the discipline on the one hand for maintaining impoverished conceptions of information, and on the other for applying deterministic models to human (living) processes.

Knowledge

Boulding distinguished mere *information* from *knowledge*, the former term denoting sensory inputs (stimuli or messages) received by the brain, the latter implying structure. *Structure* Boulding defined as "a very complex and frequently quite loose pattern, almost like an enormous molecule, with its parts connected in various ways by ties of varying degrees of strength." Knowledge, for Boulding, is "mental structure" (Boulding, [1955] 1974, p. 23). Knowledge, or "image," or "information structure," for Boulding, derived from experience: "Part of the image is the history of the image itself" (Boulding, [1956] 1961, p. 6).[12]

At any moment, information (that is, sensory stimuli) bombards a person's knowledge structure. Messages in a sense are "shot into" the image. Behavioral psychologists, in attempting to reduce behavior to mere stimulus–response, Boulding suggested, commit a grievous error in failing to consider the knowledge structure, and "especially images of the future," which for him are decisive (Boulding, 1978, p. 109).

When an organism confronts messages or sensory stimuli there are, according to Boulding, not one but four possible consequences for image or knowledge structure. First, information may pass right through the knowledge structure's interstices, leaving it quite unaffected.

Second, messages can "stick" to the knowledge structure (what he called "addition"), leaving however the basic organization intact. Rote learning, he suggested, would be an example of "addition."

Third, and more interestingly, message reception can cause reorganization, whether great or small, in the knowledge structure. For Boulding, as for Marshall McLuhan, "the meaning of a message *is* the change which it produces in the image" (Boulding, [1956] 1961, p. 7; emphasis added). Likewise, *learning* Boulding defined as a change in the knowledge structure or image (Boulding, 1970, p. 9). If a message "hits some 'nucleus' that knocks the props out of a large area of the structure," he explained further, there will result "a very radical reorganization of the mental structure" (Boulding, [1955] 1974, p. 24). Such fundamental reorganizations, he believed, are rare. Usually people resist information fundamentally at odds with their knowledge structure.

Finally, the fourth possibility concerns dimensions of certainty and uncertainty, of probability and improbability, of clarity and vagueness. Elements of the knowledge structure are not uniformly certain, probable or clear. Informational stimuli, therefore, can either clarify or obscure images; they can make things previously regarded as less certain more certain, and vice versa (Boulding, [1956] 1961, p. 10).

Stability (resistance to change) of a knowledge structure, Boulding wrote, depends in part upon its internal consistency and its arrangement. As with some crystals and molecules, minimizing internal strain lends stability to knowledge structures (Boulding, [1956] 1961, p. 13). Boulding raised the difficult question of the optimal tradeoff between stability and adaptability of knowledge structures. Clearly, on the one hand, stability (that is, insensitivity to, or critical appraisal of, message inputs) is required as otherwise "the world would dissolve into a heap of incoherent impressions—automobiles would get bigger as they approached us, rooms would change shape as we walked through them." On the other hand, however, survival also requires that knowledge "map" adequately the outside world, that it adapt as changes occur in the environment.

Boulding noted also that the concept of "an optimum degree of sensitivity of the knowledge structure, useful as it may be, begs some of the ultimate metaphysical questions" (Boulding, [1955] 1974, p. 27).

Information, perception and the sociology of knowledge

Boulding on occasion distinguished also mere information (any and all messages or sensory inputs registered on the brain) from "signals." A *signal* he defined as "a non-random event set in the middle of a succession of random events (noise)." Since "all events, however, are events," there arises the problem of discriminating between signals and noise. Boulding proposed four possibilities. First, the signal receiver ("signal detector") may correctly recognize a signal as a signal (a "hit"); second, he/she may mistake a random event for a signal (a "false alarm"); third, the receiver may mistake a signal for a random event (a "miss"); fourth, the detector may correctly perceive a random event for what it is (a "negative hit," or a "correct rejection").

For any given intensity of signal relative to noise (signal to noise ratio), there is, according to Boulding, a mathematical function "relating the probability of a hit with the probability of a false alarm under 'optimal' behavior" (Boulding, [1955] 1974, p. 25); this function he termed the "signal detection curve." Cautious receivers score few hits but also give few false alarms, whereas reckless receivers attain many hits but give also more false alarms. Furthermore, payoffs and penalties for hits and false alarms respectively influence the positioning of a signal detector on the signal detection curve:

> The detector will be more reckless the greater the intrinsic probability that the signal is present, the smaller the rewards for correct rejection and the smaller the penalties for false alarms, and the greater the rewards for hits and the penalties for misses.
>
> (Boulding, [1955] 1974, p. 25)

The implications of this theory of signal detection, according to Boulding, are several and startling. With regard to the theory of perception, for instance, "the notion of a clear psycho physiological 'threshold' of signal intensity above which the signal is perceived and below which it is not," is questioned since, in Boulding's model, "all perception is only probable, and the greater the probability of hits the greater the probability also of false alarms" (Boulding, [1955] 1974, p. 25).[13]

As well the theory has implications for the problem of the validity of knowledge. Boulding's "organic theory of knowledge," he attested, challenges the purported "objectivity" of science, since "perception of anything cannot be divorced from the valuations which surround the act of perception." Indeed, he declared, "the whole concept of a 'fact' really disappears: all that is left are messages in noisy channels, and the interpretation of these messages as 'facts' depends in part on the value system of the observer" (Boulding, [1955] 1974, p. 25).[14]

In saying this, however, Boulding did not contend that images are purely private or subjective. To the contrary, he wrote,

> Part of our image of the world is the belief that this image is shared by other people like ourselves who are part of our image of the world. In common daily intercourse we all behave as if we possess roughly the same image of the world.... Where there is no universe of discourse, where the image possessed by the organism is purely private and cannot be communicated to anyone else, we say that the person is mad.
>
> (Boulding, [1956] 1961, pp. 14–15)

Boulding, then, continued in, and amplified, the tradition known as the sociology of knowledge developed by Veblen. Like Veblen, he too posited a "selection process" whereby images interact with environment, a continual testing to segregate and eliminate the ones not "fit" for survival (Boulding, 1978, p. 20).

Knowledge for Boulding was an "organic structure"[15] that grows, mutates, is selected, even dies. Like all structures, knowledge has an "embryology," starting off simple, then growing and developing, becoming increasingly complex. At each stage of development there are only certain alternative paths open; everything builds on what has gone before (Boulding, [1956] 1961, p. 95). As Boulding expressed it, "The tree of knowledge unfolds in good order and proper succession, first the blade and then the ear, first the trunk and then the branch." Growth in this "tree of knowledge," however, is also profoundly affected by outside conditions—it is "bent by storms or encouraged by sunshine in one direction or another."

Boulding noted as well an important difference between the "metabolism" of knowledge and biogenetic metabolism: The former does not obey the laws of thermodynamics, that is, the law of conservation and the law of entropy. For Boulding this distinction is most significant, and is addressed below.

Constituents of communicatory processes

Signs and symbols

In communicatory processes, signs and symbols are carried by media ("agents of communication") to the destination. *Signs* Boulding defined as information that alters an organism's image of its immediate surroundings. For Boulding all life participates at some level in communication through signs. Plants, for instance, lean in the direction of the sun, while social insects communicate with one another through signs (Boulding, [1956] 1961, p. 45). In contrast, *symbols* impact upon the "image of the image, on the image of the future, on the image of the past, on the image of the potential or even the image of the impossible" (Boulding, [1956] 1961, p. 44). When someone speaks, our image of our surroundings changes as we receive *signs* that someone is present; but in comprehending what is said the content of our imagination also is affected, and this "same" information becomes a *symbol*. What distinguishes human society from all other animal life, according to Boulding, is the high level of symbolic communication.

Media

Modes of communication (i.e., media) carry signs and symbols to the destination. Physical systems, then, are "agents of communication." In biogenetic systems the agent or carrier is DNA, genetic information being encoded in a double helix of carbon atoms with attached atoms of oxygen, hydrogen, nitrogen and carbon. In human social systems, by contrast, modes of communication (media) change through time and these changes, for Boulding (as for others, such as Harold Innis), lie at the very heart of societal evolution.

In non-literate societies, for example, "noogenetic" communication is limited to verbal rituals, poems, legends, ceremonies, and so forth. Writing, however, inaugurated what Boulding called the "disassociated transcript" (Boulding, [1956] 1961, p. 65), expanding enormously the temporal and spatial dimensions of communication and learning (Boulding, 1981, p. 122). Without records, complex organizational continuity from place to place and generation to generation would have been impossible. Nor could decision-makers have transmitted instructions as effectively to distant peripheries. With writing, the "total body of human knowledge potentially accessible to an individual grew constantly, as each generation left its deposit.... It was no accident," Boulding concluded, "that [western or modern] science comes along with printing" (Boulding, 1981, p. 128).

Inventions subsequent to printing (for instance, cameras and sound recordings), Boulding further opined, permit direct,[16] as opposed to symbolic, transcription of aspects of life and experience, although large portions thereof—smell, taste, touch, emotions, feelings—must still be stored and transmitted "through the crowded channels of symbolic representation" (Boulding, [1956] 1961, p. 65).

Innovations in media were, for Boulding, at the heart of the "organizational revolution," by which he meant the "great rise in the number, size, and power of organizations of many diverse kinds, and especially of economic organizations" (Boulding, [1953] 1968, p. xiii). He maintained that evolving media enable organizational growth in two principal ways. First, media help overcome external constraints. Revolutions in transportation (for example, railroads, steamships, automobiles, airplanes) and in communication (telegraph, telephone, radio) "pushed back the limitations of the environment [enabling organizations] to expand farther into [their] environment" (Boulding, [1953] 1968, p. 25). Second, media like typewriters, duplicators, calculators and computers facilitate internal communication (Boulding, [1953] 1968, p. 26). Without changes in media technology, internal communication for growing organizations would become increasingly difficult: relaying information from organizations' contact points with their environment to their decision-making centers, and as well transmittal of accurate instructions from centers to their peripheries, become more difficult as the number of messages increase exponentially with firm size. Evolving media, however, alleviate such internal constraints on organizational growth by increasing both the speed of message transmittal and organizations' capacities to process information (Boulding, [1953] 1968, p. 23).

Indeed communication media help alter fundamentally geo-social/cultural structures. Over the past couple of hundred years, "the world has changed from being a set of a considerable number of fairly isolated social systems ... into something approaching a single social system" (Boulding, 1985, p. 148). Initially ocean transport enabled transoceanic migrations and world trade; subsequently the telegraph, telephone, transoceanic cables, radio, television, communication satellites and optical fibers "played an overwhelmingly important role in this transformation into a single world system" (Boulding, 1985, p. 148). Transmissions of knowledge structures have affected profoundly "architecture around the world, tastes in food and clothing, music and art, and dancing," eroding local cultures and substituting in their place "superculture" (Boulding, 1985, p. 151).

Ways of communicating

Moreover, Boulding often invoked a triad of communicatory modes consisting of threat, exchange and love to typify instances of human communication. He affirmed, "All social organizations without exception are built by processes that can be classified into these three general types..." (Boulding, 1970, p. 27).

It was Boulding's position that market exchanges are necessarily rooted either in systems of love and integration, or in systems of threat; hence, he distinguished between "economies of love" and "economies of fear" (Boulding, 1973). Understanding the social system "as a total pattern, of which economics is only a part," led Boulding to depart from economic orthodoxy, and to conceive all human communication, including the traditionally "economic," as bearing elements of threat and love. Even the *grants economy* of one-way transfers, he noted, issues from these two different motivations—love giving rise to "gifts," and threat giving rise to "tribute" (Boulding, 1973, pp. v–vi).

Information, entropy and evolution

Laws of conservation, entropy and evolution

Boulding declared that evolution "is not a determinate system like celestial mechanics because it is not an equilibrium system."[17] Rather, it involves inherently unpredictable changes in parameters on account of "the long-run importance of improbable events" (Boulding, 1981, p. 69).

Mechanical and equilibrium processes, he explained are predictable or determinate because they involve matter and energy alone, and consequently physical (mechanical) laws apply to them. Matter and energy, for example, are subject to the Law of Conservation, also known as the First Law of Thermodynamics, which states that matter/energy can be neither created nor destroyed, only rendered more or less useful.

In thus distinguishing matter/energy on the one hand from information/knowledge on the other, two opposing forces or tendencies become evident. On the one hand is the Law of Entropy, known also as the Second Law of Thermodynamics, which states that increased disorder or randomness results from any process, that there is a tendency for states to become more probable, more chaotic, less ordered, less differentiated (Boulding, 1978, p. 10). The end of the universe, according to the Law of Entropy, is but a "thin soup without form." The counter-tendency, however, is the Law of Evolution, the capacity for complexity, organization, differentiation and structure to increase over time (Boulding, 1978, p. 10). Recall that Boulding defined *production* as processes that increase material complexity (Boulding, 1978, p. 34). Evidently production, and therefore information and communication, are inherent to the Law of Evolution.

Production and changes in processes of production, according to Boulding, are possible over the long term only because of the properties of information and knowledge, and in particular the inapplicability to information/knowledge of the Law of Conservation. Unlike matter and energy, knowledge can be reproduced without limit, can be shared simultaneously by many and can grow incrementally and suddenly. Boulding declared, "It is a powerful and accurate metaphor to see the whole evolutionary process from the beginning of the universe as a process in the increase of knowledge or the information structure" (Boulding, 1978, p. 33).

Knowledge and economic development

Economic development from Boulding's perspective consists of two processes "which go in opposite directions" (Boulding, 1981, p. 73). First is the using up of known stocks of matter and energy; second is "replenishment," by which he meant "the constant growth of knowledge and discovery" (Boulding, 1981,

p. 73). Discovery of so-called fossil fuels, for instance, "represented [an] enormous expansion of the energy inputs into human societies and temporarily at least expanded the human niche to the point where we find it today" (Boulding, 1981, p. 72). Since scarcity of energy and materials constrains economic development, whereas increments to knowledge serve to "push back" constraints, Boulding concluded that:

> In interpreting history one should look for the points at which knowledge rose to the point where new energy sources and new materials were captured for the productive process. The domestication of both crops and animals typified such occasions of fundamental change, increasing the efficiency of the capture of solar energy for human purposes. The development of the steam engine was a similar step forward.
>
> (Boulding, 1978, p. 225)

On the other hand, Boulding perceived those nations mired in underdevelopment as lacking the means of storing and distributing knowledge. Indeed, in his view, the world is quickly separating into two cultures. Those individuals and countries able to adapt to and utilize modern technology are growing richer, while those unable to adapt and utilize the new media are experiencing not only the collapse of their traditional cultures due to the onslaught of the "technical superculture," but as well they are becoming ever more "disorganized, delinquent, anemic and poor" (Boulding, [1966] 1995, p. 20).

Evolutionary directionality

Evolutionary processes, while inherently unpredictable, display distinct directionality toward "complexity and toward noogenetics and consciousness" (Boulding, 1978, p. 22). Boulding regarded the universe as having undergone three great stages of development: first was *physical evolution*, culminating in the appearance of DNA; second came *biological evolution*, giving rise to life forms of increasing complexity, culminating in human beings; and finally, *societal evolution*. As Boulding noted, "these three great evolutionary processes … are not independent of each other [but] constantly interact" (Boulding, 1978, p. 30).

The "sociosphere," consisting of humans, their organizations and artifacts, interacts profusely with the biosphere, causing, for instance, extinction of some species and domestication of others. Human knowledge and evaluations have even produced "very substantial rearrangements of existing genetic material." Boulding therefore conjectured, "It may well be that biological evolution is approaching its end and that it will be succeeded by an evolutionary process wholly dominated by noogenetic processes directed by human values" (Boulding, 1978, p. 22).

Human activity has also profoundly affected the earth's physical evolution:

> It has built dams, diverted rivers, dug mines, bulldozed mountains, eroded soil, and even created earthquakes; it has polluted the atmosphere, rivers,

> lakes and oceans; it has cut down forests and substituted agriculture; it has changed climates, at least over small areas, and perhaps over the whole earth; it has even gone to the moon and left its improbable artifacts.
>
> (Boulding, 1978, p. 31)

For Boulding, we live in the middle time, the epoch of "civilization," an intermediate state for humankind separating "pre-civilization" from "post civilization." "It is furthermore a rather disagreeable state for most people living in it, and its disappearance need occasion few tears" (Boulding, [1964] 1965, p. 2).

Boulding believed that throughout the epoch of civilization there has arisen "a slowly rising stream of knowledge and organization" of a quality different from that of the civilized society within which it has grown (Boulding, [1964] 1965, p. 5). Hence, he contended, humanity is entering a new era—*post-civilization*—an epoch based on knowledge, on science and on technology, as opposed to the mechanical and industrial processes of civilization (Boulding [1956] 1961, p. 37).

While the human niche "expanded enormously" during the neolithic period, "from perhaps ten million to hundreds of million" (Boulding, 1978, p. 17), the rise of science over the past five hundred years is expanding it dramatically once again (Boulding, 1978, p. 171).

How far this expansion can continue, however, is a moot question, insofar as part of the expansion is attributable to the discovery and utilization of non-renewable resources. And there is now a continual build-up of wastes.

"Post-civilization," then, must entail new awareness, altered perceptions and transformed goals. In the previous industrial (or "cowboy") economy, the earth was perceived as boundless, both in its supply of resource inputs and in its capacity to absorb waste. In our day, high production engendered by the harnessing of scientific knowledge to industry has, however, rendered that perception obsolete and dangerous. For post-civilization the requisite image is that of "spaceship earth," our island home, where both resource inputs and the capacity of the earth to absorb waste are recognized as being finite.

This new vision carries with it altered values. In post-civilization, consumption and production are no longer to be perceived as being good in and of themselves. To the contrary, they are to be regarded as things to be minimized. As Boulding advised, in the post-civilization, spaceship-earth economy, value needs to center on the nature, extent, quality and complexity of the total capital stock, which should be maintained using as few resource inputs as possible, rather than on production, consumption and throughputs. This is a lesson, he added, that is "very strange to economists, who have been obsessed with the income-flow concepts to the exclusion, almost, of capital-stock concepts" (Boulding, [1966] 1993, p. 304).

Usually quite buoyant, Boulding on occasion entertained dark thoughts with regard humankind's future. In his view, technological modes of communication and emerging world "superculture" carry high risks. He wrote:

> There are ... profound dangers. [And particularly] there is danger ... due to the lack of isolation. All systems face eventual catastrophe, that is death. The evolutionary process has survived the death of innumerable individuals and species because of isolation and diversity, but a single world system might face universal and irretrievable catastrophe. One world could lead to no world. The one source for hope is the unexhausted potential of the human mind and the unexhausted potential of the evolutionary process itself. Any species, the human race not excepted, from an evolutionary point of view is a transmitter of the process of increasing complexity. When its work is done, it passes from the scene. How long the human race will last, we do not know. At the rate at which we have speeded up the evolutionary process, the life span of all species may be diminishing markedly. We may not have long to go. If we produce our evolutionary successor, however, we will not have been wasted.
>
> (Boulding, [1979] 1995, pp. 37–8)

Recapitulation

According to Kenneth Boulding:

> The pattern of human development is ... an extension, enlargement, and acceleration of the pattern of biological development, operating through mutation and selection. Selection is ecological interaction constantly creating new niches and destroying old ones; mutation takes the form of invention, discovery, expansions of the noosphere and the human noogenetic structure.
>
> (Boulding, 1978, p. 18)

Malthus, Veblen and Boulding

Thomas Robert Malthus maintained that important parameters, such as the Law of Population and the Law of Arithmetic Food Increase, are most difficult to alter. The perceived intractability of these two "laws" for the Malthusian system, as we have seen, flows from the scant attention Malthus paid to information/communication. Communication in the Malthusian system was confined largely to commodity exchange relations and to conjugal acts of reproduction that he perceived were instinctual (mechanical), giving rise to the "law" of population. It is true that Malthus, in revisions to his first *Essay*, significantly modified his pessimism and determinism by acknowledging the possibility that the "instinct" to reproduce could be countered by "moral restraint," a possibility stemming from the human capacity to teach, learn and communicate. In the Malthusian system, therefore, we indeed detect an incipient theory of information/communication, giving rise to the possibility (albeit an improbable one, in Malthus's view) of fundamental shifts in society's basic parameters.

Thorstein Veblen seized and elaborated upon the notion that through communication all things can change, and do so unpredictably. Veblen defined institutions as "habits of thought." For him changes in habits of thought are intrinsic to social/cultural change. Successive generations of individuals differ little in intellectual capacity or in amorphous instinctual propensity, but ways of seeing and of doing (habits of thought and of action) can and indeed do undergo cumulative change. Through his concept of institution, therefore, Veblen substituted collectivities for Malthus's individuals. Furthermore, he privileged communication in his social analysis rather than individual struggle and biologically inherited traits. In so doing he opened up possibilities for fundamental social and individual change.

Evolutionary economics awaited the abundant and seminal work of Kenneth E. Boulding, however, before information, that which flows in communicatory processes, was made a primary subject of economic analysis. Through the body of his vast work Boulding has no peer in examining information as evolutionary and organizing agent. For him only "know-how," or its equivalent in the form of improbable genetic structures, grows or evolves, thus making knowledge and information crucial for evolutionary theory and for economic dynamics. Whereas matter and energy, quantifiable and subject to the Law of Conservation, are frequently amenable to mainstream (static, equilibrium) economic analyses, of the basic factors of production (as reformulated by Boulding), only information and knowledge can increase and be negentropic. Privileging knowledge and information shifts economics from a static, equilibrium, non-evolutionary mode to an evolutionary, developmental paradigm. This is one of the fundamental implications of information for economic analysis, and a summary of Boulding's immense contribution.

Malthus, Veblen and Boulding, each in his own way, provide a counterpoint to today's prevailing neoclassicism. Malthus demonstrated that human activity, particularly biological reproduction, can outgrow the sustaining capacity of the ecosystem. Therefore, he recommended that communication, in the form of education and moral instruction, attempt to alter otherwise ineluctable social parameters. Veblen went several steps further, arguing that no social parameters are intractable, they only seem to be fixed on account of our present-mindedness due to our immersion in the present social order and its singular "habits of thought." Kenneth Boulding elucidated on information as the agent transforming social parameters and undergirding all evolutionary processes.

These three great economists give us insight as to how information/communication can be more fully incorporated into an economics that will be no longer apologetic for a crisis-prone and markedly inegalitartian order, but one rather that helps usher in a new era—more just, ameliorative and ecologically sound.

Notes

1 This article was previously published in Robert E. Babe, *Communication and the Transformation of Economics: Essays in Information, Public Policy, and Political*

Economy, Critical Studies in Communication and in the Cultural Industries, Boulder and Oxford: Harper Collins, Westview Press, 1995, pp. 159–78.

2 He is mused that he was probably the first in his family to go beyond the eighth grade (Boulding, 1992, p. 69).

3 Similarly he declared that his professional life was spent studying two questions: "First, what does it mean to say that things have gone from bad to better rather than from bad to worse? Second, how do we get to better?" (Wright, 1988, p. 295).

4 Lamarck maintained that characteristics of the genotype are modified by the phenotype it creates, now a generally discredited view with regard to biogenetic processes. According to Boulding, however, the greater the noospheric (or knowledge-based) component of evolutionary processes, the more analogous to Lamarckian-type processes evolution becomes. *Biogenetic* mutations, that is, "changes in the structure of the genes and DNA" are "highly Mendelian," wrote Boulding, whereas *noogenetic* change, that is, changes in "learned structures in organisms that are transmitted from one generation to the next by a learning process" are Lamarckian, making evolution in our day, in Boulding's view, "extremely Lamarckian" (Boulding, 1985, p. 66).

5 This is not the "information" of Shannon and Weaver's "mathematical theory of communication," however. For Boulding, information "involves not only improbability of structure, but the structure's ability to 'instruct'; that is, to be a code of selection according to a program" (Boulding, 1978, p. 13).

6 Boulding's proposal, if accepted more widely, would affect dramatically "images" of economic processes. Consider, for example, implications for the Marxian theory of class struggle, and as well for neoclassical economics and its taxonomy of factor returns into rent, wages and interest.

7 When messages confirm that a discrepancy exists between actual and ideal states, ensuing action can be of three types. Action can modify internally the ideal image, bringing it more in line with the existing state of affairs (one becomes more "realistic"). Alternatively energy may be expended on the external environment with the intent of bringing that more in line with the ideal. As a third, and probably most common possibility, action can modify both the ideal and the real. In any event, decisions or actions stem not merely from the flow of sensory stimuli, as would be the case with purely mechanical systems of cause and effect, but from "the change in context which that information provides" (Boulding, 1958, p. 90).

8 All *biological* species, Boulding maintained, are subject to the "law of diminishing growth" whereby growth rates eventually decline to zero (Boulding, 1981, p. 11). Populations that are increasing continually will normally face the specter of overcrowding, lack of food, conflict or other degradations, at which point birth rates will fall or death rates rise, establishing eventually an "equilibrium" where these two rates are equal, unless and until parameters of the niche change. The economists' famous "law of diminishing returns" is, then, but a special instance of this more general law, whose proof is established merely by noting the impossibility of growing the world's food supply in a flower pot (Boulding, 1978, p. 110).

9 On the other hand, Boulding acknowledged, populations of artifacts and organic species are alike in expanding or contracting in accordance with changes "in the total condition of the system" (Boulding, 1978, p. 69).

10 Boulding, unlike Veblen, certainly did not dismiss the possibility, or even likelihood, of teleological elements being inherent in the universe. He wrote that this, however, is an item of speculation or of faith, a proposition that cannot be confirmed "scientifically."

11 *Noogenetic* is a term Boulding derived from *noosphere*, a term first used by the Jesuit Pierre Teilhard de Chardin, whose *Phenomenon of Man* ([1955] 1970) was for Boulding particularly influential. Boulding distinguished between *biogenetic processes*—those producing phenotypes, through inherited genetic structures, and *noogenetic processes*—which refer to structures within the central nervous system of the

individual organism that must be learned from parents or other environments (Boulding, 1978, p. 14).

12 He elucidated further as follows:

> At one stage the image, I suppose, consists of little else than an undifferentiated blur and movement. From the moment of birth, if not before, there is a constant stream of messages entering the organism from the senses. At first, these may merely be undifferentiated lights and noises. As the child grows, however, they gradually become distinguished into people and objects. The conscious image has begun.
>
> (Boulding, [1956] 1961, p. 6)

13 Nonetheless, as Ian Parker in private correspondence has noted:

> Notwithstanding the probabilistic character of perception, the "threshold" notion is not necessarily obsolete. In the first place, there *are* psycho physiological limits on perception: e.g. dog whistles. Second, signals can be intensified and enhanced to sharpen the differentiation between them and noise, if it is technically feasible and economically advantageous. Third, "noise" filters can perform the same function, and/or more redundancy or repetition built into the system. Fourth, apart from all of the above, there is (in hearing experiments, for instance) a range of volumes or intensities such that a signal will *never* be reported [at low intensities or low signal-noise ratios], and *always* be reported (correctly) [at high intensities or high signal-noise ratios].

In Parker's view, Boulding described an intermediary range between the extremes beyond which, on the one hand, it is impossible to detect signals due to high noise, and on the other where signals will always be detected.

14 Elsewhere Boulding wrote that science is a subculture for direct testing of new ideas, serving thereby to increase dramatically humanity's capacity for knowledge growth. Science, however, is quite restricted in the types of ideas it can test. "We cannot do experiments on unique events, and we cannot experiment on the past." Scientific testing applies only to systems that are "stable, repeatable and divisible" (Boulding, 1981, p. 10). As with all images, scientific knowledge to survive must be born anew into the minds of each succeeding generation through the selective processes of teaching and learning (Boulding, 1970, pp. 9–10).

15 Boulding used the word "organic" to describe open systems which maintain their structure even while taking things from their environment and depositing other things into it (Boulding, [1956] 1961, p. 33). He wrote: "When I say that knowledge is an organic structure, I mean that it follows principles of growth and development similar to those with which we are familiar in complex organizations and organisms" (Boulding, [1956] 1961, p. 17).

16 As Ian Parker has noted, however, the distinction between "direct" and "indirect" is complex and ambiguous. Parker writes: "I would lean toward the view that 'cameras and sound recordings' generate *indirect, symbolic* messages (cf. Walter Benjamin *et al.*) especially once one allows for the editing process."

17 To help explain inherent evolutionary trends toward complexity and order, Boulding classified processes as being: *equilibrium processes*, in which disturbances result in dynamic processes to restore equilibrium; *cyclical processes*, in which patterns are repeated time and time again; and *cumulative processes*, where there is never a return to a previous position but in which nonetheless a consistency in the pattern of change can be detected. Most teleological processes are cumulative, as are evolutionary processes (Boulding, 1970, p. 15).

References

Boulding, K. [1953] 1968. *The Organizational Revolution: A Study in the Ethics of Economic Organization*. Chicago: Quadrangle Books.

Boulding, K. [1955] 1974. "Notes on the Information Concept," in *Collected Papers, Volume 4: Toward a General Social Science*, edited by L.D. Singell. Boulder, CO: Colorado Associated University Press.

Boulding, K. [1956] 1961. *The Image: Knowledge and Life in Society*. Ann Arbor, MI: University of Michigan Press.

Boulding, K. 1958. *The Skills of the Economist*. Toronto, ON: Clarke, Irwin and Co.

Boulding, K. [1962] 1963. *Conflict and Defense: A General Theory*. New York: Harper & Row, Publishers.

Boulding, K. [1964] 1965. *The Meaning of the Twentieth Century: The Great Transition*. New York: Harper and Row.

Boulding, K. [1966] 1993. "The Economics of the Coming Spaceship Earth," in *Environmental Quality in a Growing Economy: Essays from the Sixth RFF Forum*, edited by H. Jarrett. Baltimore: John Hopkins University Press. Reprinted in *Valuing the Earth: Economics, Ecology, Ehtics*, edited by Herman E. Daly and Kenneth N. Townsend. Cambridge, MA: MIT Press, pp. 297–309.

Boulding, K. [1966] 1995. "Expecting the Unexpected: The Uncertain Future of Knowledge and Technology," in *Prospective Changes in Society by 1980 Including Some Implications for Education*. Reprinted in *The Future: Images and Processes*, edited by E. Boulding and K. Boulding. Thousand Oaks, CA: Sage Publications, pp. 7–25.

Boulding, K. 1970. *A Primer on Social Dynamics: History as Dialectics and Development*. New York: The Free Press, Collier-Macmillan.

Boulding, K. 1973. *The Economy of Love and Fear: A Preface to Grants Economics*. Belmont: Wadsworth.

Boulding, K. 1978. *Ecodynamics: A New Theory of Societal Evolution*. Beverly Hills, CA: Sage Publications.

Boulding, K. [1979] 1995. "The Limits to Societal Growth," in *Social Growth: Processes and Implications*, edited by A. H. Hawley. Reprinted in *The Future: Images and Processes*, edited by E. Boulding and K. Boulding. Thousand Oaks, CA: Sage Publications, pp. 26–38.

Boulding, K. 1981. *Evolutionary Economics*. Beverly Hills, CA: Sage Publications.

Boulding, K. [1983] 1995. "World Society: The Range of Possible Futures," in *How Humans Adapt: A Biocultural Odyssey*, edited by D. J. Ortner. Washington, DC: Smithonian Press. Reprinted in *The Future: Images and Processes*, edited by E. Boulding and K. Boulding. Thousand Oaks, CA: Sage Publications, pp. 39–56.

Boulding, K. 1985. *The World as a Total System*. Newbury Park, CA: Sage Publications.

Boulding, K. 1992. "From Chemistry to Economics and Beyond," in *Eminent Economists*, edited by M. Szenberg. Cambridge: Cambridge University Press, pp. 69–83.

Bronowski, J. [1956] 1972. *Science and Human Values*. New York: Perennial Library.

Teilhard de Chardin, P. [1955] 1970. *The Phenomenon of Man*. Glasgow: William Collins Sons & Co., Ltd.

Wright, R. (1988) *Three Scientists and Their Gods. Looking For Meaning in an Age of Information*. New York: Times Books.

5b Comment: On "the pathologies of persuasion"

Robert E. Babe

Kenneth Boulding's "The pathologies of persuasion" appeared in a 1989 book of essays honoring John Kenneth Galbraith (Boulding 1989). For many years prior to this publication, terms cognate to persuasion—information, communication, education, knowledge, learning, teaching, adaptation, evolution—had been central to Boulding's work. By and large, however, prior to this point he had given short shrift to both "pathologies" and "persuasion."

In medicine, "pathology" is the scientific study of disease—its causes, processes and effects. In writing about "the pathologies of persuasion," then, Boulding was presumably concerning himself with "diseases" or undesirable effects stemming from persuasion. For purposes of this comment, what is most striking about the Galbraithian connection is how that, evidently, induced Boulding to confront directly *pathologies* or negativities of communication and/or persuasion.

Galbraith and Boulding, both legendary "institutional" economists, were of substantially different outlooks and dispositions. Galbraith was a skeptic whose humor often dripped with sarcasm. Boulding, although certainly not bereft of humor (his quip, the "immaculate conception of the indifference curve," aptly reappears in the "pathologies" article), was, in contrast, an idealist, a systems builder, a progressive evolutionist. Those familiar with Boulding's work will attest that he was an inveterate optimist; in his own words, he chose to study how "things have gone from bad to better rather than from bad to worse" (Wright 1988: 295). It is in his idealism and optimism that I find the likeliest explanation why both "pathologies" and "persuasion" figured so little in Boulding's writings prior to 1989.

One of Galbraith's major constructs was "The Revised Sequence," a term he used to summarize customers being routinely persuaded into desiring precisely what the "Technostructure" (the "brain" of corporations) planned to offer (Galbraith 1967: 71, 211ff.). For Galbraith, the Revised Sequence turned on its head the doctrine of consumer sovereignty which, along with its contingent postulate, "economic man" (Boulding 1989: 4), historically has been a primary "justification" for private enterprise, deregulated markets and an unfettered price system (Smith 1937; Hayek 1945). Arguably, the logic of the Revised Sequence subverts, too, the most cherished conceptions of democracy if and when it is applied to the political realm (Lippmann 1922). Boulding evidently had Galbraith's Revised Sequence firmly in mind when confronting persuasion and its "pathologies" (Boulding 1989: 5 n. 3).

In this comment I will first briefly review how Boulding treated information, communication, education, knowledge, teaching, learning and persuasion prior to writing the "Pathologies" article. Next, I will show how he altered fundamentally his approach to communication etc. in the "Pathologies" article. Then, I will show that Boulding's optimism and idealism evidently caused him to neglect some major pathologies and overlook two expansive literatures relating to them. In the final section, I assess Boulding's legacy, and in particular point to the bulwark he constructed against contemporary poststructuralist positions.

Information, communication, knowledge and persuasion in Boulding's system

Boulding was an "Enlightenment" scholar, albeit one living in the twentieth century. He believed, ultimately, in the unity of knowledge. Moreover, he maintained that increases in knowledge lead inexorably to human betterment. His understanding of and approaches to "information" and "communication" grounded, and were grounded in, these two propositions. Stated obversely, there is precious little in Boulding's work indicating that "information" or "communication" can debase and/or fracture knowledge or human society—a "poststructuralist" position.

The unity of existence in Boulding's system

Boulding confessed "to a strong interest in the integration of knowledge" (Boulding 1958: 131). Nowhere is this more evident than in his treatment of production.

Boulding defined *production*, both biological and industrial, as processes whereby an *information or knowledge structure* directs energy to transport, transform, and/or rearrange materials into less probable structures (Boulding 1978: 12, 34). When a seed germinates in the ground, its informational or knowledge structure (DNA) utilizes and directs energy to draw selectively upon nutrients or "building materials" in the soil to produce its phenotype (the plant). Similarly, a housing contractor, after studying a blueprint and comprehending the knowledge or instructions embedded therein, expends energy to assemble and rearrange materials to produce a more complex or improbable structure than had existed previously. *Production*, therefore, is essentially a *communicatory* process—a process so universal in Boulding's view that he recommended replacing land–labor–capital as economics' prototypical factors of production with the triad energy–materials–information.

Boulding understood humans, too, as being products of production processes—in two senses. First, people are produced biogenetically in accordance with information/instructions comprising their genetic structures. Second, they are produced "noogentically" when they acquire knowledge, languages, skills, customs, and so forth (Boulding 1981: 24). Whereas in biogenetic production, "information is transmitted by genes from one generation to the next," with noogenetic production "learned structures in central nervous systems or their equivalents ... [are transmitted] by a learning process" (Boulding and Boulding 1995: 27). Boulding defined both *communication* and *teaching* as "any process that transfers some kind of significant structure or pattern from one system to another" (Boulding 1985: 133). *Learning* for him comprises changes in an individual's "image" or knowledge structure (Boulding 1956: 54–55).

To summarize, Boulding proposed a unity among industrial production, biological reproduction and cultural production/reproduction; and he based this unity on a triad of constructs—information, knowledge and transmission (or communication). Boulding's remarkable insight has vast heuristic potential.

Information, communication and human betterment

In addition to championing the principle of unified knowledge, Boulding also held a seemingly unshakable belief in the inevitability of human betterment. He saw the world as being subject to the *Law of Evolution*, which he defined as the capacity for complexity, organization, differentiation and structure to increase over time (Boulding 1978: 10). He posited three major stages of development: *physical evolution*, culminating with the appearance of DNA; *biological evolution*, giving rise to life forms of increasing complexity culminating in the appearance of human beings; and *societal evolution*, based on growth in knowledge. He proposed that, although evolutionary processes are inherently unpredictable, they do display directionality toward "complexity and toward noogenetics and consciousness" (Boulding 1978: 22). Boulding maintained that in our era, changes in noogenetic structures spearhead evolutionary processes.

Boulding wrote that we live now in a middle time, the epoch of "civilization"—a period between "pre-civilization" and "post-civilization" (Boulding 1964: 2). Throughout the epoch of civilization, there has arisen "a slowly rising stream of knowledge and organization" of a quality different from that of the civilized society (Boulding 1964: 5). Hence, he contended, humanity's new era—*post-civilization*—will be knowledge-based, developing particularly from scientific knowledge and technology as opposed to the mechanical and industrial processes of "civilization" (Boulding 1956: 37). Whereas in the era of *civilization* people regarded the earth as boundless, both in its supply of resources and its capacity to absorb waste, for *post-civilization* the requisite image is that of "spaceship earth," where both resource inputs and the capacity of the earth to absorb waste are recognized as finite. Boulding largely left unaddressed, however, the role of "persuasion"—as distinct from "teaching" or "education"—in bringing about the requisite shift in values and understandings.

"Persuasion"

The term "persuasion" rarely appears in Boulding's writings.[1] In *The Image* (1956), his inaugural book on perception, communication and learning, he used the word but once:

> Changes in the image [knowledge structure] as a result of symbolic intercourse would depend, of course, on the skill of the communicators as well as on the initial situation. The whole art of persuasion is the art of perceiving the weak spots in the images of others and of prying them apart with well-constructed symbolic messages.
>
> (Boulding 1956: 134)

Equating persuasion with spotting "weak spots" in another's understanding, and "prying them apart," certainly smacks of aggressively changing the minds of other persons, as opposed to more moderately "informing," "convincing" or "educating" them.

Similarly, in *Conflict and Defense* (1962), Boulding characterized persuasion as follows:

> The whole vast art of persuasion, however, whether expressed in advertising, missionary work, government propaganda, or political-party campaigning, can be interpreted as attempts on the part of some organizations to affect the behavior of other organizations favorably to the first.
>
> (Boulding 1962: 164)

Here Boulding highlighted the notion that with "persuasion" the effort made is to convert the reader or auditor primarily to benefit the message sender, the contrast implicitly being to educators disinterestedly wishing to benefit message recipients into accepting truer or more useful (for them) points of view.

Likewise in his microeconomics textbook, Boulding noted that most advertising

> unfortunately, is devoted to an attempt to build up in the minds of the consumer irrational preferences for certain brands of goods. All the arts of psychology—particularly the art of association—are used to persuade consumers … There is very little place in the technique of advertising for the sober, truthful presentation of the qualities and prices of commodities.
>
> (Boulding 1966: 513)

In *The World as a Total System* he wrote, somewhat more expansively:

> In both economic and political life, however, there is not merely the communication of information. There is also persuasion, which can easily take pathological forms. Advertising can certainly be divided into purely

> communicative advertising, of which want ads are a fairly good example, and persuasive advertising, which is designed to change the potential purchaser's value structure in such a way as to induce an acceptance of the exchange offer that otherwise might not be taken up. Sometimes this persuasion has very little to do with the merits of the commodity itself. It appeals to all sorts of extraneous values associated with sex or prestige, or even plain human gullibility.
>
> (Boulding 1985: 143)

It is interesting that in this extract, echoing his treatment in *Microeconomics*, Boulding illustrated persuasion by pointing to advertisers marketing products through irrational associations, a depiction quite consistent with the Revised Sequence. However, here he proposed also that persuasion differs from the mere "communication of information," and that it can indeed "take pathological forms," evidently because it can be deceptive (untrue) and/or because it may use unfair (psychological) strategies.

From the foregoing extracts then, we can discern that, in Boulding's mind, "persuasion" is the dark side of communication, and stands in stark contrast to teaching/learning, which would be the enlightenment side. However, notwithstanding scattered (negative) references, the point also remains that, prior to his 1989 article, "persuasion" was at most an afterthought in Boulding's work; it seldom appeared, and when it did it served mainly to slightly dampen his ebullience in contemplating evolutionary betterment though information, knowledge and communication.

Persuasion in "The pathologies of persuasion"

Contrary to his previous writings, in "The pathologies of persuasion" Boulding not only highlighted persuasion, but also treated it much more favorably. Now, he proposed that persuasion is a "part of the human learning process," and hence, is a part of "the essence of the social dynamics of society" (Boulding 1989: 4). Here, he defined persuasion merely as an attempt to "change the mind" of another, and as modifying "the internal universe, or the image of the world which is possessed by the knower" (Boulding 1989: 4, 6), thereby making persuasion akin to teaching or education. In "Pathologies," moreover, Boulding even declared: "Persuasion plays a crucial role in all social systems [and] without it society probably could not exist" (Boulding 1989: 3). He added that persuasion is the "matrix" within which the three basic coordinating systems—threat, integration and exchange—function. He then proceeded to enumerate five "areas of life" where an active persuader/more passive persuadee relationship is vital: the family, formal education, religion, politics and business/economic life (Boulding 1989: 10–12).

Due to the importance yet uncertainty of successful persuasion, Boulding remarked, a "persuasion industry" arose, which employs all sorts of irrational appeals. It is at this point that he finally turned to the *pathologies* of persuasion

(Boulding 1989: 15). For him, the "greatest pathology of persuasion is that it may produce error;" he defined error as "images in the minds of the persuaded that *do not correspond* to something in the real world" (Boulding 1989: 15; emphasis added).

Boulding's definition of error does raise difficulties. Perhaps his phrase, "correspond to" implies that Boulding here assumed a staunchly "realist" position of "things in themselves" (*Ding ansich*), in which case if one's image does not exactly "map" the exterior world, one is in error. He illustrated his position by referring to pink elephants and how that imaginary beast has no correlate in the material world; in other words, the imaginary construct is belied by sensory experience. Hence, to be "persuaded" into believing in the existence of pink elephants is to fall into "error"—ergo, a "pathology of persuasion."

On the other hand, Boulding of course emphatically insisted that we do not confront sensory stimuli directly; rather, we process stimuli with our internal knowledge structures (or "images"). This would argue against him having adopted a strictly realist (or *Ding ansich*) position. But, again on the other hand, one senses in Boulding's work a strong insistence that through time we can and do come closer to knowing things as they "really" are:

> At the … level of scientific knowledge, of course, these regularities become explicit. They are embodied in mathematical formulae, from which precise images of the future are derived and can be tested. *The testing process, however, is crucial to the development of knowledge of all kinds.*
>
> (Boulding 1989: 8; emphasis added)

In addition to pink elephants, Boulding illustrated "error" and "pathologies" by referring to charismatic preachers, rain dancers, alchemists, Marxists, mainline economists, behavioral psychologists and marketers. Below we will have occasion to touch upon astrologers.

Significantly, however, Boulding declined to mention as a possibility of the "pathologies" of persuasion the targeting of *values* and *emotions*, and through that the odious biasing of attitudes toward entities in the real world (fascist propagandists did this, for example). To be sure, he acknowledged that "a part of our knowledge structure is a set of preferences" and added that "almost the whole preference structure of the adult has been learned … We are persuaded of our values" (Boulding 1989: 8, 9; see also Boulding 1958: 163). But values, of course, are not subject to the rigors of scientific testing; nor are "good" ones necessarily affirmed by our sensory inputs. Yet, as Boulding wholeheartedly agreed, values *are* subject to persuasion, and they do color the meanings we attach to things in the world. The role of values in our cognition undermines any *Ding ansich* postulate, and hence renders incomplete Boulding's definition of "pathology." Fascists did not try to persuade others that Jews existed where they did not, but they certainly did try to persuade people into how they should regard them—a "pathology" of persuasion if ever there was one.

Nor in discussing "pathologies" did Boulding mention systematic obscuring or censoring from consciousness things or events in the world at a distance (in terms either of time or space), and hence beyond direct sensory testing—this being, incidentally, a major component of Noam Chomsky's press criticisms (Chomsky 1989). There are, in brief, political- and economic-power issues behind what we *can* (or are allowed to) come to know, but these are not addressed in Boulding's chapter.

Boulding next remarked that in our time, "the information industry is growing very rapidly as a percentage of the total economy." Gloomily he added that this could mean that "the pathologies of persuasion [will] become more and more important" (Boulding 1989: 18). On the other hand, in concluding the article, he reaffirmed his optimism by suggesting that rapid developments in information technologies may "*countervail*" (another of Galbraith's concepts) concentrations of communicatory power. He declared: "The pathologies of persuasion are not wholly incurable and ... the very technology of information itself [may provide] countervailing power" (Boulding 1989: 19). This "countervailing power" may even arise, he suggested, from "voices in the wilderness," concluding: "There is much hope for the future" (Boulding 1989: 19).

While we may well hope that Boulding is right, one wonders whether he was not, perhaps, a touch too optimistic in placing his chips on countervailing power. Granted that "technologies of information" can be used by dissenters as well as elites, it is nonetheless surely the latter who possess the wherewithal to make their communication more pervasive and "persuasive." Much could be written on this issue, but unfortunately I must drop it here.

Neglected literatures and omitted pathologies

Boulding began his "Pathologies" article by claiming that, despite persuasion's universality and significance, it "has been much neglected, both by social scientists and by moral philosophers" (Boulding 1989: 3). He pointed specifically to orthodox economics, psychology, sociology and (as just mentioned) moral philosophy as being deficient in this regard. Several decades prior to the appearance of Boulding's "Pathologies" article, however, and contemporaneous with (and even prior to) his earliest writings on "the Image," there were available large and influential literatures on persuasion—from both social scientists and moral philosophers. It behooves the present commentator, then, to place Boulding's writings in the context of relevant scholarship then accessible but not addressed.

American communication study

American communication study was born between the wars. In 1918, upon America's entry into World War I, President Woodrow Wilson established the Committee on Public Information (CPI) as "the nation's first 'propaganda ministry' " (Glander 2000: 5).[2] The agency was deemed necessary, in part at least, due to Wilson's campaign slogan of 1916: "He kept us out of the war" (Ewen 1996:

104). George Creel, who headed the new agency, amongst other tactics enlisted the graphic arts, including the nascent movie industry, to help mobilize support for the war effort. As Stuart Ewen writes,

> Film was developing its own, unparalleled idiom of persuasion—a language that touched the recesses of inner life and spoke the uncanny vocabulary of dreams, permitting storytellers to enchant an audience silently with deep, psychologically charged ways of seeing ... Film had revealed a new, uncanny ability to transcend facticity for the purposes of persuasion, to reach a public on another, more emotional level ... Employing this powerful new tool—with all its suggestive implications—the CPI's Division of Films launched an unprecedented effort to deploy movies as implements of war.
>
> (Ewen 1996: 115)

In 1928 Edward Bernays, pioneer of US public relations, reflected on the successes of wartime propaganda, and remarked,

> [During the war] the manipulators of patriotic opinion made use of the mental clichés and the emotional habits of the public to produce mass reactions against the alleged atrocities, the terror and the tyranny of the enemy. It was only natural, after the war ended, that intelligent persons should ask themselves whether it was not possible to apply a similar technique to the problems of peace.
>
> (Bernays 1928: 28)

Bernays added: "We are governed, our minds are molded, our tastes formed, our ideas suggested, largely by men we have never heard of" (Bernays 1928: 9).

In 1939, prior to America's entry into World War II, there formed in Washington through Rockefeller Foundation funding a "Communication Seminar," attended over the next few years by some of the most notable of communication scholars, including Paul Lazarsfeld, Hadley Cantril and Harold Lasswell. The Seminar was, according to Jefferson Pooley, "a self-conscious precursor to the government propaganda campaigns of the war" (Pooley 2008: 51). The Seminar's work, also according to Pooley, had two converging agendas: "to map out the scientific study of mass communication, and to design an extragovernmental plan for combating Nazi propaganda and mobilizing war support" (Pooley 2008: 52). In July 1940 the Seminar issued a report entitled, "Research in Mass Communication," stating:

> We believe ... that for leadership to secure that consent [to engage in the war] will require unprecedented knowledge of the public mind and of the means by which leadership can secure consent ... We believe ... that we have available today methods of research which can reliably inform us about the public mind and how it is being, or can be, influenced in relation to public affairs.
>
> (quoted in Pooley 2008: 53)

The authors of the report also declared that mass communication was worthy of support as the ensuing research findings could indicate means of controlling public opinion: "Government which rests upon consent rests also upon knowledge of how best to secure consent. Research in the field of mass communications research is a new and a sure weapon to achieve that end" (quoted in Glander 2000: 46).

Once war was declared, the US government, through various departments and agencies, gathered in Washington "an invisible college of communication scholars" (Rogers 1994: 11), including: Lasswell, Cantril, Rensis Likert, Leonard Doob, Wilbur Schramm, Leo Lowenthal, Lazarsfeld, Frank Stanton, George Gallup, Elmo Roper, Ithiel de Sola Pool, Daniel Lerner, Edward Shils, Carl Hovland, Louis Gutman and Robert Merton (Simpson 1994: 26–29). Among the agencies the government set up was the Office of War Information (OWI), which comprised several divisions dealing respectively with the news, radio, motion pictures and publications/graphics. OWI created and censored news reports and radio programs, and it sponsored films (such as *Mission to Moscow* and *Song of Russia* to counter decades-long anti-Soviet propaganda) (Glander 2000: 52–53). It surveyed US public opinion, thereby assessing its successes and failures in molding opinion. Several of the social scientists who inaugurated mass communication programs in universities after the war were housed in OWI.

Wartime psychological research into opinion control, then, inaugurated communication study in the United States (Rogers 1994; Schramm 1997; Delia 1987; Pooley 2008). For both the sponsoring government agencies and for the assembled social scientists, "mass communication [was] an instrument for persuading or dominating targeted groups" (Simpson 1994: 6).

The first postwar American textbook in communication study was *Mass Communication*, edited by Wilbur Schramm (1949). In 1954, Schramm published a second textbook, *The Process and Effects of Mass Communication*, which was originally intended to be a training manual for the US Information Agency. The revised edition, co-edited by Schramm and Donald Roberts, appeared in 1971, and "for many years [was] the best-selling and by far the most influential textbook in the field" (Jansen 2008: 83, 104, n. 59). Schramm, who worked in Washington as a propagandist during the war, consulted government for two decades after the war as a cold warrior[3]; he "virtually defined what would become the dominant paradigm in the [mass communication] field for the next three decades" (Jansen 2008: 83).

Certainly propaganda, psychological warfare, underhanded techniques of persuasion (Gitlin 2007), racial stereotyping, arousal of fear and aggression, etc., would have been relevant and important "pathologies" for Boulding to have explored in the context of his model linking biological, industrial and noogenetic processes, and as well with regard to his treatment of persuasion as the commonality in exchange threat, and integrating social systems. It is interesting to speculate how these unmentioned "pathologies," and the burgeoning "how-to" social science literature, would have affected his analyses had he taken them into account.

Just to continue the story briefly: In waging wars against Panama (1989) and Iraq (1991), the US government mobilized public opinion in part by demonizing those countries' leaders, Manuel Noriega and Saddam Hussein. Without demonization, i.e., the deliberate construction of objects of hatred, it is unlikely public opinion would have supported the invasions. Contemporaneously, there were other national leaders rivaling those two on any bastardly deeds scale—Augustus Pinochet and General Suharto, for instance—but they were largely exempt from a bad press in the USA and from censure by the US government. Censorship, censure, biasing values, stereotyping, implanting false stories and enlisting emotions are tried and true weapons within the arsenal of psychological warfare, and their use can lead to hundreds of thousands, even millions, of deaths.

Theodor Adorno and the critical school

In addition to the research literature by social scientists cited above, there was also readily available at the time Boulding wrote a more philosophically and critically inclined literature on persuasion. Here, I will focus on writings of Theodor Adorno, a major figure in the Frankfurt School of Critical Theory.

Adorno (1903–1969) was a German philosopher, sociologist, musician, composer, musicologist and political economist. Son of a well-to-do Jewish wine merchant, he fled Nazi Germany for the USA prior to World War II, resettling in Germany in the early 1950s. Animating much of his work was a revulsion at and fear of anti-Semitism, ethnocentrism, authoritarianism, irrationalism, conformity and cultures of compliance. Ominously, he believed he had detected disquieting similarities between American commercial (popular) culture and German fascist propaganda through the period of roughly 1935 to 1955. With Max Horkheimer, Adorno invented the construct *the culture industry* to help describe and investigate properties and consequences of culture mass-produced and reinforced by profit-seeking institutions.

For Adorno, the astrology column of the *Los Angeles Times* was but one instance of a broader trend within commercial mass media of surreptitiously promoting audience conformity, psychological dependence, paternalism and irrationality—all of which, he believed, were conducive to strengthening fascism in America (Adorno 1974: 46). In his essay, "The Stars Down to Earth," for example, he pointed to the essentially conservative ideology promoted by the astrology column of the *Los Angeles Times*—particularly how it justified the status quo and promoted social conformity. He declared, "The column attempts to satisfy the longings of people who are thoroughly convinced that others (or some unknown agency) ought to know more about themselves and what they should do than they can decide for themselves" (Adorno 1974: 52). The column urged readers to adjust themselves "to the commands of the stars at given times," implicitly emphasizing "the individual's powerlessness" in the face of cosmic design (Bernstein 1991: 12).

More generally it was Adorno's contention that entertainment is, ipso facto, "persuasive" in the sense that "pleasure always means not to think about anything, to forget suffering even where it is shown. Basically it is helplessness." He added: "The liberation which amusement promises is freedom from thought and from negation" (Horkheimer and Adorno 1991: 144).

In "Anti-Semitism and Fascist Propaganda" (1946) and in *The Psychological Technique of Martin Luther Thomas' Radio Addresses* (2000), Adorno disclosed that American fascist propaganda, like the astrology column, was "primarily of a psychological nature" (Adorno 1946: 218). He had no difficulty identifying blatantly anti-Semitic, fascist radio commentators.[4] Although often touching on economic, political and social problems, these American fascist propagandists persuaded by playing on people's "unconscious mechanisms."

Unlike Boulding, Adorno certainly did not view accretions to knowledge and technological progress as likely emancipators of humankind. Famously, he wrote, "No universal history leads from savagery to humanitarianism, but there is one leading from the slingshot to the megaton bomb" (Adorno 1973: 320). After Auschwitz, Adorno insisted, "all talk of progress towards freedom seem[s] ludicrous" (Adorno 2006: 7).

The foregoing hardly does justice to Adorno's nuanced and voluminous thought, let alone that of the Frankfurt School. This and the preceding section may suffice, nonetheless, to establish that, before and while Boulding was engaged in his seminal work on communication, there were extant substantial literatures, one oriented toward social sciences and a second, philosophically grounded critical literature that questioned and appraised the role and uses of power and irrationality in persuasive communication. Had Boulding drawn upon either or both of these literatures, he might well have afforded persuasion much greater attention than he did, and he might even have treated persuasion's "pathologies" more extensively and less cavalierly. "Pathologies" of persuasion are a direct challenge to Boulding's "Law of Evolution," and hence to his vision for "post-civilization."

Kenneth Boulding's legacy

Kenneth Boulding was certainly correct in claiming in 1989 that there was then extant a "persuasion industry," whose function was, in part, to convince people into accepting as real things that are not there. He understandably neglected to mention, however, yet a third literature that was just then bursting on the scene, which actually denied that a "real" even exists. In this section I argue that an important legacy of Boulding's information/communication writings is the bulwark they constitute against these postmodernist/poststructuralist[5] positions.

Since the 1980s, according to Frank Webster, "postmodernism" (aka poststructuralism) has been evident in "just about every university discipline, from art history to accountancy" (Webster 1995: 163). Webster proposes that, most basically, postmodernism is "a rejection of modernist ways of seeing"; in particular, it rejects all expression—artistic, scholarly, architectural, and so forth—claiming "to represent some 'reality' behind their symbolic form" (Webster 1995: 164, 165).

Poststructuralism may have started with Jacques Derrida's deconstructionist claims that, as summarized by Ben Agger, "language produces meaning only with reference to other meanings against which it takes on its own significance; thus, we can never establish stable meanings by attempting correspondence between language and the world addressed by language" (Agger 1991a: 28). We are destined, in other words, "to remain locked up in the prison house of language" (Agger 1991a: 29).

Derrida's deconstruction and Webster's typification of poststructuralism fit well with positions staked out by writers such as Jean Baudrillard, Mark Poster and Lawrence Grossberg. For Baudrillard, for example, all signs (such as words) are simulations, not representations. For him, "the territory no longer precedes the map, nor survives it; henceforth it is the map that precedes the territory—*the precession of simulacra*—it is the map that engenders the territory" (Baudrillard 2001: 168). For Mark Poster, likewise, in the information age " 'reality' comes to be constituted in the 'unreal' dimension of the media" (Poster 1989: 85). In this electronic era, he declared: "Language no longer represents a reality, no longer is a neutral tool to enhance the subject's instrumental rationality: language becomes or better reconfigures reality" (Poster 1994: 176). For Poster, therefore, "the tendency … is to regard truth as a multiplicity, to exult in the play of diverse meanings, in the continual process of reinterpretation, in the contention of opposing claims" (Poster 1989: 15). Finally, Grossberg, in a well-known debate with Nicholas Garnham, showed his concurrence with the aforementioned poststructuralist positions:

> GARNHAM: The rejection of false consciousness within [poststructuralist] cultural studies goes along with the rejection of truth as a state of the world, as opposed to the temporary effect of discourse. But without some notion of grounded truth the ideas of emancipation, resistance, and progressiveness become meaningless. Resistance to what, emancipation from what and for what, progression toward what?
>
> (Garnham 1995: 69)

> GROSSBERG: Thus the category of false consciousness returns—actually it has never left political economy. According to Garnham, without such a notion (and the related notion of truth), intellectuals have no valid role. And [poststructuralist] cultural studies of course rejects such notions.
>
> (Grossberg 1995: 79)

For present purposes, one could justifiably substitute in the foregoing extracts Boulding's "pathologies of persuasion" for "false consciousness." In any event, it follows that in denying a "real," poststructuralists are also at odds with Boulding regarding the ultimate unity of knowledge/unity of nature. Knowledge for poststructuralists is fragmented, subjective, transitory, in flux. Fragmentation was taken to the ultimate extreme by Stanley Fish in his famous book *Is There A Text in This Class?* Paul Cobley, introducing an essay by Fish, summarizes:

> The crux of the issue is whether there are as many possible readings of a text as there are readers, or whether there may be a small number of "correct" or "legitimate" readings of a text (or even just one "correct" reading) … For Fish, the reader supplies everything; this is because there can be nothing that precedes interpretation. As soon as human beings apprehend an item in the world they have already embarked on a process of interpreting it. There can be no "given" as such.
>
> (Cobley 1996: 405, 406)

Elsewhere, I have offered rebuttal against these and other poststructuralists' claims and positions (Babe 2009: 175–93). Here it may suffice simply to note that acceptance of poststructuralist positions is to deny that persuasion can have "pathologies"; for if there is no "real," one can hardly be convinced into accepting a false belief. Moreover, poststructuralism absolves professional persuaders of any and all responsibility for what they propagate—a boon, surely, to the "persuasion industry." This latter observation may go some distance in explaining poststructuralism's appeal and broad acceptance today.

The final, and most important point is that, in my view, Boulding constructed a strong discursive bulwark against poststructuralist claims. The centerpiece of Boulding's communication theory, to recall, is *production.* By linking biogenetic, noogenetic and industrial production through their commonalities regarding information, transmission and knowledge structures, Boulding qualifies as one of the twentieth century's premier "grand narrators" (to borrow a poststructuralist phrase). Likewise, in proposing the "world as a total system," he is in complete contradistinction to the poststructuralist claim that there are no general truths, only local and personal "truths."

In contrast to poststructuralism, Boulding's mode of analysis was "ecological," both in the narrow sense of being environmentally aware and concerned, but also (and in this context even more importantly) in the broader sense of insisting that everything depends upon everything else (Boulding 1958: 154–155). Boulding rooted this interdependence on flows of information as well as on flows of matter and energy. Whereas for poststructuralists, information and communication fragment not just societies but individual psyches, for Boulding information and communication heighten interdependencies, bring entities into systems and allow systems to evolve in terms of higher complexities.

Poststructuralist Mark Poster described the postmodern era as one in which language no longer points accurately or reliably to non-linguistic reality; this is because, in his view, language has become increasingly *self*-referential. For Boulding, in contrast, we have entered the era of *post-civilization* (as opposed to postmodernism or poststructuralism), and we have done this not because language has lost its referentiality to external materiality, but because our knowledge is becoming *more* scientific, *more* holistic, *more* universal, *more* environmentally sound—*more in-tune with material reality.* Whereas poststructuralists advise that we relax in our ignorance and simply consume for our own pleasures, Boulding admonished that consumption, as an indicator of welfare, is now anachronistic, that we must pursue a sustainable economy that minimizes throughputs of matter and energy. Whereas poststructuralists claim that general or universal knowledges oppress the disadvantaged because "knowledge" is controlled by the powerful, Boulding proposed antithetically (as a true, contemporary Enlightenment thinker) that knowledge is liberating. In the specific case of environmental knowledge, arguably, it is the poor and otherwise disadvantaged that have most to gain from environmentally sound policies and practices as derived from scientific knowledge, since it is they that suffer most from environmental distresses.

Today, poststructuralism continues to wield enormous clout across multiple academic disciplines. In my view, one of the strongest antidotes to this scholarly disease—which denies even the possibility of general knowledge, and concomitantly (albeit implicitly) the possibility of rectifying injustices—is the holistic scholarship of Kenneth Boulding. Boulding's holistic communication model, which conceptually unites biogenetic, noogenetic and industrial production, and which brings together communication, information, persuasion, teaching/learning, knowledge, evolution and human progress—in contradistinction to poststructuralism's insistent fragmentation—may be his most enduring legacy.

In this comment, I have taken issue with Boulding's seemingly unbridled optimism and his relative neglect of literatures pointing to the darker side of information, communication and persuasion. However, it is not Boulding's (perhaps undue) ebullience that tests the claims of the much darker poststructuralist literature; rather, it is his holism and the integrative nature of his innovative and heuristic analysis. There *is* unity in biogenetic, noogenetic and industrial production. The world *is*, and is increasingly so, a total system. Knowledge *can* be attained, tested, taught, learned and applied for good purposes. In an age some would term postmodern, the Enlightenment voice of Kenneth Boulding is one that needs to be heard again, and again, and again.

Notes

1 Among the books perused for this section, there is no entry for "persuasion" in the indexes to the fourth edition of *Economic Analysis, Volume 1: Microeconomics* (although the word "persuade" does appear at page 513), to *Ecodynamics, A Primer on Social Dynamics* or to *The Future: Images and Processes.* There is a single reference in the index to *Conflict and Defense* and two references in the index to *The World as a Total System.* There is no index appended to *Beyond Economics, The Meaning of the 20th Century*, *The Skills of the Economist* or *The Image.* Regarding *The Image*, however, a Google word search revealed one mention (at page 134).

2 Timothy Glander reports:

> The CPI carefully prepared news stories to the various media outlets and carefully monitored these media to determine if they were, in fact adhering to the governmental line … The Espionage Act was effective in ensuring that the CPI remained the dominant organ of news and opinion during the war.

CPI also produced feature length films, such as *Pershing's Crusaders, America's Answer* and *Our Colored Fighters*, along with several short-subject films. And it sponsored the Four Minute Men.

> The Four-Minute Men consisted of 75,000 volunteers who gave official pronouncements concerning the war during intermissions at movie houses, theaters, and other public gatherings throughout the United States ... Anticipating later days when radio and television would carry simultaneous messages to various parts of the country, the speeches of the Four-Minute Men were orchestrated so that their messages were heard on, or near, the same day in all parts of the country.
>
> (Glander 2000: 6, 7)

3 Shortly after the onset of the Korean War (1950), the US Air Force sent Schramm and two others to Korea to interview anticommunist refugees and to study US psychological operations. Stemming from that excursion, *inter alia*, was *The Reds Take a City*, with a Foreword by Frederick W. Williams of the Maxwell Air Force Base, Alabama (Schramm and Riley 1951).

4 The most popular and infamous of these was the Catholic prelate Father Charles E. Coughlin (1891–1979), who for several years had a network show on CBS with audiences in the tens of millions. At the height of his popularity through the 1930s, he received on average 80,000 letters a week. According to *The Holocaust Encyclopedia*, Coughlin vigorously denounced "international bankers," defended Nazi violence as justifiable retaliation for Jewish persecution of Christians, "promoted fascist dictatorship and authoritarian government as the only cure to the ills of democracy and capitalism" and "denounced the entry of the United States into World War II, claiming that the Jews had planned the war for their own benefit and had conspired to involve the United States." See United States Holocaust Memorial Museum (n.d.).

5 The terms *postmodern* and *poststructural* will be used interchangeably. For a nuanced distinction, see Agger (1991b).

References

Adorno, T.W. (1946) "Anti-Semitism and Fascist Propaganda," reprinted in *The Stars Down to Earth and Other Essays on the Irrational in Culture* (1994), edited with an Introduction by S. Crook. London: Routledge: 218–231.

Adorno, T.W. (1973) *Negative Dialectics*, translated by E. B. Ashton. New York: Continuum. First published in German in 1966.

Adorno, T.W. (1974) "The Stars Down to Earth," reprinted in *The Stars Down to Earth and Other Essays on the Irrational in Culture* (1944), edited with an Introduction by S. Crook. London: Routledge: 46–171.

Adorno, T.W. (2000) *The Psychological Technique of Martin Luther Thomas' Radio Addresses*. Stanford, CA: Stanford University Press.

Adorno, T.W. (2006) "Progress or Regression?" Lecture delivered in 1965 at Institute of Social Research, printed in *History and Freedom*, edited by R. Tiedemann, translated by R. Livingstone. London: Polity: 3–9.

Agger, B. (1991a) *A Critical Theory of Public Life: Knowledge, Discourse and Politics in an Age of Decline*. London: RoutledgeFalmer.

Agger, B. (1991b) "Critical Theory, Poststructuralism, Postmodernism: Their Sociological Relevance," *Annual Review of Sociology*, 17: 105–131.

Babe, R.E. (2009) *Cultural Studies and Political Economy: Toward a New Integration*. Lanham, MD: Lexington Books.

Baudrillard, J. (2001) "Simulacra and Simulations," in *Jean Baudrillard: Selected Writings*, 2nd ed., edited and introduced by M. Poster. Stanford, CA: Stanford University Press: 169–187.

Bernays, E. (1928) *Propaganda.* New York: Horace Liveright.

Bernstein, J.M. (1991) "Introduction," in T.W. Adorno, *The Culture Industry*, edited by J.M. Bernstein. London: Routledge: 1–25.

Boulding, K. (1956) *The Image: Knowledge and Life in Society.* Ann Arbor, MI: University of Michigan Press.

Boulding, K. (1958) *The Skills of the Economist.* Toronto, ON: Clarke, Irwin and Co.

Boulding, K. (1962) *Conflict and Defense: A General Theory*. New York: Harper & Row, Publishers.

Boulding, K. (1964) *The Meaning of the Twentieth Century: The Great Transition*. New York: Harper and Row.

Boulding, K. (1966) *Economic Analysis, Vol. 1: Microeconomics*, 4th ed. New York: Harper and Row; 1st ed., 1941.

Boulding, K. (1970) *A Primer on Social Dynamics: History as Dialectics and Development*. New York: The Free Press, Collier-Macmillan.

Boulding, K. (1978) *Ecodynamics: A New Theory of Societal Evolution.* Beverly Hills, CA: Sage Publications.

Boulding, K. (1981) *Evolutionary Economics.* Beverly Hills, CA: Sage Publications.

Boulding, K. (1985) *The World as a Total System.* Newbury Park, CA: Sage Publications.

Boulding, K. (1989) "The Pathologies of Persuasion," in *Unconventional Wisdom: Essays on Economics in Honor of John Kenneth Galbraith*, edited by S. Bowles, R.C. Edwards and W.G. Shepherd. New York: Houghton Mifflin: 3–19.

Boulding, E. and K. Boulding (1995) *The Future: Images and Processes*. Thousand Oaks, CA: Sage Publications.

Cobley, P. (1996) "Interpretation, Ideation and the Reading Process," in *The Communication Theory Reader*, edited by P. Cobley. London: Routledge: 405–406.

Chomsky, N. (1989) *Necessary Illusions: Thought Control in Democratic Societies*. Toronto, ON: CBC Enterprises.

Delia, J. (1987) "Communication Research: A History," in *Handbook of Communication Science*, edited by C.R. Berger and S. Chaffee. Newbury Park, CA: Sage Publications: 20–98.

Ewen, S. (1996) *PR!: A Social History of Spin*. New York: Basic Books.

Fish, S. (1980) *Is There a Text in this Class?* Cambridge, MA: Harvard University Press.

Galbraith, J.K. (1967) *The New Industrial State.* Boston: MA: Houghton Mifflin.

Garnham, N. (1995) "Political Economy and Cultural Studies: Reconciliation or Divorce?" *Critical Studies in Mass Communications*, 1 (2): 62–71.

Gitlin, J.M. (2007) "Stealth Advertising: Marketing Creeps into the Evening News," *Ars Technica.* Available: http://arstechnica.com/old/content/2007/07/stealth-advertising-marketing-creeps-into-the-evening-news.ars (accessed December 26, 2010).

Glander, T. (2000) *Origins of Mass Communications Research During the American Cold War.* Mahwah, NJ: Lawrence Erlbaum Associates, Inc., Publishers.

Grossberg, L. (1995) "Cultural Studies vs. Political Economy: Is Anybody Else Bored by this Debate? *Critical Studies in Mass Communications*, 1 (2): 72–81.

Hayek, F.A. (1945) "The Use of Knowledge in Society," *American Economic Review*, 35 (4): 510–530.

Horkheimer, M. and T.W. Adorno (1991) *Dialectic of Enlightenment*. New York: Continuum; originally published in German in 1944; first English translation 1972.

Jansen, S.C. (2008) "Walter Lippmann, Straw Man of Communication Research," in *The History of Media and Communication Research: Contested Memories*, edited by D.W. Park and J. Pooley. New York: Peter Lang: 71–112.

Lippmann, W. (1922) *Public Opinion.* Reprint: Mineola, NY: Dover, 2004.

Pooley, J. (2008) "The New History of Mass Communication Research," in *The History of Media and Communication Research: Contested Memories*, edited by D.W. Park and J. Pooley. New York: Peter Lang: 43–69.

Poster, M. (1989) *Critical Theory and Poststructuralism: In Search of a Context.* Ithaca. NY: Cornell University Press.

Poster, M. (1994) "The Mode of Information and Postmodernity," in *Communication Theory Today*, edited by D. Crowley and D. Mitchell. Stanford: Stanford University Press: 173–192.

Rogers, E.M. (1994) *A History of Communication Study: A Biographical Approach.* New York: Free Press.

Schramm, W., ed. (1949) *Mass Communication.* Urbana, IL: University of Illinois Press.

Schramm, W., ed. (1954) *The Process and Effects of Mass Communication.* Urbana, IL: University of Illinois Press.

Schramm, W. (1997) *The Beginnings of Communication Research in America: A Personal Memoir*, edited by S.F. Chaffee and E.M. Rogers. Thousand Oaks, CA: Sage Publications.

Schramm, W. and J. Riley (1951) *The Reds Take a City: The Communist Occupation of Seoul.* New Brunswick, NJ: Rutgers University Press.

Schramm, W. and D.F. Roberts, eds. (1971) *The Process and Effects of Mass Communication*, revised edition. Urbana, IL: University of Illinois Press.

Simpson, C. (1994) *Science of Coercion: Communication Research and Psychological Warfare1945–1960.* Oxford: Oxford University Press.

Smith, A. (1937) *An Inquiry into the Nature and Causes of the Wealth of Nations*, edited with an Introduction by E. Cannan. New York: The Modern Library; 1st ed., 1776.

United States Holocaust Memorial Museum (n.d.) "Charles E. Coughlin," *The Holocaust Encyclopedia,* www.ushmm.org/wlc/en/article.php?ModuleId=10005516 (accessed December 7, 2010).

Webster, F. (1995) *Theories of the Information Society.* London: Routledge.

Wright, R. (1988) *Three Scientists and Their Gods. Looking For Meaning in an Age of Information.* New York: Times Books.

Poem

The Undigested Remark

The Undigested Remark
Is doomed to constant frustration,
Because he feels in the dark
About his communication.

Part VI

Power theory

6 Key text: Power in society[1]

Kenneth E. Boulding

Decision implies power and freedom

One of the fundamental differences between biological dynamics and social dynamics is the much greater importance of decision in the social system by comparison with the biosphere. This is not to say by any means that the phenomenon of decision is unknown below the level of the human race. Animals, even down to the lowly amoeba, undoubtedly possess some kind of image of at least an immediate future and choose the better future rather than the worse. It is very difficult to say where the image of the future really begins in the long process of evolution. There is no doubt that the higher animals possess it in some small degree and that they have some kind of primitive value system enabling them to make choices. The behavior of predators and of predatees is not simple, immediate stimulus and response, as perhaps the behavior of the amoeba is. It is based to some extent on expectations, particularly when we come to dogs, coyotes, raccoons, and the higher apes. There are quite active learning processes at work and many examples of cooperative behavior, which have the form of very primitive organization.

With the coming of the human nervous system, the development of societal evolution, and the vast proliferation of human artifacts, however, complex images of the future and decisions emerge, involving choice among images of the future according to some patterns of valuation, which, as we have seen, is what an economist means by "maximizing behavior." It is being conscious of an "agenda," that is, a range of possible futures, and it involves being able to order these on some scale of values and choosing the "best" from this scale.

It is only with the coming of decision as a major element in dynamics that the question of power becomes important. Unfortunately the word "power," like so many others, has a considerable range of meanings. It conjures up images of wrestling, weight lifting, bulldozing, and rocket launching, which do not necessarily gather the essence of the concept; even in physics there are anthropomorphic overtones of the concepts of force and work. All we can observe is system change. We can never observe directly the force, whatever it is, that changes it, except as far as we have internal reflections on our subjective experience of will, that is, deciding to move something, and then acting in such a way that it is moved.

As a first approximation we might define power as the change in the future state of the universe brought about by a decision. If I get into an elevator, press the button for the fourth floor, and the elevator rises to it, then by a decision to press the button, I have changed the state of the universe, though not by very much. If I had not pressed the button, the elevator would have remained on the ground floor. If the elevator had been out of order and I had pressed the button, it would still have remained on the ground floor and I would have had no power over it at all. If I had pressed the button and destroyed the whole earth, obviously I would have a great deal of power. The power of an individual decision-maker, therefore, is the amount of change in the state of the universe he can accomplish by choosing one future rather than another. If we can suppose that one choice is always to do nothing, which may not of course always be true, but is useful as a simplifying assumption, then power is the difference in the state of the universe between doing something and doing nothing.

The measurement of power is a tricky business. In the first place, a change in the state of the universe is going to be highly multidimensional in many cases. If we change A, B, C, D, and E, we can only measure the total change by some process of putting value weights on the changes in these various components. That is, we always have a problem of indexing, and with different value weights the answer might come out differently. Another even more fundamental difficulty is that all we can ever observe is what happened; we can never observe what did not happen and, if power is the difference between what did happen and what did not happen, we always have to make some kind of evaluation or estimate of what real difference the decision made. In the case of pushing the elevator button and going to the fourth floor, this is fairly easy; when it comes to things like making a law, a presidential veto, a declaration of war, or an assassination, the difference between what would have happened if the event had not taken place and what actually happened is often extremely difficult to evaluate. In this sense, power is always based on some kind of subjective estimates, rather than objective "fact," in the sense that it is not wholly subject to observation.

A concept closely related to that of power is freedom. This, again, is a concept of many meanings and many dimensions. One meaning is that of the range of choice, that is, the size of the agenda of decision. If I have no alternative, that is, if only one possible future is available for me, I am clearly not free to choose. Freedom of choice always implies alternatives. Up to a point, perhaps, the most alternatives there are, the more freedom we feel. The rich man in this sense is much more free than a poor one; the poor man cannot afford to go outside his own village, the rich man can go anywhere he likes in the world.

Another dimension of freedom is that of the absence of restrictions imposed by others. If I am conscious of a potential range of alternatives, but some of these are denied me because of the decisions of others, I feel unfree in the sense that I am dependent on the decisions of others. The power of one person may or may not limit the freedom of another, depending on the circumstances. Thus, when there are only a few cars on the road, the power that the possession of a car gives a person does not limit the freedom of others to drive, though if I get a car, it may limit your freedom to get one. If everybody has a car and roads get congested, however, then one person trying to exercise his power to drive may limit the power of others, and hence the freedom of others.[2]

Power as capacity to change the future

We can think of the total power of the human race as measured by the degree to which it can change the future. King Canute had no power over the tides. The mightiest empire has no power over the sun and the moon; even our space exploration does not change the length of the month perceptibly. Up to now we have had very little power over natural disasters—earthquakes, hurricanes, tornadoes and floods—though we do have some power in mitigating their effects and preparing for them. We have some power over the course of biological evolution. The human race has caused an appreciable number of species to become extinct before they otherwise would have. By artificial selection we have created domesticated plants and animals, corn and hogs, and so on. We have affected the gene pool of the earth somewhat, but only by selection. So far we have not been able to intervene much in genetic mutations, although this is not far off.

Our intervention in climate is still minimal. Nobody can pretend that the human race caused the last ice age, and it is clear that the earth is in the grip of very large systems, in the face of which human activity is still relatively peripheral. We do change the climate of cities a little, we do a little cloud seeding; however, we really do not know what will be the effects of our burning fossil fuels, creating contrails, or releasing freon into the atmosphere. It is a little distressing indeed that the meteorologists do not seem able to decide whether the activities of the human race are warming the earth up or cooling it down. A few years ago they were all worried about a "greenhouse effect." The rising level of carbon dioxide in the atmosphere as a result of burning fossil fuels acts as a greenhouse, letting the high-intensity radiation from the sun in, but preventing the low-intensity radiation from the surface of the earth from getting out. This of course would warm up the earth, causing the fear that the polar ice caps might melt and flood most of the land area where the human race now lives, thereby altering the patterns of world climate very profoundly. Now, however, the fear seems to be of a new ice age. The earth is cooling off very rapidly, with an almost unprecedented decline in temperature in the last 20 years, but nobody I think really knows why. We may have been suffering from slight delusions of grandeur in respect to our impact on the earth.

The uncertainty and illusions of power

When it comes to social dynamics, the extent of human power becomes a very tricky question and is not capable of easy resolution. We know certainly that some persons are more powerful than others. We will return later to the problem of the distribution of power. The decisions of most people affect themselves, their immediate families, perhaps their employers or employees, their circle of friends, and so on, but the effects do not extend much beyond this. For most people, if every decision they made in their lives had been different, their own lives would have been different, but the life of mankind would not have been changed very much. On the other hand, there are people of whom this is perhaps not true: the "great," the rulers and conquerors, political leaders, founders of religions, makers of great discoveries, and so on. The difficulty here is that we never really know what would have happened if a decision had gone the other way. In a great many decisions, even by powerful people, the major alternatives may be quite small. The powerful are hedged in by their own circumstances, their own organizations, the information which reaches them, the staff with which they are surrounded, and so on, so that their agendas are smaller than is often thought. In many cases, even if other persons had occupied their roles, the decisions would not have been very different, because it is the role rather than the person that determines the decision. This is an old and rather unresolvable argument in the interpretation of history.

On the one side, there is the "great men" theory of history, as represented, for instance, by Thomas Carlyle. This attributes great importance to the influence of powerful people, and states that history would have been very different if certain decisions had gone the other way. At the other extreme, we have a kind of mechanistic determinism to which Marxism comes very close, in which the great forces of social dynamics are regarded as virtually independent of the decisions even of powerful people, and independent pretty much of whoever occupies the roles. We could hold this position whether we believed in dialectics or in evolution, provided we hold the view that it is only larger dynamic forces that matter, so that particular human decisions can only cause ripples on the surface of the great ongoing river of history. This is a question that is very difficult, perhaps impossible, to resolve because of the principle that we can only know what happened (as far as the imperfect record permits) and never "what would have happened if." Even if we believe there are strong random elements in human history, a proposition for which a very strong case can be made, we cannot quite dismiss decisions as part of the random structure. Decisions may have random elements in them, as in a dilemma where we decide between two equally attractive alternatives by tossing a mental coin, but they also have strong nonrandom elements. Furthermore, random decisions may or may not cumulate, that is, they may either be offset by the nonrandom forces or they may cumulate into a pattern very different from what would have been the case if the random factors had gone the other way.

History is at least in part a Monte Carlo simulation with somebody throwing the dice every so often and putting in the numbers that turn up. Then how far do these random perturbations cancel each other out according to the famous law of large numbers? And how far do they cumulate to carry us over watersheds into different dynamic systems than we would have had if random shocks had not accumulated in the way that they did? Unfortunately, there is no really secure way of answering these questions. The most we can do perhaps is to suggest those parts of the total system within which neither the whims of the powerful nor the random shocks of nature make very much difference in the long run, and those parts in which we may suspect that these things do make a difference.

The "outability of truth": reality imposes itself on knowledge

One suspects, for instance, that the cumulative growth of knowledge, that is, the whole development of the noosphere and the genetic structure of human artifacts, follows an unfolding pattern, which may be speeded up or slowed down by random events or by the decisions of the powerful, but which cannot fundamentally be changed in its course in the long run simply because of what I have sometimes called the "outability of truth." Also, if we think of the growth of knowledge as the growth of structures within the human organism that correspond in some way in their patterns to structures outside it, then the structures outside it ultimately dominate the growth of the structures inside it. Just as there is a profound asymmetry between truth and lies, in the sense that lies can be found out whereas truth cannot, there is similarly an asymmetry between truth and error in the sense that erroneous images are much more likely to change in the direction of truth rather than true images in the direction of error, even though this may occasionally happen. We may indulge in occasional philosophical doubt about the existence of a real world but, if our image of the world is that we can fly by flapping our arms when we jump off the Empire State Building, the real world will break into our illusions with considerable rapidity. Superstition may be long lived, but truth is immortal and will outlive it. A small sect may cherish the belief that the earth is flat, but if any of its members becomes an astronaut or even an airline pilot, that belief will certainly have to be abandoned in practice.

There are difficulties, of course, in social systems in that beliefs about the system and images of it are an important part of the system itself. Hence, there is sometimes no objective truth to ride herd on the cavorting legions of error. In social systems, some beliefs are self-justified, at least in the short run. If everybody believes the price of stocks is going to rise, rise they will. If everybody believes there is going to be a gasoline shortage next week, they will fill up their tanks and create it. The belief that two countries are on the road to war propels them along that road and it often makes the war inevitable, even though it might not have happened otherwise. Nevertheless, the entire social system is not a product of the fevered human imagination. There are certain stabilities in its dynamic, and self-justified beliefs and expectations tend to be short run. We return to the old image of the loom: one sees these disturbances as a kind of temporary gathering of the warp, producing perhaps a hole or a blotch in the fabric, but as time goes on the fundamental patterns reassert themselves and the end result is as if the disturbance had never happened at all.

Determinism versus randomness in history

Thus, it is quite legitimate to ask whether the overall history of the human race, at least in its broad outlines, would have been very different if decisive battles of history had gone the other way. One suspects the answer is "not very much." We might have had one empire rather than another, or we might be speaking one language rather than another, but the long process of the growth of human knowledge, invention, discovery, and the development of artifacts and organizations might not have been very much affected. The common phenomenon, for instance, of simultaneous invention and discovery of the same thing by different people in different places at about the same time suggests that, when the time is ripe, the fruit will be picked, no matter who picks it. Certainly if Columbus had not discovered the American shores, some other European would have. Once the Europeans had the rudder and could set a course, and once they improved navigation to the point where they could travel 3,000 miles in a straight line, as somebody once said, "How could Columbus miss it?" It is hard to see how we could have avoided inventing the automobile about the time we did; and if Henry Ford had died in infancy, surely there would have been another person to invent the assembly line, because there were at least 200 firms already making automobiles.

Niches dominate mutations, and power changes names more than patterns

In evolutionary terms it is rarely mutation that imposes limits on evolution; it is the development of niches in the course of selection. Once a niche has been created in the slow, grinding ecological interaction of populations, it is extremely probable that some mutations will take place to fill it, simply because mutation is something of which there is very little scarcity either in biological systems or in social systems. It goes on all the time. Most mutations, of course, did not survive; they are adverse in the present structure of niches. Decisions, conflicts, fights, discoveries, inventions are all part of the mutational structure of society. Hence, paradoxically, they are not very important when it comes to the pattern of the long-run movements, although they may be important in the short run in creating disturbances. Discoveries, inventions, organizations, battles and wars, conquests and all that may determine exactly what is going to fill the niche, but they do not create the niches. Given the knowledge technology of the day, if the Carthaginians had won the Punic Wars, there would have been a Mediterranean Carthaginian Empire rather than a Roman Empire and St. Peter's might later have been built in Tunis instead of Rome, but there still would have been a Mediterranean empire facilitating the spread of Christianity, which would later collapse under the impact of migrations from Asia and so on. Power changes names, but it does not change patterns.

Power important at thresholds

On the other hand, one has to admit that there may be exceptions to this rule, particularly in the early days of an evolutionary phylum. Evolutionary potential may not be realized because of some random accident or because of some power structure and the decisions emerging from it. We cannot quite rule out the possibility that there have been times and places in which the cast of the die, the fate of the particular occupant of a powerful role, or the way in which a decision was made either failed to create evolutionary potential that might have been created or destroyed the possibility of some potential becoming actual. We see this in the case of the individual life, particularly the exceptional person. The fertilized egg that became Shakespeare certainly had a rather unusual genetic structure, no doubt a result of a chance aggregation of chromosomes. Genius does not have to be hereditary in the strict sense. It may be the result of an unusual combination of quite common genetic structures created by the constant rearrangement of genetic structures that takes place in sexual reproduction. If Shakespeare had been aborted or had died in infancy (and there must have been a quite noticeable probability that this could have happened in light of the infant mortality of the day), the history of the English language or even of English-speaking peoples might have been somewhat different. On the other hand, there may have been many mute, inglorious Miltons and Cromwells guiltless of their countries' blood in innumerable Stoke Poges.[3]

There are "threshold phenomena," which can be perceived when they do happen, but we never know how close they came to happening when they do not happen. If Hitler had died in infancy, the history of Europe in the twentieth century might have been substantially different, simply because the rise of the Nazis to power was one of these threshold phenomena that just made it over the top. If it had not been for the peculiarly charismatic nature of Hitler, there would undoubtedly have been something like a Nazi movement, but it might never have made it over the threshold to power. A very similar phenomenon is that of the critical mass, which is particularly important at the beginning of both organizations and social movements. Historians are not very much help to us here, simply because they are quite obsessed with what did happen (from their own point of view, of course, quite rightly), and their main concern is with maintaining and improving the record, and it is only what did happen that is recorded. From the point of view of understanding the record, however, it is what did *not* happen that is important, and studies of this are very rare and also very difficult.

The question as to whether power is important in human history, therefore, is something that within a wide range we must leave somewhat undecided. My personal view is that it is much less important than most historians, philosophers, social scientists, and certainly most ideologists have thought. Power is dramatic and visible and great decisions are interesting, while the aspects of the great pattern of society through space and time that are independent of power are drab, hard to perceive, undramatic, and fail to attract attention. For this very reason one suspects that power is more visible than it deserves to be and less important than most people think. That it is often important, however, cannot be denied; hence, of course, it deserves most careful study. It is particularly important to the people who exercise it and those on whom it is exercised. One can be fairly sure that locally in particular times and places power is much more significant than it is in considering the totality of the pattern through time. It is in these local times and places, however, that we all live, so we certainly cannot be blamed for being interested in power or even for overestimating its significance. It is not much comfort to us to think that what we do matters less than we thought.

Types of power: threat power

There are many different kinds of power. We can distinguish roughly three types of power corresponding to the three major social organizers of love, threat, and exchange. The first of these is threat power, often identified with what is called "force." The second is exchange power, which is the power of wealth or riches. The third is integrative power, which is the power of legitimacy or status. In popular thinking, power is often exclusively associated with threat power, both on the right and on the left. This, however, is a great mistake. Threat power is only one form of power and is in and of itself by no means the most powerful. Exchange power in its various forms is at least as important, and integrative power is probably the most important of all. Without integrative power, that is, some kind of status, role structure, or legitimacy, the other forms of power have very limited horizons and are very weak. This is often not generally recognized.

Threats, as we have seen, can be of many kinds. There are those associated with weapons, that is, with artifacts designed to give the possessor or the wielder the capability of doing harm to others. Threats only lead to power in the threat–submission system, in which case the threatener has the power to change the behavior of the threatened in what the threatener perceives as his favor. The threatened party then perceives his freedom as being diminished. Threat power is least effective when the threats are highly unspecific and generalized as, for instance, when minority groups use bombings at rather unspecified targets. Threats are most effective as power when they are specific and especially when they are not carried out but held, as it were, in reserve. Threat power is generally very ineffective unless it is linked intimately with some form of integrative power to legitimate it, as is the case, for instance, with the tax system and the law. The state has a great deal of threat power precisely because it is regarded by most people as legitimate. If the legitimacy decays, the threat power decays also. If the legitimacy of a taxing authority, for instance, is denied by a large majority of those who are liable for taxes, the authority collapses even in the face of severe sanctions, and the cost of collecting taxes rises to the point where they are not worth collecting.

Physical threat and weapons are by no means the only kinds of threat. Spiritual threats were an important source of the power of a priesthood, and even in the European middle ages the threat of excommunication by the pope could bring an emperor literally to his knees. Threats of exclusion or social disapproval and rejection are very powerful organizers of society. Most people are kept in line to follow the social mores and to obey the law more by the subtle threat system of exclusion from society, community, or valued social intercourse than they are by the sanctions of the law.

The power of nonviolence

The theory of the power of nonviolence as developed, for instance, by Gandhi and expounded in the United States by Richard B. Gregg (1966) and Gene Sharp (1973) is a very interesting example of the development of subtle forms of threat. The use of nonviolent threats as an instrument of political power is an important social invention. We have seen it used in struggles for independence, as in India, or for the rights of minorities, as in the United States with Martin Luther King and the civil rights movement. There are many different forms of nonviolent threat. The most common perhaps is that of simple withdrawal, that is, a passive defiance of the threats of the authorities whose legitimacy is being challenged, coupled with the willingness to suffer the consequences. Threat power is limited by the phenomenon noticed before, that the carrying out of a threat is often highly costly to the threatener and that, where this is so, threat–submission systems are apt to be unstable and slip into defiance. Defiance, especially if it is well organized, may be quite successful in undermining the credibility and the legitimacy of the original threat system of the authorities. Strikes, boycotts, sit-ins, demonstrations, tax refusal, and so on are as much a part of threat power as guns, bombs, and armies. The development of organized nonviolence, indeed, is perhaps one of the most significant political inventions of the twentieth century, even though it has been known in a sporadic way for a very long time. It operates partly in undermining by calm defiance the threat system of the authorities; this operates to undermine their legitimacy, particularly their internal legitimacy, that is, their morale or self image. An army or police force faced with disciplined and organized nonviolence is a little bit like the personal attacker faced with jujitsu. The violent expect violence in return. When they are met with nonviolence they are thrown off balance and their self-confidence and legitimacy tend to be undermined. Without legitimacy, however, as we have seen, threats are very ineffective, even violent threats.

It is a paradox of nonviolence, however, that it is much more effective for aggression than it is for defense. Aggression may be defined as activity directed to produce change wanted by the actor. The word aggression carries considerable overtones of illegitimacy in the English language, but it is hard to think of any other word that means the effort to produce a wanted change. Defense, on the other hand, is effort designed to prevent unwanted change. This is just as common and just as legitimate as aggression, though, as we shall see later, it always seems to produce pathological results. Nonviolence is almost always aggressive in this sense, that is, it is designed to produce the change desired by its organizers. Defense against it is often very difficult, which is why one suspects that nonviolent action in organization quite often produces violence as a reaction, though often rather ineffective violence. The effectiveness of nonviolence depends a good deal on the particular structure of the integrative system within which it is operating. It is most effective where the wielder of established threat systems, such as an occupying power or an imperial power, is in a weak integrative position. We will look at this problem a little further when we discuss integrative power.

Economic power

The second major source of power is economic power. This is not quite the same thing as exchange power, although, of course, it is closely related to it because exchange is such a central institution in economic life. Economic power is the power to command or control human artifacts, particularly those artifacts which are commodities and which participate in the processes of exchange, that is, economic goods. We do not have to limit these to goods that actually participate in exchange. There may be "provisions" (economic goods) that are human artifacts of value and significance to those who possess or control them. These may be produced for consumption and used domestically, rather than for exchange. But it is, as we have seen, the exchange phenomenon that leads to the division of labor, increase in productivity, and the massive expansion of human artifacts.

Economic power, that is, command over economic goods, comes from a number of different sources. It comes mainly from control over the factors of production that enter into the process of production of economic goods. As we have seen earlier, these consist essentially of knowledge or know-how, energy, and materials. The greatest of these is knowledge, although there are occasions in which the power to produce economic goods is limited by lack of access to energy or to materials. It is these three factors that largely determine the productivity of human activity in the production of economic goods. This is particularly true to large groups or societies. Today, for instance, the rich countries are rich and the power countries are poor mainly because the rich countries have large accumulations of knowledge and capital, which is essentially human knowledge imposed on the material world by past production, and access to large energy sources and material sources. The poor countries lack knowledge and, because of this, they also frequently lack access to energy and materials. In the rich countries the capabilities of production rest on a vast infrastructure of scientific and technical knowledge that permits these countries in these days to draw on fossil fuels through elaborate mechanisms of production and exchange, and with these to transform large quantities of materials into large quantities of economic goods. The poor countries, relying on their traditional folk knowledge, on human and animal muscles as energy sources, and on purely local materials, are able to produce very little.

A rough measure of economic power is the net output of economic goods per head or per capita real income. For any group or even any arbitrary set of people, the total income of economic goods depends on the division of total activity among (1) production for domestic use, (2) production for exchange, and (3) nonproduction, such as activity devoted to leisure or sleep, or time spent in unemployment. Suppose that out of a group of L persons we have the equivalent of L_d persons producing for domestic use, L_e producing for exchange, and L_u not producing. Then

$$L = L_d + L_e + L_u \tag{1}$$

If p_d is the productivity of domestic activity, p_e the productivity of production for export, T the terms of trade (that is, how many imports are obtained per unit of exports), and G the total of grants, gifts, or transfers (which may of course be positive or negative), the total real income Y is

$$Y = L_d p_d + L_e p_e T + G\,. \tag{2}$$

Then we have the per capita real income or economic power,

$$y = \frac{Y}{L} = \frac{L_d p_d + L_e p_e T + G}{L_d + L_e + L_u} \tag{3}$$

This is an instructive equation, showing the sources of an increase in economic power. A shift out of L_u, that is, unemployed potential, into either L_d or L_e will increase economic power, y. Shifts into production for export out of domestic production will increase only if p_e is greater than p_d. An increase in positive grants, of course, will increase economic power and so will an improvement in the terms of trade, T, that is, how much we get in imports per unit of what we give up in exports. The major long-run source of increase in economic power, however, is increase in productivity, that is, in p_d or p_e. This is the only source that can be sustained for very long. An improvement in terms of trade easily reverses itself. Shifts into more productive occupations soon exhaust themselves. The horizon on the increase of grants is fairly low. Rich countries have become rich because their productivity has been increasing so rapidly for so long. Any improvement in their terms of trade has been a minor factor, occasionally significant for short periods. Even exploitative grants to them from the poor countries have been quite small.

This formula can be applied to a single individual or family as well as to a nation or group. Here again, if in a particular occupation there are good terms of trade and good productivity in production for exchange, the individual may get richer by shifting from domestic production into exchange production, such as, for instance, going to work for an employer and getting wages with which he or she buys other things, rather than trying to produce these other things at home. Increase in productivity often comes from education, training, or an increase in skill. The grants factor in the case of an individual would include income received without any activity, which could include either welfare payments or income on property, especially pure interest or dividend income, which does not involve any management or activity factor. The richest individuals tend to have a larger income from property than they do from their own labor or activity.

Productivity and reallocation as sources of economic power

Equation 3 really points us to four types or sources of economic power. The first might be called "productive power," as reflected in the productivity coefficients p_d and p_e. This is very largely a function of the knowledge stock, although it is also a function of the availability of energy and of materials of various sorts. This is reflected, for instance, in the fertility of the land a group occupies, the natural resources to which it has access, and so on, but over the long haul the knowledge factor is really dominant. A good example is the case of Germany and Japan after World War II. The destruction of a large amount of the material base in terms of buildings, machines, and so on can be recovered very easily if the knowledge factors are not affected. Both Germany and Japan had remarkably rapid recovery from the defeat and devastation of World War II. Defeat in war may even have improved the knowledge base of the society in the sense that it got rid of a lot of powerful people, like Hitler and the Japanese military, who had very imperfect knowledge, that is, whose images of the world were very unrealistic. Many countries that in 1945, let us say, had not been devastated and had their material capital unimpaired nevertheless stagnated or developed very slowly in the next generation because the knowledge stock simply was not there.

A second rather minor source of economic power is what might be called "allocational efficiency," that is, the ability of either a person, group, or society to allocate its resources properly first between production for domestic use and production for exchange, and then in a larger sense between the lines of production among the different industries. A society willing to take advantage of the terms of trade that the world market offers is likely to develop more rapidly than one that goes in for import substitution, protecting often very inefficient domestic industry, and so on. This is not to say that absolute free trade is always the best road to riches. There are disadvantages of producing for exchange as well as advantages. Both an individual and a society have to find a proper balance between domestic production and production for export and exchange.

It is hard to assess the actual impact of this factor because it is associated with certain psychological factors that also have an effect on the growth of knowledge and productivity. "Protectionist" individuals and societies, which are suspicious of intercourse with the outside, exchange, foreign trade, and producing for others and become ingrown, inward looking, and hostile to the outside world, are very often also individual and societies that inhibit the growth of knowledge in themselves, are afraid to take risks, and stagnate in their own little self-contained package. The hippie, the drug addict, the withdrawn communitarians, the agrarian simple lifers, and the nationalist protectionist nations all have this element of withdrawal in common. They all are likely to suffer from it in the long run.

Terms of trade, monopoly, and grants as sources of economic power

The third source of economic power is reflected in the terms of trade higher the price of the things we sell and the lower the price of things we buy, the richer we are. Control over the terms of trade, however, is only achieved through monopoly power, which in turn is only achieved through control of the total sales and ultimately the total output of the export commodity. Monopoly power is very widespread in society, but in a certain sense it is not very large. For one thing, monopolies often tend to be fragile, especially when they are based on some "organization of organizations" like a cartel, which are difficult to maintain unless they are upheld by the threat power of the state. Monopolies frequently tend to be undermined by technical change, which they may indeed stimulate, in the invention of substitutes for the monopolized commodity. There are fairly strong limits to the degree to which terms of trade can be manipulated. It would be very hard, for instance, even under the most favorable circumstances such as

OPEC, the monopolistic association of the oil producers, to raise the terms of trade by much more than a factor of 2 or 3. This is a one-shot operation—once done it cannot be repeated. Productivity coefficients, on the other hand, have been doubling each generation in what are now the rich countries for a number of generations and in some fields are more than 50 times what they were 200 years ago.

Nevertheless, monopoly is important especially in the short run, and it is quite pervasive. Labor unions, especially craft unions, insofar as they can restrict entry into their occupation, exercise monopoly power, some of which they usually pass on to their employers. This is obtained at the expense of the purchasers of the commodity that they jointly produce. Professional associations like the American Medical Association also create very substantial monopoly power for the medical profession by restricting entry into medical schools. Cartels and commodity agreements may create monopoly power for the producers of particular commodities. In the past these have not been very successful, except for short periods. The oil producers are a notable exception to this rule. When the last of the oil is all gone, this will have been a very temporary episode in human history. It may have long-run results if the oil producers can invest their monopoly gains wisely. "Natural monopolies" are important in some fields, like telephones and electric utilities, where there are great technical advantages in having a single firm in one area. These are usually subject to some kind of public regulation.

Monopoly power frequently tends to be mixed with threat power. The monopolist says in effect to his customer, "If you do not pay my price, you will not get the commodity." Monopoly power can be regarded, therefore, as a use of organized threats to push the terms of trade, where there is a range of mutual benefit, toward the high price or the sellers' end of the scale. As we have seen, there is both a community and a conflict of interest in exchange, and monopoly power is a way of organizing the conflict of interest. On the other side of the picture, monopsony power is more rare, but now unknown. This is the power of organized buyers who refuse to buy from the sellers except at a price toward the buyers' end of the range of mutual benefit. Tacit or sometimes open agreements among employers in an area not to bid up wages, which Adam Smith (1937) noted, are an example. When a large corporation purchases a commodity produced by large numbers of individual producers or by a considerable number of individual countries, it may be able to set a "take-it-or-leave-it" price, which the producers simply have to follow. In the absence of organized political power, however, both monopoly and monopsony power are hard to sustain, simply because the more the power is exercised by the collective organization, the greater are the incentives for the individual member to break away.

Threat systems, as we have seen, are costly to the threatener as well as to the threatened. Monopoly power is most sustainable when there are few producers of a commodity that has very few substitutes. Petroleum, of course, is a very good example of this. On the other hand, if the monopoly power is exercised too vigorously, there are strong incentives both to discover substitutes and to increase the efficiency of the use of the monopolized article; hence the monopolists find their market shrinking. The weaker ones among the associated producers find themselves in an increasingly difficult position with shrinking markets and hence they have increasing incentives to break out of the monopoly and to offer to sell at a lower price. This has been the history of innumerable monopolies in the past; it would be a little surprising if it does not happen to OPEC in the future.

The most secure monopolies are those supported by the organized political threat system of the state, such as the monopoly of the communist party in communist countries. An interesting historical example was the sovereign monopoly of the British East India Company in India and similar state trading companies especially in the sixteenth and seventeenth centuries in Europe. Even the history of these, however, is full of disaster and collapse. The monopoly may have aroused enough antagonism to undermine the legitimacy of the political organization that supports it. This happened with the British in India. The monopoly itself may generate so much internal inefficiency, because it relies on threat power rather than exchange power, that it collapses internally in spite of its monopoly power. Most of the monopolistic trading companies suffered this fate. Even the powerful East India Company was virtually bankrupt around the mid-nineteenth century.

The fourth source of economic power is grants (G of the formula in Equations 2 and 3 earlier). They are a product partly of the threat system in the form of tribute, theft, and taxes, and partly of the integrative system in the form of gifts. Taxes are essentially part of the redistribution of economic power through the threat system, although there are elements of integrative power here as taxes, for instance, can only be collected if the threat behind them is widely regarded as legitimate. Tribute and armed robbery arise out of almost pure threat with a small integrative component. Grants in the form of gifts belong mainly to the system of integrative power, such as grants within the family from parents to children and in old age from children to parents, charitable grants to beggars, contributions to worthy causes, foundation grants, welfare payments, foreign aid, and so on.

Integrative power: role power

Integrative power is one of the most subtle and least understood of the forms of power, yet in terms of long-run social dynamics it is probably the most important. It is, however, a very heterogeneous collection of types of power, and the question could legitimately be raised whether it is too heterogeneous to deserve a name. It is, however, convenient to have a category of relationships and types of power that does not fall easily into the other two categories of threat power and economic power, recognizing that we may want to subdivide it into various sub-categories.

Perhaps the most important category of integrative power is what might be called "role power." This is the power that comes to an occupant of a role simply because he or she occupies it rather than because of any personal characteristics of the occupier. Role power is closely bound up with the legitimacy of the role, the degree to which it is accepted by those who occupy it and by those who are related to it. Thus, anybody who becomes president of the United States increases his personal power because of the role he occupies. When President Nixon resigned from office, his personal power diminished enormously. When Lenin became in effect czar of the Russian Empire, even though he did not adopt the title, his person power increased enormously. It is the role, however, that gives the power, not the person, though the behavior of the person may affect the power of the role and frequently does. If the person performs very badly, the role itself may be delegitimated and its integrative power lost.

The exact dynamic process by which powerful roles are created is a complex, puzzling phenomenon. Roles evolve essentially in the human learning process. It is the image of roles in the minds of the human race that give them their power and nothing else. Repetition is an important element in this learning process. It is constantly drilled into us that certain roles are powerful, and if we never hear anything to the contrary, we come to believe it. Once we believe it, the sheer force of habit makes it hard to disturb that belief, except under conditions of extreme dislocation.

Symbolic power

Another important aspect of integrative power is symbolic power. This is significant mainly perhaps because it is part of the learning process by which role power is developed. The symbols of role power are an important part of the process by which it is established. These are such things as the ideology of the revolutionary, the crown and the robe of the monarch, the sword of the noble, the gown of the scholar, the collar of the cleric, the vestments of the priest, the flag and the anthem of the national state, the ritual of the church, and ceremonies of all kinds such as coronations, investitures, convocations, commencements, religious rituals, marriages, funerals, festivals, holidays. These are all part of the learning process by which the structure of role power is created. Art and architecture are important in creating the settings by which symbolic power is reinforced; temples, palaces, cathedrals, and campuses are all part of the symbolic learning process—what Adam Smith called "state" in the sense of "stately." Pageants and processions and the architecture, art, and music accompanying them all reinforce the distinction and legitimacy of important and powerful roles. Much of what the American Institutionalists like Thorstein Veblen (1934) and Clarence Ayres (1961) despised as the extravagant, conspicuous-consumption, ceremonial aspects of life are in fact extremely important elements in establishing role structures. The Capitol in Washington, DC proclaims at the top of its silent voice, "I am important and what goes on in here is important." Nobody would pay much attention to a government that met in a mud hut or a chief executive that lives in a hovel—unless, of course, these too become symbols of power, as they well may.

As legitimacy becomes established through age and habit, it may no longer be necessary to symbolize it by extravagant buildings and expenditures. State universities, for instance, are now such well-established legitimacies that they tend to abandon the gowns, processions, and elegant architecture with its associations with past legitimacies, and turn to building hideous shoeboxes and granting mail-order degrees. Titles are also important symbols of legitimacy. The loss of legitimacy of a role indeed through misbehavior or incompetence on the part of previous occupants can sometimes be restored by simply changing the title—the king or emperor becomes president or chairman, or challenged by women's liberation, a chairperson. Titles, "good words," and fashionable expressions, like "the name of the game," have a kind of ecology of their own. Those who use the right words and adopt the right gestures often achieve the powerful roles.

Community power and moral power

A very important form of integrative power, which has a considerable impact on the grants economy, might be called "community power." This is the power that people or groups have because they are recognized as belonging to a larger community. The smallest community is of course the family. Membership in a family confers very substantial power on the individual, which is greater, of course, the greater the wealth and power of the family to which the individual belongs. This is reflected in the importance of the family grants economy, which may be as much as 30 percent of the gross national product in the United States (Baerwaldt and Morgan, 1973). The national community is of increasing importance, particularly in the grants economy, in effecting redistributions. Belonging to communities within the larger community, like a governing class, may be of considerable importance in determining the power of an individual in obtaining grants and privileges. On the other hand, as national states are moved toward a larger basis of participation, the poorer classes within them have tended to benefit from redistributions, especially those classes perceived as victims of discrimination, but who are recognized as being part of the community.

This might almost be called "hypocrisy power," because when the practices of a community do not conform to its professed ideals, as has been the case in the United States, for instance, in regard to racial, cultural, and sexual discrimination, the victims of this hypocrisy can use it as a moral weapon to increase their own power in the community. Thus, whatever "black power" exists in the United States is mainly integrative power of this kind. It does not rest very much on threats or economic power, but on the appeal to the principle of community that "we are all Americans together." One sees this dramatically in comparing the United States, for instance, with a country that does not make these professions of community. The blacks in the United States are Americans, even if as a group they may be somewhat underprivileged citizens. The blacks in South Africa are not South Africans at all and are excluded completely from the political community as aliens in their native land. We see the exercise of community power in a very interesting way also in the disbanded empires. The French community, for instance, has a great deal of community power. The outlying parts of the remaining French Empire, such as Cayenne, Reunion, and until recently the territory of the Azars and Issas, extract large grants from metropolitan France because they belong to the French community. Even the British Commonwealth—a weak community—had its Columbo Plan for economic aid.

In general social dynamics it is important to identify something that might be called "moral power." The development of professed moral ideals is part of the larger dynamic of symbolic and persuasive systems, which has a strong, though poorly understood dynamic of its own. Moral power arises with the development of the perception of inconsistencies between these professed moral ideals and the actual practices of a society. This can be particularly important when the professed moral ideals are enshrined in sacred documents, like the Bible or the American Declaration of Independence, with which the hypocrite can be confronted.

Role-filling mechanisms

The problem of who gets into powerful roles is another very interesting question that is important in all large organizations, whether they are institutions of political life like the state, of economic life like the corporation or bank, or of religious life like the church. It is indeed large organizations that create powerful roles. Constitutions usually specify the mechanism by which role occupants are selected. It may be by appointment in the hierarchy, as the pope appoints cardinals or the president of the United States appoints justices to the Supreme Court. It may be by election, with all sorts of conventions about who votes and how many votes are necessary, as in the case of parliamentary or congressional democracy or in the case of the cardinals electing the pope. It may be by direct threat, as in a military coup, a revolution, or the capture of the police or armed forces by an ambitious and charismatic figure. Role occupancy may also be determined by inheritance, as in the hereditary monarchy. Even when there is no inheritance by persons, as in the case of the monarchy or hereditary aristocracy, there is often a hereditary class in the sense that children born of certain parents have a much better chance of achieving powerful roles than children born of others. Another important source of role power is sacredness, as an aspect of symbolic power. How this is created and destroyed we do not really know, but historically it has been of great importance. The interaction between the icon builders and the iconoclasts throughout human history has been of considerable importance. All these methods of role occupancy must find their own legitimacy and their own place in integrative structures, in interactions which may be of great complexity.

All forms of power interact

It is very important to stress that all the forms of power interact with each other. It is very rare indeed to find any of them in a pure form. Power indeed is an ecological system. It is hard perhaps to think of its many forms and manifestations as populations, but they do interact in a highly ecological way—sometimes reinforcing each other, sometimes competing with each other, sometimes in a predative relationship. Political power is an intricate mixture of threat power, economic power, allocative power, organizational power, monopoly power, and role power. Economic power likewise develops in a complex matrix of threat and integrative structures. Role power is closely related to threats on the one hand and to economic power on the other. No single form of power is dominant at all times and places, although the importance of different forms of power varies widely from place to place and from time to time. Sacred power was important in the European Middle Ages and is still important in communist countries today. This is the power of ideology and of the unquestionable and the untouchable. Economic power rises in importance under capitalist development and occasionally subordinates the political power. The power or weakness of classes and groups, of minorities, of blacks, of women, and of the poor of the Third World are all bound up in an intricate dynamic that all the forms of power interweave. Invoking a power that does not exist may be very dangerous to the invoker and actually diminish his power. Thinking of power in terms of a single form, such as threat power, may be highly unrealistic. On the other hand, imaginative leaders may create new forms of power. The more we appreciate the subtlety and yet at the same time the very persistent patterns of the dynamics of power in society, the more likely we are to move toward those forms of power that are in fact fruitful and can move us toward the better rather than toward the worse.

Notes

1 This article was previously published as chapter 11 in Kenneth E. Boulding, *Ecodynamics – A New Theory of Societal Evolution*, Beverly Hills and London: Sage, 1978, pp. 233–252.

2 For a further discussion, see Boulding (1964).

3 Stoke Poges is supposed to be the site of Thomas Gray's "Elegy Written in a Country Churchyard." The verse quoted is:

> Some village Hampden that with dauntless breast
> The little tyrant of his fields withstood,
> Some mute inglorious Milton here may rest
> Some Cromwell guiltless of his country's blood.

References

Ayres, Clarence E., *Towards a Reasonable Society*, Austin: University of Texas Press, 1961.

Baerwaldt, Nancy and James N. Morgan, "Trends in Intra-Family Transfers," in *Surveys of Consumers, 1971–72*, Lewis Mandell, ed., Ann Arbor: Survey Research Center, Institute for Social Research, University of Michigan, 1973.

Boulding, Kenneth E., "The Dimensions of Economic Freedom," in *The Nation's Economic Objectives*, Edgar Edwards, ed., Chicago: University of Chicago Press, 1964, 107–122; reprinted in *Kenneth Boulding/Collected Papers*, Larry Singell, ed., Boulder: Colorado Associated University Press, 1973, Vol. III, 201–218.

Gregg, Richard B., *The Power of Nonviolence*, New York: Schocken Books, 1966.

Sharp, Gene, *The Politics of Nonviolent Action*, Boston: Porter Sargent, 1973.

Smith, Adam, *The Wealth of Nations*, New York: Modern Library Edition, 1937.

Veblen, Thorstein, *The Theory of the Leisure Class*, New York: Modern Library, 1934.

6a Commentary article: Global institutions for an interdependent world[1]

Paul Streeten

After a brief discussion of some necessary conditions for an international order concerned with development, a distinction is drawn, following Boulding, between the exchange system, the threat system, and the integrative system. It pays one country to put up protectionist barriers, whether others do so or not; it pays one country to build up arms, whether others do so or not; it pays one country to pollute the global air and oceans, whether others do so or not. These typical prisoner's dilemma situations call for global reforms. There is a lag between technological advance that has unified the globe and the institution of the nation state. Suggestions are made as to how to overcome this lag, when the world no longer has a dominant poker that provides the global public goods and avoids the global public bads.

Introduction and summary

It has been said that the nation has become too small for the big things, and too big for the small things. In the course of growing national integration, the state has assumed more and more functions and responsibilities. To the nightwatchman's duty of maintaining law and order and enforcing contracts have been added such responsibilities as maintaining price stability, high levels of employment and high growth rates, population policy, regional policy, industrial policy, agricultural policy, responsibility for redistributing incomes and alleviating poverty through social services, protection of the environment, physical and human resource and energy policy, and others. As a result, some of these functions have not been carried out satisfactorily, while others have been neglected. The need for a greater degree of decentralization, delegation downwards, including delegation to market forces, and participation, is not the subject of this essay. It is part of the basic needs approach to development. But the need to delegate some functions upwards, to renounce some degree of national sovereignty in order to pursue national policies more effectively, is at the heart of this essay.

A major theme of this paper is that we are suffering from a lag of institutional adjustment behind technological advance. Technologically, the world has shrunk, but our social and political arrangements have not caught up with this advance. The result has been threats of mutual impoverishment and even mutual destruction.

In analyzing the direction of needed reforms, a distinction is drawn, following Boulding, between three systems: the exchange system, the threat system, and the integrative or love system. The bulk of the economic development literature is concerned with the exchange system, in which transactions between North and South yield mutual benefits. Discussion of the threat system is largely confined to experts on military matters, but should also cover economic threats such as competitive protectionism, competitive devaluation, or investment wars. The integrative system, which calls for sacrifices by the North in the spirit of human solidarity, is not fashionable, but it is argued that without it little progress can be made. It embraces not only more and better development aid, but also changes in the rules, procedures, and institutions that are now biased in favor of the North (such as cascading tariffs that discriminate against processing in developing countries, or discriminatory rules about immigration to the industrialized countries), and more "voice" in the councils of nations for the developing countries.

Causes of the disorder

In order to understand the present international economic disorder, it is useful to remember some of the functions that any international order for economic development must fulfill. There must be, first, a source for the generation of balance-of-payments surpluses. Second, there must be institutions that fulfill three financial functions: (1) institutions that convert these surpluses into long-term development loans on commercial terms; (2) lenders of last resort to provide liquidity should confidence collapse; and (3) suppliers and withdrawers of international liquidity, according to the requirements of international trade and capital flows. There must be, third, the industrial and commercial capacity to produce, sell, and deliver the capital goods needed for development. And there must be, fourth, military power to back the economic power, to see that contracts are enforced, property rights observed, and peace kept.

These four functions had been combined until about 1970 by a single dominant power, with the rest of the world dependent on the coordination by the center. Until 1914, this power was Great Britain, which established an international order and developed the areas of recent settlement in Canada, the United States, Australia, New Zealand, South Africa, and Latin America under the *Pax Britannica.* Current account surpluses were generated by Britain, the financial institutions grew in the City of London, gold or sterling provided the reserve currency for international monetary transactions, the industrial capacity of the north of England provided the iron, steel, and capital goods, and the British navy kept world order.

There was not much of an order between the two world wars, but for a quarter of a century after the end of World War II, the *Pax Americana* established an international order centered on the mighty dollar. Current account surpluses originated from the United States, and for a time people worried about a chronic dollar shortage. New York became a rival center to London for financial transactions; the dollar replaced sterling as the world's reserve currency. Industrial capacity grew strong in the United States, and the American army enforced the

American peace. But since 1970 these functions have been fragmented, split up between different centers, without coordination. For a period, the surpluses were generated by a few desert sheikhdoms in the Gulf, joined by West Germany and, most conspicuously and recently, by Japan. As the capital surpluses of the OPEC countries dwindled away and turned into deficits with the drop in the price of oil, West Germany and Japan continued to run surpluses. And $100 billion of surpluses were unaccounted for, presumably largely unrecorded capital flight from some of the developing, debtor countries.

The concentration in the financial centers of London and New York was diluted by the mushrooming of banks in Singapore, Hong Kong, Japan, Germany, and their affiliates in the Cayman Islands, the Bahamas, and other tax havens. International liquid reserves were either too plentiful or too scarce and ill distributed, in spite of the creation of special drawing rights (SDRs). Industrial capacity increasingly shifted to West Germany and Japan, and to the newly industrializing countries. One of the most striking structural changes in the world economy has been the growth of manufacturing production and trade in an increasing number of developing countries. The military pygmies are the economic giants, whereas the military superpowers are economically weakened by their military expenditure. The four functions are dispersed among different groups of countries. The coordination arising from dominance by one country has been replaced by more or less successful forms of cooperation between countries with different degrees of power.

This breakup of uncoordinated functions provides us with the opportunity for a constructive institutional response. It allows for the replacement of the past international orders based on dominance and dependence, and on the needs of a superpower, by a pluralistic order of interdependence. International liquidity would be created according to global requirements of trade and capital flows, not according to the need to run deficits in the balance of payments of a capital-rich, reserve currency country. Financial institutions and multinational corporations would compete with one another on equal terms, and everyone would be free to buy in the cheapest and sell in the dearest markets. Many would say that such an order, even if it were desirable (which some doubt) would not be feasible. Richard Cooper has pointed out[2] that it took 50 years for international cooperation in such an obvious area as health to be achieved.

On the other hand, Robert Keohane has shown that it is easier to maintain international regimes than to bring them into being. Their continued momentum, after the power that has set them up has declined, depends on their economizing in transaction costs, on inertia, sunk costs, and absence of alternatives. This explains to some extent the continued existence of the rules and procedures set up after the war even after American power has ebbed away.[3]

Interdependence

The period of postwar US dominance was one of comparative calm, economic expansion, and commitment to development on the part of the rich countries.

The retreat from Third World commitments started in the 1970s. The two oil shocks, the election of Mrs. Thatcher in Britain and Mr. Reagan in the United States, the turning of attention to East–West issues abroad and to fighting inflation and unemployment at home, and the dominance of the international debt problem all contributed to this. At the same time, the old doctrinal wisdom on economic policy was overturned, partly as a result of internal theoretical strains. The emphasis shifted from fiscal to monetary policy, from demand management to supply management, from accelerator to interest rates as investment determinants, from public interventions to reliance on the private sector and market forces, and, somewhat earlier, from fixed to flexible exchange rates. In the same vein, there was a turn from concern for development to domestic issues.

Interdependence is often said to be large and to have increased. International trade is taken to be an indicator of interdependence, and its high, and, with some interruptions, growing values are accepted as evidence. Yet three important qualifications are necessary.

First, if we take the ratio of international trade to national income, the rapid growth in the postwar decades until 1976 can be taken to be a return to pre-1914 values. For the major countries, trade as a proportion of GNP has just about caught up with what it had been before the damage done by two world wars and the Great Depression. The ratio of exports to GNP was nearly 14 percent in 1960 and over 22 percent at the end of the 1970s, but it was about that before 1914.[4] If, however, we allow for the fact that the public sector has greatly increased, and that the prices of nontradable services in this sector have risen more than the average price level, trade as a ratio of private tradable goods has indeed increased since 1914 and continues to grow.

The second qualification is that few countries, or (in some cases) groups within countries, have participated in the benefits from growing trade, though their number has increased. The large, poor masses of the Indian subcontinent and of sub-Saharan Africa have not participated substantially in the growth of international trade.

The third qualification is that neither the volume of trade nor its rate of growth should be accepted as an indicator of economic interdependence, but rather the damage that would be done by its elimination, i.e., consumers' and producers' surpluses. Much trade is conducted in slightly differentiated consumer goods, which could readily be replaced by domestic production without great loss to consumers, judged by consumers' surpluses. This would have to be qualified only if the product differentiation were based on substantial economies of scale or yielded great benefits to consumers, so that the elimination of these lines and their replacement by domestic production would be very costly or would reduce consumers' satisfaction greatly. There may even be an excess of international trade beyond the optimum indicated by trade theory because of cross-hauling at prices that are below total unit cost for foreign sales of, say, motor cars. On the other hand, small and slowly or not-at-all growing items of trade could be of very great importance and lead to substantial losses if they were eliminated. The United States, for instance, depends strongly on imports of manganese, tin, and chromium.

Trade is, of course, only one, and not the most important, among many manifestations of economic interdependence. Others comprise the flow of factors of production, capital, enterprise, and labor across frontiers; there is the exchange of assets, of legal rights, of information and knowledge. In addition to economic interdependence, there are educational and cultural, as well as military, strategic, and political impulses that are rapidly propagated throughout the world.

Sir Arthur Lewis, when he invited us to imagine that all the developed countries were to sink under the sea,[5] suggested that, after a period of adjustment, the length of which would remain to be specified, it would not make much difference to the developing world. The same might be said about the developed countries, if the developing countries were to sink under the sea. Yet, with these qualifications, there is no doubt that interdependence has increased.

Technology and institutions

There is a demonstrated gap between the rapid advances in technical knowledge, resulting in revolutions in transport, information, and communications which have shrunk distances, on the one hand, and the political institution of the nation state, with its claim to sovereign authority and attempts to regulate the lives of its citizens and respond to their clamor for protection and insurance against the impact of interdependence on the other. It has been vividly symbolized by the shooting down of the Korean commercial airliner over Soviet territory, or by the Iranian revolution, or by the large sums of money moving across the world in response to instant information, and determining exchange and interest rates. As Stanley Hoffmann has said, the nation state has remained more obstinate than obsolete.[6] The tensions and contradictions created by this gap are at the root of the negative sum games, the mutual infliction of damage in an interdependent, though far from integrated, in some respects disintegrating, world.

The main conclusion I draw from what I have said so far is that we are suffering from a lag of institutional adaptation to the technological and political reality of the end of the twentieth century. One institution, the nation state, is still rooted in a soil over 300 years old, going back to the Peace of Westphalia, while modern science and technology have moved ahead rapidly. The dispersal and fragmentation of the four development functions have meant that opportunities have been missed, and damage has been inflicted by the uncoordinated actions of these nation states.

I do not want to be misunderstood. When I speak of institutional innovation, I do not mean additional international bureaucracies. New bodies, organizations, and forums have mushroomed. But international bureaucrats have often been an obstacle rather than a help to progress and reform, and have increased the resistance to change. Sir Herman Bondi has said that the stupidity of an organization is proportional to the cube of the number of its members. One can imagine the size of global institutions. What I have in mind by institutional innovation is rules, procedures, and organizations that have precise technical functions (such as the successful Universal Postal Union) are immune from politicization, and are publicly accountable. I agree with viewing institutions "not simply as formal organizations with headquarters buildings and organized staffs, but more broadly as 'recognized patterns of practice around which expectations converge' (Young, 1980, p. 337)."[7]

It is worth noting that these institutional responses have occurred in the private sector. The multinational corporations, the Eurocurrency market, and the transnational banks are responses to the revolution in information, communications, travel, and transport. The equivalent in the public sector can be achieved, as is shown by some successful international bodies, such as the International Communication Union, the International Civil Aviation Organization, the World Meteorological Association, and a few others. We should aim at functional solutions at the global level.

Many of the problems in the international relations of interdependence arise from a combination of the free-rider problem, Olson's problem,[8] and the prisoner's dilemma. Indeed, the free-rider or contributor's dilemma is a special case of the prisoner's dilemma. The free-rider problem exists because some of the solutions of international difficulties consist in the provision of public goods.[9] A public good is one from whose supply all those who value the good benefit, irrespective of whether they have contributed to its costs. The concept can readily be extended to cover common goals or common interests, the achievement of which benefits all, irrespective of whether they have contributed to the costs of achieving these goals or interests. The enjoyment of the good or service by one person does not detract from the enjoyment of others. In this sense, international cooperation and the prevention of international wars are public goods. So are markets and a working international monetary order with an international central bank as a lender of last resort and as a provider of liquidity. Scientific research is of this kind. An international income tax or the coordination of international fixed investment decisions fall under the same heading.

These public goods will be, however, systematically undersupplied, because any one country will not find it worth its while to take the appropriate action, relying instead on others to do so; even though the benefits would exceed the costs were all to contribute. Each country, knowing that others will not act, has no incentive to be the only one to contribute to something that benefits others. As a result, international cooperation, peace, research, international monetary stability, and world development will be undersupplied. No one contributes and everyone is worse off. The Invisible Hand, which, according to Adam Smith, coordinates the independent decisions of a multitude of individuals, could also be applied and has been applied to the unintended coordination of the actions of nation states. But this Invisible Hand that is supposed to guide the self-interest of each agent, whether individual or country, to the common good, is not to be seen in the cases discussed above.[10]

It is true that free-rider problems are not ubiquitous. Individuals may be afraid of the sanctions attached to such behavior. Or they may avoid free-riding because they believe that their contributions will make others contribute. Individuals sometimes do behave according to Kant's categorical imperative, in a manner that can be universalized. Otherwise why should anybody clap after a theater performance (assuming you don't get pleasure from clapping), or vote in a democratic election? But Kant's categorical imperative, or the notion that we should behave in the way we want others to behave, may apply less to the actions of nation states than to those of individuals. Leadership, and even hegemony, particularly by a strong superpower, and enlightened self-interest can contribute to such Kantian behavior by nation states.

The prisoner's dilemma arises because each country, in promoting its own national interest rationally, contributes to a situation in which all countries are worse off. It pays any one country to put up protectionist barriers, whether others do so or not; it pays any one country to build up its arms, whether others do so or not; it pays any one country to pollute the common air and oceans, whether others do so or not. These are typical prisoner's dilemma situations, self-damaging and possibly self-destructive. Just as public goods are undersupplied, public bads are oversupplied. No single actor has an adequate incentive to remove them. This applies to competitive protectionism, beggar-my-neighbor devaluations or deflations, the spread of inflation, investment wars, the arms race, global pollution of the air and the sea, overfishing and excessive exploitation of exhaustible resources to which no property rights are attached, and similar situations. Richard Cooper has likened the situation to a crowd in which each member, wishing to see better a passing parade, rises to his tiptoes, with the result that no one sees better but everyone is more uncomfortable.[11] What is needed is either coordination and cooperation or supra-national sanctions that force all countries to act in what will amount to their self-interest. Without such coordinated or enforced action, the outcome of nationally rational actions will be irrational damage and mutual impoverishment. For the damaging action is the best, whether other nations act similarly or not.

On the other hand, according to Coase's theorem, if, in the absence of transaction costs, and in the presence of a legal framework and full information, one country inflicts damages on another which are greater than the benefits to the first country, the injured country can enter into a contract and pay the injuring country to not inflict the injury, and be better off. Likewise, the injuring country can compensate the injured country for the damage, and still be better off. Such international compensations or bribes are in fact not common but they point, in principle, to the other extreme from that of the prisoner's dilemma. In such a world, Pareto optimal allocations would be achieved, for any deviation would give rise to joint gains, out of which losers could be compensated for accepting them.[12]

The difficulties of reaching Coase-type agreements and the dangers of ending in prisoner's dilemma situations are aggravated by four factors. First, there is no longer a hegemonic power, such as Britain before World War I, which is prepared to carry a large part of the cost of the public goods to exercise leadership to make others contribute. Second, the proliferation of independent nation states to about 160 makes agreements more difficult than in an age when fewer governments could establish a system of mutual trust or enforcement (Olson's problem). It is, however, true that most of these nations are quite small, and that coordination by a few large ones is what matters. Third, the rapid pace of social and technical change makes it more difficult to evolve the stability on which trust can be built. It has been shown that repeated games of prisoner's dilemma in similar situations tend to lead to cooperative solutions. Rapid change in the conditions on which cooperation is based prevents the formation of this kind of stability.[13] Fourth, the absence of world government and world courts makes it impossible to establish property rights, enforce contracts, and set the sanctions for failing to abide by agreements.

As Michael Lipton has said,[14] if all outcomes were noncooperative prisoner's dilemmas, no government would be possible. If all were according to Coase's theorem, no government would be needed (except for income redistribution). The actual world is between the two extremes. But the relations of nation states are nearer the prisoner's dilemma end of the spectrum, for the four reasons given above.

Three systems

In order to set up a framework for a more constructive response to the call of the South for a better world order, Kenneth Boulding's distinction between the exchange system, the threat system, and the integrative system is useful. The exchange system is based on the principle: "I do something good for you if you do something good for me." It covers the area of mutual interests. The threat system is based on the principle: "Unless you do something good for me I shall do something horrid to you." In the integrative or love system, the principles of love and duty applied to ourselves and our family are extended to other members of a wider community. We do good neither in the expectation of good in return, nor under the threat of harm, but from a sense of unity or solidarity or duty. This sense can derive from a common ideology or from a sense of community and obligation. These not only reduce the danger of too many free-riders, so that each contributes voluntarily to the common good that also benefits him, but also lead to some sacrifice for the benefit of others: genuine altruism. The three systems correspond roughly to positive-sum games, in which all participants benefit, avoiding negative-sum games, in which all would lose in the absence of coordinated action, and zero-sum games, in which one side has to make concessions for the benefit of others.

Systems can, of course, be mixed. What appears to be a genuine sacrifice in the short run may turn out to be beneficial to the sacrificer in the long run. Or the removal of the benefit (such as access to markets) can constitute a threat. Or the division of the joint gains can give rise to conflicts. This, in practice, is a particularly important obstacle to the pursuit of positive-sum games. The gains come to be accepted and only the wrangles over their division remain.

It is important to distinguish between doing what is right, and wishing to be seen to be doing right because this is in the nation's self-interest. The United States is dedicated to a value system, what Myrdal called the American Creed. It adds cohesion to American society and strength to its foreign policy. But it is an entirely different thing to say, as a paragraph in the Kissinger Commission Report on Central America does, that it is in the American national self-interest *to be seen* to be acting right. "To preserve the moral authority of the United States. To be perceived by others as a nation that does what is right *because* it is right is one of this country's principal assets." There is all the difference in the world between doing what is right because it is right, and doing it because the United States must be seen to do what is right. It is in the US national interest to be seen to act in a moral way. The first action is moral, disinterested; the second self-interested.[15]

The distinction between the three systems is useful for a clear analysis, but not for negotiations. There we have an interest in pretending that what is truly a benefit to us is a sacrifice, so that we may get concessions on other fronts.

The exchange system of mutual interests has been much promoted, especially by the Brandt Commission, the OECD, and the Overseas Development Council. Trade liberalization is the most frequently advocated policy. "Man was born free, but everywhere he is in chains." Similarly, all economists recommend free(r) trade, but everywhere there is protection.

It might be thought that, by and large, people, groups, and nations are very good in detecting and pursuing their self-interest and that not much exhortation is needed. But, as we have seen, there can be important divergencies between reaching for and achieving what is in one's interest. In some cases, the self-interested action leads to damage to oneself. We have already discussed the prisoner's dilemma and the free-rider problem. The first leads to the infliction of mutual harm, the second to the undersupply of public goods and the oversupply of public bads. In addition, the national interest may be damaged for several reasons. There can be conflict between groups with different power, articulateness, and influence, so that the more powerful influence policy more strongly, even if their gains are smaller than the losses of the less powerful, less articulate, less influential. Or there may be conflict between dispersed larger and concentrated smaller gains, or between uncertain larger and certain smaller gains, or between larger future and smaller present gains, or between perceived larger but really smaller gains. The last may be one of the reasons why the general public and policy makers are not prepared to surrender national sovereignty, even though its surrender would lead to a more effective achievement of self-interested objectives than the formal adherence to full sovereignty, autonomy, and control, in the same way in which the acceptance of traffic regulations enlarges our freedom to drive accident free, while restricting our freedom of choice. Finally, the gains to some may be much larger than the gains to others, who, though gaining a little, resent this. In any case, the distribution of gains presents quite different problems at the international level from those at the national. For any national community, a central government can tax and redistribute gains if this is deemed desirable. But without a world government, this cannot be done at the international level.

In all these cases, selfish action may not lead to the achievement of self-interest, and the achievement of self-interested objectives may involve some sacrifice in unconstrained and uncoordinated selfishness. Moreover, it would be only a fluke if the actions dictated by national self-interest were to coincide with our development objectives, whether these are accelerated growth, growth with equity, redistribution with growth, or meeting basic needs. In particular, the poorest groups and the poorest countries will tend to be left out of a strategy based on national self-interest.

Removal of the dangers of the threat system and the avoidance of negative-sum games should have a high priority, for they can lead to mutual impoverishment and even destruction: disarmament, removal of the threat of protection, and an end to beggar-my-neighbor deflation or inflation, and of "voluntary" export restraints, are clearly lines of action worth pursuing. They call for international coordination and institutional responses of the kind discussed in this paper.

It may be thought that all agreements entered into voluntarily between states must amount to positive-sum games, in which each is better off. But this is not so. Some alliances may be formed with the specific purpose, or with the unintended result, of inflicting costs on outsiders. In this case, alliances or pacts can lead to negative-sum games.

One of the reasons why agreements on avoiding negative-sum games, on reducing bads and creating anti-bads, are so difficult, is to be found in the logic of collective action, so well analyzed by Mancur Olson.[16] The larger the group, the weaker the incentive for any one member to contribute to the action that benefits all. We now have about 160 countries in the world. As a result, the public goods are not produced, or are underproduced, even though their value is greater than their costs to the group of countries as a whole. It is true that some smaller subset of countries, the Group of 5 or the Group of 7, may take responsibility for the rest, but they may also act in a way that imposes costs on others.

We can build on areas of common national interests, emphasizing mutual benefits to be derived from, e.g., resumption of orderly and equitable growth in the world economy, forswearing self-defeating protectionism, exploring ways of increasing the resources in globally scarce supply, etc. But while there is considerable scope for positive-sum games in exploring areas of common and mutual interests, and avoiding self-defeating, mutually destructive policies of the prisoner's dilemma type, there is also a "higher" interest in a world order that both is, and is seen to be, equitable, that is acceptable and therefore accepted, and that reduces conflict and confrontation.

All societies need for their self-regulation and for social control a basis of moral principles. Individuals are ready to make sacrifices for the communities in which they live. This forms the basis of the integrative system. Can this principle stop at the nation state? A belief in the harmony between self-interest and altruism is deep-seated in Anglo-Saxon thought and action. One is reminded of the eighteenth-century bishop Joseph Butler: "When we sit down in a cool hour, we can neither justify to ourselves this or any other pursuit, till we are convinced that it will be for our happiness..."[17] The only question is why it appears to be easier to identify, or at least harmonize, individual happiness with the national interest than with that of the world community. It is odd that a moral, disinterested concern by rich countries with the development of the poor is hardly ever conceded. As hypocrisy is the tribute vice pays to virtue, so professions of national self-interest in the development of poor countries may be the tribute that virtue has to pay to vice.

In the present fashion of stressing common and mutual interests, we run the danger of underestimating the power of moral or humanitarian appeals. The Netherlands, Sweden, and Norway, which have put international cooperation squarely on a moral basis, have hit the 0.7 percent aid target. It is the countries in which aid has been sold to the public as being in the national self-interest where the effort is lagging.

The common interests must also be defined in terms of different time horizons: the next year, the next five years, the next 20 years. There may be conflicts and tradeoffs between these different time spans. For example, concessionary aid to the poorest may involve economic sacrifices in the near future but, by laying the foundations for a world in which all human beings born can fully develop their potential, it contributes to the long-term interest of mankind.

One difficulty is that in democracies adults have votes, but children and the unborn do not. The fight is not only against powerfully organized vested interests, but also against all our own short-term interests that neglect the interests of future generations.

Any attempt to build cooperation for development on moral principles has to answer three questions. First, do the rich in a community have an obligation in social justice (not only in charity) to the poor, and do the poor have a just claim on the rich? Second, does mankind constitute a community in the relevant sense, or do communities stop at national boundaries? Third, does the existence of national governments not interfere with the discharge of the obligations of the rich, if such obligations exist, to the poor in the world community, if there is such a community?

The first question cannot be answered without an analysis of various theories of moral philosophy. But both utilitarianism and various types of entitlement theory would provide a basis for an obligation of the rich to contribute to improving the lot of the poor in a community. Perhaps more difficult is the case for saying that mankind does constitute a community in the relevant sense. Social contract theories might say that we need not do anything for the world community because the world community does not do anything for us, whereas the state provides protection, security, and certain other services. But even if the first two questions were answered in the affirmative, the third question presents the difficulty that the discharge of the obligation may take the form of what opponents of aid-giving have called "a redistribution of resources from the poor in rich countries to the rich in poor countries." To meet this difficulty we have to exercise our institutional imagination in finding procedures and institutions that avoid, or at least minimize, this possibility.

The "higher" interest in an acceptable world order can be defined either in moral terms or in terms of the desire to avoid negative-sum games, breakdown, and wars. Whatever the definition and justification, its aim is to transform adversary relationship into cooperation. When interests diverge or conflict, the task of statesmanship is to reconcile them. This is a task quite distinct from, and more important than, that of exploring areas of common or mutual interest. It is in this light that cooperative action to eradicate world poverty and to restructure the international economic order has to be seen.

What, then, are the requirements of a sensible international order? It will consist of negative rules of what national governments must not do, and agreements on certain positive cooperative actions. The rules of abstention will be intended to prevent negative-sum games, and the rules of action to create some public goods and avoid public bads. Ralph Bryant has called these rules "supranational traffic regulations."[18] Some critics have accused the developing countries of wishing exemption from some general rules (such as reciprocity in tariff reductions or the banning of preferential trading arrangements) to which the developed countries should adhere. The discussion about appropriate rules for international economic relations has suffered from a long-standing confusion. It is the confusion between *uniform* (sometimes also called general) principles or rules (the opposite of specific ones, and therefore necessarily simple) and *universal* principles or rules (which may be highly specific and complicated, provided that they contain no uneliminable reference to individual cases). Further confusion is caused if a third characteristic of rules is added—*inflexibility* over time—and confused with either uniformity or universality. A rule is capable of being *altered*, though it remains either uniform (i.e., simple) or universal (i.e., may have a lot of "exceptions" written into it). The "equal" treatment of unequals is not a principle of justice, and a general rule commanding it is an unjust rule. In order to prevent partiality and partisanship, rules have to be universal, i.e., not contain references to individual cases. They may not, and indeed should not, be uniform. They should pay attention to the varying characteristics and circumstances of different countries.

Those who charge the developing countries with asking for exemptions from rules are guilty of this confusion between *uniform* and *universal. Thus* a differentiated system of multi-tier preferences according to the level of development of the exporting countries may be best and most just for a group of trading countries at different stages of development. A fair system of rules also points to the differentiation in responsibilities and rights according to circumstances. Middle-income countries would not have the responsibility to give aid, but neither would they receive it. They would not have to give trade preferences, but neither would they receive them. Even finer differentiation would be possible. A country with a large balance-of-payments surplus might be asked to contribute to loans because of its foreign exchange earnings, and, if its citizens enjoy high incomes, to aid because of its income per head, but might receive trade preferences if its level of industrialization is low. The 0.7 percent aid target would be replaced by a system in which those below a certain income per head are exempted, and the percentage target rises with income per head.

There is, of course, a practical and tactical case for *simple* rules, which might overrule the case in fairness for universal (though complex) rules: they are less open to abuse and easier to police. And there may be a tactical case for uniform rules; they may be easier to negotiate. It is for such pragmatic reasons rather than on theoretical grounds that one may advocate that rules should not be too complex, and should not be changed too often.

Any specific proposal, such as nonreciprocity in trade concessions, or trade preferences would, of course, have to be examined on its merits. But the distinction between "exemption from rules" and "drawing up new rules" is logically untenable, to the extent to which the call for exemption is really a call for a set of universal rules that pays attention to the different characteristics and circumstances of different countries, just as income tax allowances for dependents or lower rates on earned than on unearned income are not "exceptions" but reflect our notions of fairness.

Those who are concerned with changing the rules of international relations are aiming partly at removing biases in the present rules, and partly at the exercise of countervailing power where at present the distribution of power is felt to be unequal. They are also concerned with counteracting biases that arise not from rules but from the nature of economic processes, such as the cumulative nature of gains accruing to those who already have more resources, and the cumulative damage inflicted on those who have initially relatively little.

In so far as the call for new rules is about strictly economic relations, there is scope for positive-sum games. But in so far as it is about national power relations between sovereign states with different and conflicting aims, power is by its very nature a *relative* concept, and what is at stake are *zero-sum games.* The demand by the developing countries for greater participation in the councils of the world and for corrections in the biases of the international power distribution is bound to diminish the power of the industrialized countries in conditions of conflict.

In addition to rules, there is a need for institutions. Let me give five illustrations of the kind of institutional reform I have in mind. First, there is the creation of an international central bank that would be able to create (and withdraw) international liquidity, both for transactions and for precautionary reasons. A panic run on the banks would cause an international financial breakdown unless an institutional arrangement existed that provided the liquidity. The General Arrangements to Borrow do this now to some extent, but a central bank would do this on a more solid and reliable basis.

The central bank would also be responsible for the growth of global reserves at a pace which gives neither an inflationary nor a deflationary bias to the world economy. In the absence of such a global authority, the competitive actions of nation states will tend to be either too restrictive, transmitting unemployment and unused industrial capacity, as each country scrambles to accumulate scarce reserves, or too expansionary, transmitting inflation throughout the world, as the reserve currency country incurs large balance-of-payments deficits to pay for economic or military ventures abroad.

Second, there is the institution of an international income tax. This could be levied progressively on GNP according to incomes per head, or, better, consumption per head so as to encourage saving, with a lower exemption limit. The tax would be collected automatically, but disbursed to developing countries according to agreed criteria. The monitoring of the fulfillment of the criteria should be done either by the developing countries themselves or by a mutually accepted transnational body.

Third, there is an international body to provide information on decisions for fixed, durable investment with long construction periods, so that we avoid the lurches from scarcity to excess capacity in steel, shipbuilding, and fertilizers that we are suffering now. It should obviously not be a super-cartel that goes in for market-sharing agreements, but a method of coordinating investment decisions.

Fourth, there is an international investment trust that channels the surpluses of the surplus countries into a multilaterally guaranteed scheme to the developing countries. It would have guarantees against inflation and exchange rate losses for the lenders. The loans would be on commercial terms to middle-income countries. At the time of this writing, Japan has become the largest lending country, with a large surplus in its balance of payments on current account. This surplus is in search of good and safe investment opportunities, which calls for the creation of appropriate institutions to convert these surpluses into long-term loans to the developing countries. This would be in the interest of Japan, which could continue its export-led growth without having either to reduce its rate of savings or to find domestic, lower-yielding alternatives; it would be in the interest of other OECD countries on whose exports some of the loans will be spent; it would be in the interest of the capital-hungry developing countries, whose resources are waiting to be mobilized by such capital flows; and it would be in the interest of the world economy, which could maintain its expansionary momentum. An interest-subsidization scheme could be grafted onto this for the low-income countries.

If this argument is accepted, the general call for Japan to raise its level of consumption or divert investment to the domestic market is seen to be misplaced. Higher consumption should not be applauded in a world that is short of savings and in need of capital. Higher domestic Japanese investment is not desirable if it is subject to declining returns. Instead of calling on Japan to reflate, we should mobilize its excess savings and channel them on acceptable terms, by long-term lending or equity capital, through either the private or the public capital markets to the developing countries.

Finally, there should be a better way of dealing with the oil price problem than the erratic, zigzag movements that we have experienced since 1973. Oil-producing and oil-consuming countries should get together and agree on a small, annual increase in the real price of oil, say 2 percent. This assumes agreement on the best guess as to the real price of oil in 20 years' time. The balance-of-payments surpluses generated by such an increase could be channeled into the investment trust proposed above. The incentives to explore for more oil, find alternatives to oil, and increase conservation would be gradual but steady. The incentives for the oil-exporting countries to use their revenue for investment in alternative productive assets would also be gradual and steady. Incentives to consumers of oil would also permit a foreseeable and gradual adaptation. There would be neither debt crises nor the sloshing around of large funds in search of remunerative and safe returns. And the world economy would be spared at least one major source of shocks and instability. Both inflation and unemployment rates would be reduced.

There is also a need for reforming the institutions charged with North–South cooperation. What has the Marshall Plan to teach us for current relations with the South? It is now generally agreed that the Marshall Plan loans to Europe were given on too soft terms, perhaps in too large amounts, but they achieved their objective of rapid European reconstruction. It has also become a platitude to say that the lessons are not applicable to the developing countries because in Europe the human capital existed, and to reconstruct with a skilled and well-motivated labor force is a much easier task than developing an underdeveloped society. But one important lesson can still be learned. Critics of both the left and the right have pointed to numerous faults of aid; in particular that it has not achieved its intended objectives, whether they are poverty alleviation, redistribution, or economic growth. They conclude that we should get rid of aid. A better conclusion might be to get rid of the faults and to evolve mechanisms that ensure that the objectives of the aid donors are achieved. The intervention of donor governments for the purpose of applying performance criteria to development aid has been regarded as inconsistent with national sovereignty, has been dismissed as intrusive, and has bred acrimony. It has also been difficult to separate objectives of accelerating development from objectives in the narrow national interest, such as export promotion, gaining votes in the United Nations, forming political alliances, or getting strategic support. Performance criteria imposed in bilateral relations by donor governments have therefore been suspect and counterproductive.

The task is then to evolve institutions that achieve the objectives of the donors and the recipients and are trusted by both sides. It is to resolve the dilemma between avoiding intrusiveness and paying respect to national sovereignty on the one hand, and responsible accounting for taxpayers' money on the other. Here the Marshall Plan has still something to teach. It is not about the speed of development, which for European reconstruction was faster than for the structural changes needed for development, nor about the terms of the aid, but about monitoring procedures. The European powers were encouraged to monitor one another's performance, and the heavy hand of the US government was kept out of it. Each government submitted a plan which was inspected, vetted, and monitored by other European governments in the Organization for European Economic Cooperation (OEEC). Controls by peers rather than supervisors is also a principle advocated in business management. A similar procedure could be adopted for groups of developing countries.

There are at least two additional options. It would be desirable to create a genuine transnational secretariat, whose loyalty would be only to the international community, that would be trusted by both donors and recipients. The staff of the present multilateral agencies does not quite achieve this, partly because the system of country quotas emphasizes national origins rather than merit, partly because the organizations are intergovernmental institutions, and partly because the recruitment, training, location, etc. of the staff of these organizations to some extent conflict with the ethos of a staff serving only the global community. In addition to having technical competence, the staff would be trained to be sensitive to social and political factors.

Finally, we might consider setting up a council of wise men and women whose task it would be to monitor the performance of both donors and recipients, and who again would be trusted by both sides. The existence of national governments that insist on the exercise of their full sovereignty at present interferes with the moral and enlightened self-interest objectives of development cooperation. Not until this obstacle is overcome can we make progress.

Notes

1 This article was previously published in *World Development*, 1989, Vol. 17, No. 9 (1989), pp. 1349–1359.
2 Cooper (1985).
3 Keohane (1984), pp. 100–103. The key question discussed in the book *After Hegemony* is "how international cooperation can be maintained among the advanced capitalist states in the absence of American hegemony" (p. 43). From that point of view, the normative position taken in this paper is naively institutionalist, but the positive position is realist, for I believe that the postwar international regimes are best explained in terms of US hegemony. Nevertheless, Keohane comes to the same conclusion, viz., that continuing cooperation is possible if built on the interests of the leading capitalist states.
4 The ratio of exports to GNP for the United Kingdom was 19.3 percent in 1913, 20.7 percent in 1976, and 21.7 percent in 1984 (28.4 percent including services); for the United States, 6.5 percent in 1913, 6.8 percent in 1976, and 6 percent in 1984 (7.4 percent including services); and for Germany 20.5 percent in 1913, 22.3 percent in 1976, and 26.5 percent in 1984 (33.5 percent including services).
5 Lewis (1970), p. 12.
6 Hoffman (1966), quoted in Keohane (1984), p. 238.
7 Keohane (1984), p. 8. The quotation is from Young (1980).
8 See below.
9 Kindleberger (1978), p. 15, and (1986).
10 Related problems have also been discussed under the concepts of "tragedy of the commons" (each agent, acting in his self-interest, contributes to social losses, such as overgrazing on a common pasture or overpopulating the globe), and "social traps" (no driver has an incentive to install a gadget that reduces pollution). These, as well as prisoner's dilemma, "collective action," and Olson's problem, are special instances of "market failure."
11 Cooper (1986), pp. 160–173.
12 Lipton (1985).
13 Axelrod (1984).
14 Lipton (1985).
15 The point is made and the quotation cited in Ash (1984).
16 Olson (1971).
17 Joseph Butler, Sermons, Sermon 11, para. 20.
18 Bryant (1980), p. 470.

References

Ash, Timothy Garton, "Back yards," *New York Review of Books*, November 22, 1984.

Axelrod, R., *The Evolution of Cooperation* (New York: Basic Books, 1984).

Bryant, Ralph, *Money and Monetary Policy in Interdependent Nations* (Washington, DC: The Brookings Institution, 1980).

Cooper, Richard N., "International economic cooperation: Is it desirable: Is it likely?" *Bulletin of the American Academy of Arts and Sciences*, Vol. 39, No. 2 (November 1985).

Cooper, Richard N., *The Economics of Interdependence: Economic Policy in the Atlantic Community* (New York: McGraw-Hill for the Council on Foreign Relations, 1986).

Hoffman, Stanley, "Obstinate or obsolete? The fate of the nation-state and the case of Western Europe," *Daedalus*, Vol. 95 (Summer 1966), pp. 862–915.

Keohane, Robert O., *After Hegemony: Cooperation and Discord in the World Economy* (Princeton, NJ: Princeton University Press, 1984).

Kindleberger, C.P., *Government and International Trade, Essays in International Finance*, 129 (Princeton, NJ: Princeton University, 1978).

Kindleberger, C.P., "International public goods without international government," Presidential address to the 98th Meeting of the American Economic Association, December 29, 1985, New York, *American Economic Review*, Vol. 76, No. 1 (March 1986).

Lewis, W. Arthur, *The Development Process* (New York: United Nations, 1970).

Lipton, Michael, "Prisoners' dilemma and Coase's theorem: A case for democracy in less developed countries?" in R.C.O. Matthews (Ed.), *Economy and Democracy* (London: Macmillan, 1985).

Olson, Mancur, *The Logic of Collective Action*, 2nd edition (Cambridge, MA: Harvard University Press, 1971).

Young, Oran R., "International regimes: Problems of concept formation," *World Politics*, Vol. 32, No. 3 (April 1980) pp. 331–356.

6b Comment: Kenneth Boulding on power

William Waller

A key essay by Kenneth Boulding on the concept of power—"Power and the Betterment of Society" (1991)—was written for a well-read audience, but not necessarily for economic and social theorists. It contains, however, a very accessible discussion of how we can move in the direction of betterment based on Boulding's extremely sophisticated theoretical system that encompasses theories of human behavior, the role of power, social valuation, conflict resolution, and the meaning of human and social betterment. In this commentary, the starting point will be explicating Boulding's theoretical system from the perspective of his theory of power.

Defining power and betterment

Few economists have made the effort to systematically study the phenomena that fall under the label of power. Of the few who have, Kenneth Boulding has explored its complexity and breadth to a much greater extent. Two factors explain the uniqueness of Boulding's approach to power. Mainstream neoclassical economists, who certainly make up the majority of economists in the Anglo-American sphere, focus almost exclusively on monopoly power in market transactions. The only power of interest in the universe of the free market is the power to set price. Other forms of power, if recognized at all, are exogenous to the economic system and the province of other forms of social theorizing, but they are not economics. Defining exogenous phenomena as "not the economy" is a well-worn theoretical element of neoclassical economics (see Jennings 1992). Even within the heterodox economic traditions, the study of power has suffered from economism—by which I mean an intense focus on economic power as the source of other power, in the form of exploitation of labor or altering prices (or more generally otherwise the terms of trade). As Boulding notes in the introduction to his book *Three Faces of Power* (1990), "The study of power as a total system, therefore, has tended to slip through the cracks between the different disciplines, and never seems to have become a discipline of its own".

Boulding undertakes an interdisciplinary examination of power as a problem in the integration of social systems understood as part of a larger biological, ecological, and physical system (Boulding 1990, p. 9). Boulding's analysis of power fills a book-length monograph. However, "Power and the Betterment of Society" (1991) includes an extensive discussion of the meaning of power and its relationship to social betterment. The focus on betterment points to the dynamic character of Boulding's conception of power as well as its connection to value theory, since betterment implies both change and the value criteria employed to evaluate whether the changed situation is a case of betterment.

Boulding asserts that power involves changes that are the result of human decisions and their resulting actions (Boulding 1991, p. 59). Power begins with a value decision—a desired change—which involves a desired future (what Boulding calls an image of the future) that we believe our actions control. If our actions result in us achieving the desired future, then we have real power. If not, we do not have power. If our "image" of the future is unrealistic, our decisions and actions will have unintended consequences and our power will be illusory. Boulding points out that we only have power within a possibility boundary that divides the world of possible images into those that are realizable and those that are not, and our image of the possibility boundary may or may not be realistic. Notice that the above definition of power takes into account the possibility that our perception of our own efficacy is wrong. In that case we may make a decision, act, and the desired image of the future may occur, but that does not mean we have power. We may, however, see the sequence of events, which are in fact unintended consequences, as being confirmation of our delusionary perception of our own possibility boundary. We have power within our actual possibility boundary—if that is large, we have a large amount of power, if it is small, our power is correspondingly small—but our perception of that boundary may or may not be realistic (Boulding 1991, p. 59).

The economy is defined as part of the sociosphere, "that consists of all human beings, the state of their bodies and the content of their minds, their potential for behavior, their artifacts such as buildings, machines, tool, pots, and clothing, their organizations, their role structures, and so on" (Boulding 1991, p. 57). The economy is the part of the sociosphere associated with provisioning (the definition of the economy employed by original institutional economists and feminist economists) by which Boulding means exchange and grants related activities. Changes in the biosphere, its subset the sociosphere, and the economy result from three kinds of change: change due to human decisions, change that occurs without regard to human decision of which we are aware, and change that occurs without regard to human decision of which we are not aware. Power is related to the first kind of change, though changes of which we are not aware are possibly the result of the unintended consequences of interactions of uncountable human decisions interacting to produce unintended changes (Boulding 1991, p. 59).

Boulding identifies "dimensions" of power. Body power involves changes that can be made by using muscles, the mind, and communication. Artifacts that are extensions of the body can extend body power. The boundary of body power may be created and altered by overlapping boundaries of body power of other individuals. This discussion of body power in "Power and the Betterment of Society" (1991) is extremely short. This is typical of discussions of power by heterodox economists—partially because of their general suspicion of theories of agency that are highly individualistic. Individual or body power is also discounted because it must be assisted or leveraged by other forms of power to become socially significant.

By way of contrast to this article, Boulding spends a great deal of time on personal power in his 1990 book *Three Faces of Power*. It includes discussions of personal forms of destructive, economic, and integrative power; all of which include components of body power and communication, but all of which are amalgams of body power with other forms of power. This parallels discussions of personal power in the work of Thorstein Veblen (see Veblen 1964) and John Kenneth Galbraith (1983).

After discussing body power, Boulding moves on to discussing exchange power, which he notes is based on structures of communication and the existence of property rights. He briefly mentions search power—the ability to explore the social environment and innovative power—the "capacity to think up something or do something that has not been thought of before" (Boulding 1991, p. 60) Up to this point Boulding's discussion has been intentionally generic. By contextualizing his analysis in terms of the biosphere and defining the economy as a generic subset of a generic sociosphere, Boulding seems to be articulating a generic taxonomy of power. But beginning with exchange power, he has moved to culturally specific territory. The history of human exchange patterns predates the notion of private property rights that co-evolved with contemporary exchange. Indeed, in most of human history, possession is a sufficient condition to allow for items to be exchanged, as it continues to be in most pawn shops in modern industrial economies. Additionally, anthropological accounts of silent trade among individuals in tribal societies is dependent upon possession and the complete absence of communication, thus having neither of the attributes associated with Boulding's characterization of exchange power but being successful systems of exchange none the less (Herskovits 1952, pp. 185–188).

Similarly, the reason for the characterization of search power and innovative power as separate and distinct categories is unclear. Search power and innovative power seems to be an expression of a combination of what Thorstein Veblen called the instincts of idle curiosity and workmanship, and what original institutional economist David Hamilton meant when he characterized the non-artifact elements of technology as organized human intelligence in action. This observation is not intended to dispute Boulding's characterization of these aspects of human behavior as manifesting a kind of power—they certainly are a way of getting work done and expressing human will—but the reason for characterizing them as separate categories and what these categories add to our understanding of power is left unexplored by Boulding. Indeed, the only discussion of innovative power in Boulding's *Three Faces of Power* (1990) is limited to a discussion of innovation as a source of monopoly power in which its scope is merely as a form of first mover advantage by firms (Boulding 1990, p. 191).

Boulding moves on to describing threat power as an important category of power. He notes it can look like a negative exchange because the actions compelled are done under duress. He argues that this is important in political processes because of the kinds of actions and rule compliance that the state compels when it exercises its police powers. He does note that these actions in particular are "legitimated in some sense" (Boulding 1991, p. 60).

The main focus of Boulding's interest in power seems to be what he calls integrative power that he claims underlies all other forms of power. Integrative power:

> is the power that arises from being an accepted member of some kind of community—the family, the church, the state, and so on. It is the power of legitimated authority, of the general acceptance of rule structures. Its dynamic is intricately related to both exchange power and threat power.
>
> (Boulding 1991, p. 60)

This conceptualization of power is similar to the conceptualization of power put forward by "original institutional economist" William Dugger (Dugger 1980, 1984, 1989).

Boulding's integrative power seems to be the power that results from the voluntary bindings and emotional ties created as a result of belonging to a social group and subscribing to its ends-in-view or purpose, and accepting the group's priorities and valuational principles. The term "integrative" seems to fit Boulding's descriptions of individual elements of power based on love, respect, and reciprocity being brought together with economic and threat power in larger social contexts such as businesses, the military, religious groups, and nation states. The similarity with Dugger's framework is clear. For both Boulding and Dugger, personal power comes from an individual who is acting in a role within a particular social institution or nexus of institutions and using their personal power to leverage the power provided by filling that particular role within the institution, allowing the structural elements and range of discretion of the social organization to be turned to personal account.

This taxonomy of power is, however, only the framework employed by Boulding in "Power and the Betterment of Society" (1991) to think about the relationship of power to betterment. Betterment for Boulding is a process of valuation. Sometimes it is a static evaluation of "whether 'this' is better than 'that'. 'This' and 'that' can be works of art, music, scenery, personalities, clothing, the whole state of ourselves..." (Boulding 1991, p. 61). But the more important element of valuational processes is assessing the impact of change. This kind of valuation, according to Boulding, involves assessing the combined impact of many small changes. The actual valuation involves the assessments by individuals, but these valuations are necessarily coordinated by the social structures in which the individuals are members and in which they participate. Many individual valuations are remarkably similar within a culture. Boulding speculates that shared values result in shared valuation over the longer period. But different subcultures might exhibit different value structures resulting in different assessments than the larger culture of which they are a part. Boulding speculates that some evolutionary process seems to be at work historically to eliminate some kinds of valuational systems or components that are inimical to the human condition.

The next step in Boulding's discussion of betterment is to survey a number of cases of valuation of economic circumstances, with particular focus on the inherent conflicts, in assessing the role of power in social betterment. Since "Power in Society" (1978) is present in this volume in its entirety, there is no reason to summarize Boulding's view of power at length here. But the conclusions that Boulding draws from these examples and his larger study of power are important to reiterate. The roads to betterment involve matters of the distribution of benefits from human activity. Additionally, how institutions distribute the power to create, the power to prevent, and the power to destroy, and the problem of how to change social institutions to promote creativity and to prevent damage while limiting destruction will remain a difficult, continuing social process. Boulding observes that enrichment of human life seems to emerge "through integrative structures that are relaxed and tolerant, gentle and liberal" (Boulding 1991, p. 73).

The role of power in Boulding's theorizing

While I have stressed some similarities of Boulding's conception of power with those ideas of original institutional economists, this should not be taken as an argument that Boulding's thinking was derived from, part of, or tied to this school of thought. Boulding theorized on a larger stage.

Human betterment, the improvement in human well-being broadly defined to include the care and maintenance of the biosphere in which human beings exist, was a constant theme in Boulding's scholarly career. Stefan Kesting (2010) traces the ties between Boulding's early critique of Paretian welfare economics to his creation of what Kesting calls Boulding's conception of welfare as an inclusive communicative process (Kesting 2010, p. 973).

Boulding abandons the notion of a preference function as used in Paretian welfare economics and replaces it with what he calls "the image" (Boulding 1997, originally 1956) Boulding describes the image as an individual's worldview created by a combination of that individual's subjective knowledge of the world, their sense of location in space and time, and their embeddedness in a web of human relations and the emotions that result from those relations. (Boulding 1997, pp. 4–6) This implies an existential theory of human behavior where behavior is motivated by the individual's image. Communication and messages received from other individuals and sensory perceptions of the environment create change to the degree that these messages, perceptions, and experiences alter the individual's image. (Boulding 1997, pp. 6–7) The individual's images are shared through conversation and discourse. Boulding asserts that organizations, cultures, and subcultures are groups that may share images. Since discourse is the mode of sharing, this defines cultures and subcultures as shared discourse communities. The image seems to fall somewhere between Durkheim's notion of a shared social collective representation and George Lakoff's notion of political frames in the United States (Durkheim 1965, p. 269; Lakoff 2009).

Stefan Kesting's (2010) and Warren Samuels' (1997) discussions of the image focus on its function rather than a description of nature, content, or creation of the image. As Samuels writes:

> The fundamental role of the image is to define the world. The image is the basic, final, fundamental, controlling element in all perception and thought. It largely governs our definition of reality, substantially and normatively, in part as to what is actual and what is possible.
>
> (Samuels 1997, p. 311; cited in Kesting 2010, p. 974)

The image necessarily is a value-laden conception of both reality and any possible future. In the case of a conflict, any resolution necessarily must involve the resolution of differences in perceptions including the value component.

The concept of the image requires that any social science incorporate explicit consideration of value principles that motivate behavior and are crucial to the construction of our perceptions. Any shared cultural understandings and experiences are the result of shared cultural images. As Kesting notes, "It is open whether the image remains stable or changes depending on the experiences of the individual and the influence of outside messages on it" (Kesting 2010, p. 975) But Boulding invokes the power of messages and communication in the alteration of images. Change in those individual and culturally shared images result from messages in the form of human communication, shared sensory experiences, and participation in discourse (either among individuals or as part of an ongoing social process). The character of the messages that is crucial to Boulding's raising the image to a shared social construct, a shared public image, is that messages shared in the process of social valuation, the process of shared analysis and consideration of alternatives, help build a shared version or component of the individual's image that allows groups of people to work together for the common good as they collectively perceive it.

Kesting then explores the role of communication in exchange and gift relationships in Boulding's (1981) work, which discusses the fact that the material flows of goods are accompanied by the important communication that includes information, threats, promises, affirmations, persuasions, and so on (Boulding 1981, p. 19; cited in Kesting 2010, p. 975). Of importance for Boulding as a theorist of power is that such activities can easily lead to misunderstanding and conflict. Conflict is not inherently good or bad; its consequences—how it is resolved—determine whether it will produce betterment or damage. Boulding sees conflict being resolved in five ways: avoidance, conquest, award, reconciliation, or compromise. Boulding's preferred way of resolving conflict is reconciliation

> in which the value systems of the images of the parties so change that they now have common preferences in their joint field: They both want the same state of affairs or position in the joint field and so conflict is eliminated.
>
> (Boulding 1962, p. 310; cited in Kesting 2010, p. 975)

Kesting again then shows the significance of this process of conflict resolution and the potential of mediation for conflict resolution and ties it to Boulding's concept of integrative power, bringing us full circle back to Boulding as a power theorist.

As Kesting notes, Boulding thought integrative power was the most important (Kesting 2010, p. 976). Integrative power is based on communication. But it is not identical to communication. The very naming of this type of power is instructive. Boulding was motivated by Galbraith's analysis of power. Boulding noted that Galbraith's categories were "roughly equivalent" to his own (Boulding 1990, p. 11). Yet Boulding did not use Galbraith's categories; instead he constructed his own. The focus for Boulding is on the power to achieve social integration that can then be used to mobilize social groups for coordinated social behavior in pursuit of common goals. Boulding's description of integrative power is based on communication within a discourse community that involves a heavily rhetorical form of social action with particular emphasis on the role of persuasion (see Robertson 1996, 1999). Boulding does not argue that the impact of communication in the form of messages that impact on individual's images creates any sort of procedural or substantive rationality. Instead, Boulding notes the importance and pervasiveness of emotional considerations in the construction of valuation criteria that strongly affect both the individual's image and the shared public image. Since these images are the basis for human behavior and the motivation for shared public action, they are parameters that create and limit opportunities for betterment.

Persuasion is the key to consensus building. The emotional component to persuasion is, according to Boulding, the capacity to be aware and appreciative of the "broader and narrower environment around a person" (Boulding 1990, p. 11; in Kesting 2010, p. 976) In addition to awareness, others need to find those environments interesting and valuable and to treat an increase in the welfare of others as an increase in their own welfare (Ibid.). These emotional relations that result in such positive outcomes are listed and ranked by Boulding in order of their intensity: reciprocity, respect, the wish and willingness to learn, sympathy, and love (Ibid.). Through social communication, messages constructed or viewed as persuasive attempt to alter individual and social images in social valuational processes. In the presence of goodwill and supporting emotional dispositions, this can lead to a consensus regarding the social action necessary to assess conditions and alter behavior in the direction of human and environmental betterment. But Boulding acknowledges that integrative power is only one kind of power and is not necessarily always constructed or used for the common good. He notes that interest groups can be built from integrative power and use it to promote their special interests at the expense of social betterment. Communication can also be used to damage and stigmatize others. Skill at communication can be used to manipulate others. This may be the most dangerous element of integrative power and the most relevant today. Boulding notes that "what is convincing is not always true, and what is true is not always convincing" (Boulding 1990, p. 119; in Kesting 2010, p. 976).

We seem to live in such an era now. Public policy discussions are dominated by references to skewed public images of what constitutes social well-being and a path to betterment. We ignore scientific evidence of environmental degradation. We ignore the actual impacts of taxation and governmental budget policies on well-being in favor of ideologically favored fantasies. Indeed, the United States in particular seems bent on policies that ensure respect; the willingness to learn, and sympathy in particular, are unsupported in our political discourse and society generally. Similarly, reciprocity is reduced to only the material and financial flows of exchange relations, ignoring all of the valuational and emotional content that Boulding describes in his characterization of exchange relations. The social situation manifest in the post-9/11 United States seems characterized by fear and accompanied by little capacity for compassion, much less expressions of love. United States citizens continue to respond to our fears with the power of destruction far too often and easily.

This leaves us in a dilemma regarding integrative power and its role in social betterment. Boulding identifies a theory of behavior that includes a path to developing power for the purpose of making progress towards human betterment. But the possibility of the process becoming a useful "alternative deliberative welfare approach" (Kesting's description of Boulding's approach) is highly dependent on social prerequisites which seem to be absent from United States culture at this time.

Assessing Boulding as a theorist

In assessing Boulding as an economic theorist who incorporated his own theory of power into his larger economic theory, two questions seem important. First, how does his work compare to other economists who took on the same challenge, namely to theoretically explain the role of power in economics and human betterment? Second, why has Boulding's theory not had a greater impact on social theorizing?

Boulding is distinct from almost all other economists who have articulated a theory of power in that his theory of power is central to his economic theorizing. In this regard, his work is most similar to William Dugger's use of power. John Kenneth Galbraith (1983), whose book on power is cited by Boulding as a motivation for his own book on power, develops his theory of power based on his prior economic theorizing—it is a result of his prior work and not, obviously, foundational to that earlier work. Adolph Berle's (1967) book on power is similarly reflective of his earlier theorizing. Thorstein Veblen's comments on the role of the vested interest in the economy and his characterization of those interests' activities as "force and fraud" certainly encompass a conceptualization that is central to the meaning of his economic analysis. Indeed, Veblen's comment on personal power relationships to a shared image in *Imperial Germany and the Industrial Revolution* is so prescient as to be chilling.

> Temperamentally erratic individuals, however, and such as are schooled by special class interest, will readily see the merits of warlike enterprise and

> keep alive the tradition of national animosity. Patriotism, piracy and prerogative converge to a common issue. Where it happens that an individual gifted with an extravagant congenital bias of this character is at the same time exposed to circumstances favoring the development of a truculent megalomania is placed in such a position of irresponsible authority and authentic prerogative as will lend countenance to his idiosyncrasies, his bent may easily gather vogue, become fashionable. And with due persistence and shrewd management come so ubiquitously into habitual acceptance as in effect to throw the population at large into an enthusiastically bellicose frame of mind. Such is particularly apt to be the consequence in case of a people whose historical traditions run in terms of dynastic strategy and whose workday scheme of institutions is drawn on lines of coercion, prerogative and loyalty.
>
> (Veblen 1964, pp. 60–61; originally 1915)

Only William Dugger's theory of power as emanating from institutional structures with valuational systems that define roles for individuals in those structures is similarly central to Dugger's theorizing as Boulding's theory of power is to his entire theoretical understanding of economies (Dugger 1980, 1984, 1989).

Therefore, as an economist who fully integrates a unique theory of power into his economic theorizing, Kenneth Boulding is almost unique. In that regard, Boulding's work is impressive.

But this comparison brings to notice that Boulding's work is integrative of a tremendous range of social science research, which leads us to the second question regarding why Boulding's theorizing has had such a small impact on social science theorizing and discourse in general and economic discourse in particular. Part of the answer is that Boulding did not contextualize his theorizing in terms of, or building upon, other scholars' research on related topics. His use of a broader understanding of exchange draws on sociological and anthropological understandings. His concept of the economic and emotional significance of gifts on individual and social images is highly reminiscent of the work of Marcell Mauss (1967). Similarly, his understanding of reciprocity, exchange as communication and possible miscommunication, is remarkably similar to the work of Bronislaw Malinowski (1967). His categorization of exchanges is consistent with Mauss' and Marshall Sahlins' (1972) notion of reciprocity as potentially both positive and negative in character.

Boulding's description of the role of image in eliminating uncertainty through the creation of habits and the elimination of nonfunctional habits is very similar to John Dewey's discussion of the social role of habits in *Human Nature and Social Conduct* (1930). Kesting also notes that Albert O. Hirschman's concepts of exit and voice (Hirschman 1970) correspond to many of Boulding's insights on conflict resolution (Kesting 2010, p. 96). We have already noted the closeness of the connection between Boulding's (1990) book on power and Galbraith's (1983) book on power. The list could go on of areas where Boulding's work closely parallels or appears very similar to the work of his contemporaries. Yet even when Boulding chooses to acknowledge those parallels and similarities, he strikes off on his own, redefining terms and recasting theoretical arguments in idiosyncratic ways. Only careful textual analysis and the passage of time will tell us if this strategy was necessary and/or useful for Boulding's theorizing. It may be that Boulding's theoretical elements of the image, conflict resolution, the grants economy, and integrative power are so unique that they had to be expressed in new language that differentiated them from other scholarly contributions. But often such efforts lead to marginalization and obscurity if the "public image" of the scholarly discourse community (in this case, social scientists, particularly economists) does not incorporate or even acknowledge the categorization schemes and definitions that a particular theorist creates in his efforts to articulate his ideas.

It is ironic that Boulding, in his book *The Image* (1997, originally 1956), dismisses Thorstein Veblen as a poor social scientist, and then proceeds to draw on Veblen's work through the rest of his career. But Veblen is most frequently described as an iconoclast, a term with two meanings: a person who attacks cherished beliefs, or a person who is a nonconformist, a dissenter, a radical. Both Boulding and Veblen read very widely in the social sciences, both struck out theoretically on their own, building their own theoretical framework for understanding, analyzing, and evaluating social and economic behavior beyond the traditional boundaries of the economics discipline. Both maintained their connection to the academic economic discourse community that sought to marginalize them. It seems Veblen's fate is to have a small but persistent and continuing impact on social and economic thinking. It is important to ensure that Boulding's theoretical contribution does not suffer the same fate of marginalization or is treated as a theoretical curio in the basement of the history of economic thought. Boulding's work on power is but part of his understanding of the economic system and is theoretically, inextricably tied to his concerns for human betterment and its connection to the environment. There is a no more important and more pressing set of economic problems to be addressed. This area of public policy, and the discourse surrounding it, is strife with conflict, misunderstanding, and the use of the power to destroy to obfuscate the significance of these problems. Boulding's work provides us with a framework to address these compelling issues in a sensible and humane way. His work is too important to be allowed to fade out of our contemporary public policy debates.

References

Berle, Adolph A. *Power*. New York: Harcourt Brace, 1967.

Boulding, Kenneth E. *Conflict and Defense: A General Theory*. New York: Harper and Bros, 1962.

Boulding, Kenneth E. *A Preface to the Grants Economy*. New York: Praeger, 1981.

Boulding, Kenneth E. *Three Faces of Power*. Newbury Park, CA: Sage, 1990.

Boulding, Kenneth E. "Power and the Betterment of Society," in *Perspective on an Economic Future*. Shripad Gopal Pendse, Ed. Westport, CT: Greenwood, 1991.

Boulding, Kenneth E. *The Image*. Ann Arbor, MI: University of Michigan Press, 1997.

Dewey, John. *Human Nature and Social Conduct*. New York: Modern Library, 1930.

Dugger, William M. "Power: An Institutional Framework of Analysis," *Journal of Economic Issues*, 14 (4), December 1980, pp. 897–907.

Dugger, William M. *An Alternative to Economic Retrenchment*. New York: Petrocelli Books, 1984.

Dugger, William M. *Corporate Hegemony*. Westport. CT: Greenwood Press, 1989.

Durkheim, Emile. *The Elementary Forms of the Religious Life*. New York: Free Press, 1965.

Galbraith, John Kenneth. *The Anatomy of Power*. Boston: Houghton Mifflin, 1983.

Herskovits, Melville J. *Economic Anthropology*, 2nd ed. New York: Albert A. Knopf, 1952.

Hirschman, Albert O. *Exit, Voice and Loyalty*. Cambridge, MA: Harvard University Press, 1970.

Jennings, Ann. "Not the Economy," in *The Stratified State*. William Dugger and William Waller, Eds. Armonk, NY: M.E. Sharpe, 1992, pp. 117–149.

Kesting, Stefan. "Boulding's Welfare Approach of Communicative Deliberation," *Ecological Economics*, 69, 2010, pp. 973–977.

Lakoff, George. *The Political Mind*. New York: Penguin, 2009.

Malinowski, Bronislaw. *Crime and Custom in Savage Society*. Totowa, NJ: Littlefield, Adams and Co, 1967.

Mauss, Marcel. *The Gift*. New York: Norton, 1967.

Robertson, Linda. "Debating Markets," *Feminist Economics*, 2 (1), 1996, pp. 93–113.

Robertson, Linda. "Rhetoric," in *The Elgar Companion to Feminist Economics*. Janice Peterson and Margaret Lewis, Eds. Northampton, MA: Edward Elgar, 1999, pp. 659–669.

Sahlins, Marshall. *Stone Age Economics*. New York: Aldine, 1972.

Samuels, Warren. "Kenneth Boulding's *The Image* and Contemporary Discourse Analysis," in *The Economy as a Process of Valuation*. Warren J. Samuels, Steven G. Medema, and A. Allan Schmid, Eds. Cheltenham: Edward Elgar, 1997.

Veblen, Thorstein B. *Imperial Germany and the Industrial Revolution*. New York: Augustus M. Kelly, 1964.

Poem

Four things that give mankind a shove
Are threats, exchange, persuasion, love;
But taken in the wrong proportions
These give us cultural abortions.
For threats bring manifold abuses
In games where everybody loses;
Exchange enriches every nation
But leads to dangerous alienation;
Persuaders organize their brothers
But fool themselves as well as others;
And love, with longer pull than hate,
Is slow indeed to propagate.

"Towards a Pure Theory of Threat
Systems," 1963, p. 434

Part VII

Evolutionary economics

7 Key text: What is evolutionary economics?[1]

Kenneth E. Boulding

In its largest sense, evolutionary economics is simply an attempt to look at an economic system, whether of the whole world or of its parts, as a continuing process in space and time. Each economy is then seen as a segment of the larger evolutionary process of the universe in space and time ... or if we want to be very Einsteinian, in four-dimensional space-time, though in economics I don't think we have to worry about that very much. The larger pattern of evolution, in this part of the universe at least, involves three stages: (1) Physical and chemical evolution produces the stars and planets, the elements, compounds, air, water, rocks, and so on. Biological evolution starts with DNA, producing living species. Societal evolution starts with *Homo sapiens* and our extraordinary capacity for knowledge, for images of the world, and for producing artifacts. As human knowledge develops into know-how, in many parts of the world now the mass of human artifacts certainly exceeds the mass of biological artifacts, and the number of different human artifacts probably exceeds the number of biological species.

An economy, of course, is part of societal evolution, though it may be affected by physical and biological evolution in some degree, through earthquakes, natural catastrophes, the geological accumulation of fossil fuels, mineral deposits, soil erosion, delta building, climate change, and the like. Soil, it should be noted, is a product both of physical and of biological evolution, and it has a very significant biological component. An economy is also a product of the larger process of societal evolution and exists in an environment of political and social institutions. The boundaries between an economy and the rest of society are not wholly clear. We generally think of an economy as consisting of activities and institutions which are organized primarily through exchange, and the production and consumption of human artifacts, which enter into some sort of accounting systems and are evaluated by some measure of value, usually money.

The description of any system in space and time—and an economy is no exception to this rule—involves, first of all, the description of the system at a moment of time, what might be called a "flashlight photograph" or "frame" of a movie. This is largely what economists think of as capital, those things existing at a moment of time on which some kind of an economic value can be put. This will include human capital, that aspect of human bodies and minds which can be evaluated in these terms, though this evaluation is often difficult. The frame also consists of such things as financial instruments, debts, promises, commitments, stocks and bonds, promissory notes, and so on. Many, though perhaps not all, of these things are described in balance sheets, which have something like a "bottom line" of net worth. A balance sheet can hypothetically be identified for each human being and all human organizations, such as families, political organizations like countries, cities, states, national states, the United Nations and its various agencies, churches, clubs, private organizations of all kinds ... all these have economic aspects which might be reflected in some sort of accounting balance sheets, though these rarely include the whole story. Some organizations, like firms and corporations, are predominantly economic, but all organizations have some kind of economic aspect.

The next stage of the description is a "movie," the succession of frames over time, in which we identify changes in the economy as we go from one frame to the next. These changes may be discontinuous, as when a baby is born or conceived or a product is produced, a death occurs or a product is consumed. Many changes also are rather continuous, like depreciation, aging, erosion, wearing out, and so on. A very important aspect of economic change is the circulation of items of capital or assets among owners. Exchange is essentially the redistribution of assets among owners. The buyer B gives the seller S a sum of money, say, $100; S gives B five shirts. B has $100 less and five shirts more in his balance sheet; S has $100 more and five shirts less. Every exchange has a ratio of exchange. In the above case, $20 per shirt. When money is one of the things exchanged, the ratio of exchange is thought of as a price.

The simplest model of an economy has strong resemblances to the simple models of a biological ecosystem. An ecosystem consists of a number of different species interacting with each other and with their environment in such a way that each species has a growth function; its rate of growth is a function of its own population and the population of each of the other species with which it interacts. If these other populations are constant, the growth of a given species will be a declining function of its population. At low populations it is easy to find food and habitats for raising the young, and it is a little harder for predators to find members of the species to eat, so that birth rates are likely to be higher than death rates and the population will grow. As it grows, however, death rates will increase, infant mortality may increase particularly, and a population will be reached at which birth rates and death rates are equal and the population ceases to grow. If the population for some reason is above this level, death rates will exceed birth rates and the population will decline. This gives us almost a Walrasian equilibrium system with n equations and n unknowns which, within certain boundaries, will have a solution.

A somewhat similar model applies to commodities, though here the genetic processes are different. A man's shirt and a woman's shirt never produced a baby shirt. Shirts are produced by processes involving human beings making plans, obtaining raw materials, spinning yarn or thread, weaving cloth, cutting and sewing the cloth into shirts, and so on, partly perhaps on farms, partly in factories and workshops, and then shipping these shirts to wholesalers and retailers. Nevertheless, shirts have a population. They are born by being produced.[2] They die by being worn out and being discarded. In terms of the genetic differences, there are functions which we can postulate which relate the total population of the stock of shirts both to their production and to their consumption. The death rate in terms of wearing out and discarding shirts may be fairly constant, though people who have a lot of shirts may not wear each one as frequently, so they may last a little longer. The birth rate of shirts through production is very much related to the total population. If this is very large, the price of shirts will be low, relative to other things, the production of shirts will be relatively unprofitable and will decline. We can easily postulate some population of shirts at which their production and consumption will be equal and the population will be stable. The function relating population of shirts to growth in the population may depend on the populations of many other things—substitutes, people's preferences, fashion, and so on. As people get richer, the number of shirts which exist may increase, and so on. Again, we end up with what looks a bit like the Walrasian equations, which may have an equilibrium if the parameters permit it.

This "demographic" equilibrium is related also to an equilibrium in the relative price structure, a model which goes back to Adam Smith. There is nothing really corresponding to this in biological systems, though there are patterns even there which look a little bit like trade, like the oxygen and nitrogen cycles, even perhaps the cycles of other elements like phosphorus. There are also cooperative relationships among species, like little fish living in the jaws of big fish, as useful parasites on the big fish. There seem to be three major types of ecological relationships as between two species: (1) Mutual competition: the more of A, the less of B; the more of B, the less of A, which is rather unstable. (2) Mutual cooperation: the more of A, the more of B; the more of B, the more of A, which tends to be rather stable. And (3) predation: the more of the predator, the less of the prey; the more of the prey, the more of the predator, which also turns out to be quite stable. There are some parallels in these relationships in the economy, but they are often hard to identify.

Price theory supposes two kinds of equilibria in the relative price structure: One is the market price structure, where many commodities are being exchanged against each other. The equilibrium market price structure is roughly equal to that which will persuade people to hold what is there to be held in the form of the stocks of these commodities. Commodities, of course, include money, financial instruments, and so on. We see this particularly in organized commodity and security markets. If a price is perceived as "too high," people on the whole will try to unload the commodity onto others. There will be more offers to sell than offers to buy and the price will fall. Similarly, if a price is perceived as too low, there will be more offers to buy than to sell and the price will rise.

Beyond the market price equilibrium, however, there is a normal or, as Adam Smith called it, a "natural" price equilibrium involving production and consumption, which, as we have seen, is something of an ecosystem. If a market price is above the "normal" price for any length of time, production of this commodity will be unusually profitable, people will go into it, production will rise, consumption will fall, the stocks of the commodity will increase, and the market price will fall. Similarly, if a market price is "too low," production will be unprofitable, production will fall, consumption will rise, the stocks of the commodity will fall, and the price will rise.

This equilibrium theory of market and normal price goes back to Adam Smith's *Wealth of Nations* and has not been much improved since, with some possible modifications regarding the impact of monopoly and oligopoly and some elegant mathematization. Adam Smith, however, went far beyond this equilibrium theory. He has a good claim to be regarded as the post-Newtonian thinker. He saw very clearly that all these equilibria were temporary, constantly undergoing change in what may be described as an evolutionary direction. The famous principle, for instance, that the division of labor depends on the extent of the market, and the extent of the market depends on the division of labor and its productivity, is a very early example of positive feedback. He also saw very clearly that increase in productivity was fundamentally a process in human learning involving skill, dexterity, and judgment.[3] He anticipated the role of research and development in increasing productivity long before this was an important factor. He also saw that this increased productivity, through the division of labor, could have adverse psychological and social consequences. Too much division of labor, too much specialization, have perverted what might be called the general learning process and produced people who fell far short of their human potential.[4] If we had followed Adam Smith's insights here, that production originated essentially in a genetic process of know-how increased by human learning, which then is able to use energy to select, transport, and transform materials into the shape of the product, economics might be further along than it is today. It happens, however, that we got trapped into what I have called a "cookbook theory" of production, that we mix land, labor, and capital, and out pops potatoes or microwave ovens. Adam Smith certainly recognized that the accumulation of capital in the shape of buildings, tools, machines, and so on was necessary in order to realize the potential of the know-how or genetic factor, and he saw that mere accumulation of capital in the absence of know-how would not produce very much.

The change in productivity of land, labor, and capital as a result of changes in human knowledge and know-how is strikingly parallel to the role of mutation in biological evolution. The genetic structure in the fertilized egg or the seed knows how to produce a mouse, a human, or a tree, though it can only do so if the appropriate materials (capital structures) in the shape of a womb, a nest, soil, and energy, whether solar or chemical, are present. Biological mutation certainly seems to be much more random than human learning, although the random factor in human learning cannot be wholly neglected. The potential for new ideas is not always realized. Biological selection is a kind of learning process. It selects those mutations which produce populations that have niches in an ecosystem. There seems to be a "time's arrow" in all this towards complexity, as there is also in the human learning process.

Evolutionary change is very strongly affected by the existence of "empty niches" in existing ecosystems, which can be filled either by genetic mutation or by migrations of species. It is very clear that Australia had an empty niche for rabbits, which because of the isolation of the continent genetic mutation had not filled, but once humans introduced rabbits, they expanded very rapidly into a very large niche. They could not have done this if there had not been foodstuffs in the shape of grass, and the niche was large because the previous evolution had not produced appropriate predators. Similarly there was no niche for automobiles in the world before the discovery of oil and the development of gasoline, which originally was the unwanted byproduct of kerosene for oil lamps. Once there was gasoline, it was hard not to invent the internal combustion engine. Automobiles have exploded over the world very much like rabbits in Australia, as they too seem to lack predators in the shape of adequate public transportation or other substitutes, though they are eventually going to run out of their food (oil).

One very fundamental principle in evolutionary processes is their profound indeterminancy. We do not know enough about physical evolution even to guess how deterministic it is. But when we get to biological evolution, it is very clear that the process is dominated by the time at which highly improbable events happen. The development of DNA may have been one of these, and the development of the human race may have been another. The empty niches in ecosystems provide opportunities for change, but there is no certainty that mutations will take place which will take advantage of these opportunities. If they do not take place, then the empty niches change, and a particular niche may disappear. These processes are very hard to study, as it is very hard to find out what didn't happen. Nevertheless, it is a great mistake to think that what did happen had to happen.

It seems fairly clear from the record also that evolution is not a continuous process, as Darwin thought, but is punctuated by catastrophes and other improbable events. The transition from one geological age to the next always seems to represent some sort of catastrophe, which led to a large extinction of species and therefore the opening up of a variety of new empty niches, some of which were filled, and, of course, others, not. Thus, if it had not been for the catastrophe, whatever it was, that exterminated the dinosaurs, it is very doubtful whether the human race would be here today, for the dinosaurs seemed well adapted to occupy the niches for large organisms. The mammals at that time all seem to have been rather small. The mammals had to get as big as we are in order to have brains large enough to be capable of what humans are capable of. Size, of course, is only a limiting factor. Mere size of brain does not necessarily produce the extraordinary capacities of the human organism, as we see in dolphins and whales. But it seems pretty certain that a mouse's brain is not large enough to develop a theory of relativity. Discontinuities in evolution do not necessarily depend even on catastrophes. The theory of punctuated equilibrium in evolution (Somit and Peterson 1989) is supported by a good deal of evidence that there have been long periods when species and ecosystems do not change very much and then quite short periods in which they change very rapidly. No one is quite sure why.

The principle of punctuated equilibrium in evolution also applies to human history and societal evolution, of which we have rather more complete records than we do of biological evolution, thanks to the capacity of human beings for creating records. Writing contains a lot more detailed information than do fossils. The human race seems to have been in a very stable culture for several tens of thousands of years in the paleolithic era. This suggests what might almost be called a "mutational equilibrium," a situation in which virtually all mutations are adverse and do not survive. In hunting and gathering societies, survival is so precarious anyway that tribes which develop innovations do not survive, and for the most part each generation reproduces the knowledge and the skills of its parents. It is puzzling, however, that this equilibrium lasted so long, with creatures genetically virtually identical with ourselves and with the same potentials for curiosity and for innovation.

The first great change, of course, seems to have been agriculture. It seems to have developed independently in at least three or four parts of the world, though we cannot be sure of this. This may have been the result of a change in the physical environment, with the ice age pushing the human race into narrower land areas, perhaps creating a situation in which, for the first time, innovations had some chance to succeed. At any rate, we do know that agriculture started, and that this led to a profound change in societal evolution, simply because agriculture produced a surplus of storable food beyond what the producers needed to support and reproduce themselves. This opened up a niche for civilization, for somebody to take the food away from the food producer and feed soldiers, builders, scribes, clothiers, and so on. The first civilizations seem to have been theocracies, with the priests persuading the farmers to give up their surplus food by threatening that if they did not perform the ceremonies, the farmers' crops would not grow. Then the priest tends to be replaced by the king and the physical threat system, as the story of the transition from Samuel to Saul in the Bible graphically describes.

Empires, however, seem to be intrinsically unstable, limited as they are in their geographical area by the cost of transport of threats. Then at their boundaries, new threat systems arise, sometimes with new technologies. With the coming of civilization, however, there seems to have been an almost irreversible overall increase in human knowledge and skills, which leads to economic development, that is, enrichment in some form, an increase in the quantity and variety of human artifacts or capital. There are positive feedback processes here: the more we know, the easier it is to know more; the more we make, the easier it is to make more; the richer we are, the easier it is to get richer. It is hard to accumulate either knowledge or capital when it takes all that we have just to stay alive and reproduce the next generation. One of the factors here may well have been an increase in the expectation of human life. When the expectation of life is only thirty years, it takes all the resources of the society just to transmit the knowledge from one generation to the next. There is nothing left over for increasing it. As the expectation of life rises, a society does not have to spend all its time simply transmitting knowledge. It can afford to spend some time in increasing it.

A very important aspect of societal evolution is the evolution of power. We are too much accustomed to thinking of power purely in terms of threat power—"You do something that I want or I'll do something that you don't want." Economic power, however, is very different from threat. It says in effect, "You do something I want and I'll do something you want." This depends, of course, on the ability to do things for other people. This is the essence of exchange. Economic power rests on the ability to expand the field of exchange and also to create exchangeables, that is, to increase productivity. It depends also on the ability to accumulate, to produce more than we consume. Too much use of threat tends to destroy threat power itself. It undermines the economic power on which the threat system rests. Plunder can only be done once. Exchange can be done many times. Overlaying both these forms of power is what I have called "integrative power" (Boulding 1989), which is the power of persuasion, legitimacy, loyalty, respect, love, and so on. If the exercise of both threat and of economic power destroys legitimacy, the foundations on which they are built will be undermined. We see many examples of this in human history—in the collapse of empires, the impoverishment which often results from military success, and the expansions of both economic and integrative power which sometimes follow from military defeat. Here again, history is so full of options not taken, niches not filled, that it is hard to generalize. Certainly the total defeat of Byzantium by the Turks in 1453 had something to do with the extraordinary expansion of Europe economically, geographically, and culturally in the following centuries, during which time Islam stagnated. On a smaller scale, the defeat of France by Germany in 1871 seems to have led to Paris becoming the cultural capital of the world for two generations, while the great cultural age of the German people seemed to be over. Sometimes the mere expansion of transportation has profound effects. The establishment of communication between the Old World and the Americas had an enormous impact on the spread of foods, diseases, and ideas.

The question then arises, if we look at economies as participants in the great evolutionary process, what kind of methodology do we use to find out about them, to perceive patterns, and to understand their great complexities? It is clear that the experimental method has very limited applicability in the study of evolutionary processes. It is very useful in exploring existing structures and highly probable events. It cannot give us a record of the past, except as data accumulate, and it cannot deal with improbable events which very rarely happen in laboratories. We have to rely, therefore, on the records of the past and on the creation of better records for the future. The record of the past, unfortunately, is an extremely small sample of the total and a sample very biased by durability, so our images of the past always have a substantial degree of uncertainty. Nevertheless, the keeping of records and the improvement of the recording process are of great importance. We saw this in celestial mechanics; the careful records of Tycho Brahe of the positions of the planets led to Kepler and Newton, and established the validity of the Copernican rather than the Ptolemaic view. Something of the same thing has been happening in the social sciences, particularly in economics, with the development of much more accurate records and particularly the development of national income statistics, which we have now had for sixty years. Simon Kuznets could well be identified as the Tycho Brahe of economics. When we examine the statistical records, it is very clear that economies are subject, like other social systems, and indeed evolutionary processes in general, to what might be called "regions of time" within which the parameters of the system are fairly stable, but at the boundaries of which the parameters change. We are very familiar with the idea of regions in geography. When we pass from land into the sea, the system changes profoundly. We are familiar with the idea of "periods" in architecture, art, and literature, like the Baroque and the Rococo in architecture, the Impressionists in art, the Romantics in literature, and so on. Social scientists have been surprisingly slow to realize that the same thing happens in social systems. If we look at the last sixty years, for instance, particularly in capitalist countries, we see the Great Depression of 1929–1933, a perfectly extraordinary dynamic, followed by the recovery from 1933–1937. Then comes the Second World War, with its enormous expansion of the war industry followed by the "Great Disarmament" of 1945–1947, when the United States, for instance, transferred over 30 percent of the economy from the war industry into civilian industry in a little over a year, without unemployment rising above 5 percent. Then from the late forties until about the middle seventies, we have a kind of golden age of economic development—increasing incomes, diminution of poverty, low unemployment, and mild inflation. Then comes the oil crisis and the cold war, the arms race, which of course, began before then. Poverty increases a little, the growth of productivity is greatly slowed down. Then we go into the eighties and the extraordinary transformations of 1989 in the socialist countries and the feeling again that we are in a new region of time. Econometrics is only useful within a region of time when the parameters are fairly stable; otherwise it represents the search for the celestial mechanics of a nonexistent universe.

Another very fundamental principle which emerges here is that in systems in which information is an essential part, exact prediction is impossible, simply because information has to be surprising. Information is not an essential part of celestial mechanics and the gravitational constant remains remarkably constant. When we go from one region of time into another in social systems, however, and in the economy, parameters change. We can only predict within rather broad limits how they are going to change.

In systems like this, graphic techniques are very valuable. Time charts are very valuable because they give a lot of indication as to when the regions of time change. What might be called "time scatter diagrams," in which the positions of two variables are plotted with the data identified, and then arrows drawn from one year to the next, can be very instructive in terms of time patterns, and may be much more valuable than conventional correlations and regressions. Statistics have a deplorable tendency to assume that parameters are constant and that means, modes, and coefficients of correlation summarize the knowledge of complex systems, which they do not. Frequently we learn more about complex systems from extreme cases than we do from more common cases. We learn about health by studying sickness. The social sciences have been very slow to catch onto this principle.

In spite of all these difficulties, however, two very important principles of the acquisition of human knowledge emerge. One is the necessity for what we might almost call fantasy for imagining possible systems. We are helped here by our capacity for perceiving identities, that is, relationships that just have to be so, such as the principle that the increase in anything is the additions minus the subtractions, or the principle that if a significant total is made up of parts, an increase in one part must be accompanied by a decrease in one or more of the others. This is the famous economic principle of scarcity. We have more complex identities, like the Fisher identity, MV = PT, in economics, or Ohm's Law in physics, that current is proportional to potential difference divided by resistance. We also perceive what might almost be called "near identities," things that almost have to be true, like the economist's theory of maximizing behavior, that people do what they think is best at the time, or the principle that disappointment of expectations leads to revision of our image of the future. These fundamental principles are useful in guiding us through the great mazes of the historical record. They are useful also in exposing fallacies, propositions that the evidence does not support.

Does evolutionary economics then lead to the evolution of economics itself? One hopes that the answer to this question is yes. I remember my old professor, Joseph Schumpeter, saying to me, "How nice economics was before anybody knew anything!" You could spin any old theory if you wanted to and nobody could check up. Now because of the improvements in the record we are improving our ability to check up on theories and images of the world, and to reject those fantasies for which there is not sufficient evidence. There is still a great deal left to be done. We still need a very substantial improvement in the day-to-day and year-to-year record of what happens. National income statistics, for instance, are quite inadequate to describe what might be called "true development." An increase in the GNP can easily be fat or cancer in the economy as an increase in body weight can also be either fat or cancer. And we do need to be sensitive to the great discontinuities of the world. We all live on mesas, table lands with cliffs around them, and it often doesn't matter very much what we do within broad limits, but we must be very careful not to fall over the cliffs. One of the greatest dangers of economics is the assumption of continuity. This is where the differential calculus breaks down. One of the great opportunities, I think, for the next few decades is the development of a mathematics which is suitable to social systems, which the sort of eighteenth-century mathematics which we mostly use is not. The world is topological rather than numerical. We need non-Cartesian algebra as we need non-Euclidean geometry, where minus minus is not always plus, and where the bottom line is often an illusion. So there is a great deal to be done. Let's get after it!

Notes

1 This article was previously published in *Evolutionary Economics*, 1991, 1: 9–17.
2 It is odd how economists tend to identify consumption with household purchases, which is nonsense. Consumption is the death of commodities. Production is their birth. Aging and depreciation may change the structure of these populations of commodities, as they do of biological populations, but we can neglect this for the moment.
3 Smith (1937, p. 10):

> All the improvements in machinery, however, have by no means been the inventions of those who had occasion to use the machines. Many improvements have been made by the ingenuity of the makers of the machines, when to make them became the business of a peculiar trade; and some by that of those who are called philosophers or men of speculation, whose trade it is not to do any thing, but to observe every thing; and who, upon that account, are often capable of combining together the powers of the most distance and dissimilar objects.

4 Smith (1937, p. 734):

> The man whose whole life is spent in performing a few simple operations, of which the effects too are, perhaps, always the same, or very nearly the same, has no occasion to exert his understanding, or to exercise his invention in finding out expedients for removing difficulties which never occur. He naturally loses, therefore, the habit of such exertion, and generally becomes as stupid and ignorant as it is possible for a human creature to become.

References

Boulding, K.E. (1989) *Three Faces of Power*. Sage Publication, Newbury Park, Ca.

Smith, A. (1937) *The Wealth of Nations*. Modern Library, New York.

Somit, A. and Peterson, S.A. (eds.) (1989) *The Punctuated Equilibrium Debate: Scientific Issues and Implications*. Cornell University Press, Ithaca. Originally published in the *Journal of Social and Biological Structures*, April/July 1989, 12 (2/3).

7a Commentary article: Kenneth Boulding

A founder of evolutionary economics[1]

Kurt Dopfer[2]

Many readers of this journal will still remember Kenneth Boulding's Richard T. Ely lecture in December 1965, when he set out against the conventional wisdom, criticized the ivory tower of orthodox economics, and called for a paradigmatic change in economic thinking. A Grand Old Man, but also *enfant terrible* of modern economics, has died recently at the age of 83.

Intellectual youth and early milestones

While still a student, Boulding wrote a paper on displacement costs, which was published in the *Economic Journal*—at the time edited by John Maynard Keynes. For two years, he studied econometrics at the University of Chicago with Henry Schultz, one of the founders of the field. Frank Knight, another teacher, helped the young graduate to further early recognition by writing an article on Mr. Boulding and the Austrians. Finally, Boulding spent a semester at Harvard, where he wrote a paper on Boehm-Bawerk for a seminar conducted by Joseph Schumpeter in which he criticized the attempt to discover conditions of equilibrium in systems that are, by their very nature, in disequilibrium. In 1934, he published an article in the *Quarterly Journal of Economics* about the application of the pure theory of population to the theory of capital—an analysis that left its traces in his future work.

Toward foundations of evolutionary economics

In his later writings, especially also in his book *Evolutionary Economics*, Boulding went beyond questioning the use of a mechanistic model in economics; rather, he developed a vision of the economy that, on the one hand, was *imbedded in a broad ecological context* and, on the other, stressed the asymmetry of time and the *global irreversibility* of economic processes.

For Boulding, it was not just a matter of rhetoric when he applied the concepts of "equilibrium" and the "invisible hand" to ecology and thus addressed the principle of self-organization. Together with N. Georgescu-Roegen (1971) and K.W. Kapp (1976), he was one of the first economists to recognize the open system character of the economy and to bring intertemporal considerations into allocation and distribution theory.

Boulding never fell into entropy-pessimism. In his evolutionary interpretation, the arrow of time not only has the direction ordained by the Second Law of Thermodynamics, but is also irreversible with respect to creativity, the origination and extension of human knowledge, gains in complexity, and morphogenesis. How information arises is of central significance in his model, not simply its procurement, diffusion, or processing. The ultimate aim of Boulding's scholarly work was a *comprehensive theory of development* designed to explain economic phenomena on the basis of evolutionary principles (Boulding 1978).

Bifurcations in the development of economic theory

In several ways, Boulding was brought into theoretical opposition to the prevailing thinking. The notion of an economic process that is time-asymmetrical and irreversible is first of all incompatible with the premises of neoclassical and Harrod-Domar growth models. He criticized the latter as useless, and he noted the obsession of economists with cookbook theories of production that purport to show the complex dynamics of development of an economy by using recipes such as take land, labor, and capital and add a bunch of innovative entrepreneurs.

With his approach to evolution, he ran into the sharpened knives of his contemporaries who had expected that the General Theory of Equilibrium would be the crowning glory of their theoretical endeavors. Already when he was a student, he challenged Schumpeter's fondness for Walras's magna carta of general equilibrium theory. In contrast to his contemporary colleagues, Paul A. Samuelson and J.R. Hicks, Boulding also viewed the ultimate attachment to concepts of equilibrium as a decisive weakness of Keynes's *General Theory*. With his LM-IS diagram, Hicks refined the analysis of equilibrium and, in his neoclassical synthesis, Samuelson joined the neoclassical theory of market equilibrium with Keynes's circulation equilibrium. The notion of equilibrium appeared to allow the integration of the independently developed and as yet unconnected results of micro and macro theory.

Though the theoretical developments were based on the feeble methodological foundations of equilibrium, they brought great renown to the representatives of what came to be called modern economics. As in the second half of the nineteenth century, when there was a split in theory formation between classical and marginalist economics, there was also a parting of the paradigmatic ways before World War II that split economics into the camps of modern *neoclassicals* and of (implicitly less modern) *heterodox economics*. Boulding did not become the *enfant terrible* until neoclassical theory became the ruling dogma (Boulding 1992).

Vistas

The history of economics could have happened differently. Today, evolutionary economics attracts increasing interest, and it could be that some day the development of theory in the last 50 or 60 years will be regarded by historians of economic thought as the *long detour of neoclassical economics*. In this perspective, the assessment of Boulding's scientific contribution must be tentative.

Boulding's lasting credit will probably result from his demonstration of the methodological untenability of the mechanistic paradigm and of the relevance of evolutionary principles for the explanation of economic phenomena.

Boulding's theoretical profile emerges from his work on the history of economic thought. While, in neoclassical interpretation, the work of Adam Smith is generally reduced to its equilibrium aspects, Boulding regarded Smith as the first post-Newtonian thinker who, viewed over the long run, specifically worked out the *disequilibratory cumulative* aspects of competitive markets. He highlights Smith's vision of a system of *positive feedbacks* in which an extension of market leads to an increase in the division of labor, which in turn expands the market. Boulding's interpretation also stresses that Smith took account of the links within the process of generation of technical progress and the growth of knowledge.

Similarly, Boulding interprets Keynes's theory of the circular flow not through the hydraulic metaphor, but on the basis of processes of positive feedback: An initial decline in investment causes a decline in profits, which leads to further cuts in investment and in turn to further shrinkage of profits, and so on. Here Boulding describes the process of *cumulative circular causation*, as put forth by Gunnar Myrdal (1976) and other institutional economists. In distinction to Boulding, however, Myrdal first wrote a book about *Monetary Equilibrium*, which rested largely on the monetary theory of Knut Wicksell and other representatives of the Stockholm school, before he recognized the deficiencies of this explanatory scheme and himself turned to evolutionary and institutional economics.

It rounds off the picture of a rich scholarly life to note Boulding's lifelong commitment to the cause of peace. He never collected large sums of money from prize award committees for his extraordinary achievements in the science of economics, nor for his activities for peace—but this in no way lessens the great worth of his work.

Notes

1 This article was previously published in *Journal of Economic Issues*, 1994, 28(4): 1201–1204.

2 The author is Professor of Economics, University of St. Gallen, Switzerland.

References

Boulding, Kenneth E. *Ecodynamics: A New Theory of Societal Evolution*. Beverly Hills, CA: Sage, 1978.

Boulding, Kenneth E. *Evolutionary Economics*. London: Sage, 1981.

Boulding, Kenneth E. "Abseits des Mainstreams: Bekenntnisse eines abtrunnigen

Okonomen." In *Okonomische Wissenschaft in der Zukunft*, edited by Horst Hanusch and Horst Claus Recktenwald. Dusseldorf: Verlag Wirtschaft und Finanzen, 1992.

Georgescu-Roegen, Nicholas. *The Entropy Law and the Economic Process.* Cambridge, MA: Harvard University Press, 1971.

Kapp, K. William. "The Open-System Character of the Economy and Its Implications." In *Economics in the Future*, by Kurt Dopfer. London and Basingstoke: Macmillan, 1976.

Myrdal, Gunnar. "The Meaning and Validity of Institutional Economics." In *Economics in the Future*, by Kurt Dopfer. London and Basingstoke: Macmillan, 1976.

7b Comment: Evolutionary economics

A framework for organizational decision-making

Robert Waters

Introduction

Kenneth Boulding's evolutionary perspective is basically a quasi-biological model that he applies to developing an image of the process of change for the whole universe. This perspective is presented in *Ecodynamics: A New Theory of Societal Evolution* (1978). However, in *Evolutionary Economics* (1981), he seeks the economic implications of biological and societal evolution. The difference between societal and economic evolution is: economic evolution is a subset and primarily focuses on the societal activities of production, consumption, distribution, and the exchange of goods.

After an Introduction, *Evolutionary Economics* contains six chapters: (1) The Basic Evolutionary Model; (2) Commodities as an Evolutionary System; (3) Evolutionary and "Mainline" Economics; (4) The Evolutionary Approach to Economic History; (5) The Economics of Energy and Entropy in Evolutionary Perspective; and (6) The Policy Implications of Evolutionary Economics. I do not plan to review the book chapter by chapter. The policy suggestions in the last chapter appear cogent, but not evolutionary economics. They appear to be more along the lines of political economy. However, I included a summary of the chapter in the text. Also, I propose to relate Boulding's evolutionary perspective to organizational decision-making, particularly by firms, to support economic development. A significant feature of evolutionary economics from mainline economics is that it is inductive rather than deductive in approach.

As he relates in the Introduction to *Evolutionary Economics*, there have been three sagas or stages of evolution: physical–chemical, biological, and societal. Each saga has resulted from the development of sufficient complexity in the prior stage. The first saga is composed of the evolution of materials, after the big bang, from the initial hydrogen universe to the development of one containing the building blocks of DNA. In addition to hydrogen, DNA requires the availability of oxygen, nitrogen, and carbon. The second saga contained the development of living organisms, from single cells to humans.

When biological evolution reached the stage at which the human nervous system existed, the third saga, societal evolution, commenced. In this phase, human biology or instinct has remained essentially stable, but evolution has continued and apparently speeded up through the accumulation of knowledge through learning. This is contained in people, and in organizations and things, which people have created.

Fundamental to human learning has been the development of language and later writing. With language, humans have been able to transfer images from one to another. A result has been the ability to coordinate human activity toward images of the future. With writing, the ability of humans to store and transfer images has been exponentially enhanced. Also, he notes (1981, 41), "All organizations, from the smallest to the largest, involve some degree of central planning...". Furthermore, organizational planning evolves from images of the future, even though the future is opaque.

At the end of the Introduction, Boulding clearly sets out his objectives for *Evolutionary Economics*. He states,

> Economic life is essentially a subset, and a fairly large one at that, of total human activity in history. We should expect it, therefore, to follow the general principles which govern the evolution of humans and human society, and we should expect it to have some peculiarities of its own. Economics deals with that portion of human activity ... which deals with the production, consumption, distribution, and exchange of economic goods. To this old taxonomy, I would add storage and enjoyment of stocks of economic goods, with production and consumption being merely the additions to and the subtractions from these stocks. We can think of economic goods, therefore, as a part of the general ecosystem of the world. Any good with an existing stock clearly has a niche of some sort, although that may be very temporary. Then, the ecological interaction provides a selective mechanism. In the case of economic goods, this is very powerfully affected by the attitudes of human beings toward them. Thus, an economic good for which there is no demand will have no niche in the system. Mutation in economic goods consists of the constant invention of new ones. This has gone on from the beginning of the human race. Many of these new goods do not find a niche and do not survive; others have a niche and expand into the system, with consequent changes in all the other niches.
>
> In the case of economic goods the ecological interaction is mediated strongly through the price system.... It is also mediated by such things as populations of financial instruments which exhibit interest rates, profit rates, and so on. These have little or no counterpart in the biosphere. We also find phenomena like unemployment, labor markets, inflation, and so on, which, have no counterpart in the biosphere. Nevertheless, we shall find the evolutionary perspective extremely illumining in explaining the ongoing processes of economic life and its political and social environment. Economics has rested too long in an essentially Newtonian paradigm of mechanical equilibrium and mechanical dynamics. Oddly enough ... economics has something to do with developing the evolutionary perspective. In a very real sense, Adam Smith and Malthus were evolutionary theorists, and so was

Alfred Marshall. It was Walras and his successors who mathematicized so successfully the Newtonian system that the evolutionary perspective was lost. This little volume is intended to provide at least a prospective for its rediscovery.

(Boulding, 1981, 17–18)

The process of change in the ecosystem

Boulding describes an ecosystem as composed of innumerable niches for different kinds of creatures and behaviors. A niche is the potential equilibrium population of a species in the ecosystem (Boulding, 1981, 31). The driving force of Boulding's systems perspective is that evolution is a process of change in genetic structure, which he identifies as mutation.[1] He believes the basic evolutionary process is the accumulation of knowledge,[2] i.e. changes in genetic structure of species. By genetic structure he meant any egg, design, or plan that contains the instructions for producing a phenotype such as a chicken, university, or building. Since the environment is composed of many niches, some of which are competitive and some of which are complementary, the interaction among them determines the potential size of each niche. At any point in time or space, there will be an ecosystem, with a given set of parameters that will move to equilibrium where the rate of growth is zero, and all niches are filled. However, equilibrium is never attained because niches open up, and sometimes are filled, sometimes not, depending on the capacity of the system for mutation; each successful mutation opens some niches and closes others. "The pattern jogs along in an immensely complex interaction of things, organizations, and people, with biological, meteorological, and geological environments, structures, and populations" (Boulding, 1978, 18).

As he indicated above, biological and societal evolution consists mainly in filling of empty niches in the course of mutation and selection.[3] Societal, hence economic, mutation results from invention, discovery, and other creative activities of humans. Whereas biological changes in DNA are largely random, often stimulated by environmental stress, societal mutations are often intentional efforts of people to create something new. The motive force may be societal or environmental stress, self-interest, curiosity, or accident. In biological selection, the members of the species that best fit the niche in terms of survival tend to fill the niche, given the environmental conditions. Societal selection is quite similar. The genetic information, which is used to produce human artifacts, is contained in human beings, human organizations, and material artifacts (Boulding, 1981, 15). Some examples of prosthetic devices containing human knowledge (genetic information) are libraries, blueprints, computers, laboratories, and so on. As in biological evolution, knowledge initiates a production process able to direct energy, to sustain temperatures, and to select, transport, and transform chemical elements into improbable structures, not only of skin, blood, and brains, but also of walls, water pipes, and computers (Boulding, 1981, 66).

Increasing complexity

There is apparently a "time's arrow" in the evolution of biological and societal species, which is reflected in change through time from simple to complex and in the development of awareness, consciousness, and intelligence. In Boulding's view, a possible explanation of the pattern of increasing complexity of species is evident in the principle that "there is always room at the top". An ecosystem may just have an unfilled niche for a species just above the level of complexity of those that constitute it. Hence, mutations toward increased complexity, and especially those toward adaptability, are likely to find new niches even in existing systems that seem rather full, and so survive (Boulding, 1978, 115).

Importance of image formation

A capacity of the human mind that is of great importance to decision-making is the ability to form complex images of the future that are a necessary prerequisite to fulfilling them. He asserts that this image-forming capacity is essential to the creation of society and human artifacts, which are the keys to economic evolution.

What makes humans different?

Human history is characterized by a phenomenon that is unknown in prehuman biological systems: niche expansion through the production of artifacts. If mutation in know-how produces a commodity for which there is no demand, it will not be produced, or, if it is produced, it will soon disappear. There will be surplus stocks of it, and these will force the price down to the point where it no longer pays to produce it. New and successful phenotypes, on the other hand, will change the ecosystem and will change niches of all the old species. Some of these niches may be reduced to zero, in which case the species become extinct. This process of the creation of new species through genetic mutation and the extinction of old species through selection has been going on now, according to Boulding, for two or three billion years. It finally produced the human race and the human race in turn has produced enormous quantities of artifacts, all following the same general principle (1981, 66).

System indeterminacy

Boulding asserts that the evolutionary model provides important insights about the future, e.g. increasing complexity through time; however, it does not lead into easy and secure predictions. Prediction of the future is possible only in systems that have stable parameters. Evolutionary systems by their very nature have unstable parameters. They are disequilibrium systems and in such systems the power of prediction, though not zero, is very limited because of the parameters themselves. Boulding wrote, "There is … a very simple non-existence theorem ... we cannot predict what we are going to know or what know-how we are going to have in the future, or we would have it now" (Boulding, 1978, 18). Later, he points out that, even though our ability to predict the future is very limited: "This is not to say that the system has no patterns. We can make rough probabilistic predictions of the future, but this is different from the exact predictions of systems, like celestial mechanics, in which the parameters remain constant" (1985, 60).

Economic development

In defense of price theory

In Chapter 3, Evolutionary and "Mainline" Economics, Boulding provides a support for the validity of price theory. He asserts:

> ...price theory can be fitted into an evolutionary framework with great ease, for there is implicit in it an ecological interaction of commodities which continually exercises a strong selective process. Those commodities are selected which satisfy an effective demand sufficient to make their production normally advantageous, and those commodities move toward extinction which fail to satisfy this criterion. Into this system, mutation constantly intrudes in the form of invention, new processes, new technologies, new commodities, new tastes, and new demands. Equilibrium in such a system is a useful intellectual construct, even though it is never found in the real world.
>
> (Boulding, 1981, 87)

Later, he repeats the theme:

> We could almost do without the equilibrium concept if we suppose that we can identify in the first place the strains on the system making the change, in the second place the relation between these strains and the changes which will ensue, and in the third place the impact of changes on the strain itself. We could perfectly well visualize a system that had no equilibrium, but in which the change took place continually, faster if the reaction to strain and the changes which are produced by it actually increase the strain, and slower where the system's reaction to strain diminishes the strain. In fact, this is what the world is like. It never has exhibited equilibrium, although there are enough quasiequilibria to justify the use of the concept.
>
> (Boulding, 1981, 91–2)

This appears confusing. If equilibrium is not to be found in the "real" world, what is its usefulness? His reply is: "Households and business firms ... move from one homeostatic (short term) state to another that is preferred" (1981, 102–3). From where does this new preferred state come? His answer: "change in expectations of the future". From where do the changed expectations come and how long do they last? His answer: "The theory of homeostasis is a very first approximation, for, as we have seen, organizations are subject to constant change, and the state which is maintained by homeostatic apparatus itself continually changes." It appears to me that he will not give up on price theory, even though his evolutionary perspective seems to invalidate it. Dopfer (1994, 1202) maintains that: "The ultimate aim of Boulding's scholarly work was a *comprehensive theory of development* designed to explain economic phenomena on the basis of evolutionary principles." This makes sense to me, and I agree! But, is conformance to price theory required to make Boulding's case? I don't think so.

Boulding (1981, 29) proposes modifying the traditional "factors of production", land, labor, and capital, used in price theory. He asserts that they are more appropriately "factors of distribution" since they are claims on the surplus from production. As substitutes, he suggests "know-how, energy, and materials", to which he adds space and time. He notes, "all processes of production require these, and they may also be limiting factors".

Policy implications

In Chapter 6, The Policy Implications of Evolutionary Economics, Boulding identifies policy as a strategy of decision-making which governs and affects future decisions. The objective of policy is to set up some kind of structure that will maximize the present value of expected future net welfare. This includes how future decisions are judged and evaluated. All individuals and organizations have policies of two types. The first is to economize the decision-making process and provide a set of rules which provide guidelines in advance for future decisions. The second type provides general guidelines rather than specific rules. The objective is to increase the chance of good decisions and diminish the chance of bad ones. As an example of the second type, he suggests taboos, i.e. prior decisions on what not to do that narrow the range of options. The number of alternative options has to be considered by the decision-maker; too many is expensive, and too few options may overlook significant ones (1981, 169–72).

Next, he states (1981, 171–2): "Government is the only agency in society that has an obligation to look at the total system…". It is expected to make decisions that are intended to better the whole society. He proposes that tradeoffs between present and future welfare impacts be compared via a discount rate. "Future welfare is discounted by some kind of subjective probability, so that a prospective high welfare that is very uncertain and improbable will have a low present value." However, he does not address the old problem; i.e. where does the appropriate discount rate come from?

He goes on to argue (1981, 172) that there is a great difference between powerful individuals and the rest. "The power of an individual can be defined as the size of the consequences of the individual's decisions in the system as a whole." The power of a decision-maker often depends on the size of the hierarchy over which he/she presides. Another form of power is the influence of some people to change the images of people that have hierarchical power and so change their decisions. These influential people may include poets, prophets, preachers, advisors, scientist, etc. Also, hierarchical power may be limited by subordinates who manage the information presented to the decision-maker.

He advances a principle (1981, 173) which he calls the "dismal theorem of political science". His definition is "that most of the skills that lead to the rise to power, unfit people to exercise it". Also, he suggests (1981, 173–4) that power passed on by inheritance, as in a hereditary monarchy, has resulted too often in poor performance, and likewise conquest and revolutions are poor training grounds for the exercise of power. Also, powerful individuals often have personal as well as organizational or societal interests. The advantage of democracy is that legislators are elected, and frequently want to be reelected. This requires persuading the majority at the next election that the incumbent has behaved responsibly by advancing the perceived interests of the electorate.

He suggests (1981, 175): "It is the asymmetry between truth and error in images of the human race that is perhaps the most basic source of societal and cultural evolution." The examination of policy by critics is a process which tends toward the continual elimination of error through time so that people's images of the world are likely to contain an increasing proportion of truth.

In policy evaluation, Boulding (1981, 176–7) identifies two problems: (1) the realism of the image of the future, and (2) the evaluation of items on the decision agenda. First, if images of the future are unrealistic, the decisions will not produce the results that are expected. If regret leads to a learning process, future images may become more realistic. Second, in evaluating policy, some kind of ethic is required which upholds community values. If the consensus breaks down, "the results are likely to be tragic, for there seems to be in any particular situation a minimum degree of consensus below which the society falls back into violence, to the detriment of all parties". Examples he provides: Cyprus, Lebanon, and Northern Ireland.

Social organizers

He offers three societal processes (1981, 177–80) by which values are coordinated: prices, policemen, and preachments. These correspond to the social organizers exchange power, threat power, and integrative power, discussed by Boulding in *Ecodynamics*, and used in Figure 7b.1 to identify the societal processes (see Note 5).

> Prices, of course, refer to the market; that is, the complex set of processes by which goods are exchanged, production is specialized and organized, and the resulting income is distributed. Out of the very diverse preferences of human beings in the market network, what emerges is not agreement in regard to preferences, but specialization and a capacity, within the limits of general scarcity, for each person to satisfy the person's own preferences

> without interfering with those of others; in fact, even helping others to satisfy their preferences.
>
> (Boulding, 1981, 177)

The market system provides a method to organize exchange with the minimum of agreement. As long as there is a demand for something at a price that pays someone to produce it, it will be produced.

Policemen (1981, 179) refer to actions of the political system based on legitimate coercion or threat. The system exacts taxes, makes government expenditures through budgets, and develops a framework of law and regulation that limits individual behavior. Since there are public goods that cannot be effectively provided or negative externalities that cannot be effectively eliminated by the market, the political system, through government, addresses them.

Preachment (1981, 180) refers to coordination of societal values, i.e. the moral and ethical system. "This is the process of social criticism of individual preferences." Boulding believes that both politics and ethics are continuous and ongoing movements that never reach equilibrium, but swing between conformity and variety.

System interaction

Figure 7b.1[4] summarizes the interaction of the nine elements of Boulding's evolutionary system and their relationships in a time context. Production of phenotypes (i.e. artifacts) involves three essential factors: knowledge, energy, and material. For production to take place, genetic structure or knowledge (contained in artifacts) must be able to direct energy, to sustain appropriate temperatures, and to transport and transform selected materials into the improbable structures of the phenotype. Examples of Things include: structures, weapons, and computers. In Organizations, the role rather than people is the essential unit, which includes: the linkage structure of tasks and communications that facilitate group cooperation. People represent the learned information in the nervous systems of individuals including the roles they assume, that is identified as the "noosphere". Additionally, there are social organizers[5] that bind the system together and also are subject to evolution. In Figure 7b.1, these are called: threat power (or policemen), exchange power (or prices), and integrative power (or preachment). According to Boulding (1989), threat was the original power that established civilization: "Do something good for me or I'll do something bad to you." Exchange power is the market, which is represented by: "Do something good for me, and I'll do something good for you." Integrative[6] power is the most abstract, but characterized by: "I'll do something good for you because I want to." As an example of integrative power, he identified the influence that religious leaders have over their adherents. He believed that in most situations, effective leaders draw on all three sources of power to implement a decision. Also, he suggests that, as time has evolved, the rate of the production of artifacts has increased exponentially.

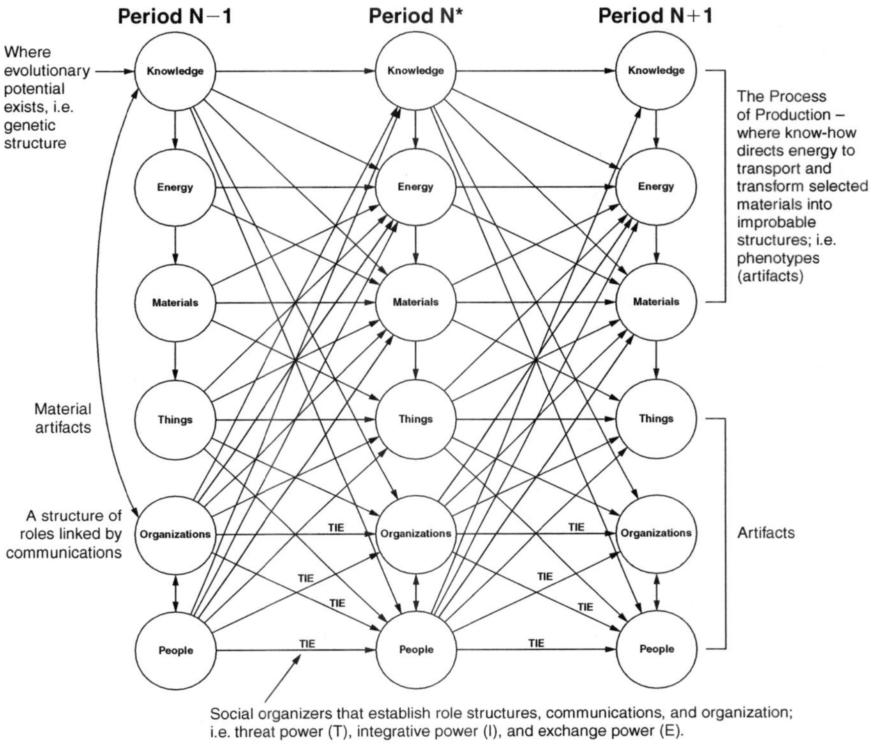

Figure 7b.1 The process of societal evolution.

With respect to the use of threat, he warns: "The perceptions of the cost of carrying out a threat are extremely important elements in the dynamics of the threat system." There must be a positive probability of the threat being carried out for the threat to be creditable. The threatened party has four choices: submission, defiance, counter threat, or flight; none of which leads to high productivity. Although he envisioned the continuing use of threat to maintain discipline in some organizations, he saw limits to its effectiveness: "Neither threats nor exchange can organize large-scale systems unless the institutions that embody them have legitimacy" (1978, 205). Legitimacy has come from persuasion by which one person, through communications, has changed the image and the value of another person in a direction that is presumably favorable to the persuader (and perhaps, the audience). Symbolic systems that have been part of the techniques of persuasion, and improvement in these techniques, may have the same kind of effect as improvements in communication and transportation have had in expanding social organization. Legitimacy has been an important product of these symbolic systems. An image of the world that makes someone important and valued and makes other people feel important and valued is likely to create legitimacy and to have survival value. He added: "One should not underestimate the importance of ceremonials. Ceremonies reinforce legitimacy and it is legitimacy that holds organizations together." Although he acknowledged that all three sources of power have an impact on cooperation, he believed more emphasis should be placed on integrative relations.

Evolutionary theory and policy

Boulding (1981, 181–2) indicates that the evolutionary model provides insight into the following issues:

1 It describes actual dynamics and provides the capability to access alternative futures which may result from particular decisions, courses of action, and policies.

2 It illuminates the relative importance of plans in reference to the environment in changing future conditions.

> The most appropriate policy or course of action … is that which makes the present value of the future greatest. If decisions are not to be frustrated and regretted, therefore, it is of greatest importance to have a realistic appraisal of the impact of any particular decision or policy on the future itself.

3 It warns against thinking of complex systems in simple terms. The first law of ecology is that action from a decision can never do only one thing; viz.:

> Any decision which changes the future will increase some good things, diminish other good things, diminish some bad things, and increase other bad things. The problem of assessment always involves an overall evaluation of these movements to see if the good that is increased and the bad that is diminished are greater than the good that is diminished and the bad that is increased.

Boulding (1981, 182) supports the introduction of environmental impact statements, as difficult and ineffective as they sometimes are, as an important mutation in political information systems. He suggests additional ones be undertaken, such as distributional impact, time impact, geographical impact, probability impact, and overall impact. He concludes:

> It is, after all, the image in the mind of a decision-maker of the overall impact upon which decisions are made. And the more information systems can assist this process, the less likely are bad decisions based on mistaken images of the future. This still does not rule out bad decisions which are made on bad evaluations.

Issues in the market economy

Boulding is also concerned about pathologies that he perceives in the market economy. (1) Left alone, it tends to inequity, which may be perceived as excessive in both welfare and income. (2) It has an inclination toward unemployment and under-utilization of capacity. After correcting for risk, when businessmen perceive that profit rates are less than interest rates for the use of their capital, they reduce investment, which then results in reduced opportunities for labor. (3) Uncertainty can also cause businessmen to reduce investment, thus reducing employment. If inequality is seen as too great, government can intervene to redistribute income and wealth through various devices, such as progressive income taxes, public education, social security, inheritance taxes, etc.

Evolutionary perspective: a framework for decision-making

To balance this discussion, I try to apply Boulding's evolutionary model to organizational decision-making, particularly within business firms and by implication to economic development. Boulding distinguishes between societal development and economic development (1981, 27): "Societal development is a process by which the human race realizes evolutionary potential for producing artifacts that is inherent in its biologically produced brains." In contrast, economic development is a subset of the evolving output of artifacts produced by humans. "It concentrates particularly on the evolution of *commodities*—that is, valued artifacts that at least potentially have the capacity for entering into exchange and transfer."

In Boulding's model, artifact production expands the knowledge base; i.e. potential, on which advances to the next level of human achievement depends. As stated, economic development occurs through mutation, (production), and selection. With selection, the enterprise or firm seeks ways to better fit its present niche. This entails investment in concepts such as customer focus; value added product and service offerings; optimum organizational scale; knowledgeable and motivated employees; mentoring and team building. Also, it would encourage investments in activities to increase knowledge to support mutation, such as idea sharing; research; continuous learning, especially from failures; education and training; career development; and job rotation.

For the firm, mutation means continuous changes in the competitive environment, which may be internally or externally generated, and in which niches are being continually created and destroyed. In the long run, all given niches tend to fill. Then, for an organization to continue to grow, it must displace its competitors in the existing niche through innovation, mergers and acquisitions. Also, it may develop or migrate to new niches. A too well-designed, i.e. too efficient, organization without slack resources does not have the capability to change when external conditions change. This may lead to extinction. The increase in number and size of industrial laboratories since World War II has been one approach for organizations to adapt to the impact of change on firms. The laboratories have served two purposes: They provide: (1) a source of new products, processes, and services for their sponsors; and (2) insight into the changing state of external knowledge, particularly science, on the niche served by the firm.

The capability to sense evolutionary changes and expeditiously respond to it is vital to survival. Although organizational planning is important to develop objectives and allocate resources, Boulding's evolutionary perspective suggests that elaborate planning systems are probably a waste of money; a better approach is flexibility and adaptability based on an informed, responsive, coordinated, and motivated people in the organization. The evolutionary perspective advocates that effort be expended in developing images of the future needs and testing the images in the real world; i.e. experiment and learn from the experiment, such as test marketing and flight testing. Most change in our images of the world, i.e. learning, is the result of failure of predictions or expectations. Since learning is the key to adaptation, the implications of failures must be analyzed and appropriate action taken. In a business organization in which there is respect for the individual, information flows are more open and the organization becomes more adaptive. The implication of Boulding's model is a strong argument for the participative style of management in organizations. Many organizations have increased employee recognition; i.e. integrative devices. Also, many leaders increase legitimacy for their organizations and themselves through donations to "good" causes, public service, and accessibility. An example of a firm that has been successful in evolving is the General Electric Company; it was founded in 1892 (Waters, 2009, 42). Over its lifetime, it has produced many new products (mutations) and developed industrial leaders for itself and other firms (selection).[7]

Conclusion

This is an attempt to provide the implications of Kenneth Boulding's evolutionary perspective to a new audience, organizational leaders and students. It asserts the nine elements of his model continually evolve. The model provides an integrated perspective on societal and economic development, and a holistic structure to evaluate many issues associated with resource allocation, in such areas as organizational planning, leadership development, research, marketing and sales, financial structure, product and process development, information systems, employee motivation, and merger and acquisition policy. Leaders that have the responsibility for the stewardship of large organizations can obtain an enhanced understanding of the dynamics affecting their situations and their role in the process by studying Boulding's evolutionary perspective.

On the validity of Boulding's evolutionary perspective

My conclusion, based on a long-term interest in the evolution of technology and organizations, is that Boulding's model is a much more realistic and dynamic description of a mixed market economy than price theory. Since price theory concerns the interaction of quantities of a good that are supplied and demanded at a given market price, ceteris paribus, the theory assumes away important parts of the problem faced by most business people. These include the dynamics generated in the market in response to evolving knowledge of science; technology; consumers; suppliers; government support, regulation, and taxes; financial, demographic, and political trends; and of course competitors. Also, there are impacts in the market from the supply and quality of available labor. Additionally, there are impacts from weather, wars, pestilence, riots, corruption, earthquakes, etc.

Boulding's model is a structure for understanding and deriving some suggestions for addressing the contingencies of the real world; whereas price theory assumes away the problem. Basically, business people do not have the required information to maximize profits in either the short or the long term. Furthermore, the data that is available can be very noisy and sometimes incorrectly specified.

Boulding works very hard to find parallel processes in biology and in sociology/economics. As pointed out in Note 1, Boulding's use of the word "mutation" as the source of change in artifacts does not correspond to its use in biology in which mutation generally means an error in the reproduction process, generally leading to the end of the process. However, I believe, as applied, his evolutionary perspective provides a significantly better model of the real economic environment than does the conventional equilibrium seeking model of price theory. Therefore, we should accept evolutionary economics as a step forward in the theory of the dynamics of a market economy and leave biological theorizing to the biologists. However, much work will be required to develop evolutionary economics into guidelines or an operational tool for decision-making in business and government. Twenty-five years after the publication of *Evolutionary Economics* (1981), Beinhocker (2006) developed a similar biologically based model directed at evolution of business firms that can be aggregated into a market economy. I believe it extends Boulding's insights.

Epilogue

Since the publication of Boulding's *Evolutionary Economics* (1981), the area of study has exploded, which a Google search of the Internet will support. Also, Wikipedia has an entry which identifies some leading contributors to and publications in the field. Similar and often overlapping ideas can be found under the subject titles of institutional economics, complexity economics, and complex adaptive systems. I found fascinating the work undertaken at the Santa Fe Institute in 1987–88 (Waldrop, 2002, 133–51 and 247–62). One outcome was the acknowledgement (Ibid., 326–7) by Kenneth Arrow that viewing the economy as a complex adaptive system was another valid way to do economics equal of status to the traditional theory. A similar process of analysis, e.g. biological modeling, used by Boulding is found in Beinhocker (2006, 11–20 and 187–379). Also, he relates subsequent activities on Wall Street undertaken by some of the economics program participants (2006, 381–414).

Two journals publishing papers in evolutionary economic theory are: *Journal of Economic Issues* (www.afee.net/division.php?page=jei) and *Journal of Evolutionary Economics* (www.springer.com/economics/journal/191).

Notes

1 Boulding's definition for the term "mutation" appears to be somewhat different from the eminent biologist Ernest Mayr (2001, 98). Mayr's position is:

> Even though all new genes are produced by mutation, most of the phenotype variation in natural populations that is available for selection is the product of recombination … The frequency of a gene in a population is in the long run determined by natural selection and stochastic processes, and not by mutation.

Whereas, Boulding (1981, 12) contends that:

> The basic source of change in the biological parameters … is genetic mutation, that is, change in the structure of the genetic instructions contained in the DNA with consequent changes in the nature of the individuals of species which these genetic instructions produce.

Boulding does not appear to recognize that most of the variation among individuals in a species originates from recombination of genes from the individual's parents and their parents, etc., not from mutation, which is most often a random event in the reproduction process that results in genetic death. However, I use Boulding's definition of mutation throughout the text to mean differentiation and amplification, as defined by Beinhocker (2006, 11).

2 Throughout his writings, with respect to genetic structure, Boulding uses the terms knowledge, know-how, and information to mean essentially the same idea.

3 I believe Beinhocker (2006, 11) is closer to the current view of the steps in evolution. He maintains that evolution consists of three steps: differentiation, selection, and amplification, which he applies to the creation of wealth. He contends: "The same process that has driven the growing order and complexity of the biosphere has driven the growing order and complexity of the 'econosphere'." Generally, presentation of Beinhocker's views appear to correspond closely to Boulding's.

4 This figure was first published by Boulding (1978, 229) and was modified by Waters (2006, 469) and for this text.

5 Boulding changed the terms for the social organizers (threat relationship, exchange relationship, and integrative relationship) presented in *Ecodynamics* (1978, 139–40 and 222–4) to the process of the coordination of values (prices, policemen, and preachment) in *Evolutionary Economics* (1981, 177–80).

6 I prefer "altruistic" or "altruism" rather than "integrative" or "preachment" for this source of power.

7 I am familiar with General Electric Company's evolution (Waters 2009, 42–3). I attempted to use my understanding of GE's history to sort events, artifacts, and people into Boulding's three elements of the genetic structure: People, Organizations, and Things. For the attempt, I first assumed that GE is a firm or organization artifact. However, I found the classification process beyond my capability. I listed the following sentence as a Thing, but it could be identified as People or Organizations. "Its medical imaging business evolved from the work of Elihu Thomson in x-rays." After some effort, I decided that my effort led to nothing of significance. As a result of touring the *Gutenberg Museum* in Mainz, it now appears to me the conditions prior, during, and after the development of the printing press could be insightfully modeled with *Figure 7b.1* on page 295.

References

Beinhocker, Eric B. (2006) *The Origin of Wealth*, Boston, MA: Harvard Business School Press.

Boulding, Kenneth E. (1978) *Ecodynamics: A New Theory of Societal Evolution*, Beverly Hills and London: Sage Publications.

Boulding, Kenneth E. (1981) *Evolutionary Economics*, Beverly Hills and London: Sage Publications.

Boulding, Kenneth E. (1985) *The World as a Total System*, Beverly Hills: Sage Publications.

Boulding, Kenneth E. (1989) *Three Faces of Power*, Beverly Hills: Sage Publications.

Dopfer, Kurt (1994) "Kenneth Boulding: A Founder of Evolutionary Economics," *Journal of Economics Issues*, vol. 28, no. 4 (Dec.), pp. 1201–4.

Mayr, Ernest (2001) *What Evolution Is*, New York, NY: Basic Books.

Waldrop, M. Mitchell (2002) *Complexity: The Emerging Science at the Edge of Order and Chaos*, New York, NY: Simon & Schuster Paperbacks.

Waters, Robert (2006) "What Happened to Boulding's Evolutionary Economics?" *Journal of Economics Issues*, vol. 40, no. 2 (June), pp. 465–72.

Waters, Robert C. (2009) "Evolution of Leadership Development at General Electric," *Engineering Management Journal*, vol. 21, no. 1 (March), pp. 42–6.

Poem

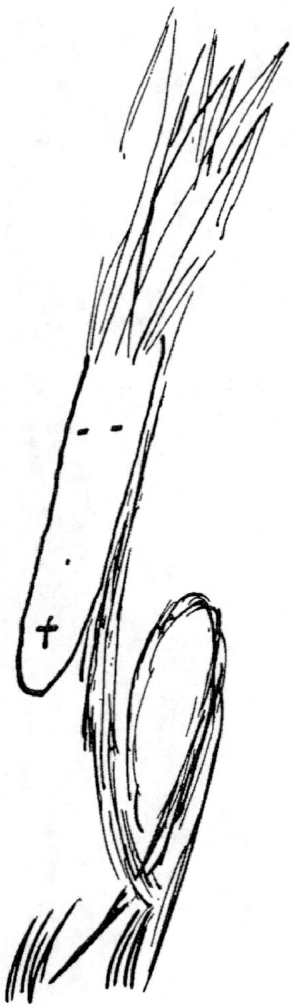

The Pirsel

The evolution of the Pirsel
Encountered once a strange reversal,
Retreating at a frightening rate
Towards the Vegetable State.

Part VIII

Institutions/institutional economics

8 Key text: Prices and other institutions[1]

Kenneth E. Boulding[2]

Economics has been a normative as well as a positive science from its very earliest days. It has always been positive in the sense of being analytical. It has always had some sort of image of what was possible and what was not. On the other hand, it has never hesitated to use this analysis to support some normative propositions about society and to suggest that some situations are better than others. This was true of the marcantilists, it was true of the English classical economists, it was true of the Marxists, and it is certainly true of the Chicago School. The institutionalists were refreshingly blatant about their normative interests. Thorstein Veblen certainly had very strong views about what he liked and what he did not like about society. John R. Commons was interested in saving capitalism by making it good, and Wesley Mitchell had no inhibitions about evaluating spending money as a backward art.

Normative science is both legitimate and dangerous. It is legitimate because the methods and ethic of science can be applied to study normative questions, both to clarify what we mean by things going from bad to better rather than from bad to worse, and to clarify the limitations within which these processes operate. It is dangerous because the norms of the investigator may act as a filter for his analytic perceptions. All thinking is partly wishful. We tend to filter out these aspects of reality which seem to challenge our norms and to overemphasize those aspects which support them, blind to what we dislike and overperceptive to what we like. Almost the only remedy for this disease is the criticism within the scientific community and the acute perception that we all have of the impact of the norms of others on their own thought, however blind we may be to the impact of our own norms on our own thought.

It is one of the tragedies of institutional economics that it reacted to what it perceived quite rightly as the implicit norms of neoclassical price theory, particularly the norm that the perfectly competitive price structure was optimal, by rejecting rather than expanding the price theory itself. This led to Veblen's case to rejection of accounting evaluations and the judgments of the financial systems on a very wholesome scale, and a corresponding uncritical adulation of the engineers. In commons this led to a failure to understand the real distributional consequences of collective bargaining, which may operate far more to redistribute income within the working class than to effect any redistribution between the working class and the capitalist class. In Mitchell it may have led to a rather sterile empiricism, even though this empiricism did lay the foundations for national income statistics. In Beatrice and Sidney Webb, who belonged to what well might be called the English institutionalist school, it led to their great book, *Industrial Democracy*, to a failure to understand the difference between the processes of inflation and deflation and the processes of relative changes in the price-wage structure.

In all these cases, one sees legitimate normative criticism lose its effect because of analytic failure. Alfred Marshall, on the other side, developed the elegant analytical framework of demand and supply analysis and was highly sensitive to its limitations, showing constantly that the real world in its dynamic variety is far more complex than any analytical scheme can represent. But by a certain failure to develop an explicit normative analysis, he left his followers an excuse to derive an implied norm of equilibrium of the price system in a way that Marshall, I think, would never really have countenanced. Since Marshall, of course, the mainstream of welfare economics—A.C. Pigou, Vilfredo Pareto, and their successors—and of the political economists—the school of Chicago and the Virginia Polytechnic Institute—have expanded price theory to more explicit normative analysis, but without breaking through into that more general normative analysis for which it seems to me the institutionalists were really striving, however unsuccessfully. A synthesis of institutionalist normative insight with neoclassical analytical sophistication would seem to me very much in order.

The set of relative commodity and factor prices is a property of the total social system. It has great importance for two reasons. First, it provides at least a first approximation set of valuation coefficients by which complex aggregates or heterogeneous elements can be evaluated. If each element has a price, it can be reduced to a sum of "dollars." Normatively, of course, the set of relative prices is only a first approximation to the "true" valuation coefficients. Unless there is a first approximation there cannot be a second, and without some sort of price set it is hard to see how we arrive at any set of social valuation coefficients which can transform heterogeneous items into a common measure of value.

The second great significance of the relative price structure is that it is an important element in determining the structure of overall terms of reciprocity. These latter are the ratio of what a person or a group gives up to the rest of society to what they receive from the rest of society. Strictly, this is the ratio of perceived utilities valued by subjective valuation coefficients. Nevertheless, the terms of reciprocity are a function of the "terms of trade," that is, the ratio of the quantities of economic goods given up to economic goods received. And this, of course, is a direct function of the relative price structure. When the relative price of wheat rises, the terms of trade of wheat farmers, and presumably their terms of reciprocity also, improve, and the terms of trade and reciprocity of the rest of us decline. The reaction to changes in perceived changes in reciprocity in terms of human behavior and activity is the generalized concept of demand and supply. If we perceive that our terms of reciprocity in a given line of activity, for example, are "low" relative to some other line of activity, we are likely to switch. When the switch is related to something we produce and give out, we are talking about supply; when the switch is related to something that we take in or purchase, we are talking about demand. The elasticity concepts can be generalized to the concept of responsiveness of activity to changes in terms of reciprocity. A large response would correspond to an elastic demand or supply; a small response to an inelastic one. Elasticity depends very much on substitutability: If there is a better opportunity we go to it; if there is not we are stuck where we are, and our activity does not change much in response to a change in terms.

The concept of the terms of reciprocity extends over the whole area of social life. In the household, for example, each party gives up something and gets something. If one party feels that a great deal is being given up and not very much is being received, the household is in danger—a couple may divorce, children may run away, a spouse may desert, and so on. Marriage counseling indeed is mainly renegotiating the terms of reciprocity in the household. The subjective nature of these terms makes it hard for each party to perceive how the other party is perceiving them, unlike relative prices and the terms of trade, which are usually very open and visible. In the labor relationship the terms of reciprocity are very important. The purchase and sale of labor involves much more reciprocity on the part of all parties than does the purchase and sale of wheat. The terms of reciprocity are extremely important in the political system. If large numbers of people perceive that they are giving up a great deal to the government and not getting much out of it, they may switch their votes, start a revolution, or emigrate, depending upon their perception of alternative opportunities. Again, the elasticity concepts are very important. Political trade-offs, logrolling, the balancing of competing objectives, and so on, all involve the same principles. In religious and charitable institutions the situation is the same. A person who is conscious of poor terms of reciprocity in his church is likely to leave it. Even the grants economy is subject to the same principle. We make a grant out of love because the direct utility loss to us of what we give up is less than the satisfaction we obtain from contemplating the other's gain. Even malevolence involves terms of reciprocity. We will damage ourselves for the satisfaction of perceiving damage to our enemy. Response to threat likewise follows much the same principles: We submit if the cost of defiance is greater than the cost of submission; we flee if the costs of flight are less than the costs of submission or defiance; we develop counterthreats if the costs are less than the costs of submission. All these, of course, in utility terms.

The concept of the market can be generalized to that of the opportunities open for selecting and switching reciprocity partners. In the economist's model of the perfect market, which is not actually a poor model for the organized commodity and security markets, there is wide and virtually costless choice of reciprocity partners, so that the terms offered by all of them cannot differ much or these would be immediate switching from one partner to another. The market price that emerges is perceived as rising from the coordination of the different evaluations of different marketers. This is the "clearing the market" principle, which states that there is some equilibrium market price at which, on balance, the people in the market are willing to hold what is there to be held. Market exchange simply rearranges the ownership of assets as sellers increase and buyers decrease their liquid assets; sellers decrease their stocks of what they sell, and buyers increase their stocks of what they buy.

Imperfection in the market is related to the lack of alternative reciprocity partners, up to the point of monopoly, where only one partner is possible. Imperfections may arise out of ignorance of alternatives or out of diversity of reciprocity offerings. I may be forced to stay with my present reciprocity partner either because I do not know of any others that are better or because there are no others that are better, simply because I have got the best (for me), and all the others are different. In a perfect market, of course, the commodity offered by all the potential partners is identical, and each party knows about all the others. What we have, however, throughout all social life is a range of perfection of the market, depending on the nature of the customs, the institutions, taboos, permissions, and encouragements of the society. The marriage market, for example, ranges from almost pure monopoly in countries where divorce is not possible, to a fairly high degree of imperfection even in permissive and loose societies because of the absence of standardization of individuals. In the market for prostitution the commodity is more standardized, and a higher degree of perfection in the market is obtained. This suggests, incidentally, that the normative appraisal of markets is not necessarily the same concept as perfection. In political structures we find a range from monopoly, in the case of the tyrant dictator who can only be removed by death, to the moderately perfect market in power in an active democracy.

There are markets of different degrees of perfection also in ideology and in ethical systems; these help to coordinate the diverse evaluations of individuals in a complex evolutionary dynamic. There may be monopoly in the case of a state church, whether of the Spanish Inquisition sort or in Maoist China, by contrast with the competitive market in religion and ideology in the democratic societies. There are degrees of monopoly and competition in the media, in the provision of information and propaganda, and so on. Within governmental structures again we have the contrast between the monopoly of highly centralized governments and a competitive system of federal, state, and local jurisdictions. It must be emphasized that monopoly is never complete, and over time it is fragile. If the terms of reciprocity are bad in one field, better terms are frequently sought in others. Where politics is unrewarding we turn to religion; where religion is unrewarding we turn back to politics. Where work is unrewarding we retreat into the family; if the family is unrewarding we escape into work. There is actually endless and all-pervasive competition in the sense of the constant search for new terms and new partners. We cannot reject the pervasiveness of competition simply because a few economists, such as Léon Walras, have worked out in great detail the implications of an extremely special case, namely, perfect competition. It would be just as absurd to deny the pervasiveness of love in society because perfect love is virtually nonexistent.

In a larger sense competition is simply ecological interaction which may be, and indeed usually is, quite unconscious. In social systems conscious competition is more important. This is the situation in which there is a conscious change in behavior and product designed to expand the niche in the general ecosystem for the party concerned through improving the terms of reciprocity, both for the party making the change and for its reciprocity partners. An improved product, for example, does precisely this. It may, of course, have an adverse effect on the producers of the inferior products. It will worsen their terms of reciprocity and shrink their social-ecological niche, but if they are adaptable, the injury will not be permanent, the improved product will be imitated, production of the now inferior product will decline, and ultimately, in the optimistic view at least, everyone will be better off, although possibly not sufficiently better off in all cases to counterbalance the costs of adjustment.

What is really significant in the critique of price theory by the institutional economists is not a criticism of its technical failures, such as the failure of the theory of perfect competition to analyze the complexity of imperfect markets, or the failure of price theory to take account of the dynamic complexity of market relations that transcend the apparent simplicity of supply and demand analysis. Rather, it is the criticism directed at the often implicit normative implications of neoclassical price theory, particularly the implication that the structure of relative prices which corresponds to perfect competition is in some sense ideal, and any departure from this is to be deplored and corrected as far as possible. This attack on the normative implications of price theory has a good deal of substance, all the more so because these normative implications are often implied rather than merely expounded. There is indeed a distressing amount of literature, in the first part of the twentieth century especially, which assumes implicitly that some kind of price equilibrium is always desirable and that disequilibrium is always to be deplored, without ever really examining the normative implications of this proposition.

Even without any very elegant apparatus of normative analysis it was easy to point out normative absurdities in the proposition that equilibrium of a perfectly competitive price structure was optimum. In the first place, its distributional impacts could be attacked as very far from optimum. Once given the distribution of property, both in physical assets and in minds and bodies, the argument of the Paretian optimum, that the structure of relative prices which corresponds to perfect competition is the only one in which moves or rearrangements cannot be made which would make some people better off and nobody worse off, is at least plausible. From a normative point of view, however, the distribution of property cannot be taken as given, simply because it is the result of an endless dynamic process, the patterns of which depend very much on the institutions of the society in regard to inheritance, family structure, integrative networks, charities, state redistributions, and so on. There is a strong tendency in the absence of offsetting institutions for property to become more unequally distributed simply because of the "Matthew principle"—"to him that hath shall be given," which means that the rich find it easier to save than the poor. There will be limits to this process, and one could postulate a long-run equilibrium of the distribution of property at which the various offsets just counterbalance the tendency for increased concentration. Such offsets might be the tendency of the rich to become profligate in succeeding generations; or the random movements of relative prices which make some people richer and some people poorer without much regard to how rich or poor they are; the pressure on other institutions, whether the church or the state, to make redistributions; and so on.

Distortions of the relative price structure away from the competitive equilibrium are frequently justified, therefore, on the grounds of more equitable distribution. These are the grounds, for example, on which we subsidize the commodities purchased by the poor and tax those purchased by the rich. The absurdities of the rich are a favorite theme of the moralists. Veblen's scathing attacks on conspicuous consumption, on the ornamental status of women, on collegiate architecture, ritual, and so on, are at least good normative preaching, however little they may contribute to the real analysis. There is something indecent about the extravagance of the rich when they use resources for frivolity that under different institutions might have relieved misery of the destitute.

There is a case on the other side. Certainly, in the age of classical civilization productivity was so low that unless there had been great inequality the peaks of human achievement in the arts, architecture, poetry, drama, and so on could never have been reached. From a normative point of view it could be argued that a society of equally squalid peasants would be worse than one with great inequality that produced the Parthenon, or Chartres, or even Versailles. Even within this framework, however, there is room for institutional normative evaluations. The splendors of the cathedrals were for everyone, the palaces were for the few. In our own day virtually everyone can enjoy the fantastic pictures from Mars, but only a few will fly in the Concorde. It is clear that the market always must be supplemented by a "grants economy" of one-way transfers and that there must be a normative evaluation of the structure of these transfers.

This problem is very closely related to another criticism of the market, namely, that it cannot provide public goods. This has always been recognized by economists, even by the most passionate advocates of the free market. The extent to which the peak achievements of humankind can be public rather than private goods is a very important institutional question, the answer to which depends to some extent on the society's technology. Mozart could never have written his music except in an aristocratic society of great inequality, but the phonograph has now made it possible for millions of people to hear it, as compared with the thousands who heard it during his lifetime.

A third normative criticism of the market and the competitive structure of relative prices is that it does not adequately provide for the right kinds of development and the best motivation for invention and technical change. This is an important defense of such institutions as trade unions, collective bargaining, and the minimum wage. These may create unemployment, and they almost certainly redistribute income away from the really poor toward the middle, but they will have the effect of directing technical change into labor-saving improvements, so they may ultimately increase the rate at which everyone becomes richer. This, of course, was the classic argument of the Webbs. It has some validity. Cheap labor, and especially slavery, may discourage labor-saving invention, for those who have the power to change do not have the will. They are rich enough. Those who might have the will to change do not have the power. My favorite example is the impact of the minimum wage of 40 cents an hour in 1936 on the peanut-shelling industry, which could only afford to pay 25 cents an hour and which simply went out of business, throwing the previous peanut shellers into unemployment. It was not long, however, before a peanut-shelling machine was invented which increased the productivity of labor to the point where the minimum wage could now be afforded, so that the peanut-shelling industry reestablished itself with a somewhat diminished volume of employment. Things, however, may not always work out this well. There is little doubt, for example, that feather-bedding on the railroads led to a diminution of this resource beyond what might have been socially desirable.

A fundamental criticism of the competitive structure of relative prices, which as far as I know was not made very explicitly by the institutionalists, is that it does not sufficiently anticipate future scarcities, changes, that is, in the relative scarcity of different outputs of the system. If a commodity, whether it be water, energy, or some materials, is relatively plentiful now but is likely to be scarce later, there is a great deal to be said for raising the relative price now, as that will encourage "economizing improvements," that is, technical change which will offset the increasing future scarcity of the input. Energy is a particularly good case in point. We have lived through a period of extraordinarily cheap energy thanks to the discovery of oil and natural gas. Indeed, in the last hundred years the real price of energy has been almost constantly declining because of the constant discovery of new sources. It seems highly probable, however, that we are facing a period of long and highly noticeable increase in the relative price of energy, and of many materials, as the cheap and easy sources are exhausted; we then must go to deeper mines, deeper wells, more inconvenient locations such as offshore drilling, or more expensive and less convenient sources, such as solar energy in its many forms.

The most sensible policy would be to make energy more expensive now, particularly through the tax system. The point is that short-run elasticities are apt to be much less than long-run elasticities. A rise in the price of energy *now* will tend to anticipate the long-run elasticity of demand in terms of conservation and increased efficiency in the utilization of energy, and it will anticipate the long-run elasticity of supply in opening up new sources. What would be really catastrophic would be to have energy remain very cheap for the next fifty years and then suddenly increase to five times its present relative price; even though we could adjust fairly easily to a fivefold increase, it would require the life span of an entire generation, and the process of rapid adjustment might be extremely costly, indeed, almost catastrophic. The competitive market alone, however, will never anticipate changes of this kind, particularly those that are fairly far in the future, not only because of time discounting but also because of uncertainty discounting. Uncertainty is much larger in the case of private decisions, which only involve a small part of the system and cannot anticipate redistributions, than it is in the case of society as a whole. In political matters, also, those who make the decisions are usually not those who bear the uncertainty, that is, who will suffer if the decision is bad. This may produce irresponsibility, but it also produces greater willingness to take what may be necessary risks.

A general normative analysis would certainly go far beyond the perfectly competitive relative price structure in its appraisals. On the other hand, no normative analysis in society can be complete without a careful analysis of the relative price structure and the impact on this of proposed changes and proposed institutions. We see this particularly clearly if we are interested in appraising the distributional impacts of any particular change in legal or institutional structures. I have been arguing that we should have distributional impact statements, much as we do environmental impact statements, which would try to estimate who would be favorably affected, and who would be unaffected by any particular change. Because of the enormous interconnectedness of the system, these would be very difficult to do, although certainly we have some skills in this regard. If they were done, the answers probably would be highly surprising because of the network character of the system, which means that change applied in one place may produce changes in other and totally unexpected places.

In social systems cause and effect are almost useless concepts in any simple sense, for innumerable causes produce innumerable effects in a mutually determined dynamic process. Even the general equilibrium models of Walras or of the ecologists are completely inadequate to handle the dynamics of the system. If there is a general equilibrium, of course, there is at least some probability that the system will move toward it, although even this is by no means certain. Even if it has an equilibrium, a complex system can easily exhibit a structure in which it moves away from the equilibrium in some of its phases and toward the equilibrium in others. Boundaries which divide these phases are extremely hard to detect until after the event. "Explode–crash" patterns of many populations of plants and animals, such as occur after a forest fire, are a good example of the complexities of the dynamics of systems of this kind. And social systems are by no means exempt. After a war or some other catastrophe, there are often extraordinary upsurges of political and religious movements which then suffer rapid decline, just like the fireweed after a forest fire.

Nevertheless, the economist must go on reiterating that the price structure is important and that it has a critical impact in determining distributional and other structures, although often in very odd ways. An example is the period 1932–1942 in the United States, when there was a spectacular rise in the labor movement, from about 3 million to 15 million members, and a large part of US industry came under collective bargaining, yet labor's proportion of national income fell sharply, simply because any impact of collective bargaining was completely swallowed up in the other movements of the society. There is no guarantee at all that collective bargaining will redistribute income away from capital income toward labor income; often, quite the reverse is the case.

I have encountered so many of these cases that I have been tempted to formulate a "law of political irony": "Everything you do to help people hurts them, and everything you do to hurt people helps them." The exceptions to this rule seem almost to be of the kind that prove it. Certainly, an enormous amount of what ostensibly is done for the poor benefits the rich. There is a classic story of the two neighboring villages in a nameless less developed country, one of which received considerable development aid, the other of which did not. The former was corrupted by the aid and ended up worse than before. The latter became so angry that it reorganized itself and began a real upsurge of development. The moral, of course, is not that we should not try to help people, but that it is a good idea to know something about it; in particular, the naïve assumption that institutions do what they are supposed to do is likely to prove very unrealistic. The market, of course, is not the only structure that holds the system together, although it is a very important part of the connective tissue of any social system, and if it is not understood, very large mistakes can be made.

We should not, of course, neglect the other networks of the system—the media, gossip, fashion, education, politics—all of which operate on principles that are rather different from that of the market. Many social processes operate much more along the lines of epidemiology than upon the model of clearing the market toward an equilibrium price. I have always suspected that the main reason why economics has been so unsuccessful in dealing with the problem of the trade-off between inflation and unemployment is that we have failed to recognize that even the structure of absolute prices is determined epidemiologically by the communications system and not by the *tatonnement* of the market. The theory of relative prices, as I have argued, is of great importance, but it is not the whole story, and the theory of the dynamics of absolute prices and wages still remains to be written.

Perhaps the most important function of the relative price system in normative analysis, as noted previously, is that it provides at least a first approximation for a system of valuation coefficients. These are absolutely necessary if the overall value of complex structures and systems is to be compared. The question which normative analysis seeks to answer is: Are things better today than they were yesterday? Between yesterday and today some things have increased, some things have diminished, some things have stayed where they are. Today is better than yesterday if the overall value in terms of our normative standard of the increase in the things that have increased is greater than the normative value of the decrease in the things that have decreased. In order to answer the question as to whether today is better than yesterday, therefore, we must have a set of valuation coefficients by which these increases and decreases can be appraised and compared. All evaluation of complex systems involves a measure of value. The only mechanism which offers a clear measure of value in our society is money. As long as there is a relative price structure, we could choose any arbitrary commodity as the "numeraire" and express the aggregate value of any collection of quantities of commodities as a quantity of the numeraire. If an orange is worth two apples, then ten apples and five oranges can be expressed as worth either ten oranges or twenty apples.

Difficulties emerge in making an overall evaluation of large, complex social systems, primarily because the system of relative prices is not necessarily the ideal from the point of view of making evaluations. This is apparent even at the statistical level, for example, when we try to compare the GNP of the USSR and the United States. Should we use Russian relative prices or US relative prices? The results would be rather different, and under some circumstances even the order of the two aggregates might be reversed. When comparing ten apples and five oranges with five apples and ten oranges, if two apples are worth one orange, the first aggregate is worth twenty apples, the second is worth twenty-five, and the second is clearly superior. But if one apple is worth two oranges, the first is worth 12.5 apples, and the second is only worth ten; the first aggregate is clearly superior.

We can add to this argument the consideration that the normatively optimum price structure is different from the actual one, as noted earlier, and if we put these values into the system the results will be different again. Unfortunately, there is no solution to this problem, even in accounting. The shift in relative values of different assets creates constant conundrums.

Nevertheless, the structure of relative prices is at least a place to start, as the first approximation when we are trying to construct overall valuation coefficients. It has an additional justification of some normative force in that the relative price structure is determined far more by alternative costs than it is by relative demands. Indeed, the latter are significant only insofar as costs are not constant, and hence a shift in demand will change alternative costs. It is the fact, in Adam Smith's famous example, that two beaver are somehow exchanged for one deer in the woods, that giving up one deer enables us to get two beaver, and giving up two beaver enables us to get one deer that determines equilibrium value of the exchange ratio in the marketplace. Relative market values, therefore, are closely connected with relative technologies and productivities. In this sense they have a kind of objective status which gives them a certain amount of normative clout. At least they are not whims, idle fancies, or even fashions, although they are the result of a long history of technological change, which itself may be evaluated normatively, as indeed is done every time we undertake technology assessment.

The second problem of overall normative evaluations is that many things in the overall pattern which we wish to evaluate do not have prices at all; hence it not only is hard to reduce them to dollars but also is regarded as improper. The law, it is true, tends to put money values on everything, including human life, promises, insults, libels, and so on, but there is a residual uneasiness in reducing everything to dollar terms. Oscar Wilde's gentleman who knew the price of everything and the value of nothing strikes a certain responsive chord. We do have a feeling somehow that there are some things which should be priceless, although we never really escape from reciprocity or trade-offs. To ask how much integrity is worth how much power may seem like an indecent question, but it is one that is answered much more often than it is asked, even though the answer may be implicit.

Part of the hostility of the institutionalists to price theory rests in the feeling that somehow money is dirty and always a little tainted and that exchange is an activity a little below the dignity of the human race. One finds this feeling particularly strong in Marx, who really hated exchange, and it is almost as strong in Veblen. Part of this attitude one might psycho-analyze as being a subconscious desire to be an aristocrat, not having to deal with the sordid necessity of working for a living, but there is unquestionably something deeper than that in human psychology. It is this which I think we have not analyzed very satisfactorily, and it accounts for a great deal of the difficulty of legitimation of the market and capitalism in general. Joseph Schumpeter, we recall, thought that capitalism was a wonderful system but that it could not survive because no one would love it. It could only survive on the integrative leftovers from the more feudal and aristocratic system which preceded it. I have an uneasy feeling that there is some truth in this. On the other hand, delegitimation of exchange could be very costly for the human race because, bad as it is, the alternatives seem to be worse in terms of centralization, dictatorship, and defenselessness against tyranny, as can be seen in the communist countries. In this regard and many others the institutionalists ask some very important questions to which neither they nor the rest of us have found answers.

Notes

1 This article was previously published in *Journal of Economic Issues*, 1977, 11(4): 809–821.

2 The author is Professor of Economics and Director, Institute of Behavioral Science, University of Colorado, Boulder.

8a Comment: A synthesis of neoclassical and institutional economic price theory?

John Groenewegen

Introduction

> It is one of the tragedies of institutional economics that it reacted to what it perceived quite rightly as the implicit norms of neoclassical price theory, particularly the norms that the perfectly competitive price structure was optimal, by rejecting rather than expanding the price theory itself.
>
> (Boulding 1977, p. 810)

Instead of expanding neoclassical price theory, the institutionalists followed, according to Boulding, their own way, which he criticized because of its lack of analytical rigor. Referring to Veblen, Commons and Mitchell, he wrote: 'In all these cases one sees legitimate normative criticism lose its effect because of analytical failure' (Boulding 1977, p. 810). This is precisely the issue that is central in the discussion between neoclassical and institutionalist economists: the neoclassicists claimed to have developed a value-free theory that showed universal laws, which can be objectively tested, whereas the institutionalists include values and norms and are more realistic in their assumptions and relevance for policy and management issues, but would lack analytical rigor.

According to Boulding (1977, p. 810), a synthesis would be the solution: 'A synthesis of institutionalist normative insight with neoclassical sophistication would seem to me very much in order.' In this contribution I will explore the possibilities of such a synthesis.

I will first make a few methodological remarks about issues related to combining different types of schools of economic thought like neoclassical (NCE) and institutional economics (IE). Second, I will discuss neoclassical price theory, explain its analytical rigor and show how the normative element is explicitly eliminated, but implicitly strongly present. Then, I will elaborate on the developments in institutional economics after Boulding's 1977 publication. Third, I will focus on new institutional economics (NIE). It will be shown how that approach is in line with the philosophy and methodology of neoclassical economics and a synthesis seems very well possible, but the possibility to take a normative analysis on board seems limited, if not absent. The fourth section addresses the school of original institutional economics (OIE), of which Veblen, Commons and Mitchell are founding fathers. I will discuss how that school in institutional economics developed, after Boulding (1977), a so-called 'social value theory', in which the normative analysis is central. However, the philosophical and methodological foundations of OIE are so different from neoclassical economics that a synthesis seems impossible, but a combination of the different theories under the umbrella of a uniting framework could be an option.

Some methodological remarks

About facts

Broadly speaking, mainstream neoclassical economics adheres to the philosophy of positivism[1]: science aims at the discovery of universal causal laws, which represent in an objective way the relationship between variables in a reality which is knowable to all scientists in the same objective way.[2] The aim of science is to reveal the Truth, which is hidden in the objects of the reality around us. In theories, like the price theory, a distinction is made between dependent (the relative prices) and the independent variables (exogenous changes in, for instance, technology, or preferences causing changes in demand or supply), which cause the changes in the prices. The causal relationship is formulated in a universal law to be tested in an objective way by (other) researchers, who will use the same objective method of deductive analysis.[3] Based on validated laws, a discipline like economics is able to make predictions like: 'if the supply is fixed and demand increases the price will go up'. Such predictions would hold anytime anywhere, but only if the assumptions stated at the beginning of the deduction are true.

In contrast to the positivist approach of mainstream science, an alternative exists, which we will call 'interpretivism'.[4] Causality is then not a straightforward matter of discovering causal laws, but consequences (also called outcomes, performances or results) are the result of complex processes, in which context specificities play a central role. A variety of mechanisms operates in a context which is specific in time and place and the process of causation results from the interaction of a number of interdependent variables and mechanisms that are 'contextual'. Instead of asking what caused the change in relative prices, the question will be more about what process emerged and evolved and how the different mechanisms interdependently made for a specific change in prices. Important is also to what extend (powerful) actors were able to design and influence the process so law-like causalities are less present.

Another important part of the interpretivist approach is the distinction between 'brute' (physical) facts and the 'interpreted' (social) facts. In the social world, facts are given meaning by the members of a community on the basis of which they act and decide and consequently constitute a social reality (see also the role of image in the theories of Boulding 1956 [1997]). Furthermore, in the interpretivist approach, the social context can also allow for autonomous individual behavior to change the context. The room to maneuver for human actors is context specific and the scientist should try to understand how and to what extent the different elements in the context 'structure' human behavior. In the case of understanding relative prices, market structures leave no, a little or plenty of room for firms to set prices. Not only market structures are important in the context, but also the socio-political and the technological structures, which can create historical lock-ins.

About values

Boulding (1977) appreciates institutional economics because of its 'normative insight', because of its insight into the role of values in economic life and economic analysis. Bush (2009) made an analytically helpful distinction between the value (being the standard of judgment), the valuation (being the application of the standard of judgment) and finally the value judgment (being the choice of value as the right standard of judgment). Introducing values into the scientific analysis raises questions about a theory being value-free, a claim made by mainstream theory with great strength. To their vision, the inclusion of values into a scientific analysis would make the analysis non-scientific, vague and imprecise. In contrast, institutional economists, who ground their theory on the pragmatist philosophy of Peirce and Dewey (see below), suggest that values can and should be included into the scientific analysis. According to institutionalists, values are always present in daily life, including that of the researcher. The point is that those values should be made explicit and subject of research and deliberation (compare Boulding on 'deliberative welfare economics' in: Kesting 2010). In a scientific analysis of values, the researcher should investigate what the consequences of the existing values are (the so-called 'is') and how those consequences hold in comparison to the desired consequences: the so-called societal objectives (the 'ought'). In a proper scientific inquiry, criteria are formulated of the appropriate values (standards of judgment). In the scientific community, open deliberation should take place about the right way to analyze the 'is' and about the consequences of applying specific values.

When the community has decided about societal objectives that are different from the 'is', then a deliberation should take place on the question of which institutional changes are necessary in order to realize the societal objectives. In other words: values as standards of judgments are not given by God or any other source and are not exogenous to the system, but part of the means and ends that actors in society decide about (Dolfsma 1997). Political debate and conflict is part and parcel of the application of (other) values because other values will give rise to other behavior with other consequences and implications for the distribution of costs and benefits (Myrdal 1944; Tool 1986). Alternatives are compared and valued using specific standards of judgment.

Above I made some remarks about the relation between facts and theory and how positivists and interpretivists differ in their ideas about facts and how science should analyze and test. Especially the role of values, valuation and value judgment differs. We will see below that NCE and NIE fit the positivist approach and OIE the interpretivist one. This has implications for the possibility to integrate theories.

Neoclassical price theory

Neoclassical economics is known as a rigorous approach: dependent variables, like relative prices, such as commodity prices, wages and interest rates, are explained and predicted by a set of independent variables, such as the technology (resulting in an efficient scale of production) and preferences of the consumers (resulting in allocative efficiency). The actors in neoclassical economics are modeled according to very specific characteristics of rationality (which makes ex ante calculation of optimal combinations possible) and rules of behavior (maximize utility and profit, minimize costs). The fully informed and knowledgeable actors are positioned in well-defined environmental structures, of which the market structure is most important. In applying the Methodology of the Scientific Research Program (Lakatos 1978) on neoclassical economics, Latsis (1976) identified the hard core, protective belt and heuristics of neoclassical economics. He concluded that the core models are all of a 'single-exit structure': given the characteristics of the actors and the situation, logically they have no other option than to calculate and 'choose' the one optimal solution, which theory predicts. This does not only hold for the model of pure and perfect competition, but also for the monopolistic and oligopolistic models with price or quantity reactions.

Boulding is positive about neoclassical price theory because of its rigor and the relative prices provide 'at least a first approximation of a system of value coefficients' (Boulding 1977, p. 819). How does such a first approximation come about? The relative prices result from a confrontation of aggregate demand and supply. In the standard neoclassical model individual actors are assumed to decide on the basis of their utility function. The utility of a good or service is the capability to satisfy wants. The actor is assumed to maximize its utility through the demand in the market. The aggregate demand in confrontation with the aggregate supply (based on individual producers, who maximize profits) results in an equilibrium price and quantity that reflects wants and scarcities. In this economic analysis the wants are given for the scientist: the individual is the starting point of the analysis and her wants are exogenous. The neoclassical theory adheres to the positive–normative dichotomy: the wants are the domain of the individual actors and exogenously given, i.e. objective facts for the scientific researcher. Preferences and valuations are a matter for the autonomous individual and just facts objectively given to the researcher. A normative analysis of those facts cannot and should not be part of scientific inquiry: the positive and the normative should be carefully separated and then, it is claimed, economics is a value-free science.

Neoclassical economics and value

Boulding points to the contribution of institutional economics to have explained the implicit normative position of neoclassical economics. It presents itself as a value-free science, but implicitly specific value judgments are applied. NCE works out of the principle of so-called 'ethical relativism' (Tool 1986): all values, criteria and preferences are relative to individuals. It is impossible to judge the values and criteria, on the basis of which the individuals choose. Wants are given and 'utility' is taken to be a stand in for values. 'Thus utility is the meaning of value in orthodox neoclassicism and price is its measure' (Tool 1986, p. 9). The Pareto optimum expresses what is 'good': making at least one person better off without making anyone else worse off. 'Better or worse' are compatible then with the ethically relative utility value theory. For the scientist, the choice of the actors is rational and as such no part of the analysis. The outcome of all decisions is then 'right' by definition: what is, is good and in that sense the normative question of how to value the outcome of the market is eliminated. Boulding points to the fundamental mistake made here:

> What is really significant in the critique of price theory by the institutional economists is not a criticism of its technical failures, such as the failure of the theory of perfect competition to analyze the complexity of imperfect markets (...) but rather it is the criticism directed at the often implicit normative implications of neoclassical price theory, particularly the implication that the structure of relative prices which corresponds to perfect competition is in some sense ideal, and any departure from this is to be deplored and corrected as far as possible.
>
> (Boulding 1977, p. 814)

Boulding refers to the fact that no 'free' market exists and that always actors choose on the basis of a specific distribution of property rights. When the outcomes of such a market are taken as 'right', then implicitly the existing power structure reflected in the distribution of property and decision rights is valued as 'right'.

This has large implications for how mainstream economists value the pure and perfect market as an optimal situation. Large part of liberalization, privatization and deregulation policies are inspired by and build upon the NCE value of the market. Note that the claims about the optimality of the market are based on a deductive analysis based on strong axioms about actors and structures. The predictions about efficient allocation in that highly abstract theoretical setting are used to recommend and defend the market in concrete economic settings.

In the following sections, I will discuss how the developments in institutional economics dealt with the questions and suggestions raised by Boulding. First, I will show how new institutional economics extended neoclassical price theory with a theory of institutions and how it remained in accord with the scientific philosophy of neoclassical economics. Second, I will discuss original institutional economics (strongly criticized by Boulding) and show how that school made the issue of values and valuation explicit.

New institutional economics

In the years after the publication of Boulding's 1977 paper, the school of new institutional economics developed strongly, with Nobel laureates like Ronald Coase, Douglass North, Elinor Ostrom and Oliver Williamson. Earlier Nobel laureates like Friedrich von Hayek, Kenneth Arrow and Herbert Simon are also considered to be institutionally oriented economists by some.[5]

Many consider NIE as an extension (or a complement) to neoclassical economics (see the introduction of Williamson 1975) and in that sense a synthesis as suggested by Boulding seems possible.

In this section, I will explain that the core of NIE works within the philosophical tradition of neoclassical economics. Figure 8a.1 shows the applicability of

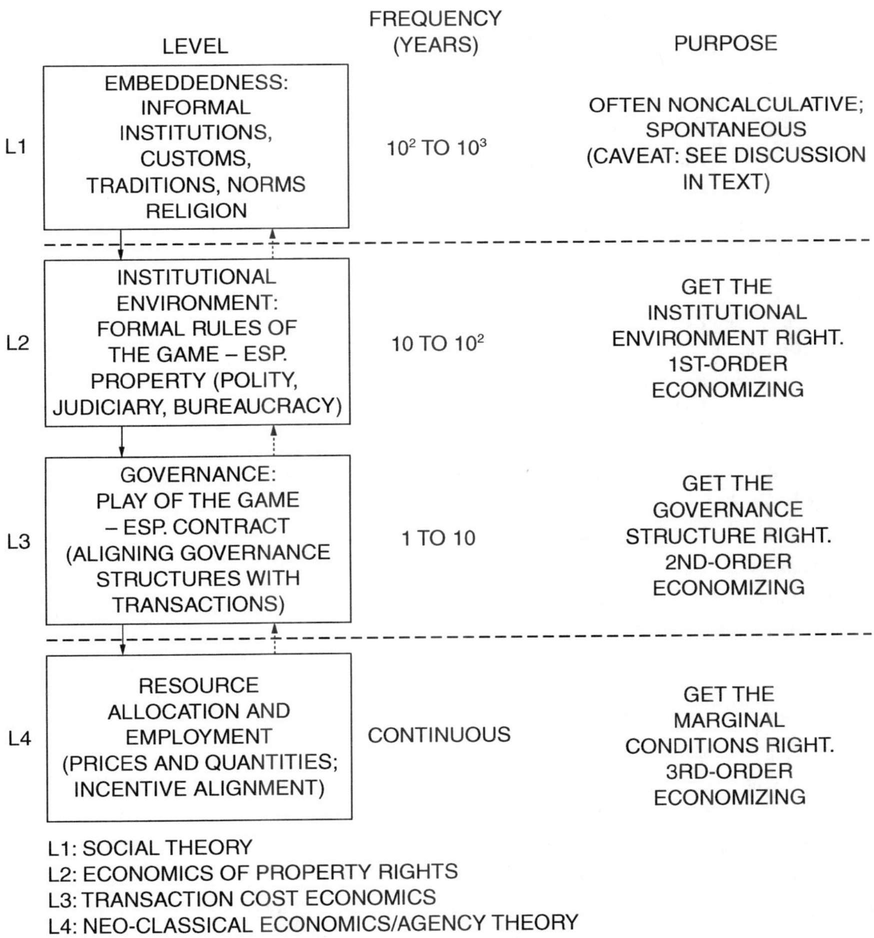

Figure 8a.1 Economics of institutions (source: Williamson 1998, p.26).

the three NIE theories: the theory of property rights (PR) is relevant for analysis at level 2, transaction cost economics (TCE) works at level 3, whereas NCE and principal-agent theory (AT) have their domain at level 4.[6] The arrows in Figure 8a.1 show 'solid' top-down relations and 'dotted' relations as feedbacks, indicating that NIE distinguishes between dependent and independent variables, but recognizes the interactions between the levels.

The theory of property rights is located at the second level of the formal institutions, TCE at the third level of the governance of transactions and the domain of neoclassical economics is located at level 4, showing that leaving the institutional environment of the higher levels to institutional economics, the economic issue of relative prices is a matter of marginal analysis. The schema suggests a complementarity between the NCE and NIE.

The first layer consists of the culture, values and norms, which are not explicitly formulated and written down, but which are internalized in the hearts and souls of the members of the community. Values and norms change slowly and are not subject to calculative behavior. Individual economic actors, and not even groups of actors in collective action, are rarely in the position to purposefully (re)design informal institutions. Informal institutions emerge, change 'spontaneously' out of the interactions of millions of actors. Individual or collective design is not relevant at this level of analysis and consequently no object of economic analysis. However, it is important to be well-informed about the informal institutions in a country, market, industry or firm, because they have a strong influence on the formal institutions at level 2.

The concept of 'first order economizing' at level 2 indicates a different nature of dynamics: formal institutions like laws and regulations are subject to 'economizing'. From an economic point of view at level 2 efficient formal institutions can be designed (laws and regulations) that provide individual actors with the right incentives to maximize profit and utility or to minimize costs. According to NIE, the central theoretical piece at level 2 is the theory of property rights. It is shown how different systems of property rights (private, public, collective and common) influence behavior of actors differently and likewise produce different outcomes. Societies that aim at efficient allocation of their scarce resources better 'get their formal institutions right', including the agencies that monitor behavior and enforce rights (judiciary and bureaucracy). The installment of clear property rights, an independent judiciary and an objective bureaucracy are the ingredients of the 'right' formal institutions.

Level 3 refers to the next step on the path of 'economizing': what are the transaction cost minimizing governance structures, such as firms, contracts, public–private partnerships, state-owned enterprises, etc., taking specific characteristics of the transaction into account? In 2009, Williamson became the Nobel laureate (together with Elinor Ostrom) for his work on governance. He showed how specific governance structures can be matched, 'aligned', with specific transactions so transaction costs are minimized. In the approach the technology, the informal and formal institutions, the characteristics of the actors and of the transaction are the independent variables.

With respect to the actors two 'attributes' are central: bounded rationality and opportunism. In that sense NIE starts from a more realistic actor than NCE, in which fully rational actors are able to design ex ante complete contracts.[7] The introduction of bounded rationality and opportunistic behavior[8] makes it possible to explain the existence of incomplete contracts and to explain why specific institutional arrangements have lower transaction costs than alternatives. A comparative institutional analysis is central in NIE. The purpose of theories of new institutional economics is to understand why modes of governance exist. How can we explain the existence of different types of contracts, of hierarchical organizations like firms, of multi-divisional firms and multinational ones, of regulation and of state-owned enterprises? The purpose of institutional theories is to provide a framework to explain these structures and preferably also to predict them. Now for theory to be able to predict, focus is needed: what is the nature of the actor and what is her rule of behavior? In institutional economics the line of reasoning of mainstream economics is maintained: the actors minimize or maximize. If we then put the actor in a theoretically closed environment we are able to predict precisely the outcome. In other words: to align a different type of transactions with a different type of governance. And that is exactly how the NIE is structured[9]; NIE applies a specific lens with which the scientist is able to focus. As Williamson (2000) explains, the TCE is in need of further extension towards a so-called zero level of cognitive maps of individual actors and towards a more dynamic interaction between organizations and technology. As discussed in Groenewegen and Vromen (1997), an extension towards more heterogeneous actors and more dynamics, in the sense that the boundaries between dependent and independent variable get blurred, sits uneasy with the rigorous analytical ambitions of TCE.

To sum up: although NCE and NIE model actors and structures somewhat differently, the philosophical underpinnings are similar. The positivist philosophy, the deductive methodology, the methodological individualistic approach, the values of competitive markets and individualistic preferences, the central role of efficiency and selection of the fittest and fitter through anonymous competition, the way of testing the theories, all that shows a large complementarity and a large potential for a synthesis.

Original institutional economics

In the USA at the end of the nineteenth century, Thorstein Veblen was the well-known institutional economist who was highly critical of neoclassical economics (NCE). In his opinion, NCE was too formal and abstract, was too static and was wrongly based on individual actors that were disconnected from their institutional environment. Until around 1945, an influential group of institutional economists dominated the development of the discipline in the USA. Clarence Ayres, Wesley Mitchell and especially John R. Commons joined Veblen in his criticism of NCE and underlined the importance of including institutions in the economic explanation (see Gruchy 1972 for details). Modeling actors as maximizing machines operating in an institutional vacuum was not considered an adequate model of economic reality.

First, OIE stresses the importance of habits in understanding human behavior (Hodgson 1988). Second, OIE stresses the capacity of human actors to deliberate and choose: actors are volitional.[10] On the one hand, habits are considered a precondition for all thought, for reasoning, containing past beliefs and experiences, and on the other hand individuals are very well capable of recognizing and shaping their habits. In other words: like values also habits are subject to valuation and can and should be changed if they result in undesirable consequences (Bromley 2006; Hodgson 2004).[11]

OIE positions human actors in an evolving institutional context. The economy is first of all a matter of the dynamics of changing institutions which influence economic behavior and vice versa. In that process, technology, values and laws interact, and economic models and theories should capture that core element of reality. Economic actors are social actors operating in specific institutional environments and markets are institutionalized structures, in which power is equally important as efficiency to understand their performance.[12] In OIE, the actors are first of all volitional actors with discretion (Tool 1986; Bromley 2006) over, among other things, prices. Prices are 'administered' (Berle and Means 1932; Tool 1993), which is a fundamentally different view on how prices come about than the neoclassical theory of relative prices.

First, attention is asked for the fact that relative prices never come about in an institutional vacuum; always power structures reflected in property and decisions structures are present and largely determine the decisions actors take. It is a fundamental mistake to present markets as neutral, anonymous mechanisms, in which individuals independently decide as if they were atoms. This might have been true for a few exceptional situations, but was certainly a misrepresentation in the times of Veblen and thereafter.

Second, markets are political constructs strongly regulated by informal and formal institutions. The rules of the game partly evolve spontaneously (especially the informal ones), but mainly result from purposeful design. The political process of institutional design is heavily influenced by societal interest groups. The process of design and redesign is characterized by struggle and conflict because a change of the rules always implies an adjustment of the distribution of costs and benefits.

Third, markets are best perceived as evolving systems in which individual and collective action results in both intended and unintended consequences. Consequently, markets are never in equilibrium, but always in a process of adaptation, transition and evolution.

In that process of constituting reality through action according to the underlying philosophy of American pragmatism, which forms the foundation of OIE, reality is not considered to be composed of objects to which the researcher has direct access, and which would allow for objective knowledge. On the contrary: in order to understand (complex) reality, people in daily life and researchers in scientific inquiry make use of 'ordering ideas', of concepts, categories and frameworks that allow for abstraction and that structure reality. The world of facts is complex and always data have to be sorted out applying specific standards of relevance (Bush 2009). In selecting the proper standards necessarily choices are made and then always values and value judgments are involved. Facts speak as far as they are considered relevant from a specific value point of view. Take the fact of a price of a good like wheat or oil. An increase in the price of these products can be considered to be caused by an increase in demand or a reduction of supply and then the price change reflects the new scarcities, stimulating actors to consume less of the product and to look for substitutes. The increase in the price can also be seen as a reflection of the use of dominant positions in the markets: powerful actors or their cartels manipulate the supply in order to increase the price. The facts about the change in the price of wheat or oil do not speak for themselves, but are theory-laden, are investigated from a specific perspective, a specific belief about how such markets function and which forces cause changes. A research from a marginalist perspective addresses other questions and collects other data than a research driven by a power perspective. The facts are sorted out based on the theories, concepts and categories that the theoretical framework provides. And the theories are chosen because of the values the (scientific) community adheres to. Facts are theory-laden and theory is value-laden.

In sum: OIE works with a framework that addresses institutional issues in a dynamic, holistic and systemic way (Wilber and Harrison 1978). In doing so the actors in the theories and models are not one-dimensionally efficiency driven, but their preferences are endogenously constituted in the process of acting.[13] Correspondingly, the environment is not only complex as in NIE, but structures in the environment are constituted mutually with the individuals and collectivities. In contrast to the methodological individualistic approach, OIE is characterized by so-called methodological interactionism, including both the interaction between actors and structures and the interaction among actors. OIE contrasts in many respects the positivist philosophy of science and adheres to the interpretivist philosophy.

According to Bush (1999, p. 895), pragmatism adheres to a realist ontology in the sense that 'it accepts things and events for what they are independently of thought' (Dewey 1925 [1984], p. 18). But pragmatism is also idealist in 'so far it contends that thought gives birth to distinctive acts which modify future facts and events in such a way as to render them more reasonable, that is to say, more adequate to the ends which we propose for ourselves' (Dewey 1925 [1984], p. 18). The phrase 'ends we propose ourselves' provides the link to the instrumental value theory, which is the opposite to NCE's given ends. Before we discuss that recent contribution of OIE we briefly explain how OIE goes about a scientific research. Not deduction, but abduction is the way to acquire knowledge. Abduction is the epistemological program of pragmatism. Raising scientific questions starts with a 'surprising' event. A fact or event is 'surprising' when the existing theory (the 'settled belief') cannot explain the fact or event. For instance, the price of oil is rising, while the production and demand are stable.

Standard market theory would predict stable prices then. Following Peirce, scientific inquiry about surprising facts should start with inference to the best available explanation. What could have caused the surprising event? Based on past beliefs and experiences and based upon imagination and deliberation, hypotheses about the explanation are formulated. The abductive syllogism is then of the form:

> The surprising fact, C, is observed
> But if A were true, C could be a matter of course
> Hence, there is reason to suspect A to be true.
>
> (Bromley 2006)

Abduction makes use of existing knowledge about relations between variables and of particular assumptions to formulate propositions (hypotheses) with the intent to explain the event. In the case of the oil price, the hypothesis could be about price-setting behavior of producers, or whole sellers. Further research could confirm the hypothesis, which could be the start of the formulation of a new theory on (oil) prices, the start of a new belief. Abduction is not only relevant in the explanation of an observed surprising fact, but also in forming hypotheses about the consequences of specific behavior that is based on a change in institutions.

Instrumental value theory

Social value theory consists of analyses of criteria and judgments in making choices about the social and economic order (Tool 1999, p. 538). Instrumental value theory is a particular formulation of social value theory in which the ideas of Peirce, Veblen, Commons and Dewey are combined. The starting point is that all theory is value-laden, relevant inquiry is and should be normative. The 'is' resulting from the maintenance of existing values should and can be compared with the 'ought': the outcome according to what society considers desirable. In a proper scientific inquiry, criteria are formulated of the appropriate values, i.e. the standards of judgment which induces behavior which results in the realization of the societal objectives. In the scientific community open deliberation should take place about the right belief to analyze the 'is', about what will be the consequences of the behavior which is based on the existing values. Likewise deliberation should take place about the necessary institutional changes, which will imply the application of other values and which will consequently give rise to other behavior with other consequences. Alternatives are compared and valued using specific standards of judgment. Following Veblen, the pragmatist institutionalists identify in every institutional structure two types of valuation: the ceremonial and the instrumental one. The ceremonial one relates to the invidious distinctions and ceremonial adequacy holds when the values serve the status quo of the existing privileges of the elite. The instrumental ones are contributing to the realization of the societal objectives.

To appraise the nature of institutions, to make distinctions between ceremonial and instrumental, there is a need of a general guiding principle that provides the fundamentals that should be taken into account. Tool (1986) has formulated a general principle saying that mankind should choose institutions and resulting behavior that 'provides for the continuity of human life and the non-invidious re-creation of community through the instrumental use of knowledge'.

From the above, one could conclude that scientific objectivity or better intersubjectivity is not about 'the elimination of all normative propositions from scientific inquiry; it is achieved through the selection of appropriate normative standards to guide inquiry' (Bush 2009, p. 299).

On integrating theories

Boulding (1956 [1997]) presented a general systems theory with a 'skeleton of science' comprised of nine levels of organization, each comprising an increasing level of complexity. From static structures via predetermined dynamics, to sociocultural systems in which human beings act and create. As discussed above, the complexity is reduced in NCE and NIE to agent–structure relations which allow for optimization, equilibrium and prediction. In OIE the complexity enters the analysis in a less reduced way, allowing for human actors and structures to be mutually constitutive.

Looking at reality in terms of increasing complexity opens a view on the relation between NCE and IE in which the one is not rejected and replaced by the other, but in which different perspectives, theories and paradigms can be complementary. Such a way of looking at the two schools in economics corresponds to the writings of original institutionalists like J.M. Clark and John R. Commons (Caldari 2010; Rutherford, 1994). Commons, for instance, saw IE coming into the picture related to a higher degree of complexity:

> I do not think that institutional economics, defined as collective action in control of individual action, is contrary to the so-called pure economics of the past, which is individual action without collective control. It is a continuation of pure economics into a higher degree of complexity.
>
> (Commons 1936, p. 241, quoted from Caldari 2010, p. 609)

One of the extensions to a more complex analysis is due to the fact that the relatively simple neoclassical type of markets, in which the actions of the participants in a harmonious way result in relative prices, is more an exception than the rule. The rule is one of conflicts and the management of conflict through the creation of order[14] is the central issue of institutional economics. So in terms of the relationship between NCE and IE, Commons suggests a continuation at a higher level of complexity: the neoclassical assumption of a 'foreordained harmony' of interest is replaced by a situation of conflict, which demands 'ordering'. One could also say that Commons considered NCE relevant for very specific conditions, in which interests of the different groups are in harmony.[15]

Also original institutionalists like J.M. Clark considered NCE and IE to be complementary; they deal with different types of reality, which demands a different approach to reality.

> Orthodox economics undertakes to interpret equilibrium: Veblen undertakes to interpret progressive change. And in the social world this is much the same as saying that orthodox economics studies the assumptions of contentment and Veblen the assumptions of discontent, both of which are undeniable facts. Since undeniable facts are difficult to ignore, the net result is very largely to call them by different names.
>
> (Clark 1921, p. 132, quoted from Caldari 2010, p. 615)

Particularly critical towards the neoclassical theory is also the OIE economist J.K. Galbraith, but he also recognizes that some assumptions of the neoclassical approach, most notably those that are required by an equilibrium framework, may be of some utility. According to Galbraith, the concept of equilibrium is valid only if the assumptions that traditional theory requires (perfect competition, maximizing attitude) are valid. These assumptions may resemble, although only roughly, a part of the economic structure of the market (mostly industries that are not susceptible to large-scale organization, such as agriculture, service industries and artistically oriented industries).

Conclusion

Boulding suggests a synthesis between NCE and IE in order to combine normative analysis with analytical rigor. Literally a synthesis would imply integration into a Grand Theory that combines the best of the two worlds. The two paradigms of NCE and IE would then merge into a new type of economics.

From the discussion above, it can be concluded that NCE and NIE belong to the same positivist paradigm and a synthesis in the sense of a melting of the theories is certainly possible. NCE and NIE work out of the same philosophy of science, the same methodology and apply the same methods; merely their specific research questions are about different issues. However, the ambition of Boulding to integrate neoclassical and institutional economics in order to integrate a normative analysis into economics can then not be realized because both NCE and NIE do not integrate values into their theory.

In the case of NCE and OIE, the conclusion from the above is that such a synthesis of a positivist and interpretivist paradigm is highly improbable, to say the least.

Instead of a synthesis, a more modest approach seems adequate, which is in accordance with Boulding's suggestion that neoclassical price theory is a good first approximation of relative scarcities. This formulation suggests that after the first approximation further complementary institutional analysis would provide a deeper insight into how markets produce relative prices, what kind of scarcities prices represent and what role values and norms play in the formation of prices.

In other words: how actors constitute prices in interaction with other actors and in interaction with technological and institutional structures. In this approach of combining NCE and IE, it is suggested that neoclassical theory should not be rejected, but should be complemented, because NCE deals only with (a very small) part of the story.

So in line with Groenewegen and Vromen (1996), it seems that a pluralistic approach towards NCE and IE is possible: different theories belonging to different paradigms can be complementary in the sense that the theories are relevant under different sets of conditions (different assumptions about market structures, about information, degrees of complexity, etc.) and in the sense that different theories are relevant for different research questions, for different 'issues'. In that case, the theories of different paradigms are not synthesized, but are combined under the umbrella of one theoretical framework. A LAT (Living Apart Together) relation instead of a marriage.

Notes

1 I describe the characteristics of the ideal type of positivism, admitting that all kinds of nuances exist under the names of post- or neo-positivism (Friedrichs and Kratochwil 2009).

2 This is known as 'ontological realism' (Friedrichs and Kratochwil 2009).

3 Deduction and induction can be formulated in logical terms like Peirce did in his example of the beans (in Houser and Kloesel 1992). It can also be formulated in terms that apply to the testing in social sciences. Then deduction is of a hypothetical-deductive kind, in which a logically derived hypothesis will be tested in an empirical setting and induction refers then to the collection of empirical case material from which a classification or typology can be constructed.

4 For our purposes, it suffices to distinguish between only two alternatives: positivism and interpretivism. Other authors make other distinctions, for example, between positivism, subjectivism and relationism (Howard 2010).

5 Gunnar Myrdal is an example of a Nobel laureate who clearly belongs to the OIE.

6 The positioning of agency theory only at level 4 is confusing: elsewhere (Groenewegen *et al.* 2010), I explained that the positive AT can be best located at level 3 and the normative one at level 4.

7 Culminating in the Arrow and Debreu (1954) 'full set of contingent claim contracts'.

8 See Groenewegen *et al.* (2010) for details.

9 Douglass North is another prominent member of the NIE. Elsewhere we have discussed that the work of North is closer to OIE then NIE (Groenewegen *et al.* 1995, 2010).

10 Much confusion exists about the role of habits and how these can be in harmony with volition. Costa and Caldas (2009) discuss clearly how in the work of especially John Dewey habits are conceived and how habits differ from the typical mechanistic stimulus–response interpretation.

11 Interesting is the question of what room is left for volition, for rational purposeful action. In this respect, the distinction between habits and routines becomes important. Dewey (1922 [1930], p. 28) explains that habits also can be inquired and tested by man, i.e. man can take distance from the habits that cause action and reflect on the consequences of the action based on specific habits. When such reflections raise doubts about the rightfulness (is the 'is' well analyzed?), or desirability of the belief (does the habit contribute to the realization of the 'ought'?), then man is in the position to inquire what is wrong about the habits causing the undesirable action and to intervene through the change of institutions (the rules of the game) to change the habit

of thought. In the case of routines man acts mechanically, without thought about the consequences and without valuation of the consequences of the routinized actions in the light of the societal goals. The real opposition is not between reason and habits, but between reasonable habits and unintelligently routinized habit.

12 Original institutional economics (OIE) was, after the emergence of NIE, also often called old institutional economics. We prefer the terminology of 'original'. Also the terminology of neo-institutionalism is used for the postwar institutionalists like John K. Galbraith, Gunnar Myrdal and others that followed the approach of the Veblen and Commons (see Gruchy 1972). In this contribution, I call the pre- and postwar institutionalists both OIE.

13 This is the core of philosophical pragmatism. In the words of Nooteboom (2012, p. 2): pragmatism 'holds that cognition, in a wide sense that includes normative judgments and goals, occurs on the basis of mental dispositions and categories that are developed in interaction with the physical and especially the social environment'. The crux of the argument is that action, practice, constitutes the actor: 'Intelligence is internalised practice' (Nooteboom 2012, p. 2).

14 Compare the 'integrative structures' of Boulding, see Kesting (2010).

15 A position also present in Ostrom (2005).

References

Arrow, Kenneth J. and G. Debreu (1954) Existence of an equilibrium for a competitive economy. *Econometrica*, 22, pp. 265–290.

Berle, Adolf A. and Gardiner C. Means (1932) *The Modern Corporation and Private Property*. New York: Commerce Clearing House.

Boulding, Kenneth E. ([1956] 1997) *The Image: Knowledge in Life and Society*. Ann Arbor: University of Michigan Press.

Boulding, Kenneth E. (1977) Prices and other institutions. *Journal of Economic Issues*, XI (4), pp. 809–821.

Bromley, Daniel W. (2006) *Sufficient Reason. Volitional Pragmatism and the Meaning of Economic Institutions*. Princeton and Oxford: Princeton University Press.

Bush, Paul D. (1999) Pragmatism. In Phillip Anthony O'Hara (ed.), *Encyclopedia of Political Economy, vol. 2: L–Z*, London: Routledge, pp. 894–897.

Bush, Paul D. (2009) The neoinstitutionalist theory of value. *Journal of Economic Issues*, 43 (2), pp. 293–306.

Caldari, Katia (2010) Institutional economics and the concept of equilibrium. *Journal of Post-Keynesian Economics*, 32 (4), pp. 601–623.

Costa Ana N. and Jose Castro Caldas (2009) Claiming choice for institutional economics. Paper presented at the EAEPE Annual Conference, Amsterdam.

Dewey, John ([1922] 1930) *Human Nature and Conduct: An Introduction to Social Psychology*. The Modern Library: New York.

Dewey, John ([1925] 1984) The development of American pragmatism. In Jo Ann Boydston (ed.), *John Dewey: The Later Works, 1925-1953, vol. 2: 1925–1927*, Carbondale, IL: Southern Illinois University Press, pp. 3–21.

Dolfsma, Wilfred (1997) The social construction of value: Value theories and John Locke's framework of qualities. *The European Journal of History of Economic Thought*, 4 (3), pp. 400–416.

Friedrichs, Jorg and Friedrich Kratochwil (2009) On acting and knowing: How pragmatism can advance international relations research and methodology. *International Organization*, 63 (Fall), pp. 701–731.

Groenewegen, J. and J. Vromen (1996) TCE and beyond: A case for theoretical pluralism. In J. Groenewegen (ed.), *TCE and Beyond*. Dordrecht/Boston: Kluwer Academic Publishers, pp. 365–380.

Groenewegen, J. and J. Vromen (1997) Theory of the firm revisited new and neo-institutional perspectives. In Lars Magnusson and Jan Ottoson (eds.), *Economics and Path Dependency*. Aldershot: Edward Elgar, pp. 33–57.

Groenewegen, J., F. Kerstholt and A. Nagelkerke (1995) On integrating new and old institutionalism: Douglass North building bridges. *Journal of Economic Issues*, XXIX (2), pp. 467–475.

Groenewegen, J., A. van Spithoven and A. van der Berg (2010) *Institutional Economics; an Introduction*. New York: Palgrave Macmillan.

Gruchy, A.G. (1972) *Contemporary Economic Thought: The Contribution of Neo Institutional Economics*. Clifton, NJ: Augustus M. Kelley.

Hodgson, G.M. (1988) *Economics and Institutions: A Manifesto for Modern Institutional Economics*. Philadelphia: University of Pennsylvania Press.

Hodgson, G.M. (2004) Reclaiming habit for institutional economics. *Journal of Economic Psychology*, 25, pp. 651–660.

Houser, N. and C. Kloesel (eds.) (1992) *The Essential Peirce*. Bloomington: Indiana University Press.

Howard, Peter (2010) Triangulating debates within the field: Teaching international relations research methodology. *International Studies Perspectives*, 11, pp. 393–408.

Kesting, Stefan (2010) Boulding's welfare approach of communicative deliberation. *Ecological Economics*, 69, pp. 973–977.

Lakatos, I. (1978) *The Methodology of Scientific Research Programmes: Philosophical Papers Volume 1*. Cambridge: Cambridge University Press.

Latsis, S.J. (1976) A research programme in economics. In J. Latsis (ed.), *Method and Appraisal in Economics*. Cambridge: Cambridge University Press, pp. 1–41.

Myrdal, Gunnar (1944) *An American Dilemma*. Oxford: Harper.

Nooteboom, B. (2012) A pragmatist theory of innovation. In H. Melkas and V. Harmaakorpi (eds.), *Practice-Based Innovation: Insights, Applications and Policy Implications*, Heidelberg: Springer, pp. 17–27.

Ostrom, Elinor (2005) *Understanding Institutional Diversity*. Princeton and Oxford: Princeton University Press.

Rutherford, M. (1994) *The Old and New Institutionalism*. Cambridge: Cambridge University Press.

Tool, Marc R. (1986) *Essays in Social Value Theory*. Armonk, NY: M.E. Sharpe.

Tool, Marc R. (1993) Pricing and valuation. *Journal of Economic Issues*, VXXVII (2), pp. 325–349.

Tool, Marc R. (1999) Instrumental value theory. In Philip Anthony O'Hara (ed.), *Encyclopedia of Political Economy*, vol. 1. London and New York: Routledge, pp. 538–541.

Wilber, Charles K. and Robert S. Harrison (1978) The methodological basis of institutional economics: Pattern model, storytelling, and holism. *Journal of Economic Issues*, XII (1), pp. 61–89.

Williamson, O.E. (1975) *Markets and Hierarchies: Analysis and Antitrust Implications*. New York: Free Press.

Williamson, O.E. (1998) Transaction cost economics: How it works; where it is headed. *De Economist*, Vol. 146, 1, pp. 23–58.

Williamson, O.E. (2000) The new institutional economics: Taking stock, looking ahead. *Journal of Economic Literature*, XXXVIII (September), pp. 595–613.

Poem

The Farmer is obsessed with Price:
So Parity's his pet device;
But now, alas, we find in Parity
The nation's most expensive charity.
Those generous contributions which
Should help the Poor, support the Rich,
Because, when Prices we uphold,
We pay the more, the more is sold.

Principles of Economic Policy,
1958, p. 313

Part IX

Spaceship earth (ecological economics)

9 Key text: The economics of the coming spaceship earth[1]

Kenneth E. Boulding

We are now in the middle of a long process of transition in the nature of the image which man has of himself and his environment. Primitive men, and to a large extent also men of the early civilizations, imagined themselves to be living on a virtually illimitable plane. There was almost always somewhere beyond the known limits of human habitation, and over a very large part of the time that man has been on earth, there has been something like a frontier. That is, there was always some place else to go when things got too difficult, either by reason of the deterioration of the natural environment or a deterioration of the social structure in places where people happened to live. The image of the frontier is probably one of the oldest images of mankind, and it is not surprising that we find it hard to get rid of.

Gradually, however, man has been accustoming himself to the notion of the spherical earth and a closed sphere of human activity. A few unusual spirits among the ancient Greeks perceived that the earth was a sphere. It was only with the circumnavigations and the geographical explorations of the fifteenth and sixteenth centuries, however, that the fact that the earth was a sphere became at all widely known and accepted. Even in the nineteenth century, the commonest map was Mercator's projection, which visualizes the earth as an illimitable cylinder, essentially a plane wrapped around the globe, and it was not until the Second World War and the development of the air age that the global nature of the planet really entered the popular imagination. Even now we are very far from having made the moral, political, and psychological adjustments which are implied in this transition from the illimitable plane to the closed sphere.

Economists in particular, for the most part, have failed to come to grips with the ultimate consequences of the transition from the open to the closed earth. One hesitates to use the terms "open" and "closed" in this connection, as they have been used with so many different shades of meaning. Nevertheless, it is hard to find equivalents. The open system, indeed, has some similarities to the open system of von Bertalanffy (1952), in that it implies that some kind of structure is maintained in the midst of a throughput from inputs to outputs. In a closed system, the outputs of all parts of the system are linked to the inputs of other parts. There are no inputs from outside and no outputs to the outside; indeed, there is no outside at all. Closed systems, in fact, are very rare in human experience, in fact almost by definition unknowable, for if there are genuinely closed systems around us, we have no way of getting information into them or out of them; and hence if they are really closed, we would be quite unaware of their existence. We can only find out about a closed system if we participate in it. Some isolated primitive societies may have approximated to this, but even these had to take inputs from the environment and give outputs to it. All living organisms, including man himself, are open systems. They have to receive inputs in the shape of air, food, water, and give off outputs in the form of effluvia and excrement. Deprivation of input of air, even for a few minutes, is fatal. Deprivation of the ability to obtain any input or to dispose of any output is fatal in a relatively short time. All human societies have likewise been open systems. They receive inputs from the earth, the atmosphere, and the waters, and they give outputs into these reservoirs; they also produce inputs internally in the shape of babies and outputs in the shape of corpses. Given a capacity to draw upon inputs and to get rid of outputs, an open system of this kind can persist indefinitely.

There are some systems—such as the biological phenotype, for instance, the human body—which cannot maintain themselves indefinitely by inputs and outputs because of the phenomenon of aging. This process is very little understood. It occurs, evidently, because there are some outputs which cannot be replaced by any known input. There is not the same necessity for aging in organizations and in societies, although an analogous phenomenon may take place. The structure and composition of an organization or society, however, can be maintained by inputs of fresh personnel from birth and education as the existing personnel ages and eventually dies. Here we have an interesting example of a system which seems to maintain itself by the self-generation of inputs, and in this sense is moving toward closure. The input of people (that is, babies) is also an output of people (that is, parents).

Systems may be open or closed in respect to a number of classes of inputs and outputs. Three important classes are matter, energy, and information. The present world economy is open in regard to all three. We can think of the world economy or "econosphere" as a subset of the "world set," which is the set of all objects of possible discourse in the world. We than think of the state of the econosphere at any one moment as being the total capital stock, that is, the set of all objects, people, organizations, and so on, which are interesting from the point of view of the system of exchange. This total stock of capital is clearly an open system in the sense that it has inputs and outputs, inputs being production which adds to the capital stock, outputs being consumption which subtracts from it. From a material point of view, we see objects passing from the noneconomic into the economic set in the process of production, and we similarly see products passing out of the economic set as their value becomes zero. Thus we see the econosphere as a material process involving the discovery and mining of fossil fuels, ores, etc., and at the other end a process by which the effluents of the system are passed out into noneconomic reservoirs—for instance, the atmosphere and the oceans—which are not appropriated and do not enter into the exchange system.

From the point of view of the energy system, the econosphere involves inputs of available energy in the form, say, of water power, fossil fuels, or sunlight, which are necessary in order to create the material throughput and to move matter from the noneconomic set into the economic set or even out of it again; and energy itself is given off by the system in a less available form, mostly in the form of heat. These inputs of available energy must come either from the sun (the energy supplied by other stars being assumed to be negligible) or it may come from the earth itself, either through its internal heat or through its energy of rotation or other motions, which generate, for instance, the energy of the tides. Agriculture, a few solar machines, and water power use the current available energy income. In advanced societies this is supplemented very extensively by the use of fossil fuels, which represent, as it were, a capital stock of stored-up sunshine. Because of this capital stock of energy, we have been able to maintain an energy input into the system, particularly over the last two centuries, much larger than we would have been able to do with existing techniques if we had had to rely on the current input of available energy from the sun or the earth itself. This supplementary input, however, is by its very nature exhaustible.

The inputs and outputs of information are more subtle and harder to trace, but also represent an open system, related to, but not wholly dependent on, the transformation of matter and energy. By far the larger amount of information and knowledge is self-generated by the human society, though a certain amount of information comes into the sociosphere in the form of light from the universe outside. The information that comes from the universe has certainly affected man's image of himself and of his environment, as we can easily visualize if we suppose that we lived on a planet with a total cloud-cover that kept out all information from the exterior universe. It is only in very recent times, of course, that the information coming in from the universe has been captured and coded in the form of a complex image of what the universe is like outside the earth; but even in primitive times, man's perception of the heavenly bodies has always profoundly affected his image of earth and of himself. It is the information generated within the planet, however, and particularly that generated by man himself, which forms by far the larger part of the information system. We can think of the stock of knowledge, or as Teilhard de Chardin called it, the "noosphere," and consider this as an open system, losing knowledge through aging and death and gaining it through birth and education and the ordinary experience of life.

From the human point of view, knowledge, or information, is by far the most important of the three systems. Matter only acquires significance and only enters the sociosphere or the econosphere insofar as it becomes an object of human knowledge. We can think of capital, indeed, as frozen knowledge or knowledge imposed on the material world in the form of improbable arrangements. A machine, for instance, originates in the mind of man, and both its construction and its use involve information processes imposed on the material world by man himself. The cumulation of knowledge, that is, the excess of its production over its consumption, is the key to human development of all kinds, especially to economic development. We can see this preeminence of knowledge very clearly in the experiences of countries where the material capital has been destroyed by a war, as in Japan and Germany. The knowledge of the people was not destroyed, and it did not take long, therefore, certainly not more than ten years, for most of the material capital to be reestablished again. In a country such as Indonesia, however, where the knowledge did not exist, the material capital did not come into being either. By "knowledge" here I mean, of course, the whole cognitive structure, which includes valuations and motivations as well as images of the factual world.

The concept of entropy, used in a somewhat loose sense, can be applied to all three of these open systems. In material systems, we can distinguish between entropic processes, which take concentrated materials and diffuse them through the oceans or over the earth's surface or into the atmosphere, and antientropic processes, which take diffuse materials and concentrate them. Material entropy can be taken as a measure of the uniformity of the distribution of elements and, more uncertainly, compounds and other structures on the earth's surface. There is, fortunately, no law of increasing material entropy, as there is in the corresponding case of energy, as it is quite possible to concentrate diffused materials if energy inputs are allowed. Thus the processes for fixation of nitrogen from the air, processes for the extraction of magnesium or other elements from the sea, and processes for the desalinization of sea water are antientropic in the material sense, though the reduction of material entropy has to be paid for by inputs of energy and also inputs of information, or at least a stock of information in the system. In regard to matter, therefore, a closed system is conceivable, that is, a system in which there is neither increase nor decrease in material entropy. In such a system all outputs from consumption would constantly be recycled to become inputs for production, as, for instance, nitrogen in the nitrogen cycle of the natural ecosystem.

In the energy system there is, unfortunately, no escape from the grim second law of thermodynamics; and if there were no energy inputs into the earth, any evolutionary or developmental process would be impossible. The large energy inputs which we have obtained from fossil fuels are strictly temporary. Even the most optimistic predictions expect the easily available supply of fossil fuels to be exhausted in a mere matter of centuries at present rates of use. If the rest of the world were to rise to American standards of power consumption, and still more if world population continues to increase, the exhaustion of fossil fuels would be even more rapid. The development of nuclear energy has improved this picture, but not fundamentally altered it, at least in present technologies, for fissionable material is still relatively scarce. If we should achieve the economic use of energy through fusion, of course, a much larger source of energy materials would be available, which would expand the time horizons of supplementary energy input into an open social system by perhaps tens to hundreds of thousands of years. Failing this, however, the time is not very far distant, historically speaking, when man will once more have to retreat to his current energy input from the sun, even though with increased knowledge this could be used much more effectively than in the past. Up to now, certainly, we have not got very far with the technology of using current solar energy, but the possibility of substantial improvements in the future is certainly high. It may be, indeed, that the biological revolution which is just beginning will produce a solution to this problem, as we develop artificial organisms which are capable of much more efficient transformation of solar energy into easily available forms than any that we now have. As Richard Meier (1956) has suggested, we may run our machines in the future with methane-producing algae.

The question of whether there is anything corresponding to entropy in the information system is a puzzling one, though of great interest. There are certainly many examples of social systems and cultures which have lost knowledge, especially in transition from one generation to the next, and in which the culture has therefore degenerated. One only has to look at the folk culture of Appalachian migrants to American cities to see a culture which started out as a fairly rich European folk culture in Elizabethan times and which seems to have lost skills, adaptability, folk tales, songs, and almost everything that goes up to make richness and complexity in a culture, in the course of about ten generations. The American Indians on reservations provide another example of such degradation of the information and knowledge system. On the other hand, over a great part of human history, the growth of knowledge in the earth as a whole seems to have been almost continuous, even though there have been times of relatively slow growth and times of rapid growth. As it is knowledge of certain kinds that produces the growth of knowledge in general, we have here a very subtle and complicated system, and it is hard to put one's finger on the particular elements in a culture which make knowledge grow more or less rapidly, or even which make it decline. One of the great puzzles in this connection, for instance, is why the takeoff into science, which represents an "acceleration," or an increase in the rate of growth of knowledge in European society in the sixteenth century, did not take place in China, which at that time (about 1600) was unquestionably ahead of Europe, and one would think even more ready for the breakthrough. This is perhaps the most crucial question in the theory of social development, yet we must confess that it is very little understood. Perhaps the most significant factor in this connection is the existence of "slack" in the culture, which permits a divergence from established patterns and activity which is not merely devoted to reproducing the existing society but is devoted to changing it. China was perhaps too well organized and had too little slack in its society to produce the kind of acceleration which we find in the somewhat poorer and less well-organized but more diverse societies of Europe.

The closed earth of the future requires economic principles which are somewhat different from those of the open earth of the past. For the sake of picturesqueness, I am tempted to call the open economy the "cowboy economy," the cowboy being symbolic of the illimitable plains and also associated with reckless, exploitative, romantic, and violent behavior, which is characteristic of open societies. The closed economy of the future might similarly be called the "spaceman" economy, in which the earth has become a single spaceship, without unlimited reservoirs of anything, either for extraction or for pollution, and in which, therefore, man must find his place in a cyclical ecological system which is capable of continuous reproduction of material form even though it cannot escape having inputs of energy. The difference between the two types of economy becomes most apparent in the attitude towards consumption. In the cowboy economy, consumption is regarded as a good thing and production likewise; and the success of the economy is measured by the amount of the throughput from the "factors of production," a part of which, at any rate, is extracted from the reservoirs of raw materials and noneconomic objects, and another part of which is output into the reservoirs of pollution. If there are infinite reservoirs from which materials can be obtained and into which effluvia can be deposited, then the throughput is at least a plausible measure of the success of the economy. The gross national product is a rough measure of this total throughput. It should be possible, however, to distinguish that part of the GNP which is derived from exhaustible and that which is derived from reproducible resources, as well as that part of consumption which represents effluvia and that which represents input into the productive system again. Nobody, as far as I know, has ever attempted to break down the GNP in this way, although it would be an interesting and extremely important exercise, which is unfortunately beyond the scope of this paper.

By contrast, in the spaceman economy, throughput is by no means a desideratum, and is indeed to be regarded as something to be minimized rather than maximized. The essential measure of the success of the economy is not production and consumption at all, but the nature, extent, quality, and complexity of the total capital stock, including in this the state of the human bodies and minds included in the system. In the spaceman economy, what we are primarily concerned with is stock maintenance, and any technological change which results in the maintenance of a given total stock with a lessened throughout (that is, less production and consumption) is clearly a gain. This idea that both production and consumption are bad things rather than good things is very strange to economists, who have been obsessed with the income-flow concepts to the exclusion, almost, of capital-stock concepts.

There are actually some very tricky and unsolved problems involved in the questions as to whether human welfare or well-being is to be regarded as a stock or a flow. Something of both these elements seems actually to be involved in it, and as far as I know there have been practically no studies directed towards identifying these two dimensions of human satisfaction. Is it, for instance, eating that is a good thing, or is it being well fed? Does economic welfare involve having nice clothes, fine houses, good equipment, and so on, or is it to be measured by the depreciation and the wearing out of these things? I am inclined myself to regard the stock concept as most fundamental, that is, to think of being well fed as more important than eating, and to think even of so-called services as essentially involving the restoration of a depleting psychic capital. Thus I have argued that we go to a concert in order to restore a psychic condition which might be called "just having gone to a concert," which, once established, tends to depreciate. When it depreciates beyond a certain point, we go to another concert in order to restore it. If it depreciates rapidly, we go to a lot of concerts; if it depreciates slowly, we go to a few. On this view, similarly, we eat primarily to restore bodily homeostasis, that is, to maintain a condition of being well fed, and so on. On this view, there is nothing desirable in consumption at all. The less consumption we can maintain a given state with, the better off we are. If we had clothes that did not wear out, houses that did not depreciate, and even if we could maintain our bodily condition without eating, we would clearly be much better off.

It is this last consideration, perhaps, which makes one pause. Would we, for instance, really want an operation that would enable us to restore all our bodily tissues by intravenous feeding while we slept? Is there not, that is to say, a certain virtue in throughput itself, in activity itself, in production and consumption itself, in raising food and in eating it? It would certainly be rash to exclude this possibility. Further interesting problems are raised by the demand for variety. We certainly do not want a constant state to be maintained; we want fluctuations in the state. Otherwise there would be no demand for variety in food, for variety in scene, as in travel, for variety in social contact, and so on. The demand for variety can, of course, be costly, and sometimes it seems to be too costly to be tolerated or at least legitimated, as in the case of marital partners, where the maintenance of a homeostatic state in the family is usually regarded as much more desirable than the variety and excessive throughput of the libertine. There are problems here which the economics profession has neglected with astonishing singlemindedness. My own attempts to call attention to some of them, for instance, in two articles (1945, 1949–1950), as far as I can judge, produced no response whatever; and economists continue to think and act as if production, consumption, throughput, and the GNP were the sufficient and adequate measure of economic success.

It may be said, of course, why worry about all this when the spaceman economy is still a good way off (at least beyond the lifetimes of any now living), so let us eat, drink, spend, extract and pollute, and be as merry as we can, and let posterity worry about the spaceship earth. It is always a little hard to find a convincing answer to the man who says, "What has posterity ever done for me?" and the conservationist has always had to fall back on rather vague ethical principles postulating identity of the individual with some human community or society which extends not only back into the past but forward into the future. Unless the individual identifies with some community of this kind, conservation is obviously "irrational." Why should we not maximize the welfare of this generation at the cost of posterity? "Après nous, le déluge" has been the motto of not insignificant numbers of human societies. The only answer to this, as far as I can see, is to point out that the welfare of the individual depends on the extent to which he can identify himself with others, and that the most satisfactory individual identity is that which identifies not only with a community in space but also with a community extending over time from the past into the future. If this kind of identity is recognized as desirable, then posterity has a voice, even if it does not have a vote; and in a sense, if its voice can influence votes, it has votes too. This whole problem is linked up with the much larger one of the determinants of the morale, legitimacy, and "nerve" of a society, and there is a great deal of historical evidence to suggest that a society which loses its identity with posterity and which loses its positive image in the future loses also its capacity to deal with present problems, and soon falls apart (Polak 1961).

Even if we concede that posterity is relevant to our present problems, we still face the question of time-discounting and the closely related question of uncertainty-discounting. It is a well-known phenomenon that individuals discount the future, even in their own lives. The very existence of a positive rate of interest may be taken as at least strong supporting evidence of this hypothesis. If we discount our own future, it is certainly not unreasonable to discount posterity's future even more, even if we do give posterity a vote. If we discount this at five percent per annum, posterity's vote or dollar halves every fourteen years as we look into the future, and after even a mere hundred years it is pretty small—only about one-and-a-half cents on the dollar. If we add another five percent for uncertainty, even the vote of our grandchildren reduces almost to insignificance. We can argue, of course, that the ethical thing to do is not to discount the future at all, that time-discounting is mainly the result of myopia and perspective, and hence is an illusion which the moral man should not tolerate. It is a very popular illusion, however, and one that must certainly be taken into consideration in the formulation of policies. It explains, perhaps, why conservationist policies almost have to be sold under some other excuse which seems more urgent, and why, indeed, necessities which are visualized as urgent, such as defense, always seem to hold priority over those which involve the future.

All these considerations add some credence to the point of view which says that we should not worry about the spaceman economy at all, and that we should just go on increasing the GNP and indeed the gross world product, or GWP, in the expectation that the problems of the future can be left to the future, that when scarcities arise, whether of raw materials or of pollutable reservoirs, the needs of the then present will determine the solutions of the then present, and there is no use giving ourselves ulcers by worrying about problems that we really do not have to solve. There is even high ethical authority for this point of view in the New Testament, which advocates that we should take no thought for tomorrow and let the dead bury their dead. There has always been something rather refreshing in the view that we should live like the birds, and perhaps posterity is for the birds in more senses than one; so perhaps we should all call it a day and go out and pollute something cheerfully. As an old taker of thought for the morrow, however, I cannot quite accept this solution; and I would argue, furthermore, that tomorrow is not only very close, but in many respects it is already here. The shadow of the future spaceship, indeed, is already falling over our spendthrift merriment. Oddly enough, it seems to be in pollution rather than in exhaustion that the problem is first becoming salient. Los Angeles has run out of air, Lake Erie has become a cesspool, the oceans are getting full of lead and DDT, and the atmosphere may become man's major problem in another generation, at the rate at which we are filling it up with gunk. It is, of course, true that at least on a microscale, things have been worse at times in the past. The cities of today, with all their foul air and polluted waterways, are probably not as bad as the filthy cities of the pretechnical age. Nevertheless, that fouling of the nest which has been typical of man's activity in the past on a local scale now seems to be extending to the whole world society; and one certainly cannot view with equanimity the present rate of pollution of any of the natural reservoirs, whether the atmosphere, the lakes, or even the oceans.

I would argue strongly also that our obsession with production and consumption to the exclusion of the "state" aspects of human welfare distorts the process of technological change in a most undesirable way. We are all familiar, of course, with the wastes involved in planned obsolescence, in competitive advertising, and in poor quality of consumer goods. These problems may not be so important as the "view with alarm" school indicates, and indeed the evidence at many points is conflicting. New materials especially seem to edge towards the side of improved durability, such as, for instance, neolite soles for footwear, nylon socks, wash and wear shirts, and so on. The case of household equipment and automobiles is a little less clear. Housing and building construction generally almost certainly has declined in durability since the Middle Ages, but this decline also reflects a change in tastes towards flexibility and fashion and a need for novelty, so that it is not easy to assess. What is clear is that no serious attempt has been made to assess the impact over the whole of economic life of changes in durability, that is, in the ratio of capital in the widest possible sense to income. I suspect that we have underestimated, even in our spendthrift society, the gains from increased durability, and that this might very well be one of the places where the price system needs correction through government-sponsored research and development. The problems which the spaceship earth is going to present, therefore, are not all in the future by any means, and a strong case can be made for paying much more attention to them in the present than we now do.

It may be complained that the considerations I have been putting forth relate only to the very long run, and they do not much concern our immediate problems. There may be some justice in this criticism, and my main excuse is that other writers have dealt adequately with the more immediate problems of deterioration in the quality of the environment. It is true, for instance, that many of the immediate problems of pollution of the atmosphere or of bodies of water arise because of the failure of the price system, and many of them could be solved by corrective taxation. If people had to pay the losses due to the nuisances which they create, a good deal more resources would go into the prevention of nuisances. These arguments involving external economies and diseconomies are familiar to economists and there is no need to recapitulate them. The law of torts is quite inadequate to provide for the correction of the price system which is required, simply because where damages are widespread and their incidence on any particular person is small, the ordinary remedies of the civil law are quite inadequate and inappropriate. There needs, therefore, to be special legislation to cover these cases, and though such legislation seems hard to get in practice, mainly because of the widespread and small personal incidence of the injuries, the technical problems involved are not insuperable. If we were to adopt in principle a law for tax penalties for social damages, with an apparatus for making assessments under it, a very large proportion of current pollution and deterioration of the environment would be prevented. There are tricky problems of equity involved, particularly where old established nuisances create a kind of "right by purchase" to perpetuate themselves, but these are problems again which a few rather arbitrary decisions can bring to some kind of solution.

The problems which I have been raising in this paper are of a larger scale and perhaps much harder to solve than the more practical and immediate problems of the above paragraph. Our success in dealing with the larger problems, however, is not unrelated to the development of skill in the solution of the more immediate and perhaps less difficult problems. One can hope, therefore, that as a succession of mounting crises, especially in pollution, arouse public opinion and mobilize support for the solution of the immediate problems, a learning process will be set in motion which will eventually lead to an appreciation of and perhaps solutions for the larger ones. My neglect of the immediate problems, therefore, is in no way intended to deny their importance, for unless we make at least a beginning on a process for solving the immediate problems we will not have much chance of solving the larger ones. On the other hand, it may also be true that a long-run vision, as it were, of the deep crisis which faces mankind may predispose people to taking more interest in the immediate problems and to devoting more effort for their solution. This may sound like a rather modest optimism, but perhaps a modest optimism is better than no optimism at all.

Note

1 This article was previously published in Herman E. Daly and Kenneth N. Townsend (eds.), *Valuing the Earth – Economics, Ecology, Ethics*, Cambridge and London: The MIT Press, 1993, pp. 297–309. Originally from *Environmental Quality in a Growing Economy*, published for Resources for the Future, Inc., by The Johns Hopkins University Press, 1966. Copyright 1966 by Resources for the Future. Reprinted by permission of the author and the publisher.

References

Boulding, Kenneth E., "The Consumption Concept in Economic Theory," *American Economic Review*, 35, no. 2, May 1945, 1–14.

Boulding, Kenneth E., "Income or Welfare?," *Review of Economic Studies*, 17, 1949–1950, 77–86.

Meier, Richard L., *Science and Economic Development*, New York: Wiley, 1956.

Polak, Fred L. *The Image of the Future*, vols. I and II, translated by Elise Boulding, New York: Sythoff, Leyden and Oceana, 1961.

von Bertalanffy, Ludwig, *Problems of Life*, New York: Wiley, 1952.

9a Commentary article: Spaceship earth revisited[1]

Kenneth E. Boulding

I have no claims to priority in the use of the metaphor spaceship earth, though I think I did think it up independently, and it was a metaphor so appropriate to its time that it would have been very surprising if somebody had not thought it up. It is still a very good metaphor, but as with all metaphors, one has to be careful with it. When a metaphor parades as a model, it can sometimes be very dangerous and misleading, particularly as metaphors are so much more convincing than models and are much more apt to change people's images of the world. The spaceship metaphor stresses the earth's smallness, crowdedness, and limited resources; the need for avoiding destructive conflict; and the necessity for a sense of world community with a very heterogeneous crew. On these grounds the metaphor is certainly as good today as it was in the 1960s. One of the paradoxes, indeed, is that we seem to be more theoretically aware of the spaceship earth model than we were in the 1960s, with the Club of Rome reports, the energy crisis, and the United Nations population conference. But this theoretical awareness does not seem to have penetrated down to the level of political consciousness in the life and awareness of the ordinary human being. It seems to be very hard to organize a long-run crisis. Certainly the ordinary American today has very little sense of crisis. Every time he turns a switch, the lights go on; every time he pulls up to a gas station, there is gas for his car. The problems of the 1970s—inflation, the arms race, rising crime rates, battered children, tax revolts, and so on—are far more political and sociological than they are related to the long-run problems of a society nonsustainable in terms of energy, materials, and pollution.

Furthermore, something has happened in the 1970s that may have an enormous potential significance for the human race or may have none at all: the development of reasonably serious proposals for space colonies. This may sound like science fiction, and there may well be some unknown factor that would make them impossible. The idea is not, however, absurd, simply because of the low energy requirements of moving materials about in empty space. On earth we need energy mainly to overcome gravity and friction.

Solar energy, the great white hope of the virtuous, does not look very much better today than it did in the 1960s, at least on the surface of the earth. It is fine for hot-water heating, moderately fine for space heating—but this is only 20 percent of our energy use. It still looks very expensive for electricity in spite of the tremendous advance in photovoltaic cells, and we are certainly no further along than we were in regard to solar-developed fuel. The essential unpredictability of knowledge and technology, of course, means that in another ten years the whole situation may look very different. The probability of our failing to solve the problem of cheap solar energy in usable forms is at least high enough to be worrying. In outer space, on the other hand, the sun never sets. Solar energy is much more available. The possibility of capturing it to transport materials from the moons and asteroids is, at least on paper, not preposterous.

Going into space, however, would be a transition for the evolutionary process as great as that involved in going from sea to land. One of the group of Princeton scientists who have been spearheading the interest in space colonies, in a paper at the American Association for the Advancement of Science in 1978, proposed, perhaps a little tongue-in-cheek, that the carrying capacity of the solar system for human beings might be one sextillion—about a billion times the present population of the earth. This, one presumes, would involve filling a wide band on either side of the orbit of the earth with space colonies using solar energy and mining the asteroids for materials. This is outrageous, but it may be no more outrageous than the whole process of evolution. Perhaps the greatest case for space colonies is that they would reintroduce isolation and variety into the evolutionary process. The most worrying thing about the earth is that there seems to be no way of preventing it from becoming one world. If there is only one world, then if anything goes wrong, everything goes wrong. And by the generalized Murphy's Law, every system has some positive probability, however low, of irretrievable catastrophe. Evolution is able to persist on the earth because of the isolation and variety of its ecosystems. Thus a total catastrophe on Krakatoa was recoverable because it did not affect the more distant ecosystems, which then recolonized the destroyed island. Similarly, the total collapse of the Mayan Empire, an early example indeed of a Club of Rome report, affected Charlemagne or the Emperor of China not at all. They knew nothing of it.

Ultimately, of course, we must face the spaceship earth on earth. Uncertainty, however, is the principal property of the future, and time horizons themselves have an irreducible uncertainty about them. Perhaps the greatest weakness of the metaphor is that the spaceship presumably has a clear destination and a mission to accomplish. It is essentially a planned economy. The evolutionary process, however, is not a significant planned economy any more than an ecosystem. The biological ecosystem is not even a community, in spite of the fact that biologists sometimes call it that, it is the wildest example of free private enterprise and does not even have a mayor. I have argued that evolution is now moving out of the *biogenetic*, that is, DNA, genes and all that, into the *noogenetic*, which is the transmission of learned structures from one generation to the next by a teaching and learning process. This is a transition that begins with the human race. It may be as profound a transition as the development of DNA itself. I get the uneasy feeling sometimes that the human race is the link between the biogenetic and the noogenetic, and we may eventually produce a self-reproducing solid-state intelligence that would be our evolutionary successor. I won't like it, having great race prejudice in favor of the human race, but we have to admit that all species are endangered and that every species is a link, even biologically, between the biogenetic know-how of the gene that preceded it and those that will follow it. It would be presumptuous of us to think that the human race is any more than a link in the great evolutionary process of the universe that moves majestically from the unknown Alpha to the even more unknown Omega.

Note

1 This article was previously published in Herman E. Daly and Kenneth N. Townsend (eds.), *Valuing the Earth – Economics, Ecology, Ethics*, Cambridge and London: The MIT Press, 1993, pp. 311–313. Written especially for the preceding edition of this book.

9b Comment: The economics of Boulding's spaceship earth

Clive L. Spash

Introduction

In the essay entitled *The Economics of the Coming Spaceship Earth*, we are presented by Boulding (1966) with an early overview and summary of the modern environmental crisis facing humanity and its roots in the total neglect of physical limits by economists. Boulding's distinctive contribution was to introduce aspects of entropy and highlight materials throughput from and to the environment, leading to a critique of the roles of growth and consumption as means of creating human well-being. He also questioned how future generations could be given voice. At the time he was amongst a small number of unassociated people making connections between social and economic systems and environmental degradation.

Almost 50 years later we are no longer in the luxurious position of being able to reflect in an abstract way about such issues, as if they only affected some distant future generation to come. The consequences of hitting the biophysical constraints are an all-too-present reality, leading to armed struggle for oil and increasing concerns over securing the supply of other resources seen as essential to national economic development. For this reason alone revisiting what Boulding had to say is of interest. Reflecting on what was recognised correctly already over half a century ago and where our knowledge has changed is also informative. This helps us gain some perspective with respect to modern social and environmental understanding. In doing so I will place the issues raised by Boulding within the context of the present field of social ecological economics.

I start by providing some background in terms of the state of environmental awareness in the USA at the time the essay was first published. This helps explain why it became a standard reading for those concerned about environment–economy interactions and was repeatedly cited and reprinted over the following decades. I then explain the central messages of Boulding's spaceship earth metaphor using both the essay and related materials. This is followed by a section critically reflecting on the weaknesses of the essay as a modern environmental critique of economic systems. In the penultimate section, I turn to the relationship with social ecological economics. First I question the links between Boulding and the ecological economics movement. Then I show how key concepts from Boulding's essay connect to social ecological economics. I close with a few remarks relating Boulding's presentation to the ecological economics community at their inaugural conference in 1990, where he discussed the role of power in addressing environmental problems.

A brief historical prelude

In the USA several elements of awareness about human society can be identified as finally coming together in the 1960s. These elements include realisation that natural systems can be devastated on a large scale by human action, fear that domestically available resources will prove inadequate, criticism of the power held by corporations and recognition of the downsides of a consumer society. Modern environmentalism then encapsulated all these different aspects which had previously remained isolated issues. However, the build-up to this synthesis was piecemeal and slow.

An event that should have triggered a greater environmental awareness was the Great Dustbowl of the 1930s. This was a prime example of human-induced environmental degradation. The human misery it created was recounted by Steinbeck (1939) in his novel *The Grapes of Wrath*. In telling that story he pointed a finger directly at the faceless banking sector and modern agricultural practices. Yet, despite such a major environmental disaster, neither the exploitation of nature nor the economic model of development were seriously brought into question. The problem of the Dustbowl was picked up by economists in the agricultural literature as how best to change farm management practices and prevent soil erosion (Ciriacy-Wantrup, 1938, 1947).

In the 1940s, World War II boosted employment and economic growth. After the war domestic resource security was a recognised policy problem. The cold war exacerbated the paranoia over securing national resource supplies in the USA and boosted military spending. This meant resource scarcity became an important priority and in 1951 President Truman established the President's Materials Policy Commission. As Jarrett (1966, p.vii) notes: "The Commission's main assignment was to inquire into whether there would be enough food and industrial raw materials at reasonable prices over the next twenty-five years to support continued economic growth and meet the requirements of national security." Amongst other things, the final report (Paley, 1952) led to the establishment of the economic think tank Resources for the Future. This organisation later became a key focus for American research on economy–environment interactions during a period when concern changed from resource quantity to environmental quality. In the 1950s consumerism and technological optimism were still the order of the day. There was no questioning of economic growth, merely concern over how to secure its continuance.

However, aspects of discontent over the modernist preoccupation with economic growth were already clear in criticisms of and warnings about the consumer society. The problems with consumerism can be found being debated in the late 1800s (e.g. Devas, 1899), and at that time Veblen (1991 [1899]) had created the phrase "conspicuous consumption". In the 1950s Galbraith (1969 [1958]) published a popular book about the newly affluent American society and its failings. This included exposing the influence of companies in creating consumer wants and the failings of a society focused on promoting private wealth to provide for the social good. As Dubos (1966, p. 32) notes, by the mid-1960s, the affluent society was being called the "effluent" society.

Environmental issues appeared in modern form, and with a public profile, after the astounding publicity surrounding Rachel Carson's (1987 [1962]) *Silent Spring*, which focused on the use of pesticides in agriculture. This had actually been shortly preceded that year by a far wider reaching environmental critique, *Our Synthetic Environment* by Lewis Herber (1962), alias Murray Bookchin. The book by Carson avoided directly addressing political and economic root causes in preference for a story centred on human–nature relationships and the need for ecological balance. The products and chemical companies responsible for damages she was denouncing were not even named (except Army Chemical Corps). Those unfamiliar with the period should remember criticism of the American way of life or its industry was subject to investigation by Hoover's FBI and libel to accusations of communism, just as today environmental activism (e.g. destroying a gas-guzzling vehicle) may be branded as terrorism.

In contrast to Carson, in *Our Synthetic Environment* Bookchin was directly concerned with how the social and economic system in the USA created pollutants and lifestyles damaging to human health and the environment. In Chapter 1, under the subtitle "man and the natural world", Bookchin stated:

> The needs of industrial plants are being placed before man's need for clean air; the disposal of industrial wastes has gained priority over the community's need for clean water. The most pernicious laws of the market place are given precedence over the most compelling laws of biology.
>
> (Herber, 1962)

His book basically disappeared and is largely unknown, Carson's is world renowned (for a comparison and explanation, see Garb, 1995). Questioning of the economic model of development from an apolitical science-based environmentalist position was apparently radical enough. Certainly in the early 1960s few professional economists can be found raising any environmental concerns.

There are two notable exceptions, Siegfried von Ciriacy-Wantrup and K. William Kapp. In his main life's work, Ciriacy-Wantrup (1952), having worked on soil erosion (see above), was mainly concerned about resource conservation, but defined resources as a very broad set including many aspects of the wider environment. A legacy of that work was the proposition of a safe-minimum standard beyond which depletion of flow resources (e.g. soil, water, plants and animals) should not go lest irreversible losses result. Kapp's work, amongst other things, explained pollution as a feature of both capitalist and socialist business enterprise, and by the early 1960s had already exploded the myth that such a prevalent phenomena could be treated as external to the economic system, rather than an inherent aspect of modern production and consumption (1950, 1963). In addition, Kapp (1961) advocated the integration of knowledge and had identified the failure to connect the biological and social sciences as in need of attention. Both Ciriacy-Wantrup and Kapp explored the institutional aspects of resource and environmental problems.

This was the context into which Boulding's essay fits and indeed why it was itself insightful. In 1965, when Boulding first presented his ideas, behind the essay, on environment–economy interactions, the literature on the topic was sparse and the connection to thermodynamics seemed lost in the past (Martinez-Alier, 1990). Boulding did not attempt a literature review, giving just four references, nor did he cite any of the above literature, despite having favourably reviewed Galbraith's book (Boulding, 1959). What Boulding did was to contribute a wide ranging semi-journalistic essay, using a powerful metaphor, at a very formative time for the debate on how economics needed to relate to environmental reality.

Boulding (1965) originally presented the ideas behind the essay to the Committee on Space Sciences as a short three-page address on 10 May 1965 at Washington State University.[1] That version entitled "Earth as a Space Ship" is very tight, critical and to the point; it also ends deriding "low-priority achievements like putting a man on the moon", which must have gone down well with the Committee! Ten months later, 8–9 March 1966, Resources for the Future held a workshop at their headquarters in Washington, DC, where Boulding presented a fuller version of his ideas. After revision of the presented papers, an edited volume appeared (Jarrett, 1966), in which the more extended and commonly known version of Boulding's essay was the opening chapter (Boulding, 1966). The earlier three-page address explicitly uses the term "Space Ship" as an analogy drawing direct comparisons with Earth systems. By the time the full essay was published a year later the term was now "Spaceship", which has changed into being a metaphor, i.e. the spaceship as an expression not literally applicable to Earth.

The spaceship earth metaphor

The original three-page address contains the key elements of concern over economic growth and the consumerist society we find today in ecological economics. The basic problem is that humanity has increased the scale of its activities to a level where pollution and resource extraction can no longer be regarded as unimportant. We cannot move to another place to escape our waste, or find new resources, as we now cover the entire planet. This has specific consequences. Societies based upon increasing consumption rates using technologies which burn fossil fuels and disperse ores, without any concern for recycling or reuse, are wasteful and short lived (Boulding, 1965, mentions a few hundred years).

A different technology is necessary to achieve a stable circular-flow of materials. Natural systems are part of the means by which materials can be concentrated. As Boulding (1965) states: "The stable high-level technology will have to rely on the oceans and the atmosphere as a basic resource from which materials may be concentrated in sufficient quantity to overcome their diffusion through consumption." Yet basic physical laws, and entropy in particular, mean continuous energy inputs are required to maintain order. As fossil fuels run out, we need new inputs of energy (he notes solar and possibly nuclear fusion). In terms of ecological systems, a symbiotic relationship with all other elements and populations of the world is recommended, although this might involve domestication and wildlife preserves.

In terms of social systems the implications are noted to be far from clear. Boulding (1965) mentions that we cannot have "cowboys and Indians" or a "cowboy ethic", a theme expanded upon in the full essay (discussed below). He rejects both unrestrained conflict and unrestricted national sovereignty. At this point he notes the comparison of Earth with a spaceship breaking-down, because a relatively small space craft is run along military lines where society is planned with a dictator in charge, and necessarily so in his opinion. In a world of ten billion a different social structure is necessary and desirable. He allows for the possibility of pricing and a market system but "of a limited and controlled kind". Institutions are required which combine the need for overall control with individual freedom and mobility. The enforcement of overall control is in reference to maintaining the social system within constraints such as population limits, while controlling for conflict and "perverse social dynamic processes" (not explained but perhaps, in light of Boulding, 1991, p. 27, a reference to such things as fashion, financial speculation and war).

Boulding is particularly critical of the poor state of human knowledge about environmental issues. He reflects on our level of ignorance about Earth systems and, amongst other things, notes the failure to resolve the question of impacts from human activity on global temperature. He is particularly critical of the state of ecology as a discipline, which he refers to as hardly beyond the level of bird-watching. He is also concerned that:

> when it comes to understanding the world social system or the sociosphere, we are not only ignorant but proud of our ignorance. There is no systematic method of data collection and processing, and the theory of social dynamics is still in its first infancy.
>
> (Boulding, 1965)

Today the level of understanding of all but the social seems to have made some considerable progress. Ecology, Earth systems and climatology have all undergone major developments over the intervening half century.

In the full-length essay, Boulding (1966) expands on these basic themes. There he introduces two similes: the cowboy economy of the past, which is contrasted with the spaceman economy of the future. The former is wasteful of resources and involves continually moving on, leaving environmental degradation in its wake. It is associated with "reckless, exploitative, romantic, and violent behavior" (Boulding, 1966, p. 9). The spaceman economy is limited in both sources of materials and pollution sinks and requires humanity living within "a cyclical ecological system which is capable of continuous reproduction of material form even though it cannot escape having inputs of energy" (Boulding, 1966, p. 9). The distinction is drawn-out further by a comparison of attitudes towards consumption. In the former throughput, and so consumption, is good, but in the latter stock maintenance for minimal input is desired, not throughput. "This idea that both production and consumption are bad things rather than good things is very strange to economists, who have been obsessed with the income-flow concepts to the exclusion, almost, of capital-stock concepts" (Boulding, 1966, p. 10). This does raise some problematic issues for Boulding in terms of how to relate to human well-being, which derives in part from the joy of throughput (see comment by Daly, 1981). In this regard he favours something which might now be regarded as a needs-based approach (e.g. see Max-Neef, 1992).

Boulding framed his primary concern about biophysical limits as a long-term problem. That is, the impact, he believed, would fall mainly, or most severely, on future generations. The question is then how current consumers of scarce resources and low entropy energy stocks can be convinced to take the needs of future generations into account? How can the unborn be given voice? No real answer is provided in the essay, but rather the issue is flagged up, requiring more attention.

The full essay also adds a relatively lengthy discussion about knowledge, its creation and loss. Knowledge is stated to be more important for humans than energy or materials (p. 6). The concept of knowledge being employed is very broadly and loosely defined and hard to grasp. As will be discussed in the next section, the explanation is far from clear or convincing and comes across as rather unscientific, speculative reflection compared to the discussion on materials and energy. Knowledge and its importance for development was something Boulding later pursued in relation to his ideas on evolutionary economics.

Shortcomings of Boulding's essay

There are actually several aspects of the essay which do not seem particularly well thought through or able to sustain some reflection. One of these is the opening claim that there has always been a frontier in the human mind and this represents a belief in a physical place to which humans can go when things get too difficult. This seems more appropriate to North American white settler mythology than a general or universal truth. The frontier did not even actually exist in North America because the country was already settled by native Americans who had to be wiped out to create the myth of an empty country full of unexploited potential. Boulding then appears to have adopted the myths of his new homeland and forgotten the European culture from whence he came, where historically most people had remained tied to local communities unless dislocated by war.

In later revisiting the spaceship metaphor, Boulding (1980 [1973]) himself recognised societies were historically isolated and this was one reason for concern over what is now termed globalisation. Where there is isolation, collapse of one society need not affect another. As he states: "the collapse of the Mayan Empire, an early example of a Club of Rome report, affected Charlemagne or the Emperor of China not at all. They knew nothing of it" (Boulding, 1980 [1973], p. 266). Human development has not then always been a matter of trashing the environment and then moving on in order to survive, as Boulding claims in his cowboy economy simile.

Indeed the fear of instability in modern society may be exactly because we have a fear of the unknown, frontiers, leaving home and hearth. Outside the local boundaries of our daily lives the world is uncertain. Historically this is reflected in stories of dark places, inhospitable lands and strange peoples. Going out into the big wide world has traditionally been threatening: "Beware! There be monsters." While globalisation, cheap flights and package holidays abroad have broken down such barriers for many, this relaxation is a relatively recent phenomenon. If there is an awareness in the collective unconscious of frontiers, it is that they are not welcoming places to go when the crisis comes, and they are as likely to bring death as be life sustaining.

This takes on more importance when we look at Boulding's technological optimism. In revisiting his metaphor he advocates colonising space (Boulding, 1980 [1973]). As per the long-running television programme *Star Trek*, space is the final frontier for the North American colonising spirit. So when Boulding advocates space colonies as a real potential future, he is doing nothing more than appeasing the critics of biophysical limits with a scientific fantasy. In doing so he readily derides the potential for solar power on Earth because in space energy flows from the sun 24 hours a day and energy transport costs are lower away from Earth's gravity. He neglects to note that, without massive material and energy inputs, space is neither an easy place to get to nor an environment in which humans can naturally survive. Boulding does himself and environmental reality no favours by such flights of fancy and would have been better off remembering his own words concluding the three-page address, that putting a man (or two) on the moon was a low-priority achievement. Indeed, the impetus for humanity sending a handful of people into space was an imperial struggle supported by the military-industrial complexes of the contestants.

The rise of nuclear power as an energy source has similar roots and, given Boulding's peace activism, his willingness to consider this option seems strange. The promise of nuclear fusion is mentioned without any caveats and fission is merely remarked upon as being limited by the available supply of fissionable materials. There is nothing about the inherently unsafe nature, toxic waste and weapons proliferation potential of nuclear energy as we know it. In a later presentation, Boulding (1975, p. 18) does briefly make these connections and is more critical.

> At the moment we seem to have put all our eggs into the rather dirty basket of the breeder reactor. I must confess I have grave doubts whether this is wise, not only because of the costs and dangers of the reactors themselves,

> but because of the enormous increase in the quantity of plutonium, the most deadly substance known to man, is not one that can be contemplated with any satisfaction, especially in light of the possibility that small organizations could make nuclear weapons.

Still, in the *Spaceship Earth* essay he remains ready to consider this and other interventionist and synthetic technologies at face value. Hence we find reference to what has become biotechnology as a possible means of harnessing energy. He refers to the biological revolution providing possible solutions by developing artificial organisms for solar energy transformation and running machines with methane-producing algae (Boulding, 1966, p. 8). This technological optimism rather runs counter to the argument for making do with what we know are the current capacities of humanity within set biophysical limits.

A related area in which the essay is open to criticism is the discussion of knowledge. This is initially compared to energy and materials, and entropy is directly stated to be applicable if "used in a somewhat loose sense". How there is meant to be some equivalence to the Laws of Thermodynamics that might cover knowledge is a mystery, and this speculation just leads to muddying the waters of scientific understanding. The discussion seems mainly to be aimed at justifying the treatment of knowledge as something of an accounting concept within a language of stocks, flows and depreciation. In fact, this accountancy approach underlies Boulding's writing in the essay. The treatment of nature as capital, and indeed the modern penchant for treating everything as readily substitutable capital, does little to address environmental problems (Spash and Clayton, 1997). Indeed buying into a neo-liberal economic ideology, where the world becomes a collection of capital assets, allows the discourse of money, banking and finance to predominate over other values, which are then more easily lost rather than preserved (Spash, 2009, 2011b).

In several respects, Boulding would not be seen as having provided the full range of arguments and concerns of modern environmentalists. For example, he does not address the social and political factors or structural issues driving economic growth and environmental degradation. Those are actually the key issues of concern today. Understanding amongst social ecological economists of the basic biophysical constraints laid out by Boulding has also improved and is more precise than in his essay.

Connecting Boulding, his spaceship and social ecological economics

The modern heterodox field of ecological economics arose to fill the gap between social and biological sciences as identified by Kapp (1961). The direct connection to Boulding's essay is the specific concern to develop the social and economic implications of biophysical reality and in particular entropy. Establishing ecological economics as a professional association took another 30 years and involved a long diversion via neoclassical resource and environmental economics (Spash,

1999). Boulding was not particularly involved in that journey, despite some early reflections on the relationships between ecology and economics (Boulding, 1950). Nor was he engaged in the decade of events during the 1980s that established ecological economics by bringing North American and European ecologists and socio-economists together; for example, he was absent from the key 1987 foundational meeting in Barcelona (Røpke, 2004).

On the basis of the *Spaceship Earth* essay, one might have expected greater cooperation and association with like-minded others, such as Georgescu-Roegen and Herman Daly. Yet, this did not happen and Boulding (1981, p. 191) himself explains why, as follows:

> Herman Daly, Nicholas Georgescu-Roegen and I, indeed, once thought of forming a society of heretics like ourselves, but it never got under way because we could not agree on the name for it, which perhaps revealed that our heresies were rather different. Georgescu-Roegen being concerned with entropy, Herman Daly with the stationary state, and I with a sustainable social evolution. This difference has persisted over the years, though in no way was it a detriment to our friendships.

The situation may not have been quite so amicable, amongst all parties, as implied. In 1971 a major work on entropy and economics was published by Georgescu-Roegen (1971) that included but a brief critical mention of Boulding. Referencing a section of a textbook by Boulding (1955, Chapter 28), Georgescu-Roegen (1971, p. 235) states his understanding of production functions encapsulates "almost every misleading notion that surrounds the conception of process in the economic literature". The following year, in the space of four paragraphs, Boulding (1972, pp. 280–281) dismissed the contents of the book with remarks apparently denying the implications of entropy for economics, although what is being dismissed is rather unclear. His comments about not being concerned for disorder are indeed senseless and empty. His other comments have little to do with the implications of entropy for economic systems, and involve a denial of an entropy theory of value. In Chapter X (which possibly Boulding had not read?), Georgescu-Roegen (1971) argues against such a reduction of economic value to a physical variable such as energy (see also Georgescu-Roegen, 1979). Perhaps we should not then be surprised to find, some years later, Georgescu-Roegen (1979, p. 1026) attacking Boulding for his inconsistency and lack of understanding of the importance of material flows. For his part, Boulding appears primarily concerned with promoting his own evolutionary ideas at the expense of others, including any ecological economic synthesis. As Martinez-Alier (1990, p. 2) states: "That there was no concerted action to create a school of ecological economics is made clear by Boulding's inane critique of Georgescu-Roegen (Boulding, 1972)."

So the sometimes noted claim of Boulding being a founder of modern ecological economics appears more as wishful thinking than fact. Any such assessment would seem unsustainable on the basis of his professional engagement, and those trying to substantiate the claim tend to appeal to the single *Spaceship Earth* essay. Boulding's move away from environmental concerns is also evident in an address entitled "Energy and the Environment", given in 1975 at the University of Wyoming, where he makes hardly any connection to environmental issues, or indeed energy, and is almost totally preoccupied with knowledge and evolutionary analogies applied to social and economic systems (Boulding, 1975). These ideas undoubtedly leading to his ecodynamic theory (Boulding, 1978). Perhaps there is a case to be made for his work on evolutionary economics being influential for some ecological economists. However, Daly (1981) can also be found gently chastising Boulding for weakening his position with respect to mainstream economics over the years, between the essay and his ecodynamics book, and offering inadequate explanations on stock/funds, flows and time (points on which Boulding, 1981, pp. 191–192, admits he has no adequate reply). Here I concentrate on the correspondence and links between the *Spaceship Earth* essay and later research by others, especially within the context of ecological economics. In doing so I will aim to point out how ideas have differed from its suggestions, where clarifications have been made and how research has progressed on related topics.

An important contribution of the essay was to raise the profile of the Laws of Thermodynamics amongst economists and their relevance for bounding social and economic systems. The First Law establishes the principle of the conservation of energy, namely that energy cannot be created nor destroyed but appears in different forms (e.g. heat, work, chemical, electrical). The Second Law concerns entropy (or unavailability of thermal energy for work) and states that in any isolated system entropy increases when energy is transformed. So, more simply, this means when using energy we irreversibly downgrade it and make it unavailable. At the same time matter becomes dispersed, degraded or disordered.

Boulding's (1966) essay was quoted in the booklet by Kneese *et al.* (1970) which developed a materials balance theory of the economy, and attempted to take some account of the First Law of Thermodynamics. Like energy, mass can neither be created nor destroyed in an isolated system. Einstein's theory of relativity equates energy to mass. The implications are simply that the mass of material inputs to the economy do not disappear upon consumption but rather are transformed into an equivalent mass of waste. As Boulding (1966, p. 5) recognised:

> From a material point of view, we see objects passing from the noneconomic into the economic set in the process of production, and we similarly see products passing out of the economic set as their value becomes zero. Thus we see the econosphere as a material process involving the discovery and mining of fossil fuels, ores, etc., and at the other end a process by which the effluents of the system are passed out into noneconomic reservoirs—for instance, the atmosphere and the oceans—which are not appropriated and do not enter into the exchange system.

The materials balance theory as applied to economics by Kneese *et al.* (1970) showed that all the prices in the economy were in need of adjustment as everything had a related externality in neoclassical economic terms. The all-pervasive nature of pollution destroyed the myth of a free unplanned market economy because prices do not reflect real resource costs and most fundamentally the wastes from production and consumption. Boulding, however, failed to make the connection to the all-pervasive nature of pollution and, near the end of his essay, recommended internalisation of externalities using taxes as the solution to what he saw as the immediate pollution problems arising from imperfections in the pricing system. He was apparently unfamiliar with the work by Kapp (1950). He also fails to recognise that appropriation of nature and the incorporation of all aspects of the environment into the exchange system are part of the problem not the solution.

Boulding (1966, p. 13) expresses concern over the lack of any serious work on the durability of products and how this might relate to the environmental impact over their economic life. The general area of the relationship of production and consumption to materials and energy has since developed, for example, in the practice of product life-cycle analysis. Ayres (1996) went on from materials balance theory to help develop the field of industrial ecology, and to explain in greater depth the connection between economic growth and useful energy or exergy (Ayres and Warr, 2005; Ayres, 1998). Others have pursued the concept of social metabolism which traces energy and materials flows through the economy and explains the process of industrialisation as exploitation of fossil fuels (Fischer-Kowalski and Haberl, 2007; Sieferle, 2001).

The Second Law concerning entropy was something explored more fully by Georgescu-Roegen (1971, 1975, 1966, pp. 66–82). Both Boulding and Georgescu-Roegen influenced Daly (1968) towards his advocacy of a steady-state economy (Daly, 1972, 1974, 1977). Georgescu-Roegen himself took a quite pessimistic stance in which the inability to recycle materials meant falling back to an agrarian society dependent upon organic agriculture and solar energy. Daly's position can be described as embracing our inevitable extinction but with the proviso of aiming for longevity on the basis of an ethic of Christian stewardship (Daly, 1974). A negative relationship between longevity and societal throughput means the higher economic growth, as we know it, the shorter humanity can be expected to survive. The idea of taking biophysical limits as serious constraints on economic activity has today become reflected in the concept of degrowth (Kallis, 2011; Martinez-Alier *et al.*, 2010).

In the discussions of the implication of these biophysical limits, the "loose" approach to language on entropy used by Boulding is problematic, and more generally such usage has been noted to have caused a period of considerable confusion in the ecological economics literature that took some time to clear-up (Baumgärtner, 1996). Boulding (1966) refers to closed and open systems but without direct correspondence to physics or the Laws of Thermodynamics. Although what he states is broadly correct, there are instances of inaccuracy. For example, the term closed systems occurs when discussing systems without any exchange of energy or matter. These are actually isolated systems in thermodynamics. Closed systems exchange energy but not matter. Earth is in practice basically (though not strictly) a closed system. Open systems exchange both materials and matter with other systems. Boundary distinctions are important because different systems have different properties. For example, while Earth is basically closed, economic and social systems are open. Boulding's (1966, p. 9) discussion of cowboy vs. spaceman economies confuses these boundaries and different systems. Clarifying such boundaries means taking into account the impacts of social and economic systems on other systems and their dependency on those systems (e.g. ecosystem, solar system).

Boulding (1966, p. 7) correctly identifies the important role of ecosystems in recycling and concentrating chemical elements and organic substances and creating low entropy materials, something Georgescu-Roegen got wrong (see also reconfirmation of this point by Bianciardi *et al.*, 1993). More recent developments have reflected the role of self-organising systems in creating order from dissipated and solar energy, but also in releasing energy through major dynamic system changes (Kay *et al.*, 1999). This links ecosystems structure and functioning to thermodynamic theory. The changing dynamic of systems is seen as highly important and especially how systems may flip due to different attractors becoming dominant. Self-organising systems may then show spontaneous coherent behaviour but suddenly change when reaching a "catastrophic" threshold (Kay *et al.*, 1999). This introduces concerns over strong uncertainty (ignorance and social indeterminacy), thresholds, non-linearity and irreversibility.

In Boulding's essay, the inevitable implication of entropy and materials dispersion was a limit on modern consumerist economies. Resources for the essential needs of future generations are being squandered on luxuries for the current rich. He might have added the current poor into the story and the failure to do so is actually a strong criticism of the essay (despite his claim others are addressing today's problems). Social inequity and harm of the innocent is not something only of concern for the future, and so explicable because people generally do not consider long time-horizons. Geographical myopia seems as prevalent as the temporal myopia which Boulding criticises. So the use of ordered forms of energy by the present rich is at the expense of the needs of the present poor, future poor and future rich. Ecological economics has an essentially social (i.e. political and distributional) aspect, hence the term social ecological economics now being used in some circles (Spash, 2011a).

The issue Boulding (1966) touches upon in his discussion of future generations is that physical laws have implications for society but what humanity chooses to do is an ethical question. The discussion of discounting contrasts with and attempts to constrain the concern for ethics and values. Mainstream economists, such as environmental economists, attempt to impose such restrictions on the debate, but these are rhetorical exercises which try to avoid the fundamental value conflicts and power struggles in society (e.g. for a discussion in the context of climate change, see Spash, 2007, 2002). The rise of the field of environmental ethics is central to understanding plural values and how they should be addressed in policy (O'Neill *et al.*, 2007). As such, ethics and value pluralism form central parts of social ecological economics (Spash, 2009). Near the end of the essay, Boulding gives a stark warning as to the consequences of failing to act ethically towards the future:

> This whole problem is linked up with the much larger one of the determinants of the morale, legitimacy, and "nerve" of a society, and there is a great deal of historical evidence to suggest that a society which loses its identity with posterity and which loses its positive image of the future loses also its capacity to deal with present problems, and soon falls apart.
>
> (Boulding, 1966, p. 11)

Concluding remarks

A spaceship earth metaphor provided an easily understandable and brief account of some key aspects of the concern, becoming increasingly acknowledged in the early 1960s, that there were some serious downsides to the American modernist technological optimism of a materialist, hedonic nirvana delivered to your door by free-market enterprise. Boulding's essay is far from perfect and contains many speculative elements and aspects which, sometimes conforming to mainstream economic thinking and/or an accountancy approach, can prevent a clear vision of environmental and social problems. Still one of the attractions of Boulding's writing is his often successful attempt to be thought provoking, and the speculative elements at least add to that. The essay is also wide-ranging and includes many ideas. The drawback of a short essay is the brevity of coverage given to those ideas, and this is unfortunately compounded because of Boulding's failure to return in any depth to the environmental challenges raised in the essay and a softening of his position on some issues. However, the essay appears to have taken on a life of its own in stimulating others.

After writing the essay, Boulding seems to have moved on to different interests, such as evolutionary economics, and did not help establish ecological economics. However, Boulding did attend the inaugural conference of the International Society for Ecological Economics in 1990, where he gave a plenary speech. His plenary address mainly concerned the potential for legitimate institutions of governance and good leadership to arise in time to tackle the impending environmental crises (Boulding, 1991). The conclusion looked towards "integrative power" by which he meant "the power of legitimacy, loyalty, respect, affection, love, truth, and so on". He concluded that in order to address environmental problems, population growth and the exhaustion of fossil fuels:

> the major element unquestionably will be integrative power, based first on the widespread knowledge that we all live on the same fragile planet, which we have now seen from outer space and to which we owe a common loyalty and affection. Unless this view is very widespread, legitimacy will not be granted to those frequently painful processes which may be necessary to prevent catastrophe.
>
> (Boulding, 1991, p. 30)

So, despite not having been active in or contributing directly to the development of ecological economics, he maintained a strong environmental concern to the end and saw the need for serious and substantive action.

As the current political and economic system pours billions into stabilising financial and banking sectors, waging wars in oil-rich countries and extracting energy from the most damaging and dangerous sources, the type of institutions and leadership required to prevent social and environmental catastrophe seem particularly lacking. Governments hark on about scientific uncertainty and call for more research rather than tackle human-induced climate change. When action occurs, it is minimal and does not address fundamental causes. The causes of greenhouse gas emissions go to the roots of the modern economic systems' failings. The biophysical basis of those failings were outlined by Boulding's essay. The social, structural and institutional aspects were largely neglected, although later partially picked up in his work on power.

Social ecological economics aims to bring all these elements together to help understand and aid the necessary transformation facing humanity. The reality of the functioning of the economy within society and society within biophysical constraints is set against the fantasy of economic growth forever. In policy circles, little has been done in half a century to address biophysical constraints, and little action seems likely without a crisis. We lack legitimate processes to achieve change in the institutional structures empowering those who benefit from, and perpetuate, the current system of accelerating environmental degradation and resource exploitation.

Note

1 Kenneth E. Boulding Papers, Archives (Box # 38), University Libraries, University of Colorado, Boulder, USA.

References

Ayres, R.U. 1998. Eco-thermodynamics: economics and the second law. *Ecological Economics* 26 (2): 189–209.

Ayres, R.U. and L.W. Ayres. 1996. *Industrial Ecology: Towards Closing the Materials Cycle*. Cheltenham, England: Edward Elgar.

Ayres, R.U. and B. Warr. 2005. Accounting for growth: The role of physical work. *Structural Change and Economic Dynamics* 16: 181–209.

Baumgärtner, S. 1996. Use of the entropy concept in ecological economics. In *Ecological Economics: Concepts and Methods*, edited by M. Faber, R. Manstetten and J. Proops. Cheltenham, England: Edward Elgar.

Bianciardi, C., E. Tiezzi and S. Ulgiati. 1993. Complete recycling of matter in the framework of physics, biology and ecological economics. *Ecological Economics* 8 (1): 1–5.

Boulding, K.E. 1950. An ecological introduction. In *A Reconstruction of Economics*, edited by K. E. Boulding. New York: Wiley.

Boulding, K.E. 1955. *Economic Analysis*. London: Hamish Hamilton.

Boulding, K.E. 1959. The Affluent Society, Galbraith, J.K. *Review of Economics and Statistics* 41 (1): 81.

Boulding, K.E. 1965. Earth as a space ship. In *Kenneth E. Boulding Papers*. Boulder: University of Colorado at Boulder Libraries.

Boulding, K.E. 1966. The economics of the coming spaceship earth. In *Environmental Quality in a Growing Economy: Essays from the Sixth RFF Forum*, edited by H. Jarrett. Baltimore: Johns Hopkins University Press.

Boulding, K.E. 1972. Toward the development of a cultural economics. *Social Science Quarterly* 53 (2): 267–284.

Boulding, K.E. 1975. *Energy and the Environment*. Laramie, Wyoming: University of Wyoming.

Boulding, K.E. 1978. *Ecodynamics: A New Theory of Social Evolution*. Beverly Hills, California: Sage.

Boulding, K.E. 1980 [1973]. Spaceship earth revisited. In *Economics, Ecology, Ethics: Essays Toward a Steady-State Economy*, edited by H.E. Daly. New York: W.H. Freeman.

Boulding, K.E. 1981. Ecodynamics: A response by the author. *Journal of Social and Biological Structures* 4 (2): 187–194.

Boulding, K.E. 1991. What do we want to sustain? Environmentalism and human evaluations. In *Ecological Economics: The Science and Management of Sustainability*, edited by R. Costanza. New York: Columbia University Press.

Carson, R. 1987 [1962]. *Silent Spring*. Twenty-fifth Anniversary Edition. Boston: Houghton Mifflin.

Ciriacy-Wantrup, S.V. 1938. Soil conservation in European farm management. *Journal of Farm Economics* 20 (February): 86–101.

Ciriacy-Wantrup, S.V. 1947. Capital returns from soil conservation practices. *Journal of Farm Economics* 29: 1188–1190.

Ciriacy-Wantrup, S.V. 1952. *Resource Conservation: Economics and Policies*. Berkeley: University of California Press.

Daly, H.E. 1968. On economics as a life science. *Journal of Political Economy* 76: 392–406.

Daly, H.E. 1972. In defense of a steady-state economy. *American Journal of Agricultural Economics* 54 (5): 945–954.

Daly, H.E. 1974. Economics of steady state. *American Economic Review* 64 (2): 15–21.

Daly, H.E. 1977. *Steady-State Economics*. San Francisco, California: W.H. Freeman.

Daly, H.E. 1981. Reflections on Boulding's "income or welfare". *Journal of Social and Biological Structures* 4 (2): 158–162.

Devas, C.S. 1899. The moral aspect of consumption. *International Journal of Ethics* 10 (1): 41–54.

Dubos, R. 1966. Promises and hazards of man's adaptability. In *Environmental Quality in a Growing Economy: Essays from the Sixth RFF Forum*, edited by H. Jarrett. Baltimore: Johns Hopkins University Press.

Fischer-Kowalski, M. and H. Haberl, eds. 2007. *Socio-ecological Transitions and Global Change. Trajectories of Social Metabolism and Land Use*. Cheltenham: Edward Elgar.

Galbraith, J.K. 1969 [1958]. *The Affluent Society*. Boston: Houghton Mifflin.

Garb, Y. 1995. Rachel Carson's Silent Spring. *Dissent* (Fall): 539–546.

Georgescu-Roegen, N. 1966. *Analytical Economics*. Cambridge: Cambridge University Press.

Georgescu-Roegen, N. 1971. *The Entropy Law and the Economic Process*. Cambridge, Massachusetts: Harvard University Press.

Georgescu-Roegen, N. 1975. Energy and economic myths. *Southern Economic Journal* 41 (3): 347–381.

Georgescu-Roegen, N. 1979. Energy analysis and economic valuation. *Southern Economic Journal* XLIV: 1023–1058.

Herber, L. 1962. *Our Synthetic Environment*. New York: Knopf.

Jarrett, H., ed. 1966. *Environmental Quality in a Growing Economy: Essays from the Sixth RFF Forum*. Baltimore, Maryland: Johns Hopkins University Press.

Kallis, G. 2011. In defence of degrowth. *Ecological Economics* 70 (5): 873–880.

Kapp, K.W. 1950. *The Social Costs of Private Enterprise*. New York: Shocken.

Kapp, K.W. 1961. *Toward a Science of Man in Society: A Positive Approach to the Integration of Social Knowledge*. The Hague: Martinus Nijhoff.

Kapp, K.W. 1963. *The Social Costs of Business Enterprise*. 2nd ed. Bombay/London: Asia Publishing House.

Kay, J.J., H.A. Regier, M. Boyle and G. Francis. 1999. An ecosystem approach for sustainability: Addressing the challenge of complexity. *Futures* 31 (7): 721–742.

Kneese, A.V., R.U. Ayres and R.C. d'Arge. 1970. *Economics and the Environment: A Materials Balance Approach*. Washington, District of Columbia: Resources for the Future.

Martinez-Alier, J. 1990. *Ecological Economics: Energy, Environment and Society*. Oxford, England: Basil Blackwell.

Martinez-Alier, J., U. Pascual, F.D. Vivien and E. Zaccai. 2010. Sustainable de-growth: Mapping the context, criticisms and future prospects of an emergent paradigm. *Ecological Economics* 69 (9): 1741–1747.

Max-Neef, M. 1992. Development and human needs. In *Real-Life Economics: Understanding Wealth Creation*, edited by P. Ekins and M. Max-Neef. London: Routledge.

O'Neill, J.F., A. Holland and A. Light. 2007. *Environmental Values*. London: Routledge.

Paley, W.S. 1952. *Resources for Freedom: Report of the President's Materials Policy Commission*. Washington, DC: United States, Government Printing Office.

Røpke, I. 2004. The early history of modern ecological economics. *Ecological Economics* 50 (3–4): 293–314.

Sieferle, R.P. 2001. *The Subterranean Forest: Energy Systems and the Industrial Revolution*. Cambridge: White Horse Press.

Spash, C.L. 1999. The development of environmental thinking in economics. *Environmental Values* 8 (4): 413–435.

Spash, C.L. 2002. *Greenhouse Economics: Value and Ethics*. London: Routledge.

Spash, C.L. 2007. The economics of climate change impacts à la Stern: Novel and nuanced or rhetorically restricted? *Ecological Economics* 63 (4): 706–713.

Spash, C.L. 2009. The new environmental pragmatists, pluralism and sustainability. *Environmental Values* 18 (3): 253–256.

Spash, C.L. 2011a. Social ecological economics: Understanding the past to see the future. *American Journal of Economics and Sociology* 70 (2): 340–375.

Spash, C.L. 2011b. Terrible economics, ecosystems and banking. *Environmental Values* 20 (2): 141–145.

Spash, C.L. and A.M.H. Clayton. 1997. The maintenance of natural capital: Motivations and methods. In *Space, Place and Environmental Ethics*, edited by A. Light and J. M. Smith. Lanham: Rowman & Littlefield Publishers, Inc.

Steinbeck, J.E. 1939. *The Grapes of Wrath*. 1st ed. New York: The Viking Press.

Veblen, T. 1991 [1899]. *The Theory of the Leisure Class*. Fairfield, New Jersey: Augustus M. Kelley.

Poems

A Conservationist's Lament

The world is finite, resources are scarce,
Things are bad and will be worse.
Coal is burned and gas exploded,
Forests cut and soils eroded.
Wells are dry and air's polluted.
Dust is blowing, trees uprooted.
Oil is going, ores depleted,
Drains receive what is excreted.
Land is sinking, seas are rising,
Man is far too enterprising.
Fire will rage with Man to fan it,
Soon we'll have a plundered planet.
People breed like fertile rabbits,
People have disgusting habits.
Moral:
  The evolutionary plan
  Went astray by evolving Man.

The Technologist's Reply

Man's potential is quite terrific,
You can't go back to the Neolithic.
The cream is there for us to skim it,
Knowledge is power, and the sky's the limit.
Every mouth has hands to feed it,
Food is found when people need it.
All we need is found in granite
Once we have the men to plan it.
Yeast and algae give us meat,
Soil is almost obsolete.
Men can grow to pastures greener
Till all the earth is Pasadena.
Moral:
  Man's a nuisance, Man's a crackpot,
  But only Man can hit the jackpot.

Published, 1956

Part X

Cultural economics

10 Key text: Towards the development of a cultural economics[1]

Kenneth E. Boulding

The founding father of economics, Adam Smith, had a strong sense of the cultural matrix of economic phenomena. One of the most interesting of the unasked questions of intellectual history is how the science of economics should have lost this sense and become an abstract discipline void almost of any cultural context. The loss of interest within the economics profession in the cultural matrix of its own discipline is a fairly continuous process, almost from the days of Adam Smith. David Ricardo, perhaps, was one of the first culprits in the process of reducing economics to a culturally free abstraction. By contrast, his great contemporary, T.R. Malthus, had a very strong feeling for the significance of culture, especially as it affected the dynamics of population. Successive editions of his great *Essay on the Principle of Population* elaborated and diversified the cultural theme. Even his much more abstract *Principles of Political Economy* (1836), a work which foreshadowed the work of John Maynard Keynes a hundred years later, was also significant in attributing to the larger cultural matrix of economic life many of the characteristics which would lead towards development or stagnation.

The work of John Stuart Mill, while in many respects it follows the abstract model of Ricardo and is not as rich as Adam Smith in its observations of economic culture, is nevertheless far from being pure abstraction, and gives a strong sense of the importance of the political and social matrix of economic life and institutions. Alfred Marshall's *Principles of Economics*, closer still to pure mechanical abstraction, represents a further movement away from the richness of Adam Smith, but its sequel, *Industry and Trade*, has a strong institutional flavor and indicates that he was well aware of the complex cultural reality that lay beneath the abstractions of demand and supply.

The marginalist school, from its very beginnings in Stanley Jevons, *Principles of Political Economy* and Auguste Walras, *Principes d'Economie Pure*, both in 1870, found the mathematics of the differential calculus and simultaneous equations highly acceptable in the push towards abstraction, and removed economics even further from its cultural matrix. The abstractions become more and more rarified as we move towards the beginnings of econometrics in the 1920s and the 1930s, where economics is reduced to equations and parameters, time series and regressions. Even Ricardo at least talked about real commodities—about corn, wine, and cloth, about employers and laborers. In modern economics, these have become *x*s and *y*s. There is no sense of the corniness of corn or the clothiness of cloth, or of any qualitative richness and variety, even in the world of commodities, and still less in the world of man.

John Maynard Keynes stands a little aside from this movement towards abstraction. He made a very important contribution in the development of abstract models, but even his models had to be straightened out by his followers. His sense of the real world, at least of the speculators and financiers which he knew so well, probably hindered him in the development of pure models, but it gives his works something of the richness of cultural detail that one feels in Adam Smith, even though in a more limited range of culture. Keynes, I suspect, has no real conception of what it was like to be either poor or working class. His own cultural setting was very much that of upper middle class dons in Cambridge.

In the present generation, as far as economic theory is concerned, abstraction has completely conquered the field. One can look in vain, for instance, through issue after issue of the *American Economic Review* to try to find anything which even remotely suggests a cultural context. The computer, if anything, has accentuated this trend. It has enabled economists to put a lot more variables together and to develop more complex models with larger numbers of equations. But it has not, on the whole, encouraged the search for new data. It has increased the quick payoffs from the analysis of old data, and by this very fact, has distracted economists from the crucial first stage of the knowledge process, which is the stage from the real world to the data. One gets a depressing feeling that the typical Ph.D. dissertation these days is done by grabbing a fist full of somebody else's data and putting it through an elaborate statistical analysis on the computer. The culmination of this movement, of course, is the use of imaginary data, which is increasingly popular. This consists of the simulation of more and more complex models, using arbitrary or even randomly generated data. In the Monte Carlo method, indeed, the table of random numbers becomes the principle source of inputs into the system. How far from the real world can one get?

A very interesting and puzzling question of intellectual history is why the American institutionalists, especially the three great names of John R. Commons, Thorstein Veblen, and Wesley Mitchell, and their later descendants, such as Clarence Ayres, failed to affect the mainstream of economic thought in the United States, when a great deal of what they were saying seems to foreshadow the cultural economics for which I am arguing in this paper. The problem is not confined to the United States, for what might be called the "European Institutionalists"—Max Weber, Sidney and Beatrice Webb, and the English Fabians—likewise failed to affect the mainstream of economic thought, although they had a profound effect on social policy and political history. As one reflects also that the New Deal of the 1930s in the United States was largely an accomplishment of the pupils of John R. Commons, the paradox of apparent political success and apparent intellectual failure becomes even more striking. One can point, of course, to certain intellectual deficiencies in institutionalist writers—Commons, for instance, was certainly deficient in literary competence, but this could not be said of Veblen, who perhaps was too competent, so that his work was admired but subconsciously dismissed as being merely aphoristic and entertaining. Mitchell, while he made enormous contributions in developing the empirical basis of subsequent economics at the National Bureau of Research, devoted his life to following a Newtonian will-o'-the-wisp in the business cycle, and never himself developed adequate theoretical models. When all this is said, however, the puzzle still remains and the answer has to lie deep in the sociology of the professions.

When one looks at the particular fields of economics, the situation seems, in places, a little better. The field which is perhaps the closest to an interest in the cultural matrix is labor economics and industrial relations, where the emphasis for a long time has been descriptive and empirical rather than analytical. There is a long tradition in labor economics in the study of the culture of the factory, of the collective bargaining processes, of the trade union organization, and so on. This indeed is perhaps the greatest contribution of the institutional economists in the United States and their counterparts in Europe. Thus, the classic studies of John R. Commons in the American labor movement and Beatrice and Sidney Webb in many aspects of English life, with their rich documentation of cultural backgrounds, are perhaps the classic expression of what might be called "cultural economics." Unfortunately, the almost complete divorce between "analytical economics" and "cultural economics" is reflected in these authors. The theoretical and analytical foundations of their work are not really adequate. Neither John R. Commons nor the Webbs really understood the processes of inflation and deflation, and this failure to appreciate larger analytical models of the economy rendered their work inadequate beyond what might be called the "micro level." At this level, however, the study of what actually goes on in the field and the factory, around the bargaining table and in union meetings, has hardly been bettered since.

Next to labor economics, the field which comes closest to cultural economics is a rather loosely defined area which might almost be called "legal economics," covered by such titles as industrial organization, government regulation of business, and various subfields such as marketing, transportation, and so on, many of which are more apt to be found in schools of business than they are in departments of economics. Such topics as the interaction of regulatory commissions with the activities which they are supposed to regulate, and the interactions of firms with each other and with the antitrust division of the Department of Justice, all reflect at least awareness that economic transactions take place in a legal and cultural setting. Even here, however, the emphasis has been on the legal rather than the cultural, on cases, judicial precedents, and the details and minutiae of the law, rather than on the behavioral component of the problem and the interaction of legal regulations with decisions at different levels and in different organizations.

There is one pioneering attempt by Cyert and March (1963) to develop a behavioral theory of the firm, which was based on some empirical study of an almost complete lack of interest on the part of all the disciplines in the learning process in the behavior of business decision-makers. This study does not seem to have been followed up. It can certainly be regarded as a pioneering work in the cultural economics of the firm, but it does not seem to have produced any descendants.

Agricultural economics has had some tradition of studying the interaction between farmers and the institutions around them, but even this in these days seems largely to have run off in the direction of abstract econometrics, and there does not seem to be the cooperation between the agricultural economists and the rural sociologists which one would hope for.

As we move towards the fields of money and banking and public finance, we find an increasing reliance on rather formalistic mechanical models and an almost complete lack of interest on the part of all the disciplines in the cultural matrix within which the institutions of money and finance operate. I have argued for years that bankers were a savage tribe who should be studied by the anthropologists rather than by the economists, and I once tried to persuade Margaret Mead to do a book on "Coming of Age in the Federal Reserve," with, I regret to say, no response at all! The culture of bankers, indeed, is more mysterious than that of the Dobuans or the Chuk-Chuks. The Navaho indeed may have a Harvard anthropologist in every family, but the Federal Reserve Board has, to my knowledge, never allowed a single one to attend the ceremonials in its marble hogan. Nobody really knows what bankers are like, what kinds of images of the world they have, what they talk about, what kind of gossip they follow, what taboos they have, and how their decisions are made. The economics of money and banking is almost entirely a matter of the analysis of published statistics and the attempt to find correlations among them. It is pure "black box" analysis with practically no attempt to pry off the lid to see what are the actual processes which produce the often very peculiar outputs.

Another area where the expansion of cultural economics might be highly useful is in the relation of the government to the economy. This is an enormous field and different parts of it tend to be cultivated with rather different instruments. Public finance, for instance, the study of government taxation, revenues, and expenditures—is frequently discussed in a rather mechanical way in terms of the impact of taxation and expenditure on the output of various commodities, on employment, on distribution of income, and so on. There is some justification for a mechanical approach here, as a good deal of the impact of public finance is in fact mechanical. The culture of the tax collector may make some difference to the efficiency with which taxes are collected, but this difference is likely to be somewhat peripheral to the major impacts of the tax and expenditure system. The anthropology of the tax collector might be just as interesting as the anthropology of bankers, but it might not be so significant in regard to its total impact on society. Where a cultural approach might be helpful would be in a study of the acceptance or legitimacy of taxation, and the study of tax resistance or tax acceptance. Societies differ widely in this regard. In the United States, for instance, taxes are paid with quite astonishing fidelity, and the system relies to a very large extent on the individual honesty of the taxpayer, though the efficiency of the Internal Revenue Service in unmasking tax evaders unquestionably has some impact. There are other societies, however, in which tax evasion is so widespread and so universal that no system of policing could possibly induce the mass of individuals to pay their legal taxes. This is really a cultural phenomenon, but as far as I know it has been very little studied.

A point at which cultural studies would be of great interest (and are somewhat neglected) is in the political decision-making process by which taxes are in fact passed into law. The actual legal tax system emerges as a result of the interaction of a number of different governmental subcultures, that, for instance, of the Treasury and Civil Service, which brings a technical point of view and a long memory of previous administrative problems to the task of formulating the details of tax administration. There is also, in the United States, the President and the Executive branch, which makes proposals to Congress, and there is Congress itself, which is the ultimate source of fiscal authority. The actual tax system emerges as a result of a long historical process, involving especially the changing culture of Congress, and this in turn reflects the changing culture of its constituencies. The processes of logrolling and political bargaining are fairly familiar. Not so familiar are the processes by which certain ideas become fashionable or unfashionable, and even certain interests become fashionable or unfashionable.

The idea that political decisions are made by the raw conflict of interests involved in the bargaining process is certainly inadequate. Interests, indeed, are often extremely hard to determine. It is extremely hard to estimate, for instance, what would be the effect on the overall distribution of income or wealth of any particular tax proposal. Any decision, even of private persons, will divide the human population into three possible groups—those who are favorably affected by it, those who are adversely affected by it, and those who are unaffected by it. In the case of the small decisions of private and unpowerful people, the third category is overwhelmingly the largest. In the case of decisions by powerful people, the power of the decision-maker could well be measured hypothetically by the size of the first two segments of the population. In most cases, however, these three boxes are empty. It is very hard to tell even how many people fall into one box or the other, and still harder to tell who these people are. It is the perception of interests, not the realities (whatever this may mean), which really affects behavior, and the perception of interest is very much a function of the culture within which the perceiver is embedded. Therefore, the way in which the culture of government changes as mistakes are made and lessons are learned, as information flows in, creating new ideas, new concepts, and new values, is of great importance in the study of the process by which decisions are actually made. A good example of a study of this kind is Herbert Stein's work on *The Fiscal Revolution in America* (1969), which shows how a combination of the failure of existing policies, and the perception of that failure, coupled with ideas about alternative policies coming in largely from the academic profession, transformed what might be called the "conventional wisdom" of American government in the space of a little over 30 years, from Herbert Hoover's tax increase in the middle of the Depression in 1932 to the Kennedy-inspired tax cut in 1964. This book indeed is one of the best examples of "cultural economics" that has been produced in this generation.

Another aspect of government interaction with the economy is regulation of private economic activity by legal prohibitions and government regulating agencies. There is a large amount of this kind of activity, ranging from regulation of labor relations by the National Labor Relations Board and similar agencies in certain specific industries, to regulatory agencies like the Interstate Commerce Commission, the Federal Communications Commission, the Securities and Exchange Commission, on to the rather looser activities of the antitrust divisions of the Department of Justice. Most of these agencies are concerned with the enforcement of prohibitions of various kinds. Thus, the law defines as illegal, certain "unfair labor practices" on the part of both employees and unions. It defines certain collusive practices as illegal under the antitrust laws. By licensing it makes such practices as running a radio station legal for some people and illegal for others. The whole problem of the cultural interaction between the regulating commissions and authorities of different kinds and the regulated is an extremely interesting subject which has not been studied as much as one would wish. Each of the commissions and agencies develops a subculture of its own, which is transmitted to each new generation of role occupants in ways that are not wholly dissimilar from the way in which a doctor transmits his culture to his successors.

It is clear that there is something, which now exists perhaps only in embryo, which deserves the name of "cultural economics." Because it has not yet taken an unambiguous form, it is obviously hard to describe it. Nevertheless, it is at least interesting to speculate what the embryo might look like if it ever lived to grow up. It may, of course, be just a mythical beast, and the fact that several promising starts seem to have come to very little suggests that it may have some genetic deficiencies which interfere with its growth in the harsh milieu of the academic community. Nevertheless, even the sketchiest attempt to describe this mythical beast portrays such a gentle and useful animal that it seems a pity not to try to bring it into the world.

Being economics, it would have to start with the phenomenon of exchange, beginning with the exchange of goods, a "good" being something that somebody wants and which has a positive marginal utility, that is, he wants more of it. There is nothing wrong with the pure economic theory of exchange as an abstract model, and indeed some anthropologists have failed to understand certain aspects of the economics of primitive societies because they have not seen that exchange was a universal phenomenon, which might be overlaid with all sorts of custom, ritual, and conventional behavior, but which nevertheless always involved some kinds of "terms of trade" or exchange ratios, which were relevant to the satisfaction of the participants and to their continued behavior in the role of exchangers. The failure to recognize the significance of the phenomenon of terms of trade is by no means confined to anthropologists. I recall once being on a committee which was considering the question of a university program in industrial relations, with a psychiatrist who was convinced that industrial conflicts could be wholly described in terms of the love life of the foreman or the frustrated sexuality of the workers, and could not be persuaded that wages had anything to do with industrial conflict. The economist, as economist, therefore, has a professional duty to point out the importance of terms of trade and, indeed, the whole structure of terms of trade that comprise the price system. This is an integral part of any set of cultural relations. Furthermore, man's experience with various terms of trade is a great cultural teacher. Even though it is a very fundamental principle of economics that no uncoerced exchange takes place without both parties believing that they benefited at the time, this leaves plenty of room for deception and regret, concepts that have very little place in formal economics. Deception, when it is found out, however, and regret, when the right lessons are drawn from it, are both very important teachers. It can hardly be said too often that we learn new things only from failure, never from success, and we learn a great deal from our failures in exchange. We buy a certain brand, and we don't like it, so we do not buy it again. We take a job, don't like it, and quit.

An enormous learning process goes on within the individual as he encounters the market, makes exchanges, whether in the labor market (where he takes a job) or in the commodity markets (where he buys things) or in capital markets (where he borrows or invests). In any of these experiences, disappointment is likely to lead to some sort of learning. The emphasis on learning is perhaps the crucial difference between mechanistic economics and cultural economics. Mechanistic economics tends to take preferences and even skills and techniques for granted, as the data or ultimate determinants of the economic process. Cultural economics must look upon both preferences, skills, and techniques as essentially learned in the great processes of cultural transmission. It may well be that one of the things which holds us up in cultural economics is the absence of any satisfactory abstract models of learning in the way, for instance, that we have abstract models of decision-making or maximizing behavior. Nevertheless, even though the models may be crude, the phenomenon is fundamental. Social learning, indeed, is the central concept of culture.

Economics has tended to restrict itself to the exchange of goods and to regard other forms of dyadic relationships, such as what I have called the "grant," that is, the one-way transfer of an exchangeable, as something a little outside the main focus of interest of economics (Boulding 1972). Cultural economics, however, would have to include all these dyadic relationships which involve exchangeables or goods, whether they conform to the traditional form of exchange or not. There are, indeed, two major forms of the one-way transfer, each of which is the door to a very large world of social organization and human relationships. One is the *gift*, which is the expression of an integrative relationship, that is, identification of the giver with the welfare of the recipient. The other is *tribute*, that is, a one-way transfer made in response to threat, a threat being a conditional undertaking to produce a negative commodity, or a bad. In its illegitimate form this is the bandit; in its legitimate form, the tax collector. I must confess that I pay my taxes mainly because, if I did not, something unpleasant would happen to me and I reckon the loss entailed by paying the taxes is less than the loss that would be entailed by suffering the sanctions of the law if I did not pay them. The threat system has a vast culture of its own, which we cannot go into here. It impinges significantly on economics, for instance, in the legal sanctions which seem to be necessary to induce people to make provision for public goods. And cultural economics will certainly recognize the complexity of the culture which surrounds the various threat relations.

The dynamics of the integrative system, which produces gifts, likewise has an interesting cultural context. Why, for instance, do we support children within the family, and, in many cultures, old people as well? These patterns of behavior are clearly learned, and arise out of the culture. In the process of the development of culture itself, however, great importance has to be assigned to *reciprocity*. This often looks very much like exchange, but it is actually something rather different. Exchange is conditional. If I give you A, will you give me B? Reciprocity is at least hypothetically unconditional, that is, I give you something out of the sheer goodness of my heart and you give me something out of the sheer goodness of yours. Reciprocity does, of course, tend to slip over into exchange and very frequently is formalized as exchange, in which case it often loses its integrative aspect. The transmission of culture depends a great deal on serial reciprocity, that is, A gives something to B, which creates a sense of obligation on B's part, which he releases by giving something not to A, but to C. We make grants to our children because we received grants from our parents. We make sacrifices for posterity because our ancestors made sacrifices for us. The only answer to the famous question, "What has posterity ever done for me?" indeed, is that our ancestors, ourselves, and our descendants are all part of a larger community of the imagination extending over time and space.

One of the most interesting questions in cultural economics is the extent to which any particular system of economic institutions will survive or fail to survive because of changes in the cultural matrix which the economic institutions produce. A related question is that of changes which spontaneous changes in the cultural institutions may produce in the economic order. We think of the time structure of society as a series of "layers" of somewhat independent systems, involving, for instance, an economic dynamic, a political dynamic, a religious dynamic, an intellectual dynamic, an artistic dynamic, and so on. Each layer has a certain independence and coherence in its own movements, but also interacts strongly at times with other layers. This contrasts with what might be called the "monodynamic" view of society, in which one of the layers, such as, for instance, the economic system, is regarded as dominant with an inherent dynamic of its own, which is not much affected by influences from outside and which, as it were, carries all the other processes of society along with it. The Marxist interpretation of history tends to be "monodynamic" in this sense. My own view is "polydynamic," in the sense that I doubt whether there is any single system which at all times dominates the others, though if there were such a system I would nominate the dynamics of the integrative system of legitimacy and community rather than the dynamics of wealth and power, for without legitimacy neither wealth nor power can be preserved.

Examples of this "polydynamic" approach would be Max Weber's theories of the impact of Protestantism in the transformation of late feudal and early capitalist society, and the views of Schumpeter regarding the instability of late capitalism and its tendency to slip over into socialism because of the inability of exchange institutions to develop an integrative matrix in terms of legitimacy, trust, acceptance, and so on, without which they cannot really function. The trouble with capitalism isn't so much that it doesn't work, as that nobody loves it! It is unloved because it depends so heavily on exchange as its social organizer, and neither merchants nor banks are capable of attracting much affection. It is reciprocity rather than exchange which creates legitimacy and community. Reciprocity, however, itself tends to be unstable and is formalized into exchange. A general theory of the interaction of the dynamic sectors of society, however, has not yet been developed and remains as a task for the future.

Perhaps the most significant attribute of a cultural economics is that it must be evolutionary. Mechanistic economics can be dynamic in the sense that it can produce models of time sequences of variables. Indeed, I would argue that dynamic mechanistic economics, as reflected, for instance, in difference equation theory, has made a small but important contribution to the development of a general social science. Mechanical dynamics, however, has sharp limitations. It depends for its predictive power on the discovery of stable parameters for its difference or differential equations. Unfortunately, in real social systems, these parameters are very rarely stable. Thus, even demography, which is perhaps the most successful of mechanical dynamics systems, has been disastrously unsuccessful in its predictions. National income economics is not much better. We have tried to solve this problem by "Ptolemization," that is, the development of increasing numbers of "epicycles" through the addition of new variables, new parameters, and new equations to our models. Unfortunately, there is not much evidence that this increase in the complexity of models has increased their predictive power, and we may be looking for the famous black cat in the dark room that isn't there. It may be, that is, that there are no stable parameters in social systems. We then have to fall back on evolutionary theory, that is, mutation and selection. There is no doubt that this is a useful, descriptive paradigm of the dynamics of society as well as the dynamics of biological evolution. In social systems the mutations consist of new ideas, new inventions (mechanical, biological, and social), new organizations, especially new species of organizations, new patterns of behavior that can be imitated by others and so on. Selection occurs in the process of total social interaction and learning. Some mutations are eliminated by bankruptcy, by conquest, by death, by the loss of legitimacy, and other selective forces. As a result of this vast melée of selective forces some things survive and some do not.

Social evolution is a good deal more complex than biological evolution. It is harder to define social species, as we do not have the delightful simplicity of biological mating. Automobiles are not produced by other automobiles as horses are produced by other horses, but by other forms of social organization, such as automobile firms. As a result of this complexity, mutation can take place at several levels. We can, for instance, have mutation which will change the rate of mutation itself, and we can have mutations which profoundly affect the selective processes. Thus, social evolution may be more Lamarckian than it is Darwinian, if only in the sense that it is harder to distinguish the genotypes from the phenotypes. There is not the nice, clear distinction between mutation in the genotype and selection in the phenotype that we have in Darwinian evolution. In social evolution, the genetic and the selective processes are much more closely interwoven than they are in biological evolution.

A good illustration of the complexity of these processes is found in the theory and history of invention, which is almost the same thing as social mutation. Inventions are clearly not "random" in the sense that all inventions have equal probability of being discovered at any time. In any particular state of the social system, some new inventions are much more probable than others, if only in the sense that a perceived "hole" in the social system is likely to be filled. In regard to invention the problem of the "levels of mutations" becomes extremely important. Thus, inventions which reduce uncertainty are likely to increase the subsequent rate of invention. We see this in the processes of economic development, where the unwillingness of people to change their ways is often closely related to a quite realistic appraisal of the uncertainties involved in so doing. Reduction of uncertainty, such as took place in American agriculture, following the development of price supports in the 1930s, may easily set in motion a large process of technical improvement and increasing productivity, as indeed in the above case it did.

The success of revolutionary movements often depends on the fact that they create uncertainties in the society which is being challenged, and hence prevent that society from making the changes which would lead to its development. The stagnation and failure of the old society then feeds the fires of revolution. Once the revolution has been accomplished, however, the success of the regime depends a great deal on its capacity to diminish the uncertainties of the society and so permit evolutionary change again.

It is highly significant that the current descendants of the American institutionalists have formed a society which they call The Association for Evolutionary Economics. The institutionalists' main criticism of traditional mechanistic economics was on the grounds that it was not evolutionary. One recalls Veblen's famous article on "Why is Economics Not an Evolutionary Science?" (in Dorfman 1919). The criticism basically is that mechanistic economics assumes that there is an equilibrium price structure, that is, an equilibrium set of all prices and money wages, in terms of trade, which is determined on the one hand by the structure of production functions, that is, what inputs produce what outputs, and on the other by the structure of preference functions, that is, what combinations of commodities are preferred to what. The demonstration, indeed, that corresponding to every set of these determinants there is only one set, or at most only a very limited number of sets, of equilibrium prices is a beautiful piece of logic and is developed at great length and with much affection in all standard textbooks. The critical question, however, is what happens if there is a divergence between the equilibrium price set and the actual price set at which exchanges are currently taking place? Mechanistic economics assumes that under these circumstances pressures will be set up to change the price set towards the equilibrium, though there are still quite serious unsolved problems as to actual machinery of this process, whether it operates, for instance, through excess demands and supplies or through excess profits or losses. The exact conditions under which a determinant solution will be reached are extremely complex and are still not wholly spelled out.

The critical question for evolutionary economics, however, is whether a disequilibrium, that is, a divergence between the actual price set and the equilibrium price set, will work back on the supposed determinants of the equilibrium as well as work on moving the actual price set towards the equilibrium. Thus, if the actual price set is not the same as the equilibrium set, this may have an effect on preferences, according to the famous "sour grapes" principle, for instance, according to which if you can't get something, you decide you don't want it. It may also affect the production functions, in the sense that if there is a commodity in excess demand, resources within the industry will be diverted away from sales towards the improvement of production and productivity; whereas if there is a commodity in excess supply, there is very little incentive to improve productivity and most of the activity will be centered on sales and marketing.

This is, indeed, a special case of a general question in the evolutionary theory which as far as I know has never been satisfactorily answered. Evolution takes place by ecological succession, that is, by irreversible changes in the determinants of the equilibrium of an ecological system. These changes may simply be irreversible physical changes, like the filling up of a pond, or they may be changes in the genetic structure through mutation. The general assumption of ecological theory is very similar to that of orthodox mechanistic economics; that if there is a divergence between the actual structure of populations of different species in an ecosystem and the equilibrium structure, those populations which are "too large" by this criterion will decline, those which are "too small" will increase, and the movements of the populations will be towards equilibrium. The critical question now, of course, is what changes the equilibrium itself, and particularly whether the existence of a disequilibrium has any impact in changing the equilibrium itself. Ecological theory seems to be in much the same state as orthodox mechanistic economics. It may well be, therefore, that the reason why evolutionary economics has been somewhat disappointing (one has to confess, it has not presented up to now a challenge to mechanistic economics which could really unseat it) is that evolutionary theory itself is in a very unsatisfactory state, and that the questions which the evolutionary economists are trying to raise are themselves still unanswered by evolutionary theory in general.

What one looks for, therefore, is a general evolutionary theory which can illuminate not only biological evolution, but cultural evolution, linguistic evolution, economic evolution, religious evolution, class evolution, family evolution, sexual evolution—anything that we would like to mention. The general outlines for such a theory, indeed, are fairly clear. It can be expressed, indeed, in three sentences: (1) The dynamic processes of any existing system will produce strain; (2) once strain increases beyond a certain threshold something will give, that is, there will be change in the parameters in the system; (3) a system gives at its weakest point, that is, what adjusts is the most easily adjustable. Any specific adjustment, however, creates further strain in other parts of the system, so the process starts all over again.

The first part of this theory is perhaps the easiest epistemologically, in the sense that it is fairly easy to detect the ongoing, regular processes of a system, and even to perceive that the strain is being increased. The second process, that of the system giving under the strain, is much harder to predict, much harder to find out about, simply because the weaknesses of the system are frequently only revealed after the event, that is, after the adjustment has been made, and are not necessarily revealed by those ongoing processes of the system which can be easily observed. The difficulty here is that what we are observing is a "threshold" phenomenon. It is often extremely difficult to find out where a threshold is until we have reached it, after which it is frequently too late. When the strain does not reach the threshold, nothing happens and it is extremely hard to observe nothing, although what does not happen is often a great deal more interesting and significant than what does. The inventions that were not made, the wars that did not happen, the revolutions that never took place, the depressions that never materialized, the crises that were avoided—these are the things that will tell us most about the social system and yet these are precisely the things which never get into the history books.

The same problem exists in biological evolution: all we know about are the mutations that were successful, at least successful enough to leave a record. There must have been thousands, perhaps millions, as many times the number of mutations that were immediately unsuccessful, and these leave no record. Consequently, it is quite impossible to estimate even the probability of things turning out the way they actually did, and we tend to have an illusion that the evolutionary record, as we find it on our own planet, had a kind of necessity about it, simply because it existed; whereas, in fact, it may have been the result of a series of extraordinarily improbable accidents. Some astronomers to the contrary, we really have no way of estimating the probability of life in other parts of the universe, simply because we have no way of estimating the probability of its having developed on our own planet. We face very much the same problem in human history. Was it, for instance, just a succession of lucky accidents that turned the dynamics of European society into science, with such incalculable consequences for all the rest of mankind?

The greatest weakness of evolutionary theory is illustrated by the fact that it is quite impossible to detect evolutionary potential at the time when it occurs. In evolution we can be wise only very long after the event. Why did the evolution of the vertebrates, for instance, proceed so much further than that, shall we say, of the octopus, who really seems to have so many advantages? Why should man have emerged out of the anthropoids rather than out of the felines, who again seem to have so many advantages? And who could have predicted at the time the enormous significance in cultural evolution of Moses or Jesus or Mohammed, or even Karl Marx? For all we know, the evolutionary potential of the twenty-fourth century is now being created in an obscure valley in the Andes and nobody will find out about it for at least a hundred years. Are the hippies an evolutionary potential which will create vast changes in life styles and demands for commodities in the next hundred years? Or are they just an unsuccessful mutation, a flash in the pan, which will produce only a little dust on shelves of the libraries, while the Mormons or Jehovah's Witnesses go on to conquer the world? It is not perhaps, therefore, too surprising that so far, at any rate, evolutionary economics has made little theoretical impact, simply because while it has a good deal to propose, it does not really have very much to say. The great English economist Alfred Marshall, who was by no means unaware of these problems, headed his great *Principles of Economics* off with Volume One; Volume Two, alas, which should have been evolutionary economics, was never written, and I think one has to confess, it is still not written, although it is still in prospect.

In a remarkable new book, *The Entropy Law and the Economic Process* (1971), one of the most erudite and imaginative of the modern economists, Nicholas Georgescu-Roegen, has raised the question as to whether the entropy concept cannot be brought in to give economics a dynamic and a sense of direction, indeed a "time's arrow." The idea is very suggestive. Economic processes, like evolutionary processes, again, are anti-entropic in the sense that they use free energy to create structures in the way of commodities and organizations, roles, professions, and so on, of increasing complexity and improbability. Evolution is the segregation of entropy, the building of little islands of low entropy and high order in the form of living organisms, artifacts, and social organizations, at the cost of creating more disorder elsewhere. It is quite tempting, therefore, to try to formulate an "entropy theory of value" in which value is identified in some sense with negentropy or order and the loss of value with the increase in entropy or disorder. This would certainly seem to make more sense than the labor theory of value, which is essentially circular; labor being defined as activity which produces value, without defining what the activity consists of.

Nevertheless, in spite of the monumental and suggestive work of Georgescu-Roegen, it seems to me that the attempt to construct an economics or any social science on the basis of the entropy concept has not so far been successful. There may be a very good reason for this lack of success. The difficulty with the entropy concept is that it is essentially negative, that is, it is a measure of disorder and the significance of the concept depends on the kind of order that is diminishing. In thermodynamics the kind of order which is diminishing is a very simple kind of order and could easily be defined, so that the entropy concept is at least moderately clear, though as Georgescu-Roegen points out, it is by no means clear that we can equate entropy, as Boltzman did, with a probabilistic-mechanistic system.

A good deal of excitement was aroused in the early days of information theory by the fact that the information measure as developed by Shannon and Weaver (1949) was formally identical with the Boltzman measure for entropy, or rather for negentropy, as information is a measure of order rather than disorder. Here again, however, the kind of order which is being measured is a very simple kind of order, very useful for Bell Telephone, for whom the conversations of a teenager and of the President of the United States over the "hot line" represent exactly the same technical problem. The concept, however, has not turned out to be very useful in the study of social communication and significance or even of knowledge. There is no "wit" as a unit of knowledge to correspond to the "bit" as a unit of information, simply because knowledge is a far more complex kind of order than information. While, therefore, we may have a fair amount of confidence that time's arrow in social as well as in biological evolution leads towards order, it is not at all clear what kind of order it leads towards, and the taxonomy of different kinds of order is a task which still remains for the future. The GNP, for instance, is a certain measure of the order of power and complexity of the society, yet this too, as we are extremely well aware these days, is highly imperfect, particularly inefficient as a measure of human welfare, and yet welfare itself involves orders of a complexity which we find extremely difficult even to describe, and still more difficult to measure.

Regretfully, therefore, I think we have to leave the entropy concept behind, as suggestive, but not ultimately very informative, simply because it cannot handle the crucial problem of cultural and economic evolution, which is that of the description and measurement of different kinds of order. To rely on the entropy concept would be rather like trying to find out about the Catholic Church by studying the people who were not Catholics. The absence of order does not really tell us very much about the order that is absent.

Perhaps the greatest achievement of mechanistic economics is the macroeconomic models which come most immediately from the inspiration of Lord Keynes. Economics, however, has had a long history of what might be called a "total systems approach," that is, looking at the economy as a totality of interrelated parts and perceiving that propositions which might be true of parts might not be true of the whole. This is implied, indeed, in Adam Smith, who was the first to develop a concept of a set of "normal," "equilibrium," or in his own term "natural" prices, a concept which was later elaborated by Alfred Marshall and Leon Walrus. In the early years of the twentieth century, Irving Fisher in the United States and Knut Wicksell in Sweden each developed systems which had implied macroeconomic models in them. As often happens in the history of science, however, the great breakthrough came as a result of a double thrust—an improvement in "economic instrumentation" pioneered at the National Bureau of Economic Research in New York by Simon Kuznets (who has just received an extremely well-deserved Nobel Prize), and the theoretical insights of John Maynard Keynes, who perceived with an almost poetic insight, first, that profits were a "widow's cruse," which would never run dry as long as they were distributed in dividends (1930 [1950]), and then the further insight in the General

Theory (1936), that there could be an equilibrium level of unemployment, at the point at which the total product of the society would just be absorbed or disposed of to households and household purchases, to government and government purchases, or to business investment—that is, a willing increase in the total capital stock of goods held by businesses. The perception that the actual quantities of product produced, consumed, invested, and so on were not the result of the decisions of individual households, businesses, or even governments, but were the result of the interaction of the decisions of all the parties to the system, is perhaps one of the most profound insights to come out of economics.

I have sometimes called these principles the "macroeconomic paradoxes." They include, for instance, the proposition that a decision on the part of individuals of a closed economy to increase their money stocks does not result itself in an increase in the stock of money, but results only in a decline in the total volume of receipts and expenditures. This follows from the principle that, whereas for an individual, receipts and expenditures are something quite different, which do not have to be equal to one another, for a closed society, receipts and expenditures are exactly the same thing as each transfer of money is a receipt at one end and an expenditure at the other. Consequently, while an individual can easily increase his money stock by spending less than he receives or decrease it by spending more than he receives, all individuals taken together cannot do this. The money stock can only be increased by increasing it, or decreased by decreasing it. It is unchanged by circulating it. These are very simple and obvious propositions, yet it is surprising how long it took for even economists to perceive them clearly.

Another of the paradoxes is the paradox of saving, that decisions to save on the part of individuals may not result in the net accumulation of capital, but may merely lead to increased unemployment and a decline in output. It is much more true to say that the aggregate decision to invest determines the volume of saving, than to say that decision to save is determined by what is available for investment, for there can be forced saving through inflation, for instance, as well as voluntary saving.

Another set of propositions which, however, are less generally accepted relate to the distribution of national income or some similar measure, as between wages or aggregate labor income and the various components of non-labor income—profits, interest, and rents. The labor market for money wages plays a surprisingly small role in this distribution. A rise in money wages can easily result in a fall in real wages and redistribution towards profits if there is an inflationary trend and prices rise faster than the money wages. This principle very severely limits the power of labor unions to redistribute income. Over the long pull, indeed, this power seems almost non-existent, and it may well be that the main impact of labor unions is to redistribute income within the working class, perhaps a little away from unorganized towards organized labor, but seems to have very little effect on the distribution of income between labor income and non-labor income. In the United States, for instance, between 1932 and 1942, there was a great rise in the power of labor unions, membership increasing four or five times, and a large part of American industry came under collective bargaining. Nevertheless, in this period the proportion of national income going to labor actually fell from about 72 percent to about 62 percent, a result of the economic recovery and the rise in investment and profits. In this area, indeed, "things are seldom what they seem." Skim milk not only masquerades as cream, but cream turns out quite unexpectedly to be nothing but skim milk.

A critical question which is not easily answered is whether there is anything in the larger framework of cultural economics, or the still larger framework of cultural science as a whole, which corresponds to these macroeconomic paradoxes. Are there things which can be said about the system as a whole, for instance, which are fundamentally different from what can be said about an individual or else part of it? Are there general cultural systems in which the sum of individual decisions produces results which are quite contrary to the intentions and expectations of any of the individual decision-makers? It is certainly tempting to look for propositions like this in the larger cultural framework. We can find them certainly in the field of the international system, especially in regard to national defense, where decisions to increase national security by increasing armaments frequently lead to the opposite result. Jay Forrester at M.I.T. has called attention to what he calls "counterintuitive results" in elaborate computer-operated dynamic models of urban development and also of the total world economy (Forrester 1969). The detailed assumptions of these models are very much open to question. One is tempted, indeed, to call them "under-the-counter intuitive assumptions," which are hidden in the mathematics and the procedures of the model, but which determine its results. Nevertheless, the principle is a sound one, that when we make models of total systems the results are very frequently counterintuitive.

A very early example of this in economics which had a wide cultural framework is the economist's attack on the old English Poor Law, beginning particularly with Malthus, on the grounds that if the poor were supported in a way that encouraged their propagation, the result would not be ultimately to relieve poverty, but rather to increase it enormously and to bring the whole society down into ruin. The counterintuitive model of 1834, then, which bore some resemblances to the rather grim models of Professor Forrester, is that if poverty is to be relieved in the long run, it must be relieved very little in the short run, and under conditions which make it both disagreeable to be on relief and also which discourage procreation. Here, again, however, one wonders if the counterintuitive model also did not contain certain errors. If the lot of the destitute could have been made a little more comfortable in nineteenth-century England, it is doubtful there would have been much more propagation, and the system might have reached a bearable equilibrium without driving the destitute into horrible workhouses.

Similar problems emerge in the situation of foreign aid to poor countries. There are circumstances, certainly, under which this could simply lead to a vast proliferation of ultimately catastrophic poverty. The medical advances of the late 1940s, which resulted in the virtual elimination of malaria in a large part of the tropics, had a totally unforeseen effect in population explosions which have made the ultimate development of these countries much more difficult. On the other hand, we have to be careful even here against under-the-counter intuitive systems. It is all too easy to make models which leave out some essential cultural variables. There have been occasions in history when a rapid rise in population has gone along with an even more rapid rise in productivity. There are other occasions, however, such as Ireland in the nineteenth century, where a rise in population has been totally disastrous, in this case, perhaps, because of foreign domination and absentee landlordism. Here I think great vigilance is needed on the part of social scientists to ensure that in the building of these models, the essential variables are not left out. Here, indeed, is perhaps the greatest task of the cultural economics that we hope is somewhere on the way.

I must confess I am not overly optimistic about a quick breakthrough into the sort of cultural economics one would like to see. Nevertheless, there is quite widespread dissatisfaction in the economics profession with the rather barren mechanistic economics and econometrics which now dominates nearly all our journals. It may be that the time is ripe for another of Mr. Kuhn's scientific revolutions (see Kuhn 1962). On the other hand, a good many revolutions have never come off; and a good many others have come off, only to be regretted later. While, therefore, I am prepared to exhibit a certain optimism, I find it hard to avoid restraining the optimism with a modicum of caution.

Note

1 This article was previously published in L. Schneider and C. M. Bonjean, eds., *The Idea of Culture in the Social Sciences*, New York: Cambridge University Press, 1973, pp. 47–64.

References

Boulding, K.E., *The Economy of Love and Fear*, Belmont, Calif.: Wadsworth, 1972.

Cyert, Richard M. and March, J.G., *Behavioral Theory of the Firm*, Englewood Cliffs, NJ: Prentice-Hall, 1963.

Dorfman, Joseph, ed., *The Place of Science in Modern Civilization*, New York: Viking Press, 1919.

Forrester, Jay, *Urban Dynamics*, Cambridge, Mass. and London: M.I.T. Press, 1969.

Georgescu-Roegen, Nicholas, *The Entropy Law and the Economic Process*, Cambridge, Mass.: Harvard University Press, 1971.

Keynes, John Maynard, *Treatise on Money*, New York: Harcourt Brace & Co., 1930; London: MacMillan & Co. Ltd., 1950.

Keynes, John Maynard, *General Theory of Employment, Interest and Money*, New York: Harcourt, Brace & Co., 1936.

Kuhn, S. Thomas, *Structure of Scientific Revolutions*, Chicago: University of Chicago Press, 1962.

Shannon, Claude and Weaver, Warren, *The Mathematical Theory of Communication*, Urbana: University of Illinois Press, 1949.

10a Comment: Culture, mind and context

The revolutionary road of Kenneth E. Boulding

Roberta Patalano

Boulding's article

Boulding's 1973 article on cultural economics opens by pointing at the gradual, though almost complete, elimination of any notion of cultural context from economic models. In his words:

> The loss of interest within the economics profession in the cultural matrix of its own discipline is a fairly continuous process, almost from the days of Adam Smith. David Ricardo, perhaps, was one of the first culprits in the process of reducing economics to a culturally free abstraction [...] The marginalist school [...] removed economics even further from its cultural matrix [...] In the present generation, as far as economic theory is concerned, abstraction has completely conquered the field. One can look in vain, for instance, through issue after issue of the American Economic Review to try to find anything which even remotely suggests a cultural context.
>
> (Boulding 1973, pp. 47–48)

The acknowledgement of a "culturally free" theory is the starting point of a contribution which follows two interconnected lines of reasoning. The first is a comparison of different branches of economic theory, according to their consideration of culture. The second is a reflection on culture and its meaning. The field in which the cultural matrix of economics is afforded more attention is labour economics and industrial relations, mostly because there is a prevalence of descriptive and empirical rather than formal models. Another promising sector is "legal economics", an umbrella under which Boulding includes several different fields of analysis, such as industrial organisation, antitrust regulation and business regulation, that, he argues,

> all reflect awareness that economic transactions take place in a legal and cultural setting [...] Even here, however, the emphasis has been on the legal rather than the cultural, on cases, judicial precedents, and the details and

> minutiae of the law, rather than on the behavioral component of the problem.
>
> (Ibid., p. 49)

As regards the "culture of the factory", a pioneering work in the cultural economics of the firm was Cyert and March (1963), although it appears not to have been developed further since then (Boulding 1973, p. 50).

Even more striking is the absence of any study of the decision processes of bankers. Indeed, we have no idea about their worldviews, the content of their conversations, the taboos to which they conform. Boulding was so persuaded by the need to analyse the anthropological and behavioural dimension of banking, in order to understand the culture which guides financial decisions, that he asked Margaret Mead to work with him on a book on this topic, but without response.[1]

Cultural economics may also produce interesting results in the study of taxation, with special regard to the phenomena of tax resistance and tax acceptance. An understanding of the process through which a citizen interprets a tax as legitimate or illegitimate may help in explaining their decision to pay or to evade. The tax system emerges—Boulding argues—as the result of a historical process which reflects changes in the cultural, political and social matrix of a country. Analogously, if we wish to understand political decisions, we cannot abstract from the evolution of the culture of government over time. The latter crucially depends on lessons that are learned from mistakes and discoveries.

Social learning is a neglected but fundamental concept of cultural dynamics. Indeed,

> the emphasis on learning is perhaps the crucial difference between mechanistic economics and cultural economics. Mechanistic economics tends to take preferences and even skills and techniques for granted, as the data or ultimate determinants of the economic process. Cultural economics must look upon both preferences, skills, and techniques as essentially learned in the great process of cultural transmission.
>
> (Ibid., p. 53)

This transmission can contribute to an explanation of institutional persistence and change, as institutions reflect the cultural matrix that exists at the time of their emergence.

Boulding also focuses on the evolutionary character that cultural economics may take and points at the concepts of mutation and selection as potentially explicative. He recognises that societal evolution is based on complex mechanisms that have yet to be fully understood. An unsolved question of evolutionary theory of particular interest concerns the way out of or back to equilibrium. What changes the equilibrium, and the nature of the relationship between equilibrium and disequilibrium, is yet to be fully explained.

The author's final remark has a methodological flavour, advising economists to avoid the risk of losing sight of the importance of culture in their models:

culture should be considered as an endogenous variable that contributes to economic dynamics through mechanisms that have been understood only partially and deserve further attention.

Cultural economics forty years later

When Boulding wrote his article in 1973, he knew that cultural economics existed only in an embryonic state and had still to free itself from a sort of ambiguity concerning its objects of inquiry. Nevertheless, he thought that it was worth speculating on the possible evolution of the field.

Looking at the literature forty years later, cultural economics seems to have followed a development which diverges from that imagined by Boulding in several important respects. The seminal survey "Where are we now on cultural economics?" by Blaug (2001) helps us clarify the point. Blaug shares the opinion of Towse (1997) about the lack of a single unifying paradigm in cultural economics, and characterises it as a largely empirical rather than theoretical subject. He then focuses on the topics that are most representative for the field and include the formation of taste in the art sector, the demand and supply functions for the arts, the equity/efficiency trade off in the organisation of museums, galleries and heritage sites, the art market and its behavioural anomalies, Baumol's cost disease and public subsidies. Interestingly, Blaug takes the coincidence between cultural economics and the economics of arts for granted and looks with suspicion on any attempt to broaden this perspective. His overture is unambiguously clear on this point:

> Cultural economics or the Economics of the Arts, as it is used to be called, may be said to have been created almost *de novo* thirty years ago by Baumol and Bowen's book, *Performing Arts: The Economic Dilemma* (1966). Since then, one or two writers have sought to widen it to embrace the "economics of culture", turning it from a sub-discipline of economics into a sub-discipline of anthropology (Klamer 1996; Throsby, 1999), but most of the literature remains wedded to the older narrower conception in which cultural economics means the economics of the performing visual and literary arts.
>
> (Blaug 2001, p. 123)

Blaug also seems to foster the coincidence between cultural economics and the analysis of the market for cultural products. Boulding, on the contrary, cast doubt on the capacity of traditional market analysis to take the complexity of cultural context into full consideration.

For Boulding, the increasing attention paid to complex models with a large number of equations has kept economists far from the cultural matrix of their discipline and, more widely, from the "real world" to which models are supposed to apply. "How far from the real world can one get?", Boulding asks (1973, p. 48), and he answers by suggesting an interpretation of culture as adherence to a specific socio-historical context, which is lost if we consider only imagined or randomly generated data. The question thus becomes methodological and relates to the degree of abstraction from reality that economists are willing to accept.

Another illuminating passage on the limits of "abstraction from the context" in economic models concerns political decisions. Let us consider, for example, political decisions that concern the choice to invest or not in a cultural sector. According to Boulding,

> the idea that political decisions are made by the raw conflict of interests involved in the bargaining process is certainly inadequate. [...] It is the perception of interests, not the realities (whatever this may mean), which really affects behavior, and the perception of interest is very much a function of the culture within which the perceiver is embedded. Therefore, the way in which the culture of government changes as mistakes are made and lessons are learned, as information flows in, creating new ideas, new concepts, and new values, is of great importance in the study of the process by which decisions are actually made.
>
> (Ibid., p. 51–52)

Analogously, economists treat exchange as an abstract phenomenon based on marginal utility. Although there is nothing wrong with this approach, it fails to recognise the cultural relations that are embedded in the process of bargaining. In particular,

> even though it is a very fundamental principle of economics that no uncoerced exchange takes place without both parties believing that they benefited at the time, this leaves plenty of room for deception and regret, concepts that have very little place in formal economics.
>
> (Ibid., p. 53)

There are also market relationships which are not mediated by the system of prices. One is the gift that represents a one-way transfer, in which the giver and the recipient share a cultural representation in which the giver has an extra-economic reason to support the welfare of the recipient. An interesting example is represented by the integrative system, that is, a cultural product, for it presupposes a hierarchy of values among the subjects to support others, for example, children and old people.

Boulding also suggests that there are some paradoxes in traditional macroeconomics that might be understood better by an analysis of the cultural context in which they take place. In his vision, they include

> the proposition that a decision on the part of individuals of a closed economy to increase their money stocks does not result itself in an increase in the stock of money, but results only in a decline in the total volume of receipts and expenditures.
>
> (Ibid., p. 62)

and the paradox of saving for which "the decisions to save on the part of individuals may not result in the net accumulation of capital" (Ibid., p. 62). Both these situations trigger a question regarding the relationship between the behaviour of individuals and that of groups.

> Are there things which can be said about the system as a whole, for instance, which are fundamentally different from what can be said about an individual or else part of it? Are there general cultural systems in which the sum of individual decisions produces results which are quite contrary to the intentions and expectations of any of the individual decision-makers?
>
> (Ibid., p. 63)

For Boulding, a traditional market analysis of cultural products cannot answer these questions. This is why he would certainly be more sympathetic to the approach proposed by Throsby (2001), who criticises economists' almost exclusive focus on cultural products. In his words, economists have limited their inquiry to the "commodification of culture" and have left aside important aspects which, however, possess an evident economic dimension. The most striking example is represented by the creativity at the basis of innovation and growth.

The *Handbook of Cultural Economics* edited by Towse (2003) has recently made another step towards the definition of a wider field of inquiry for cultural economics in consonance with Boulding's perspective. The concepts of cultural value (Klamer), cultural sustainability (Throsby) and cultural capital (Throsby) are considered part of the discipline, although they extend beyond the boundaries of the traditional approach and demand an interdisciplinary perspective which takes the sociological, anthropological and ethical dimensions of culture into account. Indeed, the concept of culture crosses multiple fields of knowledge and even in social sciences beyond economics it lacks a unique and sharp definition. An aspect that most definitions appear to share concerns its value-laden nature that orients behaviour and provides guidelines for interpreting reality. The dependence of culture on history is also widely recognised as well as its relationship with knowledge, traditions, symbols and habits.[2]

Once one considers how complex and articulated the concept of culture can be, the equivalence between cultural economics and the market for the visual and performing arts looks restrictive. Moreover, it seems to presuppose a vision of economics as a science in which historical and social dimensions are worth a sacrifice if this can improve analytical tractability. We do not deny that there may be good reasons behind such a methodological choice. Instead, we wish to highlight that this approach is not the only one possible. Moreover, it requires a quite radical departure from some of the historical roots of cultural economics, as Boulding's contributions can show (but see also Hayek 1952, 1979). As far as Boulding is concerned, we argue that a different perspective emerges by enriching his contribution with contemporary developments in cognitive and institutional economics.

Boulding's ideas forty years later

When Boulding wrote his article, Simon (1947, 1956) was refining the concept of bounded rationality and Hayek was about to be awarded the Nobel Prize. The cognitive revolution in social sciences had been settled (Gardner 1985) and times were mature for a cognitive turn in economics also.[3]

If in the period 1950–1980 there were single authors who contributed to the foundation of an innovative and still emergent field, cognitive economics today is a robust and varied research programme which involves thousands of scholars around the world. It aims at explaining and possibly modelling the behaviour of agents through hypotheses which are coherent with psychological findings. In particular it

> proposes an interdisciplinary approach to the study of human problem-solving, choice, decision-making and change, to explain the nature and evolution of organisations and economic institutions, in a context characterised by structural uncertainty. Just like psychology, neurobiology and philosophy, cognitive economics has its micro-foundations in the understanding of human mental activities and it elaborates its models in relation to these disciplines and their advancements.
>
> (Egidi and Rizzello 2003)

For cognitive economists, mind is not an exogenous variable, it has no constant value, and cannot be represented by a set of preferences or by rationality alone. Instead, rationality is only one of the cognitive mechanisms that agents can use in decision-making. Moreover, mind produces representations on which the behaviour of individuals depends (Castelfranchi 2003; Patalano 2005).

Boulding made an important contribution to the cognitive revolution in economics, which has only recently started to be appraised (Patalano 2005, 2010a, 2012; Patalano and Rizzello 2003). In particular, he developed a pioneering analysis of mental images in economic and social settings that highlights the fundamental role of imagination in the market.[4] He describes mental images as a filter through which it is possible to interpret reality. Instead of looking at the world with an empty mind, Boulding argues, we look at it from the perspective of our imagination, that is to say, from the point of view that has sedimented in our mind as a result of experience and learning.[5] From this perspective, knowledge may be compared to an "organic structure" that grows by digesting and organising stimuli from the environment. It differs from information because, while the latter can be identified with objective data, knowledge has a subjective nature, as it springs from the personal interpretation that is built up on the basis of available information. Pieces of information acquire meanings by means of an evaluation process regulated by individual images.

Although not explicitly, Boulding seems to keep this perspective very much in mind while writing on cultural economics. Many times in his 1973 article, he stresses the scant attention paid to the behavioural components of problems and the cultural background in which they settle. He points at our lack of comprehension of the organisational behaviour and mental images that orient bankers' choices. He laments the absence of consideration for learning and the mental mechanisms that allow for the legitimation of social norms.

Has anything changed in the literature since Boulding's article in 1973? In order to answer this question, we will focus on four aspects that Boulding considered as critical and underdeveloped: the behavioural components of economic phenomena, the cultural matrix of institutions, the mechanisms of learning and the process of societal evolution. As we will see, important changes have taken place that modify the picture in which cultural economics may be set.

As far as behaviour is concerned, Boulding defines the book by Cyert and Simon as a "pioneering work in the cultural economics of the firm that does not seem to have produced any descendants" (1973, p. 50); a few lines above, he describes the book as "a pioneering attempt to develop a behavioural theory of the firm" (Ibid., pp. 49–50). This is one example among many which demonstrates Boulding's view of behaviour as a component of culture. In fact, economists' burgeoning interest in the behavioural foundations of their models may be seen in a huge number of articles (especially in the last two decades). The evolution of behavioural economics seems to follow two intersecting paths: a theoretical approach in which psychological, cultural, institutional and social aspects of economic choices are considered, and an experimental approach in which some theoretical hypotheses are tested empirically. The book by Cyert and March was a mixture of these methods.

Seen through a contemporary lens, many aspects that Boulding placed in the realm of cultural economics have been developed in the behavioural field. This is the case of financial economics. Boulding observed that we have no idea of bankers' worldviews, of their taboos or their way of thinking. If some of these aspects remain a mystery, much has been done to clarify the cognitive processes that financial actors follow as well as the cognitive traps into which they fall. Behavioural finance focuses on the biases that characterise their behaviour in order to explain the anomalies which a traditional model of rational choice cannot justify (Barberis and Thaler 2003). Notwithstanding the important conclusions that have been reached so far, behavioural literature has focused mainly on individual investors, giving only partial consideration to bankers. Interesting contributions have recently addressed the role of information asymmetries and ethical concern in bankers' behaviour (Dowd 1996; Dow 2012).

A parallel interesting evolution has occurred in the legal sector. Boulding appraised the consideration of the cultural-institutional background in legal economics but lamented an excess of attention paid to the minutiae of the law. Recent developments in behavioural law and economics have overcome this problem and leave space for the consideration of the cognitive and social background which sustains or limits the reception and legitimation of laws (North 1994, 2005; Jolls *et al.* 1998; Patalano 2007a, 2010b). Among the many results that have been questioned by behavioural findings, the Coase theorem and Becker's model of criminality represent significant examples (Ulen 2006). As is well known, the Coase theorem holds that when transaction costs are zero or very low, an efficient allocation of resources will result, independently of other factors. Public intervention is thus needed to achieve an efficient allocation of legal entitlements only when transaction costs limit or impede bargaining. Although there is experimental evidence which supports this result, recent developments in behavioural economics have cast doubts on its validity. In particular, the "endowment effect", in which people place greater value on things they already possess, including entitlements, than they place on the same things when they must be purchased, has opened a different scenario. In fact, due to that effect, entitlements may remain where they are without being exchanged as easily as traditional theory presupposes.

Behavioural economics has also revealed that individuals make systematic mistakes in decision-making, impeding fulfilment of crucial predictions of traditional rational choice theory. Interesting implications concern Becker's (1968) model for which the decision to commit a crime is taken or avoided by following rational calculation, that is, by comparing expected costs and benefits of the crime. An immediate policy implication of this model is that crime could be deterred by raising the probabilities of detection and arrest. However, as criminals suffer from the same cognitive limitations as other human beings and so do political actors, the capacity of both parties to calculate and alter the costs and benefits of crime must not be taken for granted.

An emerging branch of behavioural law and economics considers the biases that affect individuals who interpret contracts and norms and aims at defining a possible way out of them (*de-biasing through the law*; Jolls and Sunstein 2006). The interesting topic of tax resistance may find a natural collocation in this emerging field. In line with Boulding's suggestions, different disciplines have already contributed to deepen our understanding of taxpayers' behaviour. For instance, sociologists have studied the role of variables such as social influences, attitudes, culture, gender and race (Cullis and Lewis 1997); psychologists have founded a field termed "fiscal psychology" (Schmölders 1959; Lewis 1982) to investigate the psychological factors that influence tax perception and acceptance. Together with values, attitudes and culture, equity and social justice that can be achieved through the tax system appear to have significant influence (Braithwaite 2003). Behavioural economics has also started offering important contributions for understanding taxpayer behaviour (James and Nobes 2003; James 2006) with particular regard to tax compliance. The role of perceived equity and fairness (Bordignon 1993) as well as that of cultural influence (Coleman and Freeman 1997) have been examined, and attempts to design policies that consider these aspects have been developed (Pommerehne *et al.* 1994; Falkinger and Walther 1991). The background of these studies is a definite way out of the traditional economic framework in which individuals are independent, selfish utility maximisers who treat taxation as they would any other transaction. Whereas in this framework, compliance or evasion are the results of an amoral cost–benefit analysis (Bernasconi 1998), behavioural analysis focuses on the mental, cultural and social dimensions that interact with rationality in determining behaviour towards taxes.

Regarding the relationship between culture and institutions, by suggesting that "one of the most interesting questions in cultural economics is the extent to which any particular system of economic institutions will survive or fail to survive because of changes in the cultural matrix which the economic institutions produce" (1973, p. 55), Boulding anticipates the core idea of North's approach by almost twenty years (Denzau and North 1994; North 1994, 2005). Mantzavinos *et al.* (2004) have recently named *cognitive institutionalism* the stream of research which originated in the work of the Nobel laureate Douglass North.[6] In this field of institutions are related to the mind because they embody the beliefs about society that individuals develop through the recurrent application of their mental schemes and structures. Moreover, both these beliefs and the mental models from which they emerge cannot be understood in isolation from the socio-cultural context in which they are developed. The reason is that culture and history are fundamental dimensions of cognition itself. An articulated relationship, connecting culture to institutions, runs through the mind of individuals.

Both Boulding and North emphasise the importance of learning. For North, learning is the mechanism through which the construction of common interpretative structures is expressed among subjects with the same social background. In his words,

> learning entails developing a structure by which to interpret the various signals received by the senses. The initial architecture of the structure is genetic, but the subsequent scaffolding is a result of the experiences of the individual—experiences coming from the physical environment and from the socio-cultural linguistic environment.
>
> (1994, p. 362)

In his Hayekian perspective, North considers culture as a factor that affects learning and favours social cohesion through the development of a common interpretation of reality. Beliefs about society become shared—at least partially—by way of repeated and prolonged interaction and constitute the basis for the shared identification of problems that institutions should try to solve. In particular,

> the process of learning is unique to each individual but a common institutional/educational structure will result in shared beliefs and perceptions. A common cultural heritage, therefore, provides a means of reducing the divergent mental models that people in a society possess.
>
> (2005, p. 27)

Learning transforms mental models through experience and mental models are transformed by learning when discrepancies between expectations about policies and results are perceived.[7]

Learning, Boulding claims, is the cornerstone of the distinction between mechanistic and cultural economics. In particular, the latter must consider preferences and skills as endogenous variables that evolve over time under the pressure of learning and its cultural transmission (1973, p. 53). Although in his 1973 article Boulding does not explore the dynamic of learning in depth, in *The Image* (1956) learning represents the key element on which the evolution of mental representation rests. More importantly, the process of learning also regards preferences and skills that must be considered as a product of experience and cultural acquisition:

> An enormous learning process goes on within the individual as he encounters the market, makes exchanges, either in the labor market (where he takes a job) or in the commodity markets (where he buys things) or in capital markets (where he borrows or invests). In any of these experiences, disappointment is likely to lead to some sort of learning.
>
> (1973, p. 53)

The attention that Boulding pays to learning is symptomatic of his general interest in the process of economic change and its still unclear mechanisms. As far as cultural economics is concerned, change should be regarded as an evolutionary process due to the roles of mutation and selection in the generation of new cultural products. In particular, for Boulding mutations are likely to produce inventions, new forms of organisations, new patterns of behaviour, while selection can reinforce or weaken emergent ideas. He also recognises that societal evolution is more complex and differs from biological evolution in important respects, being more Lamarckian than it is Darwinian.[8] The extension of Darwin's theory to culture has been developed further in recent decades and is based on the possibility of identifying a substrate that even if not genetic can replicate and be transmitted to descendants, also preserving a plurality of results for this transmission process (Hodgson 2003, 2007). Although fostering such developments, Boulding seems to be aware that they also give rise to significant problems due to the crucial differences that characterise evolution in biological and social settings, in particular when the process of change is considered.[9] As he explains, in cultural contexts, change lacks the random character that it acquires in biology and its peculiarities must be considered. Although there have been attempts to understand the process of economic change in greater depth, especially in the institutional field (North 2005; Patalano 2010b, 2011), a general theory of change has not yet been developed by the literature.

Boulding's suggestions for the future

One might reasonably ask what remains of Boulding's project for cultural economics if its core ideas have been largely developed in other fields of economic theory. We argue that it is exactly thanks to the growing consolidation of the behavioural and institutional research programme that the evolution which Boulding predicted for cultural economics is now ripe for concrete development.

The time seems right to extend the field of cultural economics and to promote a fruitful integration with other emergent branches of inquiry. Concepts that influence economic performance but are not yet well understood, such as creativity and change, might find their natural ground for analysis in such conceptual territory.

In order to show how cultural economics may benefit from the "instruments" developed by economists in other sectors of their discipline, we will focus on the relationship between culture, mind and history.

Throsby (2001) suggests two different meanings for culture. The first includes attitudes, beliefs, customs, values and habits that are shared by a social group and that define its identity, thus making it different from other groups. The second identifies culture with activities that exhibit three main characteristics: the involvement of creativity, the generation of a symbolic meaning and of some form of intellectual property. Both these definitions pay attention to the mental and the social dimensions of the cultural texture. Although they go far beyond the "cultural commodification" that economists have embraced in recent decades, they are not without roots in the history of economic thought. As is evident in his 1973 article, for Boulding, the abstraction of economic models from their cultural context is not a necessity but a critical tendency that emerged from one point on in the history of economic thought and towards which he manifests disappointment. A different perspective characterises the Austrian tradition and in particular Hayek's thought.

For Hayek, mind and culture co-evolve simultaneously and inextricably (1952, 1979). The evolution of society begins with life in small primitive groups in which individuals act on the basis of instincts that are genetically inherited. Gradually, innate responses to stimuli are replaced by rules and habits that are learned and shared by the group. It is the gradual suppression of instinct and its substitution with learned responses that give rise to cultural evolution. Among these responses, moral principles are of primary importance (Gick and Gick 2001). Within groups, learning takes the form of imitation and corresponds to a durable change in the mental structures through which individuals interpret external stimuli: new connections among neurons may emerge while non-active ones weaken and fade. Over time, the rules that are shared within a social group become part of the societal tradition and are transmitted from one generation to the other through socialisation.

In such a dynamic perspective, the evolution of culture seems to be strongly intertwined with the evolution of its psychological substrates. As also highlighted by Boulding, a key role in cultural growth is played by learning that modifies the patterns of interpreting and evaluating perceptual stimuli and pieces of information that individuals receive from the environment. By changing the cognitive structures that are involved in information processing, learning transforms the knowledge that is built up by individuals and, thus, it can lead to a modification of their behaviour. Learning is both stimulated and constrained by the cultural context in which it unfolds, for it takes place within the visions of the world that have already sedimented in society. It also has a relevant social resonance as individuals in the same context learn from each other through imitation and reinforce common patterns of interpretation and evaluation of reality (Bandura 1977). A similar approach was developed in *The Image* (1956). On the one hand, learning represents the key mechanism which allows for the evolution of mental representations that organise behaviour. On the other, the relationship between individual images and society is bi-directional and involves reciprocal influence: in fact, the persistence of given cognitive and cultural frameworks in individuals supports the emergence of a societal structure and the latter strengthens or weakens the mental images on which it rests.

In a dynamic perspective, learning represents the main endogenous process that allows for cultural evolution, which consists of the intergenerational transmission and transformation of knowledge, attitudes, values and institutions that have survived over time (Hayek 1979). Due to this process of cumulative development, culture embodies the "distilled experience of the past" (North 2005, p. 72) and transmits it through time.

From an interrelated point of view, David (1985, 1994) suggests that cultural products, including institutions, exhibit a path-dependent dynamic.[10] In particular, conventions, norms and habits that are part of the cultural context can be interpreted as an important "carrier of history" whose growth over time is self-enforcing. In fact, by giving shape to institutions and social relationships, they also shape the cognitive patterns which support their existence (Coriat and Dosi 1998; North 1994, 2005; Patalano 2007a, 2010b).

If seen through a contemporary lens, path dependence represents a sophisticated conceptual instrument through which the relationship between economic behaviour and culture can be analysed. Behaviour that agents exhibit is the result of their experience in time and of the cultural background through which they approach choice: this background affects their way of interpreting problems, framing information and finding solutions. More importantly, economic agents are not condemned to merely repeat their own or their predecessors' past choices. They can alter the course of history by enriching and transforming the cultural and psychological basis on which behaviour depends. As cultural evolution allows for the emergence of novelty, innovation and growth cannot be fully explained without a careful consideration of the cultural development that they require.

Path dependence also helps to distinguish the growth of culture from that of biological organisms. Culture is a social product and thus does not evolve randomly. There can be exogenous, unexpected shocks that occasionally modify its trajectory but, for the most part, it develops in time through a dynamic which depends on the behaviour of social actors, whether conscious or not, in response to internal and/or environmental pressures.

In path-dependent contexts, history represents the experiential base that learning transforms. It sets the bounds within which change can realise when novelty emerges and emancipation from established traditions and ways of seeing are possible. Due to the possibility of changing, at least partially, the road set by history, creativity that fosters innovation represents a cornerstone of societal evolution without which blind dependence on the past would result. *The Image* (Boulding 1956) represents a pioneering attempt to understand how creativity works in the social context and, in particular, how imagination unfolds. Recent contributions have aimed at deepening our comprehension of the emergence of novelty in economic settings (Witt 2009; Patalano 2010a, 2010b; March 2000) but research on this topic still seems to be in its infancy and deserves further development.

Concluding remarks

Boulding argues that, since the time of Adam Smith, economists have showed a progressive lack of interest towards the cultural context in which economic phenomena are embedded. He reviews the scattered attempts that have been made to contrast this tendency and suggests the areas of research that would be most promising for the emergent and still embryonic field of cultural economics.

For Boulding, there exists a fundamental link between culture and behaviour, as the latter is informed by the values and ways of seeing that are ingrained in the cultural matrix of a society and that materialise in customs, traditions and habits. Moreover, behaviour evolves through learning and learning, in its social dimension, "is the central concept of culture" (1973, p. 53). One of the most interesting questions for cultural economics concerns the influence that culture has on the emergence and the survival of economic institutions. In fact, cultural and economic evolutions are twin processes that shape each other and whose mechanisms and reciprocal influences have not yet been fully understood. Based on these considerations, Boulding tries to imagine the form cultural economics might take, and develops an interdisciplinary picture where the behavioural and institutional components of culture find a natural and recognisable place.

Although the cognitive turn in economics had already started, in 1973 economic theory was not mature enough to develop Boulding's suggestions. In contrast to his expectations, cultural economics emerged as an autonomous field of research on the blueprint of the standard microeconomic approach and has produced interesting results in recent decades. In this paper we have argued that recent achievements of behavioural and institutional economics may integrate these results, along the conceptual path that Boulding suggested forty years ago. The cornerstone of this shift of perspective is a broader definition of culture whose social, institutional and cognitive dimensions might be considered and appraised as endogenous components of economic models.

Notes

1

> I have argued for years that bankers were a savage tribe who should be studied by the anthropologists rather than by economists, and I once tried to persuade Margaret Mead to do a book on "Coming of Age in the Federal Reserve", with, I regret to say, no response at all!

(Ibid., p. 50)

2 "Culture … is that complex whole which includes knowledge, belief, art, law, morals, custom, and any other capabilities and habits acquired by man as a member of society" (Edward Tylor 1871, p. 1); "Culture means the whole complex of traditional behaviour which has been developed by the human race and is successively learned by each generation" (Margaret Mead 1937, p. 17);

> Culture consists of patterns, explicit and implicit, of and for behaviour acquired and transmitted by symbols, constituting the distinctive achievement of human groups, including their embodiment in artefacts; the essential core of culture consists of traditional (i.e. historically derived and selected) ideas and especially their attached values
>
> (Kroeber and Kluckhohn 1952, p. 357)

3 As far as economics is concerned, since the 1950s, experimental results had already been questioning the validity of the standard model of rational action (Egidi and Rizzello 2003). Moreover, interest in the mind was not a novelty for economics, as pioneering contributions in the history of thought show (Rizzello 1999).

4 In *The Image. Knowledge in Life and Society* (1956), Boulding discusses the roles of mental images in different fields of knowledge, including biology, economics, political philosophy, organisational theory, history and sociology. He interprets mental images as mental representations that guide behaviour: the latter changes if and only if the images on which it is based modify. Mental images are not neutral nor affect free: they represent subjective ways of seeing and feeling reality, contain emotions as well as beliefs. They evolve under the pressure of learning but also have intrinsic mechanisms of resistance to change that limit their evolution.

5 Boulding's approach has many interesting similarities—and some remarkable differences—with Hayek's perspective on the psychology of perception (1952). For both authors the cognitive structures of economic agents allow them to find the world significant and meaningful: in Boulding (1956) mental images are the interpretative key; in Hayek (1952) it is perception which allows for a personal reading of information that is interpreted and transformed into knowledge. See Patalano (2012) for a discussion.

6

> There is an intimate relationship between belief systems and the institutional framework. Belief systems embody the internal representation of the human landscape. Institutions are the structure that humans impose on that landscape in order to produce the desired outcome. Belief systems therefore are the internal representation and institutions the external manifestation of that representation.
>
> (North 2005, p. 49)

7 In order to isolate the key building blocks of cognitive institutionalism, Mantzavinos *et al.* (2004) have proposed the following scheme: "reality" > beliefs > institutions > specific policies > outcomes (and, thus, altered "reality").

> Reality is perceived and classified by individuals on behalf of mental models, thus giving rise to beliefs that become shared—at least partially—by way of repeated and prolonged interaction. When problems that need to be addressed are defined among the members of a society, institutions emerge as shared solutions to these problems and plan the policies that have to be performed. An important feedback mechanism which runs through the mind re-connects the results of policies to reality. Should the outcomes that are produced on the basis of existing mental models prompt a modification of such models—because they have led to unexpected results (positive or negative) or they have failed to reach programmed

targets—learning intervenes and may generate a revision (whose immediate effect will be a change in the perception of reality). In order to understand institutional evolution, it is therefore necessary to explore how perception and beliefs evolve and are socialized.

(Patalano 2010b, pp. 273–274)

8 Ten years after Boulding's article, Dawkins (1983) introduced the term "Universal Darwinism", which aimed at applying Darwinian concepts through the evolution of culture, a possibility that Darwin had also suggested with regard to language and customs (1859). As a leading voice of evolutionary economics, in the 1980s, Winter claimed that:

> Natural selection and evolution should not be viewed as concepts developed for the specific purposes of biology and possibly appropriable for the specific purposes of economics, but rather as elements of the framework of a new conceptual structure that biology, economics and other social sciences can comfortably share.
>
> (1987, p. 617)

9 Pioneering remarks on these differences are due to Penrose (1952), who argued that while in biology mutations are the product of chance and are not predictable, in humans they depend on will, awareness and thought. In other words, at least some mutations in the social context must be considered as intentional (Penrose 1952; Nelson and Winter 1982; Dosi and Nelson 1994; Rizzello 1999; Patalano 2007b). More recently it has been pointed out that, while biological mutations are exogenous and depend on unexpected shocks, in economics innovations are also generated without shocks during path-dependent dynamics (Rizzello 2004; Patalano 2007b, 2011). A further critical concept is heredity (Hodgson 2003). In the natural context, transmitted characters are an exact reproduction of the original; in a cultural setting heredity takes the form of cultural transmission; it is only partial and requires a mechanism of emancipation from its original content.

10 Path dependence requires the existence of a stochastic process that develops through time and can reach multiple equilibria. The realisation of one specific equilibrium depends on initial conditions and on the whole history of the process. In particular, small random events occurring in its dynamic maintain a permanent influence and render the evolution of the process not predictable ex-ante. Although path dependence has been initially used to interpret technological and institutional evolution, recently its cognitive dimension has been recognised (Patalano 2007b; Rizzello 2004). Knowledge that includes mental models and affective dispositions grows over time through a process that involves both dependence from the past, that is, from the pre-existing knowledge that has sedimented in society, and evolves in novel and unpredictable directions. Pioneering intuitions on this aspect are due to Hayek (1952). In *The Sensory Order*, he explains that the ability of the brain to adapt to the external environment depends on the presence of neural connections which have existed since the individual's birth but also continuously change throughout their life in response to experiences. Changes are mainly due to learning and involve the recombination of synaptic connections. Thus, in the case of the brain, the past perceptual experience that is embedded in a certain neural structure influences the present one but does not preclude the emergence of new configurations (Paller 2001; Patalano 2007b, 2010a, 2010b; Rizzello 2004).

References

Bandura, A. (1977) *Social Learning Theory*, Englewood Cliffs: Prentice Hall.

Barberis, N. and Thaler, R. (2003) "A survey of behavioral finance", in G.M. Constantinides,

M. Harris and R.M. Stulz (eds.), *Handbook of the Economics of Finance*, London: Elsevier, 1, 18: 1053–1128.

Baumol, W.J. and Bowen W.G. (1966) *Performing Arts: The Economic Dilemma*, New York: The Twentieth Century Fund.

Becker, Gary S. (1968) "Crime and punishment: An economic approach", *Journal of Political Economy*, 76: 169–217.

Bernasconi, M. (1998) "Tax evasion and orders of risk aversion", *Journal of Public Economics*, 67: 123–134.

Blaug, M. (2001) "Where are we now on cultural economics?", *Journal of Economic Surveys*, 15, 2: 123–143.

Bordignon, M. (1993) "A fairness approach to income tax evasion", *Journal of Public Economics*, 52: 345–362.

Boulding, K.E. (1956) *The Image. Knowledge in Life and Society*, Ann Arbor: The University of Michigan Press.

Boulding, K.E. (1973) "Toward the development of a cultural economics", in L. Schneider and C. Bonjean (eds.), *The Idea of Culture in the Social Sciences*, Cambridge: Cambridge University Press, 47–64.

Braithwaite, V. (2003) *Taxing Democracy: Understanding Tax Avoidance and Evasion*, Aldershot, UK: Ashgate.

Castelfranchi, C. (2003) "For a 'cognitive program': Explicit mental representations for Homo oeconomicus (the case of trust)", in M. Basili, N. Dimitri and I. Gilboa (eds.), *Cognitive Processes and Economic Behaviour*, London: Routledge, 168–208.

Coleman, C. and Freeman, L. (1997) "Cultural foundations of taxpayer attitudes to voluntary compliance", *Australian Tax Forum*, 13: 311–336.

Coriat, B. and Dosi, G. (1998) "Learning how to govern and learning how to solve problems. On the double nature of routines as problem solving and governance devices", in A.D. Chandler, Ö. Sölvell and P. Hagström (eds.), *The Dynamic Firm. The Role of Technology, Strategy, Organization and Regions*, Oxford: Oxford University Press, 103–133.

Cullis, J.G. and Lewis, A. (1997) "Why people pay taxes: From a conventional economic model to a model of social convention", *Journal of Economic Psychology*, 18: 305–321.

Cyert, R.M. and March, J.G. (1963) *Behavioral Theory of the Firm*, Englewood Cliffs: Prentice-Hall.

Darwin, C. (1859) *On the Origin of Species by Means of Natural Selection*, London: Murray.

David, P. (1985) "Clio and the economics of QWERTY", *American Economic Review*, 75, 2: 332–337.

David, P. (1994) "Why are institutions the 'carriers of history'? Path-dependence and the evolution of conventions, organizations and institutions", *Structural Change and Economic Dynamics*, 5, 2: 205–220.

Dawkins, R. (1983) "Universal Darwinism", in D.S. Bendall (ed.), *Evolution from Molecules to Man*, Cambridge: Cambridge University Press, 403–425.

Denzau, A. and North, D. (1994) "Shared mental models: Ideologies and institutions", *Kyklos*, 47: 3–31.

Dosi, G. and Nelson, R. (1994) "An introduction to evolutionary theories in economics", *Journal of Evolutionary Economics*, 4, 3: 153–172.

Dow, S.C. (2012) "Economics and moral sentiments: The case of moral hazard", in V. Neves and J. Castro Caldas (eds.), *Facts, Values and Objectivity*, London: Routledge, 17–32.

Dowd, K. (1996) "The case for financial laissez-faire", *The Economic Journal*, 106, 436: 679–687.

Egidi, M. and Rizzello, S. (2003) "Cognitive economics: Foundations and historical evolution", in M. Egidi and S. Rizzello (eds.), *Cognitive Economics*, two volumes for the series The International Library of Critical Writings in Economics, Cheltenham: Edward Elgar.

Falkinger, J. and Walther, W. (1991) "Rewards versus penalties: On a new policy against tax evasion", *Public Finance Quarterly*, 19: 67–69.

Gardner, H. (1985) *The Mind's New Science: A History of the Cognitive Revolution*, New York: Basic Books.

Gick, E. and Gick, W. (2001) "F.A. Hayek's theory of mind and theory of cultural evolution revisited: Toward an integrated perspective", *Mind & Society*, 3, 2: 149–162.

Hayek, F.A. (1952) *The Sensory Order. An Inquiry into the Foundations of Theoretical Psychology*, London: Routledge & Kegan Paul.

Hayek, F.A. (1979) *Law, Legislation and Liberty*, vol. 3, Chicago: University of Chicago Press.

Hodgson, G.M. (2003) "The mystery of the routine: The Darwinian destiny of an evolutionary theory of economic change", *Revue Economique*, 54, 2: 355–384.

Hodgson, G.M. (2007) "Institutions and individuals: Interaction and evolution", *Organization Studies*, 28, 1: 95–116.

James, S. (2006) "Taxation and the contribution of behavioral economics", in M. Altman (ed.), *Handbook of Contemporary Behavioral Economics. Foundations and Developments*, New York: M.E. Sharpe, Inc.

James, S. and Nobes, C. (2003) *The Economics of Taxation: Principles, Policies and Practice*, 7th ed., Harlow: Prentice Hall.

Jolls, C. and Sunstein, C.R. (2006) "Debiasing through law", *Journal of Legal Studies*, 35: 199–241.

Jolls, C., Sunstein, C.R. and Thaler, R. (1998) "A behavioral approach to law and economics", *Stanford Law Review*, 50: 1471–1550.

Klamer, A. (ed.) (1996) *The Value of Culture. On the Relationship Between Economics and the Arts*, Amsterdam: Amsterdam University Press.

Kroeber, A. and Kluckhohn, C. (1952) *Culture. A Critical Review of Concepts and Definitions*, New York: Vintage Books.

Lewis, A. (1982) *The Psychology of Taxation*, Oxford: Blackwell.

Mantzavinos, C., North, D.C. and Shariq, S. (2004) "Learning, institutions, and economic performance", *Perspectives on Politics*, 2, 1: 75–84.

March, J.G. (2000) *Dynamics of Rules: Change in Written Organizational Codes*, Stanford: Stanford University Press.

Mead, M. (ed.) (1937) *Cooperation and Competition Among Primitive Peoples*, New York: McGraw-Hill.

Nelson, R. and Winter, S.G. (1982) *An Evolutionary Theory of Economic Change*, Cambridge, MA: Harvard University Press.

North, D.C. (1994) "Economic performance through time", Nobel Prize lecture, *The American Economic Review*, 84, 3: 359–368.

North, D.C. (2005) *Understanding the Process of Economic Change*, Princeton and Oxford: Princeton University Press.

Paller, K.A. (2001) "Neurocognitive foundations of human memory", in D.L. Medin (ed.), *The Psychology of Learning and Motivation*, 40, New York: Academic Press, 121–145.

Patalano, R. (2005) *La mente economica. Immagini e comportamenti di mercato*, Roma-Bari: Laterza.

Patalano, R. (2007a) "Imagination and society. The affective side of institutions", *Constitutional Political Economy*, 18, 4: 223–241.

Patalano, R. (2007b) "Mind-dependence. The past in the grip of the present", *Journal of Bioeconomics*, 9, 2: 85–107.

Patalano, R. (2010a) "Imagination and economics at the crossroad. Materials for a dialogue", *History of Economic Ideas*, XVIII, 1: 167–189.

Patalano, R. (2010b) "Understanding economic change. The impact of emotion", *Constitutional Political Economy*, 21: 270–287.

Patalano, R. (2011) "Resistance to change: Historical excursus and contemporary interpretations", *Review of Political Economy*, 23, 2: 249–266.

Patalano, R. (2012) "Imagination and perception as gateways to knowledge: The unexplored affinity between Boulding and Hayek", in R. Arena, A. Festré and N. Lazaric (eds.), *Handbook of Knowledge and Economics*, Cheltenham: Edward Elgar, 121–143.

Patalano, R. and Rizzello, S. (2003) "Il concetto di *image* nel pensiero di Kenneth Boulding e le implicazioni per la teoria economica contemporanea", *Storia del Pensiero Economico*, 1, 45: 3–32.

Penrose, E.T. (1952) "Biological analogies in the theory of the firm", *American Economic Review*, 42, 5: 804–819.

Pommerehne, W.W., Hart, A. and Frey, B. (1994) "Tax moral, tax evasion and the choice of policy instruments in different political systems", *Public Finance*, 49 (supp.): 52–69.

Rizzello, S. (1999) *The Economics of the Mind*, Cheltenham (UK) and Northampton (MA): Edward Elgar.

Rizzello, S. (2004) "Knowledge as a path-dependence process", *Journal of Bioeconomics*, 6: 255–274.

Schmölders, G. (1959) "Fiscal psychology: A new branch of public finance", *National Tax Journal*, 15: 184–193.

Simon, H.A. (1947) *Administrative Behaviour*, New York: Macmillan.

Simon, H.A. (1956) "Rational choice and the structure of the environment", *Psychological Review*, 63, 2: 129–138.

Throsby, D. (1999) "Cultural capital", *Journal of Cultural Economics*, 23: 3–12.

Throsby, D. (2001) *Economics and Culture*, Cambridge, UK: Cambridge University Press.

Towse, R. (ed.) (1997) *Cultural Economics: The Arts, the Heritage and the Media Industries*, Cheltenham: Edward Elgar.

Towse, R. (ed.) (2003) *A Handbook of Cultural Economics*, Cheltenham: Edward Elgar.

Tylor, E.B. ([1871] 1976) *Primitive Culture: Researches into the Development of Mythology, Philosophy, Religion, Language, Art, and Custom*, New York: Gordon Press.

Ulen, T.S. (2006) "Behavioral law and economics: An introduction", in M. Altman (ed.), *Handbook of Contemporary Behavioral Economics. Foundations and Developments*, New York: M.E. Sharpe, Inc.

Winter, S.G. (1987) "Natural selection and evolution", in J. Eatwell, M. Milgate and P. Newman (eds.), *The New Palgrave Dictionary of Economics*, vol. 3, London: Macmillan.

Witt, U. (2009) "Novelty and the bounds of unknowledge in economics", *Journal of Economic Methodology*, 16, 4: 361–375.

Poem

Dirge For an Urban Dweller

I do not really wish to go
And dwell among the Navaho
I have rejected every plan
To live like Neolithic Man
And even when I'm feeling low
I never emulate Thoreau.

The works of Nature in the raw
Are what I have no yearning for
The unexploited wilderness
Is rather an untidy mess
Alas, it cannot be disguised
I dote on being civilized.

I like to drive, I like to fly,
I like ice cream and apple pie
Sometimes, in spite of all derision
I like to look at television
I may be crude, I may be crass
But still I'm fond of Culture (Mass).

I do not feel undue elation
Before climactic Vegetation
Unless the climax that I see
Includes the maintenance of me,
My friends, my children, and my wife
In our accustomed style of life.

And yet I get some inner qualms
From Conservationists' alarms
Perhaps my all too urban race
Has lost its biologic base
And man is clearly understood
To be too clever for his good.

Unpublished, 1970

Part XI

Grants economics

11 Key text: The micro theory of grants and granting behavior[1]

Kenneth E. Boulding

A grant is always a relationship between two or more parties. In the simple two-party relationship it involves the grantor or donor on the one hand and the recipient on the other. Thus, a grant involves at least two decisions—a decision[2] on the part of the donor to make a grant and a decision on the part of the recipient to receive it. The decision of the donor may seem to be the more significant of the two, but the decision of the recipient is by no means insignificant. There may be elements of threat in the recipient's decision to receive, just as these elements may take part in the decision of the grantor to give. It is not always unreasonable to be unwilling to receive a gift horse without looking it in the mouth. Grants can also be initiated by the recipient asking or applying for them. Therefore, if we are to perceive the special significance of the grant in the spectrum of human relationships and behavior, we must first look at the general pattern of these relationships.

Figure 11.1 illustrates a general form of the two-party relationship. Here we have two parties, *A* and *B*, which may be either persons or social organizations. *A* gives up something, x_a, which he perceives as sending x_a to *B*. When x_a arrives at *B*, however, it may be something else, x_b. Similarly, *B* sends out y_b, and *A* receives y_a. These *x*s and *y*s may be commodities, such as wheat or money; they may also be communications, information, threats, promises affirmations, persuasions, and so on. In simple commodity exchange, we generally assume that what physically leaves one party is the same as what reaches the other, that is, $x_a = x_b$ and $y_b = y_a$. Thus, *A* may transfer 100 bushels of wheat to *B*, and *B* will transfer at the same time $200 of money to *A*. However, the significance, or utility, of the exchangeables is different for the two parties. In the classical theory of exchange, it is assumed that uncoerced exchange will not take place at all unless both parties benefit—that is, unless what *A* gives up is worth less to him subjectively than what he receives, and what *B* gives up is, likewise, worth less subjectively than what he receives. Therefore, in our simple case of the sale of wheat, the seller values the money more than the wheat and the buyer values the wheat more than the money, even though the physical quantities transferred do not change in the act of transfer.

Even in the simplest two-party relations, there are more than two things transferred. Thus, the x_a, x_b, y_a, and y_b of Figure 11.1 really represent packages or

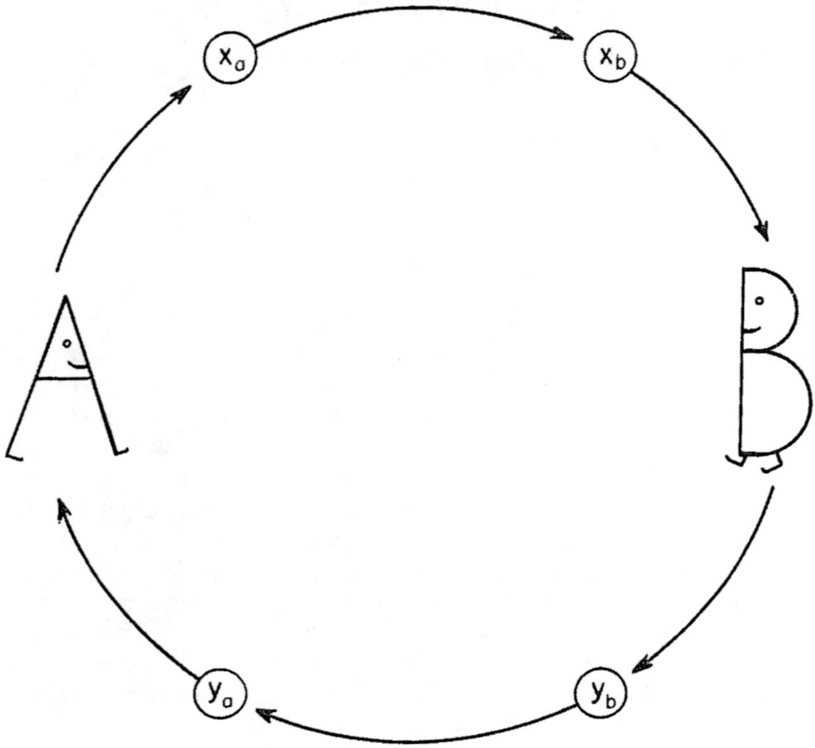

Figure 11.1 Simple exchange.

combinations of things. Even in the case of simple exchange, then, it is not merely commodities that are transferred, but also information, communications, or messages. If I pass a store window and see a shirt with a price tag on it that I would like to buy, I have perceived a message from the storekeeper saying "I am willing to give you this shirt, if you will give me this amount of money." When I go into the store, I have to communicate with the storekeeper before he will bring the shirt out of the window so the transaction can take place. It is almost impossible to think of any relationship among people in which communication does not play some part.

In communication, of course, the possibility that what leaves one party will not be what the other party receives—that is, that x_a will not be the same as x_b, and that y_b will not be the same as y_a—is very strong. *A*'s communication x_a comes out of *A*'s image of the world. When it arrives as x_b at *B*, even if it has not been transformed or distorted in the process of transmission, it has to pass into *B*'s image of the world in order to achieve significance, and the significance it has for *B* may be different from what it originally had for *A*. Such crossing perceptions are, of course, a common source of misunderstanding in communication. The situation is further complicated in that x_a depends on *A*'s image of the significance that the receipt of it will have for *B*, and *A*'s image of the significance for *B* may be very different from *B*'s image of its significance.

In many forms, even in commodity exchange, the difference between x_a and x_b and between y_b and y_a may be of great significance. We see this, for instance, in the labor market, where the exchange of labor for money is much more complex than, shall we say, the exchange of money for stocks and bonds in the financial market. Thus, if *A* is the employer and *B* is the worker in Figure 11.1, x_a represents the money wages the employer pays out, the significance to him depending on the alternative uses of the money, for instance, to improve his capital equipment. What the workers receives, x_b, even though it may represent the same number of dollars, has a very different significance for the worker. For him it represents in real terms the consumer goods he can buy with it. The y_b, which is what the worker gives up, is so many hours a day, the significance of which depends on the alternative uses of his time, either in other jobs, in self-employment, or in leisure. The y_a which the employer receives, however, acquires its significance from the product of the work, especially the marginal product, or the additional product produced by the additional work.

It is not surprising, then, that the labor market is the focus of so much conflict, waste, and anxiety, and that it creates a sociological environment that is totally different from that of the stock market or the wheat market. Even the organizations surrounding the labor market—trade unions and employees' associations, conciliators, mediators, government agencies, and so on—cannot be explained only in terms of the simple economics of monopoly power, or attempts at monopoly power, but they have to be explained largely in terms of the extreme communication difficulties involved in this type of relationship. Because of the different life experiences of workers and employers, it is very hard for either of them to put themselves in the other's place and see the world from the other's point of view. Consequently, communications are almost invariably distorted—*A*'s image of *B*'s world is very different from *B*'s image of his own world, and *B*'s image of *A*'s world is, likewise, very different from *A*'s image of it. This situation can breed an enormous amount of misunderstanding and unnecessary conflict. We should not assume, of course, that misunderstanding always increases conflict. It is probable that if people knew what the real world was like they would perceive real conflicts of interest that they may not perceive now because of misunderstanding.

To make our picture of the two-party relationship more complete, we can express it as in Figure 11.2, where the solid lines $x_a x_b$ and $y_b y_a$ represent transfers of some sort of material objects—commodities, money, or services—and the dotted lines $x'_a x'_b$ and $y'_b y'_a$ represent flows of information and communication. The grant is, then, the special case in which one of the commodity flows is zero; for example, in Figure 11.3, y_b and y_a are zero, and we are left only with the other commodity flow and with the information and communication flows.

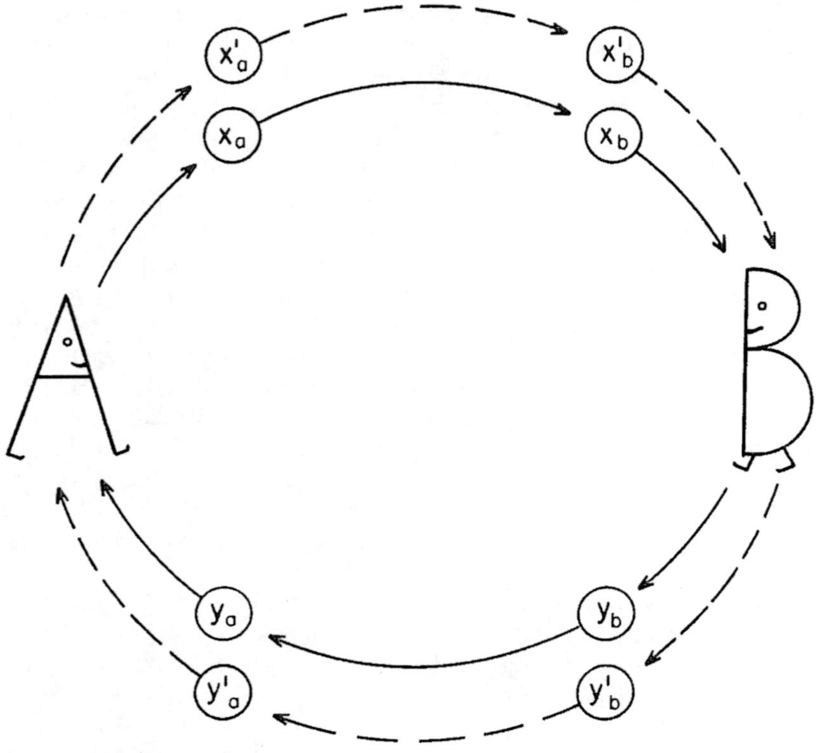

Figure 11.2 Complete exchange.

The terms of trade of the two parties is a very significant quantity in the two-party relationship. For party *A* in Figure 11.1, this quantity is y_a/x_a—that is, how much he takes in per unit of what he gives out. A rise in this number is an improvement in his terms of trade; he is getting more in for every unit that goes out. Similarly, *B*'s terms of trade are x_b/y_b. If now $x_a = x_b$ and $y_b = y_a$, which we generally assume in simple commodity exchange, then *A*'s terms of trade T_a will be the reciprocal of *B*'s terms T_b, or

$$T_a = \frac{1}{T_b}. \quad (1)$$

Thus, suppose $x_a = x_b$ = \$200, and $y_b = y_a$ = 100 bushels of wheat, where *A* is buying wheat from *B* at \$2.00 per bushel. *B*'s term of trade are \$2.00 per bushel, *A*'s are 1/2 bushel per dollar. If the price rises, say, to \$3.00 per bushel, the seller's (*B*'s) terms of trade improve, and the buyer's (*A*'s) worsen to 1/3 bushel per dollar. Under these circumstances, of course, any improvement in *A*'s terms of trade means a worsening of *B*'s terms of trade. This is the essence of the conflict

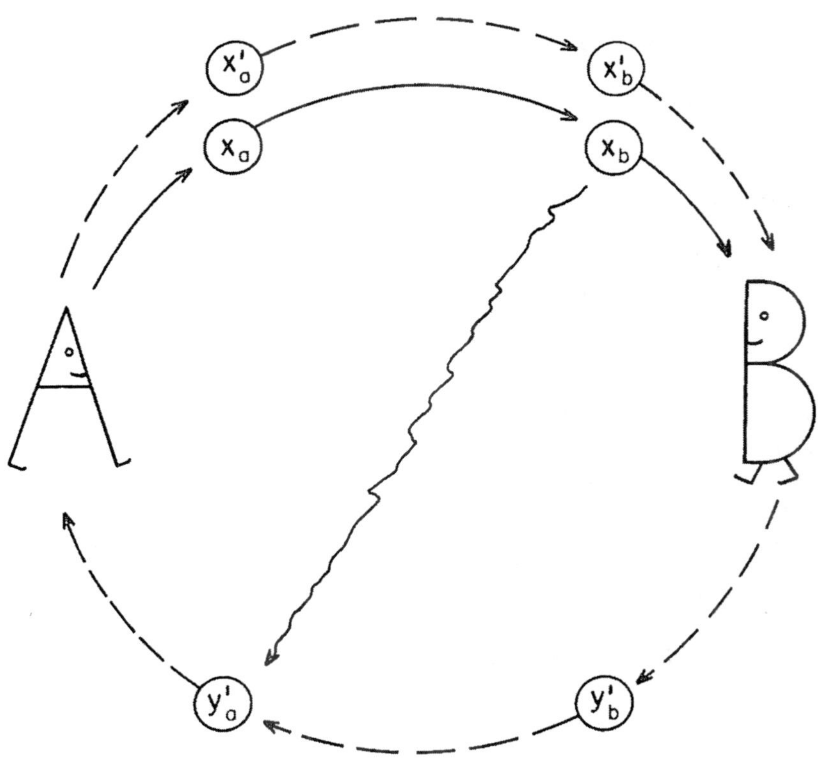

Figure 11.3 The grant.

in exchange. There is, indeed, a curious paradox about the phenomenon even of simple exchange, in that it involves both a conflict and a community of interest. There is community of interest, on the assumption that the exchange is not coerced, for the exchange will not take place unless both parties benefit. On the other hand, there may well be a conflict of interest in the terms of the exchange—that is, in the terms of trade, or the ratio of exchange. Everybody likes to have a high price for the things that he sells and a low price for the things he buys, so that any change in the structure of the relative prices will create some sort of redistribution of welfare, about which there may be conflict.

When we go to the general case of the two-party relationship, both the terms-of-trade concept and the conflict concept become much more complex. In Figure 11.1, if x_a is not equal to x_b and y_b is not equal to y_a, then the simple reciprocal relationship of equation 1 breaks down. *A* can improve his terms of trade without a worsening of *B*'s, for example, if y_a rises relative to *yb*. Thus, *A*'s and *B*'s evaluations of loss or gain in the transfer process itself are important elements. If x_b is larger than x_a and y_a is larger than y_b, we have a situation which is likely to be profitable to both parties. This, indeed, is precisely the classic theory of exchange, when x_a, y_a, x_b, and y_b are interpreted as *utilities*. On the other hand, we cannot rule out the case in which x_b is smaller than x_a and y_a smaller than y_b. In this case neither party gets as much as the other party gives up. This, of course, operates to restrict the area within which exchange is mutually advantageous. A classical example of this situation occurs when costs of transport or transaction costs are involved in the transfers. The elements of this situation are well worked out in the theory of international trade.[3] In the classical theory of exchange, the differences in utility of the two parties act, as it were, as negative costs of transport. The x_a given up by A is perhaps something he did not want very much because he has a lot of it. This factor is transformed into a much larger x_b when it arrives at B, in terms of B's utility, because this is something that B wants a good deal, perhaps because he does not have very much of it. Similar considerations hold for the *y*s.

When we look at the complete exchange of Figure 11.2, the terms of trade have to be measured by each party's evaluation of the inputs and outputs. Thus, suppose that in the estimation of party A, the total value or utility to him of x_a is $x_a v_a$. The quantity v_a is then a *valuation coefficient* somewhat analogous to a "utility price."[4] Similarly, we have valuation coefficients v_a for the output x'_a, u_a for the input y_a, u'_a for the input y'_a, and similar concepts for party B. The terms of trade T'_a for A and T'_b for B are now given by equations 2a and 2b:

$$T'_a = \frac{y_a u_a + y'_a u'_a}{x_a v_a + x'_a v'_a} \tag{2a}$$

$$T'_b = \frac{x_b v_b + x'_b v'_b}{y_b u_b + y'_b u'_b}. \tag{2b}$$

Now, of course, it would only be under very unusual conditions that the reciprocal relationship of equation 1 would hold. In the special case of the grant relationship, Figure 11.3, we suppose that y_b and y_a are zero, so that equations 2a and 2b reduce to equations 3a and 3b:

$$T'_a = \frac{y'_a u'_a}{x_a v_a + x'_a v'_a} \tag{3a}$$

$$T'_b = \frac{x_b v_b + x'_b v'_b}{y'_b u'_b}. \tag{3b}$$

The basic theoretical assumption in all these cases is that the two-party relationship will either not come into being at all or it will break down and cease to be if the utility terms of trade of both parties T'_a and T'_b are not greater than one. If T'_a were exactly equal to one, party A would be indifferent to the relationship in that A would get out of it exactly the same in utility as what he put into it. If T'_a is greater than one, A has a net gain in utility and gets more out of the relationship than he is putting into it, and hence he will be motivated to veto the relationship (we are assuming for the moment that each party has the veto power over the relationship). Just how this comes about we shall look at later. In simple exchange, where $x_a = x_b = X$ and $y_a = y_b = Y$, equations 2 reduce to equations 4.

$$T'_a = \frac{yu_a}{xv_a} \tag{4a}$$

$$T'_b = \frac{xv_b}{yu_b}. \tag{4b}$$

In equations 2, 3, and 4, putting $T'_a = T'_b = 1$ gives us two equations that define a boundary in the variable space, on the one side of which the utility terms of trade of both parties are greater than one and the two-party relation is viable. This rather simplified analysis assumes a cardinally measurable utility. As every economist knows, it is nearly always possible to reformulate the problem in terms of ordinal utilities. (I have done this in my article "Notes on a Theory of Philanthropy,"[5] in which the conventional economic apparatus of the "Edgeworth box," which is usually only applied to exchange, is extended to grants, again demonstrating that the grant from one part to another is simply a special case of the two-party relation.)

Let us now look at the grant relationship of Figure 11.3 in a little more detail. As we have seen, the grant will take place if the utility terms of trade of both parties are greater than one, or at least not less than one. For grantor *A*, this means that the loss in utility from giving up x_a must be more than balanced by the total gain in utility resulting from the output x'_a and the input y'_a. Noncommodity outputs, x'_a in this case, might consist of the release of guilt or obligation. In any case, a noncommodity output, which would carry a positive utility, would help to offset the negative utility of the commodity output. *A*'s noncommodity inputs, symbolized by y'_a, may be of many different kinds. If *A* is benevolent toward *B*, then *A*'s perception that *B*'s welfare has increased represents an increase in *A*'s welfare or utility (suggested by the wavy arrow in Figure 11.3). The more benevolent *A* feels toward *B* and the more he perceives his output x_a as increasing *B*'s welfare, the larger will be the utility value of y'_a and the more likely the transaction is to take place.

As we have seen, grants are made not only out of benevolence but also in response to threat. Thus, the noncommodity input to $A(y'_a)$ may consist of a threat from *B* that if *A* does not make the grant (x_a), *B* will diminish *A*'s utility by doing him some damage. In this case, the increase in utility represented by y'_a is a "negative negative"—that is, it is the absence of a decrease in utility that would otherwise have taken place. From the point of view of individual utility accounting, though not from the point of view of society as a whole, this may be just as effective as a positive increase in utility and may be equally influential in accounting for the existence of grants.

Looking now at *B*'s side of the relationship, x_b, *B*'s commodity input, presumably causes an increase in his utility, although this might not always be the case. That is, assuming that x_a and x_b are approximately the same thing, what *A* wants to give may not be at all what *B* wants to receive, and may, in fact, have a much greater utility for *A* than for *B*. There may also be noncommodity inputs, y_b, that have negative utility—for example, if the commodity grant is accompanied by noncommodity communications suggesting *B*'s inferiority of status or his obligations to be grateful. Indeed since grants almost always imply a superior status of the grantor to the recipient the implication is that a negative noncommodity input of utility will frequently go along with commodity grants. Indeed, there is often a good deal of humiliation involved in receiving somebody else's bounty. It should be noted that there are some exceptions to the rule—for instance, gifts made by subjects to their rulers, vassals to their lords, parishioners to their clergy, and so on. Such gifts are more likely to be a result of a threat system, whether spiritual or material, and in such systems the threatener tends to have superior status. Even the bandit or the holdup man at the moment of attack has something of the status of a lord, and the victim is his vassal. Status rewards may also play a significant part in y'_a, that is, *A*'s noncommodity inputs. If the grant made to *B* reinforces and symbolizes *A*'s higher status, then in a very real sense, y'_b is an output of status from *B* and y'_a is an input of status into *A*. Thus, a gift to a beggar or a lift to a hitchhiker may symbolize a rise of status to the donor.

Because of this potential element of threat, we should note that malevolence, as well as benevolence, may play a significant role in the grant relationship. If *A* perceives that an improvement in *B*'s status is a negative utility to *A* (makes him feel worse off), or if his perception of a worsening in *B*'s status would be a positive utility to him, then we can see malevolence at work. Under these circumstances, we may get a "negative grant"—that is, an output from *A*, even in commodity terms, that is designed to diminish *B*'s welfare rather than to increase it. This output may take the form of poison pen letters, slander, the destruction of *B*'s property, and in the extreme case, of course, the taking of *B*'s life. Negative grants, unfortunately, are still an important element in the world system, especially in the international system, where the defense industries of the various countries are mainly concerned with producing the capability of making negative grants to other countries. Negative grants, of course, are twice-cursed—they are costly to the grantor, for whom they represent utilization of resources that might have been employed in the production of positive commodities; and if the intentions of the grantor are fulfilled, they are, of course, an injury to the recipient. The record of warfare shows that negative grants are by no means uncommon.

Negative grants may not always result from malevolence. They may be executed as a kind of investment by the grantor in reestablishing the credibility of his threats. Thus, he will have the expectation of getting tribute—a commodity transferred from the other part in the future. Negative grants may also be made under conditions of benevolence, as when a parent punishes a child. It may even be true that "This hurts me more than it hurts you" and the parent is giving negative grants to the child in the expectation that the child will thereby eventually have an increase in welfare, which will then be registered, of course, as an increase in the parent's welfare.

Professional granting organizations—such as foundations, and to some extent governments—present a particularly interesting problem. The decision to set up a foundation in the first place may be analyzed as a variant of the two-party relationship of Figure 11.3. If A is the donor or establisher, and B is the foundation itself, it can be said that the donor transfers commodities, securities, or money from himself to the foundation. The noneconomic transfers may include an input of status and, of course, "benevolence" toward the foundation itself as an extension of the donor's own interests and purposes. Foundations and charitable endowments may also be set up through threat and fear; in earlier times, for instance, through the fear of hell; in modern times, through the fear of inheritance taxes and a preference for private grants over public grants enforced through taxation. All this, however, fits fairly well into the pattern of our previous analysis.

However, once the foundation is set up and a professional staff is acquired, the situation becomes different, particularly in terms of the alternative costs of the grants. When a private person makes grants for charitable purposes, the alternative cost of the grants is what he might otherwise have done with the money, such as invest it or spend it for some immediate pleasure and satisfaction in consumable goods. A foundation does not have this option. Once the commitment has been made, the funds which it has at its disposal must be granted; they cannot be used for consumption or investment, except under very unusual circumstances. A foundation, therefore, is an organization that possesses earning assets that continually provide inputs of money into the foundation's account. Beyond a certain point, however, money is a disutility to the foundation. An increase in assets, especially liquid assets, is a disutility to it and it must, therefore, reduce its net worth by making grants. Thus, a foundation is almost literally an organization that excretes money. Decision-makers of foundations have to decide to whom and for what purposes grants will be given; they rarely have the option of not making grants at all, especially where the tax laws or other laws regulate their conduct.

Foundations differ from firms in that, provided that they stay within what is usually a rather broad framework of the law, there are no very clear standards by which they or anybody else can judge whether they are being successful. A profit-making institution in a market environment has a measure of its success in its rate of profit. If it continually takes losses it will not survive, and if it makes profits there is evidence that the institution is meeting a need which can be expressed through the exchange economy—that is, it is satisfying a demand at least as well as anybody else can satisfy it. This hypothesis leaves open, of course, the ultimate social question of whether all demands are good, but at least within a certain restricted framework, there is a rather clear standard of success. Foundations have no such standards of success. No matter to whom or for what purposes a foundation makes its grants, provided that it stays within the law and it manages its investments successfully, it will survive. There is very little selective process that eliminates foundations with frivolous or unproductive purposes, in the way that there is a selective process operating to eliminate firms which do not produce something for which people are willing to pay. Because the survival of the foundation does not depend on the feedback it gets from its decisions, it has less interest in obtaining this feedback. I have sometimes called this "Edsel's law." When the Ford Motor Company produced the Edsel automobile, it soon discovered that the demand was not adequate to justify its production. There was very rapid feedback, and as a result the mistake was corrected and the Edsel withdrawn. In contrast, if the Ford Foundation produced an "Edsel" in the form of grants for purposes that were not particularly socially useful or did not produce the intended results, the Foundation might never know, or might only find out after a long time, and would probably not change its policies very much once it had this information. This absence of feedback from grants is a serious defect, which could easily lead into pathological states of the grants economy. This is one point at which the exchange economy, where feedback tends to be rapid, direct, and acted upon, has a certain advantage.

Foundations can say, of course, that "success" consists of carrying out the purposes set forth in their charters. However, these purposes are usually very vague, and the question of their social desirability remains unresolved. There are many foundations, like the famous one in St. Louis, to provide covered wagons for pioneers going westward—a purpose that is now obsolete. Although there are many other foundations whose purposes can be criticized for their low social priority, such criticisms are rarely made and are seldom effective even when they are made.

Nevertheless, there is something like a "market" in grants. Where there are a large number of grantors facing a large number of potential recipients, at least an analog of the competitive market in the exchange sector begins to appear. Something like this market exists, at least in the more developed countries, in the field of research grants. Research is widely recognized as a highly suitable activity for grant support. Scientific knowledge is a public good in that, once the discovery has been made, it is available to anyone who can understand it. This does not necessarily apply, of course, to trade secrets, classified research and patented processes, which are more of the nature of private goods; however, the principle applies extensively over the field of pure science. As it produces a public good, science almost has to be supported by the grants economy rather than through the exchange economy. What is called "science policy" is very largely a matter of who shall give what research grants to whom and with what strings attached. If there is only a single grantor, such as the government or a single agency of governing, we have a monopoly situation that may lead to an undesirable concentration of power in the hands of the grantor. Where there are many grantors and many grantees, a grantee who does not get a grant from one granting agency can try another one. Hence, the grantee is less at the mercy of the whims of any particular grantor and is much more likely to find somebody who will support his idea. The case against monopolies is just as strong in the grants economy as it is in the exchange economy. It has even been suggested that we might need an "antitrust act" for foundations, and that there should be a legal maximum size for a particular foundation, in which case the large foundations might have to split up into a number of independent smaller ones. Indeed, government regulation of foundations has some of the aspects of the regulation of private monopoly.

Insofar as grants are very intimately related with the political system, foundations could almost be regarded as a form of private government, and it is not surprising that public government looks on them with a somewhat careful and critical eye.

Another relationship that is not fully included in the previous scheme is *reciprocity*. This may look very much like exchange, as it usually involves a two-way transfer, sometimes separated by an interval of time, of commodities or exchangeables between two parties. It is different from exchange, however, in that whereas exchange is conditional ("I will give you so much of *x* if you will give me so much of *y*") and is based essentially on the acceptance of a conditional offer, reciprocity is formally unconditional, although in practice it often tends to edge across the spectrum into exchange. Thus, reciprocity can be defined as mutual grants or a pair of grants. That is, *A* gives something to *B* out of the sheer goodness of his heart and his benevolence for *B*, and *B* gives something to *A* out of the sheer goodness of his heart and his benevolence towards *A*, yet the two acts are not being formally related since neither is a formal condition of the other. Christmas presents are a good example of an activity that frequently involves reciprocity and occasionally degenerates into exchange. The unconditional nature of the operation, however, differentiates it from exchange and perhaps explains why people rarely get what they really want for Christmas.

Conditions under which it is acceptable or not acceptable to give money rather than commodity presents would make a very interesting study. The giving of a gift also conveys a message saying, in effect, "I have gone to some trouble to get you something which I think you will like." This is a message implying regard or affection, or some sort of integrative relationship. Reciprocity, even though it looks superficially like exchange, has integrative aspects that exchange does not. The fact that "commercialization" of Christmas is so widely deplored suggests that reciprocity has a function in building a sense of community and a more complex structure of personal relationships that exchange pure and simple is unable to perform. I would argue that even exchange requires a degree of integrative relationship among the parties before it can be legitimated, which is why exchange almost always develops originally out of reciprocity, and may be regarded historically as the formalization of reciprocity.

The formalization of reciprocity into exchange takes place not only because of the greater flexibility and convenience of exchange in getting what we really want, but also because it may be an escape from the status inequality implied in the grant. As we have noted, when *A* gives something to *B*, it is frequently a symbol or even a creator of higher status for *A* and lower status for *B*. When *B* reciprocates by giving something to *A*, *B* restores his and *A*'s status to what they may have been before the initial gift. Exchange, almost by its very symmetry, implies equality of status. That is, in the exchange diagram of Figure 11.2, we can interchange *A* and *B* and it makes no difference in the pattern. In the grants diagram, this is not so. The relationship is not symmetrical. Exchange has the same eyeball-to-eyeball quality about it that characterizes the threat–counter-threat or deterrence system (if you do something nasty to me, I'll do something nasty to you), although there is much less glare in the eyeballs. The social customs and the noncommodity inputs and outputs that surround the exchange process often develop because the equality of status implied in exchange may be at variance with the inequality of status recognized elsewhere in society. This accounts for the obsequiousness of the traditional shopkeeper toward his more exalted customers. He knows perfectly well that in the exchange transaction he has the superior status—having superior knowledge—but he has to disguise this fact in order to avoid offending his customers who are under the illusion that they have the superior status. In a supermarket there is no obsequiousness and only the bare rudiments of courtesy because the equality implied in paying dollars for groceries does not have to be denied. There is little difference in status between the housewife checking her groceries out and the clerk on the other side of the counter.

A very interesting aspect of reciprocity is what might be called "serial reciprocity," in which a gift from *A* to *B* creates a generalized sense of obligation on the part of *B*. This obligation is satisfied by a gift from *B*, not to *A*, but to another party *C*, who in turn satisfies his sense of obligation to another party *D*, and so on around the circle, until finally perhaps a gift comes back to *A*, and the whole process is repeated. The famous "Kula ring" of the Pacific islands is perhaps an example of this phenomenon. Some commodities circulate as gifts in one direction around a group of islands, yet another group of commodities travels in the opposite direction around the same circle. Even in modern societies, however, serial reciprocity is by no means an insignificant phenomenon. It is very important, for instance, in the relations of the generations. The debt we owe to our parents is not often repaid to them but to our children instead, who in turn pay the debt they owe us to their children and so on, one generation to the next. There is, of course, also a certain amount of deferred exchange or simple reciprocity in the relationship between the two generations. Parents support their children with grants—at least they did before the development of pension funds and social security—in the expectation that in their old age their children will support them by grants. This is reciprocity over time, rather than exchange, as it involves complex integrative relationships and is not contractually formalized. Once the support of old age is contractually formalized, of course, it ceases to be reciprocity and becomes exchange. Even the social security system, however, has a considerable element of "public reciprocity" about it and usually lacks the clear contractual exchange framework of private pensions and insurance.

One of the most important aspects of the grants economy is the role it plays in the building up of integrative structures and communities—that is, groups of people who have some feelings of identification and benevolence toward each other. The dynamics of community growth are subtle and very little understood. The one-way transfer, however, plays a very significant role in the process, partly because of the phenomenon Gouldner (1960) has called the "reciprocity multiplier," in the case of serial reciprocity. A gift may be a unilateral expression by the donor of identification with the recipient. The receipt of the gift, however, frequently creates an almost unconscious sense of obligation—perhaps, as was suggested earlier, because of the status-lowering aspects of being a recipient. If this obligation is fulfilled by a return gift, we have simple reciprocity and the circuit is closed immediately without further repercussions, even though there may be a certain buildup of integrative feeling between the two parties. If it results, however, in serial reciprocity there may very well be a multiplier effect involving more and more people in the community building operations of gift-giving, unless some sort of equilibrium is reached. We can think of the process perhaps in epidemiological terms. Thus, the original gift giver becomes a source of infection of benevolence. The infection may lose its intensity as it goes through a number of receivers and subsequent givers, but under some circumstances it may increase in intensity as it triggers off previously latent benevolent feelings. The process stops, of course, when it reaches a recalcitrant character who simply absorbs a gift without feeling any obligation to retransmit it. The gifts, incidentally, need not be commodities. They may be merely communications—smiles, courtesies, hellos, small favors, and so on.

Another source of interaction between the grants economy and the integrative system arises out of what in its pathological form I have called the "sacrifice trap." A gift helps to create the identity of the giver, and a gift either to an individual or to a cause or community identifies the giver with the recipient. Once the gift has been made, however, it is very difficult to withdraw it and also very difficult for the giver to admit that he was wrong. Thus, the gift builds itself into the identity of the giver; in pathological cases he can become trapped into a disadvantageous identification with the society, organization, or cause for which he has sacrificed. This principle causes people to throw good money after bad, to throw live soldiers after dead, new martyrs after old ones, and so on. It is very hard for a politician whose decisions have cost a large number of human lives to admit either to himself or to anybody that these decisions were mistaken. In order to justify them, he often has to throw more lives into the bottomless pit of sacrifice. Up to a point the principle may be a healthy one, for without the kind of commitment or identity which emerges from sacrifice, it may well be that no communities, not even the family, would really stay together. On the other hand, the principle easily becomes pathological, as we see in war and in certain excesses or religious or political devotion, or even in the family, where people sometimes create lives of utter misery for each other because each has sacrificed so much. Exchange has no such power to create community, identity, and commitment, perhaps because it involves so little sacrifice. This, indeed, is one of the great weaknesses of capitalism, which is organized principally through exchange. It may not be able to attract through its institutions that minimum of loyalty, devotion, and affection necessary to maintain them. Joseph Schumpeter (1942) was perhaps the first economist to point this out.

Another source of integrative weakness of exchange is its almost exclusive confinement to two-party relationships, whereas a grant system can easily be multi-party. Although the operations of the competitive market involves many parties, each transaction in the system is between two parties—a contract, for instance, in which *A* gives something to *B*, *B* gives something to *C*, and *C* gives something to *A*. Even the mechanisms that create a unified market, such as arbitrage,[6] take place in individual two-party transactions. One exchange, of course, affects others in its neighborhood, so that the exchange system does maintain something like a many-partied equilibrium. This, however, is unseen, covert, and "ecological." It appears to the individual as some outside force of nature over which he has no control, and it is not surprising, therefore, that it is hard for an exchange system to command loyalties. Nobody loves a bank in the way in which he may love a country, political party, family, or church.

By contrast, grants are easily adapted to multi-partied relationships. They are indeed the prime creator of large-scale organization. A hierarchy, for instance, is organized by grants rather than by exchange. With all the virtuous talk about two-way communication in organizations, it still remains true that in communication reciprocity rather than exchange is the only really obtainable ideal. An "order" from the "boss" is essentially a grant of information often accompanied by grants of commodities.

There are two major patterns in multi-party relationships. One is the hierarchy, as illustrated in Figure 11.4, the *P*s standing for the parties. The other pattern of multi-party relationships is the "group," illustrated in Figure 11.5, in which relationships go from all members to all other members. In both of these cases, contractual exchange is too complex and rigid a relationship to permit much complexity in multi-party patterns. What looks like exchange is frequently reciprocity. Even in the labor market, the exchange relationship is between the individual worker and the organization. The actual organization structure, if it is hierarchical, almost has to consist of one-way transfers and one-way communications. Similarly, in the group, if exchange is relied on as the social organizer, the group will soon break up into pairs, simply because it is very hard to maintain exchange transactions with large numbers of people. There will indeed be reciprocity, but this, as we have seen, is something rather different from exchange. Terms of trade—what we get per unit of what we give—are still very important in a multi-party situation, because if any one party finds that his terms of trade with the group, or with the organization, are poor he will tend to leave. Nevertheless, the terms of trade are determined in a system of reciprocity rather than in an exchange system, which is one reason perhaps why it is often difficult in these cases to correct unsatisfactory terms of trade, even when it is to the interest of the parties to do so. Thus, a man quits a company, leaves a church, or even divorces his wife because he feels that he is giving too much and getting too little. If the transactions were of simple exchange, the terms of trade perhaps could be renegotiated. Where the transactions involve reciprocity, however, negotiation and bargaining are almost ruled out by definition, and one has to rely on spontaneous changes in the flow of one-way transfers, which may be very difficult to achieve consciously. Some modern organization theorists have argued that the pathologies and inefficiencies of hierarchy could be corrected by developing exchange simulations in the middle of organizations. Whether this can really be done, however, is open to grave doubt, simply because of the sheer difficulty of organizing multi-party relationships through contract.

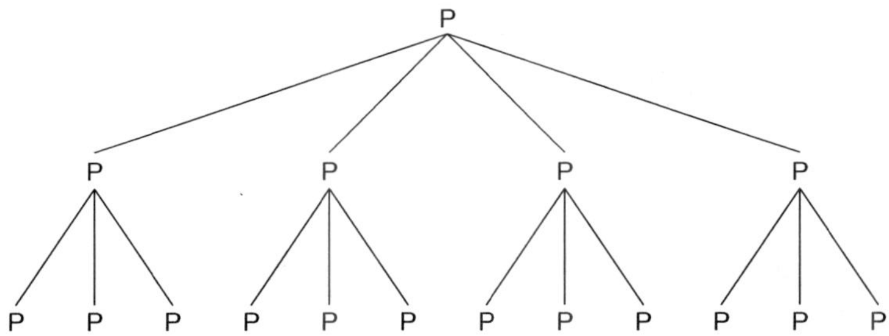

Figure 11.4 Hierarchy.

Another very significant aspect of the grants economy, which has also been neglected by economists, is the "labor grant," or the voluntary provision of personal services without charge. This covers a very large area of social life and quantitatively it may be the largest single element in the grants economy. I know of no aggregate estimates of its overall magnitude. It is perhaps significant, however, that shortly after the formation of the Association for the Study of the Grants Economy in 1969, the Association of Voluntary Action Scholars was established, as well as a *Journal of Voluntary Action Research.* There is also a Center for a Voluntary Society and a National Center for Voluntary Action in Washington, which operates "Volinflo," a partly computerized information collection, storage, retrieval, and dissemination system in this field. Voluntary action includes such things as volunteer work camps, volunteer helpers of all ages in hospitals, work done by honorary secretaries and officers of innumerable organizations, unpaid councilmen in cities, counties, townships, and political organizations of all sorts, board members of innumerable organizations, Sunday school teachers and religious workers, student volunteers of all kinds—the list could be extended almost indefinitely.

It is not always easy to tell where volunteer labor ends and leisure-time activities begin. Again, there is a wide spectrum of activity, and it is not particularly important where the actual dividing lines are drawn. There is a broad distinction between volunteer action or labor grants, which is unpaid activity designed to

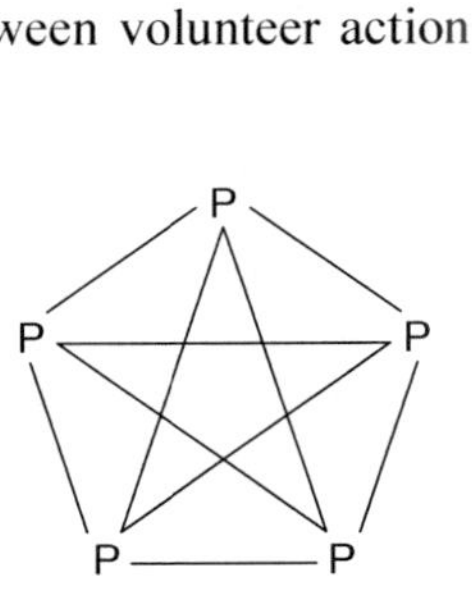

Figure 11.5 Group.

benefit somebody else, and leisure-time activity, which is designed primarily to benefit the person performing it. There is a great overlap, however. If a father takes his children camping, he is acting on his own behalf as well as on theirs, and a great deal of the satisfaction of leisure-time activity consists in some sort of reciprocity, as in the playing of games. Being a golf partner, for instance, is a service to the opponent, who might conceivably have to pay somebody to play golf with him, as well as a leisure-time activity on the part of the person involved.

The theory of volunteer action is not very different from that of grants as a whole, just as the theory of labor supply is a special case of the theory of exchange. The motivation for a labor grant, like that of any other, may be threefold. There may be personal satisfaction in simply performing the operation, a motivation that is likely to be more significant in a labor grant than in the grant of a commodity or money, simply because the activity itself may be interesting and significant to the performer and thus preferable to mere idleness and boredom. Another motivation we have already examined is benevolence—that is, identification with the welfare of the party benefiting from the labor grant. In this sense, giving service is not very different from giving money, especially if it involves a sacrifice of earnings on the part of the giver and an increase in welfare on the part of the recipient. Like all grants, labor grants will be made if the perceived "utility terms of trade" are greater than 1—that is, if the utility derived from the activity itself, plus the contemplation of increased benefits to others with whom the actor identifies and is benevolent toward, exceeds the utility cost involved in the sacrifice of alternative uses of time and their product. The total amount of voluntary labor supplied, therefore, will be that at which an extra "hour" will bring in less to the supplier, in terms of additional satisfaction either in the activity itself or in the contemplation of its benefits to others, than it costs him in terms of disagreeableness of the activity and contemplation of alternative uses of the time. There will be more volunteer labor, therefore, the more pleasurable the activity is in itself, the more it is perceived as being effective in increasing the welfare of others, the greater the rate of benevolence, and the less the value of the alternative uses of time.

There is a certain parallel to tribute involved in labor grants, such as the taxation in kind that is involved in a compulsory draft or conscription, insofar as a draft forces people into occupations that they otherwise would not be in, at wages below what would otherwise attract them. The difference between the wage that would attract them and the wage actually paid is an implicit tax, and hence, again, can be properly regarded as part of the grants economy. There have been attempts to estimate the tax involved in the draft, paid by draftees in these terms in the United States (Oi 1967). While, of course, any exact measurement is impossible, the order of magnitude certainly runs into billions. Forced labor of any kind, the corvée of medieval France, the so-called "slave labor camps" of the Soviet Union, and prison labor in the chain gang in Georgia, are examples of this kind of "tribute labor." Compulsory education is another example. In the case of minors, it could be argued that this use of threats is in the interest of benevolence and that we force children into compulsory education because they are not able at this stage to assess the advantages and disadvantages of being a student. It is hard to deny the theoretical validity of this argument, even though one may be skeptical about its application in particular cases.

An extremely interesting application of the principle of voluntary action has been studied by Professor Titmuss (1971) of the London School of Economics in regard to blood donors. In the United Kingdom the blood supply for medical purposes is almost entirely voluntary. In the United States and the Soviet Union it is largely in the exchange system, and human blood is mainly a marketable commodity. Titmuss documents with great skill the consequences of these two different policies, particularly for the quality of the blood supplied, which tends to deteriorate under conditions of the market, following a kind of generalized Gresham's Law[7]—that in the absence of differentiation for quality, bad blood drives out the good.

A very interesting question in the area of social policy issues is the nature of the adjustment when there is danger that the voluntary labor supply will be inadequate to perform a necessary function. Should one move toward increasing the supply of voluntary labor for services, which seems to have been done in Britain in blood donation, or should one go into the market and begin paying for the service, in which case there may be a change in the quality of the service itself? A church faces the same problem when it goes from a lay ministry to a professional ministry, as does any charitable organization, professional society, or club, when it moves toward professionalized management. Paid labor may be more efficient in the technical sense, but something is lost in the integrative system as we move from voluntary labor, which tends to create integrative relationships, to paid labor, where the integrative relationship is almost inevitably less.

Another social phenomenon closely related to the grants economy is inheritance, which is essentially a grant from the dead to the living. Making a will has some of the aspects of setting up a foundation. A bequest, however, is a rather peculiar form of grant. It is certainly a grant to the recipient in that it increases his net worth. It can hardly be said to diminish the net worth of the donor after he is dead, except in the sense that death removes all net worth, at least in the form of worldly goods. From the recipients' point of view inheritance, even in the narrow sense of bequests, is a sizable part of the grants economy. In a society, say, in which the life expectancy is 70 and in which there is equal distribution of wealth among age groups, about 1/70 of the total wealth of the society will be passed on by death and inheritance in each year. If the capital–income ratio is about 3, then inheritance would account for about 3/70, or about 4 percent of total income in each year. Since the aged are wealthier than the young, the proportion should be more than this—perhaps as much as 8–10 percent. We know very little about the distribution of receipts from inheritance, although this is something that would certainly be amenable to statistical investigation. A very important question in the dynamics of society is whether inheritance concentrates wealth or diffuses it. It may very easily do either, depending on the habits of will-making and the legal and tax structure. The decision-making processes involved in bequests have received astonishingly little attention from economists or other social scientists. There is a certain amount of practical legal knowledge involved, and there are even training schools that train fund-raisers for colleges and other institutions to advise potential will-makers on how to avoid taxation, in the hope perhaps that some of the taxation that is avoided will come to the advisory institution in the form of a bequest.

The theory of the bequest should not be very different in principle from the theory of grants in general, with the one proviso that the will contemplates a situation in which the grant is compulsory and its total amount is determined simply by the total net assets of the testator. The decision-making process involves only the distribution of this total among various possible recipients. This is going to depend mainly on the system of benevolence and malevolence—that is, on the nature of the integrative structure and the identification of the testator with others. The frequency with which bequests go to children and other relatives is a testimony to the powerful integrative structure of the family. On the other hand, there may also be malevolence, as when an erring child is "cut off at a shilling," or when the threat of disinheritance is used as a motivator to extract "tribute" from a potentially erring child. There are some very interesting behavioral problems here that have been studied very little. I have no figures on the proportion of total inheritance in each year which goes to family members, but it must be very large. Indeed, Professor James Morgan[8] has concluded that the family is by far the largest component of the grants economy. It is a useful indicator of the integrative norms of society that all societies have laws about the disposition of estates left intestate, almost universally leaving them to blood relations. Inheritance taxation can likewise be regarded as an expression of these norms, representing the claims of the state against the family, or private charities, on the total of inheritance grants.

Inheritance has a larger aspect than that of the mere bequest of "worldly goods." Each of us inherits from our parents language, culture, class, as well as the genetic attributes of race, genetic defects like leukemia, and more doubtfully, genetic excellences. We inherit also from the society around us cathedrals, literature, pictures, music, the great achievements of the past that are part of our heritage. The principle of serial reciprocity comes into play here, for those who are aware of this inheritance acquire a sense of community with the past and hence also with the future; they become concerned not only with conserving but also with increasing the inheritance that is passed on to the next generation. There may be very sharp personal psychological differences among individuals and among societies in the extent to which this sense of inheritance and obligation to the past is felt. If child rearing and educational processes are traumatic, the debt to the past may not be felt at all except as a burden and there would be no interest in conserving it or passing it on.

Just as there is a problem in the impact of inheritance on the distribution of wealth, so also in the larger sense inheritance may either perpetuate, increase, or diminish existing inequalities. The fact that I inherited the English language from my parents and teachers and peers is an asset to me in that English is a world language, which somebody who inherited Welsh or Basque would have to acquire. Knowledge of the English language probably has a monetary value for the individual that could conceivably be estimated. Similarly, I may inherit a religion, a nationality, and a culture, which may be of more or less value to me, and the differential inheritance of these things may easily lead toward increasing or decreasing inequality, depending on the nature of the process itself. If inheritance leads to inequality, it may be necessary to intervene, where increasing equality is a social goal. We can think of Head Start and similar remedial measures as almost equivalent to negative inheritance taxation—that is, as a kind of negative tax subsidy to those whose cultural or genetic inheritance is in some sense deficient.

It is clear that the one-way transfer, far from being something extraneous or extraordinary in the general organization of social life, is an integral and essential part of the system, without which not only community but organization and society itself would be virtually impossible. The concentration of economists on exchange as a social organizer, important as that is, has frequently blinded them to this essential fact.

Notes

1 This article was previously published as chapter 2 in K.E. Boulding, *A Preface to Grants Economics: The Economy of Love and Fear*, New York: Praeger, 1981, pp. 15–34.

2 A decision is a complex phenomenon that involves at least two elements. First, there is a selection of one from at least two alternative images of the future present in the mind of the decision-maker, and second is the decision-maker's selection of an act that he believes can bring about the chosen image of the future. Of course, the decision-maker can be in error, in which case he will be surprised at the outcome. If he learns from his surprise, his future images and future decisions will be affected.

3 See Boulding (1966).

4 If x_a = 100 bushels, at a price of \$2.00 per bushel, it would be worth \$200. If it is worth 2 "utils" per bushel ($v_a = 2$), its total value is 200 utils ($x_a v_a$), a "util" being a hypothetical unit of welfare. This illustration assumes simple *additivity* of utilities. More complex relations can be postulated but would not much change the results.

5 In Dickinson (1962) and reprinted in Boulding (1971, pp. 235–249).

6 Arbitrage is the process by which individuals take advantage of price differences in different parts of a market by buying something where the price is low and selling it to a part of the market where the price is high. This tends to raise the price where it is low and lower it where it is high, and so bring all prices in the market into consistency. A person who practices arbitrage is called an arbitrageur.

7 The principle that "bad money drives out the good" is usually called "Gresham's Law" after Sir Thomas Gresham (1519?–1579).

8 Morgan and Baerwaldt (1971, p. 20).

References

Boulding, K.E., *Economic Analysis*, 4th ed., Vol. 1, New York: Harper and Row, 1966.

Boulding, K.E., *Collected Papers*, Vol. II, Fred Glahe, ed., Boulder, Colorado: Colorado Associated University Press, 1971.

Dickinson, F.G., ed., *Philanthropy and Public Policy*, National Bureau of Economic Research, 1962.

Gouldner, Alvin W., "The Norm of Reciprocity: A Preliminary Statement," *American Sociological Review*, 25, 1960, 161–178.

Morgan, James N. and Baerwaldt, Nancy A., "Trends in Inter-Family Transfers," Paper presented at a joint session of the Association for the Study of the Grants Economy and the American Economic Association, New Orleans, December 1971.

Oi, Walter Y., "The Economic Cost of the Draft," *American Economic Review*, May 1967, 39–62.

Schumpeter, Joseph, *Capitalism, Socialism and Democracy*, New York: Harper & Row, 1942.

Titmuss, R.M., *The Gift Relationship*, London: Allen & Unwin, Ltd., 1971.

11a Commentary article: Kenneth Boulding's grants economics[1]

L. Randall Wray[2]

I will examine the basis of Boulding's claim that neoclassical economics is only a subclass of his more general approach, briefly explain his theory of the grants economy, analyze the application of this theory to the financial system, puzzle over the relative lack of institutionalist interest in this area of Boulding's work, and offer several criticisms of his approach.

Toward the grants economy

From his first publication (1932; in J.M. Keynes's *Economic Journal* as an undergraduate) to his last, Boulding was highly skeptical of neoclassical economics. He traced the origins of grants economics to his peace research in the late 1950s (Mott 1992, 365), but it is easy to place the genesis of these ideas in his early critiques of neoclassical theory in the 1940s and even the 1930s. In these critiques, he was concerned with assumptions of fully utilized, scarce resources (1932); with the transformation of economics from an analysis of the sources of wealth to a theory of distribution of fixed resources (1939); with assumptions of utility maximization as the single goal of human behavior (1952; 1954); and with marginal productivity as the basis of distribution (1935).

Boulding did not reject the notion of an equilibrium distribution, but he argued that it would depend on the institutions of society rather than on productivities (Mott 1992, 360). He recognized quite early that, in his words, "marginal theory is a set of mathematical variations on the theme that everybody does what they think is best at the time. This is almost an identity" (Mott 1992, 357). By itself, this will not take us very far because utility functions or preference relations are neither given nor independent; they are, as Thorstein Veblen argued, the *product* of human interaction, relationships, and institutions (1963, 138). Further, Boulding was very skeptical of the concept of "maximization," arguing that the *process* of carefully weighing marginal utilities would be highly disagreeable (and, indeed, fraught with the danger of error) so that there would instead "be a preference for plateaus of opportunity, where we can wander around without disaster and even large errors are not fatal..." (1952, 398). Besides,

> even the opportunity function may not be invariant to the path chosen; means determine ends, and ends means; history is irreversible, and often there are no roads back from errors committed ... it is no wonder that mankind has generally retreated from the quagmire of rationality to the solid highroads of taboo and principle...
>
> (1952, 399)

I have elsewhere (Wray 1990a) written of Boulding's preoccupation with balance sheets and stocks and, particularly, with changes in these over time. He argued that any disturbance to some sort of general equilibrium generates a process of homeostasis as all economic agents adjust balance sheets in response to the deviation of their actual from desired positions caused by primary, secondary, tertiary, and so on, disturbances to the system. Much later, he presented these ideas using a "world economic matrix," "a vast system of echoes" that attempts to trace the ultimate effects of any disturbance, although "...it is often very hard to predict what the total effect will be" (1981, 54; 1944). However, one can be sure that "those who can adjust will adjust, and those who cannot will not, so that the ultimate impact of the system in terms of distribution ends up with the nonadjustable..." (1978a, vii).

The concern with *stocks* led to his application of population theory to economics (explicitly in 1934; 1955b; 1985b, but also implicitly in 1932; 1935; 1936) and moved him toward a non-mechanistic, dynamic, *systems* perspective (Troub 1978, 52; Boulding 1957a; 1963; 1969b). Boulding helped found the Society for General Systems Research (1954), and his interest in this area eventually led to the search for an integration of the sciences on the basis of a general, evolutionary approach (1971c; 1978b; Mott 1992). In his view, individuals do not and cannot perceive raw data; rather, data are mediated through a learned process of interpretation and acceptance, and shared interpretations (or "images") of the world make social organizations possible (Troub 1978). This interest in organization led Boulding to wonder why some social conflicts lead to creative resolution, while others cannot be resolved. During an incredibly fertile period toward the end of the 1950s, Boulding helped lay the groundwork for three related research areas: conflict resolution, peace research, and grants economics. (He helped found the Center for Research on Conflict Resolution [1958] and the *Journal of Conflict Resolution*; he served as the president of the International Peace Research Society, and he helped found the Association for the Study of the Grants Economy [1969] and served as its president [Mott 1992; Pfaff 1976].) According to Boulding, during a year in Jamaica (1959–60) he hit upon the notion of an integrative system, within which conflict can be constructive (Mott 1992, 366). Components of the integrative system include status, identity, community, respect, love, hate, benevolence, and malevolence, in short, "the whole raft of social institutions which define roles in such a way that you do things because of what you are and because of what I am..." (1965b, 348; 1981, v).

Boulding claimed that a search for a *measure* of the integrative system led to the idea of a *grant*, that is, a unilateral transfer (Mott 1992, 366). However, it should be clear that his early interest in balance sheets played a role in the recognition that not all balance sheet transactions involve equal exchanges. According to Boulding, any time there is a redistribution of net worth, a grant has occurred:

> The net worth criterion can be effectively used to distinguish a grant as any two-party relationship in which an exchangeable passes one way but no exchangeable passes the other way, even though there may be nonexchangeables passing between the two parties.
>
> (1981, 2)

Grants always increase the net worth of the grantee and decrease that of the grantor; economists had ignored grants precisely because their focus on exchange led them to examine only cases in which transfers did not affect net worth (1969b).

The three systems of social organization

Further reflection, however, convinced Boulding that grants could not measure the integrative system because they could be given out of "love" or out of "fear." He thus developed an elaborate theory involving three systems of social organization presented variously as threat, exchange, and integrative systems or as the systems of fear, exchange, and love. There is admittedly some ambiguity in Boulding's presentation of his *general* theory of the integrative system because his exposition varied over time. As mentioned above, he first defined the integrative system in such a way that it would seem to include a wide range of human forces and human drives, including, as Ray Canterbery remembers, "love and hate, malevolence and benevolence, faith and fact, curiosity, commitment, pity, envy, identity, solidarity," in short, all those things that "integrate the 'group' and serve to organize interactive and collective behavior."[3] Boulding's integrative system would thus be the source of many of the institutions studied by institutionalists. In this view, the integrative system includes "hate" and "malevolence" and would seem to play an important role regardless of the form society might take. In other words, the integrative system so defined would be involved whether society were primarily organized by love, by fear, or by exchange because some social integration is always required. The earlier version of his triad of systems is, thus: fear, exchange, and love, with the integrative "system" playing a role in each. In this case, grants would form an important part of the integrative system, although they could come out of "love" or out of "fear." In the latest version of his theory (1981), however, Boulding used the term "integrative system" much more narrowly, identifying it with what he had previously called "love." In this case, the triad becomes fear, exchange, and integrative systems, and grants are involved in both the integrative and the fear systems. I will use this later version in what follows.

According to Boulding, all societies are organized through a combination of these three systems; however, historically there has been an evolution away from early dominance of the threat system to greater reliance on exchange, "an extraordinarily equalitarian institution" (1965b, 348). Presumably, further evolution will allow the integrative system to flower (1963; 1972a; 1968a; 1969b). The exchange and integrative systems will ultimately triumph over threat systems because the latter require willingness and ability to carry out the threat; eventually, either willingness or ability will fail, in which case the threat loses credibility. In a more wistful summary, Boulding says:

> Four things that give mankind a shove/Are threats, exchange, persuasion, love/But taken in the wrong proportions/These give us cultural abortions/ For threats bring manifold abuses/In games where everybody loses/ Exchange enriches every nation/But leads to dangerous alienation/Persuaders organize their brothers/But fool themselves as well as others/And love, with longer pull than hate/Is slow indeed to propagate.
>
> (1963, 147)

In the hypothesized world of neoclassical exchange, independence of utility functions and unlimited selfishness ensure the absence of benevolence and malevolence; this, in turn, guarantees that trade cannot affect the net worth of the parties to the exchange. According to Boulding, "Anything less descriptive of the human condition could hardly be imagined"; the plain fact is that our lives are dominated by interdependent utility functions (1969a, 454). This means that one is willing to reduce one's net worth to help another (benevolence) *or* to do harm to another (malevolence) (1972b). Grants, in turn, can be uncoerced—voluntarily given—(gifts or philanthropy), or coerced (tribute) through social pressure, force of law, or threats. (This is more a continuum than a dichotomy [1962]; for example, most of us voluntarily pay taxes we have approved at the ballot box because we believe these represent a legitimate method of providing government revenue while eliminating the "free-rider" problem associated with "public goods".) And just as the neoclassical relative price system of an exchange economy performs allocative, distributive, and development functions, the grants system similarly performs these functions (1969a). This is why Boulding classifies neoclassical economics as a subspecies of his more general approach; a focus on exchange alone ignores the importance of philanthropy and tribute in allocating resources, determining income and wealth, and generating economic growth. Furthermore, as discussed, Boulding acknowledges interdependence of utility functions, the social determination of preferences, the institutional basis of income distribution, and the importance of interlocking balance sheets—all of which make his approach more general.

According to Boulding, there are two kinds of communities: those of ascription (membership by birth and origin) and those of achievement (to which one belongs by choice) (1957a). The development of capitalism and the concomitant rise of the exchange system create a community of achievement, which is a precondition to full development of an integrative system, by creating opportunities and by destroying ascription communities (1957a; 1972a, 594). However, *because* exchange does not require significant interpersonal relations (for example, it does not require the sacrifice involved in a threat system or an integrative system, but it does require a minimum of trust between the parties to the exchange) it also negates community (1968a, 387). On the other hand, exchange as a *system* requires at least some of the characteristics of an integrative system to give it legitimacy. Boulding notes that nobody *loves* an exchange system (an observation he credited to Joseph Schumpeter [1981]); indeed, many types of exchange are almost universally disliked (Boulding lists as examples exchanges in the labor market, in the financial markets, in the drug and alcohol trade, and in prostitution). Thus, an integrative system is required to give legitimacy to the exchange system. In his view, as society evolved, it would place more emphasis on integrative and exchange relations and less on coercive relations.

When he was young, Boulding wanted to be a socialist. However, his study of classical economics led to appreciation of the workings of the invisible hand and to the harmonies purported to result from reliance on the price system (1957a). The Great Depression cast some doubt on his beliefs, but Keynes's *General Theory* appeared to rescue libertarianism. Boulding came to associate planning with rule by force (the threat system) and "to fear tyranny as the inevitable counterpart of large scale organization and the monopoly of the state" (1957a, 72). This led to a "new appreciation" of the impersonality of the market and to a life-long suspicion of government intervention. According to Boulding, capitalism is a "polylithic" society that allows a network of small organizations coordinated through the market systems; he compared it with an ecosystem of roughly equal individuals (1957a, 79) (although he did recognize the rapid growth of the size of organizations this century, he argued "the case for capitalism is the case for smallness of scale; the case against Communism is the case against the Brontosaurus—that beyond a certain point, increase in the scale of organization results in a breakdown of communications, in a lack of flexibility, in bureaucratic stagnation and insensitivity" [1958, 126]). On balance, however, Boulding's orientation was libertarian: "Nations are built on the solid foundations of violence and cruelty, threats and counterthreats" (1963, 147); "I am as unfriendly to great societies as I am to great men and my ideal society is one which interferes as little as possible with the ability of little people to have a little fun" (1972a, 602).

On the *other* other hand, Boulding attacked free market libertarians such as Milton Friedman by proclaiming the greatest threat to the exchange system is the claim that it can do everything (1965b). He also emphasized that a grants economy develops to correct the defects of the exchange economy by supporting those who cannot be productive, by compensating for discrimination in exchange, and so on (1976). He faulted such libertarians for their failure to understand the integrative system, which cannot be created by exchange, but only by things such as religion, education, family, or nationalism; of these the national state is "by far" the strongest integrative system in the world today (1965b, 353). Public and private grants help to develop the integrative system, bringing us closer together (1969a, 479, 482). The greatest task of social and moral sciences, according to Boulding, is to walk the fine line between "intolerable tyranny" and a society that "becomes a community which enlarges and makes more meaningful the lives of all persons within it" (1972a, 603).

Still, readers will remember Boulding's habitual skepticism and distrust of "do-gooders." He proclaimed many times his "principal of political irony": everything done to help the poor actually hurts them, and vice-versa (1976, 16). He was fond of Director's law: "Nearly all social legislation seems to result in redistributing away from the poor and the rich toward the middle" (1978a, vii). He adopted the conservative's favorite attack on the welfare system: that grants create a "dependency trap" (1981). He described the whole social democracy movement as the development of a larger grants economy, with most grants diverted to the rich and middle class; indeed, social democracy was defined as "how the government subsidizes the middle in the name of subsidizing the poor" (1978a, vii). His distrust even extended to individual do-gooders: according to Boulding, the hero is the great legitimator of the threat system; exchange is the great threat to the hero and to the saint (1968b, 399). While these statements were no doubt partially designed to shock liberals (I can remember nearly a half dozen occasions on which Boulding told me that trees are the worst polluters on earth!), they also reflected Boulding's notion of homeostasis: any disturbance to the system leads to multifarious impacts that are difficult to trace and measure. This makes it very unlikely that well-meaning policies would have desired consequences.

Although consistency is the mark of a small mind, one would like to see more from Boulding on the role of the nation state in developing the integrative system; if, as he said, the nation state is the most important integrative force, but is at the same time the greatest threat system, what are we to do? I think that in spite of his skeptical attitude, in his later years, he came down more heavily on the side of the state as integrative force (although he was always concerned with the arms race and the use by the United States of threats *internationally*). The 12 years of vindictive and disintegrative leadership of the Reagan–Bush tenure, during which *both* the tax system and the welfare system were dismantled, must have played a role in tipping the scales. This "controlled experiment" brought into sharp detail the successes of the "Great Society" through comparison with the unbridled selfishness of the 1980s. Boulding remarked that surveys "reveal that the rich in this country are a) almost inconceivably stingy and b) quite surprisingly stupid" (1965b, 352). After the Reagan–Bush experiment in redistributing income to the rich, Boulding was despondent over the lack of public *grants* funding for education, homelessness, poverty, and disintegration in the family—he argued that just a 5 percent tax increase to fund public grants would be of enormous value (Mott 1992, 370).

The failure of grants economics

While Boulding was certainly admired by many institutionalists, his work on the grants economy is virtually ignored by them. Other than a few tributes (Troub

1978; Silk 1978) and book reviews (Broder 1981; Faas 1981; Heilbroner 1975; Rasche 1981; Sichel 1981), I could find no citations in the *JEI* to Boulding's ideas on grants. He was rather ambivalent about institutionalists, too. He once received a letter from Ayres "accusing" him of being an institutionalist; although he said he would accept the accusation, one suspects he was never serious about this (1957b). He also said that although institutionalists reach the wrong conclusions, they do ask the right questions—but this was a backhanded compliment at best, for he used virtually identical words to describe Marx (for whom he had little respect) (1957b; 1978b; 1981; Mott 1992). He claimed that an early reading of institutionalist writing left him with the impression that it offered nothing but bad writing, bad temper, and sniping radicalism—a position from which I suspect he retreated only partially (1957b).

If I may be permitted a sweeping evaluation, I would say that Boulding's theory of grants economics has been a resounding failure. While most economists are probably somewhat familiar with the general outline of the argument, it was embraced by only a few, primarily conservative neoclassical economists. In a rather strange introduction to a series on the grants economy, Boulding (with Pfaff) says

> this series of volumes might almost be described as radical economics by regular economists. Most are members of the Association for the Study of the Grants Economy, and some may indeed be members of the Union for Radical Political Economy too, although most of them are not, we are sure.
>
> (Boulding and Pfaff 1972, i)

The list of "regular" economists who contributed to various volumes on grants economics reads almost like a "who's who" of the American Economics Association (Henry Aaron, Evsey Domar, Harry G. Johnson, W. Lee Hansen, Thomas Havrilesky, Patric Hendershott, Charles Schultze, Tibor Scitovsky, Jan Tinbergen, and Murray Weidenbaum).[4] Most of the contributed essays are "applied" studies, which try to measure the impact of grants resulting from government intervention into the market economy. Many are little more than tax incidence studies; others find that government intervention misallocates scarce resources—a finding that is not surprising given the free market orientation of most of the economists. In short, very little of "grants economics" has been "radical"—indeed, the research program has deviated only very slightly from that of "regular" Neoclassical economics: studies of deviations from optimal allocations of scarce resources caused by grants.

One such volume will have to serve as an example: that on grants and the financial system, edited by Boulding and Wilson (Boulding and Wilson 1978a). Boulding had identified the financial system as perhaps the most fertile area for application of his theory of grants.[5] Most of these essays are concerned with "seigniorage" through which the government and banks receive grants from the public (e.g., Johnson 1978; Klein 1978), with the "inflation tax" (Johnson 1978; Wilson 1978b), and with "implicit" grants in the form of credit guarantees and interest rate controls that "redistribute" income (Pyle 1978; von Furstenberg 1978; Weidenbaum 1978; Wilson 1978a). I found all the articles to be extremely confused: the authors neither understand Boulding's theory of grants nor do they understand the financial topics addressed.

For example, the articles on seigniorage emphasize that through their ability to create money, banks and the government are able to appropriate to themselves real goods and services; this is defined as a grant or unilateral transfer to banks or the government; and in several of the articles, there is some implication that governments, at least, are violating the rules of the game through seigniorage. Nonsense. Boulding has defined a grant as a reduction of net worth of the grantor and increase of net worth of the grantee. But "money creation" does neither: banks might purchase goods and services (although they rarely do so) by "money creation," which is merely the issue of bank liabilities. Neither the net worth of banks nor that of those who supply the goods and services to them would change at all: banks have more assets but also more liabilities, while the public has fewer goods and services but more bank deposits. The same principles hold regardless of who creates money—whether it is the government, or you, or me—and as anyone can create money, I would not deny to the government that which the lowly university employee is disposed to do (Wray 1990b).

The argument that inflation redistributes income and wealth through a series of unilateral transfers among groups also makes little sense. Inflation cannot normally lead to grants: inflation may hurt some groups in *real* terms, but real terms are irrelevant to the notion of a grant—balance sheets are kept in nominal terms only for reasons quite clear to readers of this journal. The only exception commonly encountered would be in the case of non-indexed progressive income taxes (the topic of some of the articles) where "grants" occur through "bracket creep"—indeed, it is claimed that the government purposely causes inflation in order to receive this grant. However, the authors merely assume that inflation is a discretionary variable. The "regular" response to the question of how the government causes inflation is that it is done through control over the money supply. However, as readers are aware: (1) the government has no direct control over the money supply; (2) the evidence of a correlation between "money supply" and "inflation" is extremely weak, and the theory behind the notion is even weaker; (3) even if money causes inflation, we are all as guilty as the government in causing inflation since we all create money all the time; and (4) the preponderance of evidence suggests that policymakers fear inflation more than just about anything and are willing to impose tremendous hardship domestically and internationally in the name of fighting it.

I cannot offer a definitive explanation for the failure of grants economics to catch the *attention* of those who might have made better use of it. One explanation is that there is a problem with Boulding's definition of a grant. He defined grants in an accountant's terms—if the accountant regards the transaction as involving items of equal worth, then no grant occurs. In much of his discussion (which almost always used the tools of utility analysis), however, he implied that what was important was the perception of equality by the two parties to the transaction—this is quite different. The point is that Boulding cannot have it both ways, and we can probably get further with the accountant's approach. But this means that we must dispense with the tools used by Boulding in virtually every exposition of grants economics—that is, utility, preferences, maximization, efficient allocations, and so on.

Finally, grants economics can be made much more appealing through introduction of some institutionalist principles. Boulding usually started from the assumption that resources are scarce; this led to his formulation of "Duchess's Law": "the more there is of yours, the less there is of mine" (1965a, 325), or the conclusion that every grant involves a winner and a loser; that every government intervention leads to *redistribution* of wealth rather than creation of wealth (1981, 12); that if one thing grows, it does so at the expense of another (1955a); that we must think of the earth as a spaceship in which scarcity will be the most dominant aspect of the society—and spaceships cannot afford Great Societies (1966, 320); and that if X gets a grant, Y cannot (1981, vi). On the other hand, Boulding recognized even in his first published article (1932) that this need not be the case, and he argued that if unemployed resources exist, then practically anything we want to do is virtually costless (1966). This is much closer to the institutionalist view that resources are created, rather than scarce, even though we would not want to throw out completely Boulding's ecological leanings. But the important point is that scarce resources are almost never an obstacle to improving living standards and that so long as unemployed resources exist, improvement of one balance sheet need not hurt another.

Perhaps grants can be more usefully defined as an increase of the assets of one balance sheet without an increase of liabilities of that balance sheet—there is no reason to restrict grants to cases where this is offset by a decrease of net worth of the "grantor." For example, if the federal government issues debt and provides a grant to enable a student to attend college, does it make any sense to argue that the net worth of the US government has now declined? We could argue about how this *should* be treated on the government's balance sheet (is this an investment? consumption?), but it certainly does not require that anyone must give up anything to enable that student to attend college (assuming there are empty desks in the system, which there certainly are). The *normal* case is that we all can enjoy *more*!

Like Troub (1978), I believe that part of the reason Boulding's ideas have not had a big impact is because their meaning and potential value can only be assessed from the context of the framework of his entire system of thought; however, like Heilbroner (1975), I find much of that vision rather fuzzy and some of it unappealing. In general, his analysis is ahistorical, indeed, historically inaccurate. For example, his argument that societies are originally organized on the basis of threat, but gradually evolve to organization through integrative systems, does not square with history.[6] His analysis could also have been improved through examination of anthropology; in particular, his view of social organization is similar to that of institutionalists who have examined the institution of reciprocity, such as David Hamilton (1970), but theirs is based on close examination of society, while his is apparently ignorant of anthropological studies.[7] Like Heilbroner (1975), I find the almost complete absence of discussion by Boulding of power in "exchange" relationships perplexing.[8] Similarly, Boulding rarely discussed the role played by fraud in the integrative system—but fraud is important in religion and nationalism, which he recognizes as two of the biggest integrative forces.

In spite of these reservations, I can strongly recommend Boulding's *Collected Papers* in general and his work on the grants economy in particular. At the very least, his writing is prescient, entertaining, and imaginative. I would almost be willing to say that one could learn just about everything there is to know about economics (and everything else) by reading the six volumes of his *Collected Papers*, plus his *Reconstruction* (1950). Everyone should read his first article (1932), an amazing piece for an economist at any stage, but truly remarkable for an undergraduate. Boulding tells the story of his acceptance to graduate studies at the University of Chicago, when he proudly provided a copy of this paper to Frank Knight—who responded with a note that read "Professor Knight thanks Mr. Boulding for his paper, which he thinks is as wrong and as confused as possible" (1971a, viii). We are fortunate, indeed, that this did not discourage Mr. Boulding.

Notes

1 This article was previously published in *Journal of Economic Issues* 28, no. 4 (December 1994): 1205–1225.
2 The author was a Research Associate, The Jerome Levy Economics Institute, and Associate Professor, University of Denver. He is now professor at the University of Missouri, Kansas City. The author would like to thank Ray Canterbery and Anne Mayhew for valuable comments.
3 E. Ray Canterbery, private correspondence, October 1993.
4 I do not mean to imply that all of these economists are equally neoclassical, nor are they equally "respectable" or "regular."
5 Ray Canterbery (private correspondence) disagrees, arguing that application of the grants idea to the financial system is its least fertile application. While I agree that, thus far, the theory of grants has contributed virtually nothing to our understanding of the financial system, I think that it could be applied in an interesting and informative manner if done correctly.
6 As just one example, the integrative system of tribal society gave way throughout Europe to the feudal threat system.
7 For an interesting critique, see the comments by De Reuck (1976), in which he adds a third type of transaction, mutual sharing, to Boulding's grants–exchange dichotomy. De Reuck argues that exchanges are reciprocal transactions, giving rise to exchange bonds whereby people profit from their differences. Grants are defined as unilateral transactions, giving rise to dative bonds. Finally, mutual sharing occurs within the family or the tribe, giving rise to complementary bonds whereby people profit from similarities, and through which a community of interests is developed. De Reuck goes on to argue that mutual sharing builds the integrative system, while grants would play a smaller role because the donor is usually in a position of power over the recipient. This seems to be a useful extension of Boulding's approach.
8 Exchange is frequently neither free nor equalitarian, as Boulding seems to assume. For example, the sale of labor power usually involves a degree of coercion because wages are required just to purchase the basic necessities required for life. The worker cannot enter into an exchange relationship with the employer on equal grounds.

Appendix: selected bibliography

Note: I will depart from the usual format for material taken from the Collected Papers; I will first list the volumes of the collection and will then list relevant articles from these volumes; all page numbers cited in the text refer to the reprints in the Collected Papers, but the dates cited refer to the original publication dates—which are important for understanding the evolution of Boulding's thought.

The Collected Papers of Kenneth E. Boulding, Volume 1, edited by Fred R. Glahe. Boulder, Colorado: Colorado Associated University Press, 1971a.

The Collected Papers of Kenneth E. Boulding, Volume 2: *Economics*, edited by Fred R. Glahe, 1971b.

The Collected Papers of Kenneth E. Boulding, Volume 3: *Political Economy*, edited by Larry D. Singell, 1973.

The Collected Papers of Kenneth E. Boulding, Volume 5: *International Systems: Peace, Conflict Resolution, and Politics*, edited by Larry D. Singell, 1975.

The Collected Papers of Kenneth E. Boulding, Volume 6: *Toward the Twenty-First Century: Political Economy, Social Systems, and World Peace*, edited by Larry D. Singell, 1985a.

Boulding, Kenneth E. "The Place of the 'Displacement Cost' Concept in Economic Theory." *Economic Journal* 42, no. 165 (March 1932): 137–141. Reprinted in CP(1): 3–7.

Boulding, Kenneth E. "The Application of the Pure Theory of Population Change to the Theory of Capital." *Quarterly Journal of Economics* 48 (August 1934): 645–666. Reprinted in CP(1): 11–32.

Boulding, Kenneth E. "The Theory of a Single Investment." *Quarterly Journal of Economics* 49 (May 1935): 475–494. Reprinted in CP(1): 43–62.

Boulding, Kenneth E. "Time and Investment." *Economica* NS 3, no. 10 (May 1936): 196–220. Reprinted in CP(1): 65–89.

Boulding, Kenneth E. "Equilibrium and Wealth: A Word of Encouragement to Economists." *Canadian Journal of Economics and Political Science* 5 (1939): 1–18. Reprinted in CP(1): 93–110.

Boulding, Kenneth E. "The Incidence of a Profits Tax." *American Economic Review* 34, no. 4 (September 1944): 567–572. Reprinted in CP(1): 147–152.

Boulding, Kenneth E. *A Reconstruction of Economics*. New York: John Wiley & Sons, Inc., 1950.

Boulding, Kenneth E. "Welfare Economics." In *A Survey of Contemporary Economics*, vol. 2, edited by B. Haley, 1–34. Homewood, Ill.: R.D. Irwin, 1952. Reprinted in CP(1): 369–402.

Boulding, Kenneth E. "An Economist's View of the Manpower Concept." *Proceedings of a Conference on the Utilization of Scientific and Professional Manpower*. New York: Columbia University Press, 1954, 11–26. Reprinted in CP(1): 419–432.

Boulding, Kenneth E. "In Defense of Statics." *Quarterly Journal of Economics* 69, no. 4 (1955a): 485–502. Reprinted in CP(1): 467–484.

Boulding, Kenneth E. "An Application of Population Analysis to the Automobile Population of the United States." *Kyklos* 2 (1955b): 109–124. Reprinted in CP(1): 435–450.

Boulding, Kenneth E. " Economic Theory: The Reconstruction Reconsidered." In *Segments of the Economy—1956; A Symposium*. Cleveland: Howard Allen, 8–55, 1957a. Reprinted in CP(2): 37–85.

Boulding, Kenneth E. "A New Look at Institutionalism." *American Economic Review* 47, no. 2 (May 1957b): 1–12. Reprinted in CP(2): 89–100.

Boulding, Kenneth E. "The Jungle of Hugeness." *Saturday Review* (March 1, 1958): 11–13, and 50. Reprinted in CP(2): 125–131.

Boulding, Kenneth E. "Notes on a Theory of Philanthropy." *Philanthropy and Public Policy*, edited by Frank G. Dickenson, 57–71. New York: National Bureau of Economic Research, 1962. Reprinted in CP(2): 235–249.

Boulding, Kenneth E. "Towards a Pure Theory of Threat Systems." *American Economic Review* 53, no. 2 (May 1963): 424–434. Reprinted in CP(5): 137–147.

Boulding, Kenneth E. "The Economics of Human Conflict." *The Nature of Human Conflict*, edited by Elton B. McNeil, 172–191. Englewood Cliffs, NJ: Prentice-Hall, 1965a. Reprinted in CP(2): 325–344.

Boulding, Kenneth E. "Economic Libertarianism." *Conference on Savings and Residential Financing*, 1965 Proceedings, Chicago: US Savings and Loan League, 1965b, 30–42. Reprinted in CP(2): 347–358.

Boulding, Kenneth E. "Is Scarcity Dead?" *The Public Interest* 5 (Fall 1966): 36–44. Reprinted in CP(3): 313–321.

Boulding, Kenneth E. "Grants Versus Exchange in the Support of Education." Joint Economic Committee, Congress of the United States: US Government Printing Office, 1968a, 232–238. Reprinted in CP(3): 385–391.

Boulding, Kenneth E. "The Legitimation of the Market." *Nebraska Journal of Economics and Business* 7, no. 1 (Spring 1968b): 3–14. Reprinted in CP(3): 395–406.

Boulding, Kenneth E. "Economics as a Moral Science." (Presidential Address, American Economic Association, December 29, 1968). *American Economic Review* 59, no. 1 (March 1969a): 1–12. Reprinted in CP(2): 449–460.

Boulding, Kenneth E. "The Grants Economy." *Michigan Academician* (Papers of the Michigan Academy of Science, Arts, and Letters) 1, nos. 1–2 (Winter 1969b): 3–11. Reprinted in CP(2): 477–485.

Boulding, Kenneth E. "Introduction to the Collected Papers of Kenneth E. Boulding, Volume II: Economics." CP(2): vii–viii, 1971c.

Boulding, Kenneth E. "Man as a Commodity." In *Human Resources and Economic Welfare*. New York: Columbia University Press, 1972a, 35–49. Reprinted in CP(3): 589–603.

Boulding, Kenneth E. "Towards a Pure Theory of Foundations." Supplement to *Non-Profit Report* 5, no. 3 (March 1972b). Reprinted in CP(6): 167–186.

Boulding, Kenneth E. "Equity and Distribution: The Interaction of Markets and Grants." In *Grants and Exchange*, edited by Martin Pfaff, 5–21. Amsterdam, New York, and Oxford: North-Holland, 1976.

Boulding, Kenneth E. "Preface." In *Redistribution Through the Financial System: The Grants Economics of Money and Credit*, edited by Kenneth E. Boulding and Thomas Frederick Wilson, v–viii. New York: Praeger Special Studies, Praeger Scientific, 1978a.

Boulding, Kenneth E. "Comments." *Journal of Economic Issues* 12, no. 2 (June 1978b): 535–539.

Boulding, Kenneth E. *A Preface to Grants Economics: The Economy of Love and Fear*. New York: Praeger Special Studies, Praeger Scientific, 1981.

Boulding, Kenneth E. "Puzzles over Distribution." *Challenge* (November–December 1985b): 4–10.

Boulding, Kenneth E., and Martin Pfaff, eds. *Redistribution to the Rich and the Poor: The Grants Economics of Income Distribution*. Belmont, Calif.: Wadsworth Publishing Company, 1972.

Boulding, Kenneth E., and Thomas Frederick Wilson, eds. *Redistribution Through the Financial System: The Grants Economics of Money and Credit*. New York: Praeger Special Studies, Praeger Scientific, 1978a.

Boulding, Kenneth E., and Thomas Frederick Wilson "Grants Economics in the Future of the Financial System." In *Redistribution Through the Financial System: The Grants Economics of Money and Credit*, edited by Kenneth E. Boulding and Thomas Frederick Wilson, 289–290. New York: Praeger Special Studies, Praeger Scientific, 1978b.

References

Boulding, Kenneth E. "The Place of the 'Displacement Cost' Concept in Economic Theory." *Economic Journal* 42, no. 165 (March 1932): 137–141.

Boulding, Kenneth E. "The Application of the Pure Theory of Population Change to the Theory of Capital." *Quarterly Journal of Economics* 48 (August 1934): 645–666.

Boulding, Kenneth E. "The Theory of a Single Investment." *Quarterly Journal of Economics* 49 (May 1935): 475–494.

Boulding, Kenneth E. "Time and Investment." *Economica* NS 3, 10 (May 1936): 196–220.

Boulding, Kenneth E. "Equilibrium and Wealth: A Word of Encouragement to Economists." *Canadian Journal of Economics and Political Science* 5 (1939): 1–18.

Boulding, Kenneth E. "The Incidence of a Profits Tax." *American Economic Review* 34, no. 4 (September 1944): 567–572. Reprinted in CP(1): 147–152.

Boulding, Kenneth E. *A Reconstruction of Economics*. New York: John Wiley & Sons, Inc., 1950.

Boulding, Kenneth E. "Welfare Economics." In *A Survey of Contemporary Economics*, vol. 2, edited by B. Haley, 1–34. Homewood, Ill.: R.D. Irwin, 1952.

Boulding, Kenneth E. "An Economist's View of the Manpower Concept." *Proceedings of a Conference on the Utilization of Scientific and Professional Manpower*. New York: Columbia University Press, 1954, 11–26.

Boulding, Kenneth E. "In Defense of Statics." *Quarterly Journal of Economics* 69, no. 4 (1955a): 485–502.

Boulding, Kenneth E. "An Application of Population Analysis to the Automobile Population of the United States." *Kyklos* 2 (1955b): 109–124.

Boulding, Kenneth E. "Economic Theory: The Reconstruction Reconsidered." Segments of the Economy—1956; A Symposium. Cleveland: Howard Allen, 8–55, 1957a.

Boulding, Kenneth E. "A New Look at Institutionalism." *American Economic Review* 47, no. 2 (May 1957b): 1–12.

Boulding, Kenneth E. "The Jungle of Hugeness." *Saturday Review* (March 1, 1958): 11–13, and 50.

Boulding, Kenneth E. "Notes on a Theory of Philanthropy." *Philanthropy and Public Policy*, edited by Frank G. Dickenson, 57–71. New York: National Bureau of Economic Research, 1962.

Boulding, Kenneth E. "Towards a Pure Theory of Threat Systems." *American Economic Review* 53, no. 2 (May 1963): 424–434.

Boulding, Kenneth E. "The Economics of Human Conflict." *The Nature of Human Conflict*, edited by Elton B. McNeil, 172–191. Englewood Cliffs, NJ: Prentice-Hall, 1965a.

Boulding, Kenneth E. "Economic Libertarianism." *Conference on Savings and Residential Financing* 1965 Proceedings, Chicago: US Savings and Loan League, 1965b, 30–42.

Boulding, Kenneth E. "Is Scarcity Dead?" *The Public Interest* 5 (Fall 1966): 36–44.

Boulding, Kenneth E. "Grants Versus Exchange in the Support of Education." Joint Economic Committee, Congress of the United States: US Government Printing Office: 232–238, 1968a.

Boulding, Kenneth E. "The Legitimation of the Market." *Nebraska Journal of Economics and Business* 7, no. 1 (Spring 1968b): 3–14.

Boulding, Kenneth E. "Economics as a Moral Science." (Presidential Address, American Economic Association, December 29, 1968). *American Economic Review* 59, no. 1 (March 1969a): 1–12.

Boulding, Kenneth E. "The Grants Economy." *Michigan Academician* (Papers of the Michigan Academy of Science, Arts, and Letters) 1, nos. 1–2, (Winter 1969b): 3–11.

Boulding, Kenneth E. *The Collected Papers of Kenneth E. Boulding*, Vol. 1, edited by Fred R. Glahe. Boulder, Colorado: Colorado Associated University Press, 1971a.

Boulding, Kenneth E. "Introduction to the Collected Papers of Kenneth E. Boulding, Volume II: Economics." CP(2): vii–viii, 1971c.

Boulding, Kenneth E. "Man as a Commodity." In *Human Resources and Economic Welfare*. New York: Columbia University Press, 1972a, 35–49.

Boulding, Kenneth E. "Towards a Pure Theory of Foundations." Supplement to *Non-Profit Report* 5, no. 3 (March 1972b).

Boulding, Kenneth E. "Equity and Distribution: The Interaction of Markets and Grants." In *Grants and Exchange*, edited by Martin Pfaff, 5–21. Amsterdam, New York, and Oxford: North-Holland, 1976.

Boulding, Kenneth E. "Preface." In *Redistribution Through the Financial System: The Grants Economics of Money and Credit*, edited by Kenneth E. Boulding and Thomas Frederick Wilson, v–viii. New York: Praeger Special Studies, Praeger Scientific, 1978a.

Boulding, Kenneth E. "Comments." *Journal of Economic Issues* 12, no. 2 (June 1978b): 535–539.

Boulding, Kenneth E. *A Preface to Grants Economics: The Economy of Love and Fear*. New York: Praeger Special Studies, Praeger Scientific, 1981.

Boulding, Kenneth E. "Puzzles over Distribution." *Challenge* (November–December 1985b): 4–10.

Boulding, Kenneth E., and Martin Pfaff, eds. *Redistribution to the Rich and the Poor: The Grants Economics of Income Distribution*. Belmont, Calif.: Wadsworth Publishing Company, 1972.

Boulding, Kenneth E., and Thomas Frederick Wilson, eds. *Redistribution Through the Financial System: The Grants Economics of Money and Credit*. New York: Praeger Special Studies, Praeger Scientific, 1978a.

Broder, Josef M. "Four Reviews of Kenneth E. Boulding and Thomas Frederick Wilson: *Redistribution Through the Financial System: The Grants Economics of Money and Credit*." *Journal of Economic Issues* 15, no. 1 (March 1981): 168–171.

De Reuck, Anthony. "Comment." In *Grants and Exchange*, edited by Martin Pfaff, 22–27. Amsterdam, New York, and Oxford: North-Holland, 1976.

Faas, Ronald C. "Four Reviews of Kenneth E. Boulding and Thomas Frederick Wilson: *Redistribution Through the Financial System: The Grants Economics of Money and Credit*." *Journal of Economic Issues* 15, no. 1 (March 1981): 165–168.

Hamilton, David. "Reciprocity, Productivity, and Poverty." *Journal of Economic Issues* 4, no. 1 (March 1970): 35–42.

Heilbroner, Robert L. "Kenneth Boulding, Collected Papers: A Review Article." *Journal of Economic Issues* 9, no. 1 (March 1975): 73–79.

Johnson, Harry G. "Seigniorage and the 'Inflation Tax' in an International Setting." In *Redistribution Through the Financial System: The Grants Economics of Money and Credit*, edited by Kenneth E. Boulding and Thomas Frederick Wilson, 20–37. New York: Praeger Special Studies, Praeger Scientific, 1978.

Klein, Benjamin. "Money, Wealth, and Seigniorage." In *Redistribution Through the Financial System: The Grants Economics of Money and Credit*, edited by Kenneth E. Boulding and Thomas Frederick Wilson, 3–19. New York: Praeger Special Studies, Praeger Scientific, 1978.

Mott, Tracy. "Kenneth Boulding Interviewed by Tracy Mott 28–29 March 1991." *Review of Political Economy* 4, no. 3 (1992): 341–374.

Pfaff, Martin, ed. *Grants and Exchange*. Amsterdam, New York, and Oxford: North-Holland, 1976.

Pyle, David H. "Interest Rate Ceilings and Net Worth Losses by Savers." In *Redistribution Through the Financial System: The Grants Economics of Money and Credit*, edited by Kenneth E. Boulding and Thomas Frederick Wilson, 87–101. New York: Praeger Special Studies, Praeger Scientific, 1978.

Rasche, Robert H. "Four Reviews of Kenneth E. Boulding and Thomas Frederick Wilson: *Redistribution Through the Financial System: The Grants Economics of Money and Credit*." *Journal of Economic Issues* 15, no. 1 (March 1981): 163–165.

Sichel, Werner. "Four Reviews of Kenneth E. Boulding and Thomas Frederick Wilson: *Redistribution Through the Financial System: The Grants Economics of Money and Credit*." *Journal of Economic Issues* 15, no. 1 (March 1981): 161–163.

Silk, Leonard. "The Economics of Kenneth Boulding." *Journal of Economic Issues* 12, no. 2 (June 1978): 529–539.

Troub, Roger M. "Kenneth Boulding: Economics from a Different Perspective." *Journal of Economic Issues* 12, no. 2 (June 1978): 501–528.

von Furstenberg, George M. "Distribution Effects of GNMA Home Mortgage Purchases and Commitments Under the Tandem Plans." In *Redistribution Through the Financial System: The Grants Economics of Money and Credit*, edited by Kenneth E. Boulding and Thomas Frederick Wilson, 244–266. New York: Praeger Special Studies, Praeger Scientific, 1978.

Weidenbaum, Murray L. "The Use of the Government's Credit Power." In *Redistribution Through the Financial System: The Grants Economics of Money and Credit*, edited by Kenneth E. Boulding and Thomas Frederick Wilson, 211–226. New York: Praeger Special Studies, Praeger Scientific, 1978.

Wilson, Thomas F. "Redistribution Through the Financial System: An Introduction." In *Redistribution Through the Financial System: The Grants Economics of Money and Credit*, edited by Kenneth E. Boulding and Thomas Frederick Wilson, xx–xxxiii. New York: Praeger Special Studies, Praeger Scientific, 1978a.

Wilson, Thomas F. "Identification and Measurement of Grant Elements in Monetary Policy." In *Redistribution Through the Financial System: The Grants Economics of Money and Credit*, edited by Kenneth E. Boulding and Thomas Frederick Wilson, 38–56. New York: Praeger Special Studies, Praeger Scientific 1978b.

Wray, L. Randall. "Boulding's Balloons: A Contribution to Monetary Theory." *Journal of Economic Issues* 24, no. 4 (December 1990a): 1–20.

Wray, L. Randall. *Money and Credit in Capitalist Economies: The Endogenous Money Approach*. Aldershot: Edward Elgar Publishing, 1990b.

11b Comment: A grant perspective

Boulding's grants economics revisited

Arjo Klamer

Boulding attached great importance to his notion of grants. In *A Preface to Grants Economics: The Economy of Love and Fear* (1981), he argued that grants economics covers a large field of economic phenomena and is more than, and includes, neoclassical economics. He clearly had high expectations of this idea of his. He founded, together with a few associates, the Association for the Study of Grants Economy and became its first president. A few studies appeared (e.g. Pfaff 1976) but the publication of *A Preface* turned out to be more or less the swan song of the enterprise. References in the literature dwindled rapidly. Randall Wray concludes in his 1994 review that grants economics simply failed to attract the attention of economists (Wray 1994). He blames Boulding's special and somewhat fuzzy framework.

Although I have trouble with the notion of a grant and suspect that Boulding was too much the neoclassical economist to do justice to the phenomena he had detected, I see a breakthrough in his proposal to consider a world beyond transactions. The standard neoclassical framework is directed at the analysis of exchange, or the moment that buyers and suppliers meet and agree to exchange one good for another. Boulding points out that a far greater part of the numerous interactions among people do not have such a character. People give money to beggars, they give each other presents at Christmas, and they transfer large amounts of money to authorities without a well-specified quid pro quo. Such transfers may amount, so he estimated, from 20 up to 50 percent of GDP, a conservative estimate so it seems now (cf. McCloskey & Klamer 1995).

Boulding thinks about the economy in terms of an accounting framework, so he defines a grant as a transfer from one person to another that decreases the net worth of the first and increases the net worth of another.[1] In case of an exchange, the net worth of each person will stay the same or will increase. When you buy an ice cream, you lose the money you pay but gain the ice cream. It should make you at least equally well-off. (As soon as you finish the ice cream, the situation will change once again, but what counts is the moment of exchange.) Another way of putting it, grants involve a redistribution of net worth.

One consequence of the introduction of grants is that it compels Boulding to consider the non-material goods involved. In the Preface, he notes that he hit upon the notion of grants when he was in Jamaica in the early sixties and noticed how much the people there interacted without the intermediation of money. People pay each other respect, offer courtesy, give attention, pay homage, all of which are valuable to the recipient and are making him better off. Yet such transfers are not accounted for in conventional economic analysis. Boulding sees respect, courtesy, attention, and the like as non-material goods and considers them part of what he calls a social integrative system. You might say, as economists are used to do, that here the sociological perspective enters the analysis. Boulding might have admitted as much, but would have hastened to say that the consideration of such transfers should be part of economics. He sees "grants economics supplementing, or perhaps correcting, the results of the exchange economy". (Boulding 1981, p. 11)

Another picture of the world

Boulding actually tries to alter the picture of the world that economists usually have. In addition to the exchanges that take place and to the transfers from the private sector to the public sector and back (think of taxes and social welfare), he distinguishes the grants that people give each other more or less spontaneously. To distinguish forced grants and voluntary grants, he bundles them under the label of the economy of fear and the latter under that of the economy of love. That gives the picture of the social triangle, as shown in Figure 11b.1.

He uses this picture to compare societies diachronically and synchronically. At first, societies may have moved from a system of love and threat to one that involved more exchange. When markets falter, as during the crisis in the thirties and around 2010, the move is towards the threat part (with stricter rules and tougher norms).

The picture makes one see the world in a different light. It makes one wonder, for instance, about the way societies function, or about what Boulding calls the social integration. Some degree of threat may be needed to enforce property rights, or to procure essential functions, such as roads, dikes, and education. The

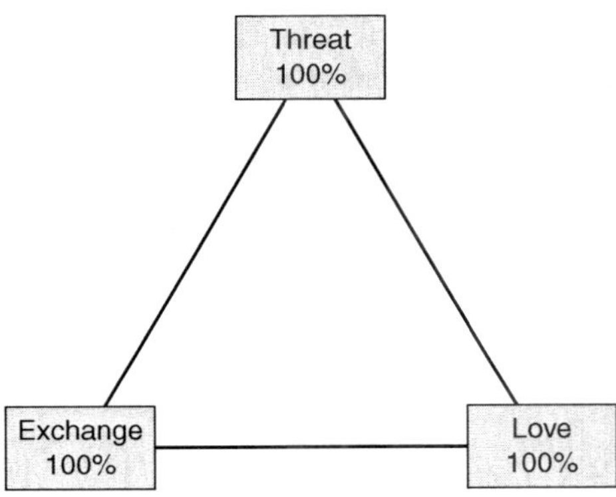

Figure 11b.1 The social triangle.

system of exchange fosters entrepreneurship and creates the space for free choice. It also tends to bring about anonymity and exploitation in the sense that other humans can become the instrument of one's own material gain. That is why the system of love is needed as a countervailing power, to allow for grants, or gifts in the spirit of friendship, family, or other types of social relationships.

It also makes one observe grants that one otherwise may not see. Boulding speaks of implicit grants. When the government rules in favor of an industry with, as the result, a rent for that industry, the customers end up handing over a grant to that industry as they will pay more than they would have before the ruling. The net worth of the customers is decreasing because of the ruling and the net worth of the companies will increase, and that is, according to Boulding's definition, a grant. Most economists identify here an externality of the ruling. Curiously, Boulding does not make the connection in *A Preface*; he does not even refer to the notion of externality. Yet, he may have had a reason to do so as there is a difference. Whereas in conventional economic analysis, externalities are considered external to the system of exchange, Boulding makes them explicit in his picture of the world. In a way he tries to make them endogenous in his model, that is, he internalizes them.

How the notion of the grant contributes to the unraveling of the neoclassical frame

Inclusion of grants in the economic model makes sense as soon as we realize that they contribute to and are part of the welfare in a society. The question is what difference the inclusion of grants makes for the usual neoclassical welfare analysis with the Pareto-optimum as focal point. The problem is immediately clear: When one person hands over a grant to another, that makes him worse off according to the definition of a grant. According to the definition of the Pareto optimum, that would mean a decline in welfare. Boulding argues that if not an increase in welfare the grant would imply an increase in overall well-being. Boulding speaks of goodness with a reference to Aristotle (1981, pp. 115–116).

That argument seems plausible when it concerns a grant that is given out of love. But how about grants that are given out of fear? Boulding finds the reasoning based on individuals maximizing their utility functions wanting at this point. He speculates that the analysis is in need of the notion of a community, his social integration system, in order to make sense of the contribution that grants based on threats (such as taxes) make to overall well-being. The payment of taxes, although not done voluntary, is agreed upon because the government can spend the tax receipts for the betterment of society as a whole. Agreement about forced grants can only be reached with a common interest at stake, that is, when there is a sense of community.

Here we see Boulding's inclination to bend the neoclassical frame to meet his theoretical needs. At another point in his analysis, he realizes that the standard assumptions of stable preferences and selfish behavior focused on the maximizing of one's own utility will not do. Yet, he does not do much more than stating as much. It is imaginable that adjustments in the sense of inclusion of preferences of others in utility functions could salvage the neoclassical frame, but such an adjustment might look too much as an ad-hoc intervention to do justice to the significance of the phenomena of the grants, at least as Boulding sees them.

Boulding's own reservations show in the titling of his book. Why would you call your book *A Preface to Grants Economics* when you have been working with colleagues for years on the project? Calling your book *The General Theory*, as Keynes, speaks of faith and shows assertiveness. Calling your book a *Preface* suggests doubts about the solidity of the theory. It may signal an invitation for elaboration but, as Randall Wray points out, it has not worked that way. The notion of the grant has not found a place in the image of economists. It has not become part of the way economists think and it has not informed and directed their research. Unfortunately so. For the phenomenon that Boulding discerned is too important to dismiss because of theoretical obstacles. It is time to wrest his insight from the neoclassical frame.

Another perspective, another framing is needed

I offer as an alternative a cultural economic perspective (Klamer 1996, 2007). This perspective looks beyond the transactions that follow the logic of the market and considers other spheres in which values are realized, such as the social sphere. (In this respect, the cultural economic perspective corresponds with Boulding's perspective.) It is inspired by observations in the cultural sector and especially on the tension that appears to exist between the cultural valuation of the arts and a financial valuation. Artists may loath the cash nexus even if they are dependent on it. They fear the compromising of cultural and artistic values when they enter a market transaction. By paying serious attention to these emotions and concerns, I became aware of the fact that the valuation of cultural values usually occurs outside the sphere of the market, at least in part. And I discovered good reasons why art works best outside the sphere of the market and that of the government. That led me towards a cultural economic perspective that is incorporating economic as well as cultural processes.

The cultural perspective concurs with Boulding's perception that important interactions take place over and beyond exchanges, or economic transactions. But my suspicion is that Boulding was held back as he clung too much to a neoclassical framing. He tried too hard to reconcile his notion of the grant with neoclassical notions of utility maximization and welfare analysis with the consequence that he did not do justice to the phenomena he had detected. I am inclined to press on and to claim that our perspective on the economy changes radically when we look beyond transactions. I find that I am in need of other concepts, a different accounting system, and for a radical change in the framing. The cultural economic perspective calls for various interventions in Boulding's neoclassical framing. I will restrict myself to three. The first is to replace the notion of a grant with that of the gift. The second is the introduction of the notion of the social good. And the third is a different picture of the world.

Gift instead of grant

The first intervention is to advance the notion of the gift to cover at least part of the domain of grants. As I noted earlier, I do not particularly care for the notion of grants. Grants remind me of foundations when they award sums of money for projects. Students receive grants from universities, Green Peace receives a grant for an educational program. But do I give a grant to my children when I am feeding and housing them? Is my paying respect to you a grant, as Boulding implies? I would not say so. The notion of the gift solves most of these problems. It has the other advantage that an extensive literature is available that discusses its characteristics (see Klamer 2003; Dolfsma *et al.* 2009).

Gifts are characteristically based on reciprocity, so it appears. An economist who is used to framing all interaction in terms of transactions may see in gift-giving a form of transaction. It is how the anthropologist Maus appears to frame the gift-giving in the Caribbean. As he clarifies in the introduction to his famous book *The Gift* (1925), his intent was to "isolate one important set of phenomena: namely, prestations which are in theory voluntary, disinterested and spontaneous, but are in fact obligatory and interested." He continues: "The form usually taken is that of the gift generously offered; but the accompanying behaviour is formal pretence and social deception, while the transaction itself is based on obligation and economic self-interest" (Maus [1925] 1960, p. 1). All his examples are drawn from studies of archaic societies, most famously studies of the potlatch of North American tribes. In the potlatch, a well-endowed member of the tribe would share his richness with the other members during a feast. The analysis shows that this generosity was enforced socially and required for one's social status within the tribe.

More recent studies bring out the complexities of the reciprocal relationships to which the phenomenon of the gift points (for a collection, see Komter 1996). A gift is not an economic exchange because of the open character thereof. The reciprocity implies that the what, how, when, and also often the from whom of the return is undetermined at the moment of the gift. The ambiguity involved is critical and calls for a context that is different from that of an economic exchange. People have to cope with the ambiguity and usually do so socially. In order to sustain a friendship, both friends need to develop a sense of what the reciprocity involves. When I make an expensive trip to help out a friend, I may not even expect a "thank you" (the offer of payment may be a betrayal of the friendship). The question is rather what I would expect him to do in return, how we maintain this sense of reciprocity in the friendship. Is it a nice gift, like a digital camera, for my birthday? Or would it be a few very important conversations that helped me get out of a difficult spot? Nobody can tell; only friends can. Their understanding of the reciprocity defines the friendship.

Gifts enable us to transfer something of value yet without the explicit measurement as in the pricing of the market (see Klamer 1996). By giving money to artists, patrons support artists without getting into a market or commercial relation. The artists may give some work by way of reciprocity, and then they may not. If they were going to price their transactions directly, the nature of the relationship changes.

Gifts can come in the form of money, commodities but also of non-material goods such as attention, respect, that is, the goods that Boulding also explicitly mentioned. They appear to play a critical role in developing and sustaining relations. The combination of non-material goods and the notion of relations brings me to the next intervention of the cultural economic perspective.

The realm of non-material goods, social goods in particular

So much of what we do, so many interactions take place outside the sphere of exchange. That is what Boulding also points out. Yet, the framing in conventional economics tends to privilege the moment of exchange. That is measured and accounted for, thus the processes that bring about critical values are too easily overlooked.

Let me give an example. When I am going with friends to a café, the accountant registers our payment at the end of our visit and the economist would focus on that payment as the transaction that took place. Boulding would quite rightly point out that a lot more is happening at the visit. I may have seriously listened to my friend's story about troubles at his job; I may even have given him valuable advice. We all may have been inspired by the atmosphere in the café; who knows, we may have met people who proved to be valuable contacts later. There is not a good reason to assume that the price that we paid for our visit is in any predictable and meaningful way related to the quality of our conversations or the importance of our encounters. A simple coffee may have been the input for a great conversation that leads to a very profitable new enterprise (perhaps another Facebook!), whereas we may have worked away a most expensive dinner with obligatory and tedious chatter.

As Boulding would point out, the visit to the café generated non-material goods such as contacts, friendship, and maybe an idea or insight. The neoclassical framing of the event would subsume all these under the heading of externalities, yet they are what the visit is all about! This shortcoming of the conventional analysis motivates my second intervention.

I propose to introduce another type of good. I will call it a social good.[2] A social good is non-material in the sense that you cannot hold it in your hands. A social good is social because it comes about in social settings. Friendship is a good example. A friendship is a good like a computer or a refrigerator in the sense that it is valuable for those who own it—it generates services like advice, companionship, support, and the like—and it is costly in terms of time and expenses. We can gain a friendship and we can lose one. People with good friends are better off than people without. Friendship is a common good because it is jointly owned. I do not own a friendship myself; I cannot buy the ownership and I cannot sell it. I share the ownership with my friend.

Social goods are clearly distinct from private and public goods. Social goods are not private because they are not privately owned. They are not collective or public either because they exclude people from enjoying them (like the non friends from friendship). They are similar to the club good that Buchanan (1965) points to, but comprise a far larger domain. All types of relationships are social goods. The sciences are a social good as they are shared by scientists. So are the arts. A neighborhood is a social good as is a tradition, a ritual, a society. When a group of people share a sense of solidarity, then that is a social good. So is a common identity. Social goods are all over. They are so obviously there, that it is remarkable the neoclassical framing tends to overlook them.

Social goods are what most human actions are all about. When I buy a house, the house is mine. The house is a private good. But the reason for buying a house is not the house itself. I want to own a house in order to create a home. The home is a social good that I share with the members of my household. Most things I buy are inputs in the "production" of my home. But I cannot buy myself a *home*.

If we were considering social goods as a category, we would immediately see that gifts serve as contributions to social goods. They are a way of gaining ownership of social goods, such as a home, the arts, the sciences, society, and friendship. Acquisition, sustenance, and strengthening of the ownership of social goods are then objectives of gift-giving or, for that matter, grant-giving. Conventional economic analysis must resort to anomalous explanations in terms of cooperative or, even worse, altruistic behavior. With the notion of social goods, it becomes perfectly clear why artists, scientists, mothers, and friends make sacrifices: they do so to secure for them important social goods.

The introduction of the notion of social goods opens a new perspective on human actions and interactions. I observe that much of what we humans do is to realize values in the form of one social good or another.

Social goods are overlooked, so I presume, because conventional accounting does not identify them and does not account for them. If we are to incorporate social goods in our frame, another system of accounting is called for.

Four spheres, four logics

Gift-giving and the generation of social goods take place outside the spheres of the market and governance. This brings me to the third intervention, and that is the introduction of two additional spheres, each of which has a distinctive logic. These are the oikos and the social sphere.

The market sphere is the sphere for the logic of exchange. Such is the logic of quid pro quo. Conventional economic analysis has a lot to say about such a logic. It is the logic of equal exchange, of reducing complexes of values to a price, of pecuniary incentives, of demand and supply, of consumer sovereignty and so forth.

The sphere of governance is the sphere for the logic of laws and rules. The logic of governance generally works by way of rules and takes the form of hierarchical and/or bureaucratic systems. This logic drives the functioning of states as much as that of (big) corporations. It is the logic of management.

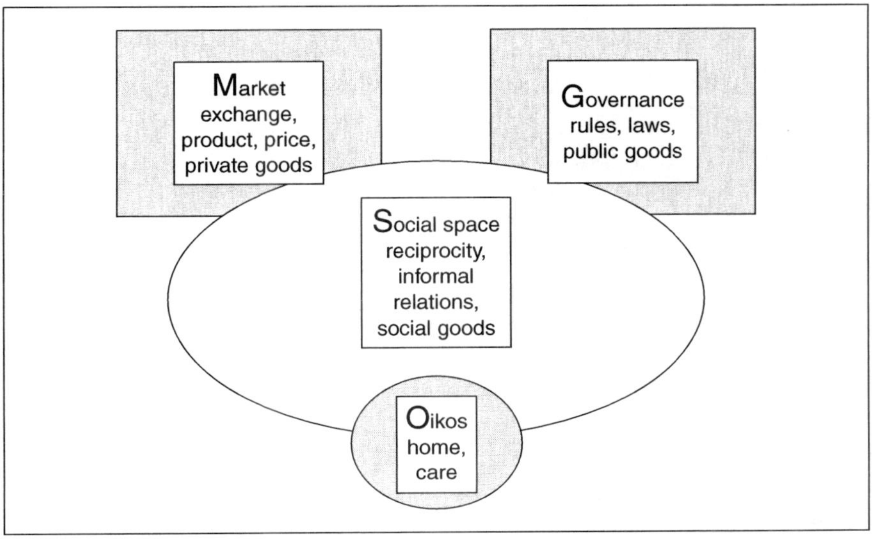

Figure 11b.2 Four spheres, four logics.

Both logics, the one of the market and that of governance, have undoubtedly played a critical and constructive role in realization of welfare all over the world. Yet they only work by virtue of the operation of two other logics: the logic of the oikos and that of the social sphere.

The logic of the oikos is at the base of each human life. The oikos stands for the sphere of essential connections that each person has with other people. In western settings, the oikos tends to be small, consisting of the single family and maybe a few other people, like grandparents. In most other societies, they tend to comprise extended relations of kinship. Anyhow, within the oikos, principles of loyalty, care, and dependency rule; they make up its logic that is, we should stress, distinctly different from the exchange logic of the market and the rule-based logic of the sphere of governance. When market logic gets applied within the oikos, usually confusion and conflict are the outcome (as becomes most obvious in cases of divorce or inheritance).

The most important sphere, however, is the social sphere. This is the sphere of informal relationships among people, of clubs, societies, friendships, neighborhoods, political parties, colleagues, scientific conversations, and arts worlds. In this sphere, social logic operates, and that is the logic of relationships, of reciprocity, of gift-giving and receiving, of social goods. When we go to the café to engage in conversation over a cup of coffee or a glass of beer, we dwell in the social sphere. Only when we step to the counter to pay the bill do we step into the market sphere. Yet when we exchange pleasantries with the barman, we are in the social sphere again. Most of our interactions outside our homes take place in the social sphere. It is a good reason to make the social sphere and its social goods explicit in our analysis.

Conclusion

The three interventions, with the gift as alternative to grants, the introduction of social goods, and the distinction of the oikos and the social sphere as two alternative spheres of interaction, serve as substantive amendments to Boulding's notion of the grants economy. Whether they serve as friendly amendments remains to be seen. They stimulate the letting-go of elements of analysis that appear to be precious to Boulding, such as the analysis in terms of individual behavior and private and public goods. But who knows, we are twenty years further on. Boulding, too, may have reached the insight that his grants economy is in need of a different perspective.

Notes

1 This was customary in the thirties, when Boulding got started as an economist. Hicks, for example, thought similarly. See McCloskey and Klamer (1992).
2 See Klamer (2007).

References

Boulding, Kenneth (1981) *A Preface to Grants Economics: The Economy of Love and Fear*. New York: Praeger.

Buchanan, James M. (1965) "An Economic Theory of Clubs." *Economica*, 32: 1–14.

Dolfsma, W., R. van der Eijk, & A. Jolink (2009) "A Source of Social Capital." *Journal of Business Ethics*, 89(3): 315–329.

Klamer, Arjo (1996) *The Value of Culture: On the Relationship between Economics and Arts*. Amsterdam: Amsterdam UP.

Klamer, Arjo (2003) "Gift Economy." In R. Towse (ed.), *A Handbook of Cultural Economics*, Cheltenham, UK: Edward Elgar Publishing, pp. 241–247.

Klamer, Arjo (2007) *Speaking of Economics: How to Get in the Conversation*, Abingdon: Routledge.

Komter, Aafke, ed. (1996) *The Gift. An Interdisciplinary Perspective*. Amsterdam: Amsterdam University Press.

McCloskey, Deirdre & Arjo Klamer (1992) "Accounting as the Master Metaphor of Economics." *European Accounting Review*, 1(1): 145–160.

McCloskey, Deirdre & Arjo Klamer (1995) "One Quarter of GDP is Persuasion." *American Economic Review*, 85(2): 191–195.

Maus, Marcel ([1925] 1960) *The Gift: Forms and Functions of Exchange in Archaic Societies*. New York: W.W. Norton.

Pfaff, Martin, ed. (1976) *Grants and Exchange*. Amsterdam: North Holland.

Wray, Randall L. (1994) "Kenneth Boulding's Grants Economics." *Journal of Economics Issues*, 28 (December): 1205–1225.

Poem

The Noble Gesture

The Noble Gesture
Is mostly vesture:
What's really him
Is pretty slim.

Part XII

Conflict resolution, peace

12 Key text: Conflict resolution and control[1]

Kenneth E. Boulding

This book has concerned itself mainly with the phenomenon of conflict as a social process that operates in many different contexts. The process clearly can be studied simply as a phenomenon of nature without any evaluation or practical conclusions. It must be confessed, however, that this study was not motivated merely by idle curiosity, even though curiosity about the nature and form of phenomena must be an important motive in any scientific and theoretical inquiry. We live in a day in which conflict, especially international conflict, threatens to get out of hand and destroy us. The theory of conflict, therefore, has practical implications, even implications about survival. We cannot leave the subject, therefore, without examining these practical implications, even though these inevitably involve us in ethical judgments.

In any given social situation or subsystem, we can perhaps postulate an optimum amount or degree of conflict. The concept is hard to specify, but it is of great importance. It relieves us immediately, for instance, from the illusion, if anyone ever possessed it, that conflict in any amount is either bad or good in itself. The evaluation of conflict has two aspects: quantitative and qualitative. In a given situation, we may have too much or too little conflict, or the amount may be just right. There is no simple operational definition of such an optimum; we must rely for our information on a complex structure of attitudes and evaluations. In a given situation, we may also have the wrong kind of conflict. Here again, there is no simple operational definition, but common speech has words that describe these qualitative differences: conflicts may be bitter and destructive, or they may be fruitful and constructive. We shall not argue here whether the qualitative difference can be reduced to quantity—whether, for instance, conflicts that are bad are so simply because there is too much or perhaps too little of them. In the absence of any clear index of the quantity of a conflict, this issue cannot be resolved. The best strategy would seem to be to go as far as we can with the concept of quantity but reserve the right to discover that conflict has more than one dimension and cannot, therefore, wholly be described in terms of simple "more or less."

We may think that a situation has too little conflict because it is dull and lacks drama. Drama is an important value in practically all cultures, and conflict is one of the most important sources of dramatic interest. Most religious and national ideologies, for instance, conceive of the universe as involving a dramatic conflict between the forces of good and evil played out on the stage of the world. In personal life also, the absence of conflict is identified with a dull, featureless existence. The institution of games and sports is evidence that, where a situation does not have enough conflict in it, conflict will be created artificially, either between individuals, as in chess, pairs as in bridge, or teams as in baseball, football, and so on. Prof. F.H. Knight is reported to have said that what people really want in the world is trouble, and if they do not have enough of it, they will create it artificially, the institution of sport being the proof.

On the other hand, there is a great deal of evidence that conflict in its non-sport aspect is usually felt as too much. Even though we may admit that some conflict is good, the word itself has a bias toward the bad. We think of the problem of conflict not usually in terms of how we get more of it but how we get less of it. We think of conflict in terms of family quarrels, separation, and divorce, or racial discrimination and race riots, or industrial disputes and strikes, or political conflict and revolution, or international conflict and war. These things we think of on the whole as bad, as tending to go too far and to get out of hand. Dialecticians like Hegel and Marx may defend conflict as a necessary instrument of change and progress, and sociologists like Simmel (1953) and Coser (1956) may defend it as an instrument of social integration, but this still has to be a defense against the common prejudice. Conflict is discord, and the opposite of conflict is harmony; the words reveal the evaluational bias in the language and in the common experience. Discord may be necessary to make music interesting and to give it drama, but its significance lies in the ability of the composer to resolve discord into some meaningful harmony, however subtle. The essence of the drama of conflict is likewise its resolution; it is not the conflict as such that makes the drama but the resolution of the conflict as a meaningful process through time. A conflict that went on and on without end and without resolution would lose even dramatic interest; it would eventually become mere noise and confusion. It is the process of conflict toward some kind of resolution which gives it meaning and which makes it good. This is true even in sports and games; a game that went on interminably without any resolution would be intolerable.

We must, therefore, look at the ways in which conflicts are resolved if we are to assess their value and if we are to evaluate the institutions by which they are controlled. What we must look for here are ways in which a particular conflict process moves toward an end. This is not to say, of course, that conflict itself comes to an end, for conflicts are continually being recreated. Each particular conflict, however, can be thought of as having a life cycle: it is conceived and born, it flourishes for a while, and then certain processes that are probably inherent in its own dynamic system eventually bring it to an end. Resolution, as we shall see, is only one way of ending conflicts, and, out of the many ways of ending conflicts, it may not always be clear which deserve the reward of being called resolution. Resolved conflicts, however, are clearly a subset of ended conflicts, and we should study the latter first.

The first method of ending conflicts is probably the commonest, though by its very nature it is also the least noticeable. This is the method of *avoidance*. The parties to the conflict simply remove themselves one from another and increase the distance between them to the point where the conflict ceases from sheer lack of contact. A man who cannot get on with his boss quits or is fired. The man who cannot get along with his country emigrates. Teams between whom the conflict has become too bitter for sportsmanship stop playing with each other. Couples who cannot get along divorce. A customer who does not like one store finds another. Two friends who quarrel separate and do not see each other again. A quarrelsome faction within a church splits from it and forms another sect. Ideological or personal conflict within a party splits it, and two parties go off from the fission. Two atoms that cannot get along in a molecule split off and go their separate ways.

Avoidance is the classical method of resolving economic conflicts through pure competition; disputes about bargains are avoided simply because there is always another bargainer to go to. Political disputes are resolved by trading votes and logrolling and by a constant ballet of shifting political partners. Racial disputes are suppressed by segregation and by seeing to it that the races do not mix or only meet under rigid and stereotyped rules of behavior. Class conflict is avoided by cultural differentiation of the classes, with different speech and behavior patterns, so that the classes also do not meet except under formal and stereotyped conditions. International conflict may be mitigated by devices like arms control, which, in effect, move the nations farther apart. Avoidance always involves putting some kind of distance between the parties. The distance need not only be physical distance, though this is the most obvious and commonest form; it may take the form of social distance, as in segregation, or epistemological distance, as when two parties deliberately cultivate ignorance of each other and avoid overt communications. The Catholic–Protestant entente in the United States almost seems to follow this pattern.

The most extreme form of avoidance is *conquest*, the second form of ending conflict, by which one of the parties is, in effect, removed to infinity, or removed from the scene, leaving the victor in sole possession of the field. An interesting asymmetry in the avoidance pattern shows up clearly at this point. There are three forms of avoidance. One party may simply remove himself from the field; the avoiding party here does all the work. Both parties may remove themselves, though this is less likely, as once one party begins to remove himself, there is little incentive for the other to move. The third form is where one party forcibly removes the other. The parent carries the howling child out into the garden and returns to the house. The trade union or the church expels a dissident faction. One nation forces another by threats to withdraw from a field of conflict. This form of avoidance usually involves a good deal more work on the part of the active party than does simple self-removal, as the active party has to remove the other and then return to the field. Conquest is the extreme case of forcible removal, in which the removed part is removed completely. In a quarrel, one man kills another. In a war, one nation exterminates another. One race or group practices genocide on another. Fortunately, these cases are fairly rare, mainly because of the amount of work involved. Conquest, of course, can take place only where one party is conditionally viable with respect to the other. Two parties that are unconditionally viable with respect to each other obviously cannot practice conquest. Even if the parties are not unconditionally viable, the cost of conquest may preclude its attempt, and some other form of conflict conclusion must be practiced.

If the parties can neither conquer nor avoid each other, some form of *procedural* resolution of conflict is likely. In procedural resolution, the parties have to stay together and live with each other; conflict, in general, may not be resolved permanently in so far as the parties continue to exist in contact, but particular conflicts may be resolved simply in the sense that they come to an end as social systems and are replaced by other conflicts and other systems. We may distinguish three types of procedural conflict conclusion. The first is *reconciliation*, in which the value systems of the images of the parties so change that they now have common preferences in their joint field: they both want the same state of affairs or position in the joint field, and so conflict is eliminated. The second is *compromise*, in which the value systems are not identical and the parties have different optimum positions in the joint field; however, each party is willing to settle for something less than his ideal position rather than continue the conflict. In compromise, this settlement is reached mutually by bargaining between the parties themselves. The third type of conflict conclusion is the *award*, in which a settlement is reached because both parties have agreed to accept the verdict of an outside person or agency rather than continue the conflict. The compromise and the award are essentially similar in that they both represent less than the ideal situation for each party; they differ mainly in the method of arriving at the settlement.

To each of the three forms of procedural conflict conclusion, there corresponds an appropriate set of procedures. Thus, reconciliation is the result of conversation, argument, discussion, or debate that leads to convergent modifications of the images of the two parties. Compromise is the end result of a process of bargaining, in which mediation and conciliation may play an important part. An award is the end result of arbitration or legal trial. Neither the three forms of settlement nor the various procedures are completely separate in practice, though there is a tendency for one form to dominate in any particular case. Frequently, however, both reconciliation and compromise go on together; indeed, some reconciliation may be necessary before compromise is possible. Consequently, there are always likely to be elements of discussion and propaganda in bargaining situations. Similarly, in arbitration cases or in court proceedings, there are often elements both of reconciliation and of bargaining before the award is handed down, and the award will not be accepted unless it has been preceded by informal reconciliation and bargaining. One of the most difficult institutional problems in the handling of conflict is how to arrange for the right proportions and the right order of these various elements of the situation. Thus, legal proceedings, such as suits, are often a poor way of handling conflicts in industrial relations, because of the difficulty of incorporating the necessary bargaining and reconciling processes in purely legal procedure. The same difficulty in marital conflict has sometimes led to the setting up of special marriage courts in which these more informal procedures can be employed.

Of all these processes, probably the process of reconciliation is the least understood, partly because very little research has been done on it and partly because of the complexity of the symbolic systems that are involved. We understand so little about the formation of value images that we can hardly be expected to understand the process by which these images are modified under the impact of mutual communication and discussion. The most we can do here is to make some suggestions and hope that social psychologists may be inspired to study this important and neglected field.

One obvious proposition is that a prerequisite to reconciliation is flexibility in the images, and especially in the value images, of the parties concerned. If the images of the two parties are completely rigid, it is clear that no process of convergence can take place. Rigidity in the image, however, may occur for a number of different reasons. The rigidity may be part of the value system of the image itself; that is, the person sets a high value on rigidity and the absence of change itself. Or the rigidity may be associated with insecurity in the valuation of the person himself; that is, he may be afraid to make any changes in the values that he puts on particular objects or goals because he sees such change as a threat to the valuation that he puts on himself. This is the problem of the identification of the image with the person, so that any change in the image is seen as a threat to the person. The person says in effect, "I am an *X*," where *X* may stand for Communist, Catholic, Pacifist, American, etc. Any attack on the *X* with which the individual identifies, then, is regarded as an attack on the integrity of the person; his value structure is not something that he has but something that he is. Thus we have, in effect, divided the value structure of a person's image into two parts: an inner core around which he integrates his personality and which holds him together and an outer shell which he holds or possesses but which does not constitute an essential part of the image of the person who does the holding or possessing. The core is rigid and not subject to small changes, though it may be subject to catastrophic reorganizations in conversion. The shell is not rigid and is amenable to the processes of modification under the stimulus of discussion and argument.

The success of the reconciliation process, then, clearly depends on how far the value structures of the parties in the field of conflict occupy the core or the shell of the value image. If the conflict is about a core value, reconciliation will be difficult or even impossible, short of very drastic experiences and conversions. If the conflict is about a shell value, change is possible, and so reconciliation is possible, though not all processes of communication lead to reconciliation. The problem is complicated by the fact that the boundary between the core and the shell is not fixed but is itself a result of the general value system and of the process of communication and argument to which the party has been subject in the past. Unskilled argumentation that seems to threaten the person of the other party may only serve to harden and widen his core of values and so make agreement all the more difficult. On the other hand, a dramatic act of renunciation symbolizing concern for the person of the rival may produce a drastic reorganization of this value structure with a shrinkage of the inflexible core and an extension of the malleable shell.

Reconciliation will presumably be easier if reconciliation itself is highly valued as a process by the contending parties. There may be an important difference in personality type between the *authoritarian* and the *reconciling* personality. The first has a very large core of particular values that he identifies with his person. Consequently, he is not interested in reconciliation but only in imposing his will and his values on others; the existence of differing values he regards as a threat to his person rather than as an opportunity for mutual learning. By contrast, the reconciling personality identifies his person not with any particular set of values or doctrines but with a learning process, a search for truth, and an interest in, and concern for, the welfare of others. Much work needs to be done on the nature of life experiences, and perhaps even genetic selection, that lead to the predominance of one type or the other in a society. One may hazard a guess that the nature of the learning experience, especially in childhood, is of great importance in this connection. Where learning is associated strongly with pain and punishment, the personality resists the learning process; consequently, it tends to integrate itself as soon as possible around a large, hard core of values and doctrines, and it resists the learning process thereafter. This is the path to the authoritarian personality. Where learning is associated with rewards rather than with punishment, the personality integrates around the idea of continued learning rather than around a core of received truth, and the reconciling personality develops. This is certainly not the whole story. There is, however, great need for further work at this point to carry forward the pioneering studies of the authoritarian personality made by Adorno *et al.* (1950).

The process of compromise through bargaining has probably received more attention than the other conflict-resolution processes. It is a process that can be more easily identified than the more subtle and less visible processes of reconciliation and, hence, is an easier object of study. It is also a process that is more subject to theoretical model building than the processes of value formation and change on which reconciliation is based. In this connection, the recent work of Schelling (1960) is of outstanding importance. Bargaining is a positive-sum game, frequently nonsymmetrical between the parties, in which there is a curious mixture of cooperation and conflict—cooperation in that both parties with a certain range of possible solutions will be better off with a solution, that is, a bargain, than without one and conflict in that, within the range of possible solutions, the distribution of the total benefit between the two parties depends on the particular solution adopted. Thus, while both parties are interested in the adoption of some solution, they have divergent interests in regard to the particular solution that is adopted. This curiously mixed character of the bargaining game gives it an unusual character and raises problems that are quite different from those of zero-sum games, which are pure conflict, or games without any problem of division of gains, which are pure cooperation.

Schelling has called attention to the importance of *saliency* in the solution of bargaining problems. Bargains can frequently be struck when there is no communication between the bargainers, simply by the tacit observation on the part of both parties of some salient feature of the situation that makes both parties settle on the salient feature itself. A man and his wife who become separated in a large department store and who have made no previous arrangements for this contingency both gravitate to the lost-and-found department if they are of a humorous turn of mind, or perhaps to the main information booth if they are more soberminded. People meet each other without prearrangement at the information booth at Grand Central Station, or at the crossroads on a map, or at noon if they are not given a time. Spoils are divided on a 50:50 basis, because this is the only division which is salient and which stands out from all the others. Even when there is communication between the bargainers, then the principle of saliency frequently governs the settlement. The reason is that, if any party stands out for a nonsalient settlement, the danger of there being no settlement at all is very large; hence, as between a high probability of consummating an agreement at the salient point and a low probability of consummating what would be, if consummated, a more favorable settlement at some other point, each party chooses the salient point as having the maximum expected value discounted for probability.

Innumerable practical applications of the principle spring to mind. In economic bargaining, whether this is two individuals bargaining about the price of a car or a house or a trade union bargaining with an employer, there is a strong tendency to settle at round numbers and at convenient splits intermediate between the offers of the two parties. The 50:50 split is, of course, a highly typical pattern; the difficulties in the bargaining process arise through the psychological problem of establishing the final offers or the range to the split. Schelling has pointed out the great advantage that an irrevocable commitment gives a bargainer, provided that it does not preclude the possibility of any bargain at all. This leads to the paradox that the weakest bargainer is frequently in the strongest bargaining position, as his very weakness gives him a commitment that would be taken away by strength. The weak have nowhere to go, no place to which to retreat, and their very weakness makes their bargaining commitments irrevocable. Thus, the sick, the aged, children, and the insane have society by the throat; their very weakness gives them an unshakeable bargaining position. They say, in effect, "Support us, or we die, and our blood will be on your heads." Because of their weakness, this is no idle threat. Similarly, the fanatical, the devotees, and the religiously committed are in a strong bargaining position because of the irrevocable nature of their commitment. Jehovah's Witnesses are in a position of great bargaining strength vis-à-vis almost any society in which they live: they cannot be coerced, because they will die rather than give up their faith and practice, as, indeed, they died in thousands under Hitler. Before the fanatic, ordinary, reasonable men are helpless: they can be moved, and the fanatic cannot. If any bargain is struck, it must be on the fanatic's terms, for no other terms are possible. When a fanatic hits a different fanatic, of course, can be struck at all.

These considerations help us to understand the role of the conciliator and mediator in the bargaining process. This role is of particular importance in labor relations, where it has been worked out most completely. It is of growing importance, however, in domestic quarrels (the family counselor, for instance, plays much the same role in family conflict that the mediator does in industrial conflict), and it also is growing in importance in international relations. The mediator role may be quite informal, as when a mutual friend tries to mediate a quarrel, or it may be more formalized, as it is in industrial relations. In any case, the role is a complex one, with a whole spectrum of possible degrees of intervention into the conflict. At one end of the scale, we have simple conciliation, in which the conciliator simply tries to clear up misunderstandings. In conflict situations, there is always ample opportunity for unnecessary incompatibility of images. Messages between the parties have to pass through an intense emotional field in which they are likely to be distorted, so that the image that each party has of the other's position may be quite false. The conciliator has the advantage of being outside the emotional field that is created by the conflict. Consequently, he can both receive and give messages to either of the parties without the kind of distortion to which direct messages are subject, By acting as a go-between, therefore, the conciliator can transmit messages between the parties with greater accuracy than is possible with direct messages and so can achieve a certain reconciliation of images that would have been impossible without him. There are, however, limits to the function of conciliation. The elimination of misunderstanding will not necessarily eliminate the conflict or produce complete reconciliation of values and images of the two parties. Indeed, there may be occasions when conciliation can actually exacerbate a conflict; each party may think, quite wrongly, that the other party agrees with him, and the clearing up of this misunderstanding may make the parties realize that their conflict is deeper than they thought. This case, however, is rare, mainly because the emotional field through which direct messages from the parties have to pass is more likely to add hostility to a message than to take it away. Hence, the parties are likely to believe that each is more hostile than he really is, and conciliation, under these circumstances, is likely to reduce hostility.

Mediation, especially as the term is used in industrial relations, implies more outside pressure brought to bear on the parties than does mere conciliation. Conciliation simply in the sense of facilitating communication between the parties may not be enough: there may still be a residum of unreconciled images, and the situation requires compromise. The mediator may have an important role to play in the actual process of agreement on the bargain, especially where there is no obviously salient position in the field to which both parties can gravitate. A skilled mediator can create saliency by bringing the weight of his authority behind a solution that he thinks would be acceptable to both parties. Sometimes the solution introduced by the mediator may be a new position altogether that neither party has previously contemplated. This may involve a new principle, that of widening the agenda.

We can perhaps distinguish three functions of the third party here, in terms of the economic theory of exchange. The function of pure conciliation is simply to see that trading opportunities are not missed in the existing field of conflict through ignorance and a failure of communication; the conciliator, in this sense, is a broker, bringing the two parties together; that is, the conciliator brings the parties to the contract or conflict curve, within the dimensions of the conflict as the parties perceive it. The second function is that of the widening of the agenda and the introduction of new variables in the field of bargaining. Two parties may have exhausted all their trading opportunities within a given set of variables, but when a new variable is introduced, new trading opportunities are opened up, and an impasse may be avoided. Even when all the trading opportunities and new variables have been exploited, however, the parties may find themselves on a conflict curve and unable to reach agreement. It is at this point that the third function of the mediator comes in, which is that of providing a salient suggestion around which a bargain may crystallize.

We have still not exhausted the functions of the mediator, however; if his suggestions do not create enough saliency in the field to permit the striking of a bargain, he may be able to introduce new elements into the field through outside pressure. He may, for instance, mobilize public opinion or threaten to mobilize public opinion on the side of one or the other of the parties, or perhaps even against both parties, and so force a sufficient reconciliation of position to permit a bargain. The impact of public opinion in the resolution of conflict by bargain is often important, but also its effects are often obscure. Each party will have reference groups, in the language of the social psychologists, whose opinion will be important to them. There will be, in fact, a series of concentric shells of reference groups ranging from the group with which the party identifies himself most strongly, which is likely to be small, to the group of the world at large, with which identification is likely to be weak. Thus, an employer is likely to be strongly influenced by the opinion of fellow employers in the same field, less strongly influenced by the opinion of employers in general, still less strongly affected by the opinion of the general public of his own country, and affected very little by opinion in other countries. A union representative will be strongly sensitive to the opinion of his fellow representatives in the same union, less sensitive to opinion in the labor movement at large, still less sensitive to opinion in the country as a whole, and so on. If a mediator can mobilize opinion in the closest and strongest reference group to the party concerned, he is most likely to have an effect; the larger and wider the reference group invoked, the stronger will an adverse opinion have to be in order to produce an effect on the party concerned.

Where mediation is unsuccessful, so that, in spite of their own and of a third party's efforts, the parties cannot strike a bargain, the third form of procedural conflict tends to take over in the form of arbitration or court proceedings, resulting in arbitration awards or court judgments. In arbitration, a preliminary bargain has to be struck, in the sense that the parties have to agree to submit to arbitration. Sometimes this can be agreed on when the terms of the bargain itself cannot be struck. A further step toward agreement is necessary, for the parties must not only agree to arbitrate but most agree on an arbitrator. This second step is often more difficult than the first. However, a profession of arbitrators has developed, especially in the United States, to meet this need in both commercial and industrial arbitration. The successful arbitrator frequently operates as mediator and conciliator as well, for the closer his award comes to what the parties might have agreed upon in the absence of arbitration, the most satisfied the parties will be, and the better the reputation of the arbitrator. It is for this reason, perhaps, that, in the area of bargaining, both in commercial and in labor relations, arbitration is frequently preferable to more formal legal procedures, which are less open to preliminary conciliation and mediation.

An interesting conclusion that emerges from the empirical study of mediation procedures is that the negotiating process develops certain formal patterns that might almost be called rituals and that attempts to bypass or to cut short these rituals often destroys the negotiating process itself (see Douglas 1957). Thus, the parties begin the proceedings by somewhat bombastic initial statements that set the initial boundaries to the negotiations. There has to be a period of withdrawal after these initial statements to make it seem as if these are genuine commitments. The parties know, however, that these are not absolute commitments; otherwise, the negotiations would simply break down. There may follow a process of trading, by which mutual concessions are made. There may be attempts at commitment by, for instance, a strike vote of a union or a tactical movement of troops in a diplomatic negotiation. There probably has to be a latent period in which the incipient settlement is forming; sometimes the settlement crystallizes out of the negotiating procedure itself and sometimes as a result of outside intervention (nucleation).

The last procedural resort, of course, is law. In part, the law performs the function of arbitration, and the judge, or sometimes even the jury, hands down an award. The law, however, has more coercive power behind it than the arbitrator, for, behind the law, stands the system of police and punishment, the apparatus of jails, and, in some societies, even the threat of capital punishment. It would take another volume to examine the social system of the law and the manner in which it operates to resolve or to fail to resolve conflicts. It is a multifaceted institution. In some respects, as in the law of torts, it acts as a third party to the disputes of private citizens, instituting a procedure of conflict to which both parties consent because it is so deeply embedded in the structure of the society to which they belong. The importance of consent is easily forgotten in well-established societies where it can be taken for granted; where it is absent, however, as it may be in societies where the legal system is imposed by an alien power or where it is controlled by one group in the society, the most elaborate apparatus of legal procedure and institutions may not resolve the personal conflicts of the society. In constitutional law, the conflict of individual citizens or private organizations with the law itself may be resolved by procedures that test the law against a written, or even an unwritten, constitution.

In criminal laws, the situation is much more complicated. Here, the law does not simply stand as an arbitrator of private quarrels but is itself one of the parties to the conflict. Much of the complexity of criminal procedure arises out of this dilemma, namely, that the law is both a party to the conflict and an agency for a settlement by award, that is, an arbitrator. In Anglo-American law, an attempt is made to resolve the dilemma by a sharp definition and differentiation of roles: the attorneys for the defense and for the prosecution symbolize the conflict; the judge and the jury symbolize the arbitration element. The conflict roles are highly stylized, as, indeed, is the whole procedure; this serves a function in resolving the dilemma imposed by the mixture of roles in the law, but it also has a cost, which may be quite high, in restricting the employment of informal mediatory and conciliatory procedure. The interaction of police, criminals, the courts, and the prisons as elements of a single social system is highly complex, and the realities often do not conform to the formal structure. Police and criminals not only have a symbiotic relationship with one another but often form part of a common subculture segregated from the rest of society. It may be, of course, that one of the most important functions of the police is to segregate the criminal subculture, even to the extent of becoming part of it, and, as long as this segregation is firm enough, the rest of the society can go about its own business. The persistence of the police–criminal complex, however, suggests that existing institutions have quite failed to solve the problem of eliminating crime. It may be, of course, that this is too ambitious an objective and that, if we limit crime to a segment of society, this is enough. On the other hand, the tendency for police and criminals to flourish together suggests that the problem of further limitation of this segment may require a rather different set of institutions from those we now possess.

Conflicts that cannot be resolved by appeal to existing law are frequently transferred to the law-making process in legislative assemblies. Here again, the proper description and analysis of the resolution of conflict in the legislative process would require another volume, if not many volumes. All political organizations have to develop a ritual of *settlement*, or decision. In an absolute dictatorship, the settlement is by the ukase of the dictator, though even the most absolute dictator presumably receives advice and hears arguments on different sides of a question. In a parliamentary democracy, the settlement is by majority vote of the legislature, perhaps with the further proviso of review by the executive or by the courts. Within the legislatures, as within the entourage of a dictator, various pressure groups will conflict. In the process of discussion and debate, positions may be modified, and a process of reconciliation goes on; in the final proposal, as it comes before the legislative body, compromise frequently plays an important part, and different groups bargain for support. The final decision, however, is of the nature of an award, except in those unusual cases where decisions are made by unanimous or virtually unanimous approval. We thus see all three of our conflict resolution procedures going forward in the legislative process.

An important distinction may be observed between *constitutional* and *legislative* settlements. A legislative conflict is settled for the moment by the passage of a law. This may not, of course, end the conflict but may merely transform it into a conflict about repeal of the first law or passage of an amending law. Legislative settlements, in this sense, tend to be temporary, though laws acquire a kind of constitutional status with the sheer passage of time and absence of successful challenge. Thus the prohibition amendment was passed and later repealed. The mere fact that it was embodied formally in a constitutional rather than a legislative change does not detract from the essentially legislative character of the enactment. The steel industry in Britain was nationalized by one government and denationalized by the next. Constitutional settlements are more fundamental and represent settlements of disputes regarding the rules of the legislative process. It may only be possible to detect the permanence of a settlement well after the event, of course. We can however, identify settlements like the American Constitution, the British settlement of 1688, and so on, as constitutional settlements. Where the legislative process is inadequate to resolve the political conflicts in a society, formal constitutional change, as in South American revolutions, sometimes takes its place, so that it is not always easy to distinguish one from the other except in the light of subsequent history.

When procedural conflict proves inadequate to deal with the intensity of the conflict in society or when there are no institutions for procedural conflict, violence is likely to result. The study of violence would again require a volume in itself; for all the importance of the phenomenon, there is surprisingly little theoretical or empirical study of it. It is not even easy to define. People can be killed or incapacitated with ulcers, and they can be injured by psychological violence just as effectively as they can with a gun. However, a distinction does not have to be clear to be important, and, at some point, there is a common-sense dividing line between procedural and violent conflict. Violence is most closely associated with conquest as a form of conflict settlement, though violence is descriptive of a conflict process rather than of a conflict settlement. It is quite possible, for instance, for conquest to be nonviolent, that is, for one party to be absorbed in another or for one organization to be dissolved by strictly procedural means. Departments are organized out of existence, countries are federated or united, organizations are laid down, and firms are bankrupted by purely procedural processes, without more than perhaps a trace of legal coercion lurking in the background.

Violence also does not necessarily lead to settlement. Indeed, it is perhaps the major evil of violence that it frequently inhibits settlement; for it often leaves no path to settlement open but conquest, and this may not be possible. Consequently, violence persists as a chronic disease of society; the procedures that might resolve the conflicts are too weak to prevent violence taking over, and violence in itself prevents the conflicts from being resolved and indeed perpetuates them. Violence, for instance, creates an atmosphere in which reconciliation is difficult and in which, indeed, each party is likely to move farther away from the position of the other. It likewise makes compromise difficult; one does not compromise with a man with a gun, and getting a gun oneself does not assist the process of compromise either. One does not negotiate from strength; one may dictate from strength, but one does not negotiate. The only place where violence may have a part to play in conflict settlement is where there is a sufficient monopoly or preponderance of violence in the hands of one party so that settlement can come about through conquest or award. Monopolies or preponderances of violence, however, seem to be unstable: where violence is not legitimated by procedures and constitutions, it tends to raise violence against it. Violence in itself, because it cannot perform the reconciling and compromising function, leads to the suppression rather than the resolution of conflict: it drives conflict underground but does little to eliminate it.

One of the great organizational problems of mankind, then, is the control of violence or, more generally, the control of conflict to the point where procedural institutions are adequate to handle it. The great course of political evolution, from the family to the tribe to the nation to the superpower, and, finally, one hopes, to the world government now in its birth pangs is testimony to the ability of human organization to extend control to wider and wider areas. It is hardly too much to say that conflict control is government, and though government has broader functions than this, conflict control is perhaps its most important single task—the one thing which it must perform or cease to be government.

A purely political and legalistic attitude toward conflict control, however, catches only half of the problem. The ability to control anything depends on two factors: the magnitude of the thing to be controlled and the skill and appropriateness of the instruments of control. It is easier to control a dog than a lion and a stream than a hurricane. The political approach is through the instruments of control—courts, legislatures, assemblies, police, and procedures. This interest and emphasis is, of course, right and necessary. It may, however, lead to a neglect of the sources of conflict itself and of the possibility of controlling conflict at its sources. Thus we need to think about institutions for lessening conflict as well as for dealing with it. One example of this is the importance of economic development in lessening economic conflict. When there seem to be abundant opportunities for increasing the pie, the problem of sharing it falls into the background. Furthermore, in a rich society, the importance of economic conflict is lessened, simply because of the decline in the marginal significance of redistributed income. A conflict about bread is going to be more severe than one about caviar.

A field in great need of further exploration is that of the sources of psychological conflict and conflict-producing images, especially in the institutions of the family, the school, and the church, where these patterns are usually set. Reform here is slow, for conflict-producing personalities tend to reproduce themselves in their children, and it is hard to break into the process of culture transmission. Something can be done, however, at the ideological level and at the level of formal education. It is at this point that more knowledge is badly needed but also that there is hope for important changes.

The biggest problem in developing the institutions of conflict control is that of catching conflicts young. Conflict situations are frequently allowed to develop to almost unmanageable proportions before anything is done about them, by which time it is often too late to resolve them by peaceable and procedural means. To catch conflicts young, however, means that these dynamic social processes which lead to ultimate breakdown have to be publicly identifiable: we cannot deal with invisibles. It is fairly easy to look back with the wisdom of hindsight and see points in history at which conflicts that ultimately became unmanageable could easily have been dealt with. Thus, the First World War might well have been scotched in the six weeks before its outbreak if communications had been better and if there had been a quite simple apparatus of mediation: it was, at least at that moment, a war that nobody really wanted, and that happened because of a dynamic process that bred misunderstandings and misinterpretations of intention. The Second World War was of a different order; it must be diagnosed not as a result of the unwanted breakdown of an essentially unstable system, like the First World War, but as the result of an epidemic of political paranoia on the part of the German nation. The processes that led to it would have had to be dealt with earlier than, say, 1939. Just when the point of no return was passed is hard to say; it may have been at the point of Hitler's reoccupation of the Rhineland, or it may have been later. To judge from the German trade statistics, February, 1937, marks the point at which the basic decision for ultimate war was taken by the German government; it was at this point that imports of certain strategic materials took a large jump.

It is easy to see that the institutions that might have prevented the two world wars were simply not present; it is more difficult to specify the institutions that will prevent a third, a possibly last, world war. Our knowledge of the dynamics of conflict processes is still primitive. Just as government efforts to prevent a business cycle may actually intensify it if poorly planned and badly timed, so efforts at conflict control may intensify the very conflicts that they are intended to control if they are based on too inaccurate knowledge of the social systems involved. Unfortunately, we cannot wait for perfect knowledge and, fortunately, we do not have to have perfect knowledge. There is some point in the growth of knowledge of social systems at which there is a net payoff for the institutions of control, and we have reason to hope that we are rapidly reaching this point in the case of conflict systems, if we have not already passed it; that is, even though, in the attempt to control conflicts, we shall make many mistakes, the successes will outweigh the failures.

The two greatest problems of control systems are first, signal detection, that is, how do we know when something needs to be done, and second, implementation, or how do we know what to do. I suspect that the signal-detection problem in conflict control is not so serious as it might seem. The problem is how to detect social situations that are in the early stages of a process that will lead eventually to destructive conflict if it is not checked. In any such detection or perception problem, there is always a chance of error. There are two types of error. We may give out a false alarm; that is, we may perceive the situation as requiring action when in fact it does not, and the problem will solve itself without action. We may give out a failed alarm; that is, we may say nothing needs to be done when in fact something should be done. It seems to be almost impossible to correct both these errors beyond a certain point; that is, if our detection system gives very few failed alarms, it will give a lot of false alarms, and we can avoid false alarms only at the cost of increasing the number of failed alarms. If both false alarms and failed alarms are costly this presents a very great dilemma. One suspects, however, that, in conflict control, false alarms are relatively cheap as compared with failed alarms; that is, the consequences of doing something that need not have been done are relatively slight, whereas the consequences of not doing something that should be done may be disastrous. There is no harm, then, in building a detection system that gives very few failed alarms, even if it gives a lot of false alarms: one can be tolerant of the false alarm. This is a very different situation from that posed by violent conflict, where false alarms and failed alarms may be equally fatal.

One would like to see an international organization for the detection of young conflict processes. The idea may seem impractical at the moment because people do not think in these terms; they think of conflicts as uncontrollable acts of God like hurricanes, and the idea of conflict control is a new one, even though the practice is as old as political organization. It was only a few years ago, however, that people thought of depressions and the business cycle in similar terms and talked about economic blizzards. Now the idea of depression control is accepted even in the most conservative circles. Similarly, one may hope that the idea of conflict control may receive equally rapid acceptance, in view of the immense crisis of conflict that we face.

The problem of implementation is, of course, much more difficult, and what to do once an incipient conflict process has been detected depends very much on the nature of the conflict itself. The problem is perhaps easiest in those areas where there are few specialized agencies for the conduct and encouragement of conflict, such as in race relations; here the counterconflict organization such as, for instance, the National Conference of Christians and Jews or the local interracial council can exercise a substantial influence. In labor relations also, conflict control is an important part of the practice of modern industrial relations, and the knowledge of industrial relations processes that has been accumulated in the course of a generation or more of study is now bearing valuable fruit. The problem is most difficult in the case of international relations, where there are specialized agencies for conflict (the armed forces) that have a vested interest in the preservation of conflict or at least of the threat of conflict, simply because conflict is the only reason for their existence as organizations. Even here, however, the sheer enormity of the cost of nuclear warfare is forcing the development of the institutions of conflict control. The current interest in arms control is a straw in the wind, and, in the case of international relations where the armed forces of the world form a social system with a dynamics of its own that is largely independent of the interests of the nations that support these forces, arms control may be nine-tenths of the problem. The problems of organization and of bargaining involved in setting up the institutions of arms control and, more generally, of international conflict control are difficult indeed; but it would be suicide for the human race to believe that they are insoluble. It has been the major theme of this work to show that conflict processes are neither arbitrary, random, nor, incomprehensible. In the understanding of these processes lies the opportunity for their control, and perhaps even for human survival. We cannot claim that our understanding is deep enough, and much work yet needs to be done, but it can and must be claimed that the understanding and, therefore ultimately, the control of these processes is possible. In that lies the present hope for mankind, for, without conflict control, all other hopes for human welfare and betterment are likely to be dashed to the ground.

Note

1 This article was previously published as chapter 15 in Kenneth E. Boulding, *Conflict and Defense: A General Theory*, Lanham, Md.: University Press of America, 1962, pp. 305–328.

References

Adorno, T.W., Frenkel-Brunswik, E., Levinson, D.J., and Sanford, N., *The Authoritarian Personality*, New York: Harper, 1950.

Coser, L., *The Functions of Social Conflict*, Glencoe, Ill.: Free Press, 1956.

Douglas, A., "The Peaceful Settlement of Industrial and Intergroup Disputes," *Journal of Conflict Resolution*, I, 69 (March).

Schelling, T.C., *The Strategy of Conflict*, Cambridge: Harvard University Press, 1960.

Simmel, G., *Conflict*, trans. Kurt H. Wolff, Glencoe, Ill.: Free Press, 1953.

12a Key text: The role of organized non-violence in achieving stable peace[1]

Kenneth E. Boulding

The last 150 years or so has been a period of quite unprecedented social change. We have seen the application of science to the technology of production and destruction, as in the chemical industry, the electrical industry, automobiles and airplanes, and nuclear power and nuclear weapons. This period has also seen profound changes in social environments and institutions, such as the rise and now, as we have seen, the decay of centrally planned economies and welfare states. There has been a spectacular increase in the expectation of human life and a decline in infant mortality, resulting in an unprecedented population explosion. The human population of the earth has more than doubled in my own lifetime.

Two social mutations which have not perhaps received the attention they deserve in this period are: the rise of areas of stable peace between independent nations; and the development of organized non-violence, associated particularly with Mohandas Gandhi and the non-violent movement for national independence in India, and with Martin Luther King and the civil rights movement in the United States, but also found in the rise of trade unionism and many, perhaps less conscious, political movements. Stable peace and organized non-violence are not unrelated to a spectacular increase in the range and the deadliness of weapons, that is, means of destruction. This process goes back a long time in human history, especially to the development of the crossbow and the cannon around the fifteenth century, with aerial warfare and the bombing of cities, the machine gun, the tank, and an order of magnitude increase in destructive power in the guided missile and nuclear warhead, especially the hydrogen bomb.

We need to look at these processes as part of the total pattern of human activity in space-time. Every person has 24 hours a day to spend, divided among various activities. Five billion human beings now on the earth have about 120 billion person-hours to spend each day, and we could divide these up among a great variety of classifications. About a third of this time is spent in sleep, about 5 or 10 per cent in eating, dressing; about 15–20 per cent in work—about half the population is in the labour force and works 8 to 12 hours a day. Perhaps 5 to 10 per cent is spent in learning processes, in school or out of it, and so on. A large proportion—perhaps 90 to 95 per cent of human time—is devoted to peaceable or what I have called 'unviolence'—ploughing, sowing, reaping, producing, buying and selling, practising the arts, playing, singing, dancing, making love, raising children, enjoying recreational activities and so on.

Some 5 to 10 per cent of human activity may be classified as 'violent' or 'preparing to be violent'. Some of this is unplanned and unorganized, an expression of rage and anger: parents abusing a child, occasional fist fights in a pub, a mob rioting and looting. Most violence, however, is organized and deliberate, particularly expressing itself in war. What might be called the 'world war industry', managed by military budgets, is something on the order of 6 per cent of the total world economic product at the time of writing, although in times of major war it goes much higher than this. In the United States, for instance, this figure was about 42 per cent in the middle of the Second World War. The proportion of the world economy going to the war industry may rise as nations get richer and think they can afford bigger military budgets. It depends on the level of hostility and perceived threat in the international system.

Like all important distinctions, the distinction between peaceful and warlike activity is a little fuzzy. There is a grey area of cold war, economic sanctions, and plain personal nastiness, but this grey area is not very large. Historians can usually tell whether country A and country B were at war or at peace on a particular date, although they may be some doubt in regard to terrorism, 'preventive strikes', and so on. I have suggested that in particular parts of the international system, and perhaps in other forms of conflict, there are four phases (Boulding 1978): one is stable war, in which war goes on virtually all the time. Southeast Asia is perhaps closest to this in the last few decades. This, however, is very costly. It is not surprising that it edges over into the second phase, unstable war, in which war is interrupted by periods of peace, although war is regarded as the norm. The Middle East perhaps would be an example in recent decades, or the Hundred Years' War between Britain and France in the Middle Ages and the Thirty Years' War in central Europe (1618–48). This, again, however, is costly and has some tendency to turn into the third phase of unstable peace, in which peace is regarded as the norm and is interrupted by wars designed to reestablish peace on the terms of the visitors. This has been a very common phenomenon in human history.

Since the middle of the nineteenth century, however, there has developed a new, fourth phase which I have called 'stable peace'—a situation among independent states in which the probability of war between any of them is so low as to be considered virtually zero. This seems to have begun in Scandinavia in the mid-nineteenth century, when the Swedes and the Danes stopped fighting each other, which they had done for many centuries. This spread to North America by about 1870, after the American Civil War, going back perhaps to the Rush-Bagot Agreement, which disarmed the Great Lakes between the United States and Canada in 1817. Also since 1848, the United States has had virtually stable peace with Mexico, with only a very minor intervention in the Mexican Revolution in the 1910s. After the Second World War, stable peace spread to Western Europe and to the Western Pacific, so that now we seem to have an area of stable pace stretching from Australia to Japan across North America to Finland, with some 18 countries who have no plans whatever to go to war with each other. This has been described as a 'security community' (Deutsch *et al.* 1957). There is surprisingly little institutional framework. The United States and Canada have the Great Lakes Commission and the Columbia River Commission. The Nordic countries have some common organizations. Now, of course, Western Europe is moving from a Common Market into a virtually frontierless community, still retaining, however, a good deal of national sovereignty. Another striking phenomenon of the twentieth century, not wholly unrelated to stable peace, has been the abandonment of empire on the part of north temperate zone powers, with the possible exception of the Soviet Union and China.

The conditions for stable peace seem to be fairly simple. They involve primarily mutual change in the national images of the nations concerned, which involves taking national frontiers off the agenda for change, except perhaps by mutual agreement. A desire to change national frontiers through violence is perhaps by far the most significant cause of international war, as we have seen recently in the case of Iran and Iraq. In the North American case, there was an edgy moment during the presidential campaign of 1839 with the slogan '54–40 or Fight', referring to the boundary with Canada. President Tyler, however, reneged on his election promises, as all presidents probably should, and the 49th parallel went peacefully, if slightly absurdly, to the Pacific. Apart from a very minor incident in the San Juan Islands, the frontier between the United States and Canada was virtually taken off everybody's agenda.

Another condition of stable peace is that there should be a certain minimum amount of intervention of each country in the affairs of the other, roughly equivalent perhaps to the degree of intervention that parents should exercise in the lives of their married children. This involves refraining from exercising some possible power, but refraining from exercising power is one of the main sources of social harmony in all fields of life.

A third possible condition is that the national state be somewhat 'desacrilized'. It should be regarded not as a sacred object demanding human sacrifice, but as a public convenience, a produce of public goods, an object of genial affection on the part of its citizens, but not regarded as something that one should either kill for or die for. This, of course, goes very much against the grain of the culture of the military, but also represents the overwhelmingly civilian character of states in the area of stable peace. They are no longer organized around the concept of victory and conquest.

Stable peace has crept up on the world almost imperceptibly, without anyone planning it consciously and without very much in the way of political movements behind it. Its origins in history indeed have been very little studied, perhaps because it has to do with changes in our images of the world that are almost unconscious. How did the murderous Viking become the modern Norwegian, or the ferocious baron, the polite courtier? How, for instance, did duelling, a very ancient violent institution, disappear in the early nineteenth century? How did we develop what might be called 'disarming behaviour', almost the Dale

Carnegie (1982) culture of 'how to win friends and influence people'? This is a history that remains to be written.

In part, the development of stable peace represents a shift in the understanding and image of the nature of power. I have argued that there are three sources of power: threat power, resting on the ability to do damage, in which A says to B, 'You do something I want or I'll do something you don't want'; economic power, an expanded form of purchasing power, which rests on the capacity to produce things that people want and the power of exchange: 'You do something I want and I'll do something you want'; and integrative power, the power of love, respect, legitimacy, community, identity, status and so on: 'You do something because of what you think I am and what I think you are'.

Threat power, perhaps because it is dramatic, is greatly overestimated. A minimum of legitimated threat seems to be necessary as a precondition of the other forms of power, for instance, in the legal system, but even here there are some points at which we probably exceed the optimum if it costs less to put up with crime rather than to try to suppress it. Naked threat is particularly ineffective. Very few people get rich by mugging. All tyrants eventually die. And conquest very rarely pays off to the conqueror. Without exception in human history, being a 'great power' has led to economic stagnation, if not decay, and the cultural stagnation. The history of civilization is one of continual expansions in the use of threat power by rulers, followed by geographic expansion (empire), which results in economic and cultural decay, and eventually decay of threat power itself, which is then taken over by some new centre of threat power, usually on the borders of the old, which again follows the same pattern of decay. The threat power of the feudal baron was outpaced by the rising economic power of the merchant and manufacturer, and the integrative power of religion and the increasingly sacred national state. Confucius, Buddha, Jesus, Mohammed, and perhaps even Karl Marx, had much greater impact on the ongoing processes of human history than did Alexander, Caesar or Napoleon.

The basic weakness of threat power is illustrated by the many examples in human history where military defeat led to economic and cultural upsurge on the part of the defeated, by comparison with the victor. Examples are numerous, but there are also some exceptions. The fall, perhaps one should say the withering away, of the Roman Empire, which had been culturally and economically stagnant from Augustus to Constantine, was followed by a slow, but continuous technological improvement in Europe, in spite of the violence of the feudal system. The defeat of the Byzantine Empire by the capture of Constantinople by the Turks in 1453 was followed by an extraordinary upsurge in Europe—the Renaissance, the rise of science, the discovery of America and Australasia, the expansion of European population around the world and the eventual reaching of the moon. The defeat of the Scots at Culloden in 1745 was followed by a remarkable economic and cultural upsurge in Scotland—the Edinburgh of the New Town, of David Hume and Adam Smith. After the defeat of France by Germany in 1871, Paris became the cultural capital of the world: music went to Paris—Debussy, Delibes, Saint-Saens; art exploded with the Impressionists;

even the French economy showed a little upsurge, perhaps even because of the German-imposed reparations. The great age of German culture followed the disastrous Thirty Years' War. Before Germany achieved the development of the national state it was extremely weak militarily, divided up among a large number of small principalities; this was the age of Kant and Hegel, Bach, Beethoven, Schumann, Goethe. It was after the defeat of Austria by Germany in 1866 that Vienna became a great cultural capital—in music and philosophy. After the defeat in 1919, Berlin produced the Bauhaus, modern architecture, and again an upsurge of art and literature, though Hitler stopped it all in 1932, by the overwhelming belief in the power of threat.

If we ask who won the Second World War economically, the answer would probably be Germany and Japan, who got rid of their military and were able to devote all their resources to getting rich. Many other examples could be given. There are also exceptions. The reaction to defeat depends on the adaptability and the creativeness of the defeated. There is something here of the Toynbean challenge and response. If the defeat is too overwhelming, creative response is difficult.

It is a very interesting question as to how far the growth of stable peace has been the result of an almost subconscious recognition of the weakness of threat and the power of economic and integrative activity. These unconscious transformations are poorly documented and hard to study, but they have great importance.

Another factor which is important in the development of stable peace is the recognition of the basic instability of deterrence or counterthreat. The persistence of threat rests in considerable part on the fact that counterthreat is a very obvious response which may be effective over short periods, but which it can be shown cannot be effective over long periods. If A says to B, 'You do something I want or I'll do something you don't want', the very obvious response of B is to say, 'If you do something I don't want, I'll do something you don't want', and to develop the means of destruction which are appropriate. This may lead in the short run to a diminution in the probability that A will carry out the threat. This is deterrence. There is a curious paradox here, however, that deterrence can only be stable in the short run, for there is some probability that it will break down and that the threats will be carried out. If the probability of the use of destructive power such as nuclear weapons were zero, they would clearly not deter anybody. It would be the same as not having them. There must be some probability, therefore, that the system of deterrence will break down. It is a very fundamental principle that, if there is some probability of anything, no matter how small, if we wait long enough it will happen.

If a probability is low enough, however, it tends to be denied. A good example of this is building in a flood plain. After a flood, people eventually forget where the flood waters reached, and go on building in the flood plain. Deterrence is a very similar system. There is some evidence that the probability of prenuclear systems of deterrence breaking down is something on the order of 4 per cent per annum, rather like a 25-year flood. The probability of nuclear deterrence breaking down may be less than this. Even if it is only 1 per cent per annum, the probability accumulates alarmingly to some 63 per cent in 100 years and 98 per cent in 400 years, very much within historic time. Yet people continue to behave as if the probability were zero. Under the present system, the major powers of the north temperate zone are under indeterminate sentence of death. Just as we can be sure that if the San Andreas fault cannot be modified San Francisco will be destroyed by an earthquake in *x* years, so if the present international system of nuclear deterrence continues, the Soviet Union, the United States, and Europe will be destroyed by nuclear war in *x* years. If the 'nuclear winter' theory is correct—and there is some probability that it may be—this catastrophe will extend to the tropics in terms of climate change, radiation and total crop failure.

Another possible response to threat is the development of defensive and protective structures against the means of destruction to the threatener—suits of armour, castles, city walls—which prevent the means of destruction from reaching their objective, so that the threat of the threatener is diminished. It is ironic that SDI, the strategic defence initiative ('Star Wars'), is implicit recognition that national defence has broken down in the nuclear age. Hardly any responsible scientists believe that SDI can be effective. Historically, the means of destruction always seem to have outrun the means of protection and defence, with profound social changes as a result. As long as the means of destruction were spears and arrows, there was some sense in having a castle or a city wall, or even a suit of armour. With the development of the effective cannon, however, no real defence against cannon was possible at a short range. Even the glacis—a sort of SDI for cannon—was not really ultimately effective and castles became either ruins or tourist attractions and city walls became boulevards. National states, however, the size of France, Sweden, Russia and Britain, were big enough to be defended, at least in part, with armies with cannon at the borders. It is not surprising that cannon led to the decline of the feudal system and the rise of the national state. The guided missile and nuclear weapons, however, have done for national states even the size of the United States and the Soviet Union what cannon did for the feudal baron. They have made national defence essentially obsolete. It would be extremely surprising if any defensive structure can really be found. Under these circumstances, the only national security is stable peace, so it is not surprising that it has come into the world. There is something to be said for national states, that they produce ecological variety in the world political system, which is very necessary for evolution. A world state could easily be a world tyranny, producing a world stagnation, so there is much to be said for national security. What has happened, however, is that national defence has become the energy of national security, and substitutes for national defence must be found.

Organized non-violence is very largely a product of the twentieth century, although what might be called 'unconscious' or 'unorganized' non-violence has been a part of human behaviour for a very long time. It is a part of the very complex set of reactions to a perceived threat when counterthreat is perceived as ineffective or too costly. One of these which accounts for a great deal of human history is flight. This depends on the principle that the capacity for destruction diminishes with increase in the distance from the destroyer. This has probably accounted for the spread of the human race around the earth, from its apparent origins in Africa. Another reaction, of course, is submission, which is very common, which is why we pay our income tax. Another is cultural absorption of the threatener. The Chinese have been remarkably good at this. Every outsider who conquered China became Chinese. This is one aspect of the strategy of communication and persuasion with the threatener.

Organized threat, however, in the form of military organizations, or even the law and police, came into existence long before organized non-violence, which required a 'founding father' or prophet, and found one in Gandhi. Organized non-violence rests partly on the use of integrative power with the threatener, embracing the threatener within a large community of interest. It is particularly effective when carrying out threat or when even submission to threat is costly to the threatener, as it frequently is. The role of the threatener has a strong tendency to produce illusions about the nature of the world. Defiance, when it is accompanied by courage and the willingness to suffer, is often very costly to the threatener who tries to carry out the threat. In India, the massacre of Amritsar, when the British-trained troops fired on defenceless protestors, helped to undermine the whole legitimacy of the British Empire in the minds of the British themselves. I remember when I was growing up in Liverpool the impact of Gandhi's visit to Lancashire, which was suffering somewhat under the Gandhi-inspired boycotts. I remember a song at the time which went something like 'We don't like the black shirts, we don't like the brown shirts, we don't like the red shirts, so here's to Gandhi with no shirt at all!' Some experiences as a child in the First World War convinced me that war was outrageous folly and murder and that I couldn't participate in it. But social pressure for regarding war as a last resort is very strong in almost all societies. It was with an extraordinary sense of excitement that I read Richard B. Gregg's *The Power of Nonviolence* ([1934] 1966) in the late 1930s, presenting Gandhianism as a viable alternative to war. The remarkable work of Gene Sharp (1973) has pointed up the potential role of organized non-violence as a substitute for military national defence and a more efficient method of counteracting threat and even invasion from abroad.

Non-violence, of course, like violence, can fail in its objectives. But if failure in both cases leads to a learning process, as it sometimes does, it will not have been in vain. Gandhi's very success in persuading the British to leave India was followed by the appalling tragedy of the Muslim–Hindu civil war, in which millions were displaced, and India and Pakistan certainly did not achieve stable peace. I once had a conversation with a leading Indian national security expert and asked him why India, once it became a national state, rejected Gandhi and became a militarized nation, almost in the pattern of nineteenth-century Europe. His answer was that 'non-violence was fine for aggression but no good for defence', an answer which, I must confess, surprised me, but also set me thinking. There is an important distinction between the prevention of unwanted change, which is what we usually mean by defence, and the achievement of wanted change, for which there seems to be no good word in the English language, as both offence and aggression have a strong offensive connotation.

Part of the strategy of organized non-violence is the persuasion of the opponent—who is not really regarded as an enemy but as a fellow inhabitant of earth—that he (or she) may be mistaken about not wanting certain change. Certainly Tapan Mukerjee's study (1972) suggests that economically the British benefited quite substantially from the abandonment of empire, even though the Falkland and Maldive incident suggests that in some British minds at any rate a costly pride in empire still lingers. Going back a little further, there is not much doubt that Britain benefited both economically and culturally from the American Revolution, although it also seems to have stimulated British imperial ambitions in the rest of the world, at least until the abandonment of empire after the Second World War.

The role of organized non-violence in preventing unwanted change needs further study. The experience of Denmark under Hitler in the Second World War suggests that a unified, fairly homogenous, well-educated nation can preserve its culture and institutions in the face of an 'alien' invasion. The corresponding experience of Norway under Hitler also suggests that, where there is internal disunity, which Quisling illustrated, the non-violent, or shall we say 'unviolent', defence of national integrity is more difficult. Even in Norway, however, the teachers' strike illustrated the relative impotence of the Nazi threat system. The question, 'Would non-violence have worked against Hitler?', which is often asked of the non-violent, is a difficult one. Hitler was something like a 1000-year flood, that is, a very improbable event that happened as a result of the combination of the Versailles Treaty, the Great Depression and the incompetence of the then-dominant powers. It is certainly very hard to prepare people for the 1000-year flood who are pretty sure it won't happen to them, but it is something we have to think about and at least lay up some reserve plans about it. At least we learned something from the Second World War, which produced a more successful peace settlement than the one in 1919, a settlement which was not punitive but which brought Japan and at least West Germany into an integrative system as partners rather than as pariahs. We need much more plain knowledge here about the role and structures of integrative power in building a community which will diminish the temptation to use threat.

A very interesting question is whether the philosophy and theory of non-violence can modify the use of violence itself, particularly in the culture of the military. Are there halfway houses between pure non-violence on the one hand, and the raw, inhumane use of military violence as we saw it not only in Hitler but in the bombings of Nagasaki and Dresden, which were almost pure genocide, almost the moral equivalent of Auschwitz? Is it absurd to think of 'Gandhizing' the military? Aerial warfare, long-range missiles and nuclear warheads essentially destroyed what might be called the traditional ethic of military culture, the ethic of courage, sacrifice and fighting with an opponent with essentially the same culture.

The effectiveness of threat depends a great deal on its specificity. The law is most effective when it is quite specific about the threats involved. 'You will be fined $10 if you park in a prohibited place.' The reason why the military are so impotent either in achieving desired change or in preventing unwanted change is that their threats are highly unspecific. 'If you do something unspecifiedly nasty to me, I'll do something unspecifiedly nasty to you.' It is lack of specificity which is one of the main reasons why deterrence always breaks down. Somebody always thinks they can get away with something. Even if we could persuade the military that their reactions to the exercise of violence should be strictly 'tit for tat', on the lines of Axelrod's (1984) theory of the prisoner's dilemma, it might be effective in limiting violence and moving the world toward stable peace. If we can persuade the military also that victory is not usually desirable, that if they feel they have to fight, a war that ends in a draw is much better than a war that is won, and that even military defeat, as we have seen, often has quite desirable consequences for the defeated, they could even become instruments for achieving stable peace and genuine national security.

There are two kinds of wars: one is the war of conquest, by which empires are created, which are only really effective for the conqueror when the conquered population is very small, scattered and at a substantially lower level of technology than the conquering party. The other kind of war is the breakdown of deterrence. Such wars are extremely costly to all parties. The earth is now so full that wars of conquest have become virtually impossible and cannot possibly benefit a conqueror, of which the impending tragedy of Israel may be an example. Wars between relative equals are always wars of the breakdown of deterrence. The only answer to this is national security through stable peace. In Gandhi's philosophy, non-violence can only be successful when it is embodied in Satyagraha, that is, truth. It is often not realized that the culture of the scientific community is profoundly Gandhian. It is based quite fundamentally on the principle that people should be persuaded by evidence and never by threat. The extraordinary success of science in expanding human knowledge is a direct consequence of this principle. When science becomes politicized, as it did in the Soviet Union under Stalin, this is a disaster for it, as seen in the Lysenko case. It is a basic principle of legal systems, also, that a judge should be influenced by the evidence presented in the court and not by either threat or bribery. In this sense, non-violence has a much wider application than what we usually think of as organized non-violence in political action. If these Gandhian principles penetrate the military, there is much more hope for the world.

Truth is the overriding concern of the scholarly community. As the scholarly community begins to understand more clearly the great complexities of the world, especially of social systems, the means by which we will abolish war—now the main priority for the human race—will become clearer. There is much work yet to be done, but if there is a will to do it, it will be done, and in that there is hope.

Note

1 This chapter was previously published in V.K. Kool, ed., *Perspectives on Nonviolence* (New York: Springer-Verlag, 1990), pp. 3–13, and was reprinted as chapter 17 in K.E. Boulding, ed., *Towards a New Economics: Critical Essays on Ecology, Distribution, and Other Themes* (Hants: Edward Elgar, 1992), pp. 225–235.

References

Axelrod, R., *The Evolution of Cooperation*, New York: Basic Books, 1984.

Boulding, K.E., *Stable Peace*, Austin: University of Texas Press, 1978.

Carnegie, D., *How to Win Friends and Influence People*, New York: Pocket Books, 1982.

Deutsch, K., Burrell, S., Kann, R., Lee, M. Jr., Lichterman, M., Lindgren, R., Loewenheim, F. and Van Wagenen, R., *Political Community and the North Atlantic Area*, Princeton, New Jersey: Princeton University Press, 1957.

Gregg, Richard B., *The Power of Nonviolence*, New York: Schocken Books, 1966; first published, 1934.

Mukerjee, T., 'Theory of Economic Drain: Impact of British Rule on the Indian Economy, 1840–1900', in K.E. Boulding and Tapan Mukerjee, eds., *Economic Imperialism: A Book of Readings*, Ann Arbor: University of Michigan Press, 1972.

Sharp, G., *The Politics of Nonviolent Action*, Boston: Porter Sargent, 1973.

12b Commentary article: Memories of Kenneth E. Boulding[1]

Anatol Rapoport

The forty-year friendship between the author and Kenneth Boulding was cemented by three affinities: (1) an intense common interest in the system theoretic approach to the philosophy of science, especially its "organismic" direction; (2) shared feeling that in its development the scientific outlook largely bypassed the introspective mode of cognition; (3) an uncompromising rejection of violence especially of its sanctioned, rationalized type, organized by power elites (war). The wide divergence of our attitudes toward religion had no effect on the intimacy and intensity of the friendship.

I first met Kenneth Boulding at the Center for Advanced Studies in Behavioral Sciences, where we were both fellows during its first year, 1954–1955. The Center was established with the view of providing young behavioral scientists with an opportunity to spend a year free of the routine obligations of academic life, such as teaching and serving on committees, presumably to contemplate the problems of their chosen field and to interact with each other. Some established behavioral scientists were also offered yearlong fellowships in the hope that the young and the mature could learn from each other.

At the orientation meeting the fellows were told about the facilities at the Center, encouraged to form groups, and invited to name fellows, if any, with whom they would especially like to collaborate and in what way. Ken named me, and I named Ken. Our common area of interest was general system theory, a way of thinking that is nurtured by insights into fundamental parallels between structures, behavior and evolution of intuitively *recognizable* sectors of reality.

The systemic paradigm

The concept of system is usually exemplified in one of two ways, one being characteristic of the method of physical sciences, the other of biological sciences. An example of a system, as it is conceived by a physicist, is the solar system. It consists of a number of bodies, which at a given moment of time are in certain positions, defined by the three coordinates of three-dimensional space, and move with certain velocities, components of speed in the three directions of the coordinate axes. Rates of change *of positions* in the different directions define the velocities; rates of change of *velocities* in the different directions define acceleration. The acceleration of each body is determined by the components of *force* in the three directions divided by the *mass* of the body. A major triumph of physical science was manifested in Laplace's treatise on celestial mechanics (1796). By means of equations expressing the interdependence of gravitational forces, positions, velocities and accelerations of the bodies it is possible, given the initial positions and velocities, to predict the positions and velocities at any moment in the future or to "postdict" it at any moment in the past. These predictions and postdictions are confirmed with uncanny accuracy.

Another example of a physical system is a mixture of substances interacting chemically in some confined space. Here a "state" of the system, corresponding to the set of positions, velocities and accelerations of the planets, is defined by the proportions of the various substances at a given moment resulting from the chemical interactions among them at a given temperature, atmospheric pressure, etc. Again, the system is characterized by the determined progression of its states from some initial to some final condition. The aim of a theory is to derive this course from basic assumptions. In the case of the solar system, these are postulated laws of motion and the mathematically defined law of universal gravitation; in the case of the chemical system, these are the laws of thermodynamics, the atomic theory of matter, etc.

I worked at that time in Nicolas Rashevsky's Committee on Mathematical Biology at the University of Chicago. Rashevsky was a pioneer in mathematical biophysics. His monograph on the subject was an extension of the methods of mathematical physics to biophysics, as they had been extended in modern physiology to biochemistry. At the time I joined the group at the Center for Advanced Studies in Behavioral Sciences, Rashevsky was working on extending the same methods to the social sciences, for example, the study of mass behavior, of competitive and cooperative interactions between individuals, groups and populations, etc. He constructed mathematical models of these phenomena of the sort that proved to be so brilliantly successful in the physical sciences.

This approach could be called *analytic* in the sense that the point of departure consists of assumed mathematically formulated interactions between the elements of a system, and the aim is to derive the time course of the state of the system as a whole. The task of general system theory based on this method is to reveal *isomorphisms* between systems of different content and similar mathematical structure. A well-known example is the isomorphism between a harmonic oscillator (a mechanical system) and an electrical system consisting of a source of electric potential, an inductance, a resistance and a capacitance in series, both being governed by the same second order differential equation. Another example is the possible isomorphism between models of the spread of a rumor and the spread of a disease in a population.

Shortly before I came to the Center I joined a group at the University of Chicago organized by Ralph Gerard and James Miller in which another direction of general system theory was being developed. A system was conceived in the spirit of biological science, namely as something analogous to a living organism. Gerard defined a system in terms of its three fundamental aspects—structure, behavior and evolution. The structure of an individual animal, for example, is at the center of interest of anatomy; its behavior is the concern of physiology; its evolution of embryology or, in the case of humans, developmental psychology. Corresponding to isomorphism in analytic system theory are analogies across the *levels* uncovered by the biologically oriented *organismic* theory.

Gerard illustrated this approach by a matrix whose rows represented levels of organization of an organismically conceived system, while its columns represented the three fundamental aspects—structure, behavior and evolution, or, as Ralph was fond of saying, being, acting and becoming. The bottom row represented the cell, a sort of fundamental biological particle. On the next level was organ or tissue. The cells were conceived as "subsystems" of organs or tissues, and these as subsystems of the organism. Organisms, in turn, can be conceived as units constituting populations, these as subsystems of species. An ecosystem is a supersystem comprising several species and is itself a subsystem of the biosphere. In the case of humans, the levels can represent successively more inclusive social groupings—a family (or a work team), an organization, a society or a nation, the international system.

One of the principal aims of the general system approach is to counteract the effects of progressive specialization in science. The tendency to develop in ever greater detail ever narrower areas of knowledge makes communication between specialists of different fields and subfields increasingly more difficult. Gerard thought that his matrix represented an integration scheme by revealing parallels between disciplines concerned with the three aspects of systems on different levels. For example, as has been suggested, anatomy is primarily concerned with the physical structure of a human individual. Behavior, such as reactions to stimuli from the environment, is the concern of psychology; the history of an individual falls into the realm of embryology or developmental psychology; the evolution of the human species into physical anthropology. On the level of society, structure is the concern of sociology, behavior of economics or political science, evolution of history. Thus, the disciplines fit into the cells of the matrix and integration of the disciplines is facilitated by the discovery of analogies between aspects of different levels of organization.

Boulding's hierarchy of systems

A seminar was organized at the Center including Ralph Gerard, Ludwig Bertalanffy, generally regarded as the founder of the theory (I believe he was the first to use the name), Kenneth Boulding and myself. At the annual meeting of the American Association for the Advancement of Science in San Francisco in December, 1954, the four of us founded the International Society for General Systems Research (now the International Society of System Sciences). The first issue of *General Systems*, the yearbook of the society, contained an article by Ken, "General Systems: the Skeleton of Science." In it Ken pictured the task of general system theory as that of exploring aspects of reality that fit into a hierarchy of *complexity* rather than a hierarchy of aggregates (organs as aggregates of cells, species or societies as aggregates of individuals, etc.). To be sure

Gerard's scheme, too, implies increasing complexity of higher levels of organization, but Boulding's is much more specific in pinpointing the crucial features of the various complexity levels. For instance:

1 The *framework* level: the "anatomy" of a system—the arrangement of its parts, such as the organization chart of a government department.
2 The *clockwork* level: adequately described by principles of mechanics. Example: the solar system.
3 The *control* level: development of feedback loops; maintenance of equilibria or steady states.
4 The "self-maintaining" level—a property of so-called open systems, beginnings to differentiation between nonliving and living states.
5 The *genetic-societal* level, exemplified by a plant—differentiation of function.
6 The *animal level* characterized by mobility and quasi-teleological behavior.
7 The *human* level—appearance of the self-image.
8 The level of *social organization.* Roles rather than persons are its "atomic constituents."
9 "To complete the structure of systems we should add a final turret for transcendental systems, even if we may be accused ... of having built Babel to the clouds. There are, however, the ultimates and absolutes and the inescapable unknowables, and they also exhibit systemic structure and relationships. It will be a sad day for man when nobody is allowed to ask questions that do not have any answers" (Boulding 1957).

Interest in general system theory was the first bond that developed between Kenneth and myself during our stay at the Center. My own conception of a system, which formed during my participation in the Chicago group, was basically consistent with Gerard's scheme. Specifically, I thought of it as apportion of reality that is recognized as "itself," in spite of the fact that its material components are constantly changing. Consider a tree, a beetle or a human being. Possibly the material constituents of each of them are completely replaced within a relatively short time; nevertheless we recognize a tree or a beetle as "itself" in spite of the changes. Most important, we are convinced that we remain "ourselves," even though every molecule in our body is replaced. We have direct "internal" evidence of this continuity through our memories. (Descartes should have said "I *remember*, therefore I am.") The importance of this holistic mode of cognition was manifested in the fundamental role classification has played in biology before the advent of evolutionary theory, inducing a conception of reality determined by awareness of similarities and differences between large organized wholes (systems).

Recognition

I sometimes illustrate the use of this "holistic" (or synthetic) method, based on recognition, where the analytic is inadequate, by the following class experiment.

I ask the students to think of two smells, say of ammonia and of garlic. After some twenty seconds, I ask whether they can almost smell each of these. They all say yes. Then I invite them to describe the difference between the two smells. No one tries. They can't even describe one of them satisfactorily in the sense that the description will elicit recognition: "Ah, that's ammonia!" or "Ah, that's garlic!" Yet every one is convinced that they can recognize each and are clearly aware of the difference. What is the process that induces this recognition?

The difference between the two modes of cognition is also exemplified by the difference between knowledge induced by observation and that induced by introspection. The preference of so-called "hard science" (in particular, behaviorist psychology) for the former and prejudice against the latter was ironically illustrated by Kenneth Boulding in a four-line stanza:

> In modern thought, (if not in fact)
> Nothing exists that doesn't act.
> So that is reckoned wisdom which
> Describes the scratch but not the itch.
>
> (Boulding 1958)

The significance of this insight for ethics and, in some respects, for religion is that it displays the basis of bonding between humans. Even though no one could describe in words the difference between ammonia and garlic or, as a matter of fact, either smell, everyone was convinced that what he or she smelled in his or her "mind's nose" was what every one else smelled. The same can be said of any "subjective" experience. There is no satisfactory way of describing in words a toothache, cold and warmth, the feel of velvet, an orgasm. Yet most of us, perhaps a vast majority, who have had such experiences are convinced that the experiences of others are identical to their own. Questions arise even with respect to analogous experiences in nonhumans. Direct comparison between those ascribed to them and our own is out of the question. Still we entertain the untested and untestable conviction that at least animals with which we communicate to a certain extent (cats, dogs, monkeys) feel in some circumstances more or less as we do. The range and firmness of this belief is something like a measure of "empathy," a concept that Max Weber used seriously in his discussion of the methodology of social sciences. In my conversations with Boulding this was a recurrent theme, which revealed to me areas of contact between my intense preoccupation with human cognition and his with religious experience.

As has been said, the organismic approach to a theory of systems is based on the concept of *recognition*, the fundamental component of perceived analogy. Indeed, the profundity of science as a mode of cognition is often manifested in the discovery of extremely far-fetched but profoundly instructive analogies between things or events that at first seem to have nothing to do with each other. Consider the following three processes: (a) a candle burns; (b) an animal breathes; (c) a nail rusts. All three are manifestations of the same process—oxidation, as in our time most adolescent schoolchildren know. But it took centuries of growth of scientific cognition to induce this insight. Or consider the following two events. (a) A bee alights on a flower. (b) A man sends a bouquet of flowers to a woman. Disparate as these two events seem, both belong in a very fundamental sense to the same category of events in the scheme of things, namely, reproduction of life: (b) is an instance of courtship, an early stage of the process; (a) of fertilization, a later stage. The organismic conception of system brings this aspect of cognition to the forefront of attention.

I mentioned the definition of a system as a portion of the world, that is, identified as "itself" in spite of material changes going on in it. This definition is not confined to organisms. It fits into the classification of populations, species, the higher taxonomic categories and in the context of human life, groups of all kinds: families, tribes, states, work teams, etc., even nonmaterial entities such as languages and religions, above all institutions. Shared interest in this conception of system (based on a generalization of the concept of organism) became one of the principal intellectual bonds between Kenneth Boulding and myself.

Preservation of "identity" as a cardinal principle of "systemness" opens the road to ever broader generalizations of the concept. Systems defined by networks of social relations and groupings bound by common goals, values or ideologies, such as the Bank of England, the Catholic Church, a regiment, the city of Rome are all systems, despite the fact that none of their human constituents of two hundred years ago is alive today.

Boulding's religious outlook

The reference to ultimates, absolutes and inescapable unknowables reflects Kenneth Boulding's profound immersion in religious thought and its linkage to his equally profound respect for the scientific mode of cognition. I believe it became the basis of our mutual "tolerance"—his for my atheism, mine for his deep religiosity. The final ideological bond between us was forged in Ann Arbor, where Ken was Professor of Economics since 1949 and where I, following my year at the Center, accepted an appointment at the newly formed Mental Health Research Institute. We shared a passionate hatred of war. It may seem strange that Boulding, so literally Christian, could be capable of such open, uncompromising hatred. But of course "hatred of hatred" is not a form of "hatred," as any one aware of the pitfalls of self-reference knows. It is only the sloppiness of everyday language that produces the illusion of incompatibility between a religion of love and hatred. Here is Boulding in the raw:

> I hate! I hate! I hate! I hate!
> I hate this thrice accursed State
> I'll smash each bloodshot German face
> That travesties the human race.
>
> (Boulding 1945)

The intensity of his passion blurs the distinction between hatred of violence (i.e. hatred of hatred) and hatred of the perpetrator. But the mood passes. I believe Cynthia Kerman, Boulding's biographer, felt directly what was going on within Ken at the time. She writes:

> But suddenly something happened to him, something inward, like an illumination. It happened, he says, at a most inappropriate moment: he was drying himself after a bath. Something broke in on him, an experiencing, almost a vision, of the suffering that Christ had taken on himself for people no better than the Germans, no better than the Bouldings. He could see again the German boys he had known as friends, and sense again the kinship with all men, in suffering, sin and hope.
>
> (Kerman 1974)

She goes on to quote his poetry:

> Hatred and sorrow murder me
> But out of blackness, bright I see
> Our blessed Lord upon the cross
> His mouth moves wanly, wry with loss
> Between the thieves alone he reigned
> (Was this one I, and that one you?)
> "If I forgive, will ye not too?"

Dismissal of "established disbelief"

I am telling this to illustrate how an ideological gulf between me (a convinced atheist) and Ken (a devout Christian) was bridged by affinity of passion. In answer to my squarely put questions, he admitted that he believed literally in Jesus's resurrection and in miracles. There was something defiant in his answer, which led me to suspect that it was not the indelible stamp of childhood experiences alone that fixed his faith. Paradoxically it seemed also a quasi-compulsion of challenging all "established beliefs," including all "established disbeliefs," all of which Ken may have subsumed under "conventional wisdom," and which he almost automatically dismissed. Perhaps he regarded disbelief in miracles as just another piece of "conventional wisdom," with which a particular form of human activity, namely, science, was saddled. In this respect, it was I, who seemed to him to be the "believer" (that is, a "disbeliever" with a negative sign attached), namely in the final dismissal of the supernatural by the scientific mode of thought. I see a bridge across the chasm that separates our respective faiths in what is to be regarded as "real" in Ken's last "level" of system organization (see (9) above): "the ultimates and absolutes and the inescapable unknowables, and they also exhibit systemic structure and relationships. It will be a sad day for man when nobody is allowed to ask questions that do not have any answers."

I accept this category of cognition if it is purged of mysticism. I conceive it as the "presently inconceivable," in the same way as the theory of differential equations was inconceivable to the early human who "did mathematics" with the aid of his twenty digits. In the same way, I see no contradiction between accepting hating of hatred and refusing to hate people. These feelings are on different levels of affect just as statements about statements are on a level different from that of statements about things or events, as Bertrand Russell once explained with admirable clarity. In a way it is these divergences that seemed to me to bring us close together. I sort of "translated" into my own language Kenneth's faith and his convictions expressed in the language of faith.

The ubiquitous trinity

By way of example, I will point to a parallel in the way Ken and I organized an important component in our ways of thinking. Besides the analogy as a mode of cognition manifested in spontaneous recognition, I believe fascination with tripartition of categories was a bond between Ken and myself. This fixation on trinities is, of course, widespread, ranging from Christian mystique to Hegel's three-stage model of cognitive progress—thesis, antithesis, synthesis—to fairy tales involving three brothers, the third being the smartest, three attempts, the third being successful, etc. To me the attractiveness of the trichotomy is in the escape it offers from the dichotomy, the "either–or" relation, preoccupation with which Korzybski (1933) called the twovalued orientation, ascribing it to the tyranny of Aristotelian logic. I see the fixation on dichotomies as a source of "us vs. them" formulations of all social ills, the often insuperable obstacle to conflict resolution.

Of my books, the earliest that expressed my most intense preoccupation with the human condition was based on a trichotomy—*Fights, Games, and Debates* (1960). In my last book (an autobiography: 1994), I discuss the three modalities of sharing as the basis of integration of humanity: the sharing of delight (in particular, appreciation of the Beautiful), a common conception of Truth (science) and a single Ethos. I believe Ken was as intensely preoccupied about the same time with the Threat–Trade–Love trichotomy, which of all his ideas influenced me most. My trichotomy dealt with three modes of conflict; his with three modes of social control. In each case, the progression marks a dimension of progress. To illustrate the parallel, I will briefly describe first my own representation of the progress, then Ken's.

In *Fights, Games, and Debates*, I pictured a fight as a conflict devoid of either a rational or an ethical component. Ordinarily a fight is assumed to be instigated by rage, hatred or the like and fuelled by "positive feedback" that is growing in intensity, which is self-driven (escalates). A dog fight is a good example. Initial growls intensify and finally explode into an attack. Hatred, rage or fear (which we attribute also to some nonhumans close to us, such as dogs) appear to be necessary components in a fight; and the only goal (if, indeed, a goal is at all envisaged) is the elimination of an opponent.

Affect is not a necessary component in a game but rationality is. Chess is a good example. Opponents in a game can be the best of friends. Their efforts are directed not at hurting or destroying the other but at outwitting him, whereby adherence to certain rules is mandatory. Moreover, success in a game necessitates not only the exercise of rational decisions but also attribution of rationality to the opponent, assuming that he, too, is able to make decisions most likely to help him win.

Finally, the goal in a debate is neither that of eliminating nor outwitting the opponent but rather *convincing* him or at least bringing his position closer to one's own. In this connection I have in mind what I call "ethical" debate, where the arguments are truly directed to the opponent rather than to third parties, as they are in a court or law, where arguments are addressed to a jury rather than to the opposing attorney, or in a legislative body, where the aim is to impress constituencies rather than convert political adversaries. A debate so conceived necessarily involves the ability to see situations from the opponent's point of view, not only with the view of assessing potential damage to oneself (as in a chess game) but also with the view of enhancing understanding and tolerance between the adversaries.

Parallels can be drawn between this trichotomy and Boulding's "Threat, Trade, and Love." Threat, most characteristic of despotic or totalitarian political systems, exercises control by intimidation: "If you do (or don't do) this, you will suffer such and such consequences." Trade exercises control by promises: "If you do this for me, I will do that for you." This mode is characteristic of market democracies. Love is a form of social control that depends on identification with others. Thus, children are normally cared for, not because they can threaten reprisals if they are not, nor because they are expected to pay, but because they are children. More generally, a member of a society based on "love" is entitled to certain amenities, assistance and so on, simply because he/she is a member. Subsequently, Boulding called the three modes of control, the "threat system," the "exchange system" and the "integrating system." The term "threat" was retained; "trade" was replaced by a synonym; "love," however, was dropped. I never asked Ken why, but I suspect he felt that the use of the term "love" might be embarrassing to some who regard themselves as scientists. Indeed "love" in this context might be misleading. It may be appropriate in references to our relations to children (especially our own) but not in references to complete strangers, which our fellow citizens usually are. The important thing in an integrating system is that beneficiaries of public goods and social services receive them not because they are "loved" but because they are integrated into the social system of which they are components. The integrating system was originally the ideal of both Christianity and communism, which may sound bizarre in consequence of the degeneration which both of these ideologies have undergone.

If I were to describe in a few words the basis of the strong affection that developed between Ken and myself during our forty-year-long association, I would say it was both the similarity of our cognitive and ethical commitments and the difference between their deep psychological roots. The similarities are conspicuous. We both were committed to the scientific mode of cognition as a way of arriving at truth and to the discovery of truth as a fundamental human value. We both rejected struggle for power, prestige, affluence, in short the pervasively assumed and accepted criteria of "success" on all levels (personal, group, corporate state), as the motivating force of effort and commitment, consistent with "human nature." Above all we were both committed to the evolutionary outlook. Among Ken's delightful aphorisms, my favorite is "Things are as they are because they got that way." On some reflection, one appreciates the profundity of this apparently inane remark. It is a bold challenge to conventional wisdom, according to which (if one takes a close look at it) "things are the way they are, because that's the way they are."

I do not identify evolution with "progress," and I don't know whether Ken thought of it in those terms. I continue to regret that I never got around to discussing this question with him in depth. I suspect, however, that Ken's view of evolution was similar to mine. That is to say, evolution provides an *opportunity* for "progress" (a movement toward the "Good") but by no means guarantees it. I tend to be rather pessimistic in this respect in the sense that I would not bet on a more or less decent future for our species, even if I were given most attractive odds against it. I believe Ken's outlook was similar. Somewhere he says that it is by no means certain that humanity is evolving along the main trunk of the evolutionary tree. Instead it may be moving out on a slim limb into a void. As for me, however, I refuse to speculate on this prospect and, above all, refuse to bet, because bets are for outside observers. Let the extraterrestrials observing us bet on what is in store for our species. I am not an outside observer; I am a member, and have a vested interest. I won't bet against my interests, no matter what odds. I think Ken felt the same way.

I sometimes experience a gnawing regret of not having had conversations with Ken about the role religion has played in the story of humankind. I am sure he would agree that it played two opposite roles: on the one hand, welding people together by bonds of loyalty (as the etymology of the word suggests) and on the other of separating them by fear and hatred. There is nothing paradoxical about this dual role, since the strongest impetus to integration is often perception of a common enemy. In this sense, religion historically performed a political function. It welded the ancient Hebrew tribes into a ruthless monolithic conquering People. Two thousand years later it fueled the ardor of the Arabs, who conquered the entire southern coast of the Mediterranean by giving the inhabitants a choice between being converted or slaughtered. However, eliminate the vision of the common human enemy and tribal religion evolves into nonproselytizing, universalist ideology (as did some pacifist Christian sects, Buddhism, the Baha'i). The key to the transformation seems to be perception of unity in diversity: unity of content, diversity of form. I think this sort of perception is another manifestation of sensitivity to analogy underlying seeming unrelated phenomena—again the ubiquity of the metaphor as the expression of insight.

It is especially the range of the unity in diversity principle (to which Ken was passionately committed) that I would have loved to discuss with him, in particular with reference to the three cardinal gratifications in human life: delight, recognition of truth and devotion to universal values. Unity in diversity is easiest to appreciate in the context of delight. Indeed the keenest delight in adult human experience is normally shared with only one person. But noninclusion in this context is not synonymous with exclusion. Tolerance of far-out diversity of customs, languages, conceptions of beauty, cuisines, etc., all sources of sensuous delight, is easiest to achieve, indeed enriches life.

In the case of devotion to truth, appreciation of unity in diversity is more difficult. Here is where religion most frequently plays out its divisive role. Ritual and mythology have served as the mortar of practically all religions from their inception. While the gradual spread of enlightened tolerance has subsumed ritual under the unity in diversity principle, reconciliation of incompatible revered myths is much more problematic. It also stands in the way of science as the most promising basis of unity firmed by universal criteria of objective truth.

Most difficult is the acceptance of the unity in diversity principle in the realm of values. In fact, in my opinion, diversity of values is incompatible with the role of the principle as a basis of integration of humanity. Yet acceptance of relativity of values was at one time, perhaps still is, a tenet of faith among cultural anthropologists. A "culture" to most representatives of this discipline is what a species is to a biologist. Intense study induces detailed familiarity, which, in turn, induces "understanding" (of how the parts fit into the whole), which often induces admiration. Many cultural anthropologists feel about "endangered" cultures the same way as conservationists feel about endangered species. This attitude seems to fit naturally into commitment to unity in diversity, but I cannot help feeling that it is incompatible with the ideal of integration of humanity. For surely veneration of violence is deeply imbedded in many cultures (manifested in war as a way of life, bloody rituals, blood vengeance as an imperative in the preservation of honor).

To summarize: The unity in diversity principle is evidently compatible with the sharing of delight. It presents problems in relying on science to provide universally acceptable criteria of truth, but perhaps diversity of beliefs of what is true is not an insuperable obstacle to the integration of humanity. In contrast, diversity of conceptions of good and evil does seem to be an insuperable obstacle. Indeed, whether a set of universal human values (which seems to be an indispensable basis of integration) exists at all is far from certain. When I assume that it exists, I sometimes feel I am indulging in wishful thinking. I have always assumed that Ken (because of his commitment to Christianity) did believe in such a set (as did Tolstoy, who identified their existence with the existence of God).

Declaration of war on the war system

The areas of thought and action in which my relation to Ken was closest were peace research and peace activism. Following our year at the Center we were together at the University of Michigan. The launching of the first satellite

("Sputnik") in 1957 was the last of three events that conferred the title of "superpower" on America's formidable adversary (the first was the explosion of the fission bomb in 1949, the second the explosion of the fusion bomb in 1953). As Ken once wrote, "in this race [between knowledge and disaster] the longer the disaster is staved off, the better chance we have of acquiring knowledge to prevent it altogether." The nature of the looming disaster was clear at the time—a war of total destruction between the Big Two. As for knowledge of how to avert it, Ken (like any member in good standing of Academe) expected it to be acquired by disciplined research. In this context, "discipline" is used in both of its senses—referring to organization of knowledge and to acquiring it by strictly rigorous (disciplined) procedures. The fifties marked the beginning of a new discipline—conflict resolution. Ken once defined three criteria that confer the title of "discipline" on a field of inquiry: there must be a literature devoted to it, a journal in which the literature is predominantly published, and it must be possible to give an examination in it. It seems that the crucial condition is the existence of a journal. Once you have a journal, literature will be produced (the existence of an outlet is a powerful stimulus). Once you have a literature, you can assign readings to students, and then you can give examinations.

The *Journal of Conflict Resolution* was launched in 1957. The Center for Research on Conflict Resolution was activated in July, 1959, but expired after a few years, partly because of lack of financial support but also because of initial opposition to it from the established political science department. Ken did not easily "make friends and influence people" in the public relations sense. At some point he minced no words in telling mainstream political scientists what he thought of their discipline. The journal, however, survived. There are now worldwide some dozens of journals dedicated to "peace and conflict studies" or research. Ken's contributions were largely from the perspective of economics (*Disarmament and the Economy* [1963], *Economics of Peace* [1972]) or from the perspective of general system theory (*Conflict and Defense* [1962]). The latter book partly overlaps with my *Fights, Games, and Debates* (1960) in devoting considerable attention to the "Richardson Process" (the dynamics of arms races).

My closest and most stimulating contact with Kenneth Boulding developed in the time of intense peace activism, that is, during the first two years of the massive intervention by the United States in Southeast Asia. It was then that both the intensity and the eloquence of his passion, reminiscent of the Old Testament prophets, drew me most strongly to him.

Immediately after bombs started to fall on North Vietnam in 1965, an elderly lady, Alice Herz of Detroit, set fire to herself, following the example of Vietnamese Buddhist monks. A group of faculty members and graduate students met to discuss possible ways of publicizing our outrage. A strike was suggested, but the idea was soon dismissed. Some 40–50 faculty members expressed support for the action, and this presaged failure, which would do far more harm than good to the emergent protest movement. Next, someone suggested devoting a class hour to acquainting the students with the background of the war in Vietnam (which had already been going on for twenty years). This idea was also dismissed. Very few of the faculty felt competent to present this information, and those who did could be easily singled out for punitive sanctions. The action might be interpreted as breach of contract, which specified the number of hours per week a faculty member undertook to teach a specified subject. Finally, the idea of the "teach-in" took shape.

The teach-in was conceived as an analogue of a sit-in strike. In the 1930s, the turbulent years of energetic union organizing, striking American workers, instead of picketing the premises, occupied them. It was much more difficult to dislodge them than to break up picket lines. The novelty of the tactic also attracted much more attention. The teach-in was like the sit-ins in that it involved occupying the premises. But breach of contract could not be easily established since those events were to take place outside the normal teaching hours.

The first teach-in took place at the University of Michigan on the night of March 24–25, 1965, from 8pm to 8am. The format was a combination of mass meetings and seminars. Lecturers and seminar leaders from several universities participated. Administration cooperated by making several lecture halls and seminar rooms available. The affair was meticulously planned along the lines of a meeting of a professional society, that is, as a tight program of lectures, workshops, etc., interspersed with plenary sessions. Of all the exciting things that happened that night, I remember most vividly and fondly the implementation of Kenneth Boulding's excellent suggestion that undoubtedly contributed to the success of the affair, namely, to provide free sandwiches and coffee to be consumed in the ten-minute breaks between the sessions. "Nothing like food to keep spirits up," Ken pointed out.

We expected a few hundred students. About three thousand showed up. There was a counter-demonstration. A dozen or two supporters of the war picketed the meetings. They carried signs urging someone to "drop the bomb" and expressing support for the President ("LBJ all the way!"). There was a bomb scare. The halls had to be cleared while they were searched. This rather raised the morale of the protesters, making them feel that they were pitted against the forces of evil. It was events like this that brought out Ken's thunderous Old Testament eloquence. I thought I was listening to Isaiah, or Themistocles or Danton.

The next day a group of people from the State Department staged a counter-teach-in. There was just one session attended by about 300. Possibly the participants of the teach-in slept all day.

The teach-in quickly spread to American and Canadian campuses. They culminated in the national teach-in in Washington, DC, on May 15, 1965. A nationwide telephone hookup broadcast the proceedings to some fifty campuses.

The last contact

In 1967, Ken went to the University of Colorado at Boulder, and three years later I went to the University of Toronto. Our face-to-face contacts were confined to conferences. We met for the last time again in Ann Arbor, in the University Hospital.

I had a heart attack during a conference of the International Peace Research Association, and Ken came to see me the next day. I told him of an interesting experience I had while I was being worked on in Emergency. I was watching with interest the several oscillographs whose wild flickerings apparently made sense to the interns working on me. At one point, one of them bent over me and asked, "How would you rate your pain on a scale from 1 to 10?" The question seemed bizarre to me, and I was tempted to say, "Do you think I carry an interval scale around on which I read off the intensity of my sensations?"

However, with deference to the gravity of the situation, I refrained from flippancy and replied meekly, "I would say about 7."

The young man seemed satisfied. In a few minutes he approached me again with the same question. The pain had subsided considerably, and I replied, "Around 4." He went on with his work. Then I recalled a paper by a Russian mathematical psychologist that apparently had some bearing on this matter. It was a model of subjective quantification of sensation that could account for just the sort of estimate of pain intensity that the intern expected me to make and incidentally also for the cross-modality experiments suggested by the psychophysical theories of S.S. Stevens. This, I pointed out to Ken, portended a break out from the confines of behaviorism—a demonstration that not only the Scratch but also the Itch is "real"! The philosophical significance of this breakthrough is immense. For is not the conviction that what I feel as an itch (or pain or ecstasy) is exactly what every other human feels, the very foundation of empathy, of identification with the Other, and consequently a solid basis for the integration of humanity?

We had a great time blurring the line between the whimsical and the dead serious. When I think of Ken, I invariably return mentally to that last conversation.

Note

1 This article was previously published in *Review of Social Economy*, 1997, 55(4): 416–431.

References

Boulding, K.E. (1945) *There is a Spirit: the Nayler Sonnets*, Nyack, NY: Fellowship Publications.

Boulding, K.E. (1957) "General System Theory—the Skeleton of Science," *General Systems* 1: 10–17.

Boulding, Kenneth E. (1958) *The Skills of the Economist*, Toronto: Clarke, Irwin & Company Limited.

Kerman, C.E. (1974) *Creative Tension. The Life and Thought of Kenneth Boulding*, Ann Arbor: The University of Michigan Press.

Korzybski, A. (1933) *Science and Sanity*, Lancaster, PA: Science Press.

Rapoport, A. (1960) *Fights, Games, and Debates*, Ann Arbor: The University of Michigan Press.

Rapoport, A. (1994) *Gewissheiten und Zweifel*, Darmstadt: Verlag Darmstadter Blätter.

12c Comment: Conflict resolution and peace

Keith Hartley

Introduction

Kenneth Boulding was a pioneer in what is now the established field of peace economics. He made important contributions to the study of conflict resolution, non-violence, disarmament and peace. These contributions were made at a time when economists were not research active in these fields. He showed how these important topics could be addressed by economists and, unlike many of today's economists, he knew how to write in a style which was readable and intelligible to both economists and to wider audiences. His aim was to apply economic thinking to producing a better world.

This chapter proceeds by briefly outlining some of the formative influences on Boulding's thinking in peace economics, followed by a review of his major contributions in the field and their relevance and impact on current thinking in the general field of defence and peace economics.

Some formative influences

Academic scholars as innovative thinkers are the result of family background, education, personal values and beliefs, family circumstances, including children, work experiences, major external events (e.g. wars), the academic research environment, personal friendships and debate with other academics.

Kenneth Boulding was born in Liverpool, England in 1910. His father was a plumber and initially he had a strict Methodist upbringing. He was educated at Oxford and held appointments at the Universities of McGill, Michigan and Colorado. He was the founder of the Centre for Conflict Resolution whilst on the faculty of the University of Michigan.

Religion was a dominant factor in Boulding's thinking. He was a devout Christian (Rapoport, 1997). His desire to model his life on Christian principles and his experiences of the First World War and its propaganda led him to the belief that he could not kill anyone nor participate in war. His childhood experiences in the First World War convinced him "that war was an outrageous folly and murder and that he could not participate in it" (Boulding, 1990: 232). By the age of 14, he was already peace-minded. Eventually, his beliefs led him to the

Society of Friends (Quakers) where he cherished the silence of the Friends Meeting and the Quaker community around the world became part of his life. He became a committed pacifist opposed to war and declared war on the war system (Rapoport, 1997). His wife, Elise, was also a Quaker. Kenneth Boulding believed that war could only be eliminated by understanding its causes: hence, his original contributions on conflict resolution, disarmament and the role of organised non-violence in achieving a stable peace (Boulding, 1962, 1963, 1990).

Conflict resolution

Boulding's starting point was that we live in a world where conflict, especially international conflict, threatens to get out of hand and destroy us. "The theory of conflict … has practical implications, even implications about survival" (Boulding, 1962: 305). The concept of an optimum amount and type of conflict is presented and illustrated, with examples ranging from family quarrels to sports, international conflict and war. Conflict is viewed as having a life cycle: it starts, it flourishes for a while and then "certain processes" bring it to an end. How can conflicts be prevented from starting, and how can they end?

Conflicts can be avoided. For example, arms control agreements are mechanisms for moving nations apart. Conflict can be ended by conquest where one party or nation forcefully removes the other. Some form of procedural resolution of conflict can emerge that is accepted by the parties. Such procedural resolution might be reconciliation, compromise or award (where both parties agree to accept the decisions of an outside agency). In some cases, such as reconciliation, much depends on individual personalities and whether they have any concern for the welfare of others. Boulding's insights into bargaining with fanatics (cf. terrorists) are revealing and relevant to today's conflicts. He concludes that "Before the fanatic, ordinary reasonable men are helpless: they can be moved and the fanatic cannot. If any bargain is struck, it must be on the fanatic's terms for no other terms are possible" (Boulding, 1962: 315–316).

Conflict can also be resolved by law. Here, interesting comparisons are made with the police–criminal complex, suggesting that existing institutions have failed to solve the problem of eliminating crime. But for international conflict, there is an absence of effective international law and institutions capable of ending international conflict. Gaps in the market arrangements for international collective action to resolve international conflicts mean that violence is a likely outcome. But violence does not necessarily lead to settlement: it can often inhibit settlement. In this context, Boulding comments that there is a surprising lack of theoretical and empirical studies of violence (Boulding, 1962: 323).

Boulding concludes that "One of the great organizational problems of mankind … is the control of violence, or more generally, the control of conflict to the point where procedural institutions are adequate to deal with it" (Boulding, 1962: 324). Here, mention is made of world government but it is recognised that the greatest problem in developing institutions of conflict control is that of catching conflicts at their outset (whilst they are young). This requires the development of conflict indicators which are available before the event. History and hindsight have identified the points where conflict was inevitable. For example, the events which led to the Second World War probably needed to be dealt with earlier than 1939 (e.g. probably 1937), but a definitive date is difficult to identify.

Institutions to prevent the two world wars did not exist. The challenge is to develop institutions which will prevent a third (and possibly last) world war. Two problems arise, namely, signal detection (how do we know when something needs to be done and how do we avoid errors) and implementation (how do we know what to do). Boulding argues for an international agency to detect conflicts at their early stages. He recognises the role of interest groups which have a vested interest in the preservation of conflict (e.g. armed forces; defence industries), simply because conflict is the only reason for their continued existence.

The conclusion is reached that the problems "...involved in setting up the institutions of arms control and, more generally, of international conflict control are difficult indeed; but it would be suicide for the human race to believe that they are insoluble". Without conflict control, "all other hopes for human welfare and betterment are likely to be dashed to the ground" (Boulding, 1962: 328).

Boulding was a peace researcher and peace activist and the 1950s marked the beginning of the new discipline of conflict resolution. He specified three criteria for conferring the title of "discipline" on a field of inquiry. It needs a literature, a journal in which the literature is published and it must be possible to give an examination in it. Once there is a journal, literature will be produced and, once a literature exists, students can be given references for readings and then examinations can be held (Rapoport, 1997). The *Journal of Conflict Resolution* was launched in 1957 and the Center for Research on Conflict Resolution was established at the University of Michigan in 1959; but the Center was short-lived due to lack of financial support and opposition from the political science department (Rapoport, 1997).

Disarmament

Boulding's work on disarmament was published shortly after his *Conflict and Defense: A General Theory* (Boulding, 1962). The focus was the world war industry as an economic problem (Boulding, 1963). The contribution was typical Boulding in showing how economics can be applied to an industry which was usually outside its scope, leading to new insights and understanding. He views the war industry's aims as the destruction of physical and human capital and reducing the age of death. The concept of the "milorg" or military organisation is introduced and compared with the firm in economic models, especially oligopoly models. Military organisations comprise national defence departments and their armed forces and form part of the military-industrial complex. But "milorgs" do not look kindly on economists.

> The efforts of Charles Hitch and other economists to introduce concepts of efficiency and economy into the American milorg are received with as little enthusiasm as the efforts of the anti-trust division of the Department of Justice are received in large corporations.
>
> (Boulding, 1963: 9)

Boulding then addresses the impact of technical change on the classical system of national defence where "milorgs" dominated their national homelands and their weapons allowed domination of surrounding areas. Long-range nuclear-armed missiles have destroyed the classical system of national defence: some nations can now destroy other nations with this new system having "…no analogue in economic life" (Boulding, 1963: 16). It is concluded that at this point, "economic theory does not seem to have much comparative advantage, although some insights may be derived from regarding the exchange of threats as analogous to the exchange of negative commodities" (Boulding, 1963: 16).

The threats to world peace and civilisation from nuclear weapons and long-range missiles means that disarmament has become economically attractive, offering large payoffs, hence the need to focus on the economics of disarmament. Here, Boulding proceeds to analyse disarmament as a bargaining problem applying the economic theory of bargaining embracing game theory and the Prisoner's Dilemma model. The analysis is expertly done but not abstract, technical and incomprehensible. It illustrates complex situations with a simple matrix comprising two countries and two choices, namely, arm and disarm, and the analysis is supported with policy-relevant applications. Possible solutions are outlined for the "dilemma of disarmament", including a shift from short-sightedness to mutual longsightedness or creating institutions to change the payoffs from disarmament (e.g. via side payments). Comparisons are made with *personal* disarmament, which has been achieved by unilateral action without any formal agreements (e.g. people no longer carry guns). Throughout, the analysis is supported by historical examples, which is an approach sadly missing from modern economics.

Boulding recognises that general and complete disarmament (i.e. the abolition of war as an organised institution) requires compensating payments for military personnel and war industries: as potential losers, these groups will form barriers to disarmament where the gainers are the "ordinary people of the world". He recognises the need for empirical studies of disarmament: for example, what are the costs and benefits of unilateral disarmament? Boulding's stress on the need for empirical work in economics is a refreshing change from the current-day emphasis by economists on abstract, highly technical, game theory models which focus on theory without empirical support and lacking in policy-relevance.

Boulding concludes on the economist's role by praising the "brilliant work" of Hitch and McKean in their *Economics of Defense in the Nuclear Age* (Hitch and McKean, 1960), "showing that economics is a way of looking at things rather than a set of precise answers" (Boulding, 1963: 27). He then argues that

> The economic way of looking at things … is a powerful corrosive of the sacred aspects of military policy. It will undoubtedly produce explosive reactions from the defenders of the sacred.… Nevertheless, when the heroic and sacred aspects of life threaten to destroy us … it is time for the grubby hand of the economist to signal a halt.
>
> (Boulding, 1963: 27)

Non-violence and stable peace

This theme starts with two developments. First, the rise of areas of stable peace between independent nations. Examples include the stable peace between Mexico and the USA after 1848 and the peace in Western Europe after 1945 and the formation of the European Union. Second, the development of organised non-violence.[1] Examples include Gandhi and the non-violent movement for Indian independence and Martin Luther King and the US civil rights movement. Boulding relates stable peace and organised non-violence to the emergence of weapons of mass destruction (e.g. aerial bombing; nuclear weapons). He guesstimates that some 90 to 95 per cent of human time is allocated to peaceful activities, with the balance devoted to violence or preparing to be violent. The world war industry based on defence spending accounted for some 6 per cent of the total world economic output in the late 1950s but this share rises during conflicts.

Boulding applied his non-violence principles to the Vietnam War when, in March 1965, he organised a teach-in at the University of Michigan. The format was a combination of mass meetings with lectures, seminars and workshops held from 8pm to 8am so as not to interfere with normal university teaching programmes. Teach-ins spread to other North American universities, culminating in a national teach-in in Washington DC in May 1965 (Rapoport, 1997).

Boulding introduced the novel idea of the four phases of conflict. First is stable war, in which war occurs continuously. Second is unstable war, where war is interrupted by periods of peace (e.g. Middle East). Third is unstable peace, where peace is regarded as the norm, which is interrupted by wars. Fourth is stable peace, where the probability of war is almost zero (e.g. Scandinavia since the mid-nineteenth century).

For Boulding, stable peace requires at least five conditions. First, a mutual change in the national images of the nations concerned, which means taking national frontiers off the agenda. Second, there should be a minimum amount of intervention of each nation in the affairs of the other state (similar to the intervention that parents exercise in the lives of their married children). Third, nation states should be "desacrilised" so that they cease to be a sacred object requiring human sacrifice and are no longer organised around the concept of victory and conquest. Such a view is alien to the military culture, which requires killing and dying for the defence of the nation state (Boulding, 1990: 228). Fourth, the growth of stable peace has resulted from recognition of the weakness of threat power and the attractiveness of economic and integrative activity. Fifth, stable peace recognises the basic instability of deterrence or counterthreat. There results a paradox, namely, that deterrence can only be stable in the short run: there is some probability that it will break down and the threat will be carried out. Boulding predicts that "if the present international system of nuclear deterrence continues, the Soviet Union, the United States and Europe will be destroyed by nuclear war in x years" (Boulding, 1990: 230). The end of the Cold War might have reduced the threat from the former Soviet Union, but there are new nuclear threats from China, India and Pakistan (and Iran?).

Boulding had that rare talent to illustrate his arguments with relevant examples. He suggests that the basic weakness of threat power is illustrated by the many examples in human history where military defeat led to economic and cultural upsurges by the defeated compared with the victor. On this basis, he suggested that Germany and Japan were the economic winners of the Second World War: they abolished their military and allocated all their resources to getting rich. Critics will claim that Germany and Japan remilitarised shortly after 1945 but both were able to "free-ride" under US military protection.

Nations will respond to threats by developing defensive and protective structures against the means of destruction. But Boulding argued that the development of missiles and nuclear weapons made national defence obsolete. In these circumstances, the only national security is stable peace. Organised non-violence is a further response to a perceived threat when counterthreat is believed to be ineffective or too costly. Gandhianism is an alternative to war (Boulding, 1990: 232). Growing up in Liverpool, Boulding remembered Gandhi's visit to Lancashire, which was suffering under the Gandhi-inspired boycotts.

For advocates of non-violence, a key question is whether it would have worked against Hitler? Boulding admits this is a difficult question and regards it as a one in 1,000 years event. But such evil dictators are probably more frequent (e.g. Stalin; Mao Tse Tung; Pol Pot; Rwanda; Congo; Gaddafi). Boulding proceeds by suggesting that the post-1945 settlements for Germany and Japan were better than the 1919 Versailles Treaty by integrating both nations into the international community. The question is also raised of whether it is possible to think of Gandhising the military. Here, he suggests some guidelines for action. First, we need to persuade the military that their reactions to the exercise of violence should be limited to "tit for tat" so limiting violence and moving the world towards stable peace. Second, we need to persuade the military that victory is not usually desirable. These are radical suggestions, not just for the military but for other central agents in national political markets (i.e. voters; governments; bureaucracies; interest groups).

Boulding concludes perceptively by stating that the academic and scientific community is basically Gandhian with its emphasis on persuasion by argument and evidence and not by threat. This principle has resulted in the success of science in expanding human knowledge.

> Truth is the overriding concern of the scholarly community. As the scholarly community begins to understand more clearly the great complexities of

the world, especially of social systems, the means by which we will abolish war—now the main priority for the human race—will become clearer.

(Boulding, 1990: 234)

Modern developments

Since the early 1960s and Boulding's contributions on conflict and its resolution, disarmament and peace, there has been a substantial economics literature which has transformed these fields of study. There have been contributions from both defence and peace economists in the form of books and journal articles. New specialist journals have been created in *Conflict Resolution*, *Defence and Peace Economics*, *Peace Research*, and *Peace Economics, Peace Science and Public Policy*. The Stockholm International Peace Research Institute (SIPRI) publishes an annual *Yearbook on Armaments, Disarmament and International Security*, which also provides valuable annual data on world military expenditure, arms production and arms transfers. SIPRI was established in 1966 to commemorate Sweden's 150 years of unbroken peace (Boulding's stable peace). It is an independent international institute for research into peace, conflict, arms control and disarmament (SIPRI, 2010). The remainder of this section reviews modern developments in the three fields of conflict, disarmament and peace. The review is illustrative of modern developments and is not meant to be a comprehensive review of the literature.

Conflict and its resolution

Boulding's criticism of neo-classical equilibrium economics finds an outlet in the study of conflict. Wars and conflict completely reverse standard economic theory. Conventional economic theory focuses on markets, voluntary exchange, equilibrium and the *creative power* of markets (producing a greater output of goods and services). In contrast, conflict is about *destructive power:* it destroys markets and creates disequilibrium and chaos. There are deaths and injuries for military and civilian personnel, whilst physical capital and infrastructure are destroyed or damaged. Markets as beneficial trading mechanisms cease to exist and are replaced by "black markets". Conflict is costly and is a major user of scarce resources which have alternative uses. Without the two world wars, there would have been much greater resources available for building hospitals, schools, houses, roads and infrastructure. And in contrast to private markets where prices allocate scarce resources, in conflict military power becomes the allocative mechanism: such power is used to achieve a re-allocation of resources between nations (e.g. theft of land; minerals; oil; water; populations).

A substantial theoretical and empirical literature has emerged on the economics of conflict, for example, Hirshleifer (1995), Garfinkel and Skaperdas (2007) on the theory of conflict. Game theory models have been applied to conflict, focusing on strategic behaviour, interactions and interdependence between adversaries. In contrast to Boulding's non-technical approach to conflict, and despite the insights they did generate, these modern models are often mathematical and abstract, lacking empirical support without any real world and historical examples and failing to address relevant policy issues on arms control and conflict resolution. Conflict involves some new applications which have also attracted the attention of economists. These include civil wars, ethnic cleansing, insurrections, terrorism and the role of corruption in conflict (Braddon and Hartley, 2011; Sandler and Hartley, 2007). An historical perspective on military history is presented in the Boulding tradition by Brauer and van Tuyll (2008).

Arms races are often regarded as a source of conflict. Boulding was especially concerned about the destructive power of nuclear weapons with their potential for mass destruction of life and civilisation. Arms races are often presented as an action–reaction process in which one nation increases its military spending in response to increases in a potential adversary's defence expenditure (Brito and Intriligator, 1995). Concerns arise that ever-increasing arms spending between nations will eventually lead to conflict. For example, during the Cold War, analysis of the arms race between the USA and the Soviet Union was topical and led to some important economic contributions to understanding arms races. However, the end of the Cold War did not lead to the end of arms races: instead there were regional arms races (e.g. Middle East; India-Pakistan; North and South Korea: Sandler and Hartley, 1995).

Conflict resolution was a central concern for Boulding. He would have welcomed the emergence of an economics literature on peace-keeping (Bove and Smith, 2011; Solomon, 2007). Preventing conflict is costly but offers long-term benefits from peace and security. International peace-keeping forces have to be created, which involves transaction costs in their organisation. They emerge from existing international organisations, such as the United Nations, the European Union or NATO, or from ad hoc arrangements between groups of nations. Boulding recognised the gap in the arrangements for international collective action on peace-keeping.

The costs of conflict show the economic benefits of conflict avoidance resulting from defence spending or peace-keeping as means of prevention. Whilst there have been some studies of the costs of conflict, there remains scope for much more empirical work in this area. Joseph Stiglitz and Linda Bilmes estimated the true costs of the Iraq conflict. They show that wars are expensive and that we need to know how expensive. Politicians have incentives to underestimate and under-report the costs of war (Stiglitz and Bilmes, 2008; Bilmes and Stiglitz, 2011). Indeed, since Boulding's early work in the field (e.g. on milorgs), an economics literature has developed on public choice which has been applied to develop models of the military-industrial-political complex. These show how the various agents in this complex behave and can influence policy on defence spending, weapons procurement and disarmament (Hartley, 2010; Smith, 2009).

Disarmament

The end of the Cold War was based on an arms control agreement which led to major disarmament and expectations of a peace dividend. For a time, there was a voluntary disarmament race as nations competed to reduce defence spending. The Soviet Union was replaced by the Russian Federation and the Warsaw Pact ceased to exist. Boulding would have assumed a similar fate for NATO, but NATO survived and acquired new members, especially from the former Warsaw Pact. But any hopes of a lasting peace were short-lived. Following the end of the Cold War, there were regional conflicts in the Middle East (e.g. first Gulf War), Bosnia and Kosovo, followed by the 9/11 terrorist attacks on the USA and the subsequent "war on terror" and the conflicts in Afghanistan and Iraq. The result was a new emphasis on defence spending and continued weapons procurement for arms industries in the USA and Europe.

Boulding's early 1960s analysis of the world war industry has become even more relevant. Today's war industry is radically different from the 1960s. The US and European defence industries now comprise an even smaller number of larger firms. The industry is dominated by such firms as Boeing, Lockheed Martin, Northrop Grumman, General Dynamics and Raytheon in the USA and BAE Systems, EADS (including Airbus), Finmeccanica and Thales in Europe. These firms have global markets and differ in their mix of military and civil products. Boeing and EADS have a large civil aircraft business compared with Lockheed Martin, Northrop Grumman and BAE Systems, which are defence specialists involved in a variety of air, land and sea systems (Brauer, 2007; Hartley, 2007; Hartley, 2012).

A policy-relevant question to be addressed is whether the defence firm has a future. Threats have changed dramatically since 1960 and new threats have emerged in the form of international terrorism, regional conflicts, so-called rogue states and the proliferation of weapons of mass destruction. Future threats are likely, so ensuring a future for defence firms; but the future defence firm of 2050 is likely to be radically different from today's arms companies. For example, continued terrorist threats will mean new market opportunities in homeland security and new surveillance techniques (Hartley and Sandler, 2003).

Boulding was especially concerned about the urgency of disarmament and the need for economic studies of its costs and benefits. Since 1960, there have been a number of such studies. A United Nations report introduced the concept of disarmament as an investment process involving both costs and benefits. Adjusting to cuts in defence spending is not costless and requires a re-allocation of resources from the military-industrial complex to the civilian sector. Such re-allocation takes time and involves adjustment costs (e.g. unemployment of resources). The report concluded that disarmament resembled an investment process with short-run costs to achieve long-run benefits. Benefits included a peace dividend from a greater output of civil goods and services as well as the public good of peace itself (UNIDIR, 1993).

Disarmament requires the conversion of resources from military to civilian use and such adjustment can be costly. Examples include converting warship building yards to some alternative civilian use (which, and is it profitable?); finding alternative uses for former military bases (e.g. housing; industrial estates) and for nuclear weapons plants (clean-up costs). Conversion raises issues about the transferability and specificity of labour and capital. Some military resources are highly transferable (e.g. military personnel with computer skills or transport aircraft pilots); others have defence-specific skills which are not marketable in the civil economy (e.g. missile operatives; submariners; tank gunners). In these circumstances, public policies are required to assist resource re-allocation. In other words, disarmament is not a simple process but raises a variety of complex adjustment problems. As Boulding recognised, such problems need to be addressed, otherwise interest groups (e.g. milorgs) likely to lose from disarmament will be major barriers to change (Brzoska, 2007; UNIDIR, 1993).

Non-violence and stable peace

Boulding considered the relationship between organised non-violence and stable peace. He recognised the need for further study of non-violence in preventing unwanted change and the task of addressing its potential in responding to the Hitler question. This is a field which remains under-researched by economists. There have been studies of revolution, insurrections, coercion and conflict (Hirshleifer, 1995; McGuire, 2006). Non-violence can be viewed as a collective action problem with its associated transaction costs of forming a relevant group and the inevitable free-riding. Events in North Africa and the Middle East in 2011 show the effectiveness of peaceful, non-violent action in achieving political change (e.g. Bahrain; Egypt; Tunisia) and such events might stimulate further research into the economics of non-violence.

There is, however, a substantial literature on peace and its stability. Boulding was one of the founders of the study of peace economics (Anderton and Carter, 2007). His world was dominated by the threat of nuclear war and not the new threats from international terrorism and suicide bombers. Nonetheless, economic studies of the arms race have contributed to new and novel insights into the concept of a stable peace showing the complexity of the impact of arms races and disarmament on war and peace. Some models suggest that not all arms races lead to war (mutual deterrence of the Cold War type). These models also suggest that some types of disarmaments might actually lead to war (Brito and Intriligator, 1995; Sandler and Hartley, 1995). More recent studies have reaffirmed Boulding's concern with the threats from nuclear weapons.

"Nuclear proliferation … could be particularly destabilizing" and whilst the Cold War is over, "…the problem of the arms race and proliferation remain important, with potential adverse consequences for the stability of the international order" (Brito and Intriligator, 1995: 159). A conclusion which would have been strongly supported by Boulding.

Conclusion

Boulding's pioneering contributions on conflict and peace and his plea for conflict control remain valid. There is an ambitious research agenda and a need for more economic studies of these problems which are vital to the future of civilisation. Boulding's legacy is that he brought these problems to the attention of economists and a wider audience and that his work will continue. This extraordinary economist has presented a challenge to future generations of economists. For all our sakes, let us hope that future generations take up this challenge.

Note

1 In his "Memories of Ken Boulding", Anatol Rapoport compares his trichotomy of Fights, Games and Debates as three modes of conflict with Boulding's Threat–Trade–Love trichotomy, which were modes of social control (Rapoport, 1997).

References

Anderton, C.H. and Carter, J.R. (2007). "A survey of peace economics", in T. Sandler and K. Hartley (eds.), *Handbook of Defense Economics, volume 2, Defense in a Globalized World*, Amsterdam: Elsevier.

Bilmes, L.J. and Stiglitz, J.E. (2011). "The long-term costs of conflict: The case of the Iraq war", in D. Braddon and K. Hartley (eds.), *Handbook on the Economics of Conflict*, Cheltenham: Edward Elgar.

Boulding, K.E. (1962). "Conflict resolution and control", in K.E. Boulding, *Conflict and Defense: A General Theory*, New York: Harper Torchbooks.

Boulding, K.E. (1963). "The world war industry as an economic problem", in E. Benoit and K.E. Boulding (eds.), *Disarmament and the Economy*, New York: Harper and Row.

Boulding, K.E. (1990). "The role of organized non-violence in achieving stable peace", in K. Kool (ed.), *Perspectives on Non-Violence*, New York: Springer-Verlag.

Bove, V. and Smith, R. (2011). "The economics of peacekeeping", in D. Braddon and K. Hartley (eds.), *Handbook on the Economics of Conflict*, Cheltenham: Edward Elgar.

Braddon, D. and Hartley, K. (eds.) (2011). *Handbook on the Economics of Conflict*, Cheltenham: Edward Elgar.

Brauer, J. (2007). "Arms industries, arms trade and developing countries", in T. Sandler and K. Hartley (eds.), *Handbook of Defense Economics, volume 2, Defense in a Globalized World*, Amsterdam: Elsevier.

Brauer, J. and van Tuyll, H. (2008). *Castles, Battles and Bombs: How Economics Explains Military History*, Chicago: University of Chicago Press.

Brito, D.L. and Intriligator, M.D. (1995). "Arms races and proliferation", in K. Hartley and T. Sandler (eds.) *Handbook of Defense Economics, volume 1*, Amsterdam: Elsevier.

Brzoska, M. (2007). "Success and failure in defense conversion in the 'long decade of disarmament' ", in T. Sandler and K. Hartley (eds.), *Handbook of Defense Economics, volume 2, Defense in a Globalized World*, Amsterdam: Elsevier.

Garfinkel, M.R. and Skaperdas, S. (2007). "Economics of conflict: An overview", in

T. Sandler and K. Hartley (eds.), *Handbook of Defense Economics, Volume 2: Defense in a Globalized World*, Amsterdam: Elsevier.

Hartley, K. (2007). "The arms industry, procurement and industrial policies", in T. Sandler and K. Hartley (eds.), *Handbook on Defense Economics, volume 2, Defense in a Globalized World*, Amsterdam: Elsevier.

Hartley, K. (2010). *The Economics of Defence Policy*, London: Routledge.

Hartley, K. (2012). "Company Survey Series: 1: BAE Systems PLC", *Defence and Peace Economics*, 23, 4, 331–342.

Hartley, K. and Sandler, T. (2003). "The future of the defence firm", *Kyklos*, 56, 3, 361–380.

Hirshleifer, J. (1995). "Theorizing about conflict", in K. Hartley and T. Sandler (eds.), *Handbook of Defense Economics, volume 1*, Amsterdam: Elsevier.

Hitch, C.J. and McKean, R.N. (1960). *The Economics of Defense in the Nuclear Age*, Oxford: Oxford University Press.

McGuire, M.C. (2006). "Memorial essays in honour of Jack Hirshleifer", *Defence and Peace Economics*, Special Issue, 17, 3, 587–690.

Rapoport, A. (1997). "Memories of Kenneth E. Boulding", *Review of Social Economy*, LV, 4, 416–431.

Sandler, T. and Hartley, K. (1995). *The Economics of Defense*, Cambridge Surveys of Economic Literature, Cambridge: Cambridge University Press.

SIPRI (2010). *SIPRI Yearbook 2020: Armaments, Disarmament and International Security*, Oxford: Oxford University Press.

Smith, R. (2009). *Military Economics, The Interactions of Power and Money*, London: Palgrave Macmillan.

Solomon, B. (2007). "Political economy of peacekeeping", in T. Sandler and K. Hartley (eds.), *Handbook of Defense Economics, Volume 2: Defense in a Globalized World*, Amsterdam: Elsevier.

Stiglitz, J.E. and Bilmes, L.J. (2008). *The Three Trillion Dollar War: The True Costs of the Iraq Conflict*, London: Allen Lane.

UNIDIR (1993). *Economic Aspects of Disarmament: Disarmament as an Investment Process*, Geneva: United Nations Institute for Disarmament Research.

Poem

The Freudian Complex

The Freudian Complex is a state
Where black is white and love is hate,
And needs analysis to prove
That white is black and hate is love.

Part XIII

Teaching economics

13 Key text: What do we want in an economics textbook?[1]

Kenneth E. Boulding

What we want in an economics textbook, of course, is economics, as we visualize and interpret it ourselves. If this represents the consensus of the profession and that consensus happens to correspond to some sort of truth, so much the better. Developing true images of complex systems, such as the economy, is elusive and is most likely to emerge out of well-conducted controversy. So I have no hesitation in expounding my own image of the economy, to which no existing textbook of the last generation conforms, not even my own.

Perhaps we might be able to agree about at least one general principle: that a textbook should have at least some combination of data and theory, that the theory should be of some help in explaining the data, and that the data should at least illustrate, if not wholly confirm, the theory. We might also agree that economics is the study of something called "the economy," and a textbook should give the student some idea of what an economy is and how it functions. We might not all agree as to just where we draw the boundary between what is the economy and what is not, but we would probably all agree that it is mainly a subset of the social system of the world. This is a system including all human beings, their structure, content, behavior, artifacts, institutions, and interactions. There is something of a no man's land between the economy and the polity, which political scientists study, and likewise between the economy and whatever it is that sociologists study, which does not seem to have a name; I have sometimes wanted to call it the "integry." It is a very fundamental principle of the world and our knowledge about it that all important distinctions are fuzzy, especially in complex systems. A very narrow definition of the economy would be "that part of society which is organized through exchange," but I myself would want to expand this to include grants and transfers, public and private capital accounting, and so on. I suspect, however, that we would find wide agreement at least about the core of the economy—that is, how society is organized through exchange.

The question of how data should be presented is an important one and quite difficult. My own inclination is for graphical analysis of statistical data, simply because the core of our imaging process is spatial and temporal. I have argued that numbers are something of a figment of the human imagination, that the real world consists of shapes, sizes, structures, patterns, fittings, and so on, and very often, though not necessarily, unless we can visualize them in some form, numbers do not convey very much. If we tell people there are five billion human beings in the world, this may not seem to imply much more than an "awful lot." If we tell people, however, that if they all joined hands they would encircle the equator about one hundred times, or if they all stood in a field, it would have to be about fourteen miles square, or if we typed out their names on a sheet of paper, it would stretch from here to China, this gives people an image of the magnitude of the system that they would not get from just looking at the number 5,000,000,000. Reducing numbers to intelligibility is indeed an art, and one that is not sufficiently practiced.

A very important thing that has happened to economics in the twentieth century has been the enormous explosion of data. I remember Professor Schumpeter saying to me even in 1933, "How nice economics was before anybody knew anything, when you could spin any old theory you wanted and nobody could check up on it." Now we certainly know much more about the overall patterns, structures, and quantities of the economy than we did at the beginning of the century, though whether we use this knowledge wisely is another matter. Also, the question of whether we know enough is very important. We may even know too much about some things and not enough about others, which is an important question for "research on research."

Once a few general principles have been established, perhaps the first question the writer of a textbook should ask is: What are we writing about? What is this "economy" that we are trying to describe, understand, and measure? We can start off by looking at the five billion human beings, all of them different and yet sharing many common characteristics. The most peculiar human being on earth is more like me than I am like a tree or even a chimpanzee. This makes thinking about the five billion a little easier, at least until we start putting them into an ecosystem, for there are an enormous number of species that are not at all like us. We look at a human being and we say, "What part of this complex structure is part of the economy, in terms of body, mind, and behavior?" His or her dreams, big toenails, the tune that is being whistled may not be much part of the economy. When, however, she goes to the store and buys something, or he takes a job and earns wages, or she employs somebody and pays wages, or he buys a bond, or she receives interest on a debt, then, aha, we are in the economy. When somebody makes up an income tax return and pays taxes, we are still in the economy. When an accountant makes out a balance sheet, this is still in the economy. When somebody goes to the voting booth, this is not so much in the economy. Whenever there is money involved, we are pretty sure we are in the economy, but I think we would also want to put barter transactions in it. As we look over the world, anything that is recognized as an exchangeable that can be exchanged for something else is certainly part of the economy. The ice at the North Pole is not part of it at the moment; ice in the grocery store is part of it.

It is very important, even for beginning students, to recognize that the economy, like everything else, is a structure in space-time. To describe any such structure, we have to start with a state description of the system at a particular moment of time. A state description of the world economy consists of a list of all things that are exchangeables or related to exchangeables. Economics is blessed, and has occasionally suffered, by having the "measuring rod of money." Part of the state description of exchangeables is their "value"—how many units of some other exchangeable one unit of a given exchangeable will exchange for. If we put all this in a matrix, it would be a square of paper stretching from here to the moon. If, however, there is a "measure of value," such as a unit of money, then we can suppose without too great a violation of reality that there is some amount of some monetary unit that can be got for any unit of an exchangeable—its price. If all exchanges are accessible (a large order), we know how much one unit of exchangeable will get for any other exchangeable. If a pound of apples exchanges for $1 and a pound of cheese for $4, then if markets are available, one pound of cheese could exchange for four pounds of apples. If then we have a price set of all exchangeables in terms of a money price, we can calculate all the other boxes in the exchange matrix.

This leads to accounting, which starts off with balance sheets. We start off with a list of the quantities of all exchangeables possessed by some person or organization. We multiply each by its money price or some equivalent in terms of what might be called a "valuation coefficient"; then we get a money value for each quantity of exchangeables. Five hundred pounds of cheese at $4 a pound will be $2,000. Some of these exchangeables are positive assets with positive money values; some of them are negative assets with negative money values. Negative assets include garbage wastes, pollution, and debts that we owe. Debts have the peculiar property that they are negative assets or liabilities in one account and positive assets in another.

Accountants are fond of showing a bottom line or net worth, which for any particular cluster of assets is the sum of the values of the positive assets minus the sum of the values of the negative assets, though negative assets are not always very well recorded. Net worths can be calculated for individuals, for families, for organizations, for corporations, for nations, and for the whole world.

There are some tricky questions here as to how we include potentials for the future in current assets. We see this in the case of the evaluation of persons. In the slave society, slaves are assets to the owner and some sort of money value can be put on them. In the nonslave society, every person is his own slave. There is no market in persons, except perhaps a little in professional sports. Nevertheless, each person is a very important part of his or her own balance sheet, depending largely on the potentials for the future. In considering what all exchangeables will exchange for, we need to remember that their potentials for the future are very important, and the whole question as to whether or how we should discount these potentials is a difficult one and a great source of controversy. The asset value of the body and mind of a person who has just gotten a good permanent job rises. That of a person who has gotten incurable cancer unquestionably falls, though by how much is very hard to say.

The capital balance-sheet structure of the economy is like a flashlight photograph. One flashlight photograph, however, does not tell us very much about a system. We have to have a succession of flashlight photographs at successive moments of time. Change is then the difference between one flashlight photograph and the immediately preceding one. A constant or steady flow is a succession of equal changes over equal intervals of time. The confusion between stocks and flows is almost endemic in economics, going right back to Adam Smith. But if we are going to have a clear picture of the total system in space-time, it is crucial that this distinction be recognized.

In describing the system, therefore, we have to describe what happens between one flashlight photograph and the next. This, of course, is "dynamics," but we have to be very careful about it. In social systems, it is a great mistake to assume that there are constant parameters of change, as there are in the solar system and celestial mechanics. Hence, theories that are modeled on celestial mechanics are apt to be misleading, especially because social systems, and the economy among them, are not determinate. The Newtonian tradition, however, dies hard. In systems that have information as an essential component—as all social systems do, and most biological systems—there is a nonexistence theorem about exact prediction. Information has to be surprising, or it is not information. This relates somewhat to the Heisenberg principle in physics. In social systems, especially, predictions tend to be self-justifying, self-defeating, or ineffective.

We need to look, then, at the changes between one flashlight photograph of the economy and the next. These are of many kinds of changes that define what we might call "events." One such event is an exchange, where, say, A gives B a car and B gives A $10,000 in cash. When we go from time 1 to time 2, we notice that A has one car less in stock and $10,000 more in cash; B has $10,000 less in cash and one more car in his stock. All exchange involves a redistribution of assets among exchangers. It is a cost-accounting convention that all exchanges are of equal values, so the net worths of the two parties are unaffected by the exchange itself, though they may be affected by the potential for the future that exchange creates.

A second type of event is production. This is a process largely internal to an organization, though, again, it may have subsequent consequences. The miller grinds wheat into flour. In his balance sheet, wheat goes down; the value of his machinery may go down as a result of wear and tear or even just aging; his cash may go down if he hired somebody to operate the mill; and his stock of flour goes up. Again, according to cost-accounting convention, the cost (the total value of what goes down) is just equal to what goes up, which is the value of the product.

A third important event is revaluation, which creates a profit or a loss. If the man who bought the automobile sells it immediately for $12,000, we have to express this as a revaluation of the automobile from $10,000 to $12,000, and then the exchange of $12,000 of automobile for $12,000 cash. His net worth goes up by $2,000, which is profit. Profit is always in some sense a net increase, and a loss a net decrease, in net worth. Similarly, if the miller sells for $1,100 the flour that has cost him $1,000 and therefore is valued at that, here again, at the moment of sale, the flour is revalued from $1,000 to $1,100 and, again, is exchanged for $1,100 cash. Revaluations do not always involve exchange. Some assets rise and some fall in what might be called "potential market value," that is, what they would bring if they were sold. Sometimes this happens through a change in the character of the asset, as when wine matures and appreciates, or when machines, buildings, clothing, and so forth, depreciate just with age. And these nonexchange revaluations under some accounting systems may appear as profit or loss.

A fourth type of event is the one-way transfer. It can take the form of a grant or theft or taxes. In a grant or gift, A gives B $100; B does not give A any tangible asset (though there may be intangible assets in terms of gratitude, or a nice smile, which the accountant does not recognize). A's cash and net worth both go down $100; B's cash and net worth both go up $100. Theft has a similar effect, unintended by the victim. Taxes are rather similar. When I pay my taxes, my own net worth goes down and the government's goes up. There may, of course, be additional intangible benefits or losses.

A fifth type of event is consumption, a concept that has caused a great deal of confusion in economics. It is sometimes used to mean household purchases, which, of course, are not consumption at all, but exchange. Money goes from the household to the store, and goods go from the store to the household. A more literal meaning of consumption is that of the destruction of capital, including goods held by households. Part of this may be thought of as costs, when something is consumed in the production of something else, such as wheat in the production of flour. When food is consumed, presumably the value of the person's body increases. Energy and materials are taken in, which are converted into muscular or mental activity and used for the replacement of depreciating structures (cells and so on). Then this energy and the materials are gradually used up, and we have to have another meal to replace what has depreciated in our bodies. From Adam Smith on, economists have regarded consumption as a process from which we get satisfaction or utility. What we get the most satisfaction out of, however, is utilization, not consumption. I get no satisfaction out of the fact that my car or my clothes are wearing out. I get satisfaction in wearing clothes or in using the car. If they wore out more slowly, that is, if their consumption were less, I would be better off. Nevertheless, we do enjoy change and variety. We enjoy eating as well as being well fed. There are good evolutionary reasons for that, so that the evaluation of consumptive change is quite complex.

A sixth change is accumulation, which is the excess of production over consumption of anything. Production adds to the stock of something; consumption subtracts from it. We could think of all existing stocks of economic goods as populations that are added to by production (which is birth) and subtracted from by consumption (which is death). If in any period, production of anything, peanuts or people, exceeds consumption, there will be an increase in the total stock. If consumption exceeds production, there will be a decrease in the stock. These might be called "derived events." The decision to accumulate may take the form either of an increase in production or of a diminution in consumption of the good in question.

A seventh event, which is more descriptive perhaps of the system as a whole than of individuals, is redistribution, that is, the change in the proportion of the total net worth of the economy held by different persons, families, groups, corporations, and so forth. This happens partly through one-way transfers, as we have seen. It also occurs, however, through the constant revaluations of changes in the price structure that are taking place all the time. Between one flashlight photograph and the next, some commodities will have risen in relative price and some will have fallen. This creates redistribution toward those who are holding those commodities that have risen in relative value and away from those who are holding commodities that have fallen in relative value.

An eighth aspect of the system, which is a little hard to visualize as an event, but which is an important part of change, is circulation. We think of this particularly in the case of money, which is constantly going from A to B, B to C, C to D, D to A, and so on all through the system. Perhaps the best way to illustrate this problem is by a class exercise in which each student is given five phony dollar bills, and when the instructor shouts "Spend," each person has to give at least one dollar bill to another. Students soon catch on to the fact that their income or rate of receipts and expenditures depends on how often the instructor shouts "Spend." Another interesting thing that happens is that the money gets redistributed. The students in the middle of the room and those who are stingier about giving money out accumulate money. Those at the edge of the room frequently lose it all. We can think of this process of money as a shifting cargo, shifting around the pockets of the balance sheets of the economy.

There is a whole penumbra of phenomena surrounding these more obvious elements of the economy that often have to be taken into consideration. What might be called "connections" are a very important part of this: who knows whom, who is employed by whom, who belongs to the same firms, governments, churches, clubs, families, schools, colleges, and so on. Another important aspect is how these clusters are formed, grow, and decline. A very striking phenomenon of the last one hundred years or so has been the rise of large-scale organizations, corporations, governments, and so on. These have tended to define the roles of their members and employees, and the roles that people accept often determine their behavior. This process is something that usually escapes formal economic theory but cannot be utterly neglected.

Another very important background to the economy is the whole institution of property, its rights or obligations, legitimacy, and so on. Exchange would be impossible without property, for each party has to have property in the things exchanged. The financial system produces immense complexity in the structure of property. The whole question of the legitimacy of concentrations of property, for instance, in land, is constantly arising. The whole question as to whether the operations of an economy tend to increase or diminish the inequality and the ownership of property is another important underground question. The whole underpinning of the economy by the legal system, such institutions as bankruptcy, regulation, and so on, cannot be neglected.

The great problem not only of a textbook but of the whole teaching–learning enterprise is: How do we reduce this immense complexity to comprehensible form? We cannot conceivably visualize all of the economic events of a single day. If we tried to receive information about the billions of transactions and economic events that take place in a single day, we would be simply overwhelmed. Knowledge always has to be gained by the orderly loss of information. This is why we have statistics, model building, and all that. One of the great functions of theory is to make complexity simple enough to be manageable. This has been one of the great tasks of science, only partially successful.

In trying to understand a complex system, our first step should be to try to identify and to recognize what might be called the "great identities" of the system. They are really truisms, and define relationships that have to be true by definition, but which nevertheless are the key to the understanding of the nature of the system. The only thing we can be sure of knowing are the identities. There are a good many of these in economics. One might be called the "demographic identity," what I have sometimes called the "bathtub theorem"—that the increase in anything is the additions minus the subtractions. Additions can be divided into births, that is, production of new objects of the population, and migration, that is, members of the population coming in from somewhere else. Similarly, subtractions consist of deaths or consumption, destruction of a member of the population, and outmigration, that is, a member of the population leaving some space that is the locus of the population or stock. This identity is true not only of human populations and populations of all living species but also of all populations of human artifacts: automobiles, screwdrivers, houses—anything that we would like to identify. Inmigration and outmigration for the artifact or commodity, of course, is trade.

Another aspect of this identity is the principle that accumulation must be equal to the production minus the consumption of anything. An economic identity that is related to the above is that in any closed system the total of all balances of payments must be equal to the change in the quantity of money in the period involved. This identity reflects the fact that every expenditure of money by one person is a receipt by another, so the only way in which total receipts can exceed total expenditures is by money being created, which, of course, it can be. The famous Irving Fisher identity, $MV = PT$, reflects the assumption that the value of what is bought is equal to what is paid for it. The quantity of money times the velocity of circulation is, by the definition of the velocity of circulation, equal to the amount spent for goods in a given period. The total value of the goods must equal the total value of the goods purchased, which is PT, that is, price times quantity. One reason why mathematics is useful in all the sciences is that it is fundamentally the study of identities.

Identities, because they cannot be violated, give us some good insights as to what is impossible in the system, such as: "We can't have more than there is." A very significant identity is that any aggregate has to be equal to the sum of its parts.[2] A good deal of what might be called the "art of economics" consists of finding what aggregates are significant and what parts of them are interesting.

Some of the charts in the Appendix illustrate the point. A good deal of model building is vitiated by the fact that either the aggregates are not very significant or the parts into which they are divided are not very significant. Thus, it is an identity that the human population is divided into the people who have red hair and those who do not, though this does not seem to be a very significant division. National income statistics, for instance, do not enable us to divide the national income exactly into labor income and nonlabor income.

No system can be completely identified by identities. All systems have what might be termed "empirical functions" and "empirical parameters." In the physical sciences, for instance, there is really no theory as to why the velocity of light is what it is. It is an empirical constant of the system and does not seem to come out of any identity, but that may be just our ignorance. In economics, indeed, and in most sciences, we have what might be called *qualitative identities* or *near identities* to which we expect exceptions to be rare. An example in economics would be the law of demand and supply—the principle that an increase in the relative price of a commodity will diminish purchases of it and increase the production of it. For ordinary commodities, this law seems very plausible, although there may be exceptions in the cases of goods that are valued simply because they are expensive. The Keynesian consumption function is another example of a plausible relationship—that the poor have to spend or consume more than their income or what they produce just in order to survive, whereas the rich can easily consume much less than their income or what they produce and so can accumulate. These qualitative relationships, however, have to be supplemented by more quantitative ones, such as the elasticity of demand or the exact value of the propensity to consume. This can be discovered only by empirical study, and also may be subject to quite unpredictable changes. All social systems, and the economy among them, are subject to inherently unpredictable changes in these quantitative parameters. For this reason, prediction, especially over longer periods, is extremely hazardous.

The theory of maximizing behavior, beloved of economists, is a good example of these problems. In one sense, it is based on what is almost a truism—that people do what they think is best at the time—and that all choice consists of the development of images of possible futures or alternative futures, the evaluation of these images, and the selection of the one that we think is best. Interesting conclusions can be drawn from this near identity in regard, for instance, to the balancing of alternatives at the margin. We have to be very careful about it, for in the first place the images of possible futures, that is, the agendas of choice, may change. In the second place, past experience may also change the valuation structures. Indifference curves, as I have often said, are not sent down from heaven, and they are, in considerable part, learned by a complex process, constantly subject to change, and rather unpredictably so. If at first you don't succeed, do you try, try again, or do you try something else? Do you learn from the immediate past or from the more distant past?

An enormous number of mistakes in economic behavior have been made because of a belief in trends. The electrical industry in this country, for instance, thought even in the late seventies that demand for electricity was going to grow at 7 percent per annum forever because it had been growing at that rate fairly steadily for a number of decades. The industry received a very rude shock in the eighties. As Keynes pointed out, there is a casino-like quality, especially about financial markets, and also about organized commodity markets. This is why they tend to generate expectational cycles. When people perceive that prices are low, they think they are going to rise, so they buy and prices do rise, which just confirms their belief, and they think they will go on rising. On the other hand, they cannot go on rising without eventually getting high, at which point people think they are going to fall, so they do fall, which confirms the prediction, and they go on falling until they get low again. What constitutes "high" and "low" is virtually impossible to predict, as the present stock market suggests.

One answer to complexity that has been much used in economics is aggregation. Examples of this would be the gross national product (GNP) or various price levels, balance-of-payments and balance-of-trade statistics, and so on. Part of this effort derives from a desire to evaluate large systems, particularly whether they are getting better or worse, or even bigger or smaller. Do we have economic growth or economic decline? In order to answer this kind of question, we have to get some sort of overall number that will measure these very large, complex, and changing aggregates. We are perhaps a little better able to do this in the economy than we are in other aspects of the social system because of the measuring rod of money. We have to be extremely careful, however, in interpreting these aggregates. If we believe in them too much, they can be misleading. Two countries, for instance, can have the same GNP according to the conventional methods of calculation, yet one could devote a large proportion of its resources to the military and have a small, very rich class and a large number of people in destitution, whereas the other could devote its resources to education and medicine and have a fairly equal distribution of income so that nobody is really destitute. We have a bit of the same problem in human growth—whether this growth is going into muscle or into fat. The only answer to this kind of question is constant reexamination of the weights that we assign to the various components of these aggregates. All aggregates are essentially obtained, like the net worth of the balance sheet, by putting valuation coefficients on the fairly homogeneous subaggregates, and these weights can easily be misleading. Some attempts have been made to develop aggregates that are a little more expressive than the GNP is of what might be called "riches," but these have not been very successful.

Price indices are even more dubious, simply because of the enormous heterogeneity of commodities and the constant change in their character and quality. A price index is supposed to tell us how many dollars we would have to have today in order to have the same purchasing power as a dollar, say, in 1920, but who can say what the price of a color television set was in 1920! The price was infinite and the quantity was zero. Unfortunately, infinity multiplied by zero is any number that we like. The recent revision in the US national income statistics, undertaken in part to account for the extraordinary change in the quality of computers in the last generation, is a case in point. There are some commodities, of course, that do not change much, such as the standard wholesale commodities—metals, grains, and things of that sort—but these things form a continually diminishing part of the economy, so that any price-level index becomes increasingly dubious. This is not to say that we should give up on aggregation indices and so on, but we should be very careful to treat them as evidence and not as truth.

An important method of simplifying the image of complex systems is the postulation of some sort of equilibrium system. If we have an equilibrium, we do not have to worry too much about how we get there. Equilibrium systems have been very important in economics, starting with the beginnings of price theory in Adam Smith's famous book 1, chapter 7, of *The Wealth of Nations*, with its distinction between market equilibrium and the long-run equilibrium, and it is clear that we do want our students to know about this. One of the very important conclusions of economics is that the relative price structure is important. There may be some range within which it can be manipulated without too much damage, but if we go beyond this range—and it is very easy to do so—then we get into very serious trouble, as societies have done innumerable times. One of the great weaknesses of centrally planned societies is that the relative price structure tends to be inflexible and distorted, constantly producing shortages, surpluses, and so on. On the other hand, it is also important that our students should know that equilibrium is a figment of the human imagination and does not really exist in the real world, though it may be approximated. The real world is a disequilibrium process, right from the time of the "big bang." I have often used the illustration of the dog chasing the rabbit, with the rabbit being the equilibrium position of the dog, but by the time the dog gets there the wise rabbit is somewhere else. The idea that we are always chasing an equilibrium that moves before us is useful and can overcome some of the illusions that obsession with equilibrium has often created.

I have sometimes said that the object of a textbook is to transmit knowledge structures from decaying old minds into decaying young ones. Without this, the human race would lose all it has learned in the last fifty thousand years in a single generation. But it does raise the question of what do we really know—are we transmitting real knowledge of the economy, for instance, or are we transmitting a lot of ritual that is useful for passing examinations? I think a textbook should give students a feeling that there is real knowledge being transmitted, and that the interaction of a large number of minds over the last two hundred or three hundred years has created a body of understanding of complex systems and of economies that did not exist before, and that as this becomes widespread it can at least prevent us from making disastrous mistakes. If we had had national income statistics and a Council of Economic Advisers in 1929, would we have done better than we did then? Could we have given information to President Hoover and to Congress that would have enabled them to offset the disastrous positive feedback process that was about to take place, which ended up with negative profits and 25 percent unemployment and an enormous amount of human misery and loss?

I would like to think that the answer is yes, that we have learned something in sixty years. But going back to Adam Smith, I often get the feeling that we have not learned very much in two hundred years. Certainly we do not want to give students the feeling that the book is closed. There is still a great deal that we do not know, but we have some chance of finding out, and perhaps our students will help us do so. The sense of being part of an ongoing process of the expansion of human images of the world toward something that could be called "truth" is something that we need to give all students. I am old-fashioned enough to believe that progress is something real, if intermittent, and that perhaps the most important thing we can give to our students is the old-fashioned feeling that they may be able to leave the world a little better place than they found it.

Appendix

The following time charts for the United States show at least part of what economics has to explain.[3] Figure 13.1 shows the major components of the gross capacity product (GCP) of the United States from 1929 to 1986 in what I have called a "layer cake diagram," in which the top line is 100 percent of the GCP and each layer shows what percentage of the total the various components

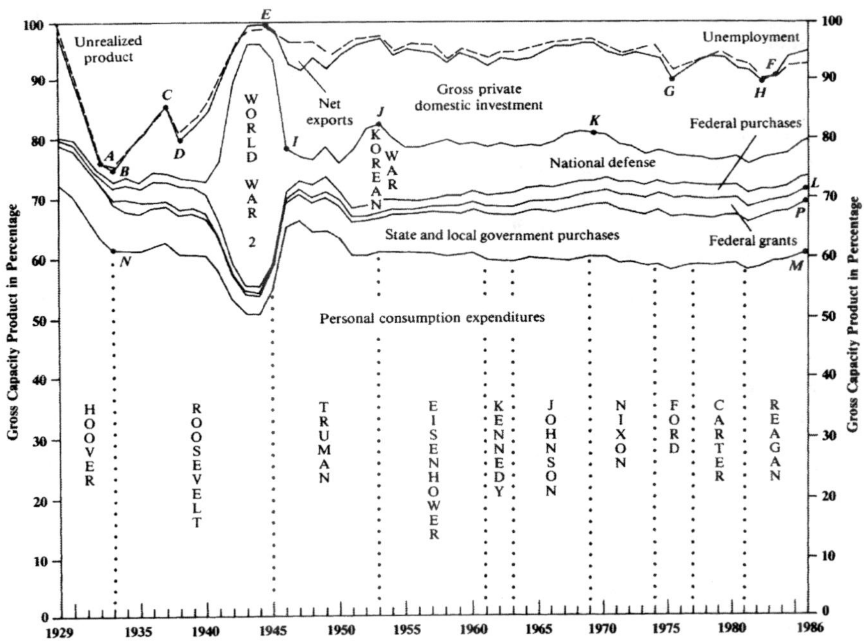

Figure 13.1 Major components of the gross capacity product, US, 1929–1986 (source: Adapted from the *Economic Report of the President*, 1986, and the national income and product of the United States, 1929–1982).

contribute. The GCP is defined as what the GNP would have been if the unemployed had been producing at the average level of labor productivity. It is by no means a perfect measure of the total size of the economy. It has the virtue of having two offsetting errors: One is that the official figures for unemployment certainly underestimate it, which makes the GCP too small. The other is that the unemployed would probably produce at less-than-the-average level of productivity, which makes the GCP too large. The GCP is equal to the GNP × 1/1 – *e*, where *e* is the portion of the labor force that is unemployed.

The top layer in Figure 13.1, then, represents unemployment or unrealized product. The percentage of unemployment is the distance between the 100 percent line and the dotted line. We see the depth of the Great Depression, when unemployment rose to about 25 percent in 1932 and 1933 (at *AB*). We see the spontaneous recovery of 1937 (from *B* to *C*) and the sharp depression of 1938 (from *C* to *D*), a puzzling episode. Then we see a virtual disappearance of unemployment during World War II (about 1944) and the rather steady level of unemployment from about 1947 on, with a small but noticeable irregular cycle.

The next layer is net exports, a very small component, which becomes net imports in 1983 (*F*). The third layer is gross private domestic investment, which could be divided into net investment and capital depreciation. We see the tremendous importance of the decline in gross private domestic investment in the Great Depression (*A* to *B*), when net investment was negative. The recovery from *B* to *C* was largely a recovery in gross private domestic investment, with a subsequent decline in the depression of 1938 (*D*). The war reduced gross private domestic investment to very low levels, so the civilian economy was probably running down somewhat during the war. Then again, beginning in the late 1940s, it was astonishingly stable, with a little inventory cycle in the 1950s, and then rather sharp dips in the mid-seventies and early eighties (*G* and *H*).

The next layer is national defense or the war industry. This is roughly equal to what is purchased with the military budget. This was less than 1 percent under Herbert Hoover, exploded to over 40 percent in World War II, and then came the Great Disarmament of about 1947 (*I*), a remarkable achievement, very little in the public consciousness, when we transferred well over 30 percent of the economy from the war industry to civilian industry in a little over a year without increasing the unemployment rate much above 5 percent. This was achieved by rapid expansion in gross private domestic investment and in personal consumption expenditures.

The Korean War is very noticeable at *J*. The Vietnam War was surprisingly small around *K*. The next rather small layer is federal civilian purchases, which have not been much more than 3 percent of the economy, although they were a larger proportion under the New Deal. State and local government purchases are shown between line *L* and line *M*. Line *LP* is federal grants, mostly to state and local governments. We see that state and local government, outside of national defense, has been much more important economically than the federal government. The large layer at the bottom is personal consumption expenditures, which, again, have been remarkably stable as a proportion of the economy since

1950. In the Great Depression (*N*), we see how personal consumption expenditures also fell and hence failed to offset the decline in gross private domestic investment, which indeed had a great deal to do with this decline. There is a complex process here of positive feedbacks that economics should certainly be able to explain. The rise in the proportion of GCP in personal consumption expenditures in the Reagan administration is noticeable, and it is certainly a result of the tax and budget deficit policy, although it has been largely offset by the rise in net imports in its effect on unemployment.

The proportionate figures of Figure 13.1 should be supplemented with the absolute figures in constant dollars of Figure 13.2, which shows the overall expansion of the American economy. The GCP increased over five times between 1929 and 1986. About half of this was increase in the labor force, and about half, increase in productivity. Certainly from 1950 on, we have had something like a "golden age."

Figure 13.3 shows another very important "layer cake," which is national income by type of income. National income itself is a rather strange aggregate, and its official components are far from ideal, but they do tell us something. Here again, this is a "layer cake diagram," showing the proportions of the components of national income. The top layer shows corporate profits, which became

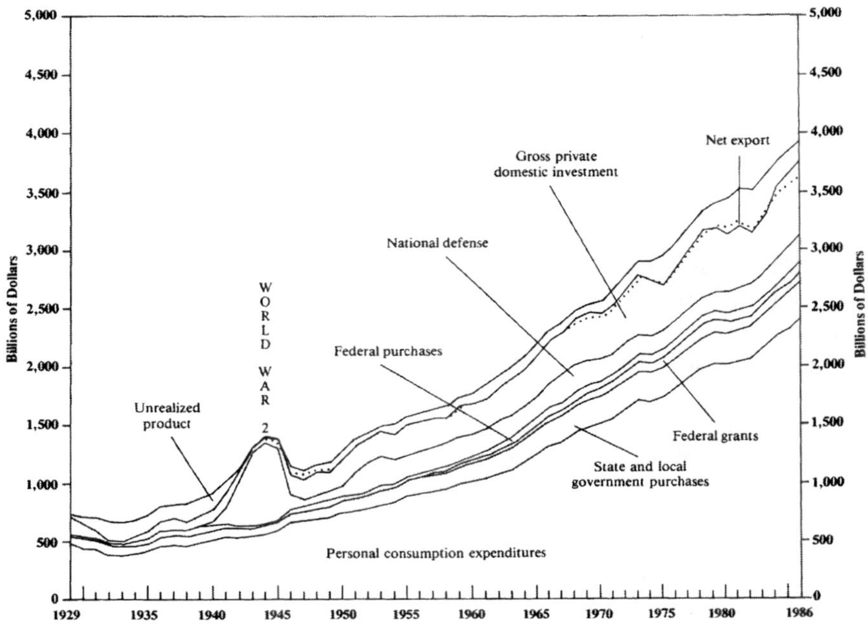

Figure 13.2 Major components of the gross capacity product in cumulative and constant 1982 dollars, 1929–1986 (source: Adapted from the *Economic Report of the President*, 1986, and the national income and product of the United States, 1929–1982).

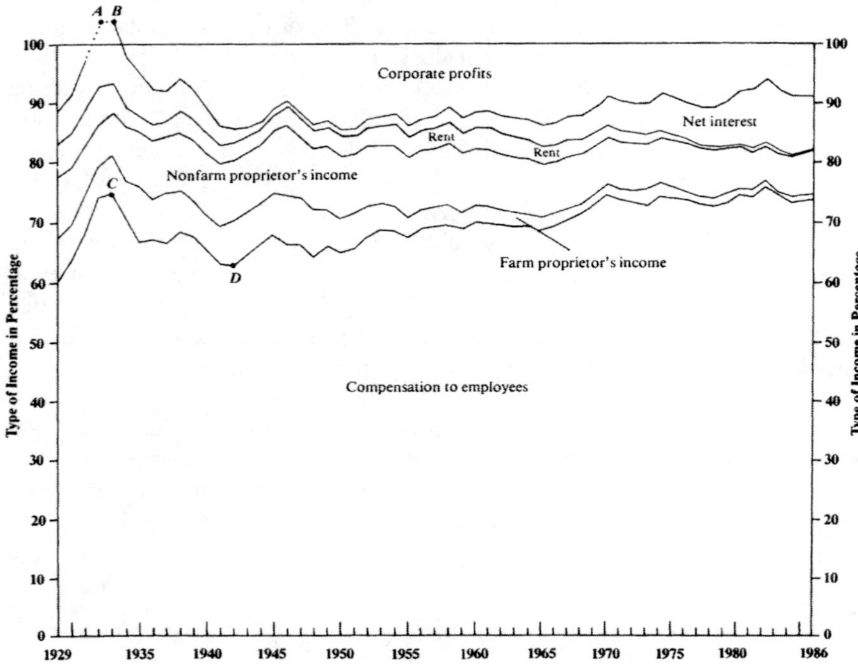

Figure 13.3 National income by type of income, US, 1929–1986 (source: Adapted from the *Economic Report of the President*, 1986, and the national income and product of the United States, 1929–1982).

negative at *A* and *B* in the Great Depression (1932–1933), recovered strikingly around 1940, but actually shrank somewhat during World War II—war is not all that good for business as a whole—recovered afterwards, and have been fairly stable since, with a rather worrying decline since the early sixties. The second layer is net interest, again a rather obscure number, but of some significance. We see it doubling in the Great Depression, when the price level was almost halved, but people continued to pay interest on their debts. The gap between profits and interest is of some significance, especially the gap between the rate of profit and rate of interest, not shown directly in this figure. For when an employer hires an employee, the employer sacrifices the interest that could have been got on the money spent on the wage in the hope of profit on the product of the work. Consequently, when, as in 1932 and 1933, profits were negative and interest was highly positive, anybody who hired anybody was either a philanthropist, a fool, or a creature of habit. It is not surprising that unemployment was 25 percent; what is surprising is that it did not go to 50 percent, causing the whole economy to collapse.

The erosion of profit by net interest since the 1960s is alarming. Profit, after all, is the reward of the productive capitalist. Interest is the reward of the lazy capitalist and is a real burden on the economy. This was negligible in the late 1940s. It is now a very severe burden, nearly 10 percent of the national income. Rent is a strange hodgepodge of items, not of much significance. Its virtual disappearance since about 1975 is a result of its redefinition. Nonfarm proprietor's income is roughly the professional and unincorporated business. This has suffered a slow decline, perhaps because of increased corporatization of the economy. The decline in farm proprietor's income, of course, represents the extraordinary technical change in agriculture, which has enormously reduced the number of proprietors. Compensation to employees, which includes fringe benefits, is interesting in that between 1934 and about 1943 (from *C* to *D*) the proportion of national income going to employees fell sharply. These were the days of the New Deal, the Wagner Act, a tremendous expansion of the labor movement, which went along with the revival of profits and a decline in the proportion of national income going to wages. This is hardly what the noneconomist would expect. I am not sure that many economists would expect it. As an explanation of the Great Depression, however, Figures 13.1 and 13.3 are very significant. The decline in profits is certainly related to the decline in investment, and the decline in investment related to the decline in profits. What we have here is a positive feedback process, which is hinted at by the diagrams, although not, of

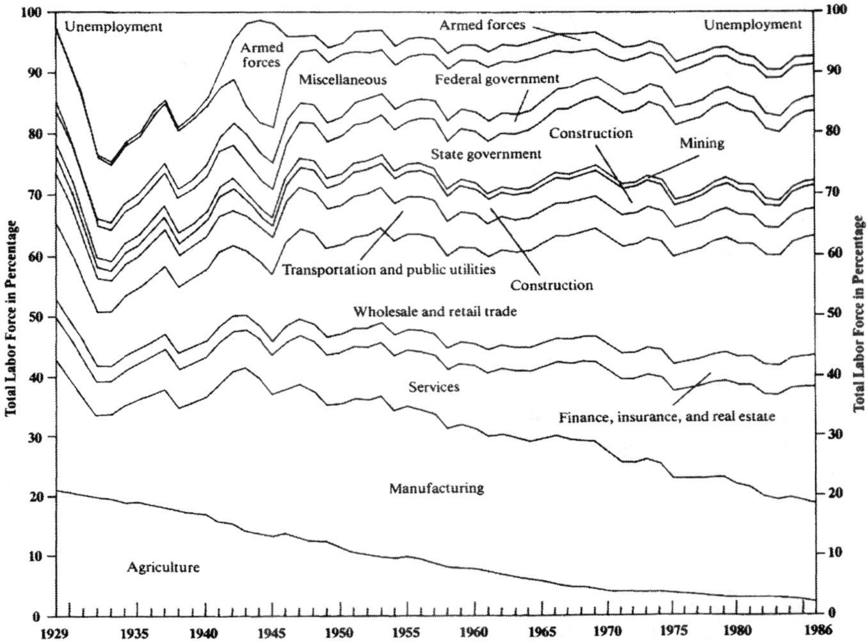

Figure 13.4 Layer cake diagram of sector employment, US, 1929–1986 (source: Adapted from the *Economic Report of the President*, 1988, 1986, and the BLS *Bulletin*, 1312–12).

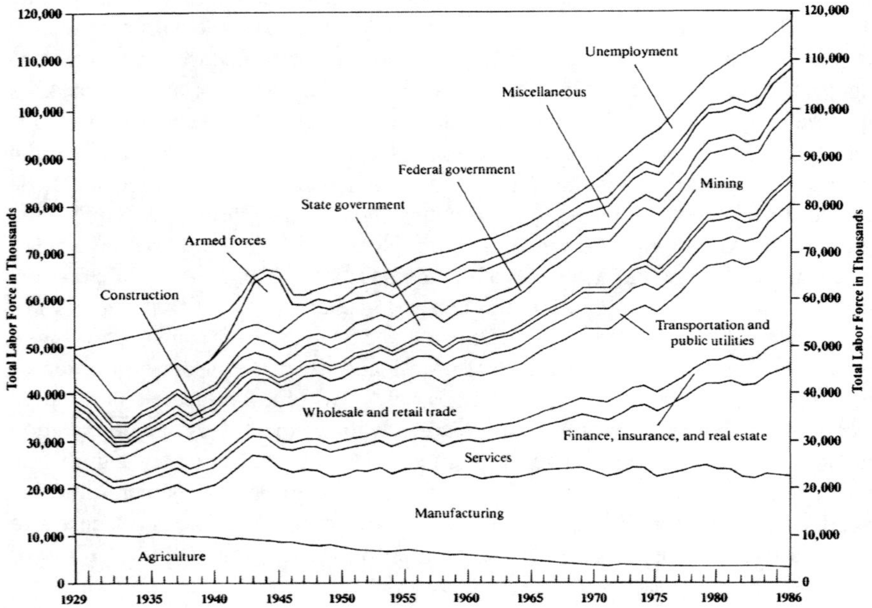

Figure 13.5 Layer cake diagram of sector employment thousands of persons 16 years or over, 1929–1986 (source: Adapted from the *Economic Report of the President*, 1988, 1986, and the BLS *Bulletin*, 1312–12).

Note
1929–1946 data includes those greater than or equal to fourteen years old.

course, fully expressed by them. Incidentally, these figures illustrate the need for an adequate theory of what might be called "macrodistribution," that is, what determines the distribution of national income by type of income. Conventional marginal productivity theory is completely inadequate. It is hard to pretend that profits became negative in the Great Depression because there was an enormous surplus of capital, or that the proportion of national income going to wages rose sharply in that period because of extreme scarcities of labor.

Figure 13.4 shows the distribution of the total labor force for the United States, expressed as 100 percent, among various classifications of occupations, including unemployment, which is the top layer. The second layer, armed forces, certainly shows World War II, but also what might be called the "mechanization" of the armed forces, as the increase in the armed forces was much less than the increase in the proportions of GCP going to the war industry. The bottom layer, agriculture, is the most striking phenomenon, declining from 22 percent of the labor force in 1929 to about 3 percent by 1986. This was a result of the extraordinary technological change in agriculture, which has enormously increased the output per worker. The second layer from the bottom, manufacturing, is interesting because it shows the closer relationship with unemployment, more than the other sectors, and also shows a long-term decline from the 1940s, although not a spectacular one. The labor force released from agriculture seems to have gone very largely into services, wholesale and retail trade (which is surprisingly large), and state government. The federal government has not expanded very much in terms of its labor force. The role of the labor force released from agriculture in increasing the per capita income of society is at least suggested by this diagram. The expanding sectors—services, wholesale and retail trade, and state government, which includes such things as education and medicine—tend to represent the expenditures of the richer sector of the economy.

The shift is shown rather dramatically also in Figure 13.5, which shows the absolute numbers in the labor force and its various segments. The total labor force has gone from about 50 million to 120 million in these fifty-seven years. Manufacturing and agriculture together have hardly increased at all. The big increases have come in services, wholesale and retail trade, and state and local government, in absolute as well as relative terms. This diagram also shows that the bulge in the absolute GCP during World War II and a corresponding bulge in personal income per capita, as we see it in Figure 13.6 at point A, is largely a result of the expansion in the labor force itself, mainly as a result of women who entered it in unprecedented numbers. Figure 13.6 does show that personal

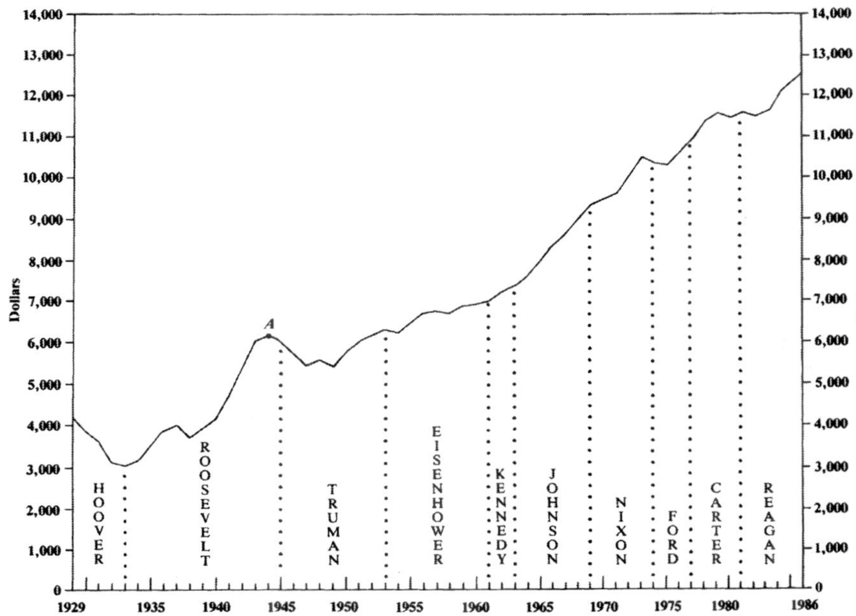

Figure 13.6 US personal income per capita, 1929–1986, in 1982 dollars (source: Adapted from the *Economic Report of the President*, 1986, and the national income and product of the United States, 1929–1982).

income per capita has increased about three times since 1929. What this means in terms of actual commodities is hard to say, but there has been a striking change in the nature and quality of commodities in this period.

Many other diagrams, showing, for instance, distribution of income, the decline in poverty from 1950 to the early 1970s and the noticeable upsurge since, the extraordinary stability of the proportionate distribution in the United States, the role of debt in all kinds of inflation, and so on, should certainly be in the textbook, which should also expand beyond the United States into the world economy, which, although data about it is much harder to get, we still have some knowledge of. The data on economic development, for instance, suggest that it is an extraordinarily complex process that relates surprisingly little to the ordinary economic variables. It seems to be much more a political and social phenomenon than an economic one. But the student in economics should also get some idea of what is not economic, as well as what is economic.

Notes

1 This article was previously published in *Journal of Economic Education*, Spring 1988, 19(2): 113–132.

2 A system is more than an aggregate, as it involves the relationship of its parts, which makes the system more complex than the sum of the parts.

3 The graphs presented in this appendix were developed by my research assistant, Dr. Jamel Zarrouk.

13a Commentary article: Kenneth Boulding's reconstruction of macroeconomics[1]

L. Randall Wray

Boulding's reconstruction of macroeconomics provides a "microfoundation" based on liquidity preference theory, a balance sheet approach, and a process of homeostasis. These microfoundations are consistent with his aggregate theory and avoid fallacies of composition—such as the paradox of thrift—as well as the "adding up" problems of marginal productivity theory. His distribution theory links income shares to the determinants of employment and output and the conditions of equilibrium of saving and investment. His definitions provide clear alternatives to the NIPA definitions adopted in "Keynesian" theory. He provides an alternative view of fiscal and monetary policies that will not prove to be impotent in the face of the ongoing conservative counterrevolution. Indeed, his theories are quite close to the modern Post-Keynesian understanding of "endogenous money," the deficit–growth relation, and the investment-saving connection, while his policy recommendations are often consistent with those of Post-Keynesians.

Let us agree that Keynesian macroeconomics is a failure. It has not been taught for so long that few living university professors are capable of doing so even if there were a text to use. It was never understood by more than a handful of economists, and probably by even fewer policy-makers. It had never offered a reconciliation of "micro" behavior with "macro" behavior—it lacked "micro foundations." It was never able to dispel the major misconceptions about the operation of the macroeconomy that had rendered economists impotent in the face of the Great Depression. And it proved to be just as useless for the formation of policy during the Great Stagflation of the 1970s as pre-Keynesian theory had been during the 1930s. It is not at all surprising that Keynesian macroeconomics is dead and that most economists and policy-makers have returned to theory and policy based on generalizations of the Robinson Crusoe "micro" experience.

Let me be clear. By Keynesian macroeconomics, I do not mean the macroeconomics of Keynes, but rather the bastard version enshrined in the popular textbooks. This version tried to "synthesize" the neoclassical micro theory of allocations of scarce resources among rational, utility-maximizing agents with the part of Keynes's theory that was easily presented through use of the National Income and Product Accounts. The synthesis was never convincing—either at the micro level or at the macro level. As neoclassical economists pointed out, the macro theory—especially that associated with policy recommendations—relied on implausible behavior of individual agents, who, for example, had to be "fooled" into mistaking "nominal" changes for "real" changes, or had to be induced to irrationally accept sticky wages and prices. At the macro level, the bastardization really could never explain why money and nominal values—which should be of almost no consequence, according to the microfoundations—are so ubiquitous and seemingly important in the real world.

The bastard ISLM model dichotomized the real and money sectors such that spending and income could increase without requiring more money—a source of confusion for generations of students who could not see how they could spend more without first receiving more money! The ISLM model also restored the old Treasury View, although in a slightly altered form, that government spending "crowds out" private spending; while the belief was that crowding-out might be acceptable under some economic circumstances, the theory perpetuated the perception that there is something basically evil about government spending. Further, while the bastard version did teach the "paradox of thrift," this was never understood by economists, their students, or policy-makers, who continued to argue that thriftiness could increase growth while government deficits soak up savings and thereby reduce growth. Indeed, the bastard version was particularly ill-suited to the study of economic growth, relying on "thriftiness" as the primary source of growth, along with population growth and some other exogenous variables to round out the theory. Finally, the bastard version had no theory of distribution of income at the aggregate level, and was eventually forced to resort to aggregate "pseudo production functions" before abandoning any attempt to explain distribution.

As mentioned above, the bastard version of Keynes attempted to wed national income accounting to Neoclassical theory. We have all been brought up on the National Income and Product Accounts, in which production equals spending equals income and, ignoring for a moment the government and foreign sectors, spending is comprised of consumption and investment, while income equals consumption and saving. By simple algebra, then, investment somewhat magically equals saving. However, the paradox of thrift tells us that we cannot increase saving by reducing consumption, and all of us know how hard it is to convince anyone of this elementary proposition. While investment and saving are said to be identically equal, they are undertaken by entirely different groups for entirely different reasons. No more than a dozen people in the world understand this. Even the better textbooks (such as that by Heilbroner and Thurow, *Economics Explained*, which I dearly love and use every quarter) get entangled in a web of confusion as they try to explain the paradox but still leave room for the argument that the "real act of saving" releases resources for "real investment" so that economic growth can occur.

Spending flows are then never to be confused with stocks such as accumulations of assets, net wealth, or money supply. We all spend years trying to convince our students that money is a stock while income is a flow, and never the twain shall meet. While it is recognized that flows can lead to stock accumulation, certainly little attention is paid to balance sheets, as almost all analysis is directed to flows. For example, in the extreme exposition of Friedman, money is dropped by helicopters to be accumulated as an asset with no offsetting liability—here, the "money flow" is entirely ignored so that the focus is on a stock (mysteriously related to flows through velocity in the equation of exchange), however, the balance sheet implication of issuing money is deemed to be entirely insignificant. The ISLM exposition is not much different: the IS curve shifts out as spending magically increases without any change of the money stock, as each dollar of the stock does overtime duty, raising velocity. Balance sheet implications of "rising velocity" are, characteristically, ignored, except as rising interest rates reduce "money demand." Alternatively, the money stock is increased at the whim of the central bank while holding spending constant. Excess money supply eventually lowers interest rates so that spending is induced. While this is not quite so mysterious as the money helicopters, there still is little concern with the balance sheet changes that must have occurred meantime. And it is not hard to see why Friedman eventually won the "great debate": it is difficult to get too far with a theory whose only real distinction from monetarism is the hypothesis that velocity might be variable. When velocity finally did become unstable in the 1970s and 1980s, this could be explained away as the result of behavioral innovations, technological change, and cash management techniques.

Further, the focus on aggregate flows made it difficult to reconcile Keynesian macroeconomics with its supposed micro foundations. Individual firms are said to maximize profits, finding the optimal combination of factors, weighing marginal productivities against given factor prices, so that in equilibrium the rates of remuneration of the factors equal their marginal productivities. The marginal productivities are the ratio of a physical output to a physical input; the rates of remuneration are a ratio of a flow of income to a measure of input. Problems involved in calculating marginal product of capital or even a return to capital are particularly severe due to heterogeneity of inputs: if one knew the value of capital inputs, one could calculate a marginal product and a profit rate; however, capital cannot be valued until the profit rate is known, so that the profit rate cannot be determined by marginal product. There are other problems, such as reswitching, that won't concern us. However, a serious problem arises because it has long been recognized that only in a very special case is it possible to attribute the total value of the product to the factors of production. In general, then, it is not possible to explain the aggregate distribution of income between "classes" or factors, for example, between wages and profits.

We are left, then, with a "synthesis" that cannot reconcile micro and macro behavior, that cannot explain distribution of income flows, that cannot explain macro growth, and that makes little attempt to explain the relations between stocks and flows. It is no wonder that the "synthesis" proved to be so difficult to understand, so useless in policy formation in the face of significant economic problems, and so weak in the face of the conservative counter-revolution that restored pre-Depression economic theory.

Let us suppose that one were allowed to rewrite the macro texts, free of the constraints of Neoclassical micro foundations and National Income and Product Accounts categories. Suppose one could redefine terms such as income, expenditure, consumption, saving, and receipts in order to offer a clear, consistent, and logical exposition of macroeconomics. The goal would be to provide an explanation of concepts such as the paradox of thrift, liquidity preference, effective demand, and money and to provide an analysis of fiscal and monetary policy at a level that could be understood by economists, students, and politicians. I submit that one could not do much better than the fourth edition of Kenneth Boulding's *Economic Analysis, Volume II: Macroeconomics* (Boulding 1966).

In private correspondence, Boulding lamented that this text "was never adequately reviewed," although it "represented a very major revision" based largely on his earlier *Reconstruction of Economics* (Boulding 1950).[2] However, as "economics obstinately refused to be reconstructed," his fourth edition was "a complete flop as a textbook" even though the first three editions (of 1941, 1948, and 1955, respectively) had been quite successful. What had happened between 1941 and 1966 was, of course, the hegemonic rise of Samuelsonian bastard Keynesianism. Boulding's exposition appeared so strange that it would have been scarcely comprehensible to anyone raised on postwar Keynesianism.

What follows is the review Boulding's exposition never received, relying heavily on the textbook, but also on the more "academic" *Reconstruction.* It is hoped that this might contribute to a reevaluation of the exposition of the economics of Keynes. I think that to some extent the followers of Keynes are trapped by the terminology and definitions adopted by the bastard Keynesians. Boulding points the way to a different exposition of Keynes's theory that I think might make it easier to explain important concepts that were never really capable of being explained clearly using the terminology of Keynesian macroeconomics.

Balance sheets, stocks, and flows

As Boulding wrote in private correspondence, "As you know, I think economists have been so obsessed by income that they miss the larger picture."[3] Further,

> I still think I was right that economics should be built around a kind of demography of commodities, with a clear distinction between the "flashlight photograph," that is, the population of goods at a moment of time, which is, of course, capital, and then going on from that to the "movie," a succession of frames or events, which, of course is income.

This view followed from his introduction of population theory to economics a half-century earlier. As he argued in 1985, "Economists obsessed with income production and consumption are rather like demographers interested only in births and deaths and not interested in the population of people" (Boulding 1985b: 6–7). Many of the problems with Keynesian macroeconomics discussed above result from the myopic concentration on births and deaths. As we shall see, Boulding's approach offers a clarifying alternative.

In the Neoclassical approach:

> The concept of the balance sheet, unfortunately, has not been employed to any extent in developing the static theory of the firm, so that as generally presented in the textbooks the firm is a strange bloodless creature without a balance sheet, without any visible capital structure, without debts, and engaged apparently in the simultaneous purchase of inputs and sale of outputs at constant rates.
>
> (Boulding 1950: 34)

This Neoclassical firm then "maximizes an odd variable called 'net revenue' of which no accountant ever heard" (Boulding 1950: viii). Boulding proposes instead to introduce

> the balance sheet as the central analytical concept of the theory of the firm, and to introduce asset preferences, especially as measured by preferred asset ratios, which hitherto have been confined almost exclusively to banking theory, as a central concept in explaining the behavior of all economic organisms.
>
> (Boulding 1950: viii–ix)

Thus, he began with balance sheets and a process he called homeostasis.

> The simplest theory of the firm is to assume that there is a "homeostasis of the balance sheet"—that is some desired quantity of all the various items in the balance sheet, and that any disturbance of this structure immediately sets in motion forces which will restore the status quo.
>
> (Boulding 1950: 27)

The balance sheet of any firm "describes the structure of the firm in terms of the various quantities of its parts. Anything that happens to a firm can be described in terms of a 'dynamic' balance sheet" (Boulding 1950: 27). Any change to the balance sheet that moves the firm away from homeostasis sets in motion "behavior on the part of the organism which tends to re-establish the desired state" (Boulding 1950: 26–27). The balance sheet at any point in time gives a complete "history" of the firm; a "moving picture of the complete balance sheet" presents a record of "every *objective* change and every *event* in the history of the firm" (Boulding 1950: 29).

This approach to the firm quite naturally provides "microfoundations" for macroeconomics.

> The balance sheet is again the basic concept: from the separate summation of business and household balance sheets, identities for gross profits (nonlabor income) and for the total wage bill are derived, the component parts of

> which are in some degree "parameters of behaviour" and which can therefore be used to construct simple models of economic equilibrium.
>
> (Boulding 1950: x)

A dynamic view of the economy follows from analysis of the process of homeostasis: as each agent tries to obtain the desired "equilibrium" balance sheet, changes to other balance sheets induce activity by other agents to adjust their own balance sheets, which generate further adjustments by others. The "moving picture" of balance sheets through time captures the macroeconomic "flows" that are the primary preoccupation of conventional economics, but without the danger of fallacy of composition.

It is difficult to see how the economic activities of one individual would not impact balance sheets of others (with the exception of the Robinson Crusoe economy), inducing secondary, tertiary, and so on, effects as others seek to obtain desired balance sheets. This is, of course, similar to, but more general than, the Keynesian "multiplier"—which focuses only on the flow effects, while Boulding analyzes flows as the "moving picture" of changes to "stocks." As Boulding argued, the multiplier requires that either the money supply increases or velocity rises, but never tells us which has happened—and the balance sheet results of these two processes should be expected to be quite different, leading to much different processes over time (Boulding 1950: 271). Indeed, if liquidity preference and the money supply are constant, then investment (or, for that matter, government spending) cannot occur to set in motion the multiplier—the bastard Keynesian IS curve cannot be shifted independently of the LM curve, as generations have been taught (Boulding 1971: 142). In contrast, Boulding's approach begins with balance sheet effects, and flows are the "moving picture" counterpart. While it might appear at first that this process would be so complex that it would be impossible to say much of anything interesting about the aggregate economy, it turns out that Boulding's process of homeostasis is quite useful for presenting Keynes's theory.

Aggregate flows: production, income, spending, receipts

Boulding defines gross production as "the process of adding to the total inventory of stock," gross consumption as "the process of subtracting from this total inventory," and the rate of real accumulation as the "difference between the rate of production and the rate of consumption," or "the rate at which the stock is increasing" (Boulding 1966: 13). Gross production is thus divided between gross consumption and accumulation; gross consumption is comprised of consumption for production (or, broadly, depreciation) and net consumption (that is, by "final consumers"). In Boulding's view, all economic agents have balance sheets and accumulate assets. Consumption is defined as destruction of assets; in general, consumption is an unintended and undesired consequence of utility-seeking behavior. "Satisfactions, therefore, must be regarded as proceeding from the stock of goods, not from their consumption" (Boulding 1966: 125). The household "accumulates" an automobile asset; this is "consumed" as the auto depreciates ("wears out"). The household does not get pleasure from the "consumption," indeed, to the degree that the auto can be "consumed" at a lower rate while still providing the auto services desired, the auto provides more pleasure and the household wealth position in each year is improved. In other words, if the useful life of an auto can be extended from five years to ten, its annual consumption is reduced so that the rate of destruction of the household auto asset is reduced (meaning that the household's wealth is higher in each of these ten years).

Saving is then defined as the net addition to total assets (accumulation), or production less consumption, or simply, the portion of output that is not consumed. This can also be called "real investment," while nominal investment equals saving plus capital gains (Boulding 1966: 123). As Boulding argued, "the concept of saving has caused a great deal of trouble in economic theory" (Boulding 1966: 121), in part because it "is equated in some sense with the idea of 'not consuming', and negative concepts of this kind always cause difficulty" (Boulding 1966: 121). The other problem has been "the confusion between saving in the sense of hoarding (accumulating liquid assets) and saving in the more proper sense of the accumulation of net worth" (Boulding 1966: 121). Boulding avoided the first error by defining consumption as destruction of assets, so that saving is the portion of produced assets that have not been yet destroyed; since production must occur first before assets can be accumulated, or saved, there is no possibility that saving is confused with refraining from activity. He avoided the second problem by carefully distinguishing between saving and hoarding. Hoarding is defined as the excess of money receipts over money expenditures (Boulding 1966: 123). Clearly "it is quite possible for an individual to be saving and dishoarding—i.e., increasing his total assets but diminishing his money assets—in the same period" (Boulding 1966: 124). An increase of "thrift" in the sense of "not spending" can never increase Boulding saving; nor can it increase aggregate hoards unless the money supply increases.

Boulding realized that his definitions are quite different from the Keynesian definitions. "Keynes defines saving as the excess of income over *consumers' expenditure*, not as the excess of income (production) over consumption" (Boulding 1966: 124). Further:

> In the United States national income accounts ... saving is defined in Keynesian terms as the difference between disposable personal income and consumers' expenditure. This underestimates, by a considerable sum, the amount of saving and investment in terms of real accumulation, as it neglects the fact that a good deal of household expenditure represents the purchase of durable goods, and for most households the value of durable goods purchased exceeds the depreciation of old household goods
>
> (Boulding 1966: 124–125)

Boulding defined a receipt as the exchange of an illiquid balance sheet item for a liquid asset, while expenditure is defined as the exchange of a liquid asset for an illiquid asset (Boulding 1950: 140). As a firm produces goods, its balance sheet shows an accumulation of inventoried assets—or an income flow. When produced goods are sold, the firm records a receipt: inventoried illiquid assets are reduced while liquid assets (for example, bank deposits) are increased. From the perspective of the employee, income is recorded as work is performed in the form of an illiquid wage claim on the firm, which is treated by the firm as a liability; when the firm pays wages, this is recorded by the employee's balance sheet as a receipt (wage claims are reduced, but liquid assets—probably a bank deposit—are increased) (Boulding 1950: 140). The firm's balance sheet will show a reduction of liquid assets (probably, a bank deposit), and a reduction of illiquid liabilities (the wage claim). Finally, when the employee purchases the output of firms, this is an expenditure that reduces the liquid assets of the employee but increases the illiquid assets on her balance sheet; the firm's balance sheet is adjusted in precisely the opposite manner. To complete the story, consumption occurs only as the purchased goods wear out; investment and saving occurred as the goods were produced (any intermediate goods destroyed in production must be netted out); and income was generated as the wage claims on the firm were accumulated, while wages are simply receipts that can be transformed as desired into illiquid assets through expenditure.

The advantage of Boulding's method is that one never confuses the act of hoarding (where money receipts exceed money expenditures) with saving and investing; one never heaps accolades on households that end a period with net money receipts (Boulding 1950: 143). Hoarding is never viewed as a public virtue, while Boulding saving (not consuming produced assets) is indeed virtuous (see Wray 1992b). "Postponed consumption" in the sense of accumulating money hoards or other financial wealth, or "thriftiness," is certainly never confused with accumulating productive assets (Boulding saving or "investing"). Indeed, because the act of hoarding by some households cannot increase the aggregate quantity of hoards, all that hoarding can do is to *redistribute* the aggregate quantity of money among households. There can be nothing virtuous about this, nor can such "thriftiness" help accumulation of productive assets nor generate real economic growth. Indeed, one could almost turn the tables entirely around and blame the thrifty for any undesired inventory accumulation: if those thrifty households had preferred to accumulate nonmoney assets, sales would have been higher and the net money receipts would have been enjoyed by firms that preferred to run down inventories. There is no "pain" in saving, no "forgone consumption" in conserving assets, as satisfaction comes not from "consuming" (destroying) assets, but from "economizing" on consumption. Saving can be accomplished only by "producing more than is consumed," but does not "necessarily involve the sacrifice of present consumption in order to increase future consumption" (Boulding 1966: 126).

Money, liquidity preference, and homeostasis

Production, consumption, saving, and income can all occur without involving money assets. In a capitalist economy, however, much production leads to the creation of wage claims that are met through expenditure of money, paying the wage bill; many transfers of assets (such as sales of inventoried goods to households) involve money receipts and money expenditures. As discussed in the previous section, when a worker works or a firm produces, income is immediately generated, although not in money form. However, economic agents are not indifferent to the form in which income is accumulated—workers prefer money receipts over wage claims on firms, while firms prefer money receipts over inventoried goods. This is at least partially due to uncertainty and resulting preference for liquid assets.

Boulding argued that the ratio of liquid assets to illiquid claims in a balance sheet is a fundamental determinant of economic behavior.[4] Indeed, each agent has a preferred liquidity ratio, deviations from which set off a process of homeostasis as agents try to obtain the desired ratio (Boulding 1950: 27). This, of course, will affect the balance sheets of others, setting off other adjustments. The liquidity ratio can be defined as the ratio of money assets to total assets held; it can vary among individuals and over the course of the business cycle. Money will tend to flow from those with low liquidity preference (who substitute illiquid assets for money assets) and to those with high liquidity preference.

When liquidity preferences (or desired liquidity ratios) rise generally, agents attempt to increase money receipts and reduce money expenditures (Boulding 1966: 75). Unless the actual quantity of money rises, the only way that higher liquidity ratios can be achieved is through falling values of accumulated nonmoney assets (Boulding 1950: 213). This, of course, is equivalent to Keynes's liquidity preference theory: as liquidity preference rises, prices of illiquid assets fall and fewer capital assets are produced, causing investment to fall and aggregate spending and income to fall through the multiplier. In Boulding's exposition, the process of homeostasis will produce falling prices of nonmoney assets as well as reduced production and accumulation rates (net accumulation may well become negative) until desired liquidity ratios are achieved. On the other hand, falling liquidity preference (or desired liquidity ratios) will cause nonmoney assets to rise in price and will increase production and net accumulation (Boulding 1966: 80; 1950: 99, 162).

However, while it is unlikely that the supply of money would increase when liquidity preference rises, falling liquidity preference would likely increase the money stock. When banks expand their balance sheets by exchanging liquid bank liabilities for the illiquid debts of their customers, the liquidity of the nonbank public increases (Boulding 1950: 271). For the most part, nonbank agents become indebted (issue nonmoney IOUs) when they plan to purchase nonmoney (illiquid) assets, and this is most likely to occur as their desired liquidity ratios fall. On the other hand, banks issue money as they purchase nonmoney (mainly financial) assets; again, this is likely to occur as bank desired liquidity ratios fall. Thus, paradoxically, the money supply expands precisely as desired liquidity ratios fall. On the other hand, when liquidity preference rises, and desired liquidity ratios rise, it is unlikely that private banks would lend (reducing their own liquidity ratios) to agents that are trying to reduce money expenditures—rather, money is just redistributed as a "shifting cargo" (Boulding 1985b: 8; 1950: 271–276).[5] In any case, Boulding's exposition is a major advance over the Bastard Keynesian treatment of money, and even over Keynes's *General Theory* treatment.

According to Boulding, the effect of an increase of the money supply depends upon who receives the money (Boulding 1950: 240). If consumers receive more money, the prices and output of consumer goods are likely to rise until desired liquidity ratios are restored—for both consumers and firms (with the created money flowing from households to firms). On the other hand, if firms receive the new money, this is likely to increase production (thus, wages and eventually sales) and accumulation of investment goods. Finally, if it is received by speculators in financial markets, the prices and perhaps quantities of financial assets will rise. Thus, it is impossible to predict whether an increase of the money supply will be associated with "inflation" (defined as the rate of growth of consumer prices, for example) unless one knows who is receiving the money, where it is being spent, and what the reactions of those receiving the money are likely to be. As "Deepthroat" might say, we must "follow the money."

Even though Boulding's homeostasis approach would appear to require overly complex analysis as we "follow the money" from one balance sheet to the next, it turns out that many quite general propositions hold that are consistent with Keynes's theory. The paradox of thrift holds: if "thriftiness" rises, or if agents try to increase money receipts without spending, undesired inventories of illiquid assets accumulate, depressing further production and accumulation, or saving. Indeed, the results are even stronger for Boulding: not only do firms reduce accumulation (or Keynesian investing), but households also reduce accumulation (or Keynesian saving) because production (and employment) declines. By focusing on balance sheets, we immediately see that as any household tries to increase money receipts, this must have an impact on another balance sheet. Keynesian liquidity preference theory follows directly from Boulding's balance sheet approach and the hypothesis about desired liquidity ratios. This is also more general than the Bastard Keynesian approach, in which liquidity preference is reduced to a demand for money that is a function of income and interest rates—an increase of income or a reduction of interest rates raises money demand in that approach. In Boulding's approach, anything that affects the size of the balance sheet or the desired liquidity ratio could set off a process of homeostasis as agents try to increase or reduce net money receipts.

Indeed, Boulding claimed that liquidity preference theory and the quantity theory of money represent two possible extremes of his own general theory. In the liquidity preference theory as it is usually presented, the quantity of money is held constant while desired liquidity ratios are changed, leading to adjustments of balance sheets as spending flows adjust through a combination of price and quantity adjustments. On the other hand, the quantity theory of money holds desired liquidity ratios constant (money demand is a function of income or transactions) as the money supply is adjusted, again leading to adjustments of balance sheets, although the focus is on the induced changes to spending flows. In Boulding's approach, because banks also have balance sheets and desired liquidity ratios, it is not appropriate to hold the money supply constant as liquidity preference changes. Adjustment is through a combination of changes to the money supply, prices, and quantities of assets accumulated; effects on flows are analyzed through changes to balance sheets.

Boulding's approach also restores a general, Keynesian liquidity preference approach to interest rates—indeed to all asset prices. In Boulding's exposition, asset prices are a function of the quantity of money, liquidity preference (or desired liquidity ratios), and the quantity of assets—all of which are variable, and, indeed, interdependent. This is a return to Keynes of the *General Theory* (expanded in his famous articles of 1937), rather than the Bastard Keynesian exposition in which "money demand" and a fixed money supply determine "the" interest rate. Boulding allows the quantity of money to increase "endogenously" as the quantity of assets increases (for example, if banks purchase some of the created nonmoney assets by issuing money liabilities); as discussed above, this is likely to occur as desired liquidity ratios fall and as production of physical assets increases. In the Keynesian terminology, as liquidity preference falls and spending increases, the money supply expands; multiplier effects on consumption spending are also expected to occur. In the Bastard Keynesian approach, an increase of spending must normally increase interest rates as income pushes up money demand in the presence of a fixed money supply. However, as Keynes had argued, this need not be the case if banks accommodate. Boulding incorporates this insight into his analysis at the beginning—those same behavioral conditions that are likely to increase spending are also likely to increase the money supply. Effects on asset prices—or interest rates—are then determined in a complex way by asset preference ratios, quantities of assets, and quantity of money (see Wray 1992a, and Boulding 1971: 133).

Monetary and fiscal policy

While Monetarists imagine helicopter money drops and impotent fiscal policy, and Bastard Keynesians make sport of shifting IS curves (fiscal policy) and LM curves (monetary policy), Boulding argues that monetary policy has to do with regulation of financial markets, while fiscal policy has to do with regulation of the quantity of money.

Like Post-Keynesians, Boulding emphasized that the central bank cannot normally control the quantity of money privately created (Boulding 1966: 112). Banks can economize on reserves and, in any case, so long as all banks grow together, none will lose reserves as "no bank loses reserves on balance except to the public" (Boulding 1966: 107). However, because the central bank can affect liquidity ratios (e.g. by issuing central bank liabilities to buy government bonds), it can influence asset prices. In addition, the central bank can regulate matters such as capital requirements, the discount rate, and required reserve ratios. Thus, according to Boulding, "What is called monetary policy is in fact 'financial' policy, i.e. actions of government which affect the structure and magnitude of financial instruments (debts)" (Boulding 1950: 282–283).

On the other hand, fiscal policy is likely to directly impact the quantity of money. When the government purchases produced assets from firms, illiquid inventories of the private sector are replaced by government money—a check drawn on the Treasury which is really nothing more than a Federal Reserve liability (or bank reserves). If the government then taxes that away, the money position of the public and the reserve position of the banks are restored—the public has reduced its inventories of goods but also reduced its tax liability by the amount of the government purchase. Even though the quantity of money has not increased (net), it is likely that a balanced budget increase of government spending will have substantial impacts on the economy because of a redistribution of money among the public. This is because it is highly unlikely that an individual's tax expenditures are exactly offset by receipts from government spending. This then sets off an adjustment process until each individual achieves his or her desired liquidity ratio, which itself has likely changed due to the balanced budget increase of spending and taxing. Thus, even balanced budgets are likely to affect the prices and quantities of nonmoney assets, and therefore Keynesian spending and income and investment and saving and consumption. The notion that government spending could be wholly impotent (policy "ineffectiveness") would seem preposterous to Boulding—he could believe that it might increase or reduce quantities and prices of goods, services and assets (including privately produced money), but the notion that government spending would have no impact on the economy would be simply implausible.

If the government instead runs deficits, then the quantity of money will have increased: "Government increases the amount of money in private hands whenever it has a 'cash deficit,' i.e. whenever it takes in from the private sector less money than it pays out" (Boulding 1950: 270). Again, this will have "multiplier" effects on production, prices, and quantities of assets and privately created money, as firms and households try to achieve desired liquidity ratios. Boulding noted that most government bonds are sold to banks, which buy assets by issuing liabilities; since their liabilities are money, sales of government bonds to banks will increase the private money supply (Boulding 1966: 244). Sales of bonds to the nonbank public will not increase the money supply (unless the public borrows from banks to finance such purchases), but are likely to redistribute money from some households to others, and so will likely affect asset prices and quantities in general. According to Boulding, the banks take up the quantity of bonds the public does not wish to hold and in this way the private money supply is increased (Boulding 1985a: 616). Private banks would be willing to purchase only a finite quantity of bonds if the aggregate quantity of reserves remained fixed. However, Boulding recognized that the main source of reserves is government deficit spending (Boulding 1985a: 617). Thus, the deficit spending creates the reserve money that is needed by banks to purchase bonds—an important point that we shall return to below.

In conclusion, fiscal policy will redistribute money with balanced budgets and will increase the money supply with deficits. Fiscal policy will indirectly influence the prices and quantities of nonmoney assets as the public and banks attempt to restore desired liquidity ratios. Through its impact on asset prices, fiscal policy also affects interest rates; however, appropriate monetary policy can mitigate any undesired effects on interest rates—and, in any case, it is not at all clear that an increase of government spending (whether accompanied by an increase of taxes or not) would generate upward pressure on interest rates: it could lower interest rates (see below).

Interestingly, Boulding's exposition is quite similar to recent Post-Keynesian work (inspired by the Chartalist approach to money) that emphasizes that government spending increases the money supply—in the form of "government money" which is primarily Fed liabilities held as bank reserves. Government taxes ensure a demand for this money (as taxes are ultimately paid in the form of bank reserves) (Knapp 1924; Minsky 1986). Because the public is likely to desire to hold some net government money reserves, taxes should be set below the level of government spending (that is, the government should normally run deficits). The government (as well as the foreign sector) is the source of net private sector financial wealth (since private sector financial assets are offset by private sector financial liabilities—again, ignoring the foreign sector as it is possible for one country to be a net creditor or debtor with respect to other countries), and it is the government deficit (expenditures less receipts) that is accumulated as private sector net financial wealth. "If we aggregate the balance sheets from the three groups (businesses, households, and government), the intrabusiness, intrahousehold, and intragovernment debts will disappear but government debt will be an asset in the balance sheets of businesses and households" (Boulding 1985b: 8). As Boulding noted, it is the total cash deficit of the government which determines the net contribution to private cash accounts; the government deficit determines the quantity of net liquid assets in private hands (Boulding 1958: 225). Because the private sector prefers to hold interest-bearing assets, the government normally "finances" most of its deficit by selling bonds to the private sector. This, however, is not because the government needs to "borrow" in order to spend in excess of tax receipts (so long as government money is demanded by the public—e.g. to pay taxes—government can always "spend" by issuing money). Rather, the government "spends" by issuing money, taxes to maintain the value of the currency (by creating a residual demand for government money), and then sells bonds as a substitute for non-interest-earning bank reserves. This allows banks to hold interest-earning government bonds rather than reserves. Indeed, if the government did not sell bonds when it runs a deficit, the excess reserves would likely push interest rates in the overnight market for reserves (the Fed funds rate) toward zero. Bond sales, then, are really part of "monetary policy," that is, are designed to allow the Fed to hit its interest rate target, and are not required to "finance" the deficit spending that has previously occurred.

This is consistent with Boulding's overall orientation: fiscal policy determines the quantity of money while monetary policy determines debt structure (including interest rates). Bastard Keynesian "crowding out" (that is, increased government spending drives up interest rates in the presence of a fixed money supply) is highly unlikely; indeed, government spending should drive interest rates down unless the government drains the money it has created through taxes or through bond sales. Nor is government deficit spending going to "absorb" private saving—the government is the only *source* of net financial saving for the private sector (again, excluding the foreign sector). As Boulding argued,

> In a period when people as a whole wish to "save"—i.e., increase their total assets—but when the increase in real assets which is economically advantageous is not great enough to supply the demand for "savings," an increase in government debt is a useful way to achieve a rise in the total net worths without accumulation of goods or inflation of prices.
>
> (Boulding 1966: 246)

Further,

> an increase in government debt results not only in an increase of total assets but also an increase in the net worths of the public. Because the desire to increase net worths in the absence of opportunities for accumulating real capital is one of the principal sources of unemployment, an increase in government debt may result in an increase in output.
>
> (Boulding 1966: 246)

To the extent that the government produces, or causes to be produced, goods to be accumulated, then real Boulding saving also occurs as the "real" counterpart to fiscal deficits. Thus, when the private sector wishes to "save" without producing the where-with-all to save (that is, "investment"), it is the responsibility of the government to provide the *means* of saving in order to prevent unemployment.

Certainly Boulding would agree that government spending could have substantial and even nefarious impacts on the economy, but these must be analyzed by carefully tracing the effects of, for example, an increase of money in the public's pockets, or a redistribution of money as the government spending and taxing activities move money to pockets of recipients and from pockets of taxpayers. However, he would reject gross aggregate analysis that argues that government spending necessarily crowds out private spending, causes inflation, or absorbs saving. As he once said, until full employment is reached, there is no aggregate cost to increasing government spending, although there would be numerous and complex micro-level costs and benefits (Boulding 1971: 7; Boulding 1966).

The "K" theory of distribution and the causes of wealth

As discussed above, Neoclassical economics hoped to derive a theory of distribution from the production process, with incomes determined by marginal productivities; this failed except under restrictive and unlikely assumptions. As Boulding argued,

> The marginal analysis ... is most instructive in dealing with the theory of the firm and with the demand, supply, and pricing of particular products and particular factors of production. It is not particularly helpful in dealing with the aggregates of the system, because its use is constantly likely to involve us in fallacies of composition.
>
> (Boulding 1971: 338)

He recognized quite early that "the distribution structure is not a result of the productive process but is in the main attributable to investment and financial processes and decisions. Investment itself is the chief determinant of profits" (Boulding 1971: 302–303). This led to the development of what he called the "K" theory of distribution:

> There is a cluster of theories that attempt to explain what determines the proportion of profits, wages, and interest in national income. These theories are associated with J.M. Keynes, M. Kalecki, N. Kaldor, and Kenneth Boulding, and some others whose names do not begin with K.
>
> (Boulding 1985b: 5)

"The K-theories suggest that the non-wage income is determined by what its recipients spend on investment, i.e., increases to the capital stock, and on their household purchases, and that wage income is the residual" (Boulding 1985b: 5).[6] Most importantly, Boulding concluded that "though production might be the result of the immutable laws of physics and chemistry, distribution was the result of human decision, and that consequently distribution could be changed within a wide range of values" (Boulding 1971: 353).

Boulding also argued that economics had erred as it turned from "the study of the Nature and Causes of the Wealth of Nations to the study of equilibrium and disequilibrium" (Boulding 1971: 93).

> [I]n the case of the "static" equilibrium of society, the condition of equilibrium is that all employments, of labour, or land, or of capital, shall be equally advantageous, in the sense that no one who can shift his resources from one occupation to another wishes to do so. This condition also tells us nothing of how wealthy the society is—it merely tells us that with the resources available, the society is as wealthy as it can be.
>
> (Boulding 1971: 94)

As economics turned from Smith's analysis of the determinants of wealth to the neoclassical analysis of the allocation of fixed scarce resources, it lost sight of the fact that resources are socially *created.* The distribution of these socially created resources is then determined by spending decisions—as capitalists direct much of the production process, they directly determine money wages (which in turn largely determine money expenditures of workers) as well as their own money expenditures. Their own expenditures return as money receipts (profits) and as well largely determine their accumulations of assets, while worker expenditures cover capitalist costs (so long as "workers spend what they get," otherwise capitalists accumulate unwanted inventoried assets).[7]

Finally, Boulding also rejected the notion that interest income is a reward for waiting, with the interest rate determined by technical conditions and the rate of time preference. As discussed above, Boulding adopted a generalized Keynesian liquidity preference theory of the determination of interest rates. The "rate of interest is not a price but is a rate of growth" (Boulding 1985b: 10), and the "rate of growth of liabilities is the rate of interest" (Boulding 1950: 281). Financial markets determine

> the price of future promises to pay specific amounts; that is, what a bond or note is. The lower the price of these instruments, of course, the higher the rate of interest, and it is the price of these instruments that is determined in the market.
>
> (Boulding 1985b: 10)

"Interest payments represent a transfer of net worth from the debtor to the creditor" (Boulding 1985b: 9). If monetary policy keeps the overnight rate high, this serves as a base for market interest rates, keeping them high and causing liabilities to grow at a high rate and reducing net worth of debtors, causing large transfers from debtors to creditors. Since firms are debtors, this causes a transfer from profit to interest, which can create "a bleak future for capitalism" because "we cannot have a profit system without profit" (Boulding 1985b: 10). Thus, "The dramatic rise in net interest from about 1 percent of national income in the mid-1940s to something like 10 percent today is about the most striking phenomenon of the American economy and has received remarkably little attention" (Boulding 1985b: 5). Indeed, it is virtually inexplicable within the confines of neoclassical orthodoxy (Americans have presumably become incomprehensibly "unthrifty" even as the amount of managed money—in pension funds, money market funds, and so on—has exploded beyond comprehension). The Boulding "K-theory" in conjunction with liquidity preference theory and his views of monetary policy offer an alternative.

Conclusion

Boulding's reconstruction of macroeconomics provides a "microfoundation" based on liquidity preference theory, a balance sheet approach, and a process of homeostasis. These microfoundations are consistent with his aggregate theory and avoid fallacies of composition—such as the paradox of thrift—as well as the "adding up" problems of marginal productivity theory. His distribution theory links income shares to the determinants of employment and output and the conditions of equilibrium of saving and investment. His definitions provide clear alternatives to the NIPA definitions adopted in "Keynesian" theory. He provides an alternative view of fiscal and monetary policies that will not prove to be impotent in the face of the ongoing conservative counter-revolution. Indeed, his theories are quite close to the modern Post Keynesian understanding of "endogenous money," the deficit–growth relation, and the investment-saving connection, while his policy recommendations are often consistent with those of Post-Keynesians.

Notes

1 This article was previously published in *Review of Social Economy*, Winter 1997, 55(4): 445–463.
2 From a letter of June 12, 1990, to the author.
3 From a letter of June 12, 1990, to the author.
4 Like Keynes, Boulding related the desire to hold liquid assets to uncertainty. Boulding's 1944 article, "A Liquidity Preference Theory of Market Prices" (reprinted in Boulding 1971: 133), "generalized" Keynes's liquidity preference theory in a direction first indicated by Townshend (and approved by Keynes) in 1937 (see Wray 1992a). While uncertainty clearly plays a role in Boulding's theory that is similar to the role it plays in Keynes's theory, it is true that Boulding did not continually refer to uncertainty in his later writings. To some extent, he appeared to simply take uncertainty for granted. I think that many followers of Keynes (particularly the Post-Keynesians) tend to focus on the role uncertainty plays in *individual* decision-making, while Boulding was more interested in the consequences for *policy-making*. That is, he continually emphasized that, due to complexity of the process of homeostasis, the impact of any policy change would be extremely difficult to ascertain. For Boulding, then, the problem was not so much that the future is "unknowable," but that it is nearly impossible to calculate.
5 This is an important asymmetry that has been noted recently by some Post-Keynesians (Dow 1993; Wray 1990).
6 Boulding credited Keynes's "Widow's Cruse" theory of profits (in the *Treatise on Money*) for the original insight, although much of Boulding's exposition (for example, in his *Reconstruction*) derived from Kalecki's approach (see, for example, Boulding 1971: 338).
7 When a government and foreign sector are added, capitalists also receive profits equal to the government's deficit and the trade surplus.

References

Boulding, Kenneth E. (1950) *A Reconstruction of Economics*, New York: John Wiley & Sons.

Boulding, Kenneth E. (1958) *Principles of Economic Policy*, Englewood Cliffs, NJ: Prentice-Hall.

Boulding, Kenneth E. (1966) *Economic Analysis: Volume II, Macroeconomics*, 4th Edition, New York: Harper & Row.

Boulding, Kenneth E. (1971) *Collected Papers, Volume One*, (ed.) Fred R. Glahe, Boulder, CO: Colorado Associated University Press.

Boulding, Kenneth E. (1985a) *Collected Papers, Volume Six: Toward the Twenty-First Century*, (ed.) Larry D. Singell, Boulder, CO: Colorado Associated University Press.

Boulding, Kenneth E. (1985b) "Puzzles over Distribution," *Challenge*, November–December: 4–10.

Dow, Sheila C. (1993) *Money and the Economic Process*, Aldershot: Edward Elgar.

Knapp, Georg Friedrich (1924) *The State Theory of Money*, London: Macmillan.
Minsky, Hyman P. (1986) *Stabilizing an Unstable Economy*, New Haven and London: Yale University Press.
Wray, L. Randall (1990) *Money and Credit in Capitalist Economies: The Endogenous Money Approach*, Aldershot: Edward Elgar.
Wray, L. Randall (1992a) "Alternative Theories of the Rate of Interest," *Cambridge Journal of Economics*, Spring, 16(1): 69–89.
Wray, L. Randall (1992b) "What is Saving, and Who Gets the Credit (Blame)?" *Journal of Economic Issues*, March, 26(1): 256–262.

13b Comment: Boulding's image of the economics textbook

A commentary[1]

Andrew Mearman

Introduction

Boulding's essay (1988)[2] is a gently persistent critique of contemporary economics textbooks, and by extension, of economics. Boulding's thesis is that: (1) economics textbooks ought to present visions (or "images") of the economy; (2) he can offer reasonably confidently (an attempt at) a true image of the economy; and (3) among contemporary attempts, "no existing textbook of the last generation ... not even my own" (113) presents this image. However, the essay aimed to defend much contemporary economic practice, albeit with some modification.

The essay has two main themes: one, the nature of the economy; two, the tools used to act informedly in it. In Boulding's view, an economics textbook should, simply, contain economics; and it should inform students about how the economy works. It would do that by presenting (where possible) true images of the economy, using some combination of theory and data. Economies are complex systems, which are difficult to comprehend; but contain a set of core "events", such as production, valuation and revaluation, distribution and redistribution, accumulation (investment), circulation and, above all, exchange. The second theme of his essay concerns economic methodology, in which Boulding offers an image of the economist as cautiously confident user of a range of useful but limited tools. Boulding echoes many of his previous works and discusses issues such as aggregation and balance sheets.

This chapter examines Boulding's essay. It does so from the perspective of economics education. We take the view that an economics textbook embodies material about the economy, economic theory, economic method and an approach to being an economist; but it also expresses an approach to education. Specifically, via the textbook, the writer aims to realise educational goals, which are prior to their choices on the content and process of teaching. Thus, the chapter considers Boulding's essay in the light of its underlying educational goals, its implications for content and teaching practice. The chapter also echoes Boulding by not focusing on economic theory. Readers focused on theory should consult Wray's excellent (1997) commentary on Boulding's theoretical insights, and elsewhere in this volume.

The chapter proceeds as follows. It will consider Boulding's comments on the nature of the economy, and on the nature of economics and economists, and their implications for the economics textbook. It will then discuss the educational aspects of Boulding's essay, including his comments on teaching technique, and the implicit philosophy of education driving his commentary.[3]

The economy

One of the striking features of Boulding (1988) is the relative absence of economic theory and economic analytical technique. This is striking in comparison with contemporary treatments, which launch into theory, perhaps via a very brief discussion of the nature of the economist. It was the case that introductory texts began with discussion of the nature and scope of economic method; but even these sections have gone. Even then, though, the *economy* was largely absent. Not completely, of course: economics textbooks have always used examples; and indeed, one of the consequences of the growth in the economics education literature following the recruitment crisis of the 1980s has been to emphasise the role of examples in stimulating engagement and communicating theory. The theory comes first though.

A feature (although not uniquely) of English is that there are different words for economy and economics. This has mixed consequences. Advantageously, the theorist ought to be clear not to reduce the economy down to their understanding of it. Perversely, though, the separation allows the theorist to neglect the economy in favour of economics and to pursue intellectual puzzles with no relevance to reality. Further, the economist can act as if separate from their object. It is clear that none of these criticisms apply to Boulding. Though he does define economics as the study of the economy, he (1966a) chastised the economics profession (via the prestigious Richard T. Ely lecture) for neglecting sectors of crucial importance, such as services and automobile production, and rejects the "positivistic fiction of a dispassionate, objective observer wholly removed from the field of observation" (Boulding, 1949: 4).

It is therefore of immediate significance that Boulding's starting point is the *economy* and its essential natures, activities and features, rather than any core *theoretical* principle(s). Boulding's position is challenging to conventional approaches which arguably prioritise technique over real-world application and relevance. In terms of an economics textbook, Boulding's approach would entail that a large proportion of the early section of such a book would be devoted to discussing the nature of the (local and global) economy. Questions of technique or theory would be postponed.

Reflecting much of his other work (principally Boulding, 1956a), Boulding views the economy as a complex system. The economy—or elsewhere, *econosphere* (Boulding, 1966b)—is a complex sub-system of the social system of the world (or *sociosphere*) (which is itself a subset of the *biosphere*). Systems theory is Boulding's *philosophical ontology*—his theory of the way the world works in broad terms. A complex system has many implications for economics: for example, because the system includes both elements and connections between them, the whole of the system is greater than an aggregate of its elements. That notion comes through strongly in Boulding's concerns about the fallacy of composition of aggregates; and in his emphasis on balance sheet analysis (1966c) (see below). Further, he explicitly refers to closed systems (119), drawing on Boulding (1956a) in particular, where he also discussed the operation of open systems, defined as self-maintaining structures (see also Boulding, 1966b: 276) and to *homeostasis*, which, as discussed at length by Wray (1997), refers to a desired state of the balance sheet.

For the teacher of economics, the notion of the world as a complex (sub-) system entails a number of challenges. Very early in the textbook and course, there would need to be a discussion of the nature of systems. This may be, for the student, necessary and illuminating (Boulding, 1956a). However, it also involves learning a new, initially abstract language of entropy, open and closed systems, positive and negative feedback, energy, matter and information exchange, throughput and the like. This language might challenge the instructor as much as the student and entail considerable unravelling. As an added set of challenges, underpinning Boulding's economics are elements of biological analogy (economic aggregates as populations [1988: 118–19]); a social theory (trends and herd behaviour [121] and custom, habit, tradition and ritual are important in economic life [1949: 7]); and psychology (preferences are learned [121]).

Overall, the complexity of beliefs supporting the economics may present a challenge to the tutor. The author of an economics textbook then faces a dilemma: explain at length the underpinning social theory; or leave the reader rather ignorant about key concepts. For Boulding, who wants economics to be useful, and wants to transmit knowledge to future generations, the first course of action would seem necessary. However, it would require great skill on the part of the writer to communicate these concepts in an engaging and sufficiently accessible way.

Economics and economists

In studying the economy, economists necessarily develop theories. Boulding (1988) says relatively little about theory. Many of his other theoretical insights are discussed elsewhere in this volume, so will not be discussed at length here. However, it is worth reiterating Wray's (1997) analysis that concepts such as liquidity preference and endogenous money play important roles in Boulding's macroeconomics, and that Boulding endorsed views redolent of recent Chartalist-inspired theories of monetary and fiscal policy.

In addition to the economy and economic theory, however, Boulding (1958) defined economics in terms of what economists are or, from Viner, what economists do. Further, Boulding holds that there are skills which are unique to economists: "there is something, however humble, which can properly be called skill among those who recognise themselves as economists" (1958: 4). Moreover, these skills have a virtue in themselves, perhaps "cultural capital"[4]: "The invention of sport is a clear testimony to the worship of skill" (1958: 2). Thus, an economics textbook ought to provide knowledge about economic methods and provide an opportunity for economists to develop their skills by working with economic systems (or some facsimile of them). Furthermore, though, Boulding talks of the desirability of "the state of mind [economics] produces" (1949: 12). That begs the question as to the nature of this state of mind. My view is that it has two main elements: a set of ways of thinking, such as in terms of systems; and a cautious confidence in the powers of economics and its methods.

On the one hand, Boulding is a believer in the progress of economics towards true images, although he admits that "[t]his proposition, I must confess, is an act of faith" (1966b: 2). This is not a faith blind to the reality of economic analysis as he sees it: "Progress in economics is going to depend on its ability to break out of these low-level systems, useful as they are as first approximations, and utilise systems which are more directly appropriate to its universe" (1956a: 96). By this he means that economic methods, though useful, do not reflect the ontology of complex systems and instead are trapped in an atomistic worldview. However, Boulding warns against relying too much on technical expertise, as "these elaborate procedures [which] may easily produce a sense of subjective certainty which is quite unwarranted by the uncertainties of the actual system" (1966a: 10). Overall then, economists must apply their theories and methods but do so in a sophisticated, cautious way. No method is infallible. That approach permeates Boulding's discussion of the skills of the economist. On every occasion that Boulding advocates a method, he also warns of its limitations.

One of the most fundamental skills of the economist is to identify their sphere of influence, i.e. the identification of what is economic (and the abstraction from the non-economic). This act is "framing", which is identified by the QAAHE (2000) as a key skill of the economist. For Boulding, "...the exercise of *any* skill depends on the ability to create an abstract system of some kind out of the totality of the world around us" (1958: 9) (emphasis in original): thus, for the economist to display their other skills, they must first demonstrate the skill of framing an economic question. Usually that entails zoning in on "...economic life itself, in the narrow sense of that part of human activity that is concerned with buying, selling, producing, and consuming," (1949: 7), echoing Boulding's consistent focus on exchange.

So, Boulding wants to distinguish "economics" either as a way of thinking, or by focusing on an area of complex, multi-faceted human lives (cf. Lawson, 2003). It is necessary to identify which part of human action to study (114). However, he also held that economists should be broader in their use of other disciplines (Boulding, 1966a); and he sees a convergence of natural and social science methods (Boulding, 1949: 4). Therefore, it would be a mistake to see Boulding's definition of economics as creating barriers between disciplines. Contrary to the apparently strict distinction between economic and non-economic, he demands that "...the student in economics should get some idea of what is not economic, as well as what is economic" (1988: 132). Overall, then, in framing an economic question, the focus of the economist should be narrow *and* broad. Boulding's approach raises interesting questions for framing: all frames would be fuzzy, contingent abstractions.

This approach presents a challenge for the teacher of economics, at two stages of the educational process: at the first, the initial engagement with the student, there is a task to explain what the subject is about, without doing so rigidly. Subsequently, in the building of a model, the student must consider what to include in it. A final pedagogical challenge is that, according to Perry's (1970) developmental psychology, students are initially comfortable with dualist thought: in this case, the notion that object *x* clearly is, or is not, economic. Boulding's fuzzy boundaries are a challenge to this dualist thought. Moving students to more "relativist" thought is difficult and must be managed carefully.

Following this framing, the economist's other skills enter. For Boulding, these skills are a mixture of technical expertise and habits of thought. Principal among them is using data effectively. The *Appendix* to Boulding demonstrates an approach to economics which begins with the clear presentation of historical economic data showing key aggregate indicators such as GNP and distributional measures. Aggregate data are a solution to complexity (121): they make the multi-faceted object comprehensible via the "orderly loss of information" (119), and provide inputs for models of, say, unemployment, which Boulding claims have been successful (1958: 23).

That is not to say that Boulding naively puts faith in aggregate data, which are often problematic. Boulding acknowledges the inadequacies of GNP as a measure of well-being and seems to applaud attempts to develop alternatives to it (122). GNP and price indices are flawed because of heterogeneity in the object (122). Despite his advocacy of historical data, Boulding notes the limitations of historical statistics in changing economies (116, 122). These problems, combined with general problems of classification (114) and specific issues such as the problem of valuing intangible assets (117), make Boulding, as enthusiastic about data as he is, also cautious. "We should always bear in mind that numbers represent a simplification of reality" (Boulding, 1989: 96). Aggregation indices should be treated as "evidence and not as truth" (1988: 122).

The fallacies of composition (1949: 10) and of aggregation were a consistent concern to Boulding and were the source of macroeconomic paradoxes, such as thrift. As discussed by Wray (1997), Boulding's solution was to use balance sheet analysis. Balance sheets encapsulate many elements of Boulding's approach. They clearly distinguish stocks from flows, which for Boulding is crucial; they provide a simple way of capturing complex data. They provide a "flashlight photograph" but are able to capture the history of the organism. Hence they reconcile static tools with the dynamic world, another theme in Boulding's work. Balance sheets also reflect Boulding's advocacy of static descriptions of an economy via valuations (115); and comparative statics methods: a series of flashlight photographs through time (166). Crucially, balance sheets also provide a basis for modelling heterogeneous individuals which is consistent with the emergent properties of the system.

So, aggregation is a useful skill of the economist, but a rather narrow one if it merely involves adding up. Consequently, part of the art of economics is identifying which aggregates are significant and which parts of them are interesting (120). That raises questions about the general problem of classification; and also about the appropriate level of abstraction chosen by the theorist. Presumably choosing good classifications which are sufficiently concrete but abstract enough to be tractable is another skill of the economist. For Boulding, "One of the most important skills of the economist, therefore, is that of simplification of the model" (1958: 19)—which he claims has been done principally through aggregation and partial equilibrium analysis (1958: 19–23). Further, the skill of the economist is in recognising that numbers are a useful simplification, but only if their meaning can be made intelligible and if they can be harnessed to enhance our vision of the world (1988: 114). Though mathematical ability is important—Boulding also identifies a command of difference equations as a core skill of the economist (1958: 27, 30)—the ability to manipulate or generate numbers is not enough. Boulding's concern here echoes contemporary concerns about whether economists are too focused on mathematical and statistical elegance and are (consequently) unable to communicate effectively.

Boulding's approach also applies to a range of conventional economic concepts and methods such as equilibrium. Boulding (1949: 8) criticises the excessive importance of the concept of mechanical equilibrium in the social sciences; yet claims that even in dynamic economic systems, the notion of equilibrium has been supremely useful in economics (1958: 14) and that it "is a notion which can be employed usefully in varying degrees of looseness" (1958: 14). Further, Boulding cites "[t]he ability to work with systems of general equilibrium [as] perhaps one of the most important skills of the economist" (1958: 15).[5] More broadly, Boulding claims that balancing alternatives at the margin is an important skill of the economist (1988: 121). Similarly, although he also disavows the notion of the utility maximiser (1949: 5; 1956b: 83–5) he identifies the theory of maximisation or rational behaviour as a special skill of the economist (1958: 27ff.).[6]

All of these tensions demonstrate the perils of being an economist and the skills necessary to be effective. For example, Boulding holds that partial equilibrium allows us to "by degrees … explore its [the system's] whole topology" (1958: 20) but warns that it can be a problem "if it is taken as an end in itself" rather than as a path to general equilibrium (1958: 21). Thus, the economist may usefully employ equilibrium but must choose the right "degree of looseness"; also, the economist must be alive to the possibility of making the wrong assessment. In complex systems, such misjudgements appear likely, but also may have significant consequences. So, the economist must recognise the peril of their situation; but act anyway.

The last paragraph suggests economist as hero. Though Boulding (1958) explores the dynamic contrast between an "economist ethic" and a "heroic ethic"—underlining the role of ethics within economics—this is almost certainly a misrepresentation of Boulding. He does, however, suggest an imperative that economists are useful. Economists, as engaged individuals, should grapple with issues they consider important (cf. Robbins, 1932): "...the act of model-building ... is not unrelated to the empirical interests of the model-builder, and the usefulness of a model depends on the degree to which it helps in interpreting the complexities of the empirical world" (1949: 5).

What are the implications of Boulding's approach to economics for the writer of an economics textbook? The economist clearly needs a range of skills: framing, abstraction, the ability to use data and statistical analysis, to use tools such as equilibrium and to be able to construct a picture of the whole economy based on partial information and great uncertainty. The economist should combine these tools with intuition in the pursuit of useful knowledge. Thus, an economics textbook must either spend a long time early on discussing the tools of the economist, or sprinkle the book with discussions of these types; and provide examples to illustrate and exercises to assess students' skills in these areas. In fact, the book probably should do both. However, it is crucial that in order to apply these skills, the budding economist needs to employ the appropriate mindset: of the engaged, humble, flexible problem-solver. The economist must recognise the limits of their subject and of the tools of analysis and capacities of mind it develops. Pedagogically this can present problems: the student can struggle if they are told that tool x is very useful, but mainly in context y, and that in this case, tool z ought to be used too. However, if such discussions are postponed, as Sutton (2000) discusses, the curiosity within students may be drummed out—as may their humility.

Teaching and learning economics

The chapter now turns to the (largely implicit) educational thrust of Boulding (1988). To reiterate: teaching approaches can be understood as containing three elements: the *what* (content, curriculum), the *how* (process, teaching technique) and the *why* (goals of education). Typically debates about economics education have focused on content-based initiatives and process-based initiatives (see Clarke and Mearman, 2003). The above discussion outlines much of what Boulding might propose for content, and he addressed process, which will be discussed shortly. Clearly both are important (Helburn, 1997). However, prior to both are the goals of education.

Following Clarke and Mearman (2003), these goals of education can be usefully divided into "liberal" and "instrumental" sets. Under a liberal perspective, education is intrinsically valuable because it develops the student's analytical, comparative and critical faculties, and in so doing generates an intellectual open-mindedness or autonomy. Instrumental education is directed towards narrower learning goals, such as the ability to solve specific problems, the retention of particular pieces of knowledge, or the development of certain skills. Further, instrumental*ist* education may be directed at broader social goals, such as the belief in a particular ideology. The distinction between liberal and instrumental approaches is—in the spirit of Boulding—best regarded as fuzzy. Instrumental education aims at the retention of facts, or theories, or methods; whereas liberal education de-emphasises all these things. However, even though it is not the goal of liberal education that students learn facts etc., it is inevitable in the educational process that this will happen. Similarly, in the process of learning facts, it is possible that students will develop critical faculties. Overall, the liberal–instrumental dichotomy is somewhat problematic but it is helpful in understanding both economics curricula and Boulding's educational philosophy.

In his first paragraph, Boulding holds that an economics textbook should contain economics. Thus a textbook should inform students about how the economy works (113). Later, he says the textbook should "transmit knowledge structures" (123). By "knowledge structures" he seems to mean knowledge of the economy—and indeed he warns against merely "transmitting a lot of ritual that is useful for passing examinations" (123). The discussion above about the economy suggests that Boulding has specific notions of what understanding students ought to have; and that this understanding is based on "events" such as exchange, and systems notions such as entropy. Boulding's concern with true images and with getting the images as correct as possible (for instance, he warns of the problem of leaving out too many variables because the economist is not familiar with them [1966b: 11]) suggests he is concerned that students learn correct theories and facts.

"Knowledge structures" could, of course, be a much more complex term. As discussed, Boulding also stresses the skills of the economist, which include theories and methods. However "knowledge structures" are defined, they suggest that education is straightforwardly about delivering specific instrumental content. Furthermore, Boulding (1949: 12) writes: "...I should like to argue the necessity for the study of economics not only for its conclusions and methods, but also for the state of mind it produces" (1949: 12). That could be read instrumentally—as the state of mind could be directed towards predetermined ends. Further, Boulding's concern to transmit knowledge from old minds to new ones (123) suggests the instrumental aim of producing new economists.

At this point it is useful to revisit Boulding on the nature and purpose of the skills of the economist. The skills themselves give us clues. As discussed above, these skills include framing, abstraction, the effective use and analysis of aggregate data, the simplification of complex systems into more simple ones; and then more specifically such skills as using equilibrium analysis (Boulding, 1958). Another term for these skills might be "threshold concepts" (Meyer and Land, 2003). A threshold concept is one which, once understood, allows the student access to higher level understanding. Notions such as opportunity cost and the margin are cited as exemplars of threshold concepts in economics, as they transform the students' understanding and allow access to a range of theories and policy analyses. Similarly, scarcity is regarded as crucial in establishing the reality of ecological limits on economic activity, which then conditions the students' thinking about all economic problems. Threshold concepts are increasingly regarded as crucial in economics teaching and inform many arguments for curricular rationalisation. Threshold concepts are dynamic in that they build intellectual capacity. In that respect, they might be regarded as consistent with liberal education. However, if they are highly specific, they might prevent open-mindedness by locking students in to particular modes of thought.

One example of the danger of learning based on thresholds is excessive mathematisation. Once schooled in mathematical technique, there is a tendency (because mathematics is regarded as being approved of and therefore its adoption is perceived as a successful strategy) for it to be used as a default. Again, Boulding is not opposed to mathematics or statistics; however, he is cautious about it. The economist must use such tools carefully. Boulding writes:

> It is clear that the building of models is not a purely mechanical process but requires skill of a high order—not merely mathematical skill but a sensitivity to the relative importance of different factors and a critical, almost an artistic, faculty in the selection of behaviour equations which are reasonable, tentative hypotheses in explaining the behaviour of actual economies.
>
> (1958: 16–17)

This rich quotation shows multiple types of skill, including criticality, artistry and sensitivity (judgement), with the goal of explaining actual economies. Relevance and usefulness are identified as crucial. The goals of education in Boulding appear to be a mixture of specific facts and other knowledge; competency in technique; habits of mind; and the development of skills. They suggest a mixture of liberal and instrumental goals of education.

Liberal education targets the development of capacities. Though "facts" may be learned, and techniques mastered, it is almost unavoidable that these learning outcomes are incidental, or at best are vehicles for achieving the wider goals. There are two main issues here: one is whether Boulding aims at capacities rather than outcomes; the second is whether Boulding as educator is prepared to change outcomes, or even more radically, to relinquish control of the process. On the first question, we have already seen that Boulding can be read as being concerned with capacities. Boulding notes: "...one often finds students who know all the right words, who can pass examinations, but have no feeling for the subject. The skill has not nucleated into an organic whole" (1958: 8). So he de-emphasises learning of facts and stresses the development of capacities. Furthermore, his overriding concern is on the stocks within the economy; the student's mental capacities are their own personal intellectual stock.

However, this intellectual stock is not built purely for its own sake. A driving concern of Boulding is that economics and economists should be useful, although he acknowledges that so far economics has not been (1966a: 9). This stress on usefulness and real-world problem solving could be interpreted as instrumental; but not necessarily. Usefulness is potentially open-ended, suggesting liberal education. Indeed, Boulding's theme of useful intervention suggests that his project was a critical one. As the theoretical interventions discussed by Wray (1997) show, Boulding appeared critical of prevailing economic orthodoxy and aimed to reshape economics. Further, Boulding's (1989) analysis of economic power had the potential to reshape key areas of economics teaching—for instance, in the area of market structure. Moreover, several of the teaching suggestions made by Boulding (1989) indicate a concern to foster critical thinking skills in his students. For example, he asked students to consider a variety of definitions of power. He invited students to think about power, in a potentially liberating way: "…the very act of thinking about power in our lives and experiences creates a process of revelation and self-analysis that may even make us look at ourselves in a new light" (1989: 259). He even asked students to do a review of his book (1989: 260) and to be as "as critical as they could…" (1989: 260). These appeals to critical thinking skills are key to developing the intellectual autonomy sought by the liberal approach.

There are further hints at a liberal approach in Boulding. Whilst education develops students' skills, the skills being developed are not the final objective, but serve other, open purposes. As already mentioned, Boulding is clear that these wider purposes will be driven by the economist's interest—what they consider important. However, these interests are not predetermined by the educator. Whereas above we argued that a state of mind could be directed towards predetermined ends and thereby be instrumental, it is also potentially anti-instrumental: it says that there are goals other than conclusions or methods which are important. In arguing this, Boulding again alludes to liberal capacities of mind.

More generally, Boulding (1988: 122) argues that equilibrium should be taught because it is a useful fiction (albeit approximable); and importantly, he holds that students should know that. Further, he draws from Adam Smith (perhaps highlighting the importance of understanding the history of economic thought) the important distinction between market and long-run equilibrium. He stresses that students ought to know this distinction (122). This position is quietly radical but is entirely consistent with Boulding's methodology discussed earlier in which conventional tools and concepts are advocated, but with caution. Educationally, Boulding is encouraging students to examine tools and concepts critically.

However, this view is contradicted by his warnings of the danger of critical thinking:

> Thinking about power and its complex manifestations may not simply lead to a better understanding of the abstract complexities of society, but may have an effect on one's own image and identity. Perhaps a warning label should be placed on the cover.
>
> (1989: 259)

Further, Boulding goes on, even more strongly, to say that "If the view of the world expressed in the book, therefore, is wrong, it could be dangerously wrong, and students perhaps should be warned of this" (1989: 259). Boulding may simply here be expressing a concern about being wrong, perhaps bearing in mind the common view that it is better to be roughly right than precisely wrong, and Keynes' warning about people being slaves of defunct economists. Alternatively,

Boulding may regard power as a concept of such importance that to get it wrong would be a serious problem, perhaps because of the resultant actions students may take if they are too strongly affected by its discussion. Thus, despite Boulding's willingness to challenge conventional economic concepts, he does not appear to embrace radical pedagogies such as Freire (1972) or Hooks, B. (1994). Further, even though Boulding stresses learning by doing, and therefore might embrace active, experiential, work- or problem-based learning, he might consider action research approaches a step too far. Further, Boulding's comments suggest some resistance to the liberal approach. That approach holds that, even if what they learn is wrong, that is acceptable because the critical capacity will have been created.

In Boulding's defence, one might argue that he simply had an understanding of the perils of working with impressionable minds. Earl (2000), Lapidus (2011) and McIntyre and van Horn (2011) all recognise the problems of challenging too quickly and too strongly students' core beliefs early in their careers. However, Boulding's claim that a textbook should "transmit knowledge structures" (1988: 123) suggests a teacher-centred approach which is at odds with contemporary student-centred philosophy.

Related to the question of criticality is the role of pluralism in teaching (see Garnett and Mearman, 2011). To what extent should an economics textbook present a single view, or should it embrace multiple perspectives, and debate? Several authors have argued for pluralist curricula on the basis that it may illuminate the world more effectively (Fullbrook, 2003); or that they generate skills such as those of critical thinking (Freeman, 2009; Mearman *et al.*, 2011). Significantly, in the opening paragraph of Boulding (1988), he expresses the hope that economics could be consensual (around truth). This aspiration towards truth is a theme of Boulding's work. However, the complexity of the world suggests that truth is elusive and that monistic approaches are less likely to capture it. Rather, a range of approaches may be required to describe and explain a complex reality. That view suggests that rival theories could co-exist.

There is some support for this view in his (1958) concern about the (non-communicative) relations between East and West in the Cold War (redolent of the paradigmism identified by Garnett, 2009). Further, there is evidence that Boulding sees multiple perspectives as important to understanding: "As a moderate Keynesian I deplore the illinformed (sic) attacks of the extreme laissez-faire economists of the von Mises' (sic) school but I must also confess that some of the questions they raise are disturbing" (1958: 5). As we have seen above, Boulding finds utility in conventional economic concepts, plus those drawn from classical economists, and as Wray (1997: *passim*) notes, from a variety of non-mainstream thinkers. There is further evidence though that Boulding considers controversy important. He thought that a consensus would "emerge out of a well-conducted controversy" (113). This might imply that Boulding favours a teaching approach based on controversy, but in the manner of a good conversation. He stresses that economists are part of debates which form an economic (conversation) akin to "family quarrels" (1958: 4), implying a closeness between the parties, and communication. Indeed, perhaps predating the contributions of McCloskey (*passim*), Boulding suggests the *need* for conversation (1958: 5–7).

Conclusion—the economics textbook

The economics textbook should contain economics. Economics is the study of the economy as a complex system; and the theories, methods and skills of the economist. The skills of the economist include a mindset of cautious confidence about established economic theories and methods. These components of economics have immediate implications for the textbook itself and for the teacher using it. Both have to communicate effectively a deep complex of concepts, yet sufficiently rooted in the reality to be useful and engaging. The textbook also actualises an approach to education, which may only be implicit but is crucial to the content and way of delivering the curriculum. This chapter has utilised the distinction between liberal and instrumental aims of education. It has been argued that Boulding's approach suggests mixed goals.

Thus an economics textbook using Boulding's template will entail several differences of approach and structure from the conventional. The Boulding model would place more emphasis on describing the economy as it is, which in turn implies that much of the early part of the book would be devoted to discussing the general nature of systems. After this, the nature and scope of economic enquiry—a topic which used to feature prominently in economics texts, but now neglected—would be discussed. The economist is a cautious practitioner who combines a variety of methods with ethical positions in the pursuit of useful explanations and interventions, perhaps through policy. Once this is all established, the book would turn to economic theory, but the theoretical framework laid out would stress many very different concepts from the conventional. Of particular importance, as discussed by Wray (1997), is balance sheet analysis, which provides the economist with coherent microfoundations for a macroeconomics of complex systems.

Notes

1 This chapter has benefitted from comments by the editors and by participants at a seminar at UWE, Bristol, on 27 January 2011. The usual disclaimer applies.

2 All references to Boulding are from 1988 unless otherwise stated.

3 Interested readers might also note Shackleford's (1991) comments on Boulding (1988). She makes two points that I do not: one, that Boulding viewed textbooks as teaching partly through stories, and two, that textbooks should allow students to access knowledge themselves. Boulding's *Appendix* lends strong support to Shackleford's first claim.

4 Following Bourdieu, cultural capital can also be a form of power.

5 If this seems highly specific, and although Boulding speaks complementarily about Walras, it seems that he means general equilibrium more broadly than any specific theory.

6 Although, as Wray (1997: 460) notes, Boulding (1971) did not regard marginal productivity theory as adequate to explain distribution, which he regarded as determined by investment and financial processes.

References

Boulding, K. (1949). "Is Economics Necessary?", *The Scientific Monthly*, 68 (4): 235–40, reprinted in *Beyond Economics: Essays on Society, Religion, and Ethics*, Ann Arbor: University of Michigan Press.

Boulding, K. (1956a). "General Systems Theory – The Skeleton of Science", *Management Science*, 2 (3): 197–208, reprinted in *Beyond Economics: Essays on Society, Religion, and Ethics*, Ann Arbor: University of Michigan Press.

Boulding, K. (1956b). *The Image: Knowledge in Life and Society*, Ann Arbor: University of Michigan Press.

Boulding, K. (1958). *The Skills of the Economist*, Cleveland: Howard Allen.

Boulding, K. (1966a). "The Economics of Knowledge and the Knowledge of Economics", *American Economic Review*, 56 (2): 1–13.

Boulding, K. (1966b). "The Economics of the Coming Spaceship Earth", in H. Jarrett (ed.), *Environmental Quality in a Growing Economy, Essays from the Sixth RFF Forum*, Baltimore: Johns Hopkins Press, reprinted in *Beyond Economics: Essays on Society, Religion, and Ethics*, Ann Arbor: University of Michigan Press.

Boulding, K. (1966c). *Economic Analysis, Volume II: Macroeconomics*, 4th edition, New York: Harper and Row.

Boulding, K. (1971). *Collected Papers, Volume One*, Boulder: Colorado Associated University Press.

Boulding, K. (1988). "What Do We Want in an Economics Textbook?", *Journal of Economic Education*, 19 (2): 113–32.

Boulding, K. (1989). *Three Faces of Power*, London: Sage.

Clarke, P. and Mearman, A. (2003). "Why Marxist Economics Should Be Taught, But Probably Won't Be", *Capital and Class*, 27 (1): 55–80.

Earl, P.E. (2000). "Indeterminacy in the Economics Classroom", in P.E. Earl and S.F. Frowen (eds.), *Economics as an Art of Thought: Essays in Memory of G.L.S. Shackle*, pp. 25–50, London: Routledge.

Freeman, A. (2009). "The Economists of Tomorrow: The Case for a Pluralist Subject Benchmark Statement for Economics", *International Review of Economics Education*, 8 (2): 23–40.

Freire, P. (1972). *Pedagogy of the Oppressed*, London: Penguin.

Fullbrook, E. (ed.) (2003). *The Crisis in Economics. The Post-Autistic Economics Movement: The First 600 Days*, London: Routledge.

Garnett, R. (2009). "Rethinking the Pluralist Debate in Economics Education", *International Review of Economic Education*, 8 (2): 58–71.

Garnett, R. and Mearman, A. (2011). "Contending Perspectives, Twenty Years On: What Have Our Students Learned?", *International Journal of Pluralism and Economics Education*, 2 (1): 2–18.

Helburn, S. (1997). "ECON 12 and the New Social Studies: Love's Labour's Lost?", *The Social Studies*, 88 (6): 268–76.

hooks, b. (1994). *Teaching to Transgress: Education as the Practice of Freedom*, London: Routledge.

Lapidus, J. (2011). "But Which Theory is Right? Economic Pluralism, Developmental

Epistemology and Uncertainty", *International Journal of Pluralism and Economics Education*, 2 (1): 82–95.

Lawson, T. (2003). *Reorienting Economics*, London: Routledge.

McIntyre, R. and van Horn, R. (2011). "Contending Perspectives in One Department", *International Journal of Pluralism and Economics Education*, 2 (1): 69–81.

Mearman, A., Shoib, G., Wakeley, T. and Webber, D. (2011). "Does Pluralism in Economics Education Make Better Educated, Happier Students? A Qualitative Analysis", *International Review of Economic Education*, 10 (2): 50–62.

Meyer, J. and Land, R. (2003). "Threshold Concepts and Troublesome Knowledge: Linkages to Ways of Thinking and Practising", in C. Rust (ed.), *Improving Student Learning – Theory and Practice Ten Years On*, pp. 412–24, Oxford: Oxford Centre for Staff and Learning Development (OCSLD).

Perry, Jr., W.G. (1970). *Forms of Intellectual and Ethical Development in the College Years: A Scheme*, New York: Holt, Rinehart and Winston.

QAAHE (2000). *Benchmarking Statements (Economics)*, London: Quality Assurance Agency for Higher Education.

Robbins, L. (1932). *An Essay on the Nature and Significance of Economic Science*, London: Macmillan.

Shackleford, J. (1991). "Review: One-Semester Introductory Economics Textbooks: Echoes and Choices", *Journal of Economic Education*, 22 (1): 55–87.

Sutton, J. (2000). *Marshall's Tendencies: What Can Economists Know?*, Cambridge, MA: MIT Press.

Wray, R. (1997). "Kenneth Boulding's Reconstruction of Macroeconomics", *Review of Social Economy*, 55 (4): 445–63.

Poem

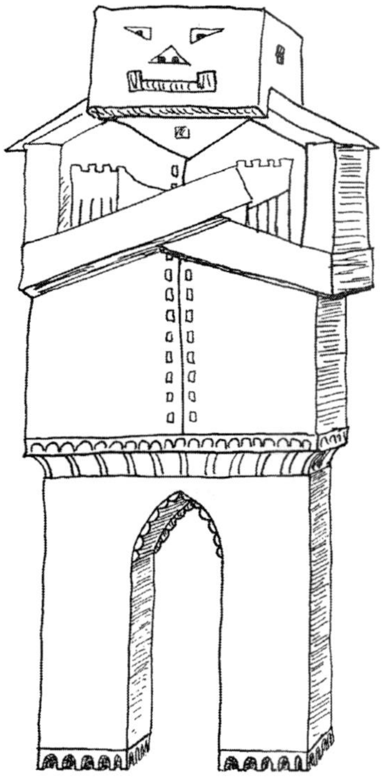

The Monumental Error

The Monumental Error
Is something of a terror,
For when you've gone and made him,
It's difficult to trade him.

Part XIV

The future of economics

14 Key text: What went wrong with economics?[1]

Kenneth E. Boulding[2]

Did anything go wrong with economics? A good many of the "mainline" economists would probably say no, or at least not very much. A survey of the profession would probably reveal that a considerable majority of economists, at least those under forty, and especially those who have just gotten tenure, would be highly satisfied with the present state of affairs. On the other hand, there are rumblings of descent, by no means united. There is still URPE, no longer as flamboyant as it was in the sixties, but still doing a certain amount of neo-Marxist complaining. There is a little group of humanist economists, the post-Keynesians, the neo-Institutionalists, the Society for Evolutionary Economics, and a few lone voices here and there, including mine. There is even a little supply-side economics on the Reaganish right.

Of all these voices, I can only speak for myself, and my own sense of uneasiness has several sources. Part of it derives from some profound uneasiness about the present state of the human race, which is unprecedented, and the failure of economics to say much about it. Some might reply that there is really nothing to say and we should not say anything. We do have, for instance, the positive probability of an almost total nuclear catastrophe as a result of the breakdown of the system of national defense. If SDI is a destabilizing pipe dream, the probability of our destruction may be rising. It could be argued, of course, that national defense is a totally noneconomic phenomenon, that economics has nothing to say about it. On the other hand, there is a rising interest in the economics of war and peace, as reflected in the recent conference in Stockholm sponsored by the International Economic Association and the Stockholm International Peace Research Institute, at which a new society with this interest was formed.

Somewhat closer to conventional economics is the problem of the ideological conflict between communism and capitalism, whatever these vague and confusing concepts mean, which is the core of the nuclear threat at the present. Economics as a discipline has remained remarkably silent about this, retreating either into a vague neo-Marxism on the part of the few or into a pretty uncritical acceptance of the very real virtues of the market without much interest in its pathologies on the part of the many. On the principle that something can go wrong with anything, it is absurd to attribute all the pathologies of the system either to the market and private property or to government intervention. And the question of the role both of the state and of the market in the economy and the interaction of the threat system and the exchange system has been very much neglected by all parties, perhaps because of the isolation of economics from political science.

Another partial failure of economics relates more to the so-called Third World, a very heterogeneous aggregate, where, however, the problem of development cannot really be separated from that of distribution, that is, who develops and where? Economists' contribution to this problem can hardly be termed an uproarious success, though neither is it a total failure. It is hard to contemplate Africa without a feeling of despair for the middle future over the next few decades. Hong Kong, with its Avis rent-a-government from the Queen, is certainly no mean tribute to the virtues of a free market, as Argentina and Egypt, to name only two cases, are no advertisement for government intervention in the market, however well meaning. All economic models of development have turned out to be much too simple and have neglected both the cultural elements and the political elements. Here again, it may be the failure of economics to transcend its self-imposed boundaries that have created the present situation of disillusionment.

An area of social pathology which has only recently become apparent, but which has been creeping up on us for a long time, is the pathology of the financial system, breaking out into view mainly in the world debt problem, but also very serious for the internal debt problem of the United States, and to a lesser extent, the rest of the developed world. The proportion of national income going to interest in the United States has risen from about 1.0 percent in 1950 to something like 10 percent today, though it may be falling a little at the moment. This is perhaps the largest quantitative change in the American economy in the last 35 years. It has received surprisingly little attention. Interest has to be treated as a necessary burden on the economy. The receivers of interest, on the whole, are very inactive, and interest greatly resembles part of the grants economy. It is almost a form of welfare to the rich and the property owners. At 1.0 percent of national income it is no great burden and is easily tolerated; at 10 percent it is a very severe burden, and eating into profit, which is the reward of the active capitalist and the employer, can easily produce unemployment and the slowing down of general enrichment.

The problem of finance is somewhat related to the more familiar problem of unemployment and inflation, the Phillips Curve dilemma, which in turn is related, though this connection is not always made, with the possible pathologies of the relative price structure, what might be called, to paraphrase an expression of Keynes, the "casino effect" of organized markets. At one end of the spectrum of competitiveness the dynamics of competitive, speculative markets creates a constant hurricane of redistribution of net worth, dividing people pretty sharply in any "day" between those whose net worth is derived from holding assets which are falling in relative value, whose net worth is diminishing, and those whose assets are rising in relative value, whose net worth is increasing. At the other end of the casino, we have the stodgy or bemired economy of imperfect markets, sticky wages, reluctant price changes, and so on. There was, after all, the Great Depression and what existed must at least have been possible then, and we cannot be sure it is impossible now. The Great Depression hovers over the imagination, at least of older people today, almost as much as does the nuclear threat. It was the Hiroshima of the market, and who knows whether it might not be repeated.

There is enough discontent here, it seems, that cannot be brushed off. I have argued indeed in the address which I gave to the British Association in 1983 on the contribution of economics to human betterment (Boulding 1984), that on the whole economics has done more good than harm. It has a potential of doing still more good however, which should be examined, and we should not be afraid to look at the possible pathologies of economics itself, with a view to some kind of eventual cure or at least mitigation. This is basically a problem in the pathologies of epistemology. How do we develop methodologies of inquiry which are appropriate to the nature of what we are inquiring about, in the sense that inquiry leads to an increase in the detection of error, and a greater probability that our image of the particular part of the world that we are investigating will map more and more closely into the real world that is the subject of the investigation?

The real world is vast and diverse and is not epistemologically homogeneous, in the sense that the same methods do not apply equally well over the whole field, and that methods which are appropriate and useful in one field may be quite inappropriate and misleading in another. Because the capacity of our minds is smaller than the universe, our image of the world is always some kind of a "muddle," that is, an abstraction from and a simplification of reality. This is true of folk knowledge. My image of the room where I am working, conveyed by the senses, is usually quite adequate for living in it, but does not contain, nor does it have to contain, the molecules, atoms, subatomic particles, radiations, and so on of which the room is composed. The models and observational methods of celestial mechanics are fine for the solar system, where the parameters are very stable. They may be quite inappropriate for the study of economic and social systems, even of biological systems, where the parameters are not stable, where the actual history of the system in space-time is dominated by the exact time at which very improbable events happened, where there are regions of time, at the boundaries of which the parameters change and where the attempt to find universal laws, therefore, is a fruitless quest because they do not exist.

While empirical observation and testing are characteristic of all epistemological systems, the exact methods again have to be tailored to the system that is being investigated. Thus, in physics and chemistry, where the parameters of the systems are very stable, both over time and over space (at least we assume so, although our experience only deals with an infinitesimally small sample of the universe), the experimental method is dominant and very successful. In celestial mechanics, the observational method has been very successful, again because of the stability of the parameters of the system. As we move into biological, however, and still more into the social, systems, change in parameters becomes very important over both space and time. All hydrogen atoms may be the same, but all human beings certainly are not. In systems like this, especially those which involve information, there are nonexistence theorems about prediction, for information has to be surprising. We are beginning to run into this even in physics and chemistry, with quantum mechanics and Prigogine's structures far from equilibrium. The social sciences are a quantum mechanics from the very beginning, full of Heisenberg principles, in which the attempt to get information out of a system changes it. Human knowledge is itself an essential part of the social system which we are trying to learn about. We cannot learn about it without changing it. This often means that the immediate past is a very poor guide to the future.

All epistemological systems start off with a perception of identities, relationships that cannot be otherwise, which are in a mathematical sense "obvious." It quite often takes a good deal of thinking to find out what is obvious. The principle of conservation and Ohm's Law are good examples in the physical sciences. What I have irreverently called the "bathtube theorem"—that the increase in anything is equal to the additions minus the subtractions—is important in all the sciences, including the social sciences. The Fisher identity in economics, MV = PT, is actually a proposition similar to Ohm's Law,

$$\text{Current} = \frac{\text{Potential Difference}}{\text{Resistance}}$$

Both are true by definition, and useful because they define meaningful concepts, like the velocity of circulation and resistance.

Then we have what I would call the "near identities," things that almost have to be true, like the second law of thermodynamics and the most probable shape of supply and demand functions, or the identity of savings and investment in Keynes' *General Theory*. Then there is the empirical world, things which could be otherwise, so we have to find out what they are and how they change. These are the parameters of the system. I know of no demonstration that the velocity of light or the gravitational constant, or any other constants of physics and chemistry, could not be otherwise in some different universe, and it is very important to find out exactly what they are in this one. Similarly, in the social sciences, as in economics, elasticities of demand and supply, rates of depreciation, the "propensity to consume," and similar parameters, differ in different times and places and have to be discovered at each time and place.

Underlying every model of the world is a taxonomy, a set of classifications into which we divide the enormous complexity of the real world. All the elements of one taxonomic set are supposed to be significantly alike and significantly taxonomic set. What is significantly alike and different, however, is often remarkably difficult to discover, especially in social systems, and a failure of taxonomy, that is, regarding things as alike which are really different and things as different which are really alike, is a main source of epistemological failure. Alchemy is a classic example of this in the physical sciences, where the elements of earth, air, fire, and water are hopelessly heterogeneous and incomparable aggregates. We never got very far in synthesizing compounds until we identified the "correct" chemical elements. The social sciences, including economics, are particularly subject to the danger of false taxonomies. This is true even in biology. Race is virtually a worthless genetic taxonomy. The genetic differences within the races are much greater than they are between them, although sociologically they may be significant, in the sense that the perception of rather trivial differences, like skin color, affects people's behavior.

Taxonomy in economics has been taken much too much for granted. The traditional taxonomy of the factors of production, for instance, is an example. Land, labor, and capital are extremely heterogeneous aggregates, not much better than earth, air, fire, and water, although they do have significance as factors of distribution. All production I have argued, whether of the chicken from the egg or the automobile from the designs and blueprints, originates from a genetic factor which might be called "know-how." The ability of the genetic factor, however, to realize its potential depends on a number of limiting factors of available energy in different forms, materials of different kinds, space, and time. This view, indeed, is implicit in Adam Smith's famous discussion of the effects of the division of labor on production, which basically takes place because of its impact on human skill and knowledge, especially that of the "philosophers" who do R & D.[3] This has been largely forgotten in modern economics. The laborer is a complex mixture with certain skills and know-how, capacity to receive and interpret information, bodily energy, and a throughput of materials. Capital is a hopelessly heterogeneous aggregate of economically significant objects of all kinds, including the laborer. Land is an aggregate of spatial position and chemical and biological potential of many different kinds. It is no wonder that attempts to form production functions in which product is regarded as a function of quantities of land, labor, and capital mixed together in a kind of cookbook recipe have not been very successful and have had to drag in the know-how concept in some form of "technology." Similarly, the theory of international trade, which regards national states as homogeneous units, is very far from the complex truth of economic geography. The taxonomy of economic organizations in economics is likewise very shaky. In the case of the firm, nobody assumes that what the firms buys is consumption, whereas we call household purchases "consumption," even if they are for durable goods. Governments have no balance sheets, no capital accounting, and so on.

The epistemological problem also underlies the whole debate about positive versus normative economics. The idea advanced by Milton Friedman that economics is "positive" if we can make predictions is very much of a half-truth. If parameters are stable and if we can identify what they are, then prediction becomes possible, and the past is a very useful guide to the future. Where parameters change, as they do all the time, prediction becomes extremely limited, and can only be attempted over a very wide range of futures, though there is no harm in having some possible futures ruled out. Uncertainty in economics, as Frank Knight pointed out so well, is not just a defect of human knowledge, but an inherent property of the system, as the development of information theory has made very clear. Any system involving information has irreducible and inherent unpredictability. This does not mean that it is totally unpredictable or random. It means that exact prediction is impossible. It is absurd to try to have an exact science in an inexact world.

Economics has never hesitated to be normative. By normative we presume dealing with human valuations and making propositions about them. The epistemological processes which develop and coordinate human images of values is highly similar, though perhaps not entirely identical, with the processes that lead to images of "fact." A process by which we detect error in propositions of fact is not very different from that by which we detect error in propositions of value. All societies involve not only preferences so beloved of economists, but also a critique of preferences, an ethos of the subculture, and a critique of the ethos of some subcultures by the larger society. This is not very different from the way in which we critique the image of a flat earth. It is true that our valuations may affect our images of fact—we may be unwilling to believe bad news—but we can also study how each affects the other. The idea that there is something called "science" which detects truth faultlessly and cannot have anything to do with valuations is an absurd byproduct of the now largely discarded logical positivism.

A very interesting epistemological question is the role of mathematics and quantification in different fields of inquiry. Mathematics is a useful way of discovering complex identities. It is indeed the study of the obvious, though what is obvious is not always immediately obvious, as the different systems of mathematics suggest. For each field of inquiry, there tends to be an appropriate mathematics, and I would certainly argue that the use of mathematics in economics has involved a type of mathematics mostly from the seventeenth and eighteenth centuries, which is not very appropriate to the field of inquiry. A Cartesian algebra and Newtonian calculus and mechanics are about as appropriate to social systems as Euclidean geometry is to Einsteinian physics and cosmology. In conventional algebra, minus minus is plus. In social systems, not doing harm is very different from doing good. The real world, even the physical world, tends to be much more topological than it is strictly quantitative. Numbers are mainly a figment of the human imagination, apart from such fundamental numbers as pi and e, and zero and one, from which all other numbers can be derived. Even the velocity of light is not a number. Conventional measurement always involves arbitrary units. Both conventional mathematics and numbers are useful crutches for the human mind and are the means for topological perceptions that we might not otherwise achieve, but it is a great mistake to confuse these abstractions with the realities.

Quantification also leads to something that might be described as "reducingism," that is, reducing complex structures and sets to single numbers. There is a certain value in this. The reality behind a single figure for the GNP, for instance, is a set of perhaps 100 million prices and quantities. The reality behind a population figure is a vast variety of human beings of different shapes, sizes, ages, skills, and capacities. These reductions are not meaningless, but their meaning has to be interpreted. The numbers are evidence, not truth. Two countries can have the same GNP or the same population and be enormously different in their structure and proportions. Two identical topological structures may have very different quantitative properties, as the famous definition of a topologist illustrates, as someone who doesn't know the difference between a donut and a cup of coffee. Yet for many purposes, the topological structures are what is significant. Maps on the whole are much better abstractions from reality than numbers. Maps are derived from numbers, such as the latitude, longitude, and altitude, of a large number of different points, and if we simply saw the numbers, they would tell us nothing.

Coming now closer to the content of economics, rather than its epistemology, we may note that whatever the economic system is, it is a structure in space-time. Consequently, it is evolutionary, subject to constant and irreversible change. The economy at a moment may be described like a frame in a movie, but the reality is not a single frame, but the movie, that is, the whole succession of frames. Newtonian mechanics is essentially the study of a system of stable parameters which is a regular structure in the four dimensions of space and time, of which celestial mechanics is a good example. Neither biological nor societal evolution is like this. Both are irreversible in time and subject to constant change of parameters, which is what mutation is all about. Curiously enough, Adam Smith has a strong claim to be the first evolutionary thinker, the first post-Newtonian model builder, for although his concept of natural price structure is very much like the concept of an ecological equilibrium, Smith also recognizes that there are irreversible processes of development, particularly through the growth of human knowledge and know-how, which constantly change the natural price structure. Malthus, likewise, really developed the concept of the ecological niche in his population theory, but also recognized that this was a function of human learning. It was no accident that reading Malthus for amusement one evening gave Darwin the idea of natural selection! Ricardo, unfortunately, represented a retreat toward more Newtonian models, which have been followed ever since, with disastrous consequences. Keynes was right in more ways than one when he said that "if only Malthus, instead of Ricardo, had been the parent stem from which nineteenth-century economics proceeded, what a much wiser and richer place the world would be today!" (Keynes 1951). Equilibrium has become a kind of holy sacrament in economics and has seriously diverted attention from the real world of Heraclitean flux. This is not to say that equilibrium is not a useful construct, but it does not exist in the real world except in very tentative and temporary forms. To quote the famous hymn, "Time, like an ever rolling stream, Bears all its sons away."

Just as Adam Smith developed both the equilibrium and the evolutionary approach, of which the latter has been largely lost, so he also saw economics as a two-fold problem, one of which was how society was organized by exchange, the other of which is how society was "provisioned," in what today would be regarded as a more ecological sense. Here again, modern economics has gone wholly toward the view of economic life as society organized by exchange, and has largely lost the sense of it being a process of provisioning of the human race, or even of the whole biosphere. Looking at it from the point of view of how society is organized through exchange, all commodities stand on equal footing. All participate in the exchange system, either actually or potentially, or they would not be commodities. Looked at in terms of provisioning, we immediately run into the concept of the food chain, so important in ecology, and very important in classical economics. Even Leontief's "input–output analysis" really misses this and regards all inputs and outputs, as it were, on the same level. The real world is not very much like a matrix. From Adam Smith even to Jevons, the food chain concept was very clear in economics. Provisioning began with the production of food. The producer of food had to be fed himself, but if he produced more food than he ate himself, then there was a surplus of food. If this were, say, oats, these could be fed to a cow, which would produce milk or meat, a different kind of food and an important addition to the diet. Fed together with leather to a shoemaker, oats would produce shoes, which in turn perhaps would enable a farmer to produce more food, thus setting up a positive-feedback process, as we would say today. Food fed to builders, together with stones and wood, would produce houses. Fed to pin makers along with steel, would produce pins. This is why "corn" played such a fundamental role in classical economics, which has been completely lost. All commodities now are just x and y.[4,5,6]

Another taxonomic and conceptual problem which has plagued economics from the time of Adam Smith, not wholly unrelated to the provisioning problem, is the confusion between stocks and flows, and the profound carelessness about the dimensions of the economic concepts. My beloved Adam Smith, I regret to say, must bear some responsibility for this. In the very first sentence of the introduction to *The Wealth of Nations* he says, "The annual labour of every nation is the fund which originally supplies it with all the necessaries and conveniences of life...." (Smith 1937, p. vii). The fund is the laborers not the annual labor, and the necessaries and conveniences of life are very largely stocks, which are certainly consumed and have to be replaced, but at many different times, not "annually." The wages fund is another muddle here. It is strange that a set of concepts that are really so simple should cause so much trouble. There is first the concept of the stock of economically significant objects, in which today we would include human bodies and minds, and also consumer capital, which Adam Smith would exclude. This is a vast ecosystem of populations of different human artifacts—loaves of bread, chairs and tables, houses, machines, roads, and so on. It may also include economically significant objects which are not human artifacts, but which are appropriable, like oil in the ground, navigable rivers, and the like. All these goods are subject to consumption in the literal sense of the word, of destruction, either by wearing out, depreciation, or by using up, that is, being transformed into other goods, as wheat is transformed into flour, flour into bread, bread into people, so on—provisions, again! Because there is consumption, there has to be production in order to maintain the capital stock. The capital stock is a population of items, production is births into this population, consumption is deaths.

Here again, we go back to Adam Smith for this neglect of household capital, which became characteristic of much subsequent economics. It took almost until Irving Fisher for us to realize that food on the fork is just as much capital as food on the grocery store shelves, or in the warehouse. Certainly the idea that consumption is equivalent to household purchases, which we find even in Keynes, is extremely misleading. Household purchases themselves depend on perceptions of the depreciation and the using up of household capital and are intended to replace such capital. Furthermore, the idea that the object of production is consumption is only partly true. What we get satisfaction from for the most part is use, not consumption. I get no satisfaction over the fact that my clothes are wearing out. I get satisfaction out of wearing them. The same goes for my automobile, my house, and even my body. On the other hand, we do also put a certain value on throughput. We like eating as well as being well fed. We like variety in our surroundings, in our clothes, and so on. The idea that we get utility or satisfaction only out of consumption is clearly ridiculous. This has led to an extraordinary neglect of information collection about the capital structure, and especially household capital, and the absurd view that it is income which is the only measure of riches. Income, of course, is related to the capital stock through length of life of the stock, that is, the time interval between production and consumption, between birth and death, and if this is fairly stable, as over short periods it is, then income is a pretty fair surrogate for the capital stock and therefore for satisfaction. But it is only a surrogate.

We see the same problem in the modern theory of the firm, which is conducted almost entirely on income statements, without any regard to the structure of the balance sheet, which may be critical in firm decisions. I have argued indeed that the simplest theory of the firm is that of the homeostasis of the balance sheet: every event changes the balance sheet structure, and behavior is simply to offset each change. Then, of course, the second approximation is change in the optimum balance sheet itself. The overemphasis on flows (income) almost to the exclusion of stocks has done a great deal of real harm and led to an underestimation of the real importance of maintenance of stocks, and has seriously perverted our image of the dynamics of the system.

Finally, perhaps the most significant unsolved problem in economics, particularly of market economies, might be called the "macro distribution problem" on the income side of the accounts, which is what really determines the distribution of some aggregate income among classes of recipients. Again, there is a taxonomic problem here, as the conventional aggregates of national income, national product, and so on and their components are not very satisfactory. Nevertheless, we can divide some national income quantity as between labor income and non-labor income, and within non-labor income as between interest and profit. There is a little question as to whether there is a place for something that might be called "rent," though this is largely an artifact of the system of national accounts, derived from certain artifacts of the private accounting system. I have argued, without much effect, for nearly forty years that there are processes at work here which I have recently called the "K theory" (Boulding 1985), as some of its major discussants have been Keynes in the *Treatise on Money* and his theory of the "widow's cruse," Kalecki, Kaldor, and Kenneth (Boulding), though others should be included. Perhaps the simplest, though not the most accurate expression is Kalecki's famous remark, which seems to belong to the Cambridge oral tradition (not even Joan Robinson could find it in writing) that "capitalists get what they spend and workers spend what they get." There is a great deal of evidence that the volume of net business investment and the degree to which the vagaries of the financial system induce the owners of capital to make household purchases have a profound effect on the proportion of national income going to profits. This is seen very clearly in 1932 and 1933, when net private domestic investment was negative, profits were negative, interest was still positive, and largely as a result, unemployment was 25 percent. This macrodistribution is a crucial question for the future of market economies. If they cannot solve it, they may eventually be replaced by centrally planned economies, which have even worse pathologies, and up to now have been unavoidably associated with excessive concentrations of political power and violations of human rights, as well as inefficient use of resources.

So much for what went wrong. Now comes the delicate question as to who did it? This is an embarrassing question. It puts one somewhat in the position of the Recording Angel, which no human should occupy, but also involves some of my very good friends and acquaintances. No individual should award an unnobeling prize. Keynes, of course, denounced Ricardo before me, so that I can hide behind that. Perhaps the real villain is the discovery of seventeenth-century mathematics some 200 years late by Cournot, Jevons, and most of all, Walras, whose elegance and brilliance set economics on a path that increasingly has become a dead end. The famous hypothesis of Benjamin Whorf that the structure of language is an important determinant of thought applies with particular intensity to mathematics, which is not even a language, but a jargon. It is remarkably deficient in verbs. It is hard to think of more than four: is equal to, is greater than, less than, or is a function of. And it, therefore, severely limits what can be talked about. It consequently deals with structures much better than it deals with processes, with equilibrium much better than with evolution. That it has its uses nobody will deny, but it also has great and largely unrecognized dangers. Sociologically, it leads into a kind of intellectual snobbery that requires every article to be prettied up in what is frequently cosmetic and unnecessary mathematics. The number of propositions, certainly about social systems, which can only be reached with the aid of mathematics is quite small. I can only think of two or three in my own work. It is sometimes useful in generalizing into complex systems. I am convinced, however, that the obsession with algebraic, nontopological mathematics has forced the main line of economics into a dead end. To break out of it, however, is difficult. The deader the end, the more it is insulated from the real world, the safer it feels, the more those people in it are going to reward each other. The only hope is that there is a real world, which not even the deadest of ends can avoid indefinitely. It is by failure that we learn, and perhaps the greatest service is to point out where the failures lie.

Notes

1 This article was previously published in *American Economist*, Spring 1986, 30, 1: 5–12.
2 Institute of Behavioral Science, University of Colorado, Boulder.
3 Adam Smith (1937), Book I, Chapter I, p. 10:

> Many improvements have been made by the ingenuity of the markers of the machines, when to make them became the business of a peculiar trade; and some by that of those who are called philosophers or men of speculation, whose trade it is not to do anything, but to observe every thing; and who, upon that account, are often capable of combining together the powers of the most distant and dissimilar objects.

4 I can hardly resist a little story at this point. I was expounding this one time to a student of Gerhard Tintner's (who had a rich Viennese accent), who said he thought Tintner was talking not about x and y, but about "eggs" and "wine."
5 One twentieth-century economist who was very much aware of the "provisioning" aspect of economics was Adolph Lowe in his book *On Economic Knowledge: Toward a Science of Political Economics*. One of my works of which I am most ashamed is a review I did of this book in *Scientific American* (1965), criticizing the provisioning approach as "Pooh Bear economics," without realizing at the time what an important and sensible approach this was.
6 Austrian economics, especially in Böhm-Bawerk, recaptured the concept of time sequence in production and consumption, but tended to lose it again in the too abstract concept of the average period of production.

References

Boulding, Kenneth E., "How Do Things Go from Bad to Better?: The Contribution of Economics" (presidential address to Section F, Economics). In: *The Economics of Human Betterment*, Kenneth E. Boulding, ed. (Proceedings of Section F, British Association for the Advancement of Science annual meeting, University of Sussex, England, Aug. 1983). London: Macmillan Press, 1984, pp. 1–14.

Boulding, Kenneth E., "Puzzles Over Distribution," *Challenge*, 28, 5, Nov./Dec. 1985: 4–10.

Keynes, John M., *Essays in Biography*, New edition, London: Macmillan Press, 1951.

Smith, Adam, *The Wealth of Nations*, New York: Modern Library Edition, 1937.

14a Comment: What went wrong with economics?

A quarter century on

Deirdre Nansen McCloskey[1]

In 1986, in one of his 1000-odd articles, this one published in *The American Economist* in connection with receiving the John R. Commons Award from the undergraduate economics honorary society, Boulding told us what had gone wrong in economics up until then. Some of what he worried about in 1986 seems dated now. The nuclear threat, whose impetus, Boulding noted, was the Cold War, has since receded, and with it the wise concern that propelled so much of Boulding's work in the public sphere. In 1986 we had lived since 1945 with the threat of nuclear Armageddon. By then our fears were perhaps not quite so vivid as in the 1950s, when American school children were drilled to hide, if the bombs fell, under their desks (the memory is the basis of a vulgar but funny spoof of a civil defense poster, which ends with "kiss your a.. good-bye"). Yet Boulding the great Quaker pacifist was still in 1986 properly fearful, a fear which in most of us had by long acquaintance dulled—even the Cuban Missile Crisis of 1962 was by then a fading memory. One can't stand to attention, or hide under one's desk, all the time. Boulding could stay alert to the reality of the threat because his fear was rooted in his solid Christian faith and his solid economic understanding, both.

Likewise his strictures in 1986 on the then and still feeble contributions of economists to understanding the nature and causes of the wealth of nations, especially in what was in those days appropriately called the Third World, have lost some of their bite. Economists, whether Marxist or bourgeois, had been giving bad advice to China and India for a long time. In China since 1978 and India since 1991, however, Adam Smith pretty much rules, and the results have been astounding. The long tradition of economics has by now earned its keep. Boulding had been saying for some time (for example, in 1964) that what was needed for the great transition to a stable, high-level technology was a "growth industry," permeating the society. That is surely correct. Look around a country like Sweden or Korea and you can see such an industry puffing away. But, as we economists all thought in 1964, he added that population needed to be controlled (though surely as a pacifist he would have been horrified at the means that governments subsequently adopted to achieve Malthusian control, following mistaken First-World ideas about limits to growth). And he added, too, that "accumulation of goods" in a capital stock is what achieves growth (Boulding

1964, p. 105). Neither is correct. The better guide to the economics of population turned out to be Julian Simon, who wrote in 1981 *The Ultimate Resource.* And the better guide to mistaken "capital fundamentalism" in foreign aid turned out to be William Easterley, who wrote in 2001 *The Elusive Quest for Growth.* But in those days of the 1980s many of us still believed in the verities of postwar development economics: stop population growth; pile up the capital; by all means *plan*. Boulding wrote later in the same essay that "the success of Japanese development is due simply to the fact that Japan [by planning] devoted a substantial portion of its resources to the growth industry, and particularly to the human resources" and then commended Max Weber's emphasis on "hard work and thrift" (1964, p. 116). Incorrect again.

Yet Boulding immediately afterwards in the old 1964 essay got it exactly right: "Mere accumulation is not enough. Economic development does not consist merely in the piling up of things, but in the accumulation of new kinds of things." Despite the ongoing attempts in New Growth Theory to make growth lie down on capital accumulation *one more time*, the argument in truth should not shock a thoughtful economist. All economists have realized since the 1870s that economics is something that happens between people's ears, and always about the future, of which Yogi Berra said: "Prediction is difficult. Especially about the future." The economists learned such truths after the 1870s from the various forms of neoclassical economics, Mengerian or Marshallian, or from institutionalism or from modern Marxism. Valuations, opinions, the image, talk on the street, imagination, expectations, hope are what drive an economy. In other words, as Boulding knew, you don't *have* to be a materialist, denying the force of ideas, just because you are an economist. Rather to the contrary. One of the leading contributors to New Growth Theory, Robert Lucas, declared that

> for income growth to occur in a society, a large fraction of people must experience changes in the possible lives they imagine for themselves and their children.... In other words ... economic development requires [in V.S. Naipaul's phrase] "a million mutinies."
>
> (2002, p. 17)

Economic growth depends mainly on Schumpeterian/Austrian innovation, which is what Boulding believed on his good days, not, as some economists and historians still believe, on classical/Marxist/Samuelsonian accumulation, reallocation, exploitation. Boulding distinguished human knowledge from know-how, the one being science, the other craft. But both drove the world, "genetically," as he would say, that is by the inheritance of skills and ideas. "Production functions involving only land, labor and capital ... never work and never explain economic development" (1990, pp. 127–128). Once upon a time the economists thought that growth depended on *physical* capital and now some think that it depends on various sorts of *human* capital. But the economist Peter Howitt has reported on a recent literature of present-day cross-country comparisons which concludes that "more than 60 percent of the cross-country variation of per-worker GDP is attributable to productivity rather than to the accumulation of physical and human capital," and over 90 percent of its growth rate (Howitt 2005, p. 7) "Thus it seems," he argues, "that almost everything to be explained by the theory lies in the Solow residual," the *A* term in Solow's classic paper of 1957. "This is part of the evidence," Howitt continues, "that inclines me towards innovation-based growth theory." It seems a sensible conclusion, and echoes Boulding's as early as 1964: "It is clear that we must look at pure science, technological change, and social invention as parts of a single pattern of development in which each supported the other" (Boulding 1964, p. 11).

That is, what matters is Boulding's "growth industry," supported by the surrounding society. The finding was anticipated by Smith, whose *Theory of Moral Sentiments* (1759 [1790]) treats of dignity, and whose *Wealth of Nations* treats of liberty. Smith believed that the obvious and simple system of natural liberty was necessary and sufficient for the (modest) growth he imagined. Kenneth Boulding was no dogmatist of laissez faire, but in view of the success of Smithian economic liberty in China and Smithian dignity in India, and our clearer understanding now of their importance in the first Industrial Revolution, I think he would have agree (had he lived to age 112) that forced or artificial capital accumulation, or forced or artificial allocation of labor, is not the ticket that we proud and rationalist economists of the 1960s thought it was.

On many of the points Boulding made in 1986, though, the essay could have been written yesterday. His warning a quarter of a century ago about "the pathology of the financial system," and in particular the burden of debt, looks prophetic, though Boulding put it in his idiosyncratic way as the problem of interest payments of all kinds, public and private, not merely the government's debt. He worried, too, about the "casino effect" of such financial markets, a worry which could not be heard very well in 1986, but rings true in these latter days: "The Great Depression hovers over the imagination ... almost as much as does the nuclear threat. It was the Hiroshima of the market, and who knows whether it might not be repeated" (1986, p. 6). In September 2008 we faced Hiroshima.

On a more strictly methodological point, Boulding was all his life correctly suspicious of "models and observational methods of celestial mechanics," which are those of modern Samuelsonian economics. They "are fine for the solar system, where the parameters are stable.... [But] may be quite inappropriate for the study of economic and social systems, even of biological systems" (1986, p. 7). His is of course an old worry about economics imitating Newton rather than Darwin. One wonders what would now be the relative prestige of mechanical as against evolutionary models if a Darwin had published *The Origin of Species* in 1687 and a Newton had not published *Principia Mathematica* until 1859.

Boulding, it should be understood, was a theorist, not an empiricist. He did not have the inclination or the patience for getting the facts exactly, precisely, forever right. As such, he was no enemy of mathematics (and neither am I, by the way, though an empiricist), unless an article is "prettied up in what is frequently cosmetic and *unnecessary* mathematics. The number of propositions, certainly about social systems, which can only be reached with the aid of mathematics, is quite small" (1986, p. 12, italics supplied). He was a producer of economic ideas, which after all is what matters in mathematical theory.

For example, he argued early and late for better accounting of what is really "consumed," that is, used up, such as ice cream, and household stocks, such as clothing or autos, that give their use value by being used, not used *up*. Getting the accounting right is the key to clear economic theorizing, as Boulding often observed. When I.M.D. Little and Milton Friedman showed that direct taxes could not be proven on a blackboard superior to indirect taxes (as economists briefly thought in the 1940s), they were using a full accounting of the use of time for work and for leisure. When Robert Barro asked if government bonds were net wealth, or when Robert Gordon noted in the national accounts that many billions of dollars of investment had been mislaid, they were using net wealth = assets – liabilities, what Boulding called The Bathtub Theorem.

He pioneered the taking of information and knowledge into the realm of economics, though the contrast between his writings on the matter and George Stigler's precise little foray in 1961 exhibits well the difference between an essentially qualitative eeconomic theorist like Boulding and an essentially quantitative economic theorist like Stigler. Still, Boulding got "knowledge" more right, mainly by *not* reducing it to "information." Stigler wanted whatever it was to be a matter of routine marginal benefit and marginal cost. Boulding observed, in a style reminiscent of the economists who have in fact gotten furtherest on the role of knowledge in the economy, the Austrians, that "there are non-existence theorems about prediction, for information has to be surprising.... Human knowledge is itself an essential part of the social system.... We cannot learn about it without changing it" (p. 7). I can heartily agree (McCloskey 1990, 2008).

For another important example, Boulding invented what he called, infelicitiously, "grants economics" (he might better have used the anthropologist's term "gifts," or even the theologian's term "grace" [see Klemm 2004]). It is an idea about the economy, but draws the attention of economists to exactly what they do not attend to when thinking of exchange alone. You know you are in a part of the economy dealing with "grants" instead of exchange when "*A* gives *B* something and *B* does not give *A* anything in the way of an economic good" (Boulding 1973, p. i). In a parent's gift to her child or the state's extraction from a citizen (the citizen being viewed as Mr. *A*) "there must be some integrative relationship between them," some sociology or politics legitimating the matter, such as The Family or The Tax-and-IRS System, an economy of love or an economy of fear. Thus courtesy, a man opening a door for a woman, say, signals the existence of a certain kind of gender relationship, for good or ill. We need both to get the whole of the society right, both the heroic gift and the sensible exchange: "Without the heroic, man has no meaning; without the economic, he has no sense" (Boulding 1958, p. 186, quoted in Silk 1976, p. 229).

An extended example: Sneering at commerce from the heights of the aristocracy or the depths of the peasantry is of course ancient and usual. Still, it is odd, since commerce itself is also ancient and usual. We all get our livings or our food and housing and books from it. Most of us literate people nowadays, and for many centuries past our illiterate ancestors, have spent most of our lives doing ... commerce. You sell your labor, you buy your bread. What's the beef?

Yet wherever we are in the social hierarchy we suspect that the other person is cheating us. If "cheating" means "leaving us with less profit than we would have had if the other was idiotically imprudent or wonderfully charitable," then every single exchange involves it. We resent the non-gift (set aside that we also sometimes resent the sheer gift, or even grace: so complicated are humans). Anxiety and irritation have always flowed from the gap between what you are willing to pay and what the seller is willing to accept. The gap characterizes all deals in the realm of exchange—wage deals, house deals, bread deals.

By the "realm of exchange" I mean the middling realm of human contact stuck, Boulding-style, between a social layer of biology and violence at the bottom and rhetoric and a social layer of the gift at the top:

In the realm of violence your satisfaction is not at issue, merely your obedience. You will be distressed that the thief has robbed you or the judge has sentenced you, but you understand the violence being applied. "If you ever go to Houston, you better walk right,/You better not stagger and you better not fight./The police will arrest you, they'll take you down./The judge will sentence you:/You're penitentiary bound." By contrast, at the far other end of human relations, the realm of rhetoric, you are after the persuasive act satisfied. When someone persuades you to believe the Pythagorean Theorem, or to believe in the mutual gains from trade, or to drive a Toyota, or to marry, or to worship, you are not anxious (buyer's remorse and the dark night of the soul aside). You have, as we say, "changed your mind."

In the middling realm of exchange, though, your mind is given—the economist's assumption of given tastes—and you try to get what gain can be achieved in a deal about goods bought and sold. But after the deal you always know that it could have been more gainful to you. In the nature of mutual advantage, you could have got a larger share of the mutual gain. There's *always* that annoying gap between what you paid and what you *could* have paid. Marshallian economists and one of their heirs, the Samuelsonian economists, call the gap between willingness to pay and willingness to accept "the sum of consumer's and producer's surplus." Marxists call it, more vividly, "exploitation" or "surplus value." It is the social gain from trade—the value created by trade—to be divided somehow into your profit and the rest of the world's profit.

Table 14a.1 The hierarchy of human contacts

Realm	*Object*	*Outcome*	*Virtues or vices*
Rhetoric	Gift	Grace, innovation	Love, faith, hope, lying
Exchange	Good	Efficiency	Prudence, justice, greed, envy
Violence	Blow	Subordination	Courage, temperance, anger
Biology	Urge	Pleasure	Gluttony, lust

The "somehow" is the source of the irritation. The amount that makes trade good for both parties also leaves both parties thinking they could have done better. In fact, either party *could* have done better, though not both. Did I get the best deal I could? Has he made a fool of me? The trouble is imagination, combined with an aversion to loss that tends to be stronger psychologically than the pleasure of gain. The psychologists call it "negativity bias." When I fork over the money for a new house, I imagine (more vividly than the utility gain) the *loss* you, the seller, have imposed on me, twice: after all, you "took" my money, and you *also took*, you rat, the larger net gain, for me, I can imagine you could have let me have … by charging less. The brain scientists observe that the amygdala, a primitive part of the brain interested in fight or flight, gets first dibs on impressions. It's necessary for quick moves for survival: jump away from the saber-toothed tiger's claw, *now*. No wonder our more advanced prefrontal cortex, which would tell us not to be so silly as to resent a mutually advantageous sale of a house, gets overwhelmed with negativity (Haidt 2006, p. 29).[2]

From reasoning of this sort, Boulding concluded early on that "Economic problems have no sharp edges. They shade off imperceptibly into politics, sociology, and ethics. Indeed, it is hardly an exaggeration to say that the ultimate answer to every economic problem lies in some other field" (*The Economics of Peace*, 1945, p. 252, quoted in Silk 1976, p. 208). Here he reflects his friendship with Frank Knight, who had been saying something similar since the early 1920s. In 1949 Samuelsonian economists took no heed of old Frank Knight or (then) young Kenneth Boulding. Attracted in 1949 after some years at Iowa State and Toronto to the University of Michigan by an opportunity for a seminar integrating the social science, Boulding found that "social scientists did not want to be integrated very much' (Harcourt 1993, p. 101).

It is appropriate to call economics since 1948 "Samuelsonian," because Paul Anthony Samuelson and his brother-in-law Kenneth Arrow (Lawrence Summers is their mutual nephew) set the tone for economics for sixty years by claiming that qualitative theorems were all that economic theory could do, quantities being left to significance tests (as Lawrence Klein, Samuelson's first Ph.D. student, urged on us). The more common labels for the school that dominates modern academic economics are wrong: "neoclassical" is wrong because the neoclassicals of the 1870s are the common ancestors of heterodox economists, like Boulding, too, and Samuelson and Arrow merely formalized one family descended from the Neoclassical Revolution; and "mainstream," another common label, is self-defeating on the lips of a heterodox economist because it condemns her by the very rhetoric to a backwater.

Boulding wasn't quite as clear as perhaps he could have been on what went wrong deep *inside* Samuelsonian economics, even if one accepts—he did not—all the premises of a Samuelsonian (or as he calls it, Walrasian) economics. Perhaps it is because he was, as I say, a theorist, an ideas person rather than a measuring person, despite his early experience with Henry Schultz at Chicago in econometrics. In little of his work does one find that obsession with How Much that characterizes the Departments of Physics or Engineering or indeed History.

The characteristic vice of Samuelsonian economic theory and its colleague, Kleinian econometrics, the very one that Boulding couldn't see because he was himself a man of qualities, is a fixation on proofs that things *exist*, on/off, yes/no, never an interest in How Much. The qualitative "existence proofs" compulsory in the *Journal of Economic Theory* reflect the education of economists in the Department of Mathematics. That the Goldbach Conjecture—that every even number is the sum of two primes—has been shown by actual calculations to be true up to 10^{18} has no charm for mathematicians: they want forever-True, Greek-style *proof*, and it annoys them that we do not even know if the Conjecture is decidable, and certainly do not know whether it is True. No science of the world, as against the sciences of existence (mathematics, philosophy, theology), cares about such profundities. The economists should be educated in their math in the Department of Physics or of Engineering, which do not care a bit about existence, or Truth, only about magnitude, or truth, showing so far as mathematics is involved merely how such-and-such an expression based on theory can be transformed into another expression better suited to observation and experiment.

One might think that econometrics would therefore come in at the end to save the day for economics as a serious science (so it is written in the formal constitution of Samuelsonian economics, brought down from the mountaintop in 1957 by Tjalling Koopmans' *Three Essays on the State of Economics Science*). Alas, econometrics does not in fact make theory into empiricism, because it in turn has become fixated on "tests of significance." Such tests are again matters of Existence, not magnitude. They purport to tell you whether an effect Exists in the date. But the data speak only of magnitude, whose relevance must be judged every time by a human, since we humans are the scientists. Nothing in the numbers themselves makes this or that regression coefficient *important*. The numbers are inputs into a human judgment, but very rarely is *sampling variability* the only relevant input.

Until economics gets over these twin fixations on the existence, on/off, yes/no, it is going to waste an awful lot of energy to no scientific point. Science is about How Much. Existence theorems and tests of statistical significance have no connection to actual findings about How Much in actual economies, despite their surface similarity to real science in their talk of x and y. A sad business. One wishes that more economists of Boulding's generation had seen how phony the existence-theorem-and-significance-test part of economics was becoming, and had stopped it, to focus, mathematically and verbally and especially quantitatively, on economic ideas measured by How Much.[3]

What, then, did Boulding say, in 1986, or whenever, that nonetheless remains helpful in thinking about the Future of Economics? In a word, "humanomics." That is the word Bart Wilson, the experimental economist, uses to label what he and I and Arjo Klamer and now many others see as the fruitful merging of the social sciences with the humanities for scientific purposes. We think humanomics is the future of a truly scientific economics. Pounding away endlessly on the Samuelsonian formula of Max U s.t. C reduces everything, simply everything, to the virtue of Prudence and its corresponding vice of Greed. It is time to get serious about human motivation, say the behavioral economists and especially the experimental economists and some now of the development economists, all of whose arguments were anticipated by the old institutional economists (remember: Boulding got the Commons prize, and admired his work), the feminist economists, and some economic historians and economic philosophers (not many of any of the categories, admittedly, and even I in my wild youth: most kept grinding away on Max U and logical positivism vintage 1922).

Boulding was in fact a pioneer of humanomics. As Leonard Silk put it,

> Boulding ... began [in *The Organizational Revolution* (1953)] to see ... society as a whole ... as subject to three organizing forces: the exchange of goods and services for mutual benefit, coercion or fear of reprisal, and love or the integration of desires and objectives.
>
> (Silk 1976, p. 19)

I would add only meaning and persuasion, as in the "rhetoric" line in Table 14a.1, to make it a fully humanistic economics. In Boulding's otherwise highly favorable review in 1948 of Samuelson's *Foundations* (I repeat, neither Boulding nor I are machine-breakers when it comes to mathematics; our complaint is deeper), he nonetheless warned of losing "art and literature where that essential ... *quality* is developed, ... its essentially humanistic and empirical quality." "Empirical" means in Greek, you know (and Boulding did, too), "having to do with experience." Not significance tests.

Boulding, for example, wisely observes that in science any model depends on a pre-chosen taxonomy, "a set of classifications into which we divide the enormous complexity of the real world.... Land, labor, and capital are extremely heterogeneous aggregates, not much better than earth, air, fire, and water" (1986, pp. 7–8). In another place he noted that "political science has never developed an adequate taxonomy of power ... [and] has been obsessed with threat power, which actually is probably the weakest of the three elements," of exchange power, love power, and threat power (Boulding 1990, p. 126; see again Table 14a.1).

The usual assumption (a false one in the halls of economic academe) is that economics only studies practical and exclusively quantitative matters, such as the Euro crisis or the Italian debt or Zurich's city income. In such a view, literature is something "higher," spiritual and verbal rather than material and countable. Such a dichotomy was very powerful during Boulding's era, and it is a tribute to his intellectual strength that he saw through it, partly, as through a glass darkly. Certainly, serious literature such as Mann's *Buddenbrooks* or Ibsen's *The Master Builder* is about the spirit, not about how to be a successful North-German grain merchant or how to build tall houses in Norway. It doesn't tell how to make money, or how to make anything much except a good, or a bad, life. Indeed, often enough even a non-serious lyric to a rock song or a non-serious film about car crashes present an artistic vision of chaos or symmetry or heroism that likewise inspires a form of life, for good or bad.

German speakers call the study of serious literature, along with history and theology and philosophy and musicology and art history, *die Geisteswissenschaften.* In English, the German word sounds weirdly spooky, "spirit sciences." We English speakers from the middle of the nineteenth century, unlike earlier English (and every other language: *scienza, science*), stopped using our science word for anything but physics and biology. The new English "meaning in ordinary use" (as the Oxford English Dictionary puts it) of the science word is very strange, and has caused all manner of strange worries about whether economics is Real Science. (Worried? Then stop using existence theorems and tests of significance, neither of which play any part in physics or astronomy.) In all other languages (Tamil, Turkish: you test it) the "science" word means "systematic inquiry," as against casual, unexplored opinion or rumor. The German language and the rest have it right. *Naturwissenschaften* and even *Wirtschaftswissenschaften* are connected at the root to *Geisteswissenschaften.* And so economics is or should become, as the French say, *une science humaine*, a systematic inquiry into humans in the ordinary business of life.

Much of genuine science, I have said, is about quantities, answering the question "How Much?" Good. We need some quantities, such as Zurich's income per head in 2012, or a quantitative sense of its startlingly lower income in 1800 (about three Swiss francs a day per person). When a science like economics gets confused it adopts techniques that do *not* answer the How Much question, and wanders off into questions of existence and non-existence better treated in mathematics or theology. At its academic level, economics has become largely a cargo-cult science and has stopped doing real measurement. By contrast with sciences like geology that measure, the humanities, *die Geisteswissenschaften*, are about *qualities*, that is, categories, asking the prior question, "What?" Vegetable or mineral? Human or animal? Male or female? What we learn from literature are chiefly categories and ethical attitudes—good and bad being categories with which humans are obsessively concerned.

But categories, what Boulding called "taxonomies," are obviously important in science, too, and he said so over and over (as, for example, in 1990). It was one of his main methodological points, and a highly humanistic one, sitting in the middle of a science of economics. You have to know what red giant stars *are* before you undertake to count them—though the mixing of quality and quantity shows in the very word "giant." You have to know what Swiss citizens *are* before you undertake to count them. You have to know the borders of Zurich—"What?"—before you undertake to measure its altitude or income or religious composition. And note the humanistic, qualitative, inquiry-into-*what* that is entailed in deciding the sub-question in Zurich whether, trivially, the question whether to use meters or feet in measuring the altitude, or—much more significantly—the humanistic, qualitative, even ethical questions involved in deciding the sub-question of what to include in "the income of the city of Zurich" or in "Protestant" or "agnostic."

Categories, then. Categories complete the link between scientific and literary studies. And categories are words, which the linguist Ferdinand de Saussure taught us a century ago to think of as contrasting pairs, such as "sheep" and "goat," or "sheep" in the field and "mutton" on the table. Consumption and investment. Information and knowledge. Accumulation and the growth industry. Exchange and the grants economy.

The sciences and the humanities depend on categories, and categories are words depending on humanly decided contrasts. The Austrian-American poet Rose Ausländer wrote, *Am Anfang/war das Wort/und das Wort/war bei Gott/ Und Gott gab uns das Wort/und wir wohnten im das Wort/Und das Wort ist unser Traum/und der Traum ist unser Leben*: "In the beginning was the Word/ And the Word was with God/And God gave us the Word/And we lived in the Word/And the Word is our dream/And the dream is our life." Truer words were never spoken. We dream of categories, in our metaphors and stories, and with them make our lives, even our scientific lives (McCloskey 1998 [1st ed. 1986], 1990, 1994). The Danish physicist Niels Bohr, who imagined the atom as a tiny solar system, said in 1927, equally truly (note: not Truly), that "It is wrong to think that the task of physics is to find out how nature *is*. Physics concerns what we can *say* about nature." We. Say. With words. *Der Traum ist unser Leben.* About *geisteswissenschaftliche* categories.

Adam Smith was Boulding's hero, as he is mine (in a lecture I can easily draw a laugh, and make a substantive point, too, about whom to read seriously, by crossing myself when I mention the Blessed Smith). "More than any other economist," Boulding wrote in an appendix to his own great if commercially unsuccessful textbook, *Economic Analysis* (another similarity in our careers; that, and stuttering; we're working on a third edition of *The Applied Theory of Price* [1985]), "with the possible exception of P. H. Wicksteed, Adam Smith embodies the liberal tradition of humane letters. The student who learns to love his quiet wit and keen but gentle observation of humanity will never generate into a narrow-minded specialist" (p. 266 of *Macroeconomics*, published as a separate volume).

There's nothing, in short, unscientific about the humanities. Boulding spoke of the "inside track" we have as social scientists because we are the very thing we study, unlike the position of the physicist studying the atom or the biologist the cell or the geologist the mountain.

> The outside track is frequently associated with scientific knowledge and the inside with folk or humanistic knowledge. The social scientist is frequently inclined to deprecate the inside track and to pretend that he operates only on the outside track. If we examine the social scientists carefully, however, we shall find that ... their theoretical models owe a great deal to the power of man to known himself from the inside.
>
> (1964, p. 59)

And how do we know ourselves from the inside? Through the arts and the humanities.

Many scientists mistakenly think that *ethical* categorization is not relevant to science: this is an echo of an attitude dating to Max Weber and adopted enthusiastically in economics during the middle of the twentieth century that fact and value are from different realms. Boulding did not agree. He realized, as many economists still do not, that "a process by which we detect errors in propositions of fact is not very different from that by which we detect error in propositions of value" (1986, p. 8; the sentence is a good example of the large virtues and occasional vices of his prose: he expresses parallel ideas in parallel form, as one should; but he was addicted as many economists and sociologists are to the hollow word "process"). About the same time as he was saying this, I was saying also to the economists that all reasoning is rhetorical. And so, Boulding and I both concluded, "The idea that there is something called 'science' which detects truth faultlessly and cannot have anything to do with valuations is an absurd byproduct of the now largely discarded logical positivism" (Boulding 1986, p. 9).

My only amendments would be that (1) the faith in a timeless and perfect Method for detecting error is Platonic, and before him Pythagorean, and is not to be blamed solely on a tiny group of Austrian philosophers in the 1920s, and that (2) despite the best efforts of Boulding and me and Amariglio and Klamer and others, economists still think it is 1922 in Philosophy Land. Boulding would have agreed that a better project than the naïve one of supposing that subjective and objective cover the epistemological territory, and that there is a Method that links the two, is to admit that all we humans know is the "conjective," that is, what we know together. We can study the conjective in our rhetoric, or as Boulding put it in *The Image* (1956), we can "discuss the growth of images [he called it 'eiconics' and I call it 'rhetoric'], both private and public, in individuals, in organizations, in society at large" (1956, p. 224).

Boulding was not a footnoter, as he himself admitted, and was likely to confidently offer up a quotation or a fact without checking it. The habit has the effect sometimes of keeping him from breaking through conventional ideas, much against his inclinations. He read widely, especially for a modern economist (born 1910), but would not go *back* to the library to get it exactly right. He was an Oxford Essayist. I can hardly in good conscience claim that essayists are a bad thing. But the Oxford version does not attend to the details—one has to get the weekly essay to one's tutor this afternoon, and so one relies on general knowledge and intellectual brilliance and a good style. No fact checking. And what is more important, no *idea* checking, no period of doubting that one's bright idea of the morning is actually true. Excellent writers in economics have the problem: I think of Keynes and Rostow and (the elder, not the younger) Galbraith. It can take a mathematical form, too. Such people (almost exclusively men: hmm) write too well, whether in words or mathematics, and especially too fluently. Boulding was all his life, I repeat, a theorist rather than an empiricist, like

Samuelson rather than Friedman. He had the theorist's lack of interest in getting the facts exactly right. What mattered, he thought, was the Image.

Yet he often lights on a beautiful and true idea. He was in this a humanist through and through. Again, the depth of his religion obviously mattered. He writes most truly that "love, in the sense of Greek *agape*, emerges as the most anti-entropic of all human relationships. It always builds up, it never tears down" (Boulding 1964, p. 146). One is reminded of 1 Corinthians 13:7–8, that favorite of Hallmark cards when understood as earthly love, *eros* or *philia*, but deeply true, as Boulding was saying, when understood as *agape*: "Love bears all things, believes all things, hopes all things, endures all things. Love never ends." Or as Boulding said to his fellow Quakers in the midst of World War II,

> true forgiveness comes only in a flood of divine love [*agape*], that wells up in our souls from places too deep to be hurt by mortal injury, love that draws us together with God and with our enemies in a healing, uniting experience.... Apart from the love of God, there is no end to the cycle of war.[4]

That is social science, making a prediction about a most material activity, war. But it is also humanistic, in the literary sense of drawing on the best that has been thought and written, and humane, too.

Thus Kenneth Ewart Boulding, and, we pray, the economist of the future.

Notes

1 Distinguished Professor of Economics, History, English, and Communication at the University of Illinois, Chicago, and Professor of Economic History, University of Gothenburg. I thank Dr. Rick Wicks of the Department of Economics, University of Gothenburg, for allowing me to use his trove of Boulding material in the writing of the essay.

2 The argument would be testable with brain scans, I suppose.

3 If you disbelieve this because your econometrics professor denies it, but are willing to think for yourself, have a look at McCloskey (1998) and Ziliak and McCloskey (2008).

4 "The Practice of Love of God," William Penn Lecture, pp. 20–21, quoted in Silk (1976, p. 207).

References

Boulding, Kenneth E. 1956. *The Image: Knowledge in Life and Society*. Ann Arbor: University of Michigan Press.

Boulding, Kenneth E. 1958. *The Skills of the Economist*. London: Hamish Hamilton.

Boulding, Kenneth E. 1964. *The Meaning of the 20th Century: The Great Transition*. New York: Harper and Row.

Boulding, Kenneth E. 1973. *The Economy of Love and Fear*. Belmont, CA: Wadsworth.

Boulding, Kenneth E. 1986. "What Went Wrong with Economics?" *The American Economist* 30 (Spring): 5–12.

Boulding, Kenneth E. 1990. "Taxonomy as a Source of Error." *Methodus* 2: 17–21.

Easterly, William. 2001. *The Elusive Quest for Growth: Economists' Adventures and Misadventures in the Tropics*. Cambridge: MIT Press.

Haidt, Jonathan. 2006. *The Happiness Hypothesis: Finding Modern Truth in Ancient Wisdom.* New York: Basic Books.

Harcourt, Geoffrey C. 1993. "A Man for All Systems: Talking with Kenneth Boulding." Pp. 93–104 in Harcourt, *Post-Keynesian Essays in Biography.* London: Macmillan.

Howitt, Peter. 2005. "Coordination Issues in Long-Run Growth." In K. Judd and L. Tesfatsion, eds., *Handbook of Computational Economics*, vol. 2, *Agent-Based Computational Economics.* Preprint at Department of Economics, Brown University.

Klemm, David E. 2004. "Material Grace." Pp. 222–245 in William Schweiker and Charles Matthewes, eds., *Having: Property and Possession in Religious and Social Life.* Grand Rapids: Eerdmans.

Koopmans, Tjalling C. 1957. *Three Essays on the State of Economic Science*. New York: McGraw-Hill.

Lucas, Robert E., Jr. 2002. *Lectures on Economic Growth.* Cambridge, Mass.: Harvard University Press.

McCloskey, Deirdre N. 1985. *The Applied Theory of Price.* 2nd ed. New York: Macmillan.

McCloskey, Deirdre N. 1990. *If You're So Smart: The Narrative of Economic Expertise.* Chicago: University of Chicago Press.

McCloskey, Deirdre N. 1994. *Knowledge and Persuasion in Economics.* Cambridge: Cambridge University Press.

McCloskey, Deirdre N. 1998. *The Rhetoric of Economics*, 2nd ed. Madison: University of Wisconsin Press.

McCloskey, Deirdre N. 2008. "How to Buy, Sell, Make, Manage, Produce, Transact, Consume with Words." Introductory essay in Edward M. Clift, ed., *How Language Is Used to Do Business: Essays on the Rhetoric of Economics*. Lewiston, NY: Mellen Press.

Silk, Leonard. 1976. *The Economists*. New York: Basic Books.

Simon, Julian L. 1981 (1996). *The Ultimate Resource*, 2nd ed. Princeton: Princeton University Press.

Stigler, George J. 1961. "The Economics of Information." *Journal of Political Economy* 69: 213–225.

Ziliak, Stephen, and Deirdre N. McCloskey. 2008. *The Cult of Statistical Significance: How the Standard Error Costs Us Jobs, Justice, and Lives*. Ann Arbor: University of Michigan Press.

Sonnet for Economics

Economist for all my working days,
I should by this time roughly know what's best
For humankind, and put to some small test
My colleagues' images of yeas and nays.
The economy, however is a maze;
To map it is a very complex quest.
Even its history mostly must be guessed
So, over this great ignorance we raise
A fantasy of markets with perfection,
Mistaking charm and elegance for truth;
But Error has a penetrating tooth
That bites when we go in a false direction.
And if our theories are mainly fictions,
It's most unwise to make exact predictions!

Epilogue

Boulding transformations?

Wilfred Dolfsma and Stefan Kesting

Boulding has extensively engaged with a range of sciences and social sciences. This volume has focused on his research that has exemplified interdisciplinary research by him. Many have argued that transformative research is likely to emanate from interdisciplinary research in particular. The question one may then ask is: has Boulding's research transformed the sciences and the social sciences in which he has been involved? The answer to this question is: yes, in a number of areas, Boulding has been transformational. Boulding has even *instigated* a number of areas for research. The latter may in particular be an indication of significance and the vast majority of scholars in any field cannot even hope to leave such a mark.

The field of ecological economics and the theme of sustainability have been transformed by Boulding. He has given an important impetus to evolutionary economic research, even when his ideas have not been as influential as they might have been. How ethics and economics intimately connect is prominently put on the agenda by Boulding, again. In addition to ecological economics, Boulding's work in the area of peace studies remains very influential—a domain he has helped start.

Some of Boulding's work has set in motion a line of thought, but the richness of the ideas proposed may not have been fully exploited. In our view, this is in particular the case for his work on grants and communication. The Association for the Study of the Grants Economy is a source of intellectual inspiration at its meetings, but remains peripheral. Communication as a theme for economists (and even some of the other main social sciences) is not seriously studied, really, and when it is, Boulding is not a source of inspiration. With an uptake of studies revolving around themes related to 'complexity', one could have expected some more attention to systems theory, and thus to Boulding's work on that as well. This has not been the case, not yet at least.

The failure to persuade the economics community of his views of teaching may be related to Boulding's complex view of how the social sciences relate and unite. Boulding has developed his research along those very lines, seeking inspiration wherever it may be found and seeking to add insights wherever his analysis took him. That is bold and courageous. At the same time, an inclination not to allow oneself to be bothered too much by the development of concepts used in particular fields may have prevented him from delving deeper than he might otherwise have done. An associative thinker, pursuing a line of thought, using carefully designed tools of the trade (i.e., precisely defined concepts), has not been Boulding's characteristic style of researching. Had he so pursued his research he might have been involved in fewer themes, but he might also have transformed more academic fields than, it now must be concluded, he has.

Again, however, transforming even a single field of scientific research is an accomplishment that few scholars can rightfully claim they have done. Boulding has transformed and created several fields of scholarly research. That is an accomplishment worthy of admiration.

Index

Page numbers in *italics* denote tables, those in **bold** denote figures